COUNTIES

Ada (B6)..............70,649
Adams (B5)............3,347
Bannock (F7)..........41,745
Bear Lake (G7).......6,834
Benewah (B2).........6,173
Bingham (F6).........23,271
Blaine (D6)..........5,384
Boise (C6)...........1,776

Bonner (B1)..........14,853
Bonneville (G6).......30,210
Boundary (B1)........5,908
Butte (E6)...........2,722
Camas (D6)...........1,079
Canyon (B6)..........53,597
Caribou (G7).........5,576
Cassia (E7)..........14,629
Clark (F5)............918
Clearwater (C3)......8,217

Custer (D5)..........3,318
Elmore (C6)..........6,687
Franklin (G7)........9,867
Fremont (G5).........9,351
Gem (B6).............8,730
Gooding (D6).........11,101
Idaho (C4)...........11,423
Jefferson (F6).......10,495
Jerome (D7)..........12,080
Kootenai (B2)........24,947

Latah (B3)...........20,971
Lemhi (D4)...........6,278
Lewis (B3)...........4,208
Lincoln (D6).........4,256
Madison (G6).........9,156
Minidoka (E7)........9,785
Nez Perce (B3).......22,658
Oneida (F7)..........4,387
Owyhee (B7)..........6,307

Payette (B5).........11,921
Power (F7)...........3,988
Shoshone (B2)........22,806
Teton (G6)...........3,204
Twin Falls (D7)......40,979
Valley (C5)..........4,270
Washington (B5)......8,576
Yellowstone Nat'l. Park (G5)..

Aberdeen (F7)............1,486
Acequia (E7)............. 125
Addie (B1)............... 15
Ahsahka (B3)...........
Alameda (F7)............4,694
Albion (E7)............. 610
Albion (mts.) (E7)...
Alexander (G7)...........
Allan (mt.) (D4).....
Almo (E7)................
Alpha (C5)...............
Alpine (G6)............. 172
Alridge (G6)...........
American Falls◉ (E7)...1,874
American Falls (res.) (F6)...
Ammon (G6)............. 447
Amsterdam (D7)......... 100
Anderson Ranch (res.) (C6)...
Archer (G6)............. 400
Arco◉ (E6)............. 961
Arimo (F7)............. 337
Arrowrock (res.) (C6)...
Ashton (G5)............1,256
Athol (B2)............. 226
Atlanta,(C6)........... 300
Atomic City (F6)...... 500
Auger (falls) (D7)..
Avery (C2)............. 350
Avon (B3)............... 6
Baker (E4)............. 150
Bald (mt.) (D5).....
Bancroft (G7)......... 495
Banida (G7)........... 140
Banks (B5).............
Bannock (mts.) (F7)
Bannock (peak) (F7)
Basalt (F6)........... 227
Bayview (B2).......... 150
Bear (B4)..............
Bear (lake) (G7).....
Bear (riv.) (G7).....
Beaverhead (mts.) (E4)...
Bellevue (D6)......... 528
Denewah (B2).......... 50
Bennett (C6).......... 10
Bennington (G7)...... 200
Berger (D7)...........
Bern (G7)............. 140
Big Creek (C4)....... 24
Big Lost (riv.) (E6)...
Big Southern (butte) (E6)...
Big Springs (G5)..... 5
Big Wood (riv.) (D6)...
Bitterroot (mts.) (D3)...
Black Pine (mts.) (E7)...
Black Pine (peak) (E7)...

◉ County Seat

Blackfoot◉ (F6)......5,180
Blackfoot (riv.) (G6)
Blackfoot River (res.) (G7)...
Blanchard (A1)...... 200
Bliss (D7)............ 126
Bloomington (G7).. 302
BOISE (B6)...........34,393
Boise (mts.) (B6)...
Boise (riv.) (B6)...
Boles (B4)............ 25
Bone (G6)............. 50
Bonners Ferry◉ (B1)...1,776
Borah (peak) (E5)...
Boulder (mts.) (D6)...
Bovill (B3)........... 437
Bowmont (B6).........
Bridge (E7)...........
Broten (B1).......... 30
Bruneau (C7)......... 100
Bruneau (riv.) (C7)...
Buhl (D7).............2,870
Burgdorf (B4).........
Burke (C2)............ 800
Burley◉ (E7).........5,924
Burmah (D6)..........
Cabinet (B1)......... 60
Calder (B2)........... 65
Caldwell◉ (B6).......10,487
Camas (F5)........... 40
Cambridge (B5)...... 354
Cameron (B3)......... 83
Canfield (B4)........ 50
Carey (E6)............1,100
Careywood (B1)...... 50
Caribou (mt.) (G6)...
Caribou (mts.) (G6)...
Carmen (E4)..........
Cascade◉ (C5)........ 943
Cascade (res.) (C5)...
Castle (peak) (D5)...
Castleford (C7)...... 500
Cavendish (B3).......
Cedar Creek (res.) (D7)...
Cedar Creek (peak) (E7)...
Centennial (mts.) (G5)...
Centerville (C6)...... 25
Central (G7)......... 120
Challis◉ (D5)........ 720
Chatcolet (B2)....... 92
Chester (G5)......... 247
Chesterfield (G7)....
Chilco (B2).......... 45
Chilly (E5)........... 84
Chubbuck (F7)....... 120
Churchill (D7).......
C. J. Strike (res.) (C7)...
Clagstone (B1)...... 15
Clark Fork (B1)..... 387
Clarkia (B2)......... 150

Clawson (G6)......... 34
Clayton (D5).......... 75
Clearwater (C3)...... 53
Clearwater (mts.) (C3)...
Clearwater (riv.) (B3)...
Clementsville (G6)... 38
Cleveland (G7)...... 135
Cliffs (B7)........... 32
Clifton (F7).......... 201
Coeur d'Alene◉ (B2)...12,198
Coer d'Alene (lake) (B2)...
Coeur d'Alene (mts.) (B2)...
Conda (G7)........... 330
Coolin (B1)...........
Copeland (B1)........ 11
Corral (B7).......... 157
Cottonwood (B3).... 689
Council◉ (B5)....... 748
Craigmont (B3)..... 594
Crane Creek (res.) (C6)...
Craters of the Moon Nat'l Mon. (E6)...
Crouch (B5).......... 60
Crystal (F7).........
Culdesac (B3)....... 175
Cuprum (B4).......... 20
Darlington (E6)..... 200
Dayton (F7).......... 287
Deadwood(res.) (C5)...
De Lamar (B6).......
Deary (B3)........... 320
Declo (E7)........... 210
Deep Creek (mts.) (F7)...
Dent (B3)............
Denver (B4).......... 29
Desmet (B2).........
Diamond (peak) (E5)...
Dietrich (D7)........ 160
Dingle (G7)..........
Dixie (C4)........... 56
Donnelly (C5)....... 595
Dover (B1)........... 385
Downey (F7)......... 748
Driggs◉ (G6)........ 941
Drummond (G5)...... 59
Dubois◉ (F5)........ 430
Duck Valley Ind. Res. (B7)...
Dudley (B2)..........
Eagle (B6)........... 500
East Hope (B1)...... 149
East Sister (peak) (C2)...
Eastport (B1)........ 108
Eden (D7)............ 456
Edgemere (B1)....... 96
Elba (E7)............ 180

Elk City (C4)........ 300
Elk River (B3)...... 312
Ellis (D5)...........
Elmira (B1).......... 128
Emida (B2)........... 125
Emmett◉ (B6).......3,067
Enaville (B2)........ 60
Fairfield◉ (D6)..... 502
Fairview (G7)....... 398
Felt (G6)............ 120
Fenn (B4)............ 57
Ferdinand (B3)..... 206
Fernwood (B2)...... 200
Filer (D7)...........1,425
Firth (F6)........... 293
Fish Creek (res.) (E6)...
Fish Haven (G7)....
Forest (B3).........
Forney (D4).........
Fort Hall (F6)......
Fort Hall Ind. Res. (F6)...
Franklin (B3)....... 467
French Creek (B4).. 65
Fruitland (B6)...... 573
Fruitvale (B5)...... 125
Gannett (D6)........ 43
Garden City (B6)... 764
Garden Valley (C5). 210
Gardena (B5)........
Gardner (F6)........
Gem (C2)............ 500
Genesee (B3)....... 552
Geneva (G7).........
Georgetown (G7)... 404
Gibbonsville (E4)... 200
Gibbs (B2)........... 35
Gifford (B3)......... 51
Gilmore (E5)........ 50
Glengary (B1).......
Glens Ferry (C7)....1,515
Goldburg (E5).......
Golden (C4)......... 100
Gooding◉ (D7)......3,099
Goodrich (B5)....... 16
Goose Creek (res.) (D7)...
Goose Creek (mts.) (E7)...
Goldstone (mt.) (E4)...
Grace (G7)........... 761
Grainville (G5)..... 30
Grand View (B7)....
Grangemont (C3)... 130
Grangeville◉ (B4)...2,544
Granite (B1)........ 150
Gray (G6)...........
Grays (lake) (G6)...
Greencreek (B3).... 51
Greenleaf (B6).....
Greer (B3).......... 127
Grimes Pass (C5)...
Grouse (E6)......... 43
Hagerman (D7)...... 520

Hailey◉ (D6).......1,464
Hamer (F6)..........
Hammett (C7)....... 350
Hansen (D7)......... 463
Harpster (C4).......
Harrison (B2)....... 322
Harvard (B3)........ 102
Hauser (B2)......... 70
Hayden Lake (B2).. 39
Hazelton (E7)....... 429
Headquarters (C3)... 300
Heath (B5).......... 15
Heglar (E7)......... 10
Heise (G6).......... 87
Henry (lake) (G5)..
Heyburn (E7)....... 539
Hibbard (G6)....... 400
Hill City (D6)...... 15
Holbrook (F7)......
Hollister (D7)...... 80
Homedale (A6)......1,411
Hope (B1)........... 111
Horse Shoe Bend (B6)... 401
Howe (F6)........... 200
Huetter (B2)........ 84
Humphrey (E5)...... 35
Hunter (peak) (D3)
Hyndman (peak) (D6)...
Idaho City◉ (C6).... 246
Idaho Falls◉ (F6)..19,218
Idahome (E7).......
Indian Valley (B5)... 50
Inkom (F7).......... 434
Iona (G6)........... 502
Irwin (G6).......... 147
Island Park (G5)...
Jerome◉ (D7)......4,523
Joseph (B4)......... 23
Juliaetta (B3)...... 365
Juniper (F7)........
Kamiah (B3)........ 812
Kellogg (B2)........4,913
Kendrick (B3)...... 409
Ketchum (D6)....... 757
Keuterville (B3).... 25
Kilgore (G5)........ 160
Kimberly (D7)......1,347
Kingston (B2)......
Kooskia (C3)....... 629
Kootenai (B1)...... 199
Kootenai (riv.) (C1)...
Kuna (B6)........... 534
Laclede (B1)........ 200
Lago (G7)........... 250
Lake (G5)........... 8
Lake Fork (B5)..... 11
Lakeview (B2)......
Lamont (G6)........ 50
Lane (G6)...........
Lapwai (B3)......... 480
Lava Hot Springs (F7)... 591
Leadore (E5)........ 159

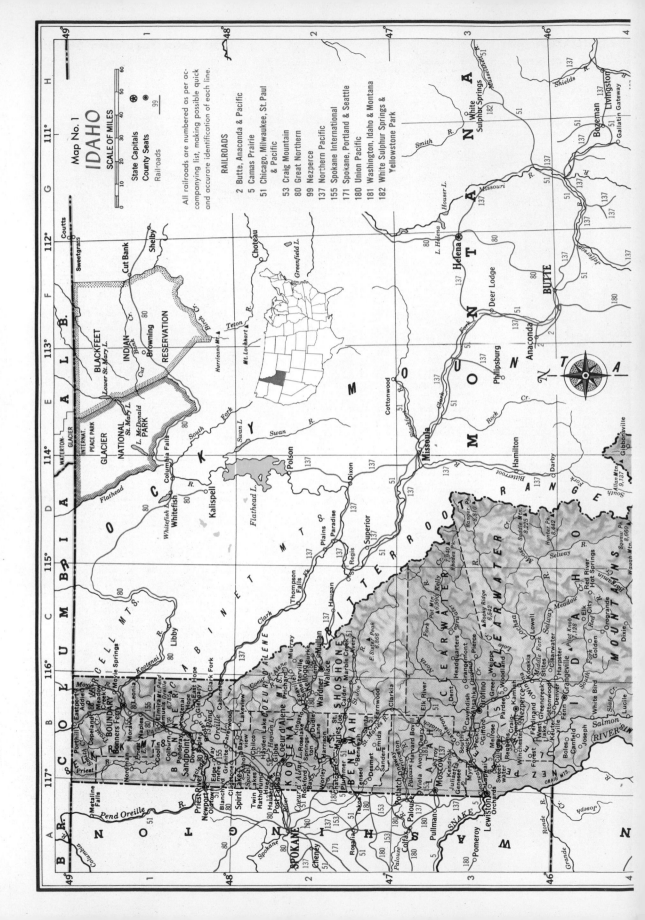

Map No. 1
IDAHO

SCALE OF MILES

State Capitals ⊛
County Seats ⦿
Railroads ——— 99

RAILROADS

All railroads are numbered as per accompanying list, making possible quick and accurate identification of each line.

2 Butte, Anaconda & Pacific
5 Camas Prairie
51 Chicago, Milwaukee, St. Paul & Pacific
53 Craig Mountain
80 Great Northern
99 Nezperce
137 Northern Pacific
155 Spokane International
171 Spokane, Portland & Seattle
180 Union Pacific
181 Washington, Idaho & Montana
182 White Sulphur Springs & Yellowstone Park

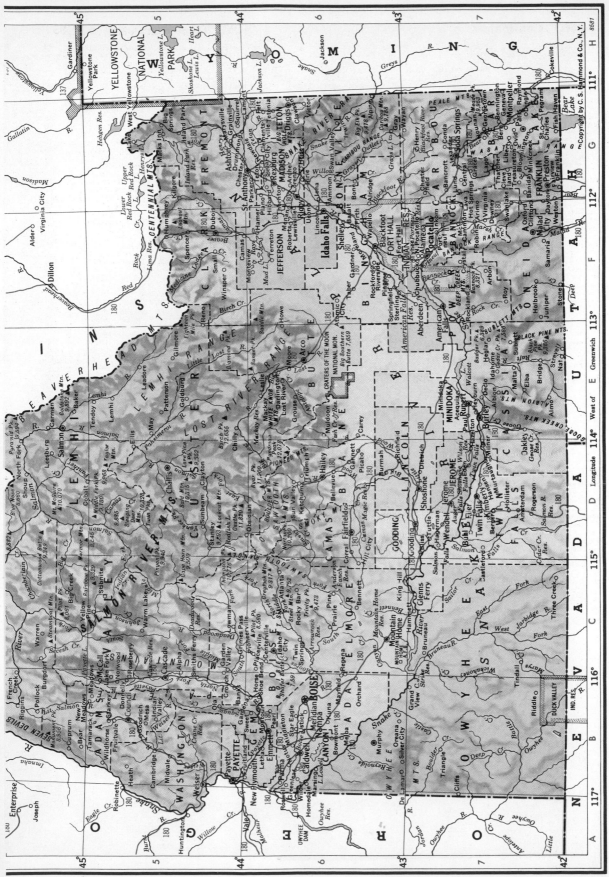

Leesburg (D4)..........	
Lemhi (E5)..............	150
Lemhi (mts.) (E5)...	
Lemhi (riv.) (E5)...	
Leonia (B1)..............	
Leslie (E6)..............	40
Letha (B6)..............	376
Lewiston◉ (A3)....12,985	
Lewisville (F6)..........	402
Liberty (G7)..............	
Lincoln (F6)..............	
Little Lost	
(riv.) (E5)	
Little Owyhee	
(riv.) (B7)	
Little Weiser	
(riv.) (B5)	
Little Wood	
(riv.) (D6)	
Lochsa (riv.) (C3)...	
Lorenzo (G6)..........	250
Lost River (E6)........	37
Lost River	
(mts.) (E5)	
Lowell (C3)..............	
Lowell (lake) (B6)..	
Lowman (C5)..........	30
Lucile (B4)..............	13
Lund (G7)..............	103
Mackay (E6)..........	760
Mackay (res.) (D6)..	
Macks Inn (G5).......	100
Magic (res.) (D6)...	
Malad City◉ (F7)....2,715	
Malta (E7)..............	518
Marble Creek (C2)..	6
Marsing (B6)..........	643
Marysville (G5).......	190
May (E5)..............	75
Mayfield (B6)..........	
Mc Call (C5).........1,173	
Mc Cammon (F7)...	578
Mc Guire (mt.) (D4)	
Meade Peak	
(mt.) (G7)	
Meadow Creek (B1)	15
Meadows (B5)..........	190
Melba (B6)..............	203
Melrose (B3)..............	5
Menan (F6)..............	430
Meridian (B6).........1,810	
Mesa (B5)..............	179
Middleton (B6)........	496
Midvale (B5)..............	231
Milner (D7)..............	
Minidoka (E7)..........	113
Minkcreek (G7)........	124
Monteview (F6)........	
Montour (B6)..........	155
Montpelier (G7).....2,682	
Monument	
(peak) (B4)	
Moore (E6)..............	256
Moravia (B1)..........	
Moreland (F6)........	250
◉ County Seat	

Moscow◉ (B3)....10,593	
Mountain Home◉	
(C6) 1,887	
Mountain Home Air	
F. Base (C6)........	
Moyie (riv.) (B1)....	
Moyie Springs (B1)..	109
Mud (lake) (F6)......	
Muldoon (E6)..........	
Mullan (C2).........2,036	
Murphy◉ (B6)........	37
Murray (C2)..........	158
Murtaugh (D7)........	239
Myrtle (B3)..............	20
Naf (E7)..............	
Nampa (B6)...........16,185	
Naples (B1)..........	
New Meadows (B4)	621
New Plymouth (B6).	942
Newdale (G6)..........	312
Nezperce◉ (B3).......	543
Nordman (B1)........	18
North Fork (D4).....	100
North Fork Payette	
(riv.) (B5)	
North Pocatello(F7)	575
Norton (peak)	
(D6)	
Norwood (C5)..........	
Notus (B6)..............	313
Nounan (G7)..........	
Oakley (D7)..........	684
Obsidian (D6)........	11
Ola (B5)..............	300
Oldtown (A1)..........	358
Onaway (B3)..........	81
Orchard (B6)..........	
Orchards (A3).........4,494	
Oreana (B6)..........	100
Orofino◉ (B3).......1,656	
Orogrande (C4)........	12
Ovid (G7)..............	200
Owyhee (mts.) (B7)..	
Owyhee (riv.) (B7)..	
Oxford (F7)..........	110
Palouse (riv.) (B3)..	
Pardee (B3)..............	
Paris◉ (G7)..............	774
Parker (G6)..........	306
Parma (B6).........1,369	
Patterson (E5)........	112
Paul (E7)..............	560
Payette◉ (B5).........4,032	
Payette (mts.) (B5)..	
Payette (riv.) (B6)..	
Peale (mts.)(G7).....	
Pearl (B6)..............	38
Peck (B3)..............	170
Pegram (G7)..........	75
Pend Oreille	
(lake) (B1)	
Pend Oreille	
(mt.) (B1)	
Pend Oreille	
(riv.) (A1)	

Picabo (D6)..............	100
Pierce (C3)................	544
Pilot Knob(mt.)(C4)	
Pine (C6)..............	
Pingree (F6)..............	102
Pinyon (peak) (C5).	
Pioneer (mts.) (D6)	
Pioneerville (C6).......	8
Placerville (C6)........	17
Plano (G6)..............	403
Plummer (B2)..........	395
Pocatello◉ (F7)....26,131	
Pollock (B4)..........	
Ponderay (B1)..........	248
Porthill (B1)..........	68
Portneuf (F7)..........	65
Portneuf (riv.) (F7)	
Post Falls (A2)........1,069	
Potlatch (A3).........1,024	
Potlatch (riv.) (B3).	
Prairie (C6)..............	150
Preston◉ (G7).........4,045	
Prichard (B2)..........	40
Priest (lake) (B1)...	
Priest River (A1).....1,592	
Princeton (B3)........	84
Purcell (mts.)(C1)...	
Pyramid (peak)(E4)	
Raft (riv.) (E7).......	
Rainbow (peak)(C4)	
Ranger (peak) (D3)	
Rathdrum (A2)........	610
Raymond (G7)........	88
Red (riv.) (C4).......	
Red River Hot	
Springs (C4)........	12
Regena (C6)..........	
Reno (F5)..............	
Reubens (B3)..........	116
Rexburg◉ (G6).........4,253	
Rhodes (peak) (D3)	
Richfield (D6)........	429
Riddle (B7)..............	35
Rigby◉ (G6).............1,826	
Riggins (B4)..........	287
Ririe (G6)..............	527
Riverside (F6)..........	
Roberts (F6)..........	341
Robin (F7)..............	165
Rockford (F6)..........	
Rockford Bay (B2)..	27
Rockland (F7)........	277
Rocky Bar (C6)........	
Rocky Ridge	
(mt.) (C3)	
Rogerson (D7)........	75
Roseberry (C5)........	
Roselake (B2)........	212
Roswell (A6)..........	92
Roy (F7)..............	25
Rupert◉ (E7).........3,098	
Ryan (peak) (D6)...	
Sagle (B1)..............	75
St. Anthony◉ (G6).2,695	
St. Charles (G7).......	363

St. Joe (B2)............	75
St. Joe (riv.) (B2)...	
St. Maries◉	
(B2) 2,220	
Salmon◉ (D4).........2,648	
Salmon (falls) (D7)	
Salmon (riv.) (B4)...	
Salmon River	
(mts.) (C5)........	
Salmon River	
(res.) (D7)	
Samaria (F7)..........	
Samuels (B1)..........	
Sanders (B2)..........	25
Sandpoint◉ (B1).....4,265	
Santa (B2)..............	
Sawtooth (mts.)(D6)	
Sawtooth (mts.)(C6)	
Selkirk (mts.)(B1)...	
Selway (riv.) (C3)...	
Seven Devils (mts.)	
(B4)	
Shafer (butte) (B6).	
Shelley (F6)..........1,856	
Shoshone◉ (D7).......1,420	
Shoshone(falls) (D7)	
Shoup (D4)..............	
Silver City (B6)........	2
Sleeping Deer	
(mt.) (D5)	
Small (F5)..............	
Smelterville (B2)...	76
Smiths Ferry (C5)...	
Smoky (mts.) (D6).	
Snake (riv.) (A3)....	
Snake River (mts.)	
(G6)	
Snake River	
(plain) (D7)	
Soda Springs◉	
(G7)	
Southwick (B3)........	200
Spencer (F5)..........	70
Spirit Lake (A2)........	823
Springfield (F6)........	435
Springston (B2)........	57
Squaw (peak) (D4).	
Squirrel (G5)..........	
Stanley (D5)..........	33
Star (B6)..............	525
Starkey (B5)..........	3
Steel (mt.) (C6)......	
Sterling (F6)..........	
Stewart (mts.)(E7)..	
Stibnite (C5)..........	717
Stites (C3)..............	227
Stone (F7)..............	170
Strevell (E7)..........	25
Sublett (F5)..........	10
Sugar City (G6)........	684
Sun Valley (D6)......	428
Sunbeam (D5)........	6
Swan Valley (G6)...	203
Swanlake (F7)........	250
Sweet (B6)..............	200

Sweetwater (B3)......	80
Taber (F6)..............	
Tamarack (B5)........	
Taylor (mt.) (D5)...	
Tendoy (E5)..........	
Tensed (B2)..........	189
Terreton (F6)..........	35
Teton (G6)..............	463
Teton (riv.) (G6)...	
Tetonia (G6)..........	232
Thatcher (G7)........	50
Thompson	
(peak) (C5)	
Thornton (G6)........	300
Three Creek (C7)...	65
Tindall (C7)..........	5
Treasureton (G7).....	
Triangle (B7)..........	35
Triumph (D6)..........	97
Troy (B3)..............	531
Tuttle (D7)..............	15
Twin (falls) (D7)...	
Twin (peaks) (D5)..	
Twin Falls◉	
(D7) 17,600	
Twin Lakes (B2)......	225
Twin Springs (C6)...	
Tyhee (F7)..............	350
Ucon (F6)..............	356
Ustick (B6)..............	200
Vay (B1)..............	80
Victor (G6)..........	431
Viola (B3)..............	150
Virginia (F7)..........	245
Walcott (lake) (E7)	
Wallace◉ (C2).........3,140	
Wapello (F6)..........	
Wardner (B2)........	772
Warm Lake (C5)......	500
Warren (C4)..........	30
Wasatch (mts.)(G7)	
Waugh (mt.) (D4)...	
Wayan (G7)..........	
Weippe (C3)..........1,000	
Weiser◉ (B5).........3,961	
Weiser (riv.) (B5)...	
Wendell (D7).........1,483	
Westlake (B3)........	35
Weston (F7)..........	382
White Bird (B4)......	
White Knob (mts.)	
(E6)	
Wilder (A6)..........	555
Wildhorse (B5)........	18
Wilson Lake	
(res.) (D7)	
Winchester (B3)......	488
Winona (B3)..........	
Winsper (F5)..........	
Wood (riv.) (D6)...	
Woodland (C3)........	
Worley (B2)..........	233
Yellow Pine (C4)....	35
Yellowstone Nat'l	
Park (H5)	

IDAHO IN THE PACIFIC NORTHWEST

IDAHO

in

the PACIFIC NORTHWEST

By

Floyd R. Barber

and

Dan W. Martin

Illustrated with photographs and maps

The CAXTON PRINTERS, Ltd.

Caldwell, Idaho

1956

Library of Congress Catalog Card No. 55-5192

Printed and bound in the United States of America by
the *Country Life Press,* Garden City, New York

Dedicated to
THE SCHOOL CHILDREN OF IDAHO
Past, Present, and Future

Preface

IN PIONEER DAYS friendly Indians often greeted white men with the exclamation, "HOW!" signifying friendship. So do we greet the school children and the other people of Idaho. It is our hope that you may find the reading of this book both interesting and helpful and that from its reading will come an even greater love and loyalty for our great and glorious state of Idaho.

THE AUTHORS

Acknowledgments

A DEBT OF GRATITUDE is hereby acknowledged to the many who have encouraged the preparation of this book and have assisted the authors by suggesting and, in many instances, supplying materials that have made the writing of the book possible. Especially are we grateful to those who have provided photographs for the illustrations. It is not possible to mention all who have helped, but we owe our special thanks to the following, whose personnel have extended themselves to aid in our project:

The Idaho State Historical Society, Boise
The Idaho Falls, Idaho, Public Library
The Pocatello, Idaho, Public Library
The Idaho State College Library, Pocatello
Idaho State Chamber of Commerce, Boise
Chamber of Commerce, Idaho Falls
Chamber of Commerce, Pocatello
Chamber of Commerce, Twin Falls
Chamber of Commerce, Grangeville
Chamber of Commerce, Moscow
Other Chambers of Commerce
Idaho State Board of Publicity and the Secretary of State, Boise
Offices of the State Auditor and the State Treasurer, Boise
State Department of Education, Boise
State Department of Forestry and the State Forester, Boise
State Fish and Game Department, Boise
State Highway Department, Boise
Boise Regional Office of the U.S. Bureau of Reclamation
Soil Conservation Service, Boise
U.S. Indian Service, Portland, Oregon, and Washington, D.C.
The following railroads: Great Northern Railway; Northern Pacific Railroad; Spokane International Railway Company; Chicago, Milwaukee, St. Paul and Pacific Railroad; Union Pacific Railroad; and the Camas Prairie Railroad.
County officers of the various counties, and especially the County School Superintendents

U.S. Forest Service, Region No. 1, Missoula, Montana

U.S. Forest Service, Region No. 4, Ogden, Utah

District Supervisors and Rangers of the National Forests in Idaho

United States Board of Geographic Names, Washington, D.C.

Senator Henry Dworshak, Washington, D.C.

State of Idaho, Military Department, Adjutant General's Office, Boise

All others who have helped in any manner to make this book possible.

It is with great appreciation and satisfaction that we report that in the eight years or more that this work has been in progress, we have not met or written to a single individual who refused to help in any way possible. This is one of the factors which has made the long and arduous task of preparing this book a pleasure, despite the time and effort involved.

To Eugene F. Hoy, of the editorial department of The Caxton Printers, Ltd., we extend our sincere thanks and appreciation for constructive criticism and aid in the final preparation of the manuscript for publication.

THE AUTHORS

Table of Contents

List of Illustrations

Introduction

IN PRESENTING A NEW BOOK in Idaho social studies, the authors have been sobered by a sense of the heavy responsibilities resting upon them. They have fully realized the need for accuracy in telling Idaho's story, for impartiality in the discussion of current issues on which people may be divided in their thinking, and for as high a degree of interest as possible in presenting what the authors regard as the most essential things that need to be told about the state.

In the preparation of the book the authors have done their best to insure accuracy. Every county and section of the state has been visited for on-the-spot observation, conferences with local residents, the examination of materials available, and meetings with state and county officials, chambers of commerce, and leaders in the field of industry. The authors have personally examined most of the published books dealing with Idaho and the Pacific Northwest, as well as scores of magazines and other sources containing pertinent information.

The aim has been to bring together in one volume as much material as possible, considering the limits placed upon the writers by the time available in school schedules for studying about Idaho and the cost of the completed book. Even so, much additional reading and research is desirable for those who wish a comprehensive knowledge of the state. The Bibliography at the end of the book suggests many sources for such reading and research.

If errors are found in this book (and no book of this nature is likely to be completely free of errors), the authors would deeply appreciate having their attention called to possible mistakes so that they may be corrected in later editions. The authors may always be contacted through the publishers, The Caxton Printers, Ltd., of Caldwell, Idaho.

FLOYD R. BARBER and DAN W. MARTIN

I Love Idaho

By

Howard P. Pinckney

MY ABODE is Idaho—the State of Shining Mountains. I love it. I love it above any State in the Union, or any section of the Universe.

I LOVE IDAHO because it offers to everyone the opportunity to live a wholesome, normal, happy, and healthy life, with access to cultural institutions of the highest order, and amid surroundings that tend to uplift, broaden, and develop.

I LOVE IDAHO because as a state it is still young, pulsing with life and vigor and the desire to achieve, yet caring for its citizens in a sane, orderly way.

I LOVE IDAHO because of its people: Openhearted, generous to a fault, with a welcome for the stranger, be he of high or low degree, that says, "Come, partake of our bounty; be one of us; help us build."

I LOVE IDAHO for the sweep of its gray sage plains that await but the vision of a dreamer, the skill of an engineer, and the hand of the husbandman to transform them to verdant meadows and green fields, with prosperous homes sheltering happy families.

I LOVE IDAHO for the lure of flashing streams, where "rainbows" challenge one's skill with rod and reel; for its mountain vastnesses where elk, and deer, and mountain sheep, and grizzly bear call the hunter.

I LOVE IDAHO for its far-flung forests, where one may go in solitude, and in the soughing of the pines, hear the whispering of nature's music.

I LOVE IDAHO for its open range, where in the long summer days the herder cares for his sheep, and in the spring the branding fires still burn, and in the fall the night herder still sings his lullaby.

I LOVE IDAHO for the majesty of its dawns, when the sun, rising, paints the eastern peaks with a radiance so glorious that the Indians, when they first beheld it, shouted "E-dah-ho!"—Shining Mountains! And the sunsets. When night lets down her purple robes and the landscape is dimmed in an effulgent glow that seems to steal away one's cares, and the things that seemed so important, or perhaps so cruel, at midday, fade into insignificance, and one rises above the petty things of life and catches a glimpse of the Infinite, and hears a whisper, "All's well."

I LOVE IDAHO for the romance of the past. Here came Captain Bonneville on his first trip of exploration; here came Lewis and Clark, led by Sacajawea, the Bird Woman; and then followed Peter Skene Ogden, and Jim Bridger and Fremont, with their sturdy following of hunters, trappers, and traders. Then the creak and clank of the wagon trains, bearing as brave and purposeful a band of argonauts as ever set forth in search of homes and high adventure, who spread into this Northwest and carved an empire that eventually was added to the Union.

I LOVE IDAHO for the future it holds. I shall not live to see the day when all its valleys and plains have been transformed, but that day will come. And to have had but a small share in its beginning will be reward enough. THAT IS WHY I love Idaho—with a love that is akin to passion. And that is why when my short day is done I should like to find a resting place not far from the music of its mountain streams and the soughing of its pines.

*   *   *   *   *

Howard P. Pinckney was one of the editors of the *Idaho State Journal,* of Pocatello. The manuscript of the beautiful prose poem you have just read was found among some papers on his desk after his untimely death, but not until after his body had been returned to his original home in Illinois for burial. It is a matter of regret that the wish he expressed in the last paragraph of his splendid tribute to Idaho could not have been carried out.

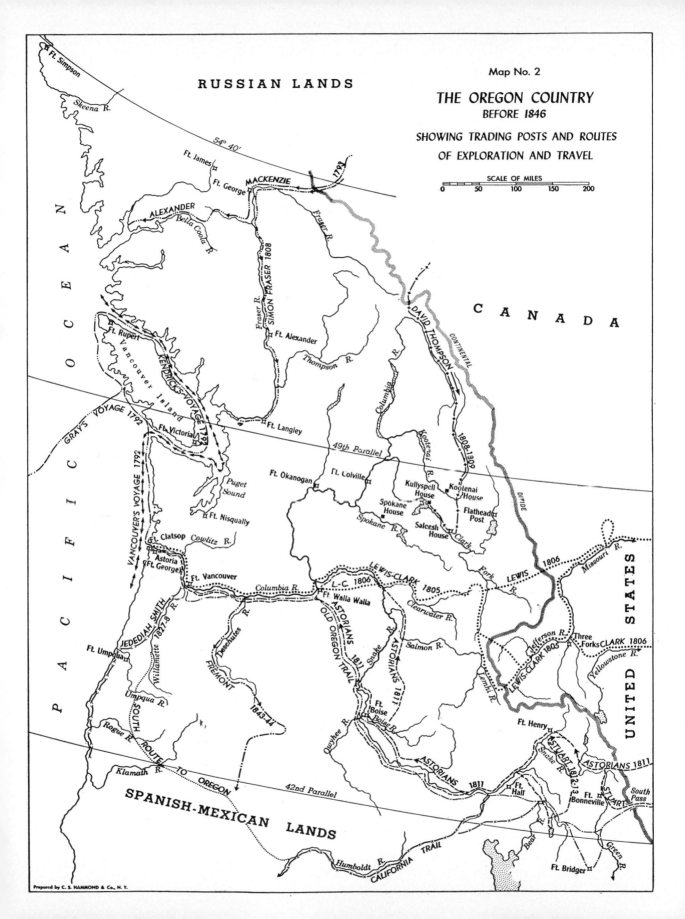

Here We Have Idaho

(General Version)

Official Idaho State Song by Enactment of 21st and 33rd Sessions of Idaho State Legislature.

Verses by ALBERT J. TOMPKINS
Chorus by MCKINLEY HELM

Music by SALLIE HUME-DOUGLAS

1. You've heard of the won-ders our land does pos-sess, Its beau-ti-ful val-leys and hills; The maj-es-tic for-ests where na-ture a-bounds, We love ev'ry nook and rill.

2. There's on-ly one state in this great land of ours, Where i-deals can be re-al-ized; The pi-o-neers made it so for you and me, A leg-a-cy we'll al-ways prize.

Music adapted from 'Garden of Paradise' and used by permission of Sallie Hume-Douglas.

Here We Have Idaho 2—2

KEEP
IDAHO
GREEN

PART ONE

IDAHO IN THE OREGON COUNTRY
(Idaho before 1863)

How the Oregon Country was discovered, explored, settled, divided, and organized; and how the finding of gold in the mountain streams laid the foundation for Idaho Territory

UNIT 1—Discovering and Exploring the Oregon Country

UNIT 2—Settling and Dividing the Oregon Country

UNIT 3—Bringing Government to the Oregon Country

Discovering and Exploring the Oregon Country

*How the Oregon Country became known to the nation and to the world
through the discoveries and explorations of seafaring men, trail blazers,
and fur-gatherers.*

LESS THAN TWO CENTURIES AGO the Oregon Country, as the Pacific Northwest was first called, was an unknown land as far as white men were concerned. A great river, spoken of as the "River of the West," the "Ourigan" of the Indians, was known to exist beyond the Rocky Mountains and to flow into the Pacific but, as far as records show, it had never been seen by people of the white race. This land of mystery was, however, soon claimed by several nations.

I. NATIONAL CLAIMS TO THE PACIFIC NORTHWEST

SPANISH SEA CAPTAINS, sailing from Spanish settlements along the coast of California more than three hundred years ago, had explored portions of the Northwest Coast and opened trade with the Indians living there. One of their main trading points was at Nootka Sound, on the west coast of Vancouver Island. Their occasional voyages and the Nootka Sound activities gave Spain a claim to the northwest region, which was further strengthened by the fact that the northern boundary of Spanish California lay along the southern border of the vast region drained by the River of the West and other streams flowing into the Pacific. The Spanish claims were established well ahead of those of other nations, but three other countries soon followed Spain's lead.

In the 1570's Sir Francis Drake, the famous Elizabethan sea dog, sailed around the southern tip of South America and northward along the western coast of the New World looking for Spanish treasure ships to capture. He went as far as the coast of northern California before turning westward across the Pacific. This voyage by Drake gave the British their first claim to the western coast of North America.

In 1728 Russia came into the picture. In that year Peter the Great, the czar of Russia, sent Vitus Bering on a voyage of exploration along the coast of Alaska. He reported that sea otters, whose skins were in great demand in the fur markets of the world, were very plentiful. Within a few years Russian trappers and traders were busily engaged along the Alaskan coast. Baranof, the greatest of the Russian traders, built his main post at Sitka, which became the capital and center of Russian activities in North America. Russia's

claim to Alaska was thus firmly established, though the Russian lands were north of the region known as the Oregon Country.

The profitable trade carried on by the Spanish and by the Russians soon attracted the attention of English sea captains. In 1778 Captain Cook, the first English trader to reach the Pacific Northwest, loaded a ship with sea otter furs and set sail for China. There, to his great delight, he was able to dispose of the skins at a huge profit. The news of his successful venture spread and soon other English traders followed Cook's example.

Learning of the great profit to be made in the fur trade, New England merchants decided to try their luck in the new region. They organized the Boston Company, which sent two ships to open trade with the Indians of the Northwest. The *Lady Washington* was commanded by Captain Robert Gray and Captain John Kendrick was in command of the *Columbia*. When they arrived off the Northwest Coast, the two commanders exchanged vessels. Captain Gray took the *Columbia* to Nootka Sound for a cargo of sea otter furs while Captain Kendrick sailed in through the Strait of Juan de Fuca and around Vancouver Island. These ships were the first vessels ever to fly the American flag over the coastal waters of the Oregon Country.

The skins loaded at Nootka were taken to China, where they were sold for a high price. Then a cargo of tea was taken on to be carried back to Boston. Thus began the famous Yankee Triangle Trade which, in turn, led to a great discovery that gave the United States a sound claim to the Pacific Northwest.

In 1792 Captain Gray sailed the *Columbia* back to the Northwest. On that voyage he discovered the mouth of a great river. In order to be certain of his discovery, he sailed about thirty miles up the mighty stream, which he named "Columbia's River," now the Columbia, in honor of his ship. He then claimed for the United States all the territory drained by the river and its tributaries. This occurred May 11, 1792, one of the most important dates in the history of the Northwest. The discovery laid a firm foundation for our claim to the vast region beyond the Rockies, a claim soon to be strengthened by the Lewis and Clark Expedition, one of the most notable journeys ever undertaken by American explorers.

II. THE LEWIS AND CLARK EXPEDITION

AT THE OPENING of the nineteenth century, France owned most of the vast region in North America lying between the Mississippi River and the Rocky Mountains. In 1803 Napoleon, the emperor of France, was in great need of money to carry on his wars in Europe; therefore, he offered to sell to the United States for fifteen million dollars all the French lands in western North America. By accepting this offer, President Jefferson more than doubled the size of the United States and extended our national boundary westward to the crest of the Rockies.

Having purchased the Louisiana Territory, as the region was called, the President was naturally curious about the new addition to the nation. What sort of country had we bought? Were there really whole mountains of rock salt, as rumor said? Was it the home of monster beasts, as many people believed? Was it suitable for agriculture? Would it support a growing population? What were its natural resources? Would its native people, the Indians, prove to be peaceable or warlike?

To find the answer to these and other questions, Jefferson appointed his able private secretary, Meriwether Lewis, to lead an expedition across the newly acquired territory. Lewis asked that another officer share in the responsibilities of the expedition and, with Jefferson's approval, wrote to his boyhood friend, William

TWO CAPTAINS OF DESTINY

CAPTAIN MERIWETHER LEWIS
(Long Knife)

CAPTAIN WILLIAM CLARK
(Red Head)

These two leaders of the Lewis and Clark Expedition conducted one of the most important explorations in history, giving to the United States a second strong claim to the Oregon Country by right of exploration. (Lewis, left; Clark, right)

Clark, inviting him to accept the position. Jefferson's instructions to proceed to the Pacific before turning back showed that our leaders were even then looking forward to the day when the United States would spread from ocean to ocean. In fact, Lewis and Clark carried secret orders from the President himself to claim all the country between Louisiana Territory and the mouth of the Columbia River for the United States.

Up the Missouri River. Leaving St. Louis in the spring of 1804, the expedition toiled up the Missouri River in a large flat-bottomed keelboat and two smaller craft. Besides the leaders, there were about forty-three other men, most of whom were soldiers. Among them were Sergeant Charles Floyd, the only man who died on the journey; Sergeant John Ordway, assigned by Captain Lewis to make a record of the events of the expedition; Sergeant Patrick Gass, who kept a daily journal of events; Sergeant Nathaniel Pryor, who was afterward to have a distinguished military career and varied experiences on the frontier; George Drouillard, also known as George Drewyer, guide and interpreter; Peter Cruzatte, a French-Canadian *voyageur* and white-water man; York, Captain Clark's huge Negro servant, an object of wonder and admiration to the Indians; and John Colter, soon to become famous as a mountain man and as the discoverer of the region which became the Yellowstone National Park. Also, there was Brewster, or Scannon, Captain Lewis's large Newfoundland dog.

The going was slow against the current, and often the men had to take to the riverbank and draw the boats upstream by pulling on ropes. But eventually the expedition reached the Mandan Indian villages, not far from the present city of Mandan, North Dakota. There they established winter quarters and built a strong stockade as a protection against possible Indian attacks.

Sacajawea. When the expedition moved on westward the following spring, it was accompanied by a French-Canadian guide and interpreter named Charboneau (SHAR'bon-o), also spelled Chaboneau. But, more important, the guide's wife also accompanied the expedition, thereby becoming the most famous Indian woman in the history of the West.

This woman was Sacajawea, a Shoshone Indian, born, according to legend, in what later became the Lemhi Valley of Idaho. When only a young girl, she accompanied members of her band over the mountains on a hunting trip into what is now southwestern Montana. There the Shoshones were attacked by a war party of Minnetaree (min-ny-TAH-ree) or Gros Ventre (grow-VAUNT) Indians belonging to the Blackfeet Nation. Sacajawea was taken captive and later sold as a slave to a Mandan Indian. Charboneau is said to have either purchased her or won her in a gambling game from her Mandan master. Captain Clark, who had a favorite nickname for most members of his party, called her "Janey."

Long Knife and the Shoshones. Leaving the Mandan encampment, the explorers traveled on westward up the Missouri and its tributaries. Passing the Great Falls and the Three Forks, they continued up the Jefferson River, named in honor of the President, and "in which," a record of the expedition said, "are a multitude of beaver." They then followed the Beaverhead River until that stream became too small for canoe travel. Abandoning the boats, they went on by what is now Horse Prairie Creek in western Montana toward a pass they could see in the mountain range ahead.

Captain Lewis and three companions pushed ahead of the main party to try to find a way across the mountains. That night they camped near the summit of the main range of the Continental Divide, now known as the Beaverhead Range. At last they had reached the very heart of the Rockies, the "Shining Mountains" of the Indians.

The next morning, August 12, 1805, dawned bright and clear, one of the important dates in Idaho history. With George Drouillard, or Drewyer, carrying the Stars and Stripes, they crossed the summit and for the first time white men stood on what was to become Idaho soil and our nation's flag proclaimed the title of the United States to the land that faced the distant Pacific. The spot where the explorers stood is now called Lewis and Clark Pass, or sometimes Lemhi Pass, where the backbone of the continent separates the drainage flowing to the Atlantic and the Pacific oceans.

That night the men camped at a spring just over the divide. The next morning they met two Shoshone women and a girl, who conducted them toward the camp of their tribe. Before reaching it, they were met by a party of warriors led by Chief Cameahwait (KAM-e-a-wait). When the women explained how they had met the white men, the chief leaped from his horse and placed his arm over Lewis's shoulder, exclaiming, *"Ah hi e!"* meaning "I am much pleased."

The Shoshoni braves went back across the mountains with the explorers and helped bring the main expedition to the Indian camp on the Lemhi River. A particularly happy event took place when Sacajawea recognized the chief of the Shoshonis as her brother, whom, of course, she had not seen or heard from since her capture many years before.

Blocked by the River of No Return. The expedition rested a week among the friendly Shoshoni while scouts tried to find a way toward the west. But wild mountains and the even wilder Salmon River, the "River of No Return," presented a seemingly impassable barrier. So the explorers, led by an Indian nicknamed "Old Toby" by Captain Clark, went downstream to Fish Creek, now the North Fork of the Salmon River. This stream they ascended and crossed over into the Bitterroot Valley in western Montana. Continuing down this valley almost to where the city of Missoula now stands, they turned to the west up Lolo Creek, then known as Traveler's Rest Creek, over an old Indian trail. With great effort they crossed the Bitterroot Mountains through what is now Lolo Pass and reached a tributary of the Clearwater River, which the Indians called the Koos-koos-kia.

On the Lolo Trail. This section of Idaho has more snow than any other part of the state. In the year 1805 the travelers found game very scarce and the snow quite deep, even that early in the fall. To add to their hardships, their guide led them too far south and they got off the so-called trail. Growing very short of

Courtesy U.S. Forest Service

Photo by M. S. Benedict

THE RUGGED SALMON RIVER COUNTRY

*This view of the rugged country through which flows the "River of No Return" helps us to understand
why Lewis and Clark gave up their plan to continue westward by way of the Salmon River.*

food, they killed a colt to provide meat. This incident led them to call the stream on which they found themselves Colt-Killed Creek. On Idaho maps of today it is shown as White Sand Creek, a tributary of the Locksa (LOCK′saw) River.

As the season advanced the snow became deeper and they found the trail badly clogged with fallen timber. Many expedition members grew ill from lack of food and the hardships of the trail, which General Howard, three fourths of a century later, called the "most terrible trail on the continent of North America." But at last they reached the Wcippc (WEE-ipe) meadows, near the present village of Weippe, in Clearwater County. There they found a Nez Perce Indian village, where friendly natives took the travelers in and fed them so generously on strange foods that many became ill.

After a short rest the party pushed on down the present Jim Ford Creek to the Clearwater River. Where the North Fork joins the main stream, they established Canoe Camp and started work on five dugout canoes, made from large, straight pine trees found growing there. They then turned the few horses they had over to friendly Nez Perce Indians and embarked in the canoes for the remainder of the journey.

From the first the leaders of the expedition had been very careful to cultivate the good will of the Indian tribes along the way. They gave many gifts to the Indians who befriended them. To the chiefs they gave, among other gifts, medals bearing on one side the likeness of President Jefferson, the Great White Father, and on the other side a picture of clasped hands, signifying friendship. Several of these old medals have been found in Indian graves, proving that the Indians treasured them highly.

To the Pacific and Back. Thanks to the Nez Perce chief, Twisted Hair, who drew a map on white elkskin showing the way they must follow down the Snake and Columbia rivers, they were able to finish their journey without serious difficulties. They arrived at the mouth of the Columbia in November, 1805, and there built the first American outpost on the Pacific, naming it Fort Clatsop from the Indian tribe living there.

In the spring of 1806 they returned to their Nez Perce friends on the Clearwater. There, in Lawyers Canyon, near the present town of Kamiah (KAM-a-i) in Lewis County, a great council was held, in some ways one of the strangest councils ever described in history. Lewis and Clark gave their messages to the

HISTORIC MARKER AT CANOE CAMP

Here, at the present village of Ahsahka (Ah-SOCK-ah) in Clearwater County, the Lewis and Clark Expedition made dugout canoes with which to complete their journey to the Pacific.

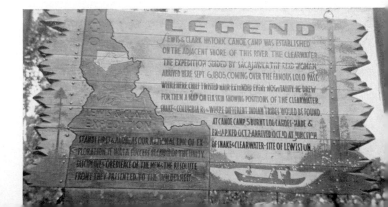

SACAJAWEA

SACAJAWEA MONUMENT IN PORTLAND, OREGON   *SACAJAWEA'S GRAVE IN WYOMING*

Sacajawea's services as interpreter and guide for Lewis and Clark gave her a secure place in history. She accompanied Charboneau to St. Louis after they returned to the Mandan villages. Sacajawea spent some time in Oklahoma, then went back to the Wind River Reservation in Wyoming. There she served her people until ripe old age, and there she died in 1884. On the sunny slopes of the Rockies she loved she "sleeps with her face toward the dawn."

Indians in English. Drouillard repeated them in French to Charboneau, who then gave them to Sacajawea in the Blackfoot dialect. Sacajawea interpreted them in the Shoshone tongue to a Shoshone warrior held captive by the Nez Perce, and he in turn gave the messages to the Indians in the Nez Perce language. One cannot help but wonder if the Nez Perces really got the messages as Lewis and Clark intended!

As soon as the melting snow permitted travel across the mountains, the expedition resumed its homeward journey. When it reached the Bitterroot Valley, it broke up into smaller parties in order to explore as much of the country as possible. These parties united again at the mouth of the Yellowstone River, then proceeded downstream to the Mandan country. There Charboneau and Sacajawea, so long the faithful friends and guides of the expedition leaders, left the party. So, too, did John Colter, who turned back with some white companions to trap the rich beaver waters through which they had passed. The main expedition continued on down the Missouri by boat to the Mandan villages and to St. Louis and a remarkably difficult and dangerous journey of more than two years and eight thousand miles came to an end.

But the effects lived on. As Olin D. Wheeler wrote in *The Trail of Lewis and Clark:*

Little did these men think, when they rounded to at St. Louis, on September 23, 1806, that they had completed the greatest exploration in modern times and that as its results were so far-reaching, so were their deeds to be treasured in the life of the Republic which they had so faithfully served; and that their children's children would be proud of the distinction which rested upon them because their grandsires were among those who crossed the continent with Lewis and Clark.

Truly, they were empire builders.

III. THE FUR-GATHERERS

THE LEWIS AND CLARK EXPEDITION proved that the Rocky Mountains and the upper reaches of streams having their sources in the Rockies abounded in beaver and other fur-bearing animals. At that time beaver fur was in great demand, for it was used in making the high beaver hats which were so extensively worn by fashionably dressed men in both Europe and America. It was, therefore, certain that daring trappers and traders would soon venture into the fur lands, braving Indians, wild beasts, severe winters, and other dangers and hardships in order to gather the plentiful peltries so greatly in demand.

The fur industry was already well established in America. Two great English companies, the North West Company and the Hudson's Bay Company, had long been active in Canada and the Red River district of what is now Minnesota and North Dakota. John Jacob Astor and his American Fur Company, with headquarters in New York City, had already built a sizable fortune in the fur business. We shall now see how these and other fur-gatherers pushed into the Oregon Country, exploring the region and opening the way for the missionaries and settlers who followed them in about a quarter century.

The North West Company and Kullyspell House. Since about 1775 the North West Company had been taking furs between the Great Lakes and the Rocky Mountains. Among the Nor'Westers, as they called themselves, were several men who were to play leading parts in the early history of the Oregon Country, including what is now Idaho. You have, perhaps, read of David Thompson, "Big Finan" McDonald, Alexander Ross, Dr. John McLoughlin, Donald McKenzie, John Day, and David Stuart. These and others were among the daring, hard-driving Nor'Westers, the first fur-gatherers to enter our land of Idaho.

The bold leaders of the North West Company were among the most remarkable explorers our continent has ever known. One of them, Alexander Mackenzie, was the first pathfinder to cross North America north of the Spanish lands, reaching what is now British Columbia and the Pacific in 1793. Writing about these men of the North West Company,[1] Robert Pinkerton gave this excellent summary (condensed) of their achievements:

They were called Roaring Nor'Westers, Thunderbolts of Montreal, and Lords of the Lakes and Forests. Never in the development of North America did a small group accomplish so much in so many ways in so short a time, in two decades exploring farther than all others in two centuries. They were a thousand miles beyond civilization before Daniel Boone went over the [Appalachian] mountains into Kentucky, and

[1]From *Blue Book* magazine for November, 1948. Used by special permission.

they reached the Pacific before Boone crossed the Mississippi. They visited the Mandans on the Missouri six years ahead of Lewis and Clark, and eight years later had opened trade with the Indians in Idaho, Montana, Washington, Oregon, and British Columbia.

In the history of Idaho, David Thompson looms as the most impressive figure among the Nor'Westers. In 1809 he came down from Canada and built a trading post which he named Kullyspell House. This was on the northeastern shore of Lake Pend Oreille, not far from the present town of Hope, and was the first building ever erected by white men on Idaho soil. Today a historical marker stands in memory of this achievement.

A short time later Spokane House, in northeastern Washington, and Saleesh House, in northwestern Montana, were built under Thompson's direction. These, with Kullyspell House, controlled trade with the Spokane, Kootenai, Pend Oreille, Coeur d'Alene, and Flathead Indians. The posts also drew trade from surrounding territory inhabited by other tribes.

Though employed by the North West Company, Thompson clearly considered himself an agent for the extension of the British Empire. Where the Snake River joined the Columbia, he posted the following notice:

Know hereby that this country is claimed by Great Britain as part of its territories, and that the N. W. Company of Merchants from Canada do hereby intend to erect a factory [trading post] at this place for the commerce of the country around. D. Thompson, junction of the Shawpatin [Snake] River with the Columbia, July 9, 1811.

Thompson's promise was fulfilled in 1818 when Donald McKenzie, a former Astorian, built Fort Nez Perces, later Fort Walla Walla, and placed Alexander Ross in charge. This post, though in the present state of Washington, was important in the history of Idaho because later trapping and trading expeditions into the Snake River country of southern Idaho often started from there.

Thompson was a careful historian and map maker. The records he made and the maps he drew of the Northwest are still valuable sources of study for modern historians and geographers. His work is found to be remarkably accurate when we understand that Thompson himself never visited much of the region included, but depended upon descriptions supplied by his trappers and by the Indians.

The Missouri Fur Company and Fort Henry. Even before Kullyspell House was built by David Thompson, the first American company to enter the fur trade in the Oregon Country was organized in St. Louis in 1808. This was the St. Louis Missouri Fur Company. Two partners in this company, Andrew Henry and Pierre Menard, led a trapping expedition to the vicinity of the Three Forks of the Missouri River in 1810. Attacks by Blackfeet Indians brought death to several trappers, among them George Drouillard, who had, as you recall, been with Lewis and Clark.

Menard, with part of the men, returned to St. Louis. Led by Henry, the rest of the trappers went up the Madison River and crossed over the Continental Divide to the vicinity of Drummond, in what is now Fremont County, Idaho. Here they apparently camped for some time in September, 1810, for boulders have been found recently which bear the following carved inscriptions: "Camp Henry" and "Sep 1810." Another stone close by has the following names carved on it, together with the date 1810:

A HENRY

T HOBACK

P MCBRIDE

B JACKSON

L CATHER[2]

After a temporary stay on Conant Creek, the party moved on to the timbered bottoms below the present city of St. Anthony and there they built some log cabins to serve as a winter shelter and headquarters while they traded with friendly Shoshone Indians. Known in history as Fort Henry, this was the second trading post in Idaho and the first in southern Idaho.

After Fort Henry was abandoned, it soon fell into decay and the location was lost. Accidentally rediscovered, on the William McMinn farm seven miles north of Rexburg, the site was excavated in 1927 and two stones uncovered. One bore the inscription "Gov't Camp 1811 H. Wells" and the other the words "Al the cook but nothing to cook." In December, 1933, Dr. M. D. Beal, John Elliot, and Milton and Clifford Mangum made further excavations which uncovered the sites of the old cabins. They also found another stone inscribed "Fort Henry 1811 by Cap. Hunt."[3] A historical marker now stands on the site of the original location of Fort Henry.

The Pacific Fur Company and the

[2]From material furnished by Margaret Hawkes Lindsley, Drummond, Idaho.

[3]From an article, "History of Fort Henry," by Samuel M. Beal, in *Seeing Idaho,* September, 1937. Published by Graves & Potter, Inc., Pocatello, Idaho.

Astorians. Organized in 1810 as a part of the far-spreading fur enterprises of John Jacob Astor, this company had a part in some of the most dramatic events in the history of Idaho and the Northwest. A ship, the *Tonquin,* was sent to the mouth of the Columbia River, where a trading post was built, called Astoria, in honor of the head of the company.

In 1810 a land expedition, led by Wilson Price Hunt, set out from St. Louis to go overland to Astoria. The Astorians, as they were called, came up the Missouri River, wintered, and then struck out westward across the present states of South Dakota and Wyoming. They entered Idaho by way of Pierre's Hole, now Teton Basin, in the fall of 1811. Stopping at abandoned Fort Henry, they made fifteen dugout canoes in which they proposed to continue the journey by water down the Snake River. Then they left their horses with friendly Indians and embarked, little dreaming of the roaring cascades and thundering waterfalls that lay below them on "Mad River," as French-Canadian boatmen often called the Snake.

They successfully passed the falls and rapids where the cities of Idaho Falls and American Falls now stand. A few miles farther down, however, near the present Milner Dam, death struck without warning. At a place they named Caldron Linn, or the Devil's Scuttle Hole, one of their dugouts was capsized and Antoine Clappine, a boatman, was drowned. Convinced by this time that the river was too dangerous to follow, they made nine caches (CASH-es), or hiding places, in which to leave most of their supplies and equipment. Then the expedition was divided into smaller parties for continuing the journey.

One party, led by Donald McKenzie, who later worked for the North West Company, followed a general northwest course and found its way through the mountains of central Idaho to the mouth of the Clearwater River. Traveling down the Snake and Columbia rivers, they eventually reached Astoria.

Ramsey Crooks, with another part of the expedition, kept to the south and west side of the Snake River until stopped by the great Snake River Canyon, below the present city of Weiser. Finding it impossible to continue through the canyon, they turned and retraced their way back upstream.

The rest of the expedition, led by Hunt himself, stayed north of Snake River and succeeded after great hardships in reaching what is now the Boise River. They crossed this stream and two others, later named the Payette and Weiser rivers. Then they, too, were halted by the terrific canyon and wild mountains of the Seven Devils country. As they returned along the stream, they were hailed by the Crooks party on the opposite bank, which then crossed the river and rejoined Hunt's men.

At an Indian village on the Weiser River the reunited party secured some horses and an Indian guide. The guide led them across the Blue Mountains to the Columbia, down which they traveled to Astoria. There McKenzie and his men, who had arrived earlier, were awaiting them.

The Astorians thus completed, after eleven months of almost continuous travel, great toil, and suffering, another of the remarkable exploring expeditions through the Northwest. The winding course they followed carried them over three thousand miles of plains, mountains, and deserts, much of it never before visited by white men. The Hunt Expedition did for southern Idaho what the Lewis and Clark Expedition did for northern Idaho: it made the region known to the outside world.

Hunt went on a visit to Russian trading posts far to the north, and while he was away the War of 1812 broke out. This event caused Astor's representatives to sell Astoria to the North West Company, as they feared the post would be captured by the British. The Astorians then broke up into small groups to explore the country, trap for beaver, and trade with the Indians.

The Reed Massacre. The Hunt explorations had shown the mountain streams to be alive with beaver. In 1813 a party of trappers under John Reed returned to what was soon to become known as the Boise River. There, early in 1814, he and his men became the victims of the first Indian massacre recorded in the history of Idaho, all of the men being slain. Madame Dorion, the wife of one of the trappers, escaped, with her two children, and made her way over the Blue Mountains to the friendly Walla Wallas, a heroic journey filled with almost unbelievable suffering and hardships. The Reed massacre and the Dorion journey were a part of the terrible price paid by the earliest pioneers in helping to pave the way for the later settlement and development of the great Northwest.

Return of the Astorians. In the summer of 1812 Robert Stuart gathered what was left of the Astorians for the return to St. Louis. Almost in reverse of their earlier journey westward, they retraced their way. Back they went across the Snake River Plains to Pierre's Hole. Then, by way of Jackson's Hole and the Hoback River, they reached Green River in western Wyoming. From Green River they crossed the Continental Divide through South Pass, which they are credited with discovering, and continued on by way of the Platte and Missouri rivers to St. Louis.

There are at least three reasons why the Astorians deserve an important place in Idaho history: (1) They spent considerable time in southern Idaho and discovered in a tragic manner that the Snake River could not be used as a water route through the Snake River Valley. (2) The establishment of Astoria and Hunt's overland expedition gave the United States an additional strong claim to the Oregon Country by right of exploration and occupation. (3) On the return journey the Astorians followed quite closely, with minor exceptions, the route of travel soon to become famous as the Oregon Trail.

The John Day Legend. Of special interest to Idahoans is the story of John Day, a member of the Hunt Expedition. Day later trapped for the North West Company in Oregon and Idaho. The John Day River in Oregon is named in his honor, as are several other places and things, including one of the residential streets in Pocatello.

Though several sites have been claimed as his burial place, it seems well established that he died in eastern Idaho in 1820. A will written by Day was probated in 1836 by his friend, Donald Mc-

Kenzie, and is on record in Chautauqua County, New York. This is the first will ever written in Idaho.

In 1935 the Idaho Falls Chapter of the Sons of the American Revolution built a monument at a site which they believe marks his grave. This is on Birch Creek, not far from State Highway 28, between Roberts and Leadore. A sign along the highway points to the location of the grave and monument.

Horse Brigades to the Snake Country. After the Pacific Fur Company sold Astoria to its English rival, the North West Company, the Nor'Westers soon extended their trapping and trading operations into many parts of the Oregon Country. To supplement the business carried on by the trading posts, they sent expeditions called horse brigades into fur-rich areas both to trap and trade with the Indian tribes inhabiting the regions. These trapping and trading journeys became known as the Snake Country Expeditions and were continued for about a score of years.

From 1818 to 1821 the Snake Country Expeditions were led by Donald ("Perpetual Motion") McKenzie. This furgatherer, called by Dr. Brosnan, in his *History of the State of Idaho,* "the ablest trapper who ever left his track along the shrub-embowered streams of Idaho," operated from Fort Nez Perces. He trapped extensively along the streams of Idaho and is credited with naming several of them.

Two famous beaver streams of that time were the two we now call the Big Wood River and Camas Creek. Trapping along the latter stream, McKenzie's men were made ill by eating the tails of bea-

FUR-GATHERERS' LAND OF PROMISE

Along lonely lakes and mountain streams in the Idaho wilderness, fur-gatherers of long ago risked their lives in constant toil and danger.

vers that had fed on certain plants. From this incident the stream was named Malade (also spelled Malad) River, *malade* being a French word meaning sick. Until fairly recent times many of the older residents called the valley basin in southern Camas County, now known as Big Camas Prairie, the Malade Basin. In fact, the old name of Malade River is still sometimes used to designate the stream above its entry into Magic Reservoir.

Do you wonder what it would have been like to have gone with a horse brigade on a trapping journey to the Snake Country? Alexander Ross, one of the great leaders of the fur-gatherers, left an account of such a journey in his famous book, *Fur Hunters of the Far West*. Here, greatly condensed, is the story of his expedition.

Ross started from Spokane House in the winter of 1824. With him he took forty men, adding fifteen more in the Flathead Indian country of what is now northern Idaho and western Montana. His band consisted of two Americans, seventeen Canadians, five half-breeds, twelve Iroquois, two Abinakas, two Nipissings, one Solteau, two Crees, one Chinook, three Flatheads, one Palouse, and one Snake Indian, as the Shoshones were usually called. About half the men were married to Indian women and took their families along. These added twenty-five women and sixty-four children to the party. The cavalcade traveled with 392 horses and made a procession more than a mile long when on the march. Imagine, if you can, feeding and caring for such a motley crew, to say nothing of directing their work!

Ross led the brigade into Montana and then traveled south up the Bitterroot Valley. Crossing the Continental Divide over what is now Gibbons Pass to the Big Hole River, he entered Idaho through the Lewis and Clark (Lemhi) Pass, the same route Lewis and Clark had followed. Traveling up the Salmon River, the expedition crossed to the headwaters of the Boise River, then known as Reed's River. The trappers worked the Boise River, Payette River, and the Weiser River territory, then moved back to the east. There they trapped the beaver colonies of the Malade (Camas Creek), Big Wood River, and Godin's (Big Lost) River. Crossing back to the Pahsimeroi River, probably through what is now called Double Springs Pass, they trapped that stream and the Lemhi River. Ross then took the expedition back to Flathead Post, in western Montana, where it was disbanded. The take

was about five thousand beaver skins, worth a sizable fortune at the high prices the furs commanded in those days.

The Hudson's Bay Company. This famous English fur company was given a charter by King Charles II in 1670 under the official name, "The Governor and Company of Adventurers of England Trading into Hudson's Bay." Having almost complete control of all the region around Hudson Bay, the company, through its factories or trading posts, carried on an extensive business in eastern and central Canada for nearly 150 years before turning its attention toward the Rocky Mountain West. In 1821 the Hudson's Bay Company and the North West Company combined. Thereafter, using the name of the older Hudson's Bay Company, the new company took over the trading posts already established in the Oregon Country by the North West Company and became a powerful rival of the American companies operating in the region.

The Oregon Country was organized as the Columbia District and placed under the charge of Dr. John McLoughlin. Fort Vancouver was built on the north bank of the Columbia four or five miles above and opposite the mouth of the Willamette River. This became the headquarters of the company, displacing Astoria, which the British renamed Fort George.

For about a score of years the Hudson's Bay Company continued the Snake Country Expeditions that had been started under the North West Company. Finan McDonald, the redheaded giant who had been Thompson's right-hand man at Kullyspell House and other trading posts, led the first horse brigade after the Hudson's Bay Company took charge. He was succeeded the following year by Alexander Ross, about whose expedition we read in an earlier topic.

The third Snake Country Expedition was led by Peter Skene Ogden, for whom Ogden, Utah, is named. This expedition, which reached the vicinity of the upper end of the Great Salt Lake, was not as successful financially as was hoped for, chiefly because American trappers and traders of the Rocky Mountain Fur Company were in the region at the same time and paid much higher prices for beaver pelts than Ogden had been authorized to give. Also, a considerable number of Ogden's men deserted him and joined the American trappers. However, Ogden led several other brigades, and his wide travel and exploration in what is now Idaho, Utah, Nevada, northern California, and other parts of the West, rank him as one of the most important leaders of the Hudson's Bay Company.

John Work, who led the expedition of 1830–31, wrote an account of his journey which is of special interest to students of Idaho history.[4] His harvest of peltries, gathered on such streams as the Wazer (Weiser), Payette, Boise, Big Lost and Little Lost rivers, and on the upper sources of Snake River in eastern Idaho and western Wyoming, brought large revenues to the company and much danger to the leader and his men. By that time the Indians were beginning to show increasing hostility toward the white trappers and traders who entered the In-

DOCTOR JOHN McLOUGHLIN

After his retirement as head of the Columbia District of the Hudson's Bay Company, Dr. McLoughlin moved to Oregon City on the Willamette River and became an American citizen.

dian country. This extract is from a letter John Work wrote after returning from his expedition: "I am happy in being able to inform you that I enjoy good health, and am yet blessed with the possession of my scalp which is rather more than I had reason to expect."

The choice of Dr. McLoughlin to head the company in the Oregon Country was a particularly wise one. For more than twenty years he controlled most of the activities, including the colorful horse brigades, of a region nearly one fourth as large as the present United States. His rule was firm but just. His friendly hos-

---

[4]*The Journal of John Work* . . . edited by William S. Lewis and Paul C. Phillips (Cleveland: The Arthur H. Clark Company, 1923).

pitality and aid to all, whether English or American, Indian or white, endeared him to almost everyone. To the Indians he was known as the "White Headed Eagle," while among the white inhabitants he earned the title of "Father of Oregon."

The Rocky Mountain Fur Company and the Rendezvous. The various fur companies, both British and American, had been the means of developing a hardy and daring breed of men who were most at home when following the fur trails of the West. Known as mountain men, they braved the severest hardships, outwitted and outfought hostile Indians, often married Indian women, and spent most of their lives in the wilderness. No dangers or difficulties were too great to face if bales of prime beaver skins promised to be the reward.

Such were the men who formed the hard core of the last great American fur company to operate in the Rocky Mountains. Very appropriately, it was named the Rocky Mountain Fur Company. Organized in St. Louis in 1823 by General William H. Ashley and Major Andrew Henry, the company sent its fur-gatherers into the mountains at the very peak of the fur harvest. In carrying on their work, they trapped every promising beaver stream in southern Idaho, western Wyoming, and northern Utah, some of them several times. They thus learned at first hand the geography of the region, a matter of the greatest importance when settlers began moving into the Northwest a little later on.

The mountain men of this organization constituted a special hall of fame for the Rockies of those years, among them the two organizers. General Ashley was for many years closely connected with the fur trade and himself led several expeditions to the Northwest. Major Henry was already famous as the builder of Fort Henry and had personally conducted several trapping and trading journeys into the Rocky Mountains. Jedediah ("Jed") Smith, the "Praying Trapper," who became a partner in the company, blazed a brilliant trail of exploration in the West for ten years before Comanche lances ended his career. The Sublette brothers, William and Milton, moved in and out among the valleys and ranges of the Middle Rockies and on the Snake River Plains. James ("Old Gabe") Bridger, the "Blanket Chief," located his famed trading post, Fort Bridger, on a tributary of Green River before the end of this golden age of the trappers. David Jackson, who gave his name to Jackson's Hole, emerged from obscurity long enough to become a partner in the company before he again disappeared into the historical mists that shroud this period. Old Pierre Tivanitagon, whose name lives on in the designation Pierre's Hole, now Teton Basin, led his Iroquois Indians into many parts of the intermountain West before being slain by the Blackfeet on the upper sources of the Missouri.

Other great names of the era were either those of men of the Rocky Mountain Fur Company or of those who had dealings with it in various ways: Hugh Glass, famed for his terrible fight with a grizzly and his incredible journey afterward; Thomas ("Broken Hand") Fitzpatrick, quartermaster of the Ashley expedition of 1823 and on whose trail wild adventure loved to lurk; Henry Fraeb and Robert Campbell; Edward Rose, the "Crow" man; James P. Beckwourth, whose *Life and Adventures* earned him the title of "gaudy liar"; Etienne Provost (or Provot), for whom Provo, Utah, is named; Mike Fink, king of keelboaters; Joe Meek and Robert Newell, both closely connected with the history of Idaho and Oregon; Colonel William Craig, Idaho's first homesteader; Kit Carson, the peerless scout and Indian fighter; and others almost equally renowned whose names we cannot mention for lack of space.

Finding it too expensive to build and maintain trading posts after the British fashion, the Rocky Mountain Fur Company invented a method that leaped into almost instant popularity after being introduced by General Ashley himself on Green River in 1825. Under this plan the company, as well as other fur-gatherers in the same general territory, held an annual meeting called a rendezvous[5] at a place agreed upon in advance. To the rendezvous came trappers and Indians to exchange their furs for traps, guns, ammunition, clothing, food, and other needed supplies, all of which were brought overland, usually from St. Louis. In addition to equipment and supplies for the trappers, there were supplies of goods intended especially for the Indian trade. Usually known among the mountain men as fofarraw (FOO-fah-raw), these consisted of colored glass beads, brightly colored cloth, ribbons, earrings, mirrors, and similar articles that appealed to the Indians' love of bright colors and trinkets.

[5]Rendezvous (REN-de-voo). An appointed meeting place; to meet by appointment.

The Green River Valley in western Wyoming was a favorite place for holding the rendezvous, but such gatherings were often held at other places. Jackson's Hole, Bear Lake Valley, Cache Valley, Salmon River Valley, and other places were scenes of these summer encampments, which usually lasted two or three weeks, or longer. The rendezvous of 1829 was in Pierre's Hole, as was also that of 1832.

The second rendezvous in Pierre's Hole, in the summer of 1832, is the most noted gathering of the kind ever held in Idaho. Present were representatives of the American Fur Company and the Rocky Mountain Fur Company, as well as free trappers, men who worked for themselves and sold their furs to whoever offered the best prices. Nathaniel Wyeth, a newcomer in Idaho but headed for undying fame as the builder of Fort Hall, was there. Toward the rendezvous Captain Bonneville was pushing with might and main, but he did not arrive until after the encampment had broken up. The Arkansas mountain man, Sinclair, leader of the free trappers, maintained a separate camp, as did large encampments of Nez Perce and Flathead Indians.

At the close of this rendezvous occurred the battle of Pierre's Hole, one of the bitterest fights between whites and Indians that ever took place in Idaho. It was brought about by a chance meeting between the newly arrived band of Blackfeet Indians and Antoine Godin, or Goddin, whose father had been killed by Blackfeet. When the parties met, Godin, and a Flathead Indian with him, killed the leader of the Blackfeet and the fight was on. The Blackfeet took refuge in a near-by wooded swamp as other trappers came racing in to aid the whites. The battle raged far into the night but the outcome was never in doubt, especially after the Nez Perces and Flatheads arrived and took part on the side of the trappers. During the fighting Sinclair was killed, Captain William Sublette received a bullet in the shoulder, and several others, both white and Indian, lost their lives. During the night the Blackfeet slipped away, leaving the mountain men and their Indian allies the victors in the bloody and useless battle.

The rendezvous flourished for almost a score of years. Constant trapping, however, soon decreased the number of fur-bearing animals so much that not enough furs could be taken to make the venture profitable. Too, silk hats became fashionable and beaver hats were no longer in great demand. As a result, most of the mountain men turned to other ways of making a living. But in its heyday (hay-day), at the height of the trapping era, there were no wilder or more picturesque assemblies on the North American continent than these annual rendezvous of the fur-gatherers in remote valleys of the Rocky Mountains.

Captain Bonneville, the Bald Chief. Among the fur-gatherers there was one who gathered more fame than furs. This was Captain Benjamin L. E. Bonneville, to whom the Indians gave the descriptive title of the "Bald Chief."

Bonneville was an officer on leave of absence from the army. He arrived in Idaho by the usual Jackson's Hole route in 1832 and returned to the East in 1835. His travels, and those of his principal aides during this three-year period, cov-

ered a large part of the Pacific Northwest, lending strength to the belief now held that he acted as an undercover agent of the United States, sent to keep a watchful eye on the Hudson's Bay Company. Among the places he and his chief agents visited in Idaho were Pierre's Hole, the Upper Snake River Valley, Portneuf Valley, Upper Cache Valley, Bear Lake Valley, the Salmon-Lemhi Valley, the Lost River section, Wood River Valley, and the Boise Valley.

It is said that the Bonneville party gave its modern name to the Boise River, which had generally been called Reed's River, after John Reed, who, with his men, had been killed there by Indians about a score of years earlier. Bonneville's men had spent some time on the desert plains north of the Snake River. When they came out on the hills overlooking the valley, French Canadians with the party exclaimed in admiration, *"Les bois, les bois! Voyez les bois!"* meaning "The woods, the woods! See the woods!" From that time on the stream has been known as the Boise River.[6] It would, perhaps, be more accurate to say that the Bonneville party popularized the name rather than originating it. The journals of Peter Skene Ogden for the years 1824–26, published in the *Hudson's Bay Book* in London in 1950, show that on Wednesday, October 19, 1825, the Ogden party "reached the waters of the River Boisse and encamped." In the same journal he also called the stream the "Rivière Boisier" and "Ried's" River. While it is probably true that the name was a refer-

[6]Hiram Taylor French, *History of Idaho* (3 vols.; Chicago: Lewis Publishing Company, 1914). Original account given in Washington Irving's *Adventures of Captain Bonneville*.

ence to the trees growing along the river, to whom we are actually indebted for its modern name may forever remain a secret.

Bonneville's explorations drew attention to the Oregon Country, particularly southern Idaho, at a time when both England and the United States were building up their claims for a final showdown on the ownership of the region. His work aroused public interest and strengthened our determination to make the Oregon Country a part of the United States.

The Boston Iceman and Old Fort Hall. A young businessman of Boston, Nathaniel Wyeth, had become interested in the profitable Triangle Trade being carried on by New England shipowners. He decided to lead an expedition overland to engage in trapping and in the trade of the Northwest. As we have seen, Wyeth and his party were at the rendezvous in Pierre's Hole in 1832. There he joined Milton Sublette's trappers and accompanied them as far south as the Portneuf River before turning west across the Snake River Plains and going on to Vancouver. At that post he learned that his ship, loaded with supplies intended for the Northwest trade, had been lost at sea.

Returning to southern Idaho, Wyeth spent some time with Captain Bonneville and attended the Green River rendezvous. There he made a contract with the Rocky Mountain Fur Company to bring a supply of merchandise to the rendezvous the following year.

Wyeth's wagons, heavily loaded with trade goods and other supplies, arrived at the rendezvous in the summer of 1834.

But the Rocky Mountain Fur Company was having a hard time making enough to pay operating expenses, and when Wyeth came with the goods, the company refused to accept them. Angered by the breach of contract, Wyeth pushed on west to Snake River. There on the bottoms, a few miles to the west of the present town of Fort Hall, he began building his trading post. In a letter written the same year to an uncle, Wyeth gave this description of the post:

. . . I have built a fort on Snake or Lewis River which I have named Fort Hall for the oldest gentleman in the concern. We manufactured a magnificent flag from some unbleached sheeting, a little red flannel and a few blue patches—and it makes, I do assure you, a very respectable appearance amid the dry and desolate regions.[7]

For about a score of years Fort Hall was the center of activities in southeastern Idaho. Its chief importance was as a stopping place on the Oregon Trail, then beginning to be recognized as the only really useful route of travel between the Mississippi and Missouri river towns and the Oregon Country. As early as 1834 missionaries were going into the Northwest, and at Fort Hall, on July 27, Jason Lee preached the first sermon ever delivered in Idaho.

Fort Boise Built to Strangle Fort Hall. The same year that Wyeth built Fort Hall, the Hudson's Bay Company sent Thomas McKay to build a post about midway between Fort Hall and Fort Walla Walla. The site he selected was near the mouth of the Boise River.

[7]From *The Correspondence and Journals of Nathaniel J. Wyeth*, edited by F. G. Young (Eugene, Oregon: University of Oregon, 1899).

OLD FORT HALL, IDAHO
reconstructed and painted by W. H. Jackson on the basis of material
red from Major Osborne Cross's report, and other descriptions of the
.e. Engraving from *Forced-Wagon Centennial and Ox-Team Days*.
Copyright 1932 by World Book Company, Publishers,
Yonkers-on-Hudson, New York.

TWO FAMOUS IDAHO TRADING POSTS

OLD FORT HALL

Built by Wyeth in 1834 as a trading post, Fort Hall was one of the most noted places on the Oregon Trail. The post was operated until 1855, then abandoned. A historic marker now shows the location.

OLD FORT BOISE

Like Fort Hall, Fort Boise was a noted stopping place on the Oregon Trail. Also like Fort Hall, no trace remains today of this frontier establishment.

There he erected the first, or temporary, Fort Boise. That the location was well chosen for trade among the Indians is shown by this extract from Nathaniel Wyeth's records of his first trip through the region, before either Fort Hall or Fort Boise had been constructed. Wyeth camped near where Old Fort Boise was built, and there he was visited by Indians anxious to trade. He wrote:

A large number of Indians were assembled around, all of whom had bundles of fish, which they were anxious to dispose of. The price of a dried salmon is a straight aul and a small fish-hook, value about one cent. . . . A beaver skin can be had for a variety of little matters which cost about twelve and a half cents; value in Boston from eight to ten dollars.[8]

After Fort Boise was built, the Hudson's Bay Company placed Francis Payette in charge of the new post with instructions to pay such prices for furs and to sell supplies so cheaply that Wyeth would find it impossible to continue in

[8]*Ibid.*

business in the Snake River country. In 1836 this policy compelled Wyeth to sell out to his rivals, at a loss, he reported, of $30,000.

In 1838 Payette built a new post, also called Fort Boise. This was near the present city of Parma. There Payette continued to represent the Hudson's Bay Company for several years. The post was never a very profitable enterprise but, like Fort Hall, it was a well-known stopping place on the Oregon Trail.

Both Fort Hall and Fort Boise were abandoned by the Hudson's Bay Company in 1855, nine years after the region had become a part of the United States. Some years later our government paid the company $650,000 in full settlement of all claims and the last English posts in what is now Idaho soon fell into decay. Now only historic markers remind us of these once busy outposts of civilization on the dry and dusty Snake River Plains, which, in their day, witnessed so much heroism and sacrifice on the part of those who staged a great drama in pioneering

American development of the Pacific Northwest.

Fort Hall to Rise Again? Largely through the efforts of the Oregon Trail Memorial Association, interest in old Fort Hall has been kept alive. In 1947 Congress passed a bill authorizing the Indian Service to construct a memorial building near the site of the old trading post. If and when built, the structure will probably serve both as a historical museum and as a place to keep alive and encourage interest and trade in Indian arts and crafts. Actual construction must await the appropriation of money sufficient to pay the cost of the building. This may not be done unless Idaho people keep the matter alive and succeed in getting Congress to set aside funds sufficient for the purpose.

Our Debt to the Fur-Gatherers. The fur-gatherers first proved the value of the Pacific Northwest. The abundant furs— sea otter along the coast and beaver on inland streams and lakes—were the basis for a huge business involving thousands of men and millions of dollars. In the course of carrying on this business, the geography as well as many of the resources of the Oregon Country became known. The men who were actively engaged in the field, which included at one time or another most of the men employed in the business of furs, gave romance, dash, and color to the history of the region by their deeds, both famous and infamous. The records they kept, scanty though they were, are almost the only history we have of that period. Many of the trails they blazed became routes of travel and transportation for emigrants who, a little later, populated the country.

Some of the fur-gatherers afterward acted as interpreters, guides, and protectors for the emigrant wagon trains. Many of them settled down to become farmers and business and professional men, strengthening the foundations of the modern and fruitful civilization which makes the Oregon Country of today a very important part of our nation and one which contributes so much to our national life.

*   *   *   *   *

The Pacific Northwest was too large in extent, too rich in natural resources, and too magnificent in scenery to remain unexplored and unknown indefinitely. In this unit we have taken a quick look at some of the men whose efforts and courage gave the world its first knowledge of the region: sailors of Spain, England, and the United States who explored portions of the Pacific coast; discoverers like Gray and Vancouver whose work established American and English claims to the region; men of the Lewis and Clark and the Wilson Price Hunt expeditions who made important overland journeys of exploration; and the fur-gatherers who laid out a network of trails which spread like a web throughout the Northwest. Some of these men lived to see the great tide of immigration begin its flow, and to know that by their labors, their sacrifices, and the blood of their comrades and coworkers, they had helped to establish a new and important part of the United States beyond the great wall of the Rocky Mountains. How this came to pass we shall see in the next unit of our Idaho story.

Settling and Dividing the Oregon Country

How the Oregon Trail came to be; how missionaries and settlers followed that historic thoroughfare to carry American institutions and the American way of life beyond the Rockies; how the United States gained the Oregon Country; and how the Mormons established permanent settlements in Idaho.

DISCOVERING A REGION or exploring it is not enough to give a nation undisputed title. The actual occupation, living on the land, is what counts in the long run. Now let us see how the Oregon Country was settled and how it was finally divided between the United States and England in a way acceptable to both.

I. SETTLEMENTS OF THE FUR-GATHERERS

IN WHAT IS NOW IDAHO the fur-gatherers established only four trading posts: Kullyspell House, Fort Henry, Fort Hall, and Fort Boise. None of these was permanent, though the last two were in operation for more than a score of years.

At several places in the Oregon Country, however, farming and stock raising were carried on in connection with the fur trade. Around Fort Vancouver, Fort Colville, and Fort Nisqually, all in what is now Washington, hundreds of acres were under cultivation. Sizable herds of cattle were maintained as well as considerable numbers of horses, hogs, and sheep.

It was the practice in some Hudson's Bay posts for trappers and others connected with the fur business to retire to farms close by when they decided to turn to other work. In this way, for example, men from Fort Vancouver moved into the valleys of the Willamette and Cowlitz rivers and began farming years before the region became part of the United States. Can you suggest reasons why similar settlements did not grow up around old Fort Hall and Fort Boise?

In the 1840's, when overtrapping and falling prices brought about a sharp decline in the fur business in the Northwest, many men who had followed the trap lines turned to farming and other occupations. The extent of agricultural development that had taken place is shown by the fact that when the United States paid the Hudson's Bay Company for its properties south of the forty-ninth parallel, the sum of $200,000 was listed as payment for agricultural properties of various kinds.

Thus, the fur-gatherers were the first actual white settlers in the Oregon Country. They proved beyond doubt that the

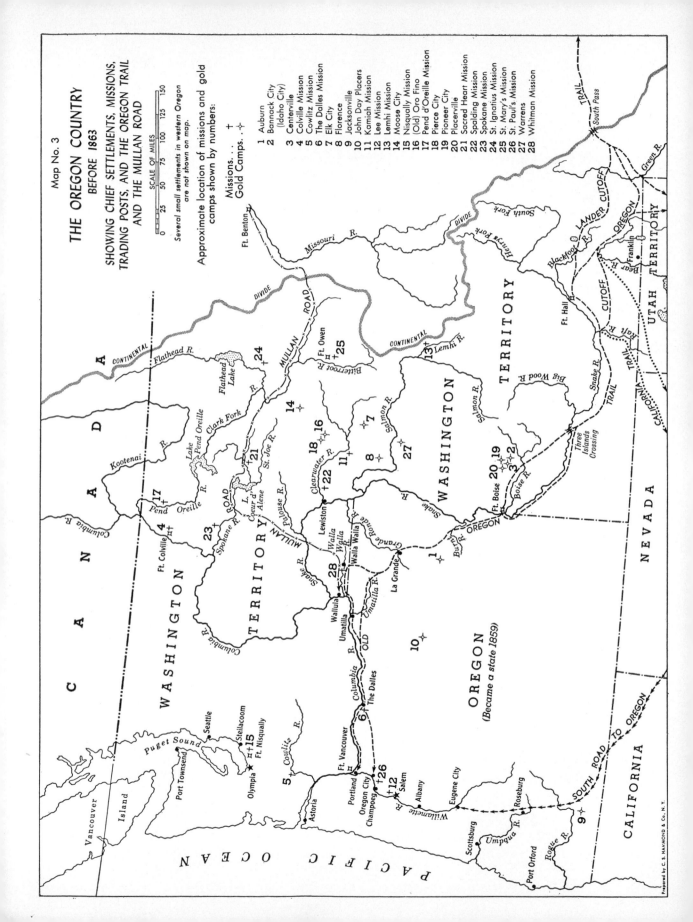

Map No. 3

THE OREGON COUNTRY
BEFORE 1863

SHOWING CHIEF SETTLEMENTS, MISSIONS,
TRADING POSTS, AND THE OREGON TRAIL
AND THE MULLAN ROAD

SCALE OF MILES

0   25   50   75   100   125   150

Several small settlements in western Oregon
are not shown on map.

Approximate location of missions and gold
camps shown by numbers:

Missions . . . . +
Gold Camps . . ✧

1	Auburn
2	Bannack City (Idaho City)
3	Centerville
4	Colville Mission
5	Cowlitz Mission
6	The Dalles Mission
7	Elk City
8	Florence
9	Jacksonville
10	John Day Placers
11	Kamiah Mission
12	Lee Mission
13	Lemhi Mission
14	Moose City
15	Nisqually Mission
16	(Old) Oro Fino
17	Pend d'Oreille Mission
18	Pierce City
19	Pioneer City
20	Placerville
21	Sacred Heart Mission
22	Spalding Mission
23	Spokane Mission
24	St. Ignatius Mission
25	St. Mary's Mission
26	St. Paul's Mission
27	Warrens
28	Whitman Mission

Prepared by C. S. HAMMOND & Co., N.Y.

region had great agricultural value, and they also made some progress in lumbering and fishing. Gradually, by word of mouth and the written accounts of a few trappers and traders, the rest of the country came to understand that a worthwhile territory lay beyond the Rocky Mountains in the Pacific Northwest.

But no matter how curious men may have been about the Northwest, there were serious obstacles that discouraged travel to that distant land. There were no roads to or through the region. Wide plains east of the Rockies were inhabited by Indian tribes, many of them warlike and hostile toward the white people. The mountains raised a high, rugged wall through which there were few good passes, and beyond the mountains lay grim and forbidding deserts. To the natural obstacles and the always dangerous Indians there was added uncertain sources of food for people and animals on the move. There was always danger that starvation or disease, or both, might strike before the long and extremely difficult journey could be completed. This did not stop the emigrants.

II. THE GREAT MEDICINE ROAD

THE GREATEST NEED that existed was for a trail or road by which travelers might follow a known course to the Rockies and on across to the Oregon Country. We discovered in our first unit that explorers, fur-gatherers, and traders had roughly followed such a course from St. Louis and Independence, Missouri, to the Columbia River. The returning Astorians closely followed this course in 1812 and 1813. Dale L. Morgan points out in his new book[1] that Jedediah Smith led a party of sixty or more men from St. Louis to the Rocky Mountains by this route in the fall and winter of 1825–26. William Sublette and Moses ("Black") Harris also traveled this way when carrying information from David Jackson to General Ashley in St. Louis. Certainly, the way was known and used before the building of Fort Hall and Fort Boise in 1834, and after the opening of these posts the development of the route was rapid. Known as the Oregon Trail, it soon became the chief route of travel to the Pacific Northwest.

Few other thoroughfares in America have been so important in history as the "Great Medicine Road," as the Indians sometimes called the Oregon Trail. In romance and adventure, as well as in usefulness, it has never been excelled. Bitter toil, hunger, sickness, fear, heartbreak, and death—all these kept pace with the plodding oxen, the complaining wheels, and the dust-burdened men, women, and children whose hopes and dreams lay at the western end of the trail or were buried in forgotten graves along its weary length. Boone's Trace through the Cumberland Gap; the National Road; the Mohawk Valley gateway in central New York; the Ohio River with its flatboats—these were famous and well-traveled routes in the Westward Movement of young America, but they were not more famous or important than the Oregon Trail.

In the *Idaho Daily Statesman* for De-

[1] Dale L. Morgan, *Jedediah Smith and the Opening of the West* (Indianapolis: The Bobbs-Merrill Company, 1953).

cember 5, 1948, Bennett L. Williams wrote:

A young and vigorous nation was on the move over one of the greatest highroads ever to mark the surface of the earth—the Old Oregon Trail. It was reaching out for more territory. Its hopes and determinations were leading a whole people onward to where their vision rested—on the shores of the Northwest Pacific. And today we know, from the record of accomplished facts, that there was no stopping that human tide until it reached that sunset goal.

In those pioneer days, road signs were few and far between. After the early 1840's, the Oregon Trail needed no sign, for thousands of wheels and millions of footprints, both human and animal, had carved its deep and bold course across half a continent. But it would have been informative, though perhaps discouraging, if there had been erected at Westport Landing, where Kansas City now is, a great signboard showing the distance to noted points along the route. We wonder how many emigrants facing such a tremendous journey, in wagons or on horseback, would have had the courage and determination to go ahead if such a sign as the following had given visible warning of the weary miles ahead:

ROAD TO OREGON	
POINTS WEST	MILES DISTANT
Junction with Santa Fe Trail	41
Blue River and St. Joseph Junction, Kansas	174
Platte River, Nebraska	316
Chimney Rock, Nebraska	571
Scott's Bluff, Nebraska	616
Fort Laramie, Wyoming	667
Independence Rock, Wyoming	838
South Pass, Wyoming	947
Green River Crossing, Wyoming	1014
Fort Bridger, Wyoming	1070
Beer Springs (Soda Springs), Idaho	1206
Fort Hall, Idaho	1288
Raft River Junction, California Trail, Idaho	1334
Three-Islands Crossing of the Snake, Idaho	1464
Fort Boise, Idaho	1585
Grande Ronde Valley, Oregon, and entrance to Blue Mountains	1736
Columbia River, Oregon	1835
The Dalles, Oregon	1934
Fort Vancouver, Washington	2020
Oregon City by South Route	2094

MAKE-BELIEVE SIGNBOARD FOR THE OREGON TRAIL

Distances are from Chittenden's *American Fur Trade of the Far West*

Importance of the Oregon Trail. Though first used by the fur-gatherers, it was as an emigrant road that the Oregon Trail was of greatest value. Emigration may be said to have begun in 1834 when Jason Lee and three other missionaries to western Oregon accompanied Nathaniel Wyeth to the site of Fort Hall. Two years later a second missionary group, consisting of Dr. and Mrs. Marcus Whitman and the Reverend Henry Harmon Spalding and Mrs. Spalding, used the route. Incidentally, Mrs. Whitman and Mrs. Spalding were the first white women to enter Idaho so far as is known.

In 1842 use of the Oregon Trail as an emigrant road began to increase rapidly. In that year Dr. Elijah White led an expedition of more than a hundred people over the road to the Willamette Valley. This was followed by the great Applegate train of a thousand emigrants in 1843. Four caravans crossed the Snake River Plains the next year. More than three thousand passed through in 1845, with additional thousands in succeeding years.

Since all these people went on through to Oregon and California, except those who stayed to "rest in unmarked graves," one might think that this great stream of human migration had but little effect on the history of Idaho. But the total effect, as we shall soon see, was to bring a large portion of the Oregon Country, of which Idaho is a part, into the United States. This alone makes the Oregon Trail and almost everything connected with it of highest importance in the history of our state.

Surveying the Oregon Trail. The great wave of settlers rolling to the Pa-

JOHN C. FREMONT, THE PATHFINDER

He made the first survey of the Oregon Trail. The fact that he was commissioned by the government to do this showed that the region was officially considered a part of the United States.

cific Northwest caused a strong demand that the United States take control of the Oregon Country. As a result, General John C. Fremont, known in western history as the Pathfinder, was sent to make a survey of the Oregon Trail. His work, completed in 1842–43, proved that the Columbia was the only large river in the Northwest that gave a practical route from the Rockies to the Pacific. Also, for the first time, the government gave official recognition to the Oregon Trail. This action strongly indicated the interest of our government in the Oregon Country and our intention to make it a part of the United States.

RABBIT-SKIN LEGGINGS

NO-HORNS-ON-HIS-HEAD

These Nez Perce Indians were members of the group of four who journeyed to St. Louis in search of the White Man's Book, the Bible. Their journey caused Christian missions to be established among the Indians of the Northwest.

III. MISSIONARIES AND MISSIONS

RELIGIONS HAVE PLAYED a great role in shaping the fate of nations and people throughout recorded history. It is not surprising, then, that Christianity, which is the principal religion of the Western World, played an important part in the history of the Oregon Country.

Search for the White Man's Book. Interest in the Indians of the Northwest was deeply stirred when a delegation of four Indians of the Nez Perce and Flathead tribes visited St. Louis in 1831. This is of special interest to Idahoans because, according to the best available information, they were Idaho Indians. Their names, translated into English, were Black Eagle or Speaking Eagle, Man-of-the-Morning, Rabbit-Skin Leggings, and No-Horns-on-His-Head. The Indians made the long journey to St. Louis because they wanted to learn more about the White Man's Book, the Bible. So great an interest was aroused that several churches in the East began to make plans for sending missionaries to work among the Indians.

Jason Lee and His Mission. The leader of the first missionary group sent to the Oregon Country was the Reverend Jason Lee. Though his mission was established in the Willamette Valley in western Oregon, he has a place in Idaho history for at least four reasons: (1) He and his associates were the first known missionaries to touch foot on Idaho soil. (2) At Fort Hall, on July 27, 1834, he preached the first sermon ever delivered in Idaho. He also conducted a funeral service while at Fort Hall for a trapper named Kanseau, who was thrown from his horse and killed while taking part in a horse race. (3) He established the first mission in the Oregon Country. (4) He went back to the East in 1839 and personally led to Oregon a party of more than fifty settlers, thus strengthening American influence in the region.

The Whitman and Spalding Missions. Following Lee, two years later, Dr. Marcus Whitman and his wife Narcissa, and the Reverend Henry Spalding and his wife Eliza, accompanied a caravan of the American Fur Company to the annual rendezvous on Green River in western Wyoming. From there they went on to Fort Hall. While there they dined on fresh vegetables from Factor Thing's garden, said to have been the first effort at cultivation of the land in Idaho. The missionaries considered the vegetables a great treat after the dried buffalo meat which they had been eating and which Mrs. Whitman described as "so filthy I could hardly eat it."

When the missionaries reached Fort Vancouver, Dr. McLoughlin showed them many courtesies and gave valuable assistance in establishing their missions. The Whitmans located at Waiilatpu, near the present city of Walla Walla, Washington. The Spaldings chose a location on the Clearwater River a few miles east of the present city of Lewiston, Idaho.

The Spalding Mission at Lapwai. When the Reverend Henry Spalding and Mrs. Spalding arrived in the Clearwater Valley in November, 1836, they found the Nez Perce Indians willing and eager to assist the missionaries in every way possible. They brought fish and other food, aided in the construction of buildings, and helped in other ways.

A site for the mission was chosen near the mouth of Lapwai (LAP'way) Creek and a crude log building was erected. From this humble beginning the mission expanded into an institution of service and usefulness whose influence is still felt among the Indians of northern Idaho, especially the Nez Perce people.

Mission Activities. Dr. C. M. Drury, in his excellent book, *Henry Harmon Spalding,* wrote that the mission activities were of four kinds: industrial, educational, medical, and spiritual; that Spalding was farmer, teacher, doctor, and preacher; and that Mrs. Spalding performed a full share of these tasks.

Spalding was not himself a doctor. But he had observed Dr. Whitman and had, on occasion, assisted him. He had made a study of the more common diseases and the simple remedies for them, and was, therefore, able to bring relief to Indian patients and assist them in recovering from the less serious ills.

The Indians were shown how to cultivate the soil and were given seed for their fields and gardens. Thus they were

"OF SUPREME HISTORICAL VALUE IN ALL IDAHO"

WHITMAN MISSION

Though not in Idaho, the Whitman Mission co-operated with the Spalding Mission and taught a better way of life to the Indians of northern Idaho and eastern Washington.

SPALDING MISSION

Here at the Spalding Mission (1836–47) occurred the first organized effort to Christianize and civilize the Indians of Idaho.

Courtesy Idaho Historical Department

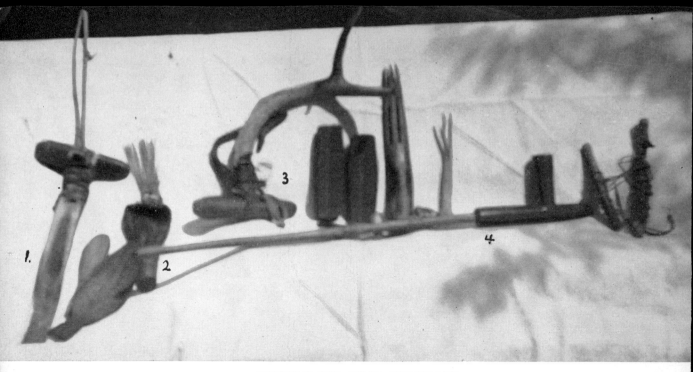

PRIMITIVE NEZ PERCE IMPLEMENTS

1. Digging tool　　　2. Broom　　　3. Rake　　　4. Pipe

(Implements posed through the courtesy of Mrs. Joe Evans, Sr., Sacajawea Museum at Spalding)

soon able to raise enough to assist substantially with the food supply. During the summer of 1838 almost a hundred Nez Perce families raised potatoes, corn, peas, and other vegetables, as well as wheat, oats, and buckwheat. They also had several cattle, hogs, and chickens from stock supplied by the mission. Later, sheep were brought in and the Nez Perce women were taught to spin the wool and weave woolen cloth. This marked the beginning of farming and stock raising in Idaho, for the Nez Perce Indians from that time on continued, at least in a small way, to practice agriculture.

The First School in Idaho. Very early in its existence the mission opened a school for the Indians. On January 27, 1837, the Spaldings started the first school ever organized on Idaho soil. Let us observe the school through the eyes of Doctor-Farmer-Preacher-Teacher Spal-

ding and compare it with the schools of today.

Here a scene commenced, more interesting, if possible, than any we had before witnessed. Nothing but actual observation can give an idea of the application of old and young, mothers with babes in their arms, grand-parents and grand-children. Having no books, Mrs. Spalding, with her numerous other cares, is obliged to supply the deficiency with her pen, and print her own books; consequently, she can spend but a short time each day in the school. But her absence does not close the school. From morning till night they are assembled in clusters, with one teaching a number of others.

Special Events at Lapwai. With great industry and zeal, activities were widened at the mission. Not only was the mission itself the first institution of its kind in Idaho, but there were recorded other *firsts* in the history of our state.

On November 15, 1837, the Spaldings' first child was born. She was named Eliza for her mother, and was the first white child born in Idaho. As a child, she was a great favorite with the Indians. She later became the wife of A. J. Warren, a rancher in eastern Oregon. She also wrote a book, *Memoirs of the West,* in which are described many incidents of her childhood and later life. Her last years, like her earliest ones, were spent in Idaho. In 1919 she passed away in the city of Coeur d'Alene, having attained the ripe old age of eighty-two years.

In 1839 a small printing press arrived at Lapwai. This was the first printing press in the Oregon Country, and was soon used to produce the first book published in the Pacific Northwest. This was a small eight-page children's book, printed almost entirely in the Nez Perce language. Other publications were a song book and parts of the New Testament, both principally in the Nez Perce dialect, or tongue.

The year 1839 witnessed two more firsts for Idaho at the Lapwai Mission. The summer of that year was very dry. In order to keep the mission garden alive a ditch was dug and the vegetable crop saved by irrigation, probably the first time in the history of the state that irrigation was used. The second event was the birth of John Henry Dix Gray, the first white baby boy born within the borders of our state. He was the child of Mr. and Mrs. William Gray, missionaries temporarily living at the Lapwai Mission.

Soon occurred another first. A combination gristmill and sawmill was constructed by Spalding, with the aid of a Mr. Blair. This mill proved of immense value, since the mission had been paying as high as $26.00 for a barrel of flour and

$35.00 for a barrel of corn meal. The mission thus became independent of outside markets for flour and meal, and provided both the mission and the Indians with the means of converting their grain into bread.

Three other children were born to the Spaldings. These were Henry Hart, Martha Jane, and Amelia Lorene. All the children lived to see the mission lands at Lapwai become successively part of Oregon Territory, Washington Territory, and Idaho Territory. All but Amelia, who died in 1889, also lived to see Idaho become the forty-third state in our nation.

Idaho's First Homesteader. In 1840 William Craig, a former mountain man, settled on a homestead near Lapwai. His wife Isabel was a Nez Perce woman, which gave Craig considerable influence among the Indians. This, as we shall soon see, proved fortunate for the Spaldings and others living at the mission.

Trouble for the Missionaries. From the first many Indians were opposed to

HISTORICAL MARKER AT THE CRAIG HOMESTEAD, NEAR LAPWAI, IDAHO

Here Colonel Craig settled Idaho's first farm and homestead.

CRAIG DONATION CLAIM
LOCATED SEPT. 15TH 1846
BY WILLIAM CRAIG MOUNTAIN
MAN AND HIS INDIAN WIFE ISABEL.

FIRST PERMANENT WHITE SETTLER IN IDAHO, 1840. FIRST
NEZ PERCE INDIAN AGENT, 1848; INTERPRETER AT WALLA WALLA
FLATHEAD AND BLACKFOOT COUNCILS, 1855. LIEUTENANT
COLONEL, WASHINGTON TERRITORY VOLUNTEERS, INDIAN WARS
1856. FIRST POSTMASTER OF WALLA WALLA, 1858. THIS WAS THE
FIRST HOMESTEAD IN IDAHO. HERE THE FAMILY OF THE
REVEREND HENRY HARMON SPAULDING WAS SHELTERED
FOLLOWING THE WHITMAN MASSACRE, 1847.

ERECTED BY COL WM. CRAIG CHAPTER No. 2.
SONS OF THE AMERICAN REVOLUTION, 1946.

EARLY MISSIONARIES

DR. MARCUS WHITMAN   REVEREND HENRY SPALDING   FATHER DE SMET   REVEREND JASON LEE

These and other missionaries who labored in the Northwest had a great influence in gaining the major part of the Oregon Country for the United States.

the missionaries. Not only did they object to the teaching of Christianity but they feared that they would finally lose their lands if more white people came into the country.

Though the missionaries were aware of the unfriendly attitude of some of the Indians, they did not allow it to interfere greatly with life at the mission or with the work that was being done. And this work was succeeding in spite of obstacles. In Eliza Spalding Warren's *Memoirs of the West* is given this picture of progress at the Spalding Mission:

The Indians were settled in homes; their crops of grain were 20,000 to 30,000 bushels a year; the cows brought by the missionaries had multiplied into numerous herds; the sheep given by the Sandwich-Islanders had grown into flocks. In the school which Mrs. Spalding taught there had been 500 pupils. A church of a hundred members had been gathered. The language had been reduced to writing. A patriarchal government had been established. They had adopted a code of laws. The Sabbath was observed. The people had been brought from the darkness of heathenism.

Tragedy Strikes at the Whitman and Spalding Missions. With staggering sud-

denness, in 1847, the trouble that had been building up among the dissatisfied Indians exploded into disaster. At the Whitman Mission both Dr. Whitman and Mrs. Whitman, together with several of their assistants, were slain in a murderous attack by the Indians. Spalding, who was on his way home from The Dalles by way of the Whitman Mission at the time, escaped only because he was warned by a Catholic priest and a friendly Indian and chose another route to his own mission at Lapwai.

A Nez Perce who had taken part in the Whitman massacre gathered a band of angry Nez Perces and tried to repeat at Lapwai what had occurred at Waiilatpu. Colonel Craig collected some friendly Nez Perces, outfaced the hostile band, and took the Spaldings to the safety of his own home. The Indians then looted the mission, destroying or carrying away much of the mission property.

These tragic events prompted the abandonment of missionary work at both missions. Guarded by friendly Nez Perces, the missionaries left for the safety of the Willamette Valley in Oregon. Not until after Idaho became a territory was missionary work again started among the Nez Perce Indians.

As the missionaries left Lapwai, Chief Timothy is said to have voiced this sad lament as he bade good-by to Mrs. Spalding:

Now, my beloved teacher, you are passing over my country for the last time. You are leaving us forever and my people, oh my people will see no more light. We shall meet no more in the classroom and my children, oh my children will live only in a night that will have no morning.

Importance of the Missions. From the Spalding and Whitman missions the Indians learned the rudiments of farming, stock raising, and homemaking. No longer did they have to depend solely upon fishing, hunting, digging camas and similar roots, and gathering wild fruits in season. As a result, they were able to give up some of their nomadic habits and have more permanent homes.

In an editorial, the *Lewiston Tribune* said:

The interesting fact is recalled that this site was voted of supreme historical value in all Idaho by the Daughters of the American Revolution. Civilization started there in 1836, when the Spaldings located their mission among the Nez Perce.

What Jamestown was to Virginia; what Plymouth Rock is to New England; what Champoeg is to Oregon, and what Waiilatpu in the Walla Walla valley is to Washington, the site of the Spalding Mission is to Idaho.

Today the mission land is a state park. In on old log building is housed part of a large and valuable collection of historical and Indian relics, gathered chiefly through the efforts of Mrs. Joe Evans, Sr. This great collection cannot be adequately displayed because of lack of space. There should be constructed in the near future a suitable museum building in which to preserve and display these priceless relics of a vanished age. Provision should also be made for a similar collection at the Lewis-Clark Normal School at Lewiston.

The Black Robes and Their Missions. About the time the American Board of Missions had the Spalding and Whitman missions well under way, the Catholic Church became interested in the Oregon Country. Quite a number of French Canadians, former employees of the Hudson's Bay Company, had settled on French Prairie in the Willamette Valley. These people were Catholics and felt a need for a church of their own faith. They therefore asked that priests be sent to establish Catholic churches among them.

The appeal was taken to Montreal, Canada, and in answer Father Blanchet and Father Demers started for Fort Vancouver. They came across the Canadian Rockies with a brigade of fur traders and embarked on the Columbia River, which they followed to their destination. In a short time they had established missions along the Cowlitz and the Willamette rivers, and made special journeys to other outposts of the Hudson's Bay Company.

Father De Smet. In 1840 Father Pierre Jean De Smet, the greatest of the Catholic missionaries, decided to see for himself what could be done to Christianize and help the Indians of the Northwest. Following the usual Oregon Trail route to Green River, he visited the 1840 rendezvous. Guided by Flathead Indians, he continued on through Jackson's Hole to Pierre's Hole. There he was met by large numbers of Indians, who had been informed of his coming, and there he performed the first Catholic church services, so far as records show, in what is now Idaho.

The fine reception given Father De Smet by the Indians convinced him that among them was a good field for missionary work. He returned to St. Louis and, the following year, came back to the Bitterroot Valley in the present state of Montana. There he established St. Mary's Mission. Later St. Ignatius Mission was built near Flathead Lake. From these, and from St. Paul's Mission in the Willamette Valley, the Catholics extended their work until several missions were operating in the Oregon Country.

The Coeur d'Alene Mission. Father De Smet's journeys carried him through the present north Idaho several times. On one of the journeys he stopped among the Coeur d'Alene Indians, who asked that a mission be provided for the tribe. Accordingly, in 1842, Father Nicholas Point chose a site and built the first Coeur d'Alene Mission on the St. Joe River, not far from the present city of St. Maries. The buildings were on low ground and high waters of the spring runoff flooded the mission. To escape future floods, a new location was chosen on the Coeur d'Alene River near the present village of Cataldo.

Sacred Heart Mission was the name chosen for the new establishment. There the famous Old Mission Church, planned by Father Anthony Ravalli, was started in 1847. Twenty-one years were required to complete the structure, which, largely for lack of nails, was put together with wooden pins.

During the more than a quarter century the Sacred Heart Mission was maintained, it played a prominent part in the history of northern Idaho and, indeed, of the entire region. Noted men, including Isaac I. Stevens, territorial governor of Washington, and Captain John Mullan, famous road builder, shared its hospitality. There Colonel George Wright, aided by the Catholic fathers, concluded a treaty with the Coeur d'Alene Indians after the Indian war of 1858. There, too, many Indian children received instruction, and their parents and other members of the tribe were assisted in many ways.

Today the Old Mission Church stands empty and forlorn. Occasional visitors still pass through its doors, and occasional pilgrimages are still made to the shrine, as Catholic authorities maintain the church in reasonably good repair. There, as at Spalding, Idaho might well establish a historical museum and restore the buildings and grounds as closely as possible to their former condition and beauty.

IV. HOW THE OREGON COUNTRY WAS DIVIDED

Both England and the United States, as you recall, had strong claims to the region known as the Oregon Country. Sailors of both nations had cruised along its shores. Both English and American pathfinders had explored the land. The fur-gatherers of both nationalities had spent years collecting the vast resources of beaver and other furs. When the fur business began to fail, trappers and traders of both countries took up land in the sheltered valleys of the Willamette–Puget Sound lowland.

Then, toward the end of the golden age of furs, missionaries came into the Oregon Country. The first missions, and the ones most active in bringing later settlers into the region, were established and largely maintained by church denominations in the United States. As a result, most of the missions became centers for spreading American influence and this had a great deal to do with bringing most of the Oregon Country within our national boundaries.

Spanish and Russian Claims Surrendered. In 1819, when Spain sold Florida to the United States, the forty-second parallel was agreed upon as the northern boundary of Spanish land in western North America. Actually, the Spanish had never established a post in the Oregon Country, though they traded at Nootka Sound on Vancouver Island off and on for several years.

Russia was not much interested, except in Alaska. In treaties made in 1824 and 1825, the Russians gave up all claims to land south of the parallel of fifty-four degrees and forty minutes (54° 40′). These treaties with Spain and Russia left England and the United States to settle between themselves the question of final ownership to most of the Pacific Northwest.

Joint Occupation Agreement. By 1818 it was clear that neither England nor the United States was willing to give up its claim to the Oregon Country. That year the two nations made an agreement that they would occupy the country jointly until some other arrangement could be made.

Starting in 1843, there came the great wave of American migration to the Willamette Valley in western Oregon. This made some form of local government necessary. The Oregon settlers met at Champoeg on the Willamette River that same year and adopted a temporary constitution and by-laws for governing the region until "such time as the United States of America extend their jurisdiction [legal control] over us." This was plain language, showing that the settlers already considered themselves part of the United States, though living outside its borders.

Fifty-Four Forty or Fight. This was the situation when James K. Polk was nominated for President by the Democrats in 1844. He strongly believed that the United States should extend unbroken from the Atlantic to the Pacific Ocean, and chose as his campaign slogan the challenging phrase, "Fifty-four forty or fight," showing that the United States claimed the whole of the Oregon Country north to the Russian lands of Alaska. It also hinted, very strongly, that the country was ready to go to war with England, if necessary, in order to settle the question.

The Oregon Treaty. In 1846 the United States Senate voted to end the Joint Occupation Agreement with England. This brought the whole question of ownership up for settlement. Since England's interest in the region was represented chiefly by trading posts of the Hudson's Bay Company, the English offered to divide the Oregon Country with the United States. The forty-ninth parallel was already the dividing line between the United States and Canada east of the Rockies; so the two nations agreed to extend the boundary west to the Pacific along that line. This agreement, known as the Treaty of Oregon, gave our nation the present states of Oregon, Washington, and Idaho, and that part of Montana and Wyoming lying west of the Continental Divide. England took the region now called British Columbia and Vancouver Island. The treaty also ended the danger of war between the two countries.

A Second Road to the Northwest. After the United States gained undisputed title to the Oregon Country south of the forty-ninth parallel, a trickle of American settlers began moving into the Columbia country now embraced in eastern Washington. Also, during the years 1855–58, Indian troubles arose that had to be settled by force of arms. These developments showed the need for an easier and faster way to get through the mountain barriers separating the headwaters of the Missouri and the Columbia rivers. The Oregon Trail, so useful to settlers in western Oregon, was too far south to be used to advantage by either military forces or settlers moving into the lands farther north.

Captain John Mullan, a West Point graduate and engineer, was commissioned to build a road from Fort Benton on the Missouri to the vicinity of old Fort Walla Walla on the Columbia River. Since machinery was largely lacking and practically all the work had to be done with horsepower and hand labor, you can readily understand what a difficult project it was. Little time was lost, however, the work being started in 1859 and completed in 1862.

The section across northern Idaho was built in 1859–60. This was the most difficult construction on the entire 624 miles of the road. It led through a densely timbered mountain country, where, for more than a hundred miles, a large force of workmen cleared a path twenty-five feet wide through the forest. Much grading had to be done, and on the Coeur d'Alene River alone a score of bridges had to be built.

While the builders were encamped at the point now marked with the Mullan Tree Monument, they held a Fourth-of-July celebration. As they fired their guns and exploded fixed charges of powder, near-by Indians took alarm and hurried to the Cataldo Mission. There they reported that the white soldiers were fighting among themselves. This has been referred to as Idaho's first Fourth-of-July celebration, though this is very doubtful, since the day has long been marked by shooting and other noisy demonstrations, especially among rural dwellers and frontiersmen. However, since that time the narrow canyon leading to the summit has been known as Fourth of July Canyon.

The Mullan Road made possible the quicker transport of soldiers and military equipment and supplies. It encouraged larger numbers of settlers to enter the Columbia country in eastern Washington. It opened up vast timber and mineral resources to later development and gave an outlet to eastern markets for the products of the region through which it passed.

Courtesy Idaho State Chamber of Commerce, Boise

MULLAN TREE

This historic tree stands beside U.S. Highway 10 east of Coeur d'Alene. Captain Mullan and party spent the Fourth of July there in 1861. A fence now surrounds the tree to prevent acts of vandalism, such as the initials carved above the Mullan inscription.

How well this pioneer road followed natural routes of travel through the region is shown by the cities now located along its course. In Idaho these include Coeur d'Alene, Wallace, Kellogg, and Mullan. Today transcontinental railroads, the Northern Pacific and the Union Pacific, and U.S. Highway 10 closely parallel the course of the Mullan Road through Idaho.

V. MORMONS SETTLE IN IDAHO

THE YEAR OF FAILURE AND TRAGEDY for the Whitman and Spalding missions saw another great religious effort succeed. In 1847 the Mormons firmly established themselves in the valley of the Great Salt Lake. There, two years later, they organized the "State of Deseret," now Utah. Their plans were to colonize the Great Basin and suitable portions of adjoining regions, including a substantial part of what is now southern Idaho.

Salmon River Mission at Fort Lemhi. The first attempt of the Mormons to spread northward beyond the Salt Lake Valley and its immediate vicinity occurred in May, 1855. Brigham Young, then president of the Mormon Church, sent twenty-seven men under the leadership of Thomas B. Smith to found a settlement in the Salmon River country. They chose a location on a tributary stream which they named the Limhi, now spelled Lemhi. They immediately constructed a number of cabins, enclosed in a stockade, which they named Fort Limhi.

After the settlers were housed, one of the first tasks was digging a ditch to bring water from the river to the land. This was the first real irrigation canal in Idaho, which, incidentally, is said to be still in use. The land was planted to peas, potatoes, turnips, and corn, but an early frost killed most of the crops. Supplies were obtained from Utah to enable the settlers to get through the winter, and twenty-two more colonists arrived.

Crops were planted again in the spring of 1856 and their luxuriant growth gave high hopes of a bountiful harvest. Those hopes were blasted when grasshoppers by the millions descended upon the fields and left them bare, requiring another trip to Utah for winter supplies.

In spite of these discouragements, the settler-missionaries held on until 1858. In February of that year Fort Lemhi was suddenly attacked by Bannock and Shoshone Indians. Two men were killed and five more wounded, and a large part of the cattle herd was driven away. Believing it impossible to carry on in the face of Indian hostility, the settlers abandoned Fort Lemhi and returned to Utah.

Franklin, Idaho's First Permanent Settlement. The work of Latter-day Saint pioneers on the Lemhi had shown the land to be fertile and irrigation possible in the valleys to the north of the Great Salt Lake. Only two years passed after the abandonment of Fort Lemhi until a second attempt was made to extend Mormon settlements to the north.

This historic event occurred April 14, 1860, while Idaho was still a part of Washington Territory. Thomas S. Smart led the first group of thirteen colonists,

HISTORIC FRANKLIN AND UPPER CACHE VALLEY

In this beautiful section of Upper Cache Valley, in what is now Franklin County, Latter-day Saint pioneers established the first permanent settlement in Idaho in 1860.

Courtesy Preston Chamber of Commerce

who selected a location and built several cabins, naming the settlement Franklin.

Work began at once to develop an agricultural community. The land was cleared of sagebrush and other small growth and plowed; irrigation ditches were dug and seed was planted. It is interesting to notice that this first permanent farming venture in Idaho was done on a community basis, farming plots being assigned to the families in tracts of one, five, and ten acres. This practice was soon changed, however, and the families became the outright owners of the land.

Before the end of the first year a church was organized. Hannah Cornish, or Comish, started Idaho's first school exclusively for white children, which she at first conducted in her own cabin. Crops, somewhat meager, were harvested, and the settlers faced their first winter with confidence born of their courage, their faith in God, and their confidence in each other. They were then unaware that they were the first settlers in what was to become Idaho, the forty-third state in the Union.

* * * * *

Explorers, trappers, fur traders, missionaries, settlers—all these, as we have seen, had a place in the history of Idaho before there was an Idaho. Their explorations, their business activities, their missionary work, their settlements, all helped to lay a foundation for the organization of Idaho Territory, an event which was soon to occur. In the next unit we shall see how the discovery of gold, and the great, boisterous mining camps that sprang up like magic in the placer gold field, made territorial organization a necessity, and how government came to Idaho.

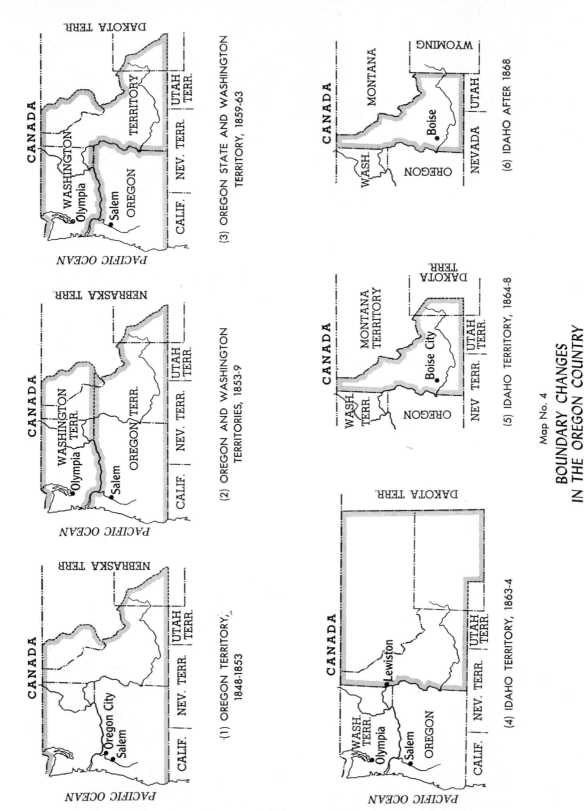

(1) OREGON TERRITORY, 1848-1853

(2) OREGON AND WASHINGTON TERRITORIES, 1853-9

(3) OREGON STATE AND WASHINGTON TERRITORY, 1859-63

(4) IDAHO TERRITORY, 1863-4

(5) IDAHO TERRITORY, 1864-8

(6) IDAHO AFTER 1868

Map No. 4

BOUNDARY CHANGES
IN THE OREGON COUNTRY

Bringing Government to the Oregon Country

How settlers in the Oregon Country governed themselves while waiting for the United States to extend the protection of its laws over them; how territorial government was organized; how Oregon became a state; how the discovery of gold made local government necessary in the gold fields; and how Idaho Territory was created.

THE TREATY OF OREGON, as we learned in the previous unit, divided the Oregon Country between the United States and England in 1846. The Stars and Stripes replaced the Hudson's Bay flag at Fort Vancouver, Fort Hall, Fort Boise, and at other Hudson's Bay posts in the region south of the forty-ninth parallel. But for some time little actual change was made in the newly won territory except in parts of the Willamette Valley, where the people had already taken the first steps in managing their own local affairs of government.

I. OREGON AND WASHINGTON LEAD THE WAY

BEFORE THE CHAMPOEG meeting in 1843, the people of western Oregon had local government of a sort and elected certain local officers. After the Champoeg meeting a provisional government was approved by the vote of the people. A governor was elected and a body of laws was adopted.

Oregon Territory Created. A bill to create Oregon Territory had been before Congress for some time, but it was not acted upon because of the fear of upsetting the balance between free states and slave states. Then, into the national capital one day in May, 1848, strode a ragged giant, a former mountain man named Joe Meek. Meek stunned the capital with news of the Whitman massacre and of the threat of Indian war hanging over the Northwest. This news brought speedy action. After several changes, the Oregon Bill was passed and Oregon Territory became a reality. The original Oregon Territory was a vast region consisting of the present states of Oregon, Washington, and Idaho, and of that part of Wyoming and Montana west of the Continental Divide. Though of immense size, the territory had a small population living mainly in the Willamette Valley.

Washington Territory Formed. For five years no change was made in Oregon Territory. But even before the United States gained title in 1846, there had been some settlement by Americans north of the Columbia River in the Cowlitz River–Puget Sound lowland. After Oregon Territory was created, this movement of settlers gained in volume. To meet the demands of the settlers, Washington Territory was created. The northern boundary was the forty-ninth parallel between the United States and Canada, and the southern border was the Columbia River and the forty-sixth parallel. Approximately the northern half of Oregon Territory was thus cut off and organized as Washington Territory in 1853.

During the six-year period, from 1853 to 1859, both Oregon and Washington territories tried to provide local government by creating counties. Oregon Territory set up a vast county between the Cascade Range and the Rocky Mountains which was named Wasco County. This, of course, included what is now southern Idaho. Washington Territory, in 1858, created another huge county named Shoshone County, which extended over what is now northern Idaho. By this time, however, both Fort Hall and Fort Boise had been abandoned and in all southern Idaho no white people lived. In the north the Coeur d'Alene mission was the only settlement housing any white people.

Statehood for Oregon. In 1859 Oregon became a state, with its present boundaries, being the first state created in the Pacific Northwest. This made an-

other change in territorial boundaries necessary. That portion of Oregon Territory east of the new state was attached to Washington Territory, which then included all of what is now Idaho. This was the situation existing when the discovery of gold on a tributary of the Clearwater River in 1860, and of other gold strikes which followed in quick succession, brought a stampede of frenzied fortune hunters to the mountains of northern and central Idaho.

Results of the Gold Discoveries. The gold rush brought an immediate need for local government. In 1861 the legislature of Washington Territory created three counties to meet this need: old Shoshone County with changed boundaries, Nez Perce County, and Idaho County. These included nearly all of the present state of Idaho north of the Payette River. A year later the discovery of gold in Boise Basin led to the creation of Boise County by the Washington territorial legislature of 1862–63.

The gold camps, however, were so far from the territorial capital at Olympia that communication was difficult and very slow. Under such circumstances it was only natural that people living in the mining districts should wish to withdraw from Washington Territory and have a government of their own.

II. IDAHO'S GOLDEN FOUNDATION

THE CREATION OF IDAHO TERRITORY was a direct result of gold discoveries in the eastern part of Washington Territory in the early 1860's. The three years between that event and the organization of Idaho Territory saw the occurrence of many of

the most dramatic events of Idaho's colorful history.

Oro Fino, "Fine Gold." Captain E. D. Pierce, a veteran of the Mexican War, heard rumors of gold along the Clearwater and on its feeder streams on the

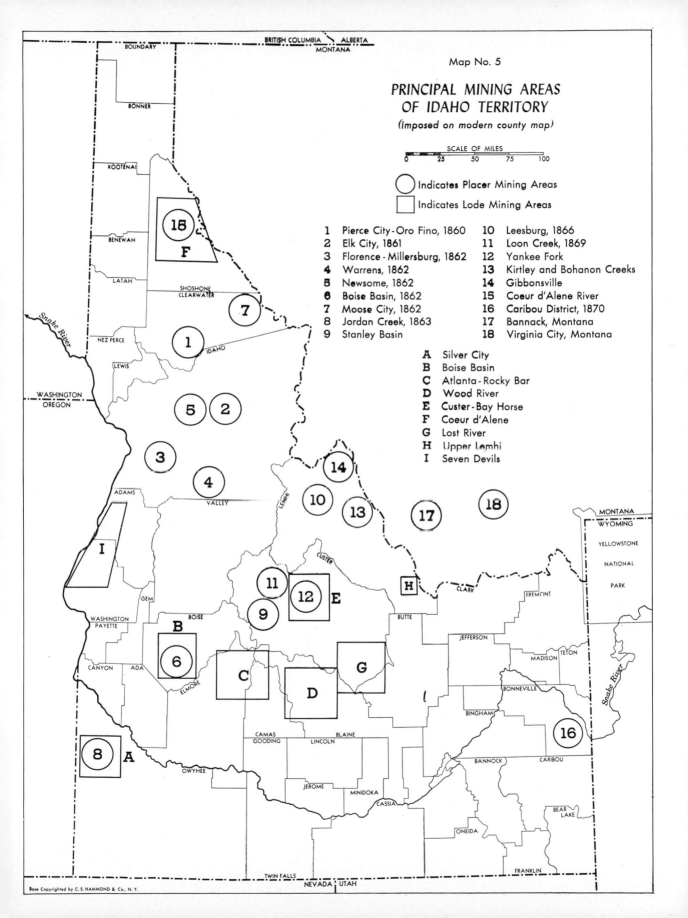

Map No. 5

PRINCIPAL MINING AREAS OF IDAHO TERRITORY

(Imposed on modern county map)

SCALE OF MILES

0   25   50   75   100

◯ Indicates Placer Mining Areas

▢ Indicates Lode Mining Areas

1 Pierce City-Oro Fino, 1860
2 Elk City, 1861
3 Florence-Millersburg, 1862
4 Warrens, 1862
5 Newsome, 1862
6 Boise Basin, 1862
7 Moose City, 1862
8 Jordan Creek, 1863
9 Stanley Basin
10 Leesburg, 1866
11 Loon Creek, 1869
12 Yankee Fork
13 Kirtley and Bohanon Creeks
14 Gibbonsville
15 Coeur d'Alene River
16 Caribou District, 1870
17 Bannack, Montana
18 Virginia City, Montana

A Silver City
B Boise Basin
C Atlanta-Rocky Bar
D Wood River
E Custer-Bay Horse
F Coeur d'Alene
G Lost River
H Upper Lemhi
I Seven Devils

western slopes of the Rocky Mountains. He had visited the Nez Perce country in 1858, but apparently did nothing more than look at the region. Two years later he was back at the head of a chosen band of gold hunters. Guided on a roundabout course by Jane, daughter of the friendly Nez Perce chief Timothy, he and his men reached a tributary of the Clearwater River now known as Orofino Creek. There, early in August, 1860, a prospector named Wilbur Bassett rolled up the curtain on a new act in the drama of Idaho. Scooping some sand into his gold pan, he washed out the first placer gold, so far as history shows, ever mined in the state.

The exact date is not firmly established in history. Defenbach thought it was probably the twelfth of August. He described the day in these arresting words:

Down at Franklin, the first crops were ripening under the summer sun; the new babies, Johnny Reed and the Frew twins, were being moved from their natal wagon boxes into the still unfinished log cabins.

At Salmon Falls, on the south side of the Snake across from Hagerman, the wagons of the Otter train were still in smoking ruins. On the hill between Weiser and Huntington the scalped and mangled bodies of the Van Norman family lay beside the Oregon Trail.

Such was the dawn of the new day. Around the little spot where Pierce, Jane, and Bassett stood, there were a year later more than seven thousand white men.

Of one thing, however, we are sure. The party's discovery of placer gold was the beginning of a new era in Idaho's history. The North Idaho Scenic-Land Association described it in these words:

Pierce is a red-letter historical spot in Idaho because it marks the place in Clearwater County where the opening scenes in the modern history of Idaho were staged. At Orofino (Creek) was enacted what can well be called the event which rang up the curtain on a train of events which ushered in the creation of Idaho Territory. On the late afternoon of an August day in 1860, the Captain E. D. Pierce party camped near the mouth of a small stream called Canal Gulch, which flows into Orofino Creek, a branch of the Clearwater River. After a trout and bacon supper on this sultry "yellow evening" a prospector, Wilbur F. Bassett, jokingly told his campfire friends that he was going to see if there was gold in the sands under the grass roots of that lonely mountain meadow. Within a few moments after his departure with shovel and pan, prospector Bassett dug up a shovelful of dirt that contained flour-like particles of fine gold— "Oro Fino." This has been described as the most important single event in Idaho history.

Seldom does an important mineral discovery anywhere in the world long remain a secret. It is almost as if the very winds carry the news to the four corners of the earth. So it was on this occasion, and hundreds of prospectors flocked to the Clearwater. By special arrangement between the government and the Nez Perce Indians, the miners were allowed to enter the field peaceably.

Pierce City, now Pierce, named in honor of the leader, was established almost at once. A few miles up the creek another large camp, old Oro Fino, grew up. But in a short time the placers, never extensive, were exhausted. Oro Fino was abandoned, but the name lives on in Orofino Creek and in the beautiful little city at the junction of the creek with the Clearwater River, now the county seat of Clearwater County. Pierce itself is not now a mining town, but is a center for lumbering and national forest work.

Idaho's First City. The easiest way to reach the Clearwater mining district was by river steamer up the Columbia and Snake rivers. The first steamer to arrive was the *Colonel Wright*. It reached the mouth of the Clearwater in 1861 and ascended that stream a few miles to Big Eddy, where Captain Baughman unloaded his supplies.

A trader named Seth Slater started a tent store and settlement, naming it Slaterville. Because of the swiftness and shallowness of the Clearwater, the place was soon abandoned and a new settlement was started where the Clearwater joins the Snake. There Slater again set up his store, and Idaho's first city was under way.

The new settlement was named Lewiston, in honor of Captain Meriwether Lewis. Steamboats loaded with supplies, miners, prospectors, and adventurers arrived at frequent intervals, and the town grew rapidly. Lewiston immediately became the distribution point for the gold district. New gold strikes added to the excitement and a constant stream of new arrivals poured in.

By 1862 Lewiston was a thriving city. The advantages of its location caused it to grow by leaps and bounds as the gold fever swept the region. In 1863, when Idaho Territory was established, Lewiston became the temporary capital.

Other North Idaho Gold Camps. The diggings on Orofino Creek, though they produced millions of dollars' worth of gold dust, were not unusually rich, averaging slightly more than twenty-five cents to the pan. Expenses were high, and impatient prospectors soon spread out through the region in search of richer dirt.

Elk City and Newsome, 1861–62. High up toward the head of the South Fork of the Clearwater River, a band of prospectors from Pierce City found another placer field. In a high meadow near the mouth of Elk Creek, gold paying as high as twenty-five cents to the pan was found.

The new discovery drew the usual rush of hopeful gold seekers. The town of Elk City was laid out and soon had a population estimated at two thousand or more. As had happened at most of the other discoveries, the richest gold was soon gleaned and in time Elk City joined the ranks of "ghost towns," though it has never been entirely deserted.

Soon after the Elk Creek discovery, gold was found along near-by Newsome Creek in 1862. As at Elk City, a town was laid out which was soon an important supply point. There is no record as to the actual gold production, but it must have been considerable, as the Chinese miners who followed the whites are known to have gathered more than $800,000 in rewashing the ground after mining by the whites had practically ceased.

Florence and Millersburg, 1862. Among the miners at Oro Fino there was a reckless, black-haired young man who had been a pony-express rider. He left his claim in Rhodes Gulch and was with one of the first parties to arrive in the next gold field discovered after Elk City. There, in 1862, near the head of Slate Creek, a small tributary of Salmon River, was found the richest placer field ever discovered in Idaho; perhaps the richest, while it lasted, ever found in the United

These reports may have been exaggerated, but they certainly indicate that the Florence diggings were extremely rich while mining was at its peak.

Gambler's Luck. Almost as extraordinary as the Florence placers were those discovered in 1862 by James Warren, whom the historian Bancroft described as "a shiftless individual, a petty gambler, miner and prospector." Near the place now called Warren in the southern part of Idaho County, he uncovered one of the richest placer fields in Idaho.

Warrens, unlike most of the early gold camps, was both deep and rich. Mining there has continued, except for short intervals, ever since the original discovery. Today the district is still a fairly heavy producer of placer gold.

Moose City. High on the western slope of the Bitterroot Range, where the North Fork of Clearwater River has its sources, an unknown prospector found rich placer gold on Moose Creek. Another wilderness gold camp sprang up and had a short but exciting existence. At one time Moose City, the main camp, had a population estimated as high as nine thousand. Now only a few ruins mark the site of this once roaring town as the Clearwater wilderness reclaims its own.

Discoveries in Southern Idaho. Famous though Pierce City and other gold camps of North Idaho were, new discoveries in southern Idaho were soon to overshadow them. Both placer gold in much greater quantities than the Orofino, Elk City, and Florence camps, and silver of dazzling richness were soon to be uncovered in southern Idaho.

"Don't Let Them Scalp Me, Mose!" In Elk City there was a miner named Moses Splawn. A Bannock Indian who sometimes visited the camp became friendly with Splawn and told him of a place to the south where the shiny metal was plentiful.

In 1862 Splawn decided to search for the place the Indian had described. In August he and George Grimes, with a small prospecting party, were in the Boise Basin on a small tributary of Boise River now known as Grimes Creek. After they made camp, one of the party, D. H. Fogus, took up a shovelful of dirt to test. To his surprise and delight, it yielded about fifteen cents in gold.

Thus was made the original discovery of placer gold in the Boise Basin, estimated to have produced between one hundred and three hundred million dollars before the placers were considered so exhausted as to be no longer profitable. As a matter of fact, the district still pays its golden rewards to dredge miners using modern methods.

The first discovery was made about where the village of Centerville now stands in Boise County. The prospectors then moved upstream and found richer ground. There they started mining in earnest, and while so engaged were attacked by Indians. George Grimes was fatally wounded by a treacherous Shoshone guide and soon died, his last words being, "Don't let them scalp me, Mose!" Today a monument marks his resting place and his name is further honored in the name of the creek on which he made the final payment of the price so often demanded of those pioneers who opened the door of opportunity for those who followed them.

Discoveries in other parts of the basin

PIERCE CITY

Pierce City (now Pierce). Here in 1860 the first gold discovery was made, ushering in the Golden Decade.

EARLY-DAY MINING

An arrastre used in early-day mining near Pierce City on Silver Creek.

IDAHO CITY

This was Idaho's largest city during the Golden Decade. It is now the county seat of Boise County.

proved that the district was both large and rich. Towns quickly mushroomed at the sites of the main strikes. In October, 1862, Pioneer City, or Pioneerville, was established. A month later Centerville was begun. Placerville, Buena Vista, and Bannack City, whose name was soon changed to Idaho City, followed. Before the end of 1863 Boise County had a population of over fifteen thousand, most of them living in the new El Dorado[3] discovered by Moses Splawn and his party only a little more than a year earlier.

"Forty-Eight Hour Insanity for Owyhee." According to legend, at some time in the 1840's a party of emigrants on the Oregon Trail reported that they had found a place where they could have picked up "A blue bucket full of nuggets." Why they did not do so certainly makes the truth of the legendary story a matter of grave doubt, but the rumor was repeated from time to time, as rumors of lost mines so often are.

In 1862 a prospector named Turner led a party from the Boise Basin south across Snake River into the Owyhee Mountains, searching for the mythical Blue Bucket Mine. His search was not successful, but it stimulated others to try their luck in the same area.

A year later Michael Jordan, with a party of twenty-nine prospectors, found profitable placer ground on a tributary of the Owyhee River. They located claims, named the small stream Jordan Creek, and went to Placerville with the story of their discovery.

The usual mad rush followed. The more than two thousand men who stormed the discovery quickly made an-

[3]El Dorado. A region rich in gold.

other discovery—that practically all the profitable ground had already been staked out by the original finders. Disappointed men by the hundreds returned to Boise Basin or went to other regions. This led a California newspaper to describe the events as "a special forty-eight hour insanity for Owyhee."

But the newspaper was wrong. The discouraged prospectors who left Jordan Creek were unknowingly leaving behind them mineral wealth far beyond their wildest dreams. But that is part of a later story which will be told as we follow the fortunes of Idaho through its territorial years.

Other Gold Fields in the Northwest. Idaho was not the only part of the Northwest in which gold was found. Important discoveries were made in southwestern and eastern Oregon, in northeastern Washington, in British Columbia, and in western Montana. However, only the Montana mines at Bannack and Virginia City were as famous and drew as many prospectors and miners as those in Idaho.[4]

Idaho's Gold Harvest. Have you ever wondered how rich the gold fields of early Idaho really were, how much gold they produced, how they rewarded the hardy men who toiled to harvest the shining treasure? No one knows, no one ever knew, the total yield of Idaho gold.

The lowest estimate gives the value of gold from the leading placer mining districts as close to one hundred and forty million dollars, almost half of this coming from Boise Basin. Other estimates run a great deal higher. James H. Hawley, once

[4]Bannack and Virginia City were in Idaho Territory until Montana Territory was created in 1864.

governor of Idaho, wrote in his *History of Idaho:*

It is generally agreed among those best acquainted with the subject, that $300,000,000 in gold dust was mined in Boise Basin alone from the discovery until the close of the year 1880, at which time bar, creek, and gulch mining had practically ceased.

No matter whether we accept the lowest figure, the highest estimate, or, as was probably true, one somewhere between the two extremes, we must agree that Idaho's golden harvest was indeed a magnificent contribution to the wealth of the territory and the nation.

The reason for Idaho's gold is found in the geography of Idaho. The first part of the answer lies far back in our geographical and geological history. Geologists, people who are skilled in reading from layers of earth and stone the story of the past, tell us that during long periods of time there was intense volcanic activity in the western part of North America. During that time the Rocky Mountains were formed and the surface of Idaho changed from seas and swamps to the mountains and plateaus we have today.

During that time, also, rock layers deep in the earth became extremely hot from volcanic heat and pressure. Gold and some other minerals were melted from the rocks in which they were originally distributed and flowed into seams and openings to form mineral veins. Later, these rock masses gradually cooled through hundreds of thousands, even millions, of years. Rain, snow, ice, and wind, the tools of erosion, wore down the surface, exposing these great rock masses. Today they lie on or near the surface of the mountains of central and northern Idaho, and are known as the Idaho Batholith, or the Mother Lode. The great batholith, covering thousands of square miles, is composed mainly of igneous, or heat-formed, granite rocks, which contain most of our gold deposits.

Later in our geological history, especially during the Glacial Epoch, or Ice Age, the rock masses were eroded and ground up. Great glaciers pushed them to lower elevations and water rushing with great force from the melting ice carried the gold-bearing rocks and gravel into mountain valleys, where they were distributed and deposited. These placer fields, as we have already seen, were the golden foundation on which Idaho Territory was founded.

Life in Idaho's Placer Gold Camps. The gold camps introduced a way of living that was in most respects different from other ways, a way peculiar to the mining camps and one that disappeared in Idaho with their passing. Because of this, it is worth while for us to obtain a general insight into how life was lived there. What sort of men opened the great gold placers of the territory? What classes of society did they represent? How did they live and work? What use did they make of their leisure time? What methods did they use to preserve order and protect life and property?

Gold Camp People. H. L. Talkington, formerly head of the History Department of the Lewiston Normal School, wrote in his fine narrative, *Heroes and Heroic Deeds of the Pacific Northwest:* "A mining camp was composed of men from every walk of life, from every state and territory in the Union, and from every nation on the globe."

Defenbach wrote of those coming to the Boise Basin: "The motley crowd contained not only miners, but merchants, packers, rangers, sporting men, lawyers, and an occasional preacher."

A large proportion of the men were experienced prospectors and miners, men who had learned their trade in the diggings of California, Colorado, Oregon, Washington, and British Columbia. The gold fever was in their blood, and every new discovery was a magnet drawing them to its glitter.

There were, however, many other kinds of people drawn to the camps: young men without previous experience looking for adventure and possible wealth; storekeepers and traders with their stocks of goods; sawmill men, blacksmiths, teamsters, carpenters, and laborers drawn by the certainty of employment at good wages; saloonkeepers, gamblers, and dancing girls; a limited number of wives and children of men who found it possible to take their families with them; and the usual riffraff, both men and women, who tagged along in the hope of defrauding honest men of their hard-earned gains.

How the Miners Worked and Lived. Placer gold in Idaho was usually found in sand, gravel, and boulders of stream beds and in the bars and benches along the streams. It was taken by a variety of methods, panning, sluicing, and using the rocker being the most common. By any method, the dirt and sand were washed away, leaving the heavier gold behind.

The work was extremely tiring. Since it could be most successfully carried on during the warmer weather when streams were free of ice and the ground was not frozen, the men worked long hours and had little time for anything else as long as conditions were favorable for mining.

The homes of the miners were of the simplest kind. Many were tents; some were rude log shacks. A few were caves or holes dug into the hillside. Such furniture as they contained was nearly always homemade. Much of the cooking was done over outdoor fires. Since the homes were considered temporary makeshifts, little thought was given to making them attractive.

Stores, saloons, and other similar business enterprises were usually housed in larger and better quarters. In camps that gave promise of longer existence, saloons and other so-called places of entertainment were sometimes large and well built, and some of them were well supplied with fine furniture and fittings.

When families began moving into the camps, the presence of women and children was usually shown by greater attention being given to making the homes more attractive and sanitary. A few of the most prosperous placer towns even constructed schools, churches, and lodges for the social needs of the people.

Their Daily Bread. Distances from markets and the high costs of transportation made food items costly and often scarce. Flour, bacon, beans, coffee, lard, and salt were staple foods. They were sometimes supplemented by such things as butter, eggs, dried fruits, onions, rice, syrup, and sugar.

Fish and game were not served as often as might be assumed. They were, no doubt, fairly plentiful, but men who toiled from daylight to dark had little time to fish and hunt. With good wages being paid for all kinds of labor, footloose men found it safer and more profitable to work for wages than to follow the chase. Indians often lurked around, and some of them were only too willing to ambush single hunters and fishermen, or even small parties that strayed away from the camps.

Travel and Transportation. As you can readily imagine, getting to and from the gold camps and bringing in supplies and equipment were big undertakings. Roads were lacking and supply points were far distant.

Saddle horses were used for those who could afford them, but much travel was on foot. Such meager supplies as could be carried on men's backs often constituted the complete food and equipment brought into the camps.

Trails were soon opened to the main camps and trains of pack horses and mules were used for transport. Later still, roads were constructed and wagons and stages brought in goods and passengers. High prices were charged for all kinds of transportation. Even letters were expensive, the charge for a single letter sometimes being as much as $1.50.

Amusements and Recreation. Man's natural desire for amusement and entertainment found outlets in various ways. Reading was limited, since books and newspapers were scarce. Bibles were not uncommon, but other books were few.

Sometimes plays and other theatrical entertainments were staged, usually by local talent. Most camps made some attempt at holding religious services, though these were by no means regular. Such fraternal organizations as the Masons and Odd Fellows organized lodges and held meetings. Shooting matches, wrestling, foot racing, and similar sports were engaged in.

By far the most popular forms of amusement were furnished by the saloons, gambling houses, and dance halls. All three were frequently combined in one large building or tent. Some men in the camps drank intoxicating liquors. Gambling games and devices of all kinds were well patronized, and crooked gamblers gained possession of much of the hard-earned gold dust gathered during working hours. Some of the gambling establishments, however, worked on percentages and tried to run honest games. Dancing girls, often known as "hurdy-gurdies," were found in most of the saloons.

Gradually the wives and children of miners, merchants, doctors, lawyers, and other professional men and workers moved to the gold camps in increasing numbers, especially into the semipermanent towns of the Boise Basin. Though never very numerous, these pioneer women comprised the best social elements and were mainly responsible for the establishment of churches, schools, and similar institutions of community improvement. The presence of such families gave substance and permanence to the region and aided in making it a land of homes instead of merely a stopping place in which to spend some time, or perhaps reap a quick fortune.

Early Law and Order. Before 1863 there was no legal government in Idaho. Even after Idaho Territory was created, it took some time to get the machinery of government set up and working satisfactorily. For example, it was not until 1864 that the first legal court trial in the territory was conducted at Lewiston, resulting in the conviction and hanging of the murderers of Lloyd Magruder.

As soon as miners and prospectors arrived in numbers at the site of a new discovery, one of their earliest group actions was the organization of a miners' court. In an open meeting they adopted a set of rules suitable to local conditions and elected officers to see that the rules were enforced. These officers were usually a judge to conduct hearings and render judgment, a recorder to make necessary records, and an executive officer similar to a sheriff or a marshal.

All sorts of cases were tried in the miners' courts. There were usually lawyers or ex-lawyers among the miners who were willing to act as attorneys. The accused or the accuser could usually demand and get a jury trial if willing to personally pay the jurors for their time. Finally, if either party to a trial was dissatisfied with the verdict, he could appeal the case to a mass meeting for final judgment.

To meet rising lawlessness, which miners' courts were sometimes unable or unwilling to prevent, secret groups known as vigilance committees were organized. Holding secret meetings, the vigilantes passed judgment on evildoers and then proceeded to carry out the judgment, which was often death. These committees were successful in breaking up such bands as the Plummer gang in Virginia City and in driving many outlaws from Florence and other mining camps of the territory.

Another group of vigilantes was active in Payette Valley. Ranchers there were beset by horse thieves and the regular forces of law and order could not, or did not, meet the situation. The ranchers organized the Payette Vigilance Committee and took matters into their own hands. They quickly broke up the thieves' headquarters at Picket Corral on Payette River and the outlaws speedily departed for parts unknown, to trouble the valley no more.

As late as 1865–66 vigilance committees in Idaho City and Boise City were necessary because the regular peace officers were either hand in glove with the criminal elements or were afraid to enforce the laws. They hanged a notorious killer, broke up a gang making counterfeit gold dust, and made the towns unsafe places in which to practice murder, robbery, and other forms of outlawry.

Defenbach wrote that during their operations in Idaho, vigilance committees hanged twenty-seven thieves and murderers and broke up or drove out many gangs of desperadoes. Certain it is that when criminal leaders and their gangs received the dread warnings signed "3–7–77" or "X X X," they usually lost little time in putting as many miles as possible between themselves and the vigilantes. Just what these signatures meant is a point on which there is some difference of opinion, but it is said that "3–7–77" referred to a grave three feet wide, seven feet long, and seventy-seven inches deep.

III. IDAHO TERRITORY CREATED

IDAHO'S PLACER GOLD had fulfilled part of its mission in our history. It had drawn the eyes of the nation to our mountains and valleys. It had created conditions that made it necessary for Congress to take steps to provide a government closer than that of Washington Territory, with its capital, Olympia, hundreds of miles distant from the gold fields.

How the Territory Was Organized. The first important step toward creating a separate territory was taken when a group of influential men met in the gold camp at Oro Fino to consider plans. Following this meeting, William H. Wallace, Washington Territory's delegate to Congress, and Dr. A. H. Henry went to the national capital. With the help of Congressman John R. McBride, of Oregon, they succeeded in having the necessary bill introduced in Congress. After considerable delay, the Idaho Organic Act creating Idaho Territory was passed in both the House and the Senate. It was signed by President Abraham Lincoln on March 3, 1863, and the separation from Washington Territory became complete.

As originally created by Congress, Idaho Territory was a huge region of about 320,000 square miles which included all the present states of Idaho and Montana and all of Wyoming except a small rectangle in the southwest corner. It was, however, soon reduced to a more reasonable size. In 1864 Montana Territory was created and the Wyoming portion of Idaho Territory was attached to Dakota Territory, with the exception of a narrow strip along the western border. Four years later, in 1868, Wyoming Territory was created, Idaho and Wyoming

Territories being given the same boundaries they now have as states.

Choosing the Name "Idaho." While the bill to create the new territory was before Congress, there was lively debate over giving it a suitable name. When Representative James M. Ashley, chairman of the Committee on Territories, introduced the bill he suggested the name Idaho. However, when the bill was passed by the House, it read "to provide a temporary form of government for the territory of Montana."

In the Senate, Senator Wilson, of Massachusetts, proposed striking out the name Montana and substituting the name Idaho. Senator Harding, of Oregon, agreed. He explained that Idaho in English means "gem of the mountains," and was, therefore, a better name for the mountainous region where the gold camps were located. This argument pleased both the Senate and the House, and Idaho became the official name of the new territory.

It is interesting here to consider the meaning of the word Idaho as explained by John E. Rees in his book, *Idaho Chronology, Nomenclature, Bibliography:*

"Idaho" is a Shoshoni Indian exclamation. The word consists of three parts. The first is "Ee," which in English conveys the idea of "coming down." The second is "dah," which is the Shoshoni stem or root for both "sun" and "mountain." The third syllable, "how," denotes the exclamation and stands for just the same thing in Indian that the exclamation mark (!) does in the English language. The Shoshoni word is "Ee-dah-how," and the Indian thought thus conveyed when translated into English means, "Behold! the sun coming down the mountain."

*　*　*　*　*

So passes in parade the creation of Oregon and Washington territories, statehood for Oregon, and the tempestuous gold camps of early Idaho, with all their hustle and confusion, their strangely mixed social groups, and their hopes and heartbreak. In these camps met the best and the worst, the highest and the lowest types of humanity. But because of them, Idaho Territory came into existence and a firm foundation was laid for nearly three decades of territorial growth and development which was finally climaxed by statehood and full membership in this Federal Union we call the United States of America.

KEEP

IDAHO

GREEN

PART TWO

IDAHO TERRITORY IN
THE GROWING WEST
(*1863–1890*)

How Idaho Territory grew in
population and wealth as its
resources were developed; how
its people created new counties
and communities to serve local
needs; and how mining, farming,
stock raising, and other occupations
made Idaho's pioneer people generally prosperous and
largely self-sufficient during our territorial years

UNIT 4—Territorial Government in Action

UNIT 5—Geographical Advantages of Idaho

UNIT 6—Physical Idaho and Its Settlement

UNIT 7—Idaho's Indian Citizens

UNIT 8—Marching Toward Statehood

Territorial Government in Action

How the people of Idaho Territory established self-government under the provisions of the Idaho Organic Act and laid a firm foundation for state government later.

IDAHO TERRITORY WAS CREATED in 1863. At that time the United States was engaged in a terrible civil war to determine whether the nation should remain united or be divided. Two years later the surrender of General Robert E. Lee and the Confederate armies gave proof that the nation would endure.

But the Civil War left many scars, some that even yet have not been wholly healed. As we continue with the story of Idaho, we shall see that the after effects of the war, and of the troubled years of the Reconstruction Period that followed, were felt even here. Our problems of territorial government were made more difficult because individuals and groups who had opposed each other during the war had carried their differences with them across the Rockies when they came West. As a result, government in Idaho Territory was not always as successful as it might have been under more favorable circumstances.

I. THE IDAHO ORGANIC ACT

WHEN A NEW TERRITORY is added to the United States, the usual method is for Congress to pass an "organic act," which describes the boundaries of the territory and lists the various provisions under which it shall be governed. As we have seen, this was the method used in creating Idaho Territory.

The Idaho Organic Act was a fairly short law consisting of only seventeen sections. It is important to us in Idaho because it provided almost complete self-government for the territory and laid the foundation for state government later.

What the Organic Act Provided.

The Organic Act set up for Idaho Territory the three-way plan under which the national government, territorial governments, and state and local governments all operate. This consists of the three co-equal departments of government, known as the executive, the legislative, and the judicial departments, all working together, but with each largely independent of the other two. This plan, first given in detail in the Constitution of the United States, has proven the best system of government ever used in the entire history of the human race to insure liberty to the people and to protect them in their rights and privileges.

The Executive Department. Under the Idaho Organic Act, executive, or administrative, power was centered in a territorial governor, appointed by the President of the United States for a four-year term. To assist the governor, a territorial secretary, also appointed by the President, was provided.

It was the duty of the governor to see that the laws passed by the territorial legislature were faithfully carried out, and to govern the territory for the best interest of its people. The secretary kept the official government records, and, in the absence or lack of a governor, he became acting governor.

The Legislative Department. The legislative or lawmaking department of Idaho Territory consisted of a council and a house of representatives. It was the duty of the legislature to make suitable laws for governing the territory. These, as we have just seen, were to be put into effect by the governor and other executive officers. The members of the legislature were elected by the vote of the people of the territory.

To represent Idaho Territory in Congress, a territorial delegate was elected by the people every two years. Though not having the right to vote, he was, nevertheless, a very important part of our territorial government, being Idaho's spokesman in Congress.

The Judicial Department. This department consisted of a territorial supreme court and various lower courts. The justices, or judges, of the supreme court were appointed by the President of the United States. The judges of the lower courts were elected by the people. The duties of the judicial department

were much the same as they are today, mainly to conduct the trials of persons accused of violating the law, to punish those found guilty, and so to protect the lives and the property of the people.

Other Provisions. Among the other provisions of the Organic Act, two were of outstanding importance. These related to certain public lands and to the Indian tribes living in Idaho.

Sections 16 and 36 of the public, or government, land in each township were set aside to be used for helping establish and maintain public schools. These lands have all through the years been an important source of income for our system of education. As the lands were sold or rented, the income was placed in a special fund known as the endowment fund, and from this fund our schools today draw a considerable part of their revenue.

You will understand this better if you remember that a township is six miles

6	5	4	3	2	1
7	8	9	10	11	12
18	17	16	15	14	13
19	20	21	22	23	24
30	29	28	27	26	25
31	32	33	34	35	36

A TOWNSHIP

Area 6 miles by 6 miles, or 36 square miles. Each section is 1 mile square and contains 640 acres.

square and consists of thirty-six sections, each section containing 640 acres. The illustration on page 58 will show you the public land sections set apart for the schools. Do you know of any school land near your own home?

The Organic Act protected the Indians of Idaho Territory by requiring territorial officers and courts to faithfully obey all Federal laws and rules applying to the Indians. At that time they were considered wards[1] of the United States, though only a few of the Idaho Indians had then been provided with reservations.

All in all, the Organic Act was a good law. Under its provisions Idaho made large gains in population, wealth, and progress during its twenty-seven years as a territory.

II. GOVERNMENT PROBLEMS AND OBSTACLES

THE NEW TERRITORY faced many difficulties. It was a huge region of more than 320,000 square miles. It had vast areas of mountains, treeless plains, and lands so arid as to be almost true desert. It was almost wholly lacking in population in its early years, except in the mining camps and in the mountain valleys close to the Mormon settlements in Utah. Too, the territory was a long way from the developed regions of the East and Middle West, from which it must draw heavily for settlers and supplies if it were to make material progress. From the east it was reached only by the Oregon Trail and the Mullan Road. The Missouri River offered the only navigable waterway from the east, while the Snake River was the only useful water outlet to the west.

Pressing problems had to be met and dealt with. Thousands of new settlers were needed to establish industries and develop the natural resources. Roads had to be built to provide facilities for travel and transportation. Law and order needed to be extended as fast as new areas were settled. Schools were necessary for the children of the communities. In parts of the territory the Indians were hostile and bitterly opposed to whites entering the country. These problems and many others required wise and united leadership, backed by the loyal co-operation of the people. Unfortunately, such leadership and co-operation were not always forthcoming.

First Territorial Officers. Under the provisions of the Organic Act, President Lincoln named a set of territorial officers. William H. Wallace, who had been active in getting Idaho Territory created by Congress, was appointed the first governor of the territory. As his assistant in the executive department, William B. Daniels was named as territorial secretary.

President Lincoln also appointed the three justices of the supreme court. To these posts he named Sidney Edgerton, Samuel C. Parks, and Alexander C. Smith. George C. Hough was appointed United States attorney for the territory, with D. S. Payne as United States marshal, or peace officer. These appoint-

---

[1]Ward. A person not allowed to manage his own business affairs; one for whom the government acts as guardian.

ments, both executive and judicial, were important because the officers named had to bring legal government to a wild and remote land, and upon the foundations they laid, later officers must build.

Governor Wallace reached Idaho in July, 1863. He named Lewiston as the temporary capital, the selection of a permanent capital being the duty of the territorial legislature not yet in existence. The governor had a census, or count of the population, taken for the purpose of dividing the territory into three judicial districts and for the election of members of the legislature. He set the date for Idaho's first election on October 31, 1863. Then, receiving the Republican party's nomination for territorial delegate in Congress, Wallace resigned as governor, having served only a few months of the term to which he was appointed.

By the laws of the territory, the territorial secretary, William B. Daniels, became acting governor. He was inaugurated December 9, and his inaugural address was described by Dr. Brosnan in his *History of the State of Idaho* as "one of our best-written state papers."

The First Territorial Legislature. The first territorial legislature convened, or met, December 7, 1863, in Lewiston.

Acting governor Daniels, in his message to the lawmakers, recommended the following: That the Nevada Code be used as a guide in making laws for the territory; that steps be taken toward the establishment of a system of public schools; that laws be passed to control gambling and to forbid the sale of intoxicating liquor to Indians; and that the legislature keep the appropriation of money to carry on the work of government as low as possible.

A majority of the members of the first legislature belonged to the Democratic party, while Daniels, the acting governor, was a Republican. Partly for this reason, no doubt, the lawmakers paid little attention to the governor's recommendations. In passing laws they followed the California Code instead of the Nevada Code and in other ways showed their independence. This was, perhaps, desirable to a certain extent, since our three-way plan of government intended the three departments of government to be coequal and more or less independent of each other. Do you think, however, early government in the territory might have been better if the governor and the legislature had worked together more closely?

Though the laws enacted by the first territorial legislature fell short of the

MEETING PLACE OF FIRST TERRITORIAL LEGISLATURE

In this building the first territorial legislature of Idaho met in Lewiston in 1863 and enacted the first laws for the territory.

governor's recommendations and went against his wishes in many respects, nevertheless they made a good beginning. The legislature changed the boundaries of Shoshone, Nez Perce, Idaho, and Boise counties and created Owyhee, Oneida, and Alturas counties in what is now Idaho; it authorized ten counties east of the Rocky Mountains in what soon became Montana Territory; created the offices of territorial treasurer, auditor, and superintendent of public instruction; provided that each county should have a board of three county commissioners, a probate judge, county clerk, auditor and recorder, sheriff, assessor, surveyor, and superintendent of schools; authorized the counties to construct public roads; granted special rights to private individuals for building and operating toll roads, bridges, and ferries; requested each county to construct and maintain a jail; gave special city charters to Boise City and Lewiston; and passed a few small appropriation bills. Thus we see that the first legislature established a pattern of government which, in many respects, is still followed very closely in our state.

Republican Governors vs. Democratic Legislatures. In government, as in other co-operative endeavors, success

depends a great deal on how well the various departments of government work together for the common welfare. If the legislative and executive branches, for example, do not work together, the people usually are the losers. This condition has often existed in our national government and it was a condition that prevailed during much of Idaho's territorial period.

Many of the people who came to Idaho during the gold excitement, and later, were from the Southern and Border States. A majority of them sympathized with the South during the Civil War and the Reconstruction Period that followed the war. In politics they belonged to the Democratic party.

But the Republicans were in control of national affairs during most of Idaho Territory's existence. The Presidents were Republicans and they, naturally, appointed Republicans as governors, territorial secretaries, and as other officers. The members of the legislature, however, were elected by the people and, as we have seen, a majority of them were Democrats. Too, our delegate in Congress was in most cases a Democrat. This set the stage for a more or less constant struggle between the governors on the one hand and the legislatures on the other.

This conflict sometimes seriously interfered with government in Idaho. Governor Lyon, for instance, was ridiculed by his political opponents so much that whatever influence he might have had was practically destroyed. In scorn his opponents wrote and spoke of him as "Cale of the Dale,"[2] and on occasion used even less complimentary terms. Another governor, David W. Ballard, was discourteously treated by the legislature, which sent him an insulting note saying that when his advice was required it would be called for. Still later Governor Mason Brayman, a really able man, aroused so much anger during the Indian wars by his strong opposition to military leaders that his usefulness in Idaho was just about ended. Though these were outstanding examples of differences between the executive and legislative departments during our territorial period of history, they were by no means the only ones. It is, of course, impossible to know to what extent progress in Idaho was hindered by such conflicts.

Idaho Echoes of Reconstruction Days. On the whole, Idaho Territory had few very able or successful governors, though there were exceptions to this general rule. The first two were appointed by President Lincoln and both had had successful records before coming to Idaho. The first, William H. Wallace, served only a few months before resigning to enter Congress as Idaho's first territorial delegate. His successor, Caleb Lyon, did not live up to the reputation he had built for himself. He proved to be a vain, self-important person much given to long, flowery speeches, one who had little

ability to govern the wild and often lawless territory placed under his charge. He made enemies of the people of northern Idaho by favoring the removal of the capital from Lewiston to Boise. A little later he went back to the East and was accused of improperly using government funds placed in his hands for the benefit of Indian tribes. His death before the investigations were completed brought the case to an end but left his name under a cloud.

The assassination of President Lincoln in 1865, shortly after the close of the Civil War, threw national affairs into disorder and ushered in the era in our history known as the Reconstruction Period. During this time, as you learned in your study of United States history, scheming politicians called carpetbaggers controlled the former slave states. Greed and dishonesty in public affairs were common practices in the Southern States and dishonest officials wasted and stole huge sums of public money.

Idaho Territory was not wholly free from the carpetbagger type of public official. A territorial secretary disappeared with a large sum of money appropriated to pay the expenses of government. Other officers, including a few of the governors, as well as elected officers in some of the counties, were accused of using their offices for personal gain. Unfortunately, some of these accusations were true. Others, however, had little if any basis in fact, but grew out of political quarrels and enmities that blazed so high that they caused at least one leader to be shot to death at Idaho City and a territorial delegate in Congress to challenge a governor of Idaho to fight a duel.

[2] "Cale of the Dale." Short for Caleb Lyon of Lyonsdale, as he often signed letters and other papers.

The Office of Governor Scorned.
Governor Ballard followed Governor Lyon. When Ballard's term expired in 1870, President U. S. Grant did not easily find anyone willing to serve the frontier territory for the meager salary of $2,500 a year which the office paid. One after the other he appointed three men, all of whom refused the position. The fourth, Thomas B. Bowen, came to Idaho, stayed about a month, and then resigned.

Grant's fifth effort was more successful. He named Thomas W. Bennett, who took office in 1871. Bennett seems to have had very little regard for public opinion or the dignity of his position, sometimes going on drinking parties with like-minded companions. In spite of that, he was direct and levelheaded in discharging his duties. An example of his common sense is revealed in these words used in addressing the legislature regarding taxes:

Taxation at best is one of the heavy burdens of any people, and when it is laid recklessly and unreasonably, it becomes almost unbearable, and kindles a spirit of insubordination[3] and unrest. Public confidence becomes weak, enterprise dies out, and business stagnates.[4]

After Bennett's term expired, President Grant again had trouble finding a governor for Idaho Territory. He appointed David P. Thompson, but soon removed him for neglect of duty. His next appointment, Mason Brayman, became so unpopular in Idaho as a result of differences between himself and the legislature and the military leaders during the Indian wars in 1877 and 1878 that he re-

signed after serving about half his term. John P. Hoyt was next appointed, but he refused to accept.

Later, President Arthur named John B. Neil as governor of Idaho, and he served three years before being removed for political reasons. He was followed by John N. Irwin, who came, stayed about a month, and departed. So little did he consider his services to Idaho worth that he refused to accept any salary for the time he served.

William M. Bunn, known as the "Dude Governor," was the next and last in the unbroken line of Republican governors. He was described as "arrogant and egotistical," meaning that he was dictatorial, highhanded, and had a very high opinion of his own importance. He made several bitter enemies during the year he held the office.

A Political About-Face. In 1885 Grover Cleveland, the first President the Democrats elected after the Civil War, promptly removed Bunn as governor and appointed Edward A. Stevenson to take his place. Stevenson thus had the honor of becoming the first and only Democrat ever to serve as territorial governor of Idaho.

But, "Believe it or not," as Ripley would have said, the very year that the Democrats elected a President, Idaho voters did an about-face and elected a Republican legislature, so that the same old division between the executive and the legislative branches of territorial government continued. In spite of that, Stevenson's appointment pleased the people of Idaho. He was widely known, not only in Idaho but throughout the West, where he had had a long career in

[3]Insubordination. Disobedience, revolt, rebellion.
[4]Stagnates. Comes to a stop; becomes slow and inactive.

public service. A strong and influential Republican newspaper published the following comment:

> The appointment [of Stevenson], we believe, will meet with general satisfaction. It is the first appointment of a citizen of Idaho for governor. Colonel Stevenson is an old resident of the territory and thoroughly identified with the interests of the people.

Stevenson seems to have pleased most of the people, except in the southeastern part of the territory where the Mormon question was a burning issue. The Mormon Test Oath Law and a law creating the University of Idaho were the outstanding acts of the territorial legislatures meeting during his term as governor. These will be discussed in a later topic.

Governors and Legislators Bury the Hatchet. The year 1889 brought calm to the troubled seas of Idaho politics. Cleveland was defeated for re-election as President in 1888, and the Republicans returned to power with the election of President Benjamin Harrison. The people of Idaho also elected another Republican legislature and for the first time in our territorial history the governor and a majority of the lawmakers belonged to the same political party.

President Harrison named George L. Shoup, a strong Republican, as the last territorial governor of Idaho. Shoup, like Stevenson, was an Idaho resident, well known and respected by both Republicans and Democrats for his services and honorable career in the territory. By that time it seemed clear that statehood for Idaho was near at hand and most activities of the territorial officers were directed toward bringing that event to a successful conclusion. With the appointment of Shoup and the election of a Republican legislature, the political division between the executive and the legislative branches of government came to an end and Idaho's last year as a territory was one of political peace.

Acting Governors. Under the Organic Act the territorial secretary became acting governor when, for any reason, the office of governor was vacant. Since Idaho's eleven territorial governors served an average of about two and a half years of their four-year terms, it is plain that the secretaries often had to assume the governors' duties.

Notable among the secretaries was Edward J. Curtis. At intervals he served as governor from 1869 almost to the time Idaho became a state. One of the most popular and levelheaded men of the territorial period, Curtis actually served as governor for a total time longer than any of the regularly appointed governors. His work was generally so satisfactory that seldom was he criticized, even by leaders of the Democrats. He deserves to be remembered among the few able governors chosen to serve Idaho during territorial years.

III. IDAHO'S TERRITORIAL LAWMAKERS

A SINGLE BOOK, unless very large, would not hold all the laws enacted by the fifteen legislatures that met while Idaho was a territory. By far the greater part of these laws dealt with routine or ordinary matters, such as tax laws and laws appropriating money for various governmental activities. They were necessary but they were mainly concerned with the unexciting business of the everyday affairs of government. Like most laws enacted over quite a period of time, some were good, some were not good, and some had little effect one way or another.

The Capital Dispute. One of the earliest laws passed by the territorial legislature almost caused the territory to be divided. The Organic Act left the duty of naming the territorial capital in the hands of the legislature. In carrying out this duty the lawmakers ran head on into trouble.

When Idaho Territory was first created, Lewiston was the most important city in the territory. It had, therefore, been chosen as temporary capital. But by 1864 southwestern Idaho, which included the famous Boise Basin and Silver City mining districts, had by far the largest part of Idaho's population. Newly established Boise City was already showing promise. With these facts in mind, the second territorial legislature, meeting in Lewiston in December, 1864, enacted a law making Boise City the permanent capital of the territory.

The law caused great anger among the people of northern Idaho. Lewiston, thoroughly aroused, determined to hold the capital by force, if necessary. Governor Caleb Lyon, fearing he would be prevented from leaving Lewiston, announced that he was going duck hunting. He then set off down Snake River in a canoe. By special arrangement he had a carriage waiting downstream to take him to Walla Walla. Having got out of Lewiston by this trick, the governor then made his way to Boise City.

After Lyon's departure, Silas Cochran, the territorial secretary, became acting governor. He was immediately placed under arrest by the sheriff of Nez Perce County, and a suit was started in the courts to decide whether the Capital Removal Act was constitutional or not.

Judge Aleck Smith decided in favor of Lewiston, but a new territorial secretary, Clinton DeWitt Smith, refused to obey the court order. With the help of United States soldiers from near-by Fort Lapwai, he forcibly took possession of the territorial records and transferred them under guard to Boise City. Later the territorial supreme court reversed Judge Smith's decision and declared the Capital Removal Act legal and constitutional.

This officially ended the dispute and

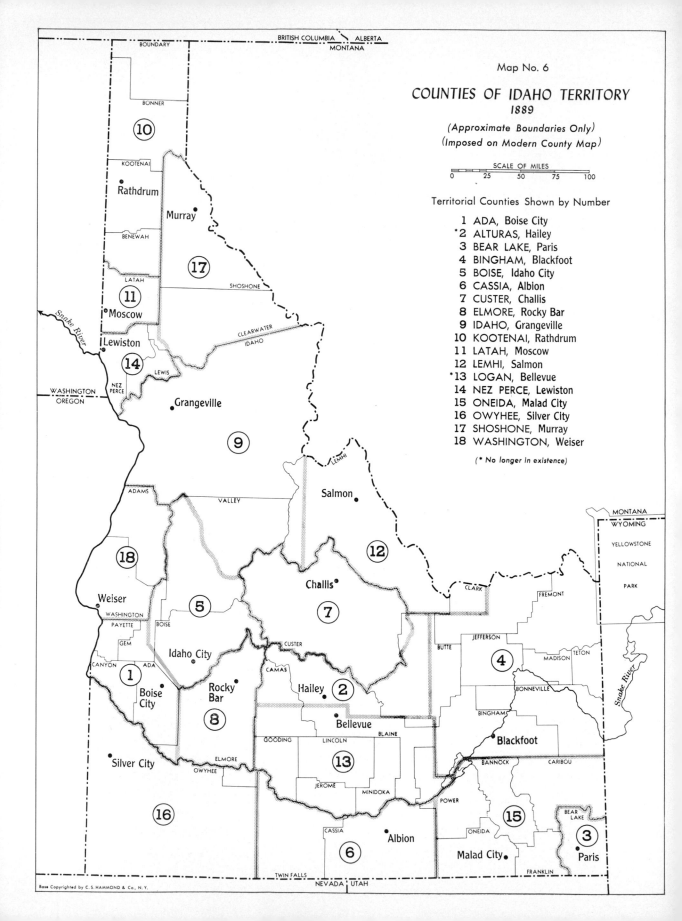

Map No. 6

COUNTIES OF IDAHO TERRITORY
1889

(Approximate Boundaries Only)
(Imposed on Modern County Map)

SCALE OF MILES
0   25   50   75   100

Territorial Counties Shown by Number

1 ADA, Boise City
*2 ALTURAS, Hailey
3 BEAR LAKE, Paris
4 BINGHAM, Blackfoot
5 BOISE, Idaho City
6 CASSIA, Albion
7 CUSTER, Challis
8 ELMORE, Rocky Bar
9 IDAHO, Grangeville
10 KOOTENAI, Rathdrum
11 LATAH, Moscow
12 LEMHI, Salmon
*13 LOGAN, Bellevue
14 NEZ PERCE, Lewiston
15 ONEIDA, Malad City
16 OWYHEE, Silver City
17 SHOSHONE, Murray
18 WASHINGTON, Weiser

(* No longer in existence)

Base Copyrighted by C. S. HAMMOND & Co., N.Y.

Boise City became the permanent capital. But the ill feeling stirred up resulted in rather serious differences between northern and southern Idaho. In the middle 1860's an attempt was made to create Columbia Territory from northern Idaho, eastern Washington, and western Montana. In 1873, 1875, 1877, and 1878, other efforts were made to separate northern Idaho from the rest of the territory. A final effort nearly succeeded when, in 1886, Washington applied for statehood with the counties of northern Idaho attached. This bill passed both houses of Congress but President Cleveland, on the advice of Governor Stevenson, refused to sign it, thus preserving the boundaries of Idaho as they are today.

New Counties. One of the most important duties of the territorial legislatures was to provide local government for a constantly increasing population. This was done by creating new counties as the need for them arose.

As we have already seen, the four counties authorized by the legislature of Washington Territory were in existence when Congress created Idaho Territory in 1863. These were Shoshone County, with the county seat at Pierce City; Nez Perce County, with Lewiston as the county seat; Idaho County, having the county seat at Florence; and Boise County, with the county seat at Idaho City.

We have also seen how the first Idaho territorial legislature made certain changes in the boundaries of these four counties and added Owyhee, Oneida, and Alturas counties to the list. Owyhee and Oneida counties comprised the vast region south of Snake River between the Oregon-Idaho boundary and the Continental Divide in what is now western Wyoming. Ruby City was the first county seat of Owyhee County, but in 1866 the county government was moved to Silver City, which by that time had practically absorbed Ruby City. Soda Springs was the original county seat of Oneida County, but Malad City soon displaced Soda Springs as the seat of county government.

North of Snake River new gold discoveries were made around the headwaters of Boise River, Big Wood River, and Salmon River. Alturas County was created to provide government for the miners and stock raisers moving into the region. The small mining village of Esmeralda was named the county seat, but before the county was actually organized the county seat was changed to Rocky Bar, another small mining town. Today even the location of Esmeralda is not definitely known, though it is believed to have been on or near the South Boise River not far from the mouth of Feather River, in what is now Elmore County. Because of the uncertainty as to its actual location, Esmeralda is sometimes spoken of as "Idaho's lost county seat."

In 1863 a company of soldiers camped on what is now called Government Island, in the Boise River near the present city of Boise. There they built barracks for a permanent military encampment. A few weeks later Boise City was surveyed and a town started. The new city almost immediately became the main supply point for the mines in Boise Basin and a trading center for farmers and stockmen settling in the Boise Valley. Therefore, in 1864, the second territorial legislature created

Ada County from the western part of Boise County and established the county seat at Boise City. The same year, as you remember, the territorial capital was moved from Lewiston to Boise City, and the new settlement was well started on its way to becoming the leading city of Idaho, a rank it still holds.

Two years later rich placer gold was found on Napias (NA′pi-us) Creek in the Salmon River Mountains and the boom city of Leesburg sprang up almost overnight. A supply point was established at the junction of the Salmon and Lemhi rivers. There, in 1867, Colonel George L. Shoup and a group of businessmen laid out Salmon City. This town became the county seat of Lemhi County, formed from the eastern part of Idaho County to provide local government for the mining camps of the district.

In the meantime Mormon settlers from Utah continued to move into the mountain valleys of southeastern and south central Idaho. This led to the creation of Bear Lake County in 1875, with the county seat at Paris, and Cassia County in 1879, with Albion as the county seat.

While Boise Valley was filling with settlers, there was a considerable movement of stockmen down the Snake into the valleys of the Payette and Weiser rivers. By 1879 so many people had moved into this area that the legislature provided Washington County for their local needs, establishing the county seat at Weiser Bridge. A little later the seat was moved to the new town of Weiser, which was by that time the principal settlement in the region.

Hard times struck Idaho Territory in the 1870's as a result of the so-called silver panic, during which the price of silver dropped so low that most of the silver mines of the West were forced to close, including those in Idaho. For this reason, population increased quite slowly for a few years. No other new county was created until 1881. In that year Custer County was organized from parts of Alturas and Lemhi counties to provide for new mining and stock-raising districts in the upper Salmon River country. Challis was made the county seat of this county.

As early as 1864 the territorial legislature of Idaho authorized the formation of Kootenai County in the Idaho Panhandle, the seat of government to be located at Seneaquoteen (SĔN′ĕ-AH′ quŏ-teen), a trading post below Lake Pend Oreille on the Pend Oreille River. Not for seventeen years, however, until 1881, were there the fifty residents needed to sign a petition to actually organize the county. Then the necessary steps were taken and Kootenai County became a reality, with Rathdrum as the county seat.

Only two more counties followed in the next seven years. Bingham County was drawn from the northern part of Oneida County in 1885, and Blackfoot was chosen as the county seat. Three years later, in 1888, Latah County was created from part of Kootenai County and unorganized territory in northern Idaho. The county seat of this county was located at Moscow. An odd fact about Latah County is that it was created by a special act of Congress, the only county in Idaho having that distinction.

The mining region around the headwaters of Boise River was so rich and productive that several good mining towns had grown up there. The county seat of Alturas County had been moved to Hailey, which was too far away from the upper Boise River district to be reached without great loss of time and considerable travel difficulties. Accordingly, Elmore County was created from the southwestern part of Alturas County in 1889, and Rocky Bar once more became a county seat, an honor it was to lose again when the seat of county government was moved to Mountain Home, located on the Oregon Short Line Railroad.

Only one more county came into existence during Idaho's territorial period. This was Logan County, formed of the southern two thirds of what remained of the once huge "Empire of Alturas," as Alturas County was sometimes called. Most of the central and southern part of the county was a semidesert, but around the county seat at Bellevue, in the northern part, were some of the richest mines of the territory.

Many changes in county boundaries, as well as many new counties, were still to be made. We shall learn about these in later units telling of events after Idaho became a state.

The Mormon Test Oath Law. The Mormon people had extensive settlements in Utah and southern Idaho. The Mormon Church at that time permitted polygamy (po-LIG-a-mĭ), or the practice of allowing men to have more than one wife. Of course, most Mormon men were not polygamists, but enough were to cause widespread criticism of the church.

Congress passed the Edmunds Act in 1882 forbidding polygamy in the United States and its territories. Three years later the territorial legislature of Idaho passed the Mormon Test Oath Law. This law forbade anyone to vote, hold public office, or serve on juries in Idaho who practiced polygamy or belonged to an organization that permitted it.

The immediate effect of this law was to deprive thousands of Mormons in Idaho Territory of their full citizenship, since merely by belonging to the Latter-day Saints Church they were assumed to be guilty under the law. Hundreds of Mormons were arrested, fined, and imprisoned during the eight years the law was in effect.

In 1890 the leaders of the Mormon Church issued a proclamation calling on all Latter-day Saints to end the practice of polygamy and to obey the laws of the nation and of the territories, states, and communities in which they lived. In 1893 the legislature of Idaho, which had then become a state, restored full citizenship to the Mormons and brought a peaceful end to the only serious conflict that has ever arisen between church and state in Idaho.

A Happy Ending. We usually enjoy stories that have a happy ending. The story of the fifteenth and last territorial legislature ends in that manner. As territorial government was drawing toward a close in Idaho, the legislature passed a law authorizing the University of Idaho and locating the institution at Moscow. This was not only a great step forward in education but it pleased the people of northern Idaho and helped to decrease the long-standing anger that had existed among the people of that part of the territory as a result of the moving of the capital from Lewiston to Boise a quarter of a century earlier.

* * * * *

Thus, briefly, have we traced the rise of government in Idaho Territory. From vigilance committees and miners' courts to laws enacted, administered, and judged by legally established departments of government—all this was a part of our orderly progress from the rip-roaring mining camps of the Golden Decade to the settled life of a commonwealth standing at the doorway of statehood. In our next two units we shall take a closer look at the natural resources and advantages Idaho could offer its citizens, and at events and developments which, during territorial years, laid so solid a foundation for our present well-being as a state. We shall find much in both units to strengthen and confirm our faith in Idaho, the state we proudly call home.

Geographical Advantages of Idaho

How the location, size, surface, climate, and natural regions of Idaho influenced its development as a territory and state.

"HISTORY WITHOUT GEOGRAPHY is like a body without bones." How true this old quotation is! History is the record of a people—how they live, the kinds of work they do, their day-by-day accomplishments. Nothing else so shapes and controls a people's history as their physical environment, or the natural conditions of the region in which they live—its size, location, elevation, surface, climate, and natural resources—in short, its geography.

Idaho is a good example of how physical environment influences ways of living. Fertile soils and a favorable climate have made parts of the state into outstanding farming sections. Mountain forests encourage lumbering and the manufacture of forest products. A great variety and richness of minerals have placed Idaho among the great mining regions of the nation and of the world. Abundant rivers provide water for irrigation and hydroelectricity. Scenic attractions and wildlife make us the envy of less favored states.

In order to understand the development of Idaho as a territory and, later, as a state, we need to know its geography. What natural regions does it contain? What kind of surface does it have? What is its climate like? What type of vegetation does it produce? What are its principal natural resources? We shall better appreciate Idaho's many advantages and the opportunities it offers its citizens as we discover the answers to these and numerous other questions connected with the geography of the state in which we live.

I. MOTHER NATURE'S WORK IN IDAHO

THE EARTH'S STORY, as told by the rocks, proves that Mother Nature has been busy for a very long time preparing Idaho as a home for man. The geology of Idaho is a very interesting story, but it is too long to tell here. However, a few glimpses into the long ago will help us understand our geography better and show us how we benefit in many ways from Mother Nature's work through the ages.

An Ancient Treasure Chest. One of the best examples of how our Idaho of today benefits very greatly from nature's work in past ages is found in the northern part of the state. For a very long period of time, perhaps hundreds of millions of years, this region lay at the bottom of an ancient sea. For long ages earth, sand, and gravel washing down from higher land bordering the sea were spread over

ZINC PLANT OF THE BUNKER HILL AND SULLIVAN MINE AT KELLOGG

In the "Old Rocks" of northern Idaho are almost inexhaustible resources of silver, lead, and zinc dating back to the Pre-Cambrian Era, hundreds of millions of years ago.

SIMPLOT FERTILIZER PLANT AT POCATELLO

Marine fossil deposits in the phosphate rocks of southeastern Idaho show how Mother Nature's work in past ages became the basis for many modern industries.

the sea bottom until the sediments were hundreds and, in places, thousands of feet in thickness.

Later the sea bottom was elevated and became mountains. The sedimentary deposits gradually hardened into stone and became the "Old Rocks" now found in northern Idaho and western Montana. In these areas are located the huge deposits of silver, lead, copper, zinc, and other minerals that have placed the Coeur d'Alene district of northern Idaho and the Butte district of Montana among the richest mining regions of the world.

Phosphate, Gift of Ancient Seas. Today the nation and the world are looking to southeastern Idaho for a large share of the phosphate rock used in the manufacture of fertilizers and certain chemicals so necessary in our modern civilization. These phosphate deposits, the greatest in the United States, are another of nature's gifts and date back about two hundred million years.

At that time a vast shallow sea or arm of the ocean stretched far northward from southern California to the Arctic regions, filling a great valley or trough where the Rocky Mountains now stand. This sea swarmed with countless myriads of shellfish and other forms of marine life. For millions and millions of years these sea creatures lived, died, and added their remains to the ooze which in time covered the sea floor to a depth of hundreds of feet. When the bottom of the sea became dry land, the sediments hardened and became the rocks in which are found Idaho's almost limitless phosphate resources. These rocks are now the basis of new mining and manufacturing industries that add millions of dollars annually to the business and industrial life of the state.

Building the Western Mountains. Millions of years ago Mother Nature began her great labor of building the Western mountains. The forming of these mountains gave us our splendid scenery, much of our gold, silver, and other minerals, and caused great changes in the climate of the Pacific Northwest.

First to be lifted were the Sierra Nevada and the Cascade mountains of California, Oregon, and Washington. These ranges cut off the direct sweep of winds from the Pacific and brought important climatic changes to the region east of the mountains. The weather became colder and drier and the seas and swamps began to slowly dry up. Today the regions we call the Great Basin and the Columbia Plateau lie in the "rain shadow" of these Western mountain ranges. This means that the mountains steal much of the moisture from the westerly winds as they move up the western slopes of the mountains. As a result, successful farming in most parts of these great natural regions is possible only by the use of irrigation.

For millions of years Mother Nature's mountain-building work continued. Volcanic activity was very great. The terrific heat and pressure within the earth caused minerals contained in the rocks to melt and run together, forming the beds, veins, and deposits of gold, silver, copper, and other hard metals now so widely distributed in the mountains of Idaho and other parts of the West.

Paving the Northwestern Plains with Lava. During the periods of greatest volcanic activity, vast quantities of molten lava were forced to the surface in many

Courtesy U.S. Bureau of Reclamation, Region No. 1, Boise

parts of the Northwest. There the lava flows spread out to form the fields of lava rock now found in many places between the Sierra Nevada–Cascade ranges and the Rocky Mountains.

As ages passed, the great sheets of lava exposed on the surface began to decompose or break up to form soil. Today these soils are among the most fertile in the nation. They make the Snake River Valley and other parts of the Columbia Plateau notable farming regions where natural precipitation is sufficient to grow crops or where irrigation water can be carried to the farms and ranches.

Ancient Lakes and Lake Beds. Another kind of work done by Mother Nature in the last few million years caused lakes to form in Idaho and other parts of the West. Though most of these lakes no longer exist, they have, nevertheless, been of great value to the people now living where their waters once covered the land.

The greatest contribution the ancient lakes made to the Idaho of today is the rich alluvial[1] soil now found where the lakes once existed. On such old lake beds Idaho's earliest agricultural settlements were made. There, too, some of the leading farming communities have grown up, as well as several of our most important cities.

Ice Sheet and Mountain Glaciers. You have read of the great ice sheet which once covered the northern part of North America, similar to the icecap that now covers Greenland. In Idaho the ice sheet reached as far south as the southern end of Lake Coeur d'Alene. At the same time great glaciers filled most of the mountain valleys in other parts of the Northwest.

The ice sheet and the glaciers made some very important changes in our part of the West. They carved out valleys and basins, dammed streams, and created many of the beautiful lakes now found in northern Idaho. They left glacial soils around Lakes Pend Oreille and Coeur

[1]Alluvial (al-LU-vi-al). Deposited by water.

d'Alene and spread much of the silt or finely ground soil later washed down into Kootenai Valley. They pulverized mineral deposits and helped spread the gold dust and nuggets whose discovery in modern times led directly to the creation of Idaho Territory. The ice also had a great deal to do with shaping much of the beautiful scenery for which our state is noted.

This short story of Mother Nature's work in Idaho and the Northwest is only a hurried view. But we have suggested enough to show how deeply we are indebted to the past and how modern man is indeed the heir of the ages.

II. THE SIZE AND LOCATION OF IDAHO

HAVE YOU EVER WONDERED how Idaho compares in size with other states and with some of the important nations of the world? Could it ever support a population of millions, as some of the states and nations do?

The Size of Idaho. Among the states, Idaho ranks twelfth in size. The two states most nearly the size of Idaho are Kansas, slightly smaller, and Minnesota, just a trifle larger. In the Old World Great Britain, which includes England, Scotland, and Wales, is only a little larger than Idaho.

According to the 1946 map of Idaho prepared by the United States Geological Survey and the Idaho Bureau of Mines and Geology, the state is about 483 miles long from north to south and 310 miles wide along the southern boundary. Across the narrowest part of the Panhandle, where Idaho joins British Columbia, it measures about forty-five miles.[2]

The United States Census Bureau gives the total area of Idaho as 83,557 square miles. This is greater than the combined area of our nine smallest states: Rhode Island, Delaware, Connecticut, New Jersey, Massachusetts, New Hampshire, Vermont, Maryland, and West Virginia. Our largest county, Idaho County, could hold within its borders the three smallest states and have left over enough land for a few good-sized farms.

Idaho's Favorable Location. Three facts about Idaho's location explain much of its progress and growth. These are: (1) its latitude, or distance from the Equator; (2) its location on the western slope of the Rocky Mountains; and (3) its situation on natural routes of travel to the coastal cities and regions of the Pacific Northwest.

Distance from the Equator. If you examine any good map of North America or of the United States, you will find that the forty-fifth parallel crosses Idaho almost in the exact center of the state. This shows that Idaho is located almost exactly halfway between the Equator and the North Pole. This insures a truly temperate climate, known to be best for promoting health and giving energy and ambition to the people living in such a climate. A temperate climate is best, too, for a great variety of the most valuable food crops, some of which do not thrive in tropical regions. Can you name Idaho's

[2]The *World Book Encyclopedia* gives the north-south length of Idaho as 490 miles and its greatest width as 305 miles.

leading food crops? Are these crops also grown extensively in hot lands?

On the Western Slope of the Rockies. Idaho lies wholly on the western slope of the Rocky Mountains. Since the prevailing winds of the Temperate Zone are from the west, we have more rain and snow as a rule in Idaho than falls in states located on the eastern slope of the mountains. Why is this important to us?

You remember, no doubt, that a great warm ocean current, the Japan Current, moves southward off the western coast of the United States. Winds that cross this current are somewhat warmed and take up moisture from the ocean. As a result, though Idaho is more than three hundred miles inland, our winters are somewhat milder and the summers a little cooler than they would be without the moderating influence of the westerly winds.

Crossed by Natural Routes of Travel. Our state lies squarely across lines of travel from the Middle West and the East to the Pacific Northwest. Both through the Snake River Valley in southern Idaho and the Purcell Trench in northern Idaho, railroads and highways form a transportation network. Idaho thus has a large share in the great tide of travel, trade, and transportation flowing back and forth across the nation.

Also, from Idaho, mountain valleys and passes lead north and south, giving direct routes into Montana and British Columbia on the north and to the Southwest and the great coastal cities of California on the south. From earliest territorial days to the present these natural routes of travel across Idaho have been extensively used by passing travelers and they are employed today to move the products of Idaho's farms, ranches, mines, and forests to market.

III. ELEVATION AND SURFACE

FEW OF THE STATES have greater differences in elevation and surface than Idaho. These in turn have great influence over our climate, vegetation, and the ways in which we live.

Height Above Sea Level. All of Idaho lies between the elevation of Lewiston, 783 feet,[3] and the summit of Mount Borah, 12,655 feet. In general, most of the state is between 2,000 and 10,000 feet above sea level. Lewiston is the only city lower than a thousand feet, while only about half a hundred peaks rise above

the ten-thousand-foot level.[4] The northern part of the state is somewhat lower than the southern part, with the average elevation of the state as a whole not far from five thousand feet.

Our Varied Surface. Idaho lies in the Rocky Mountain Region and in the Columbia Plateau, except for a small section in the southeast. Only a little more than half the state is mountainous. The rest consists of plateaus and valleys. Practically all the surface belongs to one or another of the six following types.

[3]Source: *Climate and Man,* the 1941 Yearbook of the U.S. Department of Agriculture. The *Idaho Encyclopedia* gives the elevation as 747 feet.

[4]Appendix Table 1 lists the fifty-two highest peaks in Idaho, as compiled from the *Idaho Encyclopedia* and U.S. Forest Service bulletins.

Young Rugged Mountains. Much of Idaho's surface is made up of young, rugged mountains, cut by deep canyons and gorges. The ranges along the Idaho-Montana border and those of central Idaho are examples of this type of surface. Few roads penetrate such regions, which are now of value chiefly as watersheds, grazing sections, and protective areas for wildlife. They contain much timber and minerals, but transportation difficulties hinder their development.

Rolling Prairie Plateaus. The Clearwater Plateau, the Ashton Plateau, the Weiser Plateau, and a few smaller parts of the state are rolling prairie uplands. These are usually foothill belts that border mountainous districts. They are among our best general farming, dry-farming, and grazing sections.

Semiarid Plateaus. Bordering the Snake River Valley proper and in other parts of southern Idaho are broad, treeless, semiarid plateaus covered with desert types of vegetation. These dry regions are thinly settled except for scattered spots where irrigation is practiced. Their greatest value is as grazing lands for cattle and sheep.

Lava Plateaus. Several barren plateaus between the Snake River and the mountains of central Idaho are wholly or largely covered with lava, the result of past volcanic activity. Grazing is the only use of these plateaus, except for some scenic attractions such as the Craters of the Moon National Monument.

River Valleys. The great open plains of the Snake River Valley represent another type of Idaho's varied surface. These are lower than the bordering plateaus. The soils usually produce abundant crops when placed under irrigation. This type of surface extends up the valleys of other rivers entering the Snake River Plain. In these valleys are found our heaviest concentration of population and industry, as well as most of our cities and towns.

Other valleys in various parts of the state furnish fertile farming lands, though on a very small scale compared with the

THE AWESOME SHOSHONE GORGE OF THE SNAKE RIVER

Here the Twin Falls–Jerome Bridge, one of the highest in the West, crosses the Snake.

Snake River Valley. Many of our streams in the mountainous regions have little or no valley land along them, but flow in narrow, rugged canyons.

Old Lake Beds, Mountain Basins, and Glacial Valleys. These land types are found widely scattered in various parts of the state. Some of our best farming sections are in such areas, though usually small in size. Others are mainly grazing districts. A few, such as Stanley Basin in central Idaho, are too high for farming, but supply grazing during the warm season. A few of the high, glacial valleys are scenic attractions, though they are usually remote and not easily reached, except by the more hardy hunters and vacationists.

IV. CLIMATE

LYING BETWEEN FORTY-TWO AND FORTY-NINE DEGREES north latitude and in the belt of westerly winds from the Pacific, Idaho has a favorable temperate climate. But location is not, perhaps, the strongest influence in its climate. Both temperature and precipitation, the two most important factors in climate, depend to a large extent on elevation, or altitude above sea level.

Elevation and Climate. In *Climate and Man,* the 1941 Yearbook of the United States Department of Agriculture, we find this explanation of Idaho's climate:

So far as temperature and precipitation are concerned, altitude is in general a more important factor of control than latitude in the climate of Idaho. The entire state lies within the region of prevailing westerly winds and is affected in a marked degree by the influence of the Pacific Ocean, so that its climate is milder than its latitude and altitude would indicate. It is considerably milder than that of states lying in the same latitude east of the Continental Divide, the lofty ranges of which frequently serve as barriers against the cold waves and blizzards that occasionally sweep down from the Canadian Northwest.

In the highest mountains we find the coolest weather and, usually, the greatest precipitation, this being deposited in largest quantities as rain or snow on the western slopes of the mountains. The lower elevations are generally both warmer and drier than the uplands.

Winds and Climate. Except in summer and early fall, the winds reaching northern Idaho are well supplied with moisture from the Pacific. As a result, that part of the state has an average annual precipitation of from twenty to forty inches. In summer, however, the winds are warmed by the Columbian Plains after crossing over the Cascade Mountains, so they provide less rainfall during the warm season.

Southern Idaho is drier than northern Idaho because the winds in summer blow for longer distances across the south Columbian and Great Basin plains before reaching Idaho. Then they continue on across the Snake River Plains, usually holding what moisture they have until they begin rising to pass over the ranges of the mountains of central and eastern Idaho. Lying thus in the rain shadow of the California and Oregon mountains, the plains of southern Idaho are dry in summer. Even in winter they often receive only a light covering of snow. Precipitation increases as the moving air reaches the mountains. This is fortunate, as the increase in moisture provides the mountain watersheds with the rain and snow they need to furnish water for irrigation during the growing season.

Local storms over much of the state are common, especially in the mountains. These are caused by comparatively warm air in the valleys being displaced by colder air from the heights. The rising air is quickly cooled as it rises, clouds form, and often rain or hail falls in summer. In the colder seasons the precipitation usually takes the form of snow.

Length of Growing Season. The length of the growing season largely determines the kinds of crops that may be raised in Idaho. The growing season is shorter in high elevations than it is lower down. A good many mountain valleys and basins in Idaho have fertile soil and sufficient moisture, but are located too high for successful farming. In these high-altitude locations, the growing season is usually less than three months, with frost likely to occur at any time. In the lower parts of the state the average growing season is from four to five months, and in a few favored locations even more. This is long enough to mature many of the Temperate Zone field crops, fruits, and vegetables.

Climatic Zones of Life in Idaho. Both plant and animal life are greatly affected by elevation and climate. Different kinds of plants and animals choose to live at different elevations and under differing climatic conditions. Human life, too, is forced to yield to the demands of these important factors.

Some of our highest peaks reach above the timber line. There trees do not grow, though some bushes and shrubbery are usually found. Somewhat lower we find small, stunted trees fighting for existence against unfavorable environment. Still lower, evergreens and aspens decorate the mountain slopes. Along the streams willows, birches, and cottonwoods are common in the southern part of the state, with mixed growth in the north. In the drier regions such desert vegetation as sagebrush and juniper are the rule.

In a similar way, wildlife shows a preference for different altitudes. Mountain sheep and goats spend much of their time among the crags and peaks. Deer and elk frequent high ranges in summer, dropping to lower elevations as snow blankets the ridges and makes food harder to secure. Moose and most fur bearers prefer to stay along the waterways, but water and food seem more important than elevation in deciding where they spend most of their time.

Birds, too, have their choice locations. Waterfowl seem to prefer the lower streams and lakes, while such birds as eagles and some species of grouse are lovers of the heights.

People, like plants and animals, have definite notions about where they establish their homes. In general, they do not choose to live above the mile-high level, though communities have grown up in higher locations where natural resources made such locations profitable places in which to live. Milder temperatures, longer growing seasons, and a greater variety of plants which can be grown all combine to keep most Idaho people below the five-thousand-foot level.

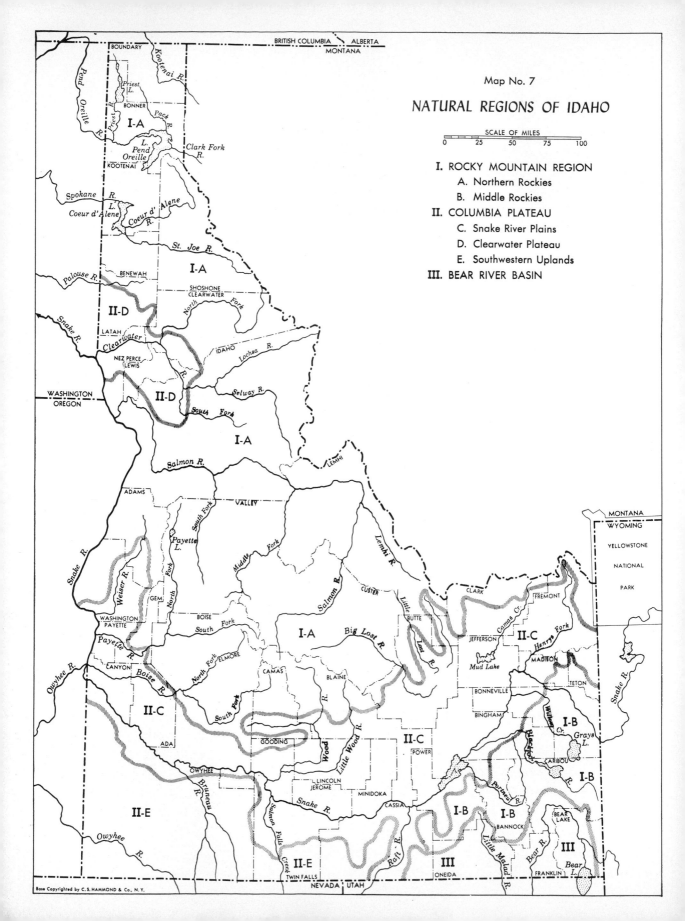

Map No. 7

NATURAL REGIONS OF IDAHO

SCALE OF MILES
0   25   50   75   100

I. ROCKY MOUNTAIN REGION
   A. Northern Rockies
   B. Middle Rockies
II. COLUMBIA PLATEAU
   C. Snake River Plains
   D. Clearwater Plateau
   E. Southwestern Uplands
III. BEAR RIVER BASIN

V. NATURAL REGIONS ENTERING IDAHO

IF YOU LOOK AT MAP NO. 7, "Natural Regions of Idaho," you will see that Idaho shares in three of the more than a score of great natural regions into which the United States is divided. These are the Rocky Mountain Region, the Columbia Plateau, and the Great Basin.

The Rocky Mountain Region. When the Lewis and Clark Expedition reached Idaho in the summer of 1805, it found the way west barred by the rugged mountain ranges that crowd most of Idaho north of the Snake River Valley. These ranges are part of the Rocky Mountain Region.

Idaho's Rocky Mountain Region is an area of approximately 45,000 square miles, more than half the total area of the state. By far the greater portion is in the region north of the Snake River Valley. This belongs to the province of the Northern Rockies. The remainder is in eastern Idaho and is part of the Middle Rocky Mountain Region.

The Rocky Mountain Region has vast resources of minerals, timber, water, grazing lands, wildlife, scenery, and recreational areas. There are small but fertile farming districts in some of the mountain valleys and on the Lakes Plateau of the Panhandle. However, lack of transportation and travel facilities in most of the region has prevented extensive development and use of the resources except in limited areas.

There are good highways and railroads in the northern part of Idaho. There river valleys and low passes through the mountains lead into a fine natural transportation route consisting of the Purcell Trench and the Spokane River Valley. Similar conditions exist in the southern part of the Rocky Mountain Region bordering the Snake River Plains where narrow valleys used by railroads and highways open gateways into the mountains.

But these roads on the north and south

PACK TRAIN IN IDAHO'S MOUNTAIN REGION

Much of the Rocky Mountain Region of Idaho is so rugged that no roads have been constructed there. The pack train is still the principal means of transportation in such areas.

leave the vast interior highlands of Idaho's mountain region almost untouched by modern methods of transportation. Only a few access roads, constructed principally by the Forest Service, and a few landing fields, built where there is enough level land for a small aircraft to land and take off, provide modern travel and transportation facilities.

For most of the region the pack train, horses or mules with burdens lashed to their backs, is still the only method except hiking by which remote places may be reached. Numerous trails along the watercourses, or hewn from the sides of steep mountains, lead to many parts of the wilderness. Over these trails pack outfits move with supplies for Forest Service posts, sheep camps, hunting and fishing lodges, small mines, and other wilderness outposts.

Mining, lumbering, stock raising, and farming are the chief basic industries. There has been extensive development of recreational areas around Lakes Pend Oreille and Coeur d'Alene in northern Idaho, Payette Lake in central Idaho, in the noted Sun Valley playground, and on a smaller scale in other parts of the region. The wildlife resources are not equaled by any other natural region of the state.

What reasons can you give why this is, in general, Idaho's most sparsely populated natural region? With a total population in 1950 of approximately 100,000 persons, the entire Rocky Mountain Region had only ten cities or towns with more than one thousand people each. The largest was Coeur d'Alene, the only one with superior natural advantages that ranked among the top ten cities of Idaho in size.

The Snake River Region. Second in size but first in economic importance among the natural regions of Idaho is the Snake River Region. Lying in southern Idaho, it is part of the huge Columbia Plateau that covers most of Oregon, Washington, and Idaho between the Cascade Mountains and the Rockies.

This comparatively dry region includes a little more than two fifths of the total area of Idaho. Its extent is more than 30,000 square miles, a territory larger than any one of our eight smallest states and more than the combined area of the five smallest together.

The surface of the region is remarkably varied. There are true plains with deep, loamy soil of great natural richness. Along the streams are narrower strips of bottom land. In other portions are elevated plateaus, where the few streams that enter this thirsty land have carved deep canyons whose nearly vertical walls of lava often hide the waters from the searching eye of the noonday sun. North of the Snake River, in the central part of the plains, is a remarkable lava plateau where bleak and forbidding floors of naked lava cover the surface and rob it of any usefulness except as a scenic area or a scientific curiosity.

South of Snake River lofty ranges of mountains rise from the desert floor. Some of the peaks reach an elevation of eight thousand to nine thousand feet, a few even more. These mountains lend variety to the landscape, provide excellent grazing on their slopes, and furnish dependable watersheds where streams have their sources.

CARROTS GROWN FOR SEED

Southern Idaho grows a large share of the nation's garden and vegetable seed.

In this natural region live about 400,-000 people, almost 70 per cent of Idaho's total population. It contains seventeen of the twenty-five largest cities of the state, including the top five: Boise, Pocatello, Idaho Falls, Twin Falls, and Nampa.

What has caused this natural division, consisting of roughly one third of the state, to become the home of about two thirds of the people? There are several reasons for this.

By far the greatest resource of the Snake River Region is its productive soil. By means of irrigation large tracts of land have truly been made to "blossom as the rose." Acre for acre, these famous farmlands produce equal to the best and better than most. It is no mere figure of speech when we call the Snake River the "Nile of Idaho," for not even the valley of the Nile produces crops in greater variety and abundance than does the Snake River

CHERRY BLOSSOM TIME IN PAYETTE VALLEY

From garden seed to tree fruits, the Snake River Valley excels.

Valley where man has conquered the desert and brought life-giving water to quench the thirst of the land.

Grazing is extensively practiced in many sections where water is not available or where the surface is unfavorable for irrigation. Grazing is further encouraged by the fact that there is still much public land which constitutes a large unfenced open range for great numbers of sheep, cattle, and horses, though the last are not so valuable as in the days before automobiles and tractors became common.

A third thing contributing to the population and development of this region is the natural roadway for travel and transportation which the Snake River Valley provides. From the time a hundred years and more ago, when emigrants began pouring into the Pacific Northwest, the main routes of travel have followed this valley. Today railroads, highways, and airlines use this great roadway built by nature. Along their courses cities have grown up, industries of many kinds have been established, and large numbers of people have built their homes.

A fourth consideration is the tremendous volume of water that enters or passes through the Snake River Valley. Its streams are all part of the Snake River system and together they furnish a great and constant flow. They supply water for irrigation and for domestic use. They fill the needs of cities and towns. They rotate giant turbines which convert the power of the water into electricity, used for energy and illumination in the homes and for many industrial purposes.

A fifth attraction of the Snake River Region is its great wealth of scenic wonders. Casual travelers passing through might think of it as barren and unattractive. But this is not so. We certainly cannot list as unattractive such marvels as Shoshone Falls and Shoshone Canyon; the Craters of the Moon National Monument; the Thousand Springs in Hagerman Valley; Cassia City of Rocks and Gooding City of Rocks, with their fantastic formations; and a host of other unusual natural features.

Though wildlife does not rival in most respects that of the Rocky Mountain Region, there is still much to draw sportsmen afield. Migratory waterfowl, especially ducks and geese, are plentiful. Chinese pheasants, or "chinks," are abundant in parts of the valley. Deer abound in some of the mountainous sections of the Snake River Region. Some notable fishing waters draw large numbers of nimrods to try their luck with rod and reel.

When important bodies of agricultural land or other natural resources are developed, other industries soon follow. There have to be mercantile enterprises to sell all sorts of things people need and to purchase surplus products. Banking institutions deal in money, the lifeblood of industry. Manufacturing and processing establishments such as meat-packing plants, butter and cheese factories, milk canneries, sugar factories, and food-canning and processing plants work up

Ektachrome by Eliot Porter

THE MOUNTAIN BLUEBIRD IS IDAHO'S OFFICIAL STATE BIRD

the raw materials of the farms and ranches. To move these raw materials to the factories, the finished products to market, and to bring in merchandise from the outside, transportation systems are developed. Railroads and highways are constructed. Warehouses and depots are built in convenient locations close to them.

All these related business interests call together large numbers of people. These people need many things. There must be carpenters and masons, painters and plumbers to construct their homes; hotels and restaurants; barbershops and beauty parlors; garages and workshops; doctors, nurses, and hospitals; and scores of other kinds of commercial and service establishments, together with the people to operate them.

The people of such communities have other interests besides their daily work. They need schools to educate their children. They want churches in which to follow their chosen forms of worship. They require lodges and social organizations of various kinds to enable them to live more usefully and to enjoy life more completely.

All these things make up the pattern of living in the Snake River Region. Taken together, they show why this region has such a large part of the people and the industries of Idaho.

The Clearwater Plateau. Like the Snake River Region, the Clearwater Plateau is part of the greater Columbia Plateau. It is a hilly or gently rolling tableland with an area of about 3,500 square miles. Adjoining both Oregon and Washington, it extends eastward on both sides of the Clearwater River, from its junction with the Snake, for a distance of about fifty miles.

The general elevation of the plateau is from two thousand to three thousand feet. Its streams for the most part flow in deeply carved valleys and canyons. These valleys are the lowest part of Idaho, being slightly less than eight hundred feet elevation where the Clearwater joins the Snake at Lewiston.

The Clearwater Plateau is a land of great natural fertility. To the basic soil of decomposed lava has been added loess (LO-es) or wind-blown silt from the plains of the Columbia to the westward. This loess, carried in by the prevailing westerly winds, has been deposited in considerable depth over most of the region.

Much of the plateau was originally grasslands, though some portions supported fine forests of commercial timber. Some timber remains, but the most valuable has been removed for lumber and other purposes.

The climate of the plateau is favorable for agriculture. The average summer temperature is not far from seventy degrees and the growing season extends from four to six months. There is usually enough precipitation to grow crops without the aid of irrigation. This is fortunate, because the rolling surface would be difficult to irrigate successfully, even if water were available for that purpose. There are, however, a few places in the valleys where irrigation is used to increase the yields and to produce more than one crop on the land during the growing season. This is especially true around the city of Lewiston, where market gardening and fruit growing are important industries.

HARVESTTIME ON THE CLEARWATER PLATEAU

The rounded prairie hills and rolling plateau are well suited to the use of machinery. This, with fertile soil, a favorable climate, and good transportation facilities, has made the region a notable farming section.

Courtesy Grangeville Chamber of Commerce

The Clearwater Plateau is one of Idaho's finest farming regions. Its prairies are famous for wheat and peas. Other small grains and hay are grown in quantity. It ranks among the best in the state as a stock-raising district. Dairying brings in a heavy income. Its low valleys, where a Mediterranean type of climate prevails, are heavy producers of vegetables and fruit.

In 1950 the population of the Clearwater Plateau was approximately 65,000. This was only about one sixth of the population of the Snake River Region, but in density of population this region ranks first in the state, having an average of about eighteen persons per square mile. This is because the plateau does not have great areas of desert, wasteland, and rugged mountains, such as are found in the southern part of the state and in the Rocky Mountain Region. As a result, people are found quite generally distributed throughout the whole plateau region.

The Great Basin. The third great natural region touching Idaho is the Great Basin, named by John C. Fremont, who explored parts of it more than a hundred years ago. No drainage from this great natural region of about 200,000 square miles ever reaches the ocean. Only an area of about 2,500 square miles in southeastern Idaho, lying within the Bear River drainage basin, is part of this great natural region.

The Great Basin in Idaho is much like the Snake River Region. Both lie in the rain shadow of the Sierra Nevada–Cascade ranges, hence are generally arid or semiarid in climate. Both have mountain ranges separated from each other by fairly wide, dry valleys. Both lack timber resources except in a few favored locations in the mountains where moisture, principally snow, furnishes natural conditions favorable to the growth of trees. In both, farming and stock raising are the principal occupations. Both depend on irrigation for best success in farming, but both have dry-farm areas where wheat is successfully grown. Both produce in general the same kind of farm products. Both are sparsely populated except where irrigation has caused the development of prosperous farming communities.

The population and industries of the Bear River Basin, the name usually given to Idaho's small share of the Great Basin, are mainly centered in five valleys: the Upper Cache Valley in Franklin County, Bear Lake Valley in Bear Lake County, Gem or Gentile Valley and the Upper Portneuf Valley in Caribou County, and Malad Valley in Oneida County. Among the earliest parts of Idaho to be settled, these are today successful farming, dairying, and stock-raising communities.

The remainder of this region is occupied by mountains, among which are a few small valleys and basins. These are given over almost wholly to the livestock industry. Very extensive phosphate deposits are found and phosphate mining and processing are now important.

Bear River, the principal stream, is heavily used for both irrigation and the production of hydroelectric energy. Power plants are located near Soda Springs, Grace, and at points lower down the river toward the Utah state line.

Bear Lake and its vicinity draw large numbers of visitors, attracted by the scenic beauty and the recreational advantages found there. The lake is one of the most beautiful in the West and the summer climate is ideal. Summer homes and public and private campgrounds line the lake shore, particularly on the western margin.

The 1950 population of the Bear River Basin was approximately 27,000. Preston, Malad City, Montpelier, and Soda Springs were the only cities with more than a thousand people. Preston, the largest, ranked seventeenth in size among the cities of the state.

* * * * *

We have now seen how Mother Nature has given Idaho many natural advantages as a home for man. The important natural resources—soil, water, trees and other vegetation, minerals, wildlife, scenery, and recreational advantages—have been mentioned and will be considered more fully in later units. How best to use these advantages is a problem that challenges us as we grow into adult citizenship. The more we learn about our state, the better prepared we are to live happy and successful lives in the Idaho that lies ahead.

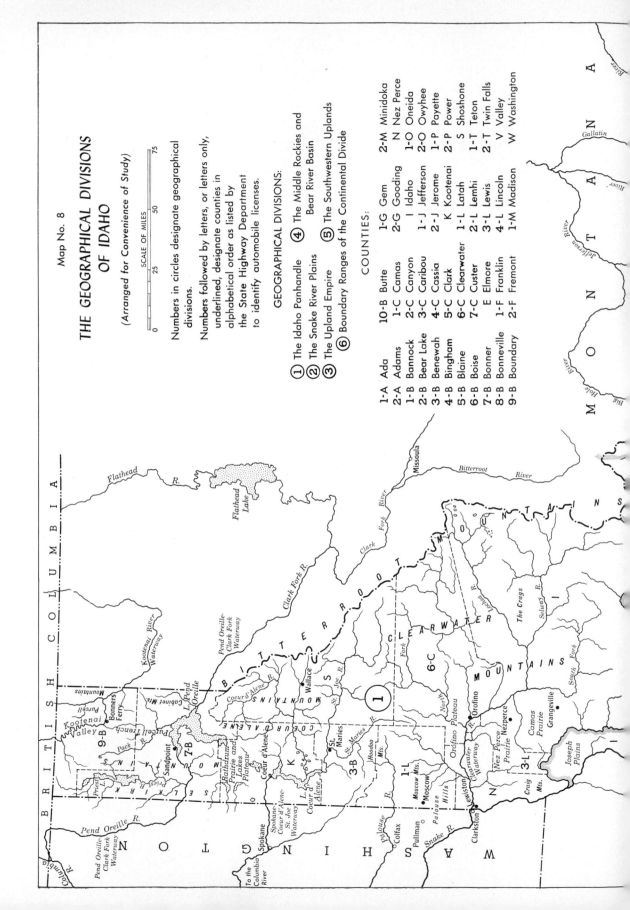

Map No. 8

THE GEOGRAPHICAL DIVISIONS OF IDAHO

(Arranged for Convenience of Study)

SCALE OF MILES

0 25 50 75

Numbers in circles designate geographical divisions.

Numbers followed by letters, or letters only, underlined, designate counties in alphabetical order as listed by the State Highway Department to identify automobile licenses.

GEOGRAPHICAL DIVISIONS:

① The Idaho Panhandle   ④ The Middle Rockies and Bear River Basin
② The Snake River Plains
③ The Upland Empire   ⑤ The Southwestern Uplands
⑥ Boundary Ranges of the Continental Divide

COUNTIES:

1-A Ada	10-B Butte	1-G Gem	2-M Minidoka
2-A Adams	1-C Camas	2-G Gooding	N Nez Perce
1-B Bannock	2-C Canyon	I Idaho	1-O Oneida
2-B Bear Lake	3-C Caribou	1-J Jefferson	2-O Owyhee
3-B Benewah	4-C Cassia	2-J Jerome	1-P Payette
4-B Bingham	5-C Clark	K Kootenai	2-P Power
5-B Blaine	6-C Clearwater	1-L Latah	S Shoshone
6-B Boise	7-C Custer	2-L Lemhi	1-T Teton
7-B Bonner	E Elmore	3-L Lewis	2-T Twin Falls
8-B Bonneville	1-F Franklin	4-L Lincoln	V Valley
9-B Boundary	2-F Fremont	1-M Madison	W Washington

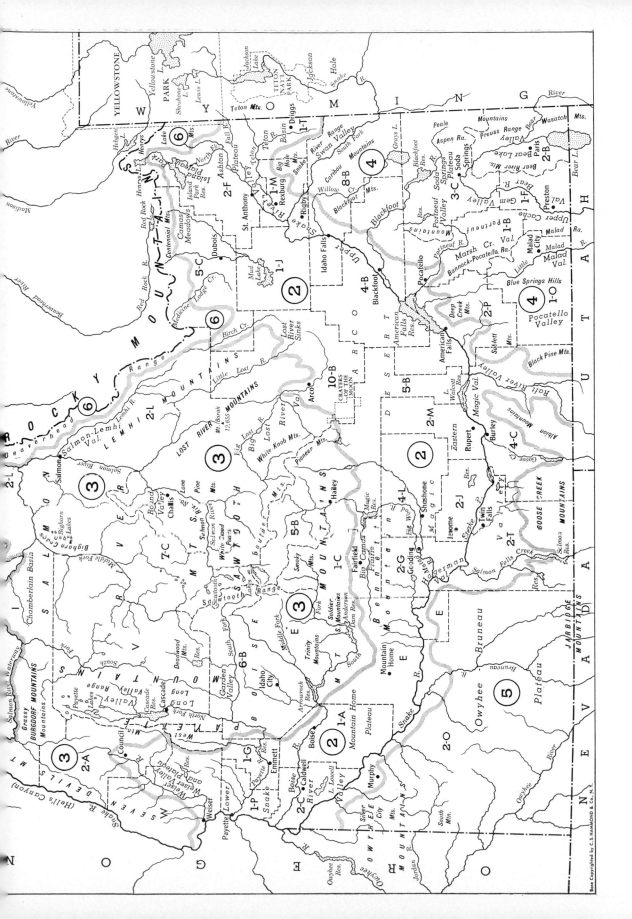

Physical Idaho and Its Settlement

How the physical features of Idaho, its mountains and plateaus, its valleys and plains, its streams and lakes, influenced its territorial settlement and development.

THE PHYSICAL FEATURES OF IDAHO, its mountains and plateaus, its valleys and plains, its streams and lakes, had much to do with its settlement and growth. This was true in the territorial years and it is still true today. Let us see what the most important of these features are.

A careful study of Map No. 8, "Geographical Divisions of Idaho," shows that the state naturally divides into six general geographical divisions. Each of these divisions has a certain unity because of its location, its natural resources, or the ways in which its people live. In the order in which they are discussed, these geographical divisions are: (1) the Panhandle Region of northern Idaho; (2) the Snake River Valley; (3) the Upland Empire, the mountainous region between the main east-west canyon of the Salmon River and the Snake River Valley; (4) the Middle Rockies and the Bear River Basin in southeastern Idaho; (5) the Southwestern Uplands; and (6) the Boundary Ranges of the Continental Divide.

I. THE IDAHO PANHANDLE

HAVE YOU EVER WONDERED just what part of Idaho is included in the Panhandle? The question is answered in this quotation from *Northern Idaho Forest Resources and Industries,* Publication No. 508 of the United States Department of Agriculture:

Northern Idaho, separated from southern Idaho by natural barriers, chief of which is the very deep canyon of the Salmon River, is a comparatively distinct unit of 12.5 million acres making up the Panhandle of the state. It includes nine complete counties and the greater portion of Idaho County.

If you are among the thousands of girls and boys who live north of the Salmon River, you already know a great deal about the Panhandle. You know about its far-spreading evergreen forests, its rich mines, its fertile farming lands. Probably you, or some member of your family, has followed its big-game trails and camped and fished along its beautiful lakes and streams. There are, indeed, many interesting things to discover about this geographical division, which includes only a little less than one fourth the total area of the state of Idaho.

Panhandle Mountains and Plateaus. Six main mountain groups and three smaller ones, all parts of the Northern Rockies, are located in the Panhandle.

The six main groups are the Selkirk Mountains, Purcell Mountains, Cabinet Mountains, Coeur d'Alene Mountains, Bitterroot Mountains, and Clearwater Mountains. The three small groups are the Hoodoo Mountains, Moscow Mountains, and the Craig Mountain group.

These mountains are not so high as those south of the Salmon River. Their summits are, in general, between five thousand and eight thousand feet, though a few are considerably higher. Most of them are heavily forested. Many rivers and smaller streams rise there, and in them are some of the best-known fishing and big-game areas of the West. Their mineral resources are very great, especially in the lead-silver-zinc belt of the Coeur d'Alene Mountains.

The preceding unit, you recall, discussed the Clearwater Plateau, largest and best of the agricultural districts of northern Idaho. The Lakes Plateau, a much smaller region, extends from the southern end of Lake Coeur d'Alene to Lake Pend Oreille and the Pend Oreille River.

On Map No. 8, find the Palouse Hills, the Nez Perce Prairie, the Camas Prairie. These are the best farming sections of the Clearwater Plateau, just as they are among the best in Idaho and the Pacific Northwest. We shall learn more about these rich regions as we read later units.

While the Lakes Plateau does not rival the Clearwater Plateau either in size or fertility, it is nevertheless a successful farming district, especially the Rathdrum Prairie section. Portions of both the Lakes Plateau and the Clearwater Plateau are important for lumbering.

Panhandle Waterways and Valleys.

Lying directly in the path of Pacific winds, the Panhandle is well supplied with lakes and streams. Three of the state's largest lakes and four large rivers are in the region and two other rivers border it. No other part of Idaho has such great water resources.

Largest of the Panhandle waterways is the Pend Oreille–Clark Fork system. The Clark Fork River enters Idaho through the picturesque Cabinet Gorge and pours its waters into Lake Pend Oreille, our largest lake. As the Pend Oreille River it resumes its journey at the western end of the lake and is soon joined by Priest River, coming down from Priest Lake to the north. Then the full volume of the great river rushes on across northeastern Washington to join the mighty Columbia.

Cutting across northeastern Idaho is the Kootenai River. Coming from Canada by way of northwestern Montana, this large river soon returns to Canada. The short portion in Idaho is important chiefly because of the fine farming lands along its valley between Bonners Ferry and the Canadian line.

Farther south is the great waterway consisting of the Spokane River, Lake Coeur d'Alene, and the Coeur d'Alene and the St. Joe rivers. The latter two rivers are the lake's chief tributaries, while the Spokane serves as the outlet through which the waters escape to the Columbia. Lake Coeur d'Alene, one of the most beautiful lakes in the Northwest, ranks next to Lake Pend Oreille in size.

The Clearwater River is entirely in Idaho. The main stream and its chief tributaries, the North Fork, South Fork, Lochsa (LOCK'saw), and Selway, sweep like a great open fan from the high Bit-

VIEW OF LAKE PEND OREILLE

In water resources, the Panhandle exceeds any other part of Idaho. Little used for irrigation, the rivers and lakes of northern Idaho are most valuable for their great recreational areas and the rivers as sources of hydroelectricity.

Courtesy Idaho Secretary of State and State Board of Publicity

terroot ranges along the Idaho-Montana border. Except along its lower course, the Clearwater system drains a vast wilderness of evergreen forests and is noted for its fish and big-game resources as well as for its great forests of white pine, cedar, and other valuable trees.

The Palouse River has only its upper waters in Idaho. It drains the country along the border between Latah and Benewah counties. On these upper Palouse watersheds are some of the finest forests in the state.

The Salmon River forms the southern boundary of the Panhandle, but only its northern tributaries are in this region. These short streams, coming down through deep canyons to the parent river, are not of great importance now, but in early territorial years rich placer strikes on some of them once led thousands of gold seekers to their high basins.

Settling the Panhandle. You no doubt remember that the first farming in Idaho was done at the Lapwai Mission between the years 1837 and 1847 under the direction of the Reverend Henry Spalding. The Nez Perce Indians learned from the missionaries how to raise crops. From that time on some of them continued to

cultivate the soil, at least to the extent of growing a few vegetables for food.

In 1840 Colonel William Craig developed the first farm homestead in Idaho on Sweetwater Creek, above the present town of Lapwai. Had conditions been favorable, other settlers might have taken up land. The Indians, however, opposed white settlement and land seekers did not enter the Clearwater region until more than a score of years later.

The Mullan Road across northern Idaho had been finished just before the discovery of gold on Orofino Creek in 1860. This opened the way for settlers to come to northern Idaho. To make their coming safer, the Indians were soon placed on reservations. As a result of these things and the gold discoveries, settlers started coming into various parts of the Panhandle.

Mining Settlements. As we learned in Unit 2, the earliest settlements in the Panhandle were made by gold miners. Mining towns which grew up were, however, practically abandoned when placer gold could no longer be found in paying quantities. Pierce City, which later turned to lumbering and forestry, is the only one of these early towns to survive, though some of the others have usually had a few residents most of the time.

In the 1880's prospectors found gold along the streams flowing into the Coeur d'Alene River in Shoshone County. In the surrounding mountains rich mines of silver and lead were soon discovered. As a result of these discoveries Murray, Eagle City, Wallace, Wardner, Kellogg, Mullan, and Kingston were settled. All but Eagle City are still mining centers in the rich Coeur d'Alene mining district.

Agricultural Settlements. It did not take long after the first mines were opened for the soil to begin to attract interest. The first land placed under cultivation was near Lewiston, but during the 1860's stockmen and farmers began to settle along the lower Salmon River and in the Clearwater Plateau on both sides of the Clearwater River. The first agricultural settlements in Latah County were in the Palouse Valley and around Moscow and Genesee in 1869–71, the

number of settlers steadily increasing after that time.

South of the Clearwater, communities were also being settled. Cottonwood and Mount Idaho were way stations on the road from Lewiston to the mines. As early as 1863 stockmen began settling the Camas Prairie, and in the middle 1870's the town of Grangeville was established.

In other parts of the Panhandle, settlements also began to spring up. About 1875 the Weippe (WEE-ipe) Prairie was settled in what is now Clearwater County. North of Lake Coeur d'Alene, Westwood, now Rathdrum, was settled in the early 1870's and the Rathdrum Prairie began to fill with people. What is now the city of Coeur d'Alene really began as a military post, Fort Coeur d'Alene or Fort Sherman, in 1879, though a settlement had been made there two years earlier.

Bonners Ferry, on the Kootenai River, began as a miners' crossing on the Wild Horse Trail to British Columbia in 1864.

Courtesy U.S. Bureau of Reclamation, Region No. 1, Boise

MORNING MINE NEAR WALLACE

Except in the Clearwater Plateau, minerals and timber are the most important resources of the Panhandle. The Morning Mine is only one of the many productive mines of the "billion-dollar triangle."

WHITE PINE FOREST IN NORTHERN IDAHO

The white pine is Idaho's most valuable tree. The largest continuous stand of virgin white pine in the United States is in the Clearwater Mountains of the Idaho Panhandle.

Courtesy U.S. Forest Service   Photo by K. D. Swan

Sandpoint was a store and trading post as early as 1880.

The Northern Pacific Railroad was completed across the Panhandle in 1882. This encouraged immigration, and the great forest resources near the railroad began to be developed. However, there was little actual settlement or development north of Rathdrum Prairie until after Idaho became a state in 1890.

II. THE SNAKE RIVER VALLEY

A DESERT THAT IS NOT A DESERT, the Snake River Valley has forged ahead of all other parts of Idaho in population and economic development. Since about two thirds of the people of the state live in that region, you girls and boys who read this book have about two chances in three of living there yourselves. If so, you already know of its fertile irrigated districts, its spreading plains and plateaus where sheep and cattle graze, its young, bustling cities, its rapidly growing industries, and how its people live. No doubt you already know many interesting things about the valley which this book does not even mention, because you have traveled through it and have seen for yourselves what it is like. Isn't that a delightful way to study geography!

What the Snake River Valley Is Like. In the preceding unit we discovered many interesting things about the Snake River Region. The great crescent-shaped Snake River Valley in southern Idaho, more than four hundred miles long, is the heart of that region. From mountain ranges bordering the valley on the north to other ranges on the south, the distance is generally from fifty to seventy-five miles, with no part of the valley less than twenty-five miles across.

Plateau belts crossing the valley in a north-south direction naturally divide it into three somewhat separate districts, each separated from the other districts by these natural uplifts of land. These districts are (1) the Upper Snake River Valley, extending from below American Falls upstream to Teton Basin and the Island Park country; (2) the central section now generally known as Magic Valley, which reaches westward down the valley to approximately the western boundaries of Twin Falls and Gooding

Courtesy U.S. Bureau of Reclamation, Region No. 1, Boise

SNAKE RIVER VALLEY'S GREATEST RESOURCE

The rich volcanic soil is the greatest natural resource of the Snake River Valley. There live two thirds of Idaho's people, most of them dependent directly or indirectly on the products of the soil.

counties; and (3) the Lower Snake River Valley, including the remainder of the region to the upper end of the great canyon below Weiser. This portion of the valley overlaps into Oregon, adding a fertile region almost as large as that on the Idaho side of the Snake.

In addition to the valley lands proper, there are special subregions in each of the three main sections of the Snake River Valley. These are really separate natural regions of their own, though all are part of the greater valley to which they belong.

The Upper Snake River Valley has six such subregions worthy of special mention. Briefly described, these are: (1) Teton Basin, a picturesque agricultural and livestock-raising valley over six thousand feet in elevation, lying along the Wyoming border under the western rim of the magnificent Teton Peaks; (2) Island Park Plateau, a timbered region around the headwaters of the North Fork of Snake River, that is the outstanding recreational area of eastern Idaho; (3) Ashton Plateau, a fertile region of rolling prairie lands along the North Fork and Fall River in southern Fremont County; (4) Camas Meadows, a hay and livestock oasis on Camas Creek in the eastern part of Clark County; (5) the Mud Lake irrigated district in central Jefferson County; and (6) the Arco Desert, Butte County's land of big buttes and lost river sinks, in which the Atomic Energy Commission has its experimental atomic plants.

The Magic Valley section of the Snake River Valley has three special sub-regions: (1) the Lava Plateau in Butte, Blaine, Minidoka, and Lincoln counties, in which is located the Craters of the Moon National Monument; (2) Big Camas Prairie, a noted wheat and live-stock basin in the southern part of Camas County; and (3) beautiful Hagerman Valley in Gooding and Twin Falls coun-ties below Shoshone Canyon, one of the natural wonders of Idaho.

Considered part of the Lower Snake River Valley are two special regions: (1) the Mountain Home Plateau, which, ex-cept for a small irrigated district around the city of Mountain Home, is a sage-grown grazing district stretching through the southern part of Elmore and Ada counties; and (2) the Weiser Valley and Plateau. The last-named region consists of the Middle and Upper Valley of Weiser River and the rolling hills and tablelands bordering the valleys. It is a general farming and livestock region of considerable importance.

Along the margin of the Snake River Valley, both north and south of the river, are small valleys opening upon the main valley from the bordering mountains and plateaus. On the north from east to west are Medicine Lodge and Birch Creek val-leys in Clark County, Big Lost River and Little Lost River valleys in Butte County, and Big Wood River and Little Wood River valleys in Blaine County.

Six valleys of considerable importance open upon the Snake River Valley from the south. These are the lower Portneuf Valley in Bannock County, Bannock Creek and Rock Creek valleys in Power County, Raft River and Goose Creek val-leys in Cassia County, and Bruneau Val-ley in northeastern Owyhee County.

All these "feeder valleys" are, in gen-eral, hay and livestock regions. They have about the same kind of climate and vegetation as the Snake River Valley. In fact, the United States Geological Sur-vey considers them as extensions of the main Snake River Valley.

Snake River, the Nile of Idaho. The Snake is the queen river of the northern Intermountain Region of the Western States and one of the truly great rivers of North America. Its length of more than a thousand miles ranks it eighth among the rivers of the United States. The tremendous volume of water that feeds its hundreds of miles of irrigation canals and turns the huge turbines of its hydroelectric plants gives it an economic value that places it among the top rivers of the continent.

Between its sources in and near Yel-lowstone National Park and its junction with the Columbia River in southern Washington, the Snake drops a vertical distance of more than one and a quarter miles. In doing this it flows through sev-eral remarkable canyons and thunders over great falls and cascades.

The highest of the cataracts is Sho-shone Falls, near the city of Twin Falls in south central Idaho. Higher than Niagara, this is one of the great scenic spectacles of the West in the spring when the Snake is at flood stage, and the sight draws thousands of visitors to view the awesome wonder.

There are remarkable canyons along the Idaho section of Snake River. The upper and lesser of these is the deep and majestic Shoshone Gorge along the northern border of Twin Falls County. Deeply carved in old basaltic lavas, its almost black walls tower hundreds of feet above the winding river, a tribute to the irresistible power of erosion during the long march of the ages. At the lower end Shoshone Gorge opens up to form the strikingly beautiful Hagerman Valley, in which are the scenic Thousand Springs, undoubtedly an outlet for the lost rivers that disappear in the lava wastes of the Snake River Plain and the vast underground lake that underlies most of the Upper Snake River Valley and Magic Valley.

The second and greater canyon is the Grand Canyon of Snake River, under the western rim of the Seven Devils Mountains. The wildest and most primitive portion of this canyon is Hell's Canyon, which the North Idaho Scenic-Land Association describes in these words:

The boast is made about the Grand Canyon of the Colorado that within the space of twenty miles the terrain falls 5,000 feet. [By comparison] Hell's Canyon has an average depth of 6,600 feet and the span is from four to nine miles. At one place it is more than 8,000 feet from the highest point to the bottom of the canyon. Even in midsummer, sunshine strikes the river for only seven hours a day; the rest of the time a twilight gloom covers the roaring waters.

Snake River is, then, a great irrigation river, a famed recreational stream, and a very great source of electrical power. These, and the fertility of Snake River Valley soils, give this river a value so great and enduring that it cannot even be closely estimated.

Many Idaho tributary streams add their waters to the Snake. From the north side comes Henrys Fork, or North Fork, the only surface stream to join the main river until the Malad is reached in Hagerman Valley, an air-line distance of more than 150 miles. From the east and south more tributaries join: the Blackfoot, Portneuf, Raft, Salmon Falls, and Bruneau rivers, with a goodly number of smaller streams. In the Lower Snake River Valley the Boise, Payette, and Weiser rivers add their waters on the Idaho side of the Snake.

Settling the Snake River Valley. We

MINIDOKA DAM ON SNAKE RIVER

Water is another great natural resource of the Snake River Valley. From such reservoirs as this one near Rupert water is drawn to irrigate almost two million acres of fertile Snake River Valley soil, soil as fine, perhaps, as any in the nation.

have seen that the discovery of the Boise Basin gold fields in 1862 attracted thousands of people to the diggings. Among those who came were many who saw the agricultural possibilities of the Snake River Valley.

In that same year Congress passed the Homestead Act. This law gave 160 acres of free land to citizens of legal age who would live on the land five years and make certain improvements. The law made it easy to secure land, and the near-by mining camps assured profitable markets for farm products. Almost immediately settlers began taking up choice land where water was easily led into canals to irrigate fields and pastures.

Settling Boise Valley. Boise City was the first organized community in the Lower Snake River Valley. In 1863 Boise Barracks was built on Government Island as a military post to protect miners and settlers from Indian attacks. That same year a group of men laid out a townsite, and in 1864 Boise City became the permanent capital of Idaho Territory.

From 1862 to 1870 the settlement of Boise Valley was rapid. Within two years nearly all the best land below Boise City had been claimed. Star and Middleton were villages down the valley from Boise City. Far down, in the section known as Lower Boise, settlements were also spreading and Notus and Riverside, or Keeney's Ferry, were early trading points not far from Old Fort Boise, though that historic post had been abandoned about a decade earlier.

The country on the south side of Boise River, between that stream and the Snake River farther south, was settled somewhat later. In 1883 the Oregon Short Line Railroad was finished across the territory. Caldwell, sometimes called Bugtown and Hamburg, was laid out on the railroad. East of Caldwell a townsite was established in a settlement then called New Jerusalem. The new town was named Nampa, after Chief Nampuh, or Bigfoot. Both these places grew rapidly, and in 1950 Caldwell was ninth and Nampa fifth in size among Idaho cities.

Cupid as a Colonizer. Settlement in the Lower Snake River Valley was given a big boost in the early years of the Golden Decade by the arrival of several wagon trains of emigrants from Missouri and Arkansas. Among the newcomers were quite a number of girls of marriageable age. In a land where men outnumbered women by, perhaps, a ratio of a hundred to one, the arrival of attractive and beautiful girls always created a sensation.

William J. McConnell, in his *Early History of Idaho,* thus describes the events that followed the arrival of the emigrant trains at Boise City:

. . . a camp was established on the riverbank near the outskirts of the town, where acquaintances were formed, and during the evenings which followed, sitting around their smouldering camp fires, plans for the future were made by the older people, while the girls and their visitors from town formed groups of two beneath the blinking stars. . . .

These fathers grim had guns. . . . So every vow made on that river bank was kept . . . and ere the slim young moon . . . had grown to full, many a young bachelor had been bound in hymeneal [wedding] ties. . . . Of the marriages resulting from these speedy courtships, I have yet to learn of a divorce. Many of the immigrants of that year located in Boise valley, while a few crossed the divide to Payette. . . .

All these early settlers enacted a prominent and honorable part in the development of the then new territory. Many of their children are still residents of Idaho, and have reason to be proud of the record they inherited from their ancestors who, having crossed the continent during those turbulent days, devoted their lives to honest industry, and finally went to their rest respected and loved by all.

Payette and Weiser Valleys. Payette Valley was settled about the same time as Boise Valley. Picket Corral, Martinsville, and Falk's Store were located a few miles up the valley. Martinsville was renamed Emmettsville, later shortened to Emmett. Now the county seat of Gem County, it is the second largest city in Payette Valley.

Near the mouth of Payette River, Bluff's Ferry began operations in 1866. When the railroad was built, a new settlement called Boomerang was started not far from the ferry. This soon became Payette, now the largest city and main business center of Payette Valley.

Settlers also moved into Weiser Valley in the 1860's. A ferry was in operation across the Snake River at Farewell Bend, now Olds Ferry, in 1863. That same year settlers established themselves near the mouth of the Weiser River, and when a bridge was built across the river, the settlement was named Weiser Bridge. A townsite was laid out in 1877 and the name was shortened to Weiser. This has always been the chief city and business and social center of Lower Weiser Valley.

Farther up the Weiser Valley settlers began homesteading in the late 1860's and the 1870's. Three towns, Midvale, Cambridge, and Council, were soon established. These are still the chief business and community centers for Middle Valley and Upper Valley of the Weiser, where hay, grain, and fruit growing, along with stock raising and lumbering, are the principal dependence of the people for their living.

Elsewhere in the Lower Snake River Valley, settlements were few and far between. Glenns Ferry, where the Glenn brothers had a ferry over the Snake as early as 1865, became a railroad division point on the Short Line Railroad in 1897, when farming and ranching began along the valley. King Hill and Mountain Home, which began as stage stations on the emigrant road, were moved to new locations on the railroad and both became railroad points.

South of the Snake, Bruneau Valley, called in Mrs. Hawes's book the "Valley of Tall Grass," was settled first. Not, however, until the cattle boom of the 1870's did the valley show much increase in population. From that time on, cattle and horse ranches dotted the region. The Three Creek district in southern Owyhee County and the Oreana district on the south side of Snake River were centers of ranching activity. Bruneau became the principal town and social and business center of a livestock district thousands of square miles in area.

Settling the Upper Snake River Valley. Barzilla W. Clark, one-time governor of Idaho, wrote in his book, *Bonneville County in the Making,* "Fort Hall was established near the mouth of the Portneuf River in 1834, but even in 1860 the Upper Snake River Valley was still a region of unknown extent and unguessed resources." That was the situation when, in 1862, rich gold fields were discovered in what was soon to become western Montana. A freight and stage-coach line connecting Salt Lake City with the mining camps caused a number of settlements to grow up in eastern Idaho.

The most important of these points was on Snake River, near the present city of Idaho Falls. As early as 1863 a ferry across the river was in operation a few miles north. Two years later Taylor's Bridge, sometimes called Anderson's Bridge, was built where the city now stands. Soon named Eagle Rock, this was the earliest permanent settlement in the whole of the Upper Snake River Valley.

In the main, the story of the settling of the valley is the story of the Mormon migration into southeastern Idaho. But a few settlers began drifting in before the wave of Mormon settlers became a major movement. Stockmen came in with herds of horses and cattle, followed by rustlers, who lived largely by stealing from the herds, and from other herds being driven through from farther west to markets in Montana and Wyoming. The forks of the Snake and Teton Basin were favorite hide-outs for the thieves, who continued to ply their trade well through the 1870's. It was of this period that Dr. Beal, in his *History of Southeastern Idaho,* wrote:

The decade of the seventies was the twilight period between the temporary and the permanent settlers and was, therefore, the time of transition from the half-lawless to the more orderly social relations.

In 1868 the Fort Hall Indian Reservation was established, with headquarters at Fort Hall Post, the second Fort Hall, on Lincoln Creek a few miles east of the present city of Blackfoot. From that time on a few white people were located on the reservation in connection with work among the Indians.

Between 1877 and 1879 the Utah &

HOME FROM THE RANGE

Millions of acres of plateau grazing lands are a third great natural resource of the Snake River Valley.

Northern Railroad was constructed across eastern Idaho. Railroad settlements grew up at Eagle Rock, Blackfoot, Pocatello, the present Fort Hall, and other points. Too, the coming of the railroad led to more rapid colonization of the upper valley.

In 1881 Eagle Rock was made a railroad division point, with general railroad shops, and almost overnight it became the leading city of the upper valley. Blackfoot was laid out in 1878, Rexburg in 1883, Rigby in 1884, and St. Anthony and Driggs in 1889. By the end of the last territorial decade, in addition to these main towns, a score or more of small villages and towns that are still community and trade centers of the upper valley were settled.

The building of the Oregon Short Line across southern Idaho in 1882–83 had already made Pocatello the most important rail point in Idaho because east-west and north-south lines met there. When, in 1887, the railroad shops from both Eagle Rock and Shoshone were moved to Pocatello, its future was assured. A tract of two thousand acres was secured from the Fort Hall Reservation, which then extended much farther south than it now does, and the Pocatello townsite was laid out in 1889. From that beginning it moved steadily forward to become the most important transportation, industrial, business, and education center, as well as the largest city, in eastern Idaho.

Settlement of Magic Valley. Though the mid-portion of the Snake River Valley in Idaho was not known as Magic Valley until fairly recent years, that name is now applied to an area of approximately ten thousand square miles. In a booklet published by the Twin Falls Chamber of Commerce, we find this statement:

Magic Valley embraces eight highly productive counties in which approximately 600,000 acres of rich lava ash soil are under irrigation with water from a never-failing source, the mighty Snake River.

These counties are Twin Falls and Cassia counties south of Snake River and Minidoka, Jerome, Gooding, Lincoln, Camas, and Blaine counties north of the Snake, the last two being only partly in the Snake River Valley.

As in the Upper Snake River Valley, the first settled spots in Magic Valley were stations and river crossings on the freight and stage roads. The most noted of these was the Rock Creek Station, southeast of the present city of Twin Falls, established in 1863. It was the first permanent settlement in the entire valley.

The real settlement of Magic Valley began with the coming of cattlemen in the late 1860's. Several large cattle outfits established ranches in the Raft River country and other grazing districts south of the Snake. About the same time, or slightly later, sheep outfits began building up herds both north and south of the river. The Big Camas Prairie section, in what is now Camas County, and the feeder valleys where Big Wood and Little Wood rivers enter the plain, were among the early livestock districts.

When the Oregon Short Line Railroad crossed the plateau north of the Snake, Minidoka and Shoshone, the latter first called Naples, were railroad stations. Gooding, once called Toponis, and Bliss were established about the same time. Shoshone and Gooding became prosperous cities and are now county seats of Lincoln and Gooding counties respectively.

In general, the Middle Snake River Valley region was not much settled during Idaho's territorial years. It was not, in fact, until after the turn of the century, when irrigation projects were developed on a large scale, that the Magic Valley began its remarkable growth.

III. THE UPLAND EMPIRE OF CENTRAL IDAHO

LAND OF ADVENTURE well describes the great mountainous region lying between the Salmon River on the north and the Snake River Valley on the south. In the *Social Studies Guide* for the schools of Idaho, prepared under the direction of the State Board of Education and the State Curriculum Committee, this region is thus described:

Central Idaho, often referred to as the great Upland Empire, contains a wealth of almost untouched native agriculture, stock raising, dairying, timber, and mineral wealth. It is one of the very few western frontiers left to the enterprising, hardy, even adventurous-souled, pioneers of today.

These mountains border the fertile Snake River Plains and are the birthplace of the rivers on which the plains depend for much of their irrigation water. This alone would make them extremely valuable, even if they had no other value. About this region, now largely included in national forests, the United States Forest Service says:

The group [of mountains] forms the northern boundary of a great treeless semiarid area of millions of acres extending across the southern part of the state and into Utah, Nevada, and Oregon. The existence of such a great reservoir of valuable timber, forage, water, fish, game, and recreational advantages is of material benefit to the population of this region, as well as to the country in general, supplying timber, forage, and a steady flow of water for irrigation, power purposes, and recreation. If adequately protected and properly managed, these resources will last indefinitely.

Mountains of the Upland Empire. These mountains, through which prospectors hopefully roved, have never had all their boundaries definitely shown on maps; neither have many parts been officially named. However, the Upland Em-

Courtesy Tommy Barrett's Camera Shop, Pocatello

IN THE PRIMITIVE AREA

In the land of adventure in central Idaho a thousand thrills await the hardy souls who venture there.

Massive mountains, deep canyons, and wild waters are typical of much of the Upland Empire in central Idaho. Though having many natural resources, the difficulties of travel and transportation hold back the development of the region.

Courtesy U.S. Forest Service

pire contains ten groups or systems of mountains. In approximate order of size, beginning with the largest, these are: (1) the Salmon River Mountains; (2) the Sawtooth Mountains; (3) the Payette Mountains;[1] (4) the Boise Mountains; (5) the Seven Devils Mountains; (6) the Lemhi Mountains; (7) the Lost River Mountains; (8) the White Knob Mountains; (9) the Burgdorf Mountains;[1] and (10) the Lone Pine Mountains.[1]

These ten mountain groups embrace an area of approximately 20,000 square miles. As a whole, this is the wildest and most rugged part of the state, as well as the highest. By name the *Idaho Encyclopedia* and the United States Forest Service list fifty-two peaks in Idaho which are over ten thousand feet high. All but seven are in the Upland Empire. Six, headed by Mount Borah, 12,655 feet, tower above twelve thousand feet and another fourteen are higher than eleven thousand feet. (See Appendix Table 1.)

The Salmon River Mountains are second in size among Idaho mountain groups, being exceeded only by the Clearwater Mountains in the Panhandle. However, both the Lost River Mountains and the Sawtooth Mountains have higher peaks. The Lost River Range has all the peaks in the state that are over 12,000 feet, except Mount Hyndman, in the Pioneer Range of the Sawtooth Mountains.

In and bordering the mountains of

[1]Not officially named, but given these names by local residents.

central Idaho are many noted scenic and recreational areas. The Salmon River Mountains are bordered on the north by the mighty Salmon River Canyon and contain the so-called Impassable Canyon of the Middle Fork, the Idaho Primitive Area, the Bighorn Crags and Cathedral Rocks and many other attractions. In the Sawtooth Mountains are the magnificent peaks of the Sawtooth Range, the Sun Valley recreational area, and scores of beautiful lakes. Bordering the Seven Devils Mountains on the west is the Grand Canyon of the Snake, including the almost unbelievable Hell's Canyon. These are only a few of the scenic wonders and recreational areas of these central mountain groups.

Waterways of the Upland Empire. In the mountains of the Upland Empire, eight Idaho rivers have their origin.

There are the sources of the Salmon, Boise, Payette, Weiser, Big Wood, Little Wood, Big Lost, and Little Lost rivers. Three of them, the Salmon, Payette, and Boise rivers, all have tributaries that rise in an area less than six miles square high in the Sawtooth Range.

The River of No Return. The Salmon River, largest tributary of the Snake, is in some ways one of the most remarkable rivers of the West. Its entire length of about 420 miles is in rugged country and for most of this distance it runs through a series of deep and picturesque canyons. From its source to its junction with the Snake near the lower end of Hell's Canyon on the Idaho-Oregon border, the river falls about eight thousand feet.

The terrific gorge through which the Salmon crosses central Idaho has had a strong influence in the history of the territory and the state. The canyon divides the Panhandle from the rest of the state. Almost impassable in territorial years, it is still a very serious barrier to travel and communication between northern and southern Idaho.

Irrigation Rivers. Though the Salmon is of considerable use for irrigation, it is less used at present than the other rivers mentioned, except Little Lost River. Together, these and their tributaries supply water for almost a million acres of land, most of it in the Snake River Valley. The Boise and Payette rivers are also being used to produce hydroelectricity, but irrigation water is by far their greatest contribution to the state.

Lakes and Lake Basins. In the mountains of central Idaho are several remarkable groups of lakes. The two most important are the Payette Lakes and the Sawtooth Lakes. The former are grouped around the heads of the North Fork of the Payette River in Valley County and the latter are on both sides of the Sawtooth Range of mountains. Three groups of lesser importance are the Bighorn Lakes in the Bighorn Crags of the Salmon River Mountains, the Trinity Lakes group in the Trinity peaks of the Boise Mountains, and the Seven Devils Lakes.

The name Payette has been given to two lakes of the Payette group, consisting of a score or more in all, most of them small. Payette Lake proper is the largest of the group. Little used in territorial years, it is now the center of a recreational and lumbering region. The lake, with its surrounding shores, is the heart of the famous mile-high playground, the most popular recreational center of western Idaho and the home of the fabled sea monster, "Sharley."

The Sawtooth Lakes, about two hundred in number, are around the headwaters of the Big Wood, Salmon, Payette, and Boise rivers. Like the Payette group, these lakes were almost unknown and little used in our territorial period. Probably most popular of the group now for recreational uses are Alturas Lake and Redfish Lake, though others are frequently visited.

Territorial Settlements in the Upland Empire. Do you believe in ghosts? No other part of Idaho has so many ghost towns as the Upland Empire. Practically all these came into existence as mining settlements before Idaho was a state. Some are well worth visiting, while even the sites of others show no traces of their former occupancy.

HAPPY BEAR VALLEY FISHERMEN

The waterways of the Upland Empire are among the best recreational waters in the United States. To the headwaters of these streams large numbers of salmon come to spawn and die in one of nature's strangest dramas.

Courtesy Idaho Fish and Game Department

A roll call by present counties of the central mountain region lists most, but not all, of the ghost towns once inhabited by Idaho pioneers. Adams County had Cuprum and Helena. In Blaine County were Alturas, Jacobs City, Bullion, Doniphan, Muldoon, Sawtooth City, and Vienna. Boise County had Banner, Centerville, Pioneerville, Placerville, and Quartzburg. Custer County lists Alder City, Bay Horse, Bonanza, Cliffton, Custer, Loon Creek, and Oro Grande. Carrietown was in Camas County. Elmore County supplied Esmeralda and Rocky Bar. Lemhi County was the location of Leesburg, Grantsville, Smithville, and Summit City. Roosevelt and Thunder City were in Valley County. Washington County had Mineral and Ruthburg. If you look closely at the Great Seal of Idaho, you will find pictured on it the old stamp mill at Ruthburg.

Of course, not all the mining settlements ceased to exist. County seats in the Upland Empire that began as mining towns or supply points for mining districts are Arco in Butte County, Challis in Custer County, Hailey in Blaine County, Salmon in Lemhi County, and Idaho City in Boise County. Other settlements that were mining towns and are still in existence, though some of them are now almost deserted, are Atlanta, Bellevue, Clayton, Featherville, Ketchum, Stanley, and Warren.

Can you suggest why farming communities in the Upland Empire were few during our territorial years? The principal reason, of course, was the scarcity of good farming land. Is that still true today?

Among the farming districts of the region, the Salmon-Lemhi Valley was the first to be settled. Salmon, then called Salmon City, got its start in the years 1866 and 1867. Between 1879 and 1885 stockmen and farmers settled in the Big Lost River Valley. After Challis was established in 1876, ranching and farming began in Round Valley,[2] in which the town is located. Numerous mines in the Wood River country brought stockmen

[2]Another Round Valley is located south of Long Valley on the North Fork of Payette River.

into these valleys late in the 1870's and 1880's, and Hailey, Ketchum, and Bellevue were established.

The last important agricultural district in the Upland Empire to be settled during territorial years was Long Valley, along the North Fork of the Payette River in Valley County. In the early 1880's, Van Wyck and Crawford were established. These were later absorbed by Cascade, and today that town and McCall are the principal commercial and social centers of the Long Valley farming, stock-raising, lumbering and recreational area, one of the few such districts in the Upland Empire.

IV. THE MIDDLE ROCKIES AND THE BEAR RIVER BASIN

BOTH THE ROCKY MOUNTAIN REGION and the Great Basin enter southeastern Idaho. In fact, these natural regions overlap. What are these regions like? What are their chief physical features? On what natural resources could the pioneer settlers build for the future? These questions were partly answered in Unit 4. Now let us discover more about this part of Idaho.

Mountains of Southeastern Idaho. Groups and ranges of the Middle Rockies, a part of the great Rocky Mountain Region, occupy Idaho east of the Snake River Valley from Teton Basin to Utah. These include the Big Hole Mountains and the Snake River Range north of the South Fork of Snake River; the Caribou Mountains, Blackfoot Mountains, Portneuf Mountains, and Peale Mountains between the South Fork of Snake River and Bear River; and the Bear River Range of the Wasatch Mountains in the great U-bend of Bear River in the southeast corner of the state.

Though these mountains are as an average less lofty and rugged than those of the Northern Rockies in the Upland Empire, they do have much high and rugged country. Nearly a score of the summits are well over nine thousand feet. Meade Peak, north of Montpelier, with a height of 9,953 feet, is the highest point in Idaho's Middle Rockies.

Westward from the Middle Rockies to Raft River Valley, south of the Snake River, are several ranges that are part of the Great Basin ranges extending northward almost to Snake River. These are the Pocatello-Bannock Range, Malad Range, Blue Springs Hills, Deep Creek Mountains, Sublett Range, and Black Pine Range. Though much like the Middle Rockies of eastern Idaho in appearance, these mountains are not quite so high nor do they contain the rich phosphate deposits so plentiful in the Middle Rockies.

Waterways of Southeastern Idaho. Five rivers provide most of the water used in the Middle Rockies and Bear River Basin of Idaho. These are the South Fork of Snake River, Blackfoot River, Portneuf River, Bear River, and Malad River. All are used for irrigation, and two, South Fork and Bear River, are important producers of hydroelectricity.

Bear River and Portneuf River valleys provide a natural route of travel and transportation from southwestern Wyoming to the Snake River Valley. From

BEAR LAKE VALLEY— BEEF AND DAIRY LAND

"The sun-soaked valley of the Bear is opulent and beneficent, full of hollows weighted with tasseled grasses and dotted with smacking-fat meadow lands. Down through the years this long slow valley has come unchanged as to its essentials of comfort and well-being."
—from Irene D. Paden's The Wake of the Prairie Schooner

Courtesy W. W. Brown & Son's Willowdale Holstein Farm, Liberty, Idaho

earliest days to the present they have been the best and most used gateways to the Pacific Northwest from the central and eastern parts of the nation. The Oregon Trail followed this historic route, and today, the Union Pacific Railroad and Highway 30 North, the Oregon Trail Highway, carry a tremendous flow of travel and commerce across the region.

Territorial Settlements in Southeastern Idaho. We have already seen that the Mormons established the first permanent settlement in Idaho at Franklin in 1860. In less than ten years the Upper Cache Valley was dotted with Latter-day Saint communities at Clifton, Weston, Dayton, Preston, Oxford, and other places in the valley.

Other Mormon pioneers were extending agricultural settlements in the Bear River Basin. In Bear Lake Valley, Paris was established in 1863. In rapid order came Montpelier, Bloomington, St. Charles, and other communities in Bear Lake County, nearly all of these being settled within a score of years or less.

At Soda Springs General Connor built a military post in 1863 to protect emigrants and settlers and in 1864 this settlement became the county seat of Oneida County, an honor it was soon to lose. From this point settlements spread down Bear River. The largest of these, Grace, is still the principal business and community center of Gentile Valley, now more generally known as Gem Valley.

Though an earlier attempt had been made, not until 1864 was colonization successful in the Malad Valley. In that year Malad City was settled, and in 1866 the county seat of Oneida County was moved there from Soda Springs. Its location on the western route of the freight and stagecoach road from Salt Lake City and Ogden to the mines of western Montana made Malad City an important point. It still remains the second city in size in Idaho's Bear River Basin, being exceeded only by Preston.

The eastern route of the Salt Lake–Montana freight and stage road passed through the valley of Marsh Creek, the principal tributary of Portneuf River. A station was established at Harkness Toll Bridge, where McCammon is now located. General settlement followed the building of the Utah & Northern Railroad in the late 1870's, and ranches and farms soon extended the length of Marsh Creek Valley.

The early settlers of southeastern Idaho were chiefly cattlemen and farmers. During territorial years, mining did not become a very important business in the Middle Rockies–Bear River Basin region. However, in 1870, placer gold of considerable richness was discovered in the mountains east of Grays Lake by a miner known as Caribou Fairchild and a rush to the district followed. Caribou City, once having a population of 1,500 or more, and Keenan City, somewhat smaller, were boisterous mining towns until the placers ceased to be profitable. Then these places joined the ghost towns that are now only reminders of a vanished era in the Idaho story.

V. THE SOUTHWESTERN UPLANDS

GOLD AND SILVER, magic words in the Idaho story! As they were the direct cause of the first development of both the Panhandle and the Upland Empire, so, too, did they lead to the earliest development of the Southwestern Uplands.

Look at Map No. 19 and notice that the southwestern part of the state is largely a plateau region, with here and there mountains rising above the plateaus. This region extends along the southern border of Idaho from the Raft River Valley all the way to Oregon. A semidesert, the region attracted few settlers in early days, and to this day it remains largely an unsettled, semiarid wilderness.

Mountains, Plateaus, and Waterways. Four groups of mountains are found in this region. From east to west they are the Albion Mountains in Cassia County, Goose Creek Mountains in Cassia and Twin Falls counties, Jarbidge Mountains, entering slightly into the southwestern corner of Twin Falls County and the southeastern corner of Owyhee County, and the Owyhee Mountains in the western part of Owyhee County. In the Albion Range, Independence Peak and Cache Peak, both well over ten thousand feet, are the highest Idaho points south of the Snake River.

The remainder of the Southwestern Uplands consists of high, gently rolling to hilly plateaus of little value except for grazing and wildlife. On the south these plateaus gradually rise to become part of the mountain groups, while on the north they fall away to merge with the Snake River Valley. The largest of these plateaus is the Bruneau-Owyhee Desert, extending from Twin Falls County to the Oregon boundary and beyond.

Only three streams of any particular size water this thirsty region. They are Salmon Falls Creek in western Twin Falls County, Bruneau River in eastern Owyhee County, and the Owyhee River, which cuts diagonally across the southwestern corner of Owyhee County on its way from Nevada into Oregon, where it curves back to join the Snake River almost opposite the mouth of Boise River. Like most streams in southern Idaho, these are of value principally for irrigation.

Settling the Southwestern Uplands.

We have seen that in 1862–63 important discoveries of gold and silver drew large numbers of people into the Owyhee Mountains. The placer gold that first attracted attention was soon completely overshadowed by the opening of fabulously rich silver mines. Ruby City was laid out in the silver district and named the county seat of Owyhee County. It was soon absorbed by Silver City, which then became the county seat and for many years remained a rich and world-famous mining center.

In the late 1860's and in the following decade, herds of Texas longhorn cattle were trailed into the country. Soon large cattle outfits dotted the region from Raft River Valley to Oregon and this territory became a part of the Old West, with its gun-toting, hard-riding cowboys and its freedom from wire fences, the "pet peeve" of the old-time cattleman.

Some farming, too, began in favored valleys. The village of Albion was settled in 1869. Ten years later Cassia County was cut from the eastern part of Owyhee County and Albion became the county seat of the new county. Bruneau Valley was settled about the same time and the village of Bruneau became a business and social center. Though not actually on the uplands, this village was, nevertheless, always very closely related to the live-stock business, and it belongs to the up-lands at least as much as it does to the Snake River Valley.

No towns except those mentioned ever grew up in the Southwestern Uplands. A few small settlements were established here and there, serving the great terri-torial cattle, horse, and sheep ranches. However, so far as actual settlement is concerned, the Southwestern Uplands remain to this very day practically a no man's land, visited only by stockmen, sportsmen, and prospectors.

VI. BOUNDARY MOUNTAINS OF THE CONTINENTAL DIVIDE

THE MAIN CHAIN OF THE ROCKY MOUN-TAINS forms part of the boundary line between Idaho and Montana for more than 250 miles. The three boundary ranges are the Beaverhead Range, Cen-tennial Mountains, and Henrys Lake Mountains. Their crest, with many peaks from 8,000 to 11,000 feet high, is part of the Continental Divide, separating the headwaters of the Missouri River and its upper tributaries on the east from those of the Columbia River system on the west.

Mountain passes suitable for railroads and highways are few in these ranges. Transportation difficulties and long, se-vere winters discouraged settlement in the few valleys found there. However, cattlemen were making some use of the good grazing lands before the end of the territorial period. Salmon City was the only territorial town on the Idaho side of these lofty ranges, and to this day it is the only place of importance in Idaho that is closely connected with these boundary ranges. Recent discoveries of large phosphate resources in these moun-tains hold a promise for future develop-ment.

* * * * *

Now that the physical Idaho our terri-torial pioneers found has passed in re-

**FORT HALL INDIAN
RESERVATION**

*INDIAN TRIBAL COURT IN
SESSION*

Tribal courts meet to determine
local affairs and matters of
tribal policy.

Courtesy U.S. Indian Service

view before us, we have a better understanding of the problems they had to
meet and solve if they were to prosper.
In spite of the great natural resources of
Idaho, the close of the territorial period
found many regions undeveloped and
largely unsettled. Barriers to travel and
transportation presented by the rugged
mountains, wide semiarid plains and plateaus, swift, rushing rivers, and deep
gorges and canyons, caused the people to
concentrate in certain favorable locations. Too, until the last territorial decade
the fear of Indian uprisings discouraged
settlement in many parts of the territory.
In the following units we shall see how
the march of events in territorial Idaho
paved the way for statehood.

Idaho's Indian Citizens

How different ways of life brought Indians and whites into conflict; how reservation life made the Indians wards of the government; and how the Indians are moving toward citizenship and political and economic equality.

LIKE A RED THREAD, the tragic story of the Indians runs through the history of Idaho, and of the New World as well. It is a hopeful sign that the story grows brighter with the passing years as the Indians gradually adapt themselves to the white man's civilization. In doing this they are breaking away from the ancient traditions of their race and building for themselves a stronger and a better way of life than they have had before, at the same time earning for themselves a respected position in the social and economic life of the nation of which they are a part.

What role have the Indians played in the history of the Northwest and of Idaho? How have they and the whites dealt with each other? What progress have they made in the past? What does the future hold for them? In this unit we shall try to become better acquainted with the Indians and their past and endeavor to gain a more sympathetic understanding of their problems and of their hopes for the future.

I. IDAHO'S FIRST INHABITANTS

THE INDIANS BELONG in any history of Idaho. Before the ships of the white men cruised along the shores of the North Pacific, before any white man had set foot on Idaho soil—indeed, before the name Idaho was spoken or written, the Indians were here. Their lodges were pitched beside the lakes and rivers. Their hunting bands and war parties threaded the plains and mountains. At night the light of their council fires twinkled in answer to the twinkling stars. Their music echoed the yapping wails of the coyote and the trail song of the wolf.

Indian Picture Writing. The past of the American Indian is, for the most part, hidden. Not even the Indians themselves know much about their origin or from whence they came. The Indians of Idaho, like those in many other parts of the continent, left records on the rocks. These are both pictographs, painted with durable colors, and petroglyphs, carved into the rocks.

Unfortunately, since the death of John E. Rees, of Salmon, generally regarded as Idaho's outstanding historian on Indian life and customs, there seems to be

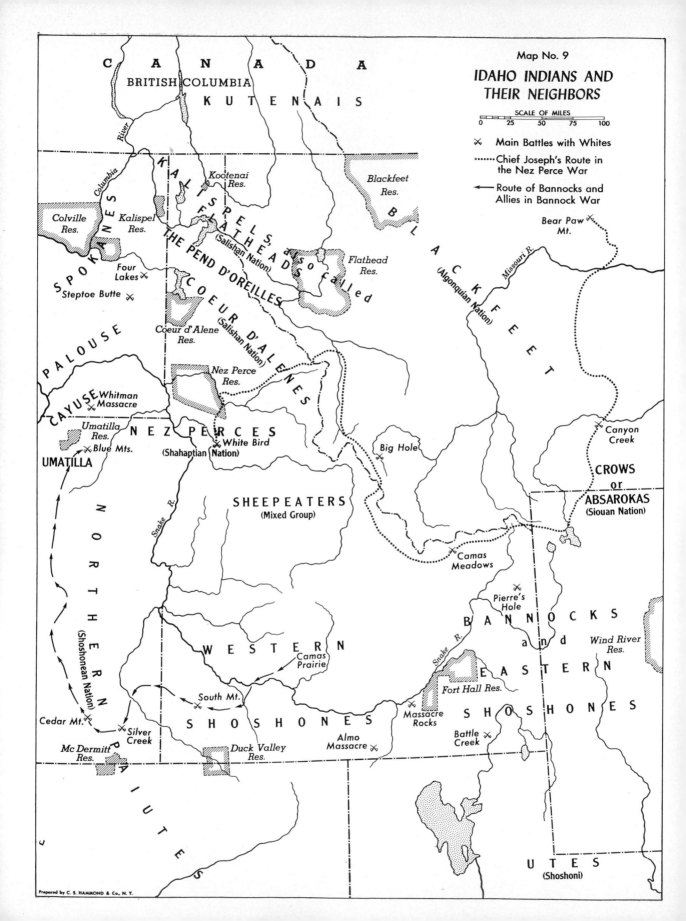

Map No. 9

IDAHO INDIANS AND
THEIR NEIGHBORS

SCALE OF MILES
0   25   50   75   100

✕ Main Battles with Whites

········ Chief Joseph's Route in
the Nez Perce War

← Route of Bannocks and
Allies in Bannock War

CANADA
BRITISH COLUMBIA
KUTENAIS

Columbia River

SPOKANES

Colville
Res.

Kalispel
Res.

Four
Lakes ✕

Steptoe Butte ✕

KALISPELS, also called

THE PEND D'OREILLES

Kootenai
Res.

FLATHEADS
(Salishan Nation)

COEUR D'ALENE
(Salishan Nation)

Coeur d'Alene
Res.

Flathead
Res.

Blackfeet
Res.

B L A C K F E E T
(Algonquian Nation)

Missouri R.

Bear Paw ✕
Mt.

PALOUSE

CAYUSE

Whitman
Massacre ✕

Umatilla
Res.

Blue Mts. ✕

UMATILLA

Nez Perce
Res.

NEZ PERCES
(Shahaptian Nation)

✕ White Bird

Big Hole ✕

Canyon ✕
Creek

CROWS
or
ABSAROKAS
(Siouan Nation)

N O R T H E R N
(Shoshonean Nation)

Snake R.

SHEEPEATERS
(Mixed Group)

Camas ✕
Meadows

Pierre's ✕
Hole

BANNOCKS
and
EASTERN

Wind River
Res.

W E S T E R N

Camas
Prairie

Snake R.

Fort Hall Res.

Cedar Mt. ✕

South Mt. ✕

S H O S H O N E S

Massacre
Rocks

S H O S H O N E S

Silver ✕
Creek

McDermitt
Res.

Duck Valley
Res.

Almo ✕
Massacre

Battle ✕
Creek

P A I U T E S

U T E S
(Shoshoni)

Prepared by C. S. HAMMOND & Co., N. Y.

no one who can interpret the pictures and carvings left by the original inhabitants in so many parts of the state. We do have some of Rees's interpretations, notably those in the Blackfoot Public Library, and in a few other places. Samples of these are shown in the illustration you see opposite. From them you can gain a dim understanding of what these picture writings are like.

Where the Idaho Indians Lived. Tribes of four Indian nations or language groups lived in that part of the Pacific Northwest which is now included in Idaho. These were the Shoshonean, Shahaptian, Salishan, and Kootenaian, or Kitunahan, nations. All were hunting Indians, and not until they were placed on reservations during the territorial period of Idaho's history did they begin the change to an agricultural economy, except in a limited way among the Nez Perce groups. The general areas in which these Indians lived are shown on Map No. 9, "Idaho Indians and Their Neighbors," which accompanies this unit.

The Shoshoni Tribes. In the southern part of what is now Idaho lived the Shoshoni Indians, part of a great Indian nation scattered over many parts of the West. Four tribes made up the Idaho groups of this nation. These were the Bannocks, the Lemhis, the Sheepeaters, and the Shoshones proper.

The Eastern Shoshones, with whom the Bannocks were closely allied but not actually a part, ranged the Upper Snake River Valley and the mountains and valleys of eastern Idaho, western Wyoming, and northern Utah. They also frequently crossed the Continental Divide on hunting trips, especially for buffalo.

Courtesy Idaho Historical Department

INDIAN PICTURE WRITING IN IDAHO

These pictures, usually on cliffs, canyon walls, walls of caves, and on smooth boulders, are fairly numerous in some parts of Idaho. They are especially plentiful in certain areas along the Snake and Salmon rivers. Do you know of any Indian picture writing near your own home?

The Lemhi Indians made the Lemhi and Upper Salmon River Valleys their main home. They, too, often traveled over the Continental Divide into southwestern Montana on hunting trips. You recall, no doubt, that it was on such a journey that Sacajawea was taken prisoner by a war party of Indians from east of the mountains.

The Tukuarika Indians seem to have lived in and around Yellowstone Park in

SHOSHONI INDIAN SUN DANCE

This traditional Indian festival is still an annual event in southern Idaho. It is chiefly a cleansing ceremony and a prayer to the Great Spirit for health and strength. Once forbidden to the whites, it is now a public affair and is attended by large numbers of tourists and other interested observers.

early times. Later they moved into the deep and remote canyons of the Salmon River Mountains, from which they seldom emerged. There they were joined by refugee Indians from other tribes, becoming known as the Sheepeaters, probably because mountain sheep and mountain goats formed a considerable part of their diet.

The Western Shoshones occupied the Lower Snake River Valley in western Idaho and eastern Oregon and the mountain valleys and basins along the Boise, Payette, Weiser, Bruneau, and Owyhee rivers. Indian Valley and Council Valley, along the Weiser River, were traditional meeting places for holding tribal councils and meeting other tribes for trade and for social activities of various kinds.

The only domesticated animals possessed by the Shoshoni were the horse and the dog. Both were used as beasts of burden as well as for food when other meat was lacking. The tribes of eastern Idaho were especially well sup-

plied with horses, which was an advantage when going on hunting expeditions to the buffalo country and in the numerous encounters with the Crows and other hostile tribes to the east.

The religion of the Shoshones and other Northwestern tribes, if religion it can be called, was a mixture of nature worship and superstition. Their festivals seem to have been both religious and social in their nature. Among the religious festivals the sun dance, also common among the tribes of the Great Plains, was probably the most important. The sun dance is still an annual affair among the Indians of southern Idaho, though of late years it has been open to attendance by white people and has become largely commercialized.

The Nez Perce Indians. These Indians belonged to the Shahaptian family or group, whose range was from central Idaho along the Clearwater and lower Salmon rivers into Oregon and Washington. The principal Idaho tribe was the

Nez Perce Indians. They were given that name by French Canadians. It means "pierced nose," and may have been bestowed because the Indians wore ornaments in the nose. In fact, Lewis and Clark called them "Pierced Noses" and mentioned that some of the tribesmen wore nose ornaments. The custom, however, was not general and seems to have disappeared before white people came to live among the Nez Perces.

These Indians were well supplied with horses, which, in fact, constituted their main wealth. They were, therefore, well equipped for long hunting trips. They often went on expeditions to the buffalo country of western Montana, following the Lolo and Nez Perce trails which led eastward through the Bitterroot Mountains.

Among the Nez Perce horses was a spotted breed known as Palouse horses because they grazed over the green hills along the Palouse River. These horses were superior in speed and stamina to ordinary Indian ponies and are said to have been a main reason why Chief Joseph was able for so long a time to elude the white soldiers sent to subdue his tribesmen in the Nez Perce War. Descendants of these horses, now called Appaloosa, are being raised in considerable numbers and are becoming popular among horse fanciers of the Northwest.

Like other intermountain Indians, the Nez Perces lived mainly by hunting and fishing. Probably the best proportioned physically of the Indians of the Northwest, they were strong, brave, and self-reliant. Inclined to live in peace, they were seldom involved in battle unless, as

Photos by Mr. John Vaninetti
Courtesy Northern Idaho Indian Agency, Lapwai, Idaho

MODERN INDIAN FARMING METHODS

Above—This boy is proud to show the garden of Jonas Frank, because he helped to care for it. Below—Modern haying equipment purchased and in use by Harry McCormack, near Lapwai, Idaho

sometimes happened, they were attacked by other tribes when away from home on their frequent hunting expeditions.

Salishan Tribes. Two small tribes belonging to the Salishan language group of Indians lived in the lakes region of northern Idaho. These were the Skitswish people around Lake Coeur d'Alene and the Kalispel Indians around Lake Pend Oreille. They were closely allied to the Flathead Indians of western Montana and were sometimes spoken of as Flatheads.

The Skitswish, who called themselves "camas people," were named the Coeur d'Alene Indians by the French Canadians. The name is said to have meant "awl-heart," "heart-like-an-awl." It is believed to have referred to the sharp bargains they tried to drive with the fur traders who sometimes visited the tribe.

The Kalispel Indians were also given a special name by the French Canadians. These trappers and traders called them the Pend d'Oreille Indians, meaning "earbob," or "earring," Indians, from shell ornaments some of them wore in their ears. In the post journal of Spokane House, in the files of the Hudson's Bay Company, reference is made to these Indians. Michael Bourden, leader of the Snake Country Expedition of that year, had just returned and the journal records the event in these words: "About sun down Bourdon [or Bourden] arrived from the Snake Country. He had left seven of his freemen [free trappers] at the Ear Ring Indians."[1]

The Kootenai Indians. These Indians occupied the lands along the Kootenai River in British Columbia, northern Idaho, and northwestern Montana. They were known as "river people" and obtained much of their food from the waterways along which they lived. Later they came into possession of horses and made some progress as hunting Indians. The Idaho tribe was always small, never numbering more than a few hundred.

Map No. 9, "Idaho Indians and Their Neighbors," which accompanies this unit, will give you a better understanding of where the Indian tribes lived, as well as indicate the territory of the principal neighboring tribes. The location of battles between whites and Indians and the reservations on which our Indian citizens now live will help round out the story of the Indians in Idaho. These matters will be discussed in the pages which follow.

II. EARLY RELATIONSHIP WITH THE WHITE RACE

THE RED AND WHITE RACES have, we know, not always lived at peace with each other. In the years when our country was filling with white settlers, there was much enmity and deadly fighting between the races. For this, neither race was wholly to blame.

The Indians blamed the white people for taking possession of land that had always been claimed by the Indians; for killing or driving away the game on which the Indians depended for food; for spreading drunkenness and disease among the tribes; and for cheating the

Indians in trade, particularly in underpaying for furs sold to the white trappers and traders.

Unfortunately, many of these charges were true. On the other hand the whites asserted that the Indians made little use of the land; that they were thieving and treacherous, cruel and bloodthirsty, and often at war with each other as well as against the whites; and that they were the main obstacles standing in the way of settlement. Many of these claims were also true.

Their Opposite Ways of Life. The truth is that opposing ways of life made lasting peace between the two races impossible until one or the other had ob-

[1]Dale L. Morgan, *Jedediah Smith and the Opening of the West* (Indianapolis: The Bobbs-Merrill Company, 1953) pp. 120–21.

tained absolute mastery. Let us take a look at some of the most striking differences between the races.

Land Ownership. The white method of land ownership was for each family to own its own home. The Indians, most of whom neither knew nor cared about agricultural activities, had no reason for individual land ownership. Instead, tribal lands were common property for the use of all members of the tribe on equal terms.

Property Rights. White people generally secured private property by purchase, trade, or making what they needed. The Indians considered it a mark of bravery and skill to take by force or stealth what they needed or wanted, or, as white people call it, to steal.

Hunting and Fishing. Both races hunted and fished. But the Indians followed these occupations solely as a means of getting food, and apparently never for sport. The whites also fished and followed the chase as a means of securing food, but they also hunted and fished for sport, often killing far beyond their needs. This was bad for the future supply of wildlife and, as a result, was deeply resented by the Indians.

Cultivating the Soil. Indians did not till the soil; at least, Idaho Indians did not do so before the coming of white men. But the settler's ax laid low the forest, his plow uprooted the grass. As the wild pastures shrank, the buffalo, the elk, and the deer decreased rapidly in numbers. Wildlife not destroyed outright was driven farther away and the Indians were thus deprived of their main source of food.

When white men first came to Idaho, they came largely as explorers and traders. This at first caused the Indians little or no alarm. In fact, they seem to have welcomed the whites in friendship and to have extended what aid they could. Later, as more and more white people entered the Indian country, trouble between the races began to build up.

Open War. Gradually the two races found themselves more and more opposed to each other. When emigrants began passing through the Indian lands in numbers, the tribes grew fearful that they would lose their ancestral homes to the invaders. Occasional bands of warriors began to attack wagon trains and other small groups of travelers, and soon fighting flared all along the frontier.

War in the Palouse Country. As we have already seen, the first Indian outbreak resulted in the wiping out of the Whitman Mission and the abandonment of the Spalding Mission. An uneasy peace of eleven years followed the Whitman massacre. In 1858, however, some white miners were killed in eastern Washington by hostile Indians, and Colonel Steptoe led an expedition into the Indian country in an attempt to overawe the tribes. His action brought out the warriors of the Palouse, Spokane, Yakima, and Coeur d'Alene tribes in force and after the battle of Steptoe Butte, near the present town of Rosalia in eastern Washington, the expedition was compelled to retreat.

Faced with the prospect of a wholesale Indian uprising in the Northwest, General Newman S. Clark, in command of the Department of the Columbia, sent Colonel George Wright with a strong force to settle the trouble. In the battle of Four Lakes, near the present city of

Spokane, the Indians were defeated and severe punishment was meted out to their leaders. This ended Indian attempts to openly resist the whites until the Nez Perce War broke out nineteen years later.

Attacks Along the Great Medicine Road. The home territory of the Bannock and Shoshone Indians lay squarely across the Oregon Trail. The Indians, observing the thousands of emigrants traveling the white man's Great Medicine Road, grew very restless and this unrest spread to other tribes. Later, when gold was discovered in Idaho, great numbers of white people began crowding in to try their luck in the gold fields.

Small bands of Indians caused considerable trouble in the Boise Basin and surrounding sections during the first year of the gold rush. Matters grew so serious that Captain Jeff Standifer organized a group of volunteers to get rid of the troublemakers. The Indians entrenched themselves in a rocky area between Indian Creek and Blacks Creek, not far from the present county line between Ada and Elmore counties. There Standifer's men surrounded them and in the ensuing battle killed about sixty, almost the entire band. This action freed the Boise Basin area from further Indian raids and attacks.

Chief Pocatello's band of Bannock Indians was openly hostile. They began attacking wagon trains, killing the emigrants, burning the wagons, and killing or driving away the livestock. On Almo Creek, in what is now Cassia County, a train of sixty wagons was destroyed and about three hundred emigrants were slain. Another wagon party was ambushed at Massacre Rocks west of American Falls. Other parties of emigrants were attacked and killings occurred at various points all the way west into Oregon, among them the Ward, Otter, and Van Norman massacres.

Following the Almo massacre the Bannocks went into winter encampment near the Mormon settlement at Franklin. Their threatening attitude led the Mormons to appeal to military authorities for protection. General Connor was sent from Fort Douglas at Salt Lake City with a detachment of soldiers. In January, 1863, a savage battle occurred on a creek a few miles from the present city of Preston, since named Battle Creek. The fight resulted in the death or capture of almost the entire band of hostiles, including most of the women and children as well as the warriors. Once more the Indians learned the hard way that it was useless to oppose the whites, and peace again prevailed throughout Idaho.

Only a small number of the Eastern Shoshones were engaged in the hostilities that had taken place. The main body of Indians, led by Chief Washakie, carefully kept out of the fighting. This attitude paid off for the Indians when the government made a treaty with them in 1863 recognizing their right to a large part of the territory they claimed, and the government extended to southern Idaho the same policy that had already been worked out with the Nez Perce Indians of northern Idaho.

Ektachrome by Ross Hall

THE IDAHO WHITE PINE IS THE STATE TREE

Idaho white pine and tamarack are shown in this picture, taken near "Niggerhead" on Lake Coeur d'Alene

III. THE RESERVATION SYSTEM

As EARLY AS 1786, the United States began the practice of allotting or setting aside certain lands to be the property of Indian tribes. This is known as the reservation plan, and it was the method used to regulate Indian interests in Idaho and the Northwest.

Reservations in Idaho. The first Indian reservation in Idaho was set aside for the Nez Perce Indians in 1855. It was at first an enormous territory extending from the Blue Mountains in Oregon to the Bitterroot Mountains in Idaho. Later, after gold was discovered in the Nez Perce country, a new treaty was made which greatly reduced the Indian lands and established the present Nez Perce Reservation, with headquarters at the town of Lapwai.

The Fort Hall Reservation in southeastern Idaho was next to be created. It was set aside in 1869 by order of President Ulysses S. Grant for the Shoshoni and Bannock tribes of eastern Idaho, and soon most of the Indians made their homes on the reservation.

Then in succession came the Coeur d'Alene Reservation in 1873, the Lemhi Reservation in 1875, and the Duck Valley or Western Shoshone Reservation in 1877. These, with a 4,105-acre allotment for the small band of Kootenai Indians in Kootenai River Valley in northern Idaho, provided reservation lands for all the Indians of Idaho.

The establishment of reservations did not, however, immediately solve the Indian problem. The tribes could not at once forsake the old freedom and the old habits of traveling to favorite camping and hunting grounds as they had been accustomed to do for perhaps hundreds of years. Neither did the reservation plan at first offer the Indians the means of living in reasonable comfort and security. They still needed the game, the fish, and the wild fruit and roots to supplement their often scanty reservation fare. For several years roving parties of Indians continued to leave the reservations to visit favorite camping grounds. It was only natural that these trips, as well as other unsatisfactory developments, should lead to trouble.

There followed in Idaho Territory the so-called Indian wars. The danger from Indians had delayed the settlement and development of various parts of the territory. Farmers, stockmen, prospectors, and miners hesitated to strike into the wilderness or to take up land far from the protection of settlements already established.

The Nez Perce War. The first serious outbreak came among the Lower Nez Perces living in the Wallowa Valley in northeastern Oregon. These Indians had been given a reservation of their own on orders of President Grant. A little later the order was canceled and the reservation was abolished. The nontreaty Nez Perces, so called because they had not signed the agreement creating the original Nez Perce Reservation, were ordered to move to the Idaho side of the Snake River and join the reservation Indians.

The nontreaty Indians were angered by the demand. After some delay, however, they grudgingly agreed to the move on the advice of Chief Joseph, their head chief. After they had completed the move, some of the young warriors attacked and killed some settlers along the lower Salmon River. The following telegram gives a quick picture of the outbreak:

"NEZ PERCE AGENCY, I.T.
JUNE 17, 1877

"THE NON-TREATY INDIANS COMMENCED HOS-TILITIES ON THE 14TH INST. UP TO DATE, 29 SETTLERS ARE REPORTED MURDERED AND FOUR INDIANS KILLED. GENERAL HOWARD IS HERE IN COMMAND. THE HOSTILES NUMBER ABOUT 100 STRONG, AND ARE REPORTED TO HAVE GONE TO THE SALMON RIVER COUNTRY AND MAKING FOR THE WEISER IN SOUTHERN IDAHO. TROOPS ARE IN PURSUIT AND WE ARE ABOUT 12 HOURS BE-HIND. THE RESERVATION INDIANS ARE TRUE TO THE GOVERNMENT. A COMPANY IS FORMED UNDER THE HEAD CHIEF, AND ARE PROTECTING KAMIAH AND EMPLOYEES. NO NEWS FROM THE INDIANS NORTH OF HERE.

WILKIUS, *Inspector*
JOHN B. MONTEITH, *Indian Agent*."

Thus, in June, 1877, began the Nez Perce War. Chief Joseph almost at once showed his genius as a military leader. A series of desperate battles began with the battle of White Bird, near the present village of that name. Joseph then led his band across the plateau to the Clearwater River near the town of Kamiah, where the two-day battle of the Clearwater was fought. The Nez Perces retreated over the Lolo Trail into the Bitterroot Valley of western Montana and crossed the Continental Divide to the Big Hole River. There they successfully beat off an attack by General Gibbon and crossed back over the Beaverhead Range into the Lemhi Valley in Idaho.

Then Joseph started east on a round-about course which was intended to carry the Nez Perces to safety in Canada. After entering Montana, they were attacked by Colonel Sturgis. In the battle of Canyon Creek, the soldiers were unable to win a decisive victory. As Joseph's band headed north, General Howard telegraphed Colonel Miles, stationed in eastern Montana, to cut off the retreat. In this Miles was successful and the warriors, together with the women and children of the band, were trapped between the forces of Colonel Miles and the pursuing forces of General Howard at Bear Paw Mountain. There Joseph, after a terrific fight, gave up, closing a speech of surrender with these words: "Hear me, my chiefs, I am tired; my heart is sick and sad. From where the sun now stands, I will fight no more forever!"

After the war the survivors of the non-treaty Indians were sent first to Oklahoma and, later, to the Colville Reservation in Washington. There Joseph, the Red Napoleon of the Northwest, died about twenty-five years later, and there the remnants of the Lower Nez Perce still live.

Chief Joseph, whose Indian name meant "Thunder-Rolling-over-the-Mountains," had the true spirit of frontier America. His outlook on life was in many respects in complete harmony with what we call today the "American way of life." This spirit was well shown when he said, "Let me be a free man, free to travel, free to stop, free to work, free to trade where I choose, free to follow the religion of my fathers, free to talk and think and act for myself."

The Bannock War. Hardly had the last shot been fired in the Nez Perce War when the Bannock War began in southern Idaho. White settlers had taken land on the Big Camas Prairie, which for generations had been a major source of the camas roots which were used as food by the Indians. Fort Hall Bannocks, under Chief Buffalo Horn, visited the camas beds in 1878. Finding that settlers were pasturing hogs, cattle, and horses on the meadows and that the hogs were rooting up and eating the camas bulbs, the Indians, in anger, went on the war path.

Striking southwest and raiding as they went, it was the purpose of the Indians to arouse the tribes of southwestern Idaho and southeastern Oregon to unite and try to sweep the white people from the territory. They destroyed the stage station at King Hill and crossed the Snake on the ferryboat at Glenns Ferry, where they killed two wagon freighters who were camped there. Going on and crossing Bruneau Valley, they reached a creek, since called Battle Creek, in Owyhee County. There they were met by volunteer white forces at South Mountain, in Owyhee County, and in the ensuing battle Buffalo Horn was killed.

Moving on into Oregon, the Bannocks were joined by restless Paiutes, Umatillas, and Western Shoshones. Chief Egan, a Umatilla, took over the leadership after vainly trying to persuade the Indians to give up the enterprise and return to their respective reservations. The soldiers caught up with the hostiles on Silver Creek, a tributary of the Owyhee River. In this struggle, sometimes called Battle Mountain, Chief Egan was seriously wounded in a personal fight with Colonel Robbins, but succeeded in making his escape. A few days later the battle of Cedar Mountain occurred in the same general area, after which the Indians retreated.

Courtesy E. A. Brininstool

CHIEF JOSEPH, NEZ PERCE LEADER

Chief Joseph, sometimes called the Red Napoleon, is considered one of the foremost Indian leaders and military strategists of the United States.

The main band, several hundred strong, headed for the John Day country, while smaller raiding bands killed and burned at isolated ranches and settlements. General Howard, fresh from his victory over the Nez Perces, pushed the Indians closely and brought them to bay in the Blue Mountains. In the battle that followed the Indians were badly beaten. About the same time a small force of Umatilla Indians who had joined the soldiers succeeded in killing Chief Egan, who was recovering from his wounds, together with a number of his most devoted followers. These reverses ended the Bannock War, the warriors breaking up into small groups and gradually returning to their reservations.

The Sheepeater War. In 1878 the Sheepeater Indians, excited by the Bannock War, attacked white settlers along the South Fork of the Salmon River and killed a few of them. Soldiers were sent into the region and after two small fights the Indians gave up and were transferred to reservations.

With the danger of Indian attacks removed and peace following a half century of unrest and outbreaks on the part of the Indians, the way was completely open at last for white development of the Northwest. In Idaho settlement went forward at a steady pace and by the close of the territorial period the Indian troubles were only a memory.

Most Idaho Indians still live on reservations. Some changes have been made in the interest of greater efficiency in administration. The Lemhi Reservation was abandoned and the residents there were given land allotments on the Fort Hall Reservation. The administrative offices of the Coeur d'Alene Reservation were moved to Lapwai on the Nez Perce Reservation, and this office now supervises the affairs of the Kootenai Indians living on a land allotment in Kootenai Valley near Bonners Ferry.

IV. A NEW DAY FOR THE INDIANS

THE OFFICE OF INDIAN AFFAIRS, a bureau or division of the United States Department of the Interior, still has considerable control over Indian affairs. It has, however, in many ways improved the condition of the Indians, and in this it has had the help of the tribes, themselves deeply interested in bettering their opportunities. Congress has actively co-operated in various programs and has aided by making appropriations for the purpose of helping the Indians.

Indian Citizenship Act. Feeling that the time had come for all Indians to assume greater responsibilities and be less dependent on government help, the Indian Office recommended and Congress enacted the Indian Citizenship Act of 1924 in the following language:

Be it enacted by the Senate and the House of Representatives of the United States of America in Congress assembled, that all non-citizen Indians born within the territorial limits of the United States be, and they are hereby, declared to be citizens of the United States.

By this law all Indians not already citizens were raised to citizenship and the ward status or condition of the Indians was practically wiped out except for certain controls over property.

Indian Reorganization Act. About ten years after the Indians were granted citizenship, the Wheeler-Howard Act was passed by Congress. This law, usually called the Indian Reorganization Act, allows the Indians a large measure of self-government and self-direction in managing personal and tribal affairs. The

INDIAN CRAFTSWOMAN AND HER WORK

"Among manual crafts and arts in the United States, by far the most important ones, in creative potentiality, are those of the Indians."
—*Harold L. Ickes, Secretary of the Interior.*

purposes of the law were well stated by Harold L. Ickes, then Secretary of the Interior, who wrote:

Fundamentally, the Reorganization Act is a declaration by the Government that the Indian as a race shall have the opportunity to live on; that the Indian civilization, as an element of human culture, shall live on. It means that the life of the Indian shall be part and parcel of those cultures and interests which constitute the United States.

No group in America today faces challenges or opportunities more exciting and commanding than those facing the Indians under the new policy.

Large natural resources still ample for many tribes, now await planned and cumulative[2] use by Indians.

Among manual crafts and arts in the United States, by far the most important ones, in creative potentiality,[3] are those of the Indians.

None of the groups in the United States has stronger traditions or a more democratic organization for public service than the Indian tribes.

Things done by the Indians now and in the years immediately ahead, under the authorities

[2]Cumulative. Collective; for the whole group.

[3]Potentiality. Possible development.

and aids of the Reorganization Act, may have their effect upon our whole population, and upon the life of the millions of Indians beyond our national frontiers.

All Indians of Idaho have accepted the terms of the Reorganization Act and are operating under its provisions, which, briefly, are: (1) The tribe or tribes adopt or reject the law by their own vote. (2) If accepted, a constitution and by-laws are drawn up and adopted, much as a state constitution or any other basic body of laws is made. (3) The group operating under the local constitution and by-laws then organizes itself as a lawful corporation, with power to engage in various kinds of enterprises.

It is worthy of note that the Indian reservations of southern Idaho are of the type known as "closed reservations," while those of northern Idaho are the "open reservation" type. On open reservations the Indians are, in general, governed by state laws the same as other citizens of Idaho, though there is still some tribal authority in special matters. On closed reservations there is a local police organization which assists in law enforcement and the enforcement of special rules and ordinances enacted by the tribal council, and which co-operates in various ways with state and local authorities.

In order to carry on the activities authorized under the Reorganization Act, most reservations are divided into districts, much as a city is divided into wards. Each district elects a representative to serve on a central council or governing body, usually called the tribal council.

Such tribal councils have rather wide local powers, all of which, however, must be stated in the constitution or by-laws. Typical duties and powers are to regulate the use and sale of tribal property; conserve and supervise natural resources; encourage and develop Indian arts and crafts; protect health and provide social and recreational opportunities; make agreements with government agencies on matters relating to the welfare of the tribe; consult with the Department of the Interior and with the Indian Bureau concerning appropriations and projects for the reservation; create, maintain, and supervise tribal funds to be used for stated purposes; and make and enforce ordinances for maintaining law and order.

As part of the Reorganization Act, Congress appropriated a large sum to be used as a revolving fund; that is, a fund to be drawn upon and used by the Indians and to be repaid by them. Tribes that are incorporated may borrow from the revolving fund for many purposes: organizing co-operative business enterprises; increasing the size and improving the quality of herds of livestock; purchasing additional lands; loaning money to individual Indian borrowers for various productive purposes. Loans from the revolving fund, however, must be approved by the reservation superintendent, a feature of the law some Indians dislike.

The chart that follows on the next page shows how the revolving fund works and how it renews itself.

V. TODAY'S INDIAN CITIZENS

TODAY'S INDIAN CITIZENS are proving themselves. In many ways they are showing to the world that they are worthy of full brotherhood in our America of today. Large numbers of them are officials and employees of the Indian Service, among them reservation superintendents; school superintendents, principals, and teachers; specialists in agriculture, livestock, and forestry; trained health and welfare workers; and many others.

In both the first and second World Wars, Indians took an active part. In the second World War about twenty thousand Indians enrolled in the armed forces, and Indian women were well represented in services connected with the war effort. Their investments in war bonds and other securities ran into millions of dollars. Thousands of them worked in war industries. Livestock and food production were increased. Victory gardens were extensively cultivated.

In combat our own Idaho Indians had

THE CHART THAT FOLLOWS SHOWS HOW THE REVOLVING FUND WORKS AND HOW IT RE-NEWS ITSELF.

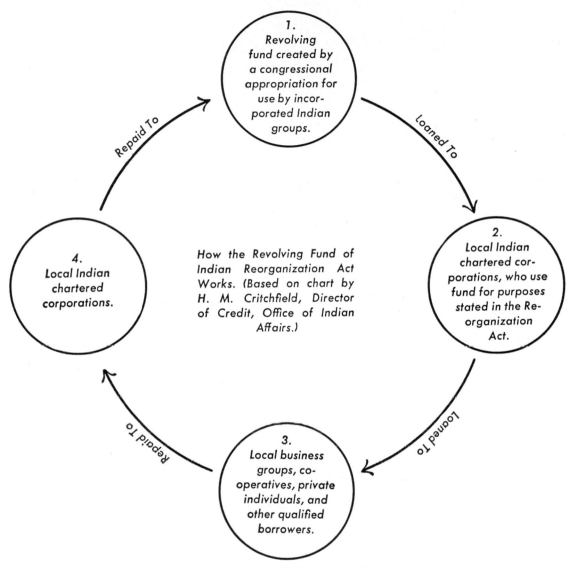

CHART NO. 1   CHART OF INDIAN REORGANIZATION ACT REVOLVING FUND

a good record in both World Wars. In World War II seven were killed in action and fifteen were wounded. They also shared in the Korean war and are represented in most branches of the military forces. When we remember that the total Indian population of Idaho is less than four thousand, including men, women, and children, we can see they conduct themselves with courage and patriotism when they have an opportunity to serve their country.

They also contributed greatly in wartime production of crops and livestock. According to the *Statistical Supplement* for the fiscal year ending June 30, 1945,

Courtesy Western Shoshone Subagency, Owyhee, Nevada

near the end of World War II, issued by the Office of Indian Affairs, Idaho Indians accounted for these totals: agricultural and grazing land operated by Indians, 368,152 acres; cash value of livestock owned, $1,466,768; cash realized from the sale of livestock, $399,856.

Figures for the Fort Hall Reservation showed that Indians operated about five thousand acres of irrigated land, which produces heavy crops of alfalfa, potatoes, and sugar beets. In northern Idaho Nez Perce, Coeur d'Alene, and Kootenai Indians harvested about nine thousand acres of wheat and other crops. Shoshone and Paiute Indians on the Duck Valley Reservation probably added little to the crop total except hay, as they specialize in raising beef cattle. Both the Fort Hall and Duck Valley beef herds are high-grade and purebred stock, ranking among the largest and best herds in the West.

In home life, our Idaho Indians are showing a steady rise toward higher standards of living. Comfortable homes, many of them having electric lights, power, running water, and modern conveniences, are replacing the unsanitary and unsatisfactory homes that were the rule not so long ago. Health standards have risen and personal and community cleanliness are receiving attention. The death rate has been greatly reduced and our Indian population is on the increase.

Indian arts and crafts are providing specialty goods such as decorative pottery, ornaments and jewelry, baskets, blankets, rugs, and beaded articles of deerskin such as gloves, moccasins, belts, and other garments. They also make cornhusk bags, Indian dolls, and a great variety of novelties. This work is especially important on the Coeur d'Alene Reservation, though done considerably on all of them.

In education the Indians are making progress, but there are still some serious obstacles in the way. Language difficulties in homes where English is not spoken is one of the great drawbacks, particularly on the Fort Hall and Duck Valley reservations in southern Idaho. Irregular attendance at school is also a serious hindrance. Most of the Indian children are enrolled in regular public schools in the state, and a considerable number go on to college and to special schools of higher education. Law, medicine, music, art, literature, teaching, forestry, the ministry—in all these fields and many more, Indians are proving their abilities.

Considerable numbers of Idaho Indians are members of the various Christian church organizations. But many of our Indians, both in Idaho and in the Northwest as a whole, believe much as they did before white men came among them. The quotation here from a member of the Yakima tribal delegation, sent to Washington, D.C., to confer with the Indian Committee of the House of Representatives, gives as clear a picture, perhaps, as has ever been made defining the "natural religion" of the Indians:

The American Indians have a peculiar religion or philosophy. They hold in reverence the natural resources of the land: the earth or soil, the fish in the streams and rivers, the timber on the mountains, the minerals and rocks in the ground, the vegetation and things that grow upon the earth. These things are sacred to the Indians, and have been from time immemorial. These are the things for which we fought in the early days. . . . Therefore, when these things are threatened, it really means that the objects of our religion are threatened.

Idaho has followed the lead of the Federal government in granting citizenship to the Indians. In 1950 the people approved an amendment to the state constitution giving the Indians the right to vote, to hold office, and to serve on juries. This amendment removed the last barrier and admitted our Indians to full citizenship in the state.

* * * * *

A new day seems, indeed, to have dawned for our Indian citizens. Several national and international Indian organi-

Courtesy Tommy Barrett's Camera Shop, Pocatello

INDIAN HOME LIFE IN IDAHO

Both the new and the old contribute to home comfort in most Indian homes.

zations are aiding the Indians to move forward to better things, the most important being the National Congress of American Indians. But most important of all is the help the Indians are giving themselves through their own local organizations and co-operative efforts.

If Idaho Indians, who but a little more than a century ago were living in a Stone Age civilization, continue to progress during the next few decades as they have in the last half century, they should soon become completely their own masters in every right and duty that is the birthright of each American citizen.

Marching Toward Statehood

How the people of Idaho Territory lived and worked together, laying a firm foundation for the privileges, duties, and responsibilities soon to be theirs as citizens of the forty-third state in the Union.

THE WEST WAS ON THE MARCH during the last half of the nineteenth century. Fourteen new states, all but one west of the Mississippi, joined the Union. We shall now see how Idaho Territory shared in the great Westward Movement and how the people of the territory established a firm foundation for statehood.

I. GROWTH IN POPULATION

POPULATION IS A YARDSTICK by which we may measure the growth of a region. Soon after Idaho Territory was created in 1863, a special census showed the population to be 21,116. By 1870, when the first United States Census was taken in the territory, there had been a decrease to 14,999, a loss of almost one third of the people.

This seven-year period is the only census period in Idaho's history that has registered a decrease in population. There were at least three reasons for this loss: (1) The placer mines were becoming exhausted and lode mining was still in its infancy. (2) General knowledge about Idaho Territory and its resources had not spread widely to other parts of the nation. (3) Transportation difficulties made migration to Idaho a matter of extreme hardship.

Beginning in the 1870's, Idaho's population began a slow but steady climb. The last territorial decade saw the trickle of people into the territory grow into a flood as population increased almost threefold, from 32,610 in 1880 to 88,548 in 1890.

Reasons for the Rapid Increase in Population. Nine factors were largely responsible for the great increase in population during the last dozen years or so of our territorial period. These were (1) the Mormon migration into southeastern Idaho; (2) favorable Federal land laws making it easy and inexpensive to acquire land; (3) removal of the danger from Indians by defeating them in war and placing them on reservations; (4) the development of lode, quartz, or hard-rock mining; (5) the extensive open range for cattle, horses, and sheep; (6) the great and almost untouched timber resources; (7) the abundance and cheapness of rich farming land; (8) the coming of railroads; and (9) the development of irrigation.

The Mormons were quick to realize

that southeastern Idaho and the Snake River Valley were great farming and livestock regions. By 1890 about one third of the total population of the territory consisted of Latter-day Saints living in Bear Lake, Bingham, Cassia, and Oneida counties, then the only counties in that part of Idaho.

Three Federal laws encouraged land ownership. These were the Homestead Act, the Desert Land Act, and the Timber and Stone Act. Under these laws hundreds of thousands of acres of government land were given free as homesteads or purchased at the low price of $1.25 per acre.

We learned in Unit 7 how the Indians were defeated in war and placed on reservations. This made it safe for white settlers to move into all parts of the territory and establish homes. Later topics in this unit will show how population growth and industrial and social progress were able to move forward so rapidly. New gold discoveries followed each other in rapid succession. A real beginning was made in farming, especially vegetable gardening, because of the high prices for which such products could be sold. Because of its mountainous surface and its great expanse of plains and plateaus, transportation developed slowly in Idaho, but individuals and companies were encouraged to build up easier and better facilities for travel.

Territorial Counties, Cities, and Towns. An earlier unit on counties showed that Idaho Territory contained eighteen counties at the close of the territorial period. These included two that no longer exist, Alturas and Logan counties. During most of this time population was fairly well divided among the agricultural counties of eastern and southwestern Idaho and such mining counties as Alturas, Boise, Custer, Elmore, Lemhi, Owyhee, and Shoshone. But in the last ten years there was a strong shift to the agricultural sections, and by 1890 fully two thirds of our people were living in the agricultural counties.

Certain conditions bring about the establishment and growth of cities. Among these are: (1) points where natural land routes such as navigable rivers and long open valleys converge on good ocean harbors; (2) the junction of navigable rivers; (3) points where natural routes of transportation meet or cross; (4) the concentration in relatively small areas of especially rich natural resources; and (5) convenient locations in regions that can supply raw materials for manufacturing, a good supply of workers for the factories, and a good market for manufactured products.

Few places in Idaho met these conditions. Only the Snake River Valley and the Purcell Trench provided really good natural routes of travel and transportation. The wide, open spaces and the rugged mountains for which Idaho is noted favored, and still favor, a rural rather than an urban, or city, way of living. In fact, in 1890 there were only fifteen incorporated towns and villages in the entire territory. Of these, not one was large enough to be classed as a city under the definition adopted by the Census Bureau, which does not list as a city any place having fewer than 2,500 people. The table that follows names all the incorporated towns. Are any of them now among the state's largest cities?

Table No. 1

INCORPORATED PLACES IN IDAHO TERRITORY, 1890

Rank	Place	Population	Territorial County in Which Located
1	Boise	2,311	Ada
2	Montpelier	1,174	Bear Lake
3	Weiser	901	Washington
4	Paris	893	Bear Lake
5	Bellevue	892	Logan (now Blaine)
6	Wallace	878	Shoshone
7	Lewiston	849	Nez Perce
8	Caldwell	779	Ada (now Canyon)
9	Grangeville	540	Idaho
10	Coeur d'Alene	491	Kootenai
11	Nampa	347	Ada (now Canyon)
12	Genesee	282	Latah
13	Mountain Home	233	Elmore
14	Rathdrum	218	Kootenai
15	Albion	179	Cassia

There were, in addition to the incorporated places, perhaps two score small towns and villages that had not yet set up local governments as legal municipal corporations. They did, however, have schools, churches, stores, and other institutions and some of them were well known in the territory. Some were, in fact, larger and more important than most of the incorporated places. Among them were Blackfoot, Emmett, Idaho Falls, Pocatello, Preston, and Rexburg, now among the leading cities of the state.

II. TERRITORIAL MINING

PLACER GOLD WAS THE MAGNET that first brought an inrush of people to Idaho. Mining continued to be the most important industry of the territory for almost two decades following the first discovery of gold in 1860, but the type of mining changed after the first few years.

Later Placer Gold Discoveries. The Golden Decade, as an outstanding Idaho historian, Byron Defenbach, has called the years from 1860 to 1870, saw the richest placer ground pretty well worked out. But occasional strikes continued to be made, some of them astonishingly rich.

In 1866 a party of prospectors led by F. B. Sharkey found rich placer gold along Napias (NA'pi-us) Creek in the western part of what is now Lemhi County. This led to the establishment of Leesburg, named in honor of General Robert E. Lee by the discoverers, who had been on the side of the South in the Civil War. A mile away sympathizers of the North established the rival town of Grantsville, named for General Grant. In a (more or less) peaceful contest, Grantsville was absorbed by Leesburg, and, in this instance at least, the South was triumphant over the North. The combined settlements once had a population estimated at seven thousand, but as production declined Leesburg joined the ranks of ghost towns. The region still produces some placer gold but is no longer an important mining section.

In 1869 gold was discovered on Loon Creek, a tributary of the Middle Fork of the Salmon River. There, in the space of about three years, gold dust and nuggets estimated at a half million dollars were gathered. Later the town was turned over to the Chinese, most of whom were killed when Indians attacked the settlement. Today, practically no trace remains of this once prosperous mining camp.

"Caribou" Jack Fairchild, F. McCoy, and F. S. Babcock found placer gold in the mountains east of Grays Lake in 1870. Two good-sized towns, Caribou City and Keenan, were settled, but both were deserted after a few years when the placers no longer paid a profit for the miners. During the time they were worked, however, they were estimated to have yielded several million dollars' worth of gold.

The discovery of placer gold along the Coeur d'Alene River and its tributaries in 1881–82 by Andrew J. Prichard drew a frenzied rush of miners to a new district in the Panhandle. Such boom towns and camps as Eagle City, Beaver, Murray, Delta, and several others sprang up. These followed the boom-and-bust pattern of most of the early gold camps of

Courtesy Charles Herndon, Salmon, Idaho

LEESBURG, A TYPICAL IDAHO GHOST TOWN

Located in 1866 and said to have produced millions in gold dust and nuggets, Leesburg now stands alone and practically deserted in a high basin of the Idaho Batholith west of the city of Salmon. Trailer and jeep add a modern touch.

Idaho Territory and had relatively short lives.

Quartz Mines of Territorial Idaho. Not long after Michael Jordan's gold discoveries in Owyhee County in 1863, fabulously rich silver ores were found in the same district. Some of these assayed as high as five thousand dollars per ton and sold for four dollars per ounce just as they came from the mines. Silver City and its surrounding mines became world famous and millions of dollars of outside capital were poured into the development of such mines as the War Eagle, Ruby Jackson, Paymaster, Owyhee Treasury, and others. The district remained very prosperous until the panic of the 1870's forced the mines to close. Mining continued more or less for a good many years, but the district never regained its former greatness and it is now practically deserted.

Some quartz mines were opened in Boise Basin, but it was around the headwaters of Boise River that the richest mines were found. The Rocky Bar–Atlanta district produced heavily for several years. The Ida Elmore Mine paid an average return of $270 per ton in gold by the crude methods of handling ore then in use. Little mining is now being done and the 1950 census failed to list any of the once booming towns of this district among the inhabited places of the state.

A new kind of lead ore called galena, usually mixed with silver, was discovered in paying quantities in the Wood River region of Alturas, now Blaine and Camas counties, and an important mining development followed. Among the noted mines were the Minnie Moore, North Star, Muldoon, Bullion, Carrietown, Vienna, Galena, and others. The Minnie Moore alone produced about four million dollars in its first two years of operation, and the entire district is said to have yielded more than a million dollars a year until several years after Idaho became a state. The Wood River district is still one of the active mining districts of the state.

The Upper Salmon River region in Custer County was another famous gold-mining district of the territory. The General Custer, the Bayhorse, and the Charles Dickens mines were very profitable, as were several others not so well known. The discoverer of the Charles Dickens Mine is said to have pounded out ten thousand dollars' worth of gold in a single month, using only a hand mortar for the work. Like the Wood River galena district, this gold-mining section paid over a million dollars a year for several years.

Another silver-lead-copper mining district was developed in Custer County in the Lost River area. In the White Knob Mountains west of the present town of Mackay were the boom towns of Cliff, Era, and Cliffton, all of which now belong among the ghost towns of the Upland Empire.

During the late 1870's, several quartz mines were developed in Lemhi County. One of these was the Viola Mine near the head of Lemhi River. This became one of the most famous lead mines of the world and for several years produced about one fourth of all the lead mined in the United States.

For one reason or another, mining ceased to be very profitable in the mountainous area of central Idaho. However, some mining has been done in various parts of the region ever since the original discoveries in territorial years. The region is known to have vast deposits of minerals of various kinds, and it is possible—in fact, probable—that mining will again become the most important industry of the Upland Empire, just as it was in the territorial period of our history.

The Coeur d'Alene Mining District. Last and richest among the lode-mining districts of Idaho is the world-renowned silver-lead-zinc district along the upper

RUINS OF GENERAL CUSTER MINE

Before it was worked out and abandoned, this famous mine produced more than six million dollars' worth of gold. The discovery of rich quartz mines in various parts of Idaho Territory was one reason for the rapid increase in population.

Courtesy U.S. Forest Service

reaches of the Coeur d'Alene River and its tributaries. This began, as we have seen, with the discovery of gold, but this metal was soon made insignificant by the amazing richness of the silver and lead mines.

The original discovery was made by Noah Kellogg, for whom the city of Kellogg is named. The great Bunker Hill and Sullivan mines resulted from the first discovery, but soon afterward three men, Carten, McDonald, and Seymour, located the Tiger and Poorman lead mines. These are only a few of the many mines that now make this district one of the greatest mining regions of the world.

Romantic legends of the early Coeur d'Alene district kept pace with the mineral development. One of the most famous stories concerns the discovery of the Bunker Hill Mine by Kellogg. There are several versions of the story, but the one that follows is, perhaps, the most interesting and it is founded on fact.

Kellogg, a poverty-stricken prospector, was grubstaked by Dr. J. T. Cooper and a building contractor named Peck. Kellogg loaded his supplies on a stray burro, or "mountain canary," that was roaming loose in the neighborhood. While prospecting in Milo Gulch, Kellogg allowed the burro to stray some distance away. When he found the missing animal, it dislodged a piece of rock in its efforts to escape capture. The peculiar appearance of the rock drew Kellogg's attention and so led to the discovery of the great mine.

The actual circumstances of the discovery will probably never be known. The following humorous poem by an unknown author may be as accurate as any other account:

FAMOUS JACK

This thriving town of Kellogg,
  'Bout sixty years ago,
Was just a wide place in the road,
  With none to come and go.

Then came a man with loaded pack,
  Noah Kellogg, so they say,
With all his goods upon a jack,
  Which he allowed to stray.

Next early morn he cast about
  To find his hobbled mule,
And though he hunted up and down,
  He could not find the fool.

HECLA STAR MINE

In the "Old Rocks" of the Idaho Panhandle are stored the mineral wealth that has made the Coeur d'Alene mining district one of the richest in the world.

Courtesy George A. McDowell, Inspector of Mines

At last he spied him on a ridge,
  And climbed up to him there.
The mule in flight kicked up a rock,
  Which looked almighty queer.

The story's long, it would, I fear,
  A ponderous volume fill—
Suffice to say the jackass found
  The famous Bunker Hill.
  —Author Unknown

(From *Gems of Thought and History of Shoshone County,* sponsored by Allied Fraternities of Shoshone County.)

After Kellogg's discovery, the men who had grubstaked him brought suit for a share in the mine. In the trial that followed, they were awarded $76,000 as their share. The mine was soon sold for $1,500,000 and the prospector, Noah S. Kellogg, received $300,000 for his share of the property. We are not told what

reward the burro received. Surely the animal was entitled to release from further toil and the finest of pastures and care for as long as life lasted!

By the time Idaho became a state, placer mining had pretty well ended, except in a very few locations. Hard-rock mining, on the other hand, was a growing industry. The hard times in the West in the 1870's, partly caused by the fact that the government had stopped the coinage of silver, had been offset by the increasing use of silver in industry and by government purchases of silver at fixed prices. As a result, the miners had generally prospered during the last territorial decade. Mining, though by that time second to agriculture in importance in Idaho, was a main support for the economic life of the territory.

III. TERRITORIAL FARMING AND STOCK RAISING

EVEN BEFORE CAPTAIN PIERCE'S DISCOVERY of gold on Orofino Creek, a begin-

ning had been made in farming and stock raising in southeastern Idaho. There the

THE OPEN RANGE

Millions of acres of unfenced wild pastures led to the growth of the livestock business during Idaho's territorial years.

Courtesy Pocatello Chamber of Commerce

Mormons had dug a ditch to carry water to small fields around Franklin. The stampede to the gold camps caused crops, especially vegetables, to be planted in suitable places close to the camps because of the high prices for which such products could be sold.

Mormons Extend the Boundaries of Zion. In earlier units we learned of Mormon settlements in southeastern Idaho. These were all farming and livestock settlements, and the Latter-day Saints were Idaho's first actual farmers. Of course, Colonel Craig, who did not depend entirely on his homestead in the Clearwater country for a living, and the Nez Perce Indians, who at that time were still more hunters than agriculturists, farmed in Idaho before the Mormons settled at Franklin.

By the end of the territorial period Mormon homes and farming villages dotted the region from Utah to Montana and from the central portion of the Snake River Valley eastward to Wyoming. In these settlements farming and stock raising went hand in hand. The Mormons were among the first settlers in Idaho to seriously undertake the improvement of beef cattle, the first to develop dairying on a commercial scale, and the first to use dry-farm methods of cropping land not suitable for irrigation.

Farming and Ranching Near the Mining Camps. While the Mormons were extending farming settlements in eastern Idaho, similar developments were taking place in the valleys of southwestern Idaho. The farms and ranches there partially supplied the food requirements of the mining towns and furnished many of the horses needed for travel and transportation.

In view of the great need for horses, it was natural that horse ranches were among the first livestock developments in southwestern Idaho. Though such ranches were established in many parts of the region, the lower valleys along the Payette and Weiser rivers were favored locations. There nourishing grasses were plentiful and the winters were so mild that little winter feeding was required.

It was soon discovered that the valleys of southwestern Idaho were ideally adapted to the growing of fruit and vegetables. Soon most of the farms had their own vegetable gardens and small family orchards. Commercial orchards began to claim attention as early as 1864, when Thomas Davis set out an apple orchard. A little later General Cartee established a nursery, the first in Idaho, near Boise City. By 1870 a number of orchards were in production, and the close of the territorial period saw this part of Idaho well established in the commercial fruit and vegetable business.

Agriculture in the Panhandle. We have seen that Lewiston, started in 1861, quickly became the main distribution point and leading town of northern Idaho. It was natural that among the early settlers there were some who were interested in the agricultural possibilities of the region.

The Reverend Henry Spalding had planted apple trees at his mission, and some of these were still bearing when Lewiston was settled. This encouraged Wesley Mulkey to start an apple orchard near Lewiston in 1863. His venture was successful and apples from his orchard were soon sold in mining settlements along the Salmon River and in western Montana. Others followed Mulkey's lead and the Lewiston area became noted for its fruit, a distinction it still holds.

Fruit raising, stock raising, and farming engaged the attention of more and more people as the Panhandle began attracting settlers other than miners. In the 1870's a sizable agricultural industry grew up in the Clearwater valleys and in the Palouse country to the north. A few cattle, horses, and sheep were making use of the natural grasslands of the Nez Perce and Camas prairies in the southern part of the Clearwater Plateau. Cattle from northern Idaho were driven to The Dalles on the Columbia, where they were loaded on cattle boats and shipped to market up and down the Pacific coast.

Texas Longhorns in Idaho. Romance and legend have grown up around the Chisholm Trail and other great western trails over which cattle from the plains of Texas were driven to railroad points in Kansas and Nebraska. But the Chisholm Trail was a mere picnic excursion compared to the cattle trails leading to the Snake River Plains and the Southwestern Uplands of Idaho.

As early as 1866 Charles S. Gamble and associated cattle interests brought a large herd of Texas cattle into the Raft River Valley and founded the Shirley Company. This herd, and others coming soon afterward, were driven northward to the vicinity of the old Oregon Trail, which they then followed in a general way into southern Idaho.

In 1869 Con Shea and associates, owners of the Ox-Yoke brand, purchased a huge herd of ten thousand Texas longhorns to drive to the upland pastures of Owyhee County. This great cattle drive required months to reach its destination in southwestern Idaho. For many years the defile used by the Shea cattle to reach a watering place on Snake River was known as the "Con Shea Watering."

OFF TO TOWN

Cowboys head for town to break the monotony of long days and hours on the cattle range.

A letter,[1] written at Silver City in 1869, shows how important the cattle business had already become in that part of the territory.

Silver City, I. Ty.
October 12, 1869.

Mr. A. H. Webb, Assessor,
  Silver City, I. Ty.

Dear Sir;—

Droves of cattle from Texas have arrived in Owyhee County and have been turned loose upon the fine range grass. . . . Most of these cattle are now feeding southwest of Silver City and number from 6000 to 7000 head. Doubtless the stock will winter well as there is an abundance of feed and a large amount of open range for them. In another large herd many of them are owned by some of Owyhee's largest cattle men, namely Edw. Bass, Robt. Enos, Con Shea, Miller, Bugbee and others, some of the 2000 head just arrived belonging to them. The Bruneau section is furnishing feed at present. The cow hands recently paid Silver City a visit where they relaxed from their long drive and were shown some of the sights of this mining camp. They amply sampled some of the wet goods as they were evidently very dry and had parched throats after the long dusty drive; many washed the alkali from their throats with Silver's best which had a splendid effect in clearing their vocal cords. They quieted down before morning with little damage done. Owyhee will be enriched by the addition of these cattle to the assessment roll.

Yours truly,
SETH CATLIN.

Big cattle outfits were scattered from eastern Oregon through what are now Owyhee, Twin Falls, and Cassia counties, eastward to the Raft River Valley and southward into Nevada. The largest of these was the Sparks-Harrold (also spelled Harrell) Shoe Sole spread. This outfit was for many years said to be the largest cattle company in the West.

Other parts of the territory important for cattle were the Wood River and Lost River ranges, the Custer County and

[1]James R. Keith, "When the Long Horned Cattle of Texas Came to Idaho Territory," Idaho State Historical Society, *Sixteenth Biennial Report, 1937–38* (Boise, Idaho, 1938), p. 49.

LONGHORN CATTLE

Immense herds of longhorn cattle once roamed the ranges of southwestern Idaho, south of Snake River. Not good beef animals, the longhorns did not hold their own with better beef types that displaced them about the close of the territorial period.

Lemhi County regions of central Idaho, the Mormon country of eastern and southeastern Idaho, the Upper Snake River Valley, and the Clearwater Plateau of northern Idaho. The longhorn cattle, however, were pretty well limited to the south side of Snake River. In other parts of the territory better grades of beef animals were brought in from the Middle West and from the Montana and Wyoming ranges. The Upper Snake River Valley was particularly active in this movement for the improvement of cattle herds.

Sheep and Horses Share the Wild Pastures. The livestock industry of Idaho Territory was by no means limited to cattle. John Hailey, a prominent business and political leader of southern Idaho, brought in several bands of sheep in the late 1860's. The dry ranges, with desert-type vegetation, proved ideal for sheep raising. These animals soon spread to many parts of the Snake River Valley and its bordering plateaus and uplands, especially after the Oregon Short Line Railroad was completed across the territory.

Since cattle and sheep do not successfully share the same range, cattlemen were angered by the coming of sheep. This sometimes led to trouble between the sheepmen and cattlemen. In his *History of Idaho,* James H. Hawley wrote:

Disputes naturally arose; there was fierce jealousy between the cattlemen and the sheepmen, and frequent battles occurred for the possession of water holes and choice feeding grounds, and many serious crimes were committed which intensified the harsh feelings between the rival stockmen. . . . These troubles lasted for many years and until new conditions developed and new policies were adopted.

The most famous episode in range disputes occurred in Cassia County after Idaho became a state, but the conditions which caused this and similar troubles developed while Idaho was still a territory. Therefore, the tale is worth telling here.

Two sheepherders were murdered at a lonely camp in the Goose Creek Mountains. A cowboy named Jack Davis, commonly called "Diamond-Field Jack," was arrested and charged with the killing. In a sensational trial he was found guilty and was sentenced to death. He was steadfast in denying that he had any part in the affair, so his death sentence was changed to life imprisonment. In 1898 a man named Bower swore that he and another man named Gray got into a fight with the sheepherders and that Gray

A REMINDER OF THE HOLY LAND

This beautiful scene on the Clearwater Plateau reminds us of Bible stories of the Holy Land. From early territorial years, sheep have shared the Idaho ranges with cattle and horses.

killed them in the resulting gun battle. Soon after this Diamond-Field Jack was pardoned and soon left the state. After an adventurous life in California and Nevada, he was struck and killed by a taxicab in Las Vegas, Nevada, a few years ago.

Horses, too, were raised in large numbers. These animals were in demand for farm and ranch work, wagon and stagecoach transportation, pack trains for use in the mountains, for general travel and pleasure, and for the United States Army. In the Bruneau country Kitty Wilkins, the "horse queen of Idaho," operated a number of large horse ranches. Similar ranches were located in other parts of the territory. Al West, a pioneer settler of Big Lost River Valley, tells of assisting in driving great herds of horses from central Idaho to railroad points along the Missouri River in the Dakotas. Some of the most colorful events of our territorial history were connected with outlaw bands who stole hundreds of horses and cattle and drove them eastward to markets beyond the Rockies.

Decline of the Great Ranches. The wide, unfenced open range was the main factor in establishing Idaho Territory as a livestock region. Distance from markets was the greatest drawback, but this was partly overcome when railroads were built. As we have seen, cattle from northern Idaho were driven to the Columbia River and shipped by steamer. In southern Idaho great cattle drives were made to Winnemucca, Nevada, and Cheyenne, Wyoming, two main shipping points and markets of those days.

Big-scale ranching as a business received a severe setback in the winter of 1886–87. Cold weather started very early and soon snow blanketed the entire region so deeply that livestock could not get to the dry grass under the snow. At that time, of course, very little hay was cut for winter feed. The weather turned bitterly cold and all streams, including Snake River, froze over. So heavy were the losses of livestock that many ranchers were ruined financially and saw the work of years go glimmering as countless frozen corpses littered the ranges. Many ranchers were either unable to start over or lost heart and moved away.

Too, conditions were changing. Many homesteads were being taken by farmers and small ranchers and larger tracts were acquired under the Desert Land Act. Some of the best rangelands were fenced and the open range was limited to less desirable pasture lands. Soon after Idaho was admitted to statehood, most of the great ranches were broken up and farmers and small ranchers took over the main livestock industry, a condition that still prevails throughout most of Idaho.

Territorial Farming. With Mormon settlements spreading through eastern Idaho, and with lands rapidly coming under cultivation in the valleys of south-western Idaho and on the Clearwater Plateau, agriculture became the leading industry of Idaho Territory. Irrigation in southern Idaho was the greatest single factor promoting the rapid advance of agriculture, but this story is saved for use in Unit 15.

Though not extensively practiced in territorial years, the method of farming known as dry farming began early in our history. As new land suitable for irrigation grew scarcer, farmers turned to the benches and foothills bordering the valleys. They discovered that by using special methods of cultivation they could raise good crops, especially of wheat, on such lands. The method was first developed in the Malad Valley of Oneida County and spread from there to other suitable areas. Today dry farming has grown so great that it is the basis of an enormous wheat production in many parts of southern Idaho and accounts for a very substantial part of our annual wheat crop, perhaps Idaho's most valuable crop year in and year out.

IV. TERRITORIAL TRANSPORTATION AND COMMUNICATION

ONE OF THE BIG TASKS a new country faces is the building of roads and the development of means of transportation and communication. Because of its extensive mountains, its spreading plains and plateaus, where water was often scarce, and its great distances, Idaho encountered many difficulties in these fields of endeavor.

Early Stage Lines. For almost a score of years after Idaho became a territory, no railroads entered the region. To transport passengers, carry mail and express, and ship out gold and silver, stage lines were started. Two lines reached Boise Basin from the west, coming from the Columbia River by way of the old Oregon Trail. Ben Holladay, called the "stagecoach king," opened a branch of the Overland Stage Line from Salt Lake City to The Dalles, passing through Idaho by way of the Malad and Raft River valleys, the Snake River Valley, Boise City, and then on west to the Columbia.

Another stage line reached from Salt

STAGECOACH ON ROAD

Travel by stagecoach in territorial Idaho was a sort of endurance contest for both travelers and horses.

Lake City to Virginia City, Montana, passing through eastern Idaho along the general route now followed by the Union Pacific Railroad from Ogden to Butte. This line crossed the Snake at Eagle Rock, now Idaho Falls.

As other mining and agricultural districts were opened, stage lines were extended. Before the close of the territorial period a network of such lines served most settled parts of the territory.

Traveling by stage was not a pleasant way of seeing Idaho. Not only were the roads rough but the stages were usually overcrowded and accommodations along the routes were few and generally unsatisfactory. Dust in summer, mud in spring and fall, snow in winter, plus mosquitoes and rattlesnakes in the warm season, were regular discomforts. Occasionally road agents, or bandits, held up stages and robbed the passengers.

Such a journey was, in fact, a sort of endurance contest, as we can see from an account by C. C. Clawson, a prominent pioneer of southern Idaho:

When the driver called *all aboard!* they [the horses] rose to their hind legs with accord and as the whip cracked, lurched into a run. Our necks being partially dislocated by this performance, we spent the next few miles in a blurred haze of sagebrush and sapphire sky, trying meanwhile to make the seats of the coach and our spinal columns conform to each other, while the wheels of the vehicle were conforming to the ruts and chuck holes of the road.

Toll Roads and Bridges. To encourage individuals and companies to construct transportation facilities, the territorial legislatures for several years granted franchises, or special rights, to those who would build and operate toll roads, bridges, and ferries, collecting fares from travelers using them. Before many years passed, the counties assumed the duty of building and maintaining roads, but toll bridges and ferries were common even after statehood.

Several noted ferries were Bonner's Ferry, on the Wild Horse Trail crossing of the Kootenai River; Lewiston Ferry, across the Snake River at the mouth of the Clearwater River; Olds' Ferry, on the Snake River below Weiser; Walters' Ferry, at the Snake River crossing on the road from Boise City to Silver City; Glenns' Ferry, near the famous Three

TOLL BRIDGE AND FERRY

Replica of Idaho's first toll bridge. At Eagle Rock, now Idaho Falls, J. M. Taylor built the first toll bridge in Idaho in 1863. It was an important stopping point on the road from Salt Lake City to the mines at Bannack and Virginia City in western Montana.

REMINGTON FERRY ON SALMON RIVER

Many ferries were in operation in territorial Idaho. Travelers using these ferries paid toll charges, permitted by law, to aid travel and transportation.

Island Crossing of the Snake River on the Oregon Trail; Montgomery's Ferry and Starrh's Ferry, on the Snake River near the present cities of Rupert and Burley; Gibson's Ferry and Central Ferry, on the Snake River near Blackfoot; and Taylor's Ferry, on the Snake River at Eagle Rock, now Idaho Falls. The last was soon displaced by Taylor's Bridge, the first toll bridge in Idaho. Many of the other ferries operated for a number of years, some for a considerable time after Idaho became a state.

Bullwhackers and Mule Skinners. Freight into and from Idaho Territory was hauled mainly in wagons, though river boats carried much freight to and from Lewiston in the Clearwater country.

An enormous volume of supplies and equipment came in by that method and a considerable amount of products went out the same way.

Drivers of ox teams were called bull-whackers, while mule skinners drove teams of mules. Such freight outfits usually consisted of three wagons hitched in a string. The lead wagon was largest, the middle or swing wagon was somewhat smaller, and the third or tail wagon was smallest. The usual load for such an outfit ranged from fifteen thousand to twenty-five thousand pounds. Each team consisted of from twelve to twenty animals, which were generally guided by a jerk line held in the hands of the driver. Drivers of ox teams usually walked beside their teams and guided them by Gee! (turn to the right), Haw! (turn left), and Whoa! (stop).

Let's Take a Steamboat Ride! Strange as it sounds, steamboats played a considerable part in Idaho's early history. River steamers regularly ascended the Snake to Lewiston. The first boat to do so was the *Colonel Wright*, but scores of others made regular or occasional trips to transport passengers and supplies.

Other steamboat lines operated on Lake Pend Oreille and Lake Coeur d'Alene. River boats of shallow draft ascended the Coeur d'Alene River to the vicinity of Cataldo, where supplies for the mines were unloaded and hauled the rest of the way in wagons. Boats also went from Lake Coeur d'Alene up the St. Joe River a considerable distance.

A steamboat, *The Idaho,* made regular trips up the Snake River from Lewiston to Pittsburg Landing, some distance above the mouth of the Salmon River. Another Snake River steamer, the *Shoshone,* operated along that stream in the Lower Snake River Valley. Undoubtedly one of the wildest steamboat rides ever taken in Idaho, or anywhere else for that matter, was when the ship's owner decided to take the *Shoshone* down river to Lewiston through the notorious Hell's Canyon. It got through, but left various parts behind in the rapids and waterfalls through which it passed.

The Iron Horse. The first railroad to enter Idaho Territory was the Utah & Northern, built from Brigham City, Utah, to Franklin in 1873. Slowly this line was extended northward and by 1881 had reached Butte. It opened up the rich resources, afforded better and faster

SEAPORT SCENE?

Steamboat travel and transportation was important in North Idaho in territorial years. This picture shows steamboats tied up at St. Maries, chief port on the St. Joe River. From Ruby El Hult's Steamboats in the Timber (1952).

travel and transportation, encouraged rapid settlement, and improved living conditions for the people of eastern Idaho. In the 1880's this line was purchased by the Oregon Short Line Railroad.

Between 1882 and 1884 the Oregon Short Line was built through the Snake River Valley. This line connected the Union Pacific main line through Granger, Wyoming, with the Oregon-Washington Railroad and Navigation Company at Huntington, Oregon, and was, in effect, a main-line railroad crossing Idaho from east to west. It also connected with the Utah & Northern at McCammon and followed the same route westward to Pocatello, where the lines again separated.

The railroads were of great value to stockmen and miners, as well as to farmers and businessmen in general. Perhaps their greatest service to Idaho was to bring about the rapid settlement of the rich agricultural sections of southern Idaho. Irrigation was beginning to come into its own and a wave of land-hungry settlers followed the Iron Horse, firmly establishing Idaho as a great farming and livestock region.

Before the Oregon Short Line tapped southern Idaho, the Northern Pacific completed its main line to the Northwest coast. This occurred in 1880–82 and was of tremendous value to the northern part of the territory. With direct access to outside markets, the Panhandle rapidly filled with settlers attracted by the fertile soils, the immense mineral wealth, and the vast timber resources of that region.

Several branch railroads were also constructed before Idaho became a state.

The Coeur d'Alene Railway and Navigation Company, which already had a steamboat service between the city of Coeur d'Alene and the old Cataldo Mission, built a narrow-gauge railroad from Cataldo to Wallace to complete their service to the rich Coeur d'Alene mines. The Oregon-Washington Railroad and Navigation Company built a railroad around the southern end of Lake Coeur d'Alene to Wallace and a second line to Moscow. The Oregon Short Line constructed branch lines from Shoshone to Ketchum and from Nampa to Boise. This line to Boise was a bitter disappointment to the residents of that city, who had asked for and expected a main-line cutoff through the capital. An editorial in the *Statesman* scolded the railroad company for its action and referred to it as the "Oregon Crooked Line."

Rapid Communication. The pony express and the overland stage were the earliest regular means of communication and travel between southern Idaho and the outside. In the north, river steamers to Lewiston and post riders to points farther north gave limited communication service to the Panhandle.

Soon after the Civil War a telegraph line was constructed across Utah, and the Deseret Telegraph Company built a line to Franklin, opening Idaho's first telegraph station in the Franklin Co-op Store in December, 1868. Eight years later news of the Custer Massacre was sent to the nation from this station, having been carried by a rider from Fort Hall. A little later the telegraph wire was strung northward from Franklin to Montana and a station was opened at Eagle Rock. A telegraph line from Winnemucca to Boise, by way of Silver City, was completed in 1875.

The first telephone line in Idaho reached Franklin from Utah in 1868. In the next few years telephone service spread slowly among the larger settlements in Idaho. However, as late as 1884, Boise, the largest territorial town, had less than three dozen telephones. Rapid communication did not become general until the transcontinental railroad lines crossed Idaho, making telegraph and telephone service a necessity in some parts of the territory.

V. TERRITORIAL SCHOOLS AND SOCIAL PROGRESS

EDUCATION HAS ALWAYS been considered necessary in our American way of life. Idaho Territory, of course, carried forward this national tradition. As soon as children became part of our population, schools were provided for their welfare.

Church Schools. We have already seen that the first school in Idaho for white children was organized at Franklin. In all Latter-day Saints communities the education of the children was considered of first importance. Church schools were operated, supported in part by the church groups and in part by tuition fees paid by the parents. But about 1870, school districts began to be organized. Trustees were chosen and teachers were required to have teachers' certificates issued by the county superintendents. Better buildings were constructed and teaching equipment and supplies were improved.

Schools, similar in many ways to our high schools of today, were established. Fielding Academy was started in Paris, Bear Lake County, in 1877. Soon other Mormon church schools were organized by Oneida Stake in Preston, Bannock Stake in Rexburg, and Cassia Stake in Oakley. Ricks Academy, the academy in Rexburg, is now Ricks College, and is still operated by the Latter-day Saints Church. The other three academies later became part of the public-school system of Idaho.

Other churches, too, operated schools:

TERRITORIAL SCHOOL IN IDAHO

Education was not neglected in territorial Idaho. The educational needs of children were supplied by private schools, church schools, and public schools.

the Episcopal Church in Boise; the Catholics in Idaho City and at their missions at Slickpoo, Cataldo, and Desmet; the Presbyterians at Lapwai and Kamiah; and the Methodists in Lewiston. There were small church schools in a few other localities, but such schools were never numerous. As public schools became generally established, most of the church schools closed, only the Catholics continuing to conduct special schools of their own.

Tuition or Subscription Schools. The following item in a Boise newspaper in 1877 shows that not all children depended on the public schools:

SELECT SCHOOL—Mrs. F. S. Blake gives notice that she will open a select school in her school house on Seventh Street on the 2nd of September. Mrs. Blake is well known as a popular teacher, and her location is very convenient for many children.

In these private schools the parents of children attending paid tuition charges sufficient to cover the teacher's salary and the operating expenses of the school. Such schools were not common, but they served a useful purpose in a day when the public schools were not yet well established.

Public Schools. From our beginning as a territory, the public schools received attention. We have already seen that the Organic Act made some provision along that line by setting aside public land sections 16 and 36 in every township for the support of education.

The first territorial legislature, meeting in Lewiston in 1863, provided for the office of territorial superintendent of schools and for county superintendents.

In 1864 the second territorial legislature established a system of common public schools.

J. A. Chittenden, the first territorial superintendent, reported in 1865 that there were 1,239 children of school age in the territory, nearly all of them in Boise and Ada counties. He also reported twelve schools in operation, four of them private schools.

Graded and High Schools. As the population increased, the schools kept pace with other developments. The legislature created the Boise and Lewiston independent school districts in 1881. A year later Boise opened the first public high school. Lewiston and Moscow followed Boise's lead in 1890, but to Boise goes the honor of having the only public high school during our territorial period.

University of Idaho. In 1889 the last territorial legislature authorized the establishment of the University of Idaho at Moscow and appropriated $15,000 to purchase the necessary grounds and have plans drawn for suitable buildings. The university was not, however, ready for use until two years after Idaho became a state.

Churches and Their Work. High among cultural and educational institutions we must place the churches. We in America generally believe that along with the cultivation of the mind must go also the teaching of right living, or morality. That, in our plan of things, belongs jointly to the home, the school, and the church.

The Presbyterian Church has been a leader from the earliest days of the opening of the Pacific Northwest. Even after the Spalding Mission was abandoned in

1847, the church did not lose interest. Spalding returned to Lapwai in 1871 and renewed his work among the Nez Perce Indians. His death in 1874 ended the career of Idaho's first and perhaps greatest religious leader.

Just before Spalding's return to Lapwai the McBeth sisters, Sue and Kate, went to the Nez Perce Reservation as teachers and missionaries, continuing their activities for many years at Lapwai and Kamiah. Kate became famous both for her work among the Indians and for her book, *The Nez Perces Since Lewis and Clark*.

The Presbyterians organized a church in Moscow in 1880 and a little later another church in Boise. Their interests soon were extended into other parts of the territory. In a later unit we shall see how their actions were broadened to include the field of religious education.

The Catholic Church was also very active in Idaho. Churches were built at Idaho City, Placerville, Centerville, Pioneer City, and in other places. Boise City was made headquarters and the Boise Diocese was authorized in 1868. We have already seen that the Sacred Heart Mission was moved from Cataldo to Desmet in 1878, where it continued to serve the Coeur d'Alene Indians until it was destroyed by fire in 1936. The Catholics also continued their service to the Nez Perce Indians through their mission at Slickpoo.

The Episcopalians were among the earliest church denominations to enter Idaho Territory. The Reverend Michael Fackler built a small church in Boise in 1864. Three years later Bishop Daniel S. Tuttle, one of the most remarkable men in the territory, started his work here. Before he left Idaho to become Bishop of Missouri in 1886, he had established Episcopal missions in Boise, Blackfoot, Silver City, Idaho City, Lewiston, Bellevue, Hailey, and Ketchum.

Other denominations were also active during our territorial years. The Methodists, who assisted in maintaining the early missions, built their first church in Boise, soon followed by churches in other parts of the territory. The Baptists organized churches at Moscow, Boise, Payette, and Weiser, beginning in 1876.

From our earliest days, the Church of Jesus Christ of Latter-day Saints, usually called the Mormon Church, has stood above other Idaho churches in membership. Beginning at Franklin in 1860, their settlements spread through the southern and eastern parts of the territory. Before Idaho became a state, their meetinghouses were found in all important communities from central Idaho to Wyoming and from the Upper Snake River Valley to Utah.

Territorial Newspapers. Newspapers are recognized as being among the most important agencies in spreading knowledge, shaping public opinion, and bringing about effective co-operation for the general welfare and benefit of all. Nearly half a hundred newspapers were started in Idaho during territorial years. Most of them had relatively short lives, but a few have had long and honorable service. Quite a number of them are still serving the needs of their communities and of the state.

One newspaper, the *Golden Age,* began publication before the creation of Idaho Territory. Published in Lewiston

from 1862 to 1865, it was Idaho's first newspaper. It was soon followed by the *Boise News,* established in Idaho City, then Bannack City, in 1863, and the *Idaho Statesman,* which made its appearance in Boise City in 1864. The *Boise News* changed its name to the *Idaho World,* continuing under that name for more than fifty years. As the *Idaho Daily Statesman,* the first daily paper in Idaho, the *Idaho Statesman* is still carrying on in Boise. One other paper, the *Owyhee Avalanche,* was published as a weekly in Silver City for more than half a century before being discontinued. Perhaps your hometown newspaper is among those started in territorial years.

You will find a fairly complete list of territorial newspapers in Appendix Table 2, in the back of this book.

Institutions for the Unfortunate. One of the ways in which a community, state, or nation may be judged is by the care it gives its unfortunate citizens. These naturally fall into three classes: (1) the wrongdoers and criminals, who must be confined for their own good and for the welfare of society; (2) the mentally sick, the nervously unbalanced, and

the insane; and (3) those unable to care for themselves and who have no one able or willing to take care of them.

Prisons. County jails were built early in our territorial period to protect the people against lawlessness. But the territory soon had need of a larger prison, and in 1867 Congress appropriated $40,-000 to construct a territorial prison at Boise. This institution has found a steady usefulness. The territorial prison was given to Idaho when it became a state. Now greatly enlarged and improved, it is the state penitentiary.

Asylum for the Insane. Before 1884, Idaho citizens who were mentally ill were cared for by relatives or friends, or were housed in an Oregon institution under a contract between Idaho Territory and the state of Oregon. But in 1885 money was appropriated for constructing an asylum at Blackfoot. This building was finished and put into use in 1886. Now greatly enlarged and modernized, it is known as the Idaho State Hospital South.

Care of the Poor. It was the custom during territorial years for the various counties to care for their own citizens who

IDAHO PENITENTIARY TODAY

Prisons are necessary for two reasons: (1) to confine, and (2) to reform, if possible, those who violate the law.

TERRITORIAL PENITENTIARY

The first penitentiary was begun as a federal prison about 1868. When Idaho became a state, the United States gave the penitentiary to the state.

required public assistance. The counties sometimes provided poorhouses in which such persons were permitted to live. Sometimes the care of such persons was contracted for by other people willing to take them for fixed sums paid by the counties. Modern methods are very different, and later topics will show the changes that have taken place in the care of our needy citizens.

Fraternal, Social, and Civic Organizations. Life in Idaho today is elevated and enriched by a large number of social and fraternal organizations that provide special help and services for their members. Many of these began in our territorial years.

Among early fraternal societies, the Masons and Odd Fellows were first and most important. The first Masonic lodge was opened in Lewiston in 1862 and other lodges quickly followed in Idaho City and Boise City. Idaho City had the first Odd Fellows lodge. Soon both organizations spread to the leading territorial towns. Today these and other fraternal societies are found in nearly every part of Idaho.

The G.A.R., or Grand Army of the Republic, made up of Union veterans, had posts in several territorial towns. The Grange, a strong national organization of people interested in rural life, was active in Idaho as early as the 1870's. The Columbian Club, an organization of Boise women, took the lead in many movements for improving living in the territory. A horticultural society did a great deal to encourage fruit growing and it helped organize county fairs to display Idaho products.

Another important territorial organization was the Historical Society of Idaho Pioneers. Its purpose was to collect and preserve historical documents and relics. It turned its valuable collection over to the Idaho Historical Society when that organization was created by the legislature several years after Idaho became a state.

VI. BUSINESS AND INDUSTRIAL DEVELOPMENT

FARMING, STOCK RAISING, MINING, AND LUMBERING, Idaho's chief basic industries, had a vigorous beginning in our territorial period. These have been, and still are, so important to our people that they will be considered in separate units in a later section of this book.

Hand in hand with the development of these industries based on Idaho's natural resources, growth in other lines of work helped give most communities in the territory a well-rounded way of life. Among these supplementary occupations were banking, merchandising, and manufacturing, and all began early in our territorial history.

Banking. Though business expansion in Idaho Territory, especially in mining, demanded large financial outlays, much of the money was provided from outside the territory. Banks were slow in getting started, largely for three reasons: (1) There were no laws concerning the organization and operation of banks in Idaho until after it became a state. (2) The larger and more valuable mining properties were mainly owned by wealthy men in San Francisco, New York, and other large cities. (3) It was common practice, especially in the earlier part of the territorial period, to pay for almost all kinds of purchases and services with raw gold, most of the larger stores and business houses having gold scales for weighing the dust.

Banking began, however, in the 1860's. The First National Bank, the first bank in Idaho, was organized in Boise City in 1867. By the close of our territorial period banks were operating in Lewiston, Idaho Falls, Caldwell, Pocatello, Moscow, Hailey, Malad, and a few other territorial towns. Do you think modern business could be successfully carried on if there were no banks?

Panics and Hard Times. Industry in Idaho did not, however, enjoy uninterrupted prosperity. Three times the territory, in common with the rest of the nation, suffered from panics, periods of scarce money and unusually hard times, known today as depressions. The first began in 1857 and lasted about three years. The second, beginning in 1873, resulted in the closing down of most of the silver mines in the territory and throughout the West. The third and least severe was in the late 1880's.

During these periods of hard times, most productive work slowed down or came to a complete stop. Farmers and stockmen were unable to sell their products for enough to come out even, and many of them went broke. Banks failed, causing a lack of money to carry on ordinary business, forcing mines to shut

DOUBLE-END STORE IN BLACKFOOT

Perhaps unique among territorial stores was Danielson's double-end store in Blackfoot, built to accommodate cowpunchers who liked to ride in at the front to make their purchases and out at the rear when their business was finished.

down and many business institutions to close their doors.

Merchandising. The buying and selling of food, clothing, and other things, usually handled through wholesale and retail stores, is called merchandising. It is a very necessary part of community life and grew up in Idaho as soon as there were enough people to create a demand for such establishments.

The first stores were probably opened in the Mormon settlements in southeastern Idaho. But about the same time, Seth Slater started a store in Lewiston. Other stores were opened almost immediately as gold discoveries brought into existence Pierce City, Elk City, Florence; the towns of the Boise Basin; and Boise City, chief supply point for the basin settlements. From these beginnings merchandising spread with new settlements until many parts of the territory boasted large retail stores carrying in stock almost everything the people of the territory needed or wanted.

Manufacturing. Sawmills and flour mills were the pioneer manufacturing establishments of Idaho Territory. Sawmills were in operation in Boise Basin as early as 1864, but not until the Northern

EVOLUTION OF A FLOUR MILL

Left. Old flour mill at Malad, built in 1867. It has been in continuous use since that time and has been enlarged and modernized.

Right. The same mill as it is today. This suggests the importance of wheat in Idaho, both in territorial years and in our own times. The rolling process for manufacturing flour was introduced in 1891, the original stones being burr stones.

Courtesy Crowther Brothers Milling Company, Malad City

Pacific Railroad crossed the Panhandle did lumbering become big business. Can you suggest reasons why this was true?

Flour mills and gristmills, or mills for grinding grain, were built in most farming districts. Since territorial farming was carried on mainly in the valleys of southeastern Idaho, the Upper and Lower Snake River valleys, and on the Clearwater Plateau, such mills were naturally located in these farming regions.

Other manufacturing was based principally on the products of the farms and ranches. Meat packing and the making of dairy products were among such territorial manufacturing enterprises.

A pioneer manufacturing establishment of special interest was the Oneida Salt Works. Opened in 1866 at Salt Springs in the eastern part of what is now Caribou County, these vats were soon turning out close to a million pounds of salt annually. As many as three hundred freight wagons were used in transporting the salt to markets in Idaho and Montana territories. The building of the Utah & Northern Railroad enabled the territories to secure salt from Salt Lake City at a much cheaper price, and so forced the Oneida Salt Works to close.

*   *   *   *   *

So we come to the year 1890. The curtain was about to fall on an era in Idaho history. The forty-third state was about to add its star to Old Glory's field of heavenly blue. What had Idaho given and what had it yet to give to make it worthy of statehood? Here are a few of its great contributions:

A stream of gold from Idaho placer fields helped the Union weather the storm of civil war and preserve undivided the world's greatest experiment in government "of the people, by the people, and for the people." A steady flow of silver, lead, and gold helped to supply the metal needs of the nation after the placer gold was largely exhausted. Vast timber resources supplied the construction needs of the territory and furnished a surplus for other regions where such resources were lacking. Our fertile soils, both irrigated and nonirrigated, added very substantially to the food supplies of the nation. Far-spreading reaches of grassy plateaus, plains, and mountain slopes furnished pasturage for great herds of cattle and horses and flocks of sheep. Within our borders was mountain scenery as grand as any in the land. Roaring rivers and thundering waterfalls held a promise of almost limitless power for future needs. Our wildlife was so great and varied that even in territorial days it was the envy of less favored regions. Most important of all, Idaho Territory was a fresh frontier land where the people already here and many others yet to come could turn their energies to almost any field of endeavor that appealed to their individual desires and interests. These were, and still are, some of Idaho's contributions to our own life and to the life of America and the world.

Color photo by Ansgar Johnson
IDAHO'S OFFICIAL STATE FLAG

KEEP
IDAHO
GREEN

PART THREE

**IDAHO IN THE NATION
AND
IN TODAY'S WORLD**
(*1890 to Present*)

How Idaho won its
place among the
states; how the people
assumed their responsibilities
as a co-operative and self-
governing part of the Union;
how they have kept pace in a
rapidly changing nation and world;
and how they are making their contribution to the American way of life in
the Atomic Age

UNIT   9—The Forty-Third State: Its Political Story
UNIT 10—Idaho's Growth in Its Geographical Setting
UNIT 11—Educational and Social Progress
UNIT 12—Significant Events in State and Nation
UNIT 13—Our Constitutional Freedoms, Rights, and Duties
UNIT 14—Our Three-Way Plan of Representative Government
UNIT 15—Using Our Land and Water Resources
UNIT 16—Using Our Forest and Mineral Resources
UNIT 17—Using Our Wildlife and Recreational Resources
UNIT 18—Conservation: Key to Idaho's Future

The Forty-Third State: Its Political Story

*How Idaho gained statehood and how political activities and parties
have influenced our progress as a state.*

WHEN A TERRITORY asks for admission as a state, Congress always considers the possible results of admission. Which political party is strongest in the territory? If admitted, will its senators and representatives in Congress strengthen or weaken the party in control in the nation? Is the territory wealthy enough and its population large enough to support a state government? These and other questions are sure to be brought up for discussion.

I. HOW STATEHOOD WAS WON

BEFORE 1890 IDAHO TERRITORY had grown rapidly both in population and in wealth. The people believed they were ready for statehood. The question was brought to a head when Governor Stevenson issued a call for a convention to prepare a constitution. However, his term as governor ended before any action could be taken.

The Constitutional Convention. George L. Shoup succeeded Stevenson as territorial governor of Idaho in 1889. The new governor also called for a constitutional convention. Delegates were chosen by the people in June, 1889, and they met in Boise City July 4.[1] After more than a month's work they completed the draft of the constitution to submit to the people. They also sent a memorial to Congress asking that Idaho be admitted to statehood, giving the following reasons for their request: The people of Idaho Territory had been loyal and had obeyed the Constitution and the other laws of the United States; the population and resources of Idaho had greatly increased; the territorial system of government was contrary to many of the basic principles of representative government and was, therefore, undemocratic. This last statement was a reference to the fact that the governor and a number of other officers were appointed by the President, rather than elected by the people of the territory.

On November 5, 1889, the people approved the new constitution by a majority of about seven to one. The action removed the last obstacle and cleared the way for Congress to act on Idaho's application for statehood.

A New Star for "Old Glory." In December, 1889, in Washington, there was introduced an Idaho statehood bill in the

[1]See Appendix Table 3 for a complete list of delegates to the Idaho Constitutional Convention.

Senate. Early in January, 1890, a similar bill was introduced in the House of Representatives by Congressman Struble of Iowa.

In Congress Idaho's admission was opposed on three grounds: (1) That the Mormon Test Oath, which was required of all Mormons before they were given the right to vote, was contrary to the Constitution of the United States; (2) that Idaho's constitutional convention had not been legally convened, or called together; and (3) that the population of the territory was not enough to justify the election of two senators to the United States Senate.

In spite of these objections, Delegate Dubois and other congressional members were able to bring the question to a vote and Struble's Idaho Admission Act successfully passed both houses of Congress. It was signed July 3, 1890, by President Benjamin Harrison and Idaho became the forty-third state in the Union.

II. POLITICS AND POLITICAL PARTIES

A CARPETBAGGER TYPE OF OFFICER, as we saw in Unit 4, was sometimes appointed to office in Idaho Territory. Idaho's admission as a state, however, brought important changes. As a state Idaho came completely under the control of its own citizens, who elected the people who filled public office. Political parties became more useful than they had been in territorial days, as policies urged by the parties determined largely who should be elected to fill the offices and what course the state government should follow.

The Two-Party System. In the United States, political power has generally been shared and divided between two main political parties. This has proven good for the country because, when the party in control showed a strong tendency toward becoming too highhanded in its methods and began to disregard the welfare of the people, the voters chose officers from the opposing party to replace them. This insures that the people themselves always hold the balance of power and causes the party in power to be more responsive to the will of the people.

Various other plans are used in many countries. In some, as in Russia, only one political party is allowed and people have only the limited choice of voting for or against the candidates nominated by the one ruling party. In some other countries people are divided into blocs or groups representing various kinds of industries or various economic differences among the people. Several countries in Europe follow this general plan, the result being that governments change so often that no set plan or policy is followed long enough to show whether it will succeed or not. Such countries, France being a typical example, often change their governments every few months, causing confusion and constant unrest among the people.

We in the United States firmly believe that the two-party system of our Republic is far superior to other so-called democratic plans of government. Its strong points are that our officers serve set terms of office, thus having time to prove their worth; and we can—and do —switch parties often enough to keep both of them constantly on their toes and doing the best possible job they can of serving the people while they are in office.

Idaho's Major Political Parties. Which are you, a Democrat or a Republican? Perhaps you aren't yet old enough to have made up your mind. Before you boys and girls finally decide which political party to join, you really should find out what the parties believe in, what they stand for. A good way to do this is to learn about their past accomplishments. Another good way is to read their political platforms, telling what they propose to do if their candidates for such important offices as President of the United States and governor of the state are elected.

Ever since Idaho became a territory, the Democratic and Republican parties have been most powerful in electing candidates for public office. Since statehood, these parties have generally been about equal in strength in Idaho. This has been fortunate for us, because the parties have changed control frequently enough to keep both of them alert to serve the people to the best of their ability. As a result, there has been comparatively little crookedness and corruption in government in Idaho, either on the state or the local level.

The Democratic Party. The Democrats have the oldest political party in the United States. Under that name it came into existence in 1824 when Andrew Jackson first ran for President. Four years later the party was strong enough to elect Jackson by a large majority and it has remained a powerful influence in the nation ever since. Frequently it has elected the President, and its party members have often had a majority in Congress.

In Idaho the Democrats have elected nine of our twenty-three state governors, and they have shared about equally with the other major party in electing senators and representatives to Congress. The party has also frequently had a majority of state senators and representatives in our state legislature.

The Republican Party. This party was organized a few years before the outbreak of the Civil War, its chief purpose then being to prevent the spread of slavery. Its members were at first drawn chiefly from an older party, the Whigs, but it gained strength very rapidly as slavery became the most serious problem facing the nation. In 1860 it was strong enough to elect Abraham Lincoln President of the United States. Like the Democratic party, it is today one of the two great political parties in Idaho and in the nation.

In our state the Republicans have held a slight edge over the Democrats in electing state officers. Fourteen governors and a little more than half our members of Congress have been Republicans. But for many years the parties have been so closely balanced that control of the state offices has passed frequently from one party to the other.

Minor Political Parties. From time to time other political parties have been formed in the United States and in Idaho. But these have never been strong enough alone to elect their candidates. Sometimes they have drawn enough strength from one of the major parties to elect an occasional officer, but such events have been rare in Idaho history.

Leading minor parties have been the Populists or People's party, the Prohibition party, the People's Democratic party, the Silver Republicans, the Socialist party, the Progressive or Bull Moose party, and the second Progressive party. The last was organized mainly by Henry A. Wallace, who had served as Vice-President under President Franklin D. Roosevelt.

Idaho's First State Government. Under the terms of the Idaho Admission Act, George L. Shoup, the last territorial governor, continued in office as the first state governor. One of his earliest acts was to call a special election to choose state officers and a representative to Congress.

Both political parties prepared for the election by holding state conventions and nominating candidates. In the first state election, held October 1, 1890, the entire Republican ticket was chosen by a small margin. George L. Shoup was elected governor and Willis A. Sweet was sent to Congress as a member of the House of Representatives. No senator was elected, since at that time Idaho's senators were chosen by the state legislature, as was done in the other states.

III. IDAHO'S MEMBERS OF CONGRESS

FROM STATEHOOD TO 1955, Idaho has been represented in the United States Senate by eighteen different men, ten Republicans and eight Democrats, though Senator Heitfield, nominally a Democrat, was elected by the Populist and Democratic fusion vote. To the House of Representatives we have sent seventeen different members, ten of whom have been elected by the Republicans.

Our Senators. Idaho, like every other state, sends two senators to the United States Senate, the upper house of Congress. They are elected for six-year terms. They are not elected the same year unless a vacancy occurs. In that case, the governor appoints someone to serve until the next general election. Thus it sometimes happens that both senators are elected the same year, one for the regular six-year term and the other to finish out an unexpired term.

Almost without exception the men who have served Idaho in the Senate have been able, patriotic, and honorable men of whom we can justly be proud. They usually acted with the welfare of the whole nation uppermost in their decisions. Four of them, George L. Shoup, James H. Brady, Frank R. Gooding, and Charles C. Gossett, served as governors of the state before they were sent to the Senate. One, William J. McConnell, was elected governor after his term as senator expired. Two of them, D. Worth Clark and Henry Dworshak, served in the House of Representatives before moving on to the upper house.

A Three-Cornered Battle. The first state legislature of Idaho engaged in one of its greatest legislative battles when it selected our first United States senators. It chose George L. Shoup and William J. McConnell, both Republicans, to fill the long and short terms respectively. Since the short term would expire before another meeting of the legislature, that body named Fred T. Dubois, another Republican, for the regular term when Mc-

Connell's term should expire in 1891. One faction of the legislature objected to Dubois and chose William H. Clagett to succeed McConnell. Since both men claimed election, the question was finally carried to the floor of the Senate. Having the power to seat or refuse to seat members, the Senate decided in favor of Dubois.

Shoup and Dubois. George L. Shoup, the first Idaho senator to serve a full six-year term, already had a distinguished record. Civil War officer, Indian fighter, and member of the Colorado constitutional convention before coming to Idaho, his career here carried him to new heights. His service in the Senate was a fitting climax to his career.

Fred T. Dubois may fittingly be described as the stormy petrel of Idaho politics. He first became well known as an anti-Mormon editor in Blackfoot and was the most active leader in having Mormons denied the right to vote or hold office in Idaho unless they would first sign the Mormon Test Oath. Later, after a stormy service as United States marshal in Idaho, Dubois served two terms as territorial delegate in Congress, where he worked earnestly to have Idaho admitted to statehood. Elected to the Senate by the first state legislature, he served twelve

IN THE HALL OF FAME

GEORGE L. SHOUP   WILLIAM E. BORAH

These two senators are the only Idahoans whose statues stand in the Capitol Building in Washington, D.C., the one in Statuary Hall and the other in the Senate Connection.

years and became one of the most noted leaders in the long fight to have silver ranked with gold as standard money of the United States. Dubois, the county seat of Clark County, is named in his honor.

Six Senators Who Died in Office. Six of Idaho's senators died in office while still serving their state and nation. These were Weldon B. Heyburn, in whose memory Heyburn State Park is named; James H. Brady, who helped develop irrigation and power projects in eastern and southern Idaho; Frank R. Gooding, industrialist and stockman for whom Gooding and Gooding County are named; William E. Borah, Idaho's most famous orator; John Thomas, rancher and businessman of Hagerman Valley and Gooding County; and Bert H. Miller, who had served as attorney general for Idaho. All except Miller were members of the Republican party.

The most famous of these six senators was William E. Borah. Although a Republican, he did not always stick to the party line, but sometimes voted with the Democrats on matters on which he did not agree with the Republicans. He served continuously from his first election in 1907 until his accidental death, resulting from a fall in his home in Washington, D.C., in 1940. During his service of thirty-three years he won an international reputation as an independent statesman who refused to be bound by tradition or party views. He fought powerfully and effectively for what he believed to be right, and more than any other senator kept the United States from joining the League of Nations after the first World War. This, many people believe, was a mistake, but it illustrated Borah's independent thinking and acting.

Borah first became known as a great orator when he made the chief argument for the prosecution during the trial in which Harry Orchard was convicted of the murder of a former governor, Frank Steunenberg. His speeches in the Senate made his fame world wide. When word spread in the national capital that the "Lion of Idaho" was beginning to roar, every available space in the Senate galleries and corridors quickly filled with eager listeners.

By his great ability, his long service, his independence of action, and his brilliant eloquence, Senator Borah gave our state prestige and influence in national and international affairs. After his death his statue was placed in the Senate Connection of the Capitol.

Short-Time and Single-Term Senators. Four Idaho senators served less than a full term in the Senate. William J. McConnell served from his election by the legislature in 1890 until March 4, 1891. The other three, Kirtland I. Perky, John F. Nugent, and Charles C. Gossett, were appointed by the governors to fill unexpired terms of senators who had died in office.

Henry Heitfield, James D. Pope, D. Worth Clark, and Glen H. Taylor each served single terms as senators from Idaho. Heitfield, the only Idaho member of Congress ever elected by a minor political party, the Populists, was swept into office by the great free-silver movement, so strong in the silver-mining states in the 1890's. Pope, a Democrat, was appointed to head the Tennessee Valley Authority (TVA), an office he still holds, when his term as senator expired. Clark, also a Democrat, who recently died in Los Angeles, served two terms in the House of Representatives before being elected to the Senate. Taylor, sometimes called the "Cowboy Senator," was nominated for Vice-President in 1948 by the short-lived second Progressive party and dropped out of politics temporarily following his defeat for that office. However, in the 1954 election he tried to make a comeback on the Democratic ticket by running for the Senate against Senator Henry C. Dworshak, but was overwhelmingly defeated.

Idaho's Present United States Senators. In 1954 Idaho was represented in the United States Senate by Henry Dworshak, of Burley, and Herman Welker, of Payette, both Republicans. Senator Dworshak, who had already served several terms in the House of Representatives, was elected in 1946, defeating Senator Charles C. Gossett, who had been appointed to fill the seat left vacant by the death of Senator Thomas. He was defeated in the 1948 election by Bert H. Miller, a Democrat. However, Senator Miller died in 1949 and Dworshak was appointed to fill out the term until the 1950 election. In 1950, he was elected to fill the short term expiring Jan. 3, 1955, and was again elected in 1954 for the term expiring in 1961. Senator Welker's term runs until January 3, 1957, an election for this post being required in 1956.[2]

Our Representatives in Congress. Representatives sent to Congress by the states serve two-year terms. The number of representatives a state has depends on its population. Idaho, being one of the states with a relatively small population, has only two representatives in Congress, one elected from each of the two congressional districts in the state. (See Map of Congressional Districts which follows.)

The people of the various states often elect the same senators and representatives to Congress term after term. It is not unusual for members to serve twenty years or more. This is not a bad practice as a general rule. Membership on important congressional committees is usually given to the senators and representatives who have served longest in Congress. This is known as the seniority system. You can readily see that the longer a member of Congress serves the more valuable he becomes to his state and to Congress if he is an able and honest public servant.

Four members of the House of Representatives served Idaho a total of almost seventy years. These men were Burton L. French, a Republican from Moscow, who served from 1903 until 1933 with the exception of two two-year terms when he failed to be re-elected; Addison T. Smith, a Republican from Twin Falls, elected successively from 1913 to 1933 except the term of 1915–17; Compton I. White, a Democrat from Hope, in northern Idaho, who served several terms; and Henry Dworshak, who, as we have seen, served several terms before gaining a seat in the Senate.

Others sent from Idaho to the House of Representatives were Willis Sweet, Edgar Wilson, James Gunn, Thomas Glenn, Thomas Hamer, Robert McCracken, Thomas Coffin, D. Worth Clark, Abe Goff, and John Sanborn.

[2]See Appendix Table 4 for a complete chronological list of Idaho's senators and representatives in Congress since statehood.

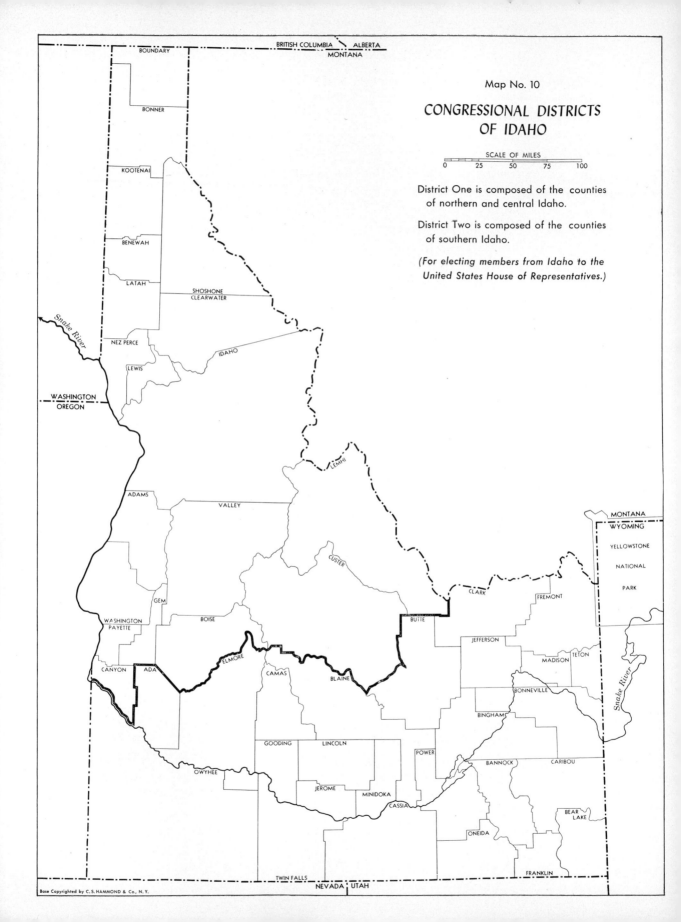

Map No. 10

CONGRESSIONAL DISTRICTS
OF IDAHO

SCALE OF MILES

0   25   50   75   100

District One is composed of the counties
of northern and central Idaho.

District Two is composed of the counties
of southern Idaho.

*(For electing members from Idaho to the
United States House of Representatives.)*

BRITISH COLUMBIA   ALBERTA
MONTANA

BOUNDARY

BONNER

KOOTENAI

BENEWAH

LATAH

SHOSHONE
CLEARWATER

NEZ PERCE

IDAHO

LEWIS

Snake River

WASHINGTON
OREGON

LEMHI

ADAMS

VALLEY

CUSTER

MONTANA
WYOMING

YELLOWSTONE

NATIONAL

PARK

GEM

BOISE

CLARK

FREMONT

BUTTE

WASHINGTON
PAYETTE

JEFFERSON

MADISON   TETON

CANYON   ADA

ELMORE

CAMAS

BLAINE

BONNEVILLE

BINGHAM

Snake River

GOODING   LINCOLN

POWER

OWYHEE

BANNOCK   CARIBOU

JEROME

MINIDOKA

CASSIA

BEAR
LAKE

ONEIDA

TWIN FALLS

FRANKLIN

NEVADA   UTAH

Base Copyrighted by C. S. HAMMOND & Co., N.Y.

Courtesy Idaho Historical Department

Elected in 1950 were Dr. John T. Wood, of St. Maries, and Hamer Budge, of Boise, both Republicans. Budge was re-elected in 1952, but Dr. Wood was de-feated by his Democratic opponent, Mrs. Gracie Pfost, of Nampa, who now, in 1955, represents Idaho from the First District.

IV. IDAHO'S STATE GOVERNORS

TWELVE STATES AND THREE FOREIGN COUNTRIES were the birthplaces of Idaho's twenty-three governors (1890 to 1955).[3] Few things give greater emphasis to the youthfulness of our state than the fact that only one of these governors, C. Ben Ross, was a native son of Idaho. Iowa was the native state of Frank Steunenberg, James H. Hawley, John M. Haines, C. A. Robins, and Robert E. Smylie. Born in Pennsylvania were George L. Shoup, John T. Morrison, and James H. Brady. Barzilla W. Clark and Chase A. Clark, brothers, were natives of Indiana. William J. McConnell was born in Michigan, Frank Hunt in Kentucky, Charles C. Moore in Missouri, H. C. Baldridge in Illinois, C. A. Bottolfsen in Wisconsin, Charles C. Gossett in Ohio, and Arnold Williams and Len B. Jordan, in Utah.

Norman B. Willey, who completed Shoup's unexpired term as governor, was born in New York. A bachelor, he went to California as a mine superin-tendent after his short service as governor. There his health failed and the legisla-ture of Idaho, hearing that he was in need, made a special appropriation for his assistance, the only such instance in the history of the state.

The foreign-born governors were Frank R. Gooding, born in England; Moses Alexander, a native of Germany; and D. W. Davis, whose birthland was Wales. The last three especially illustrate how the United States is truly a land of opportunity in which ambitious and ca-pable people can rise to high position re-gardless of the places and circumstances of their birth.

The Governor's Influence in State Affairs. How much power does the gov-

[3]For a list of Idaho's governors since statehood, see Appendix Table 5.

ernor of Idaho have? That is a question whose answer must remain in doubt, for much depends upon the personality and leadership of the individual who holds the office. Certainly, the governor does have considerable influence, as these facts will show.

The Governor as a Party Leader. By virtue of his office, the governor is the leader of his party in the state. Though the actual work of leadership is usually left to others, such as state and county committee members, the governor is usually consulted before important party decisions are reached. However, purely party matters do not take too great a share of his time, for he is the governor of all the people of the state regardless of their political beliefs and is honor bound to govern for the benefit of all.

Legislative Messages. When the legislature meets in regular or special session, it is the duty of the governor to make recommendations concerning what, in his opinion, the legislature should do regarding the enactment of laws. He prepares or has the budget prepared as an estimate of the amount of money needed to operate the state government for a two-year period, and he sometimes suggests ways in which the money may be raised.

We need to remember, however, that it is the legislature that exercises the real control over state affairs. The legislature makes the laws, raises the money to carry on the work of government, and by means of appropriation bills directs how the money shall be spent. In the field of legislation, the governor's part is limited to the advice he may offer, his veto powers over bills passed by the legislature, and his power to call the legislature into special session.

Appointive Powers. The governor appoints commissioners and other directors for many of the departments of state government. In this way he exercises much control over state affairs. The department heads he appoints are answerable to him and he may remove them if they fail in their duty or refuse to carry out his recommendations. Both they and the governor, however, are bound by law and can do nothing that is contrary to the laws of the state.

Commander of the National Guard. The governor is commander in chief of the state militia, usually called the Na-

Courtesy State of Idaho, Military Department

STATE MILITIA IN SUMMER ENCAMPMENT

Idaho National Guardsmen and equipment pass in review during a summer encampment.

tional Guard. This is made up of volunteers who may be called to active duty in case of an emergency. Only very rarely does the governor call out the militia, leaving its actual command and management in the hands of military officers who are given that responsibility.

Link Between State and Federal Government. The governor is the agent, the go-between, for the state and the Federal government. Either the state or the Federal government may take the lead in affairs that require the co-operation of the state and the national government, but in all cases the governor, or someone he appoints, is the state agent in such matters, unless, of course, they are matters already covered by law.

The Governors' Conference. There is an organization of governors called the Governors' Conference, organized in 1908. This includes all the state and territorial governors of the United States. The first conference was called by President Theodore Roosevelt. Meeting annually, this conference of governors has had a great influence in improving state governments and promoting interstate co-operation. It carries on its work mainly through an executive committee of seven governors, elected annually by the conference.

The governors of the eleven Western states and of Alaska and Hawaii have an informal organization, the Conference of Western Governors. This group usually meets twice a year to consider matters of special interest to the West and to plan co-operative action along various lines.

The Governor's Mansion. The governors of Idaho often found it difficult to secure suitable living quarters in the capital for themselves and their families. To solve this problem, the legislature, in 1947, appropriated $45,000 to purchase, repair, furnish, and maintain an official residence for the governor. The Department of Public Works, to whom this duty was entrusted, purchased a spacious and lovely home in Boise. There the governor is required by law to reside during his term of office.

The Governor's Mansion is located at 1805 North Twenty-first Street and it provides a suitable and comfortable home for the governor and his family.

Ansgar Johnson photo

THE GOVERNOR'S MANSION

The governor is required by law to live in this lovely home in Boise during his term of office. Governor Robins was the first governor to live here.

There is a saying that "Home is where the heart is" and a bit of our hearts will always be found in the dwelling which shelters Idaho's first family.

Interesting Items About Our Governors. Aside from their official acts, our governors are of interest because of personal items or situations that were unusual and pertained to them individually. These are not necessarily important from a historical point of view, but they may, nevertheless, linger in our recollection when more important things are forgotten.

George L. Shoup held the office of governor less than two years, but in that time served under three different regimes. He was our last territorial governor. Then, after Idaho was admitted as a state, he was governor under the terms of the Idaho Admission Act until an election could be held. Finally, when the special election was held, he was chosen by the vote of the people as Idaho's first elected governor. Too, he is the only Idaho governor to be honored by having his statue in Statuary Hall in the National Capitol.

William J. McConnell was our first schoolteacher-governor; the first and only one who walked to the state because he felt himself financially unable to afford any other method of getting here; the first to be elected to two terms; and the first depression governor, one who served during a period of hard times.

Frank Steunenberg, the second two-term governor, was the first to be elected by the Democrats. The youngest governor Idaho ever elected, he was also our first war governor, serving during the Spanish-American War. He was the first

Courtesy Idaho Historical Department

FRANK STEUNENBERG: IDAHO'S MARTYRED GOVERNOR

Because he called out the Idaho National Guard to preserve order and protect property during the Coeur d'Alene riots, Steunenberg was murdered by Harry Orchard, an agent of radical groups active in northern Idaho mining and lumbering camps in the 1890's.

governor to exercise his constitutional authority as commander in chief of the National Guard, calling this force out for duty during the Coeur d'Alene labor riots. He was the only governor to be assassinated, being murdered after his term of office expired because of his leadership in bringing law and order to the strife-torn Coeur d'Alene mining district.

Frank W. Hunt was the first veteran of foreign wars to become governor and the first to be elected on a fusion ticket—that is, a union of two or more political parties. Nominally a Democrat, he was also supported by the Populists and the Silver Republicans.

Frank R. Gooding, a native of England, was our first foreign-born governor. The third governor elected for two terms, he was the only one of our governors to have either a city or a county named in his honor. Incidentally, his election and service was in violation of the laws of the state because he was not a citizen of the United States at the time. When he sought election later to the United States Senate, the error was discovered. Gooding then became a naturalized citizen and in 1921 was elected senator from Idaho.

James H. Brady was the first governor to invest his personal fortune in Idaho projects. The Mountain Home Irrigation Project owed its early development largely to his faith and efforts, as did electrical power projects in eastern Idaho.

John T. Morrison was our first college-graduate governor, holding degrees from two eastern universities. He was also governor when the first large-scale irrigation projects under the Carey Act began.

James H. Hawley, a Democrat, was the first governor nominated under the primary election law. He also had the distinction of winning the governorship when all other state officers elected were Republicans. Too, he was the first lawyer to become a governor of Idaho. He called the first special session of the legislature in our state. He was the author of a fine history entitled *History of Idaho, the Gem of the Mountains*. Because of his unusually long and distinguished career in the state, he was known by the descriptive title, "Idaho's Grand Old Man."

John M. Haines had the honor of signing the law creating the State Board of Education, the greatest unifying and directing force in Idaho's system of public education. His, too, was the very disagreeable duty of seeing that legal punishment was swift and sure when the state treasurer in his administration embezzled $100,000 in state funds.

Moses Alexander, a native of Germany, was our second foreign-born governor. He was the first and only person of Jewish descent ever to occupy the governor's chair. On him fell the heavy duty of directing the affairs of Idaho during the first World War. The fourth governor to serve two terms, he was also the only governor to own and operate a chain of stores retailing men's wearing apparel.

D. W. Davis, from the small country of Wales, was our third and last foreign-born governor. Like each of the other foreign-born governors, he was elected to a second term. His fame rests on the "Governor's Cabinet," Davis's plan for the reorganization of the state's administrative departments. This plan, with certain changes to keep it up to date with changing times, is still a principal feature of Idaho's state government.

During Charles C. (Charley) Moore's two terms as governor, the American Falls dam and reservoir were almost completed. Though this was a Federal project under the direction of the United States Bureau of Reclamation, the state and state officers co-operated as fully as possible in the work. Before his election as governor, Moore had served two terms as lieutenant governor.

H. C. Baldridge duplicated Charley Moore's record of serving two terms as lieutenant governor, followed by two terms as governor. This record, and that of Governor Moore as well, was made possible by an era of good times that began during World War I and lasted for more than a decade.

C. Ben Ross, first elected in 1930, was the second Democrat to become governor since 1903. Five things made him perhaps the most unusual governor we have ever had. (1) He was the first, and to date, the only governor born in Idaho. (2) He was the only governor to be elected for three terms. (3) He sponsored our present Direct Primary Law for nominating candidates for public office. (4) He secured the passage of our first and only sales tax, giving rise to the famous and often-heard expression, "A penny for Benny." (5) He served Idaho during the early and difficult years of the depression and aided in many of Franklin D. Roosevelt's New Deal activities here. Before becoming governor he was mayor of Pocatello, Ross Park being named in his honor. A final odd fact about him was that he would never reveal his age.

Barzilla W. Clark and Chase A. Clark were the only brothers ever to serve as governors of Idaho. What makes their careers more unusual is the fact that both served as mayor of Idaho Falls, moving on from that office to the governor's chair. It is said that the plans that led successively to the office of mayor and then to that of governor for the two brothers were hatched in a chickenhouse. In this case it almost seems that they successfully upset the old saying, "Never count your chickens before they are hatched."

C. A. Bottolfsen was the first veteran of World War I to become governor, and the only one elected to two terms that were not consecutive. He pushed through the state legislature the highly argumentative five-dollar automobile license law, praised by some as a boon to poorer families and condemned by others as the chief robber of our highway funds. (This law was repealed by the 1955 legislature.) Bottolfsen is one of the nation's outstanding parliamentarians, being frequently called from his home in Arco to preside over meetings of the National Education Association and other organizations. He is now (1955) administrative assistant to Senator Welker and makes his home in the nation's capital.

Charles C. Gossett suffered the ironic fate of falling victim to his own worthy ambitions. Soon after Gossett's election as governor, Senator John Thomas died, leaving an Idaho vacancy in the United States Senate. Gossett resigned as governor and was succeeded by the lieutenant governor, Arnold Williams. Thereupon Williams appointed Gossett to the Senate to complete Thomas's unexpired term. This action boomeranged, for when Gossett stood for re-election to the Senate in 1946, the voters turned him down and elected his opponent, Henry Dworshak.

Arnold Williams, who, as we have seen, succeeded Gossett as governor, has the unique distinction of being Idaho's one and only Mormon governor. The political clouds that blotted out Gossett's career brought a like fate to Williams. Nominated by the Democrats in 1946, he lost the governorship to his Republican opponent, Dr. C. A. Robins. During his partial term as governor, however, he called the legislature into special session and it enacted the Teachers' Retirement Law, a bill which has been of great benefit in attracting desirable young people to the teaching profession and holding them in that work.

Like Ross, Dr. C. A. Robins had five unusual facts connected with his service. (1) He was the first governor elected to a four-year term under a 1944 amendment to the state constitution. (2) He was the first governor from the Panhandle in fifty years and the second to be elected from northern Idaho. (3) He was the first physician to fill the governor's chair. (4) He was the first to live in the state-owned governor's mansion. (5) He signed into law the far-reaching School Reorganization Act, believed by many people to be the greatest forward step in education in the entire history of our state.

Len B. Jordan was the second Utah native to become governor of Idaho. A graduate of the University of Oregon, he came to Idaho and engaged in business in Idaho County. It is something of a coincidence that both he and Dr. Robins, whom he followed, are the first two four-year governors, the first two who could not succeed themselves in the governor's office because that is prohibited under the Four-Year Tenure Law, and that both are from the Panhandle, the first to be elected from northern Idaho since Governor McConnell's term expired in 1897. Also, both are Republicans. Of interest, too, is the fact that the Jordans' first home in Idaho was below Hell's Canyon of the Snake River, where they operated a sheep ranch and where their children were born and raised. As schools were not available, the children were taught by Mrs. Jordan, who, like

Courtesy Idaho Power Company

IDAHO POWER COMPANY'S C. J. STRIKE DAM AND POWER PLANT ON THE SNAKE RIVER SOUTH OF MOUNTAIN HOME

The development was completed in 1952 and has a generating capacity of 90,000 kilowatts.

her husband, is also a college graduate.

After Jordan's term as governor expired, he became a member of the Joint Internal Commission, composed of citizens of the United States and Canada and organized to pass on problems concerning rivers and lakes in which both nations have an interest. President Eisenhower appointed him to this position before his term as governor expired.

Robert E. Smylie was elected governor in 1954. Representing the Republican party, he defeated his Democratic opponent, Clark Hamilton, formerly a state senator from Washington County. He began his administration in January, 1955, with the distinction of having been the second youngest candidate ever elected as governor of Idaho, the only one to go from the office of attorney general to the governor's chair, and the only one who is a graduate of an Idaho college, having received his degree in 1938 from the College of Idaho.

*   *   *   *   *

Let us take pride in the fact that Idaho's record as a state has always been good and that our members of Congress, our governors, and practically all our other state officers have been honorable and faithful public servants. Idaho has been and still is a law-abiding state, free from evil groups such as have attained control in some less fortunate states from time to time. If we all take our duties of citizenship seriously, if we always vote for officers whose public record and personal conduct are above reproach, we shall continue to keep Idaho among the states whose political records are clean and whose affairs are honestly managed for the best interests of their people.

Idaho's Growth in Its Geographical Setting

*How and why Idaho counties increased in number; principal industries
of the counties; growth of cities, towns, and villages; how the counties
were named.*

THE SAME GEOGRAPHICAL FACTORS that caused the development of Idaho Territory have been mainly responsible for its continued growth and development as a state. These are, as you learned in Units 5 and 6: (1) a favorable temperate climate; (2) a choice location on the western slope of the Rocky Mountains; (3) an area which ranks it among the dozen largest states of the Union; (4) a share in three of the natural physiographic[1] regions of the United States; (5) a great variety in elevation and surface features; (6) large bodies of fertile soils; (7) a great number of streams and lakes; (8) extensive forests; (9) rich and varied mineral resources; (10) large areas of natural grazing lands; (11) outstanding scenic and recreational attractions; and (12) exceptional wildlife resources.

Idaho's people have been of a kind to make good use of our favorable geographical factors. The state has been peopled by a bold, frontier type of Americans accustomed to thinking and acting for themselves, yet co-operating with each other in matters of general welfare. In this unit we shall see how our people have established communities to serve their economic and social needs.

I. OUR FORTY-FOUR COUNTIES

EIGHTEEN COUNTIES were in existence when Idaho became a state in 1890. Twenty-eight more counties have been organized since that time. Two counties, Alturas and Logan, were abolished when the legislature created Blaine County in 1895. This gives us the forty-four counties we now have. For quick reference, the table that follows lists them in alphabetical order, showing the year they were established, their population according to the 1950 census, the county seats, the population of the county seats, and the county designations for automobile license plates. For a comparison of the taxable wealth of the counties, see Appendix Table 13.

Why Counties Increased Rapidly Until 1919. If we consider the growth in population from 1890 to 1920, we shall understand the principal reason for the increase in counties during these years. When Idaho was admitted as a state in 1890, our population was, in round numbers, 88,000. During the first decade of statehood the population almost doubled,

[1]Physiographic (FĬZ-ĭ-ō-GRĂF-ik). Pertaining to the earth and its physical features.

Table No. 2

COUNTIES OF IDAHO

County	Year Created	Area Sq. Mi. 1954	Population 1950	County Seat	Population County Seat 1950	Auto License
Ada	1864	1046	70,649	Boise	34,393	1A
Adams	1911	1377	3,347*	Council	748	2A
Bannock	1893	1124	41,745	Pocatello	26,131	1B
Bear Lake	1875	988	6,834*	Paris	774*	2B
Benewah	1915	791	6,173*	St. Maries	2,220*	3B
Bingham	1885	2072	23,271	Blackfoot	5,180	4B
Blaine	1895	2649	5,384	Hailey	1,464	5B
Boise†	1863	1913	1,776*	Idaho City	246*	6B
Bonner	1907	1736	14,853*	Sandpoint	4,265*	7B
Bonneville	1911	1846	30,210	Idaho Falls	19,218	8B
Boundary	1915	1275	5,908*	Bonners Ferry	1,776	9B
Butte	1917	2240	2,722	Arco	961	10B
Camas	1917	1057	1,079*	Fairfield	502*	1C
Canyon	1891	580	53,597	Caldwell	10,487	2C
Caribou	1919	1747	5,576	Soda Springs	1,329	3C
Cassia	1879	2544	14,629	Burley	5,924	4C
Clark	1919	1751	918*	Dubois	430	5C
Clearwater	1911	2522	8,217*	Orofino	1,656	6C
Custer	1881	4933	3,318*	Challis	728	7C
Elmore	1889	3062	6,687	Mountain Home	1,887	E
Franklin	1913	667	9,867*	Preston	4,045*	1F

County	Year			County Seat		Ref
Fremont	1893	1819	9,351*	St. Anthony	2,695*	2F
Gem	1915	555	8,730*	Emmett	3,067*	1G
Gooding	1913	722	11,101	Gooding	3,099	2G
Idaho†	1861	8515	11,423*	Grangeville	2,544	I
Jefferson	1913	1089	10,495*	Rigby	1,826*	1J
Jerome	1919	593	12,080	Jerome	4,523	2J
Kootenai‡	1881	1256	24,947	Coeur d'Alene	12,198	K
Latah‡	1888	1090	20,971	Moscow	10,593	1L
Lemhi	1869	4585	6,278*	Salmon	2,648	2L
Lewis	1911	478	4,208*	Nezperce	543*	3L
Lincoln	1895	1203	4,256	Shoshone	1,420	4L
Madison	1913	473	9,156*	Rexburg	4,253	1M
Minidoka	1913	750	9,785*	Rupert	3,098*	2M
Nez Perce†	1861	847	22,658	Lewiston	12,985	N
Oneida	1864	1191	4,387*	Malad City	2,715*	1O
Owyhee	1863	7648	6,307	Murphy§	100	2O
Payette	1917	403	11,921	Payette	4,032	1P
Power	1913	1411	3,988	American Falls	1,874	2P
Shoshone†	1858	2609	22,866	Wallace	3,140*	S
Teton	1915	459	3,204*	Driggs	941*	1T
Twin Falls	1907	1942	40,979	Twin Falls	17,600	2T
Valley	1917	3678	4,270	Cascade	943*	V
Washington	1879	1475	8,576*	Weiser	3,961	W

*Population smaller than in 1940.

†Originally created by Washington territorial legislature.

‡Authorized in 1864 but not organized until year shown above.

§Village unincorporated. Population shown is for voting precinct.

reaching more than 160,000 in 1900. It just about doubled again between 1900 and 1910, exceeding 320,000. In the succeeding ten years, about 110,000 more people were added to our population. With an increase of close to 340,000 people in thirty years, the state needed many more counties so that the people could have more effective control of their local governments.

No new counties have been formed since 1919, but several changes have been made in county boundaries. If changes are made, they are always decided by the vote of the people after the legislature enacts a law authorizing a special election for deciding proposed changes. The most recent change of importance occurred in 1948 when 581 square miles, then in the eastern part of Bannock County, seceded and joined Caribou County.

Size and Population of Idaho Counties. It is always interesting to compare Idaho with other states and to compare the counties of the state with each other. We have already learned that Idaho is among the larger states. Now let us look briefly at our counties from the standpoint of size and population.

In the forty-eight states of the Union there are, approximately, three thousand counties. Though some of these are very large, most are small, the average size of counties the nation over being close to one thousand square miles. By way of general comparison, Idaho's forty-four counties average close to two thousand square miles each, about double the size of the nation's average county.

Idaho and Owyhee counties are the largest in our state, having 8,515 and 7,648 square miles respectively. Idaho County is about the same in size as the total area of the three smallest states, Rhode Island, Connecticut, and Delaware, and Owyhee County is only slightly smaller. Name other large counties with an area of three thousand square miles or more. (See table.)

At the other extreme are Payette, Teton, Madison, and Lewis counties, all less than five hundred square miles in area. Other counties well under the national average in size are Gem, Canyon, Jerome, Franklin, Gooding, Minidoka, Benewah, and Nez Perce. Close to the national average in size are Ada, Bear Lake, Jefferson, and Latah counties.

In population, the average county of the United States has about fifty thousand people. In Idaho the average is a little more than twelve thousand, less than one fourth the national average. Can you suggest some reasons why this is so?

Ada County, with a population of more than seventy thousand, is far ahead of any other county. Next comes Canyon County, with more than fifty thousand people. These are the only two counties in Idaho that exceed the national average in population. Two other counties, Bannock and Twin Falls, are approaching the national average but are still well below it. What cities help to boost the population of Ada, Canyon, Bannock, and Twin Falls counties?

Far down at the other end of the line stands Clark County which, in 1950, counted only 918 souls. Camas and Boise counties, with a few more than one thousand people each, are a little better off. What reasons can you give for the small population of these counties?

II. COUNTY RESOURCES AND INDUSTRIES

ON WHAT OCCUPATION do more people of your own county depend than on any other kind of work? The answer to this question depends mainly upon the natural resources your county has, or, at least, those that are most used. What are they?

As we become better acquainted with our counties, we shall discover that they fall into economic groups: agricultural, grazing, lumbering, mining, and so on. Of course, no county is limited to only one occupation, but we shall find that in practically every county one main occupation ranks above others in importance.

Agricultural Counties. When the United States Census of 1950 was released, it showed that two counties in Idaho ranked among the one hundred leading agricultural counties of the United States. These were Twin Falls and Canyon counties, ranking fifty-seventh and sixty-first respectively in the nation. Total sales of farm products in these two counties amounted to approximately fifty million dollars in 1949, the year for which census statistics were collected.

Standing next to the top-ranking counties in order of total farm production of all kinds were Bingham County in third place, Bonneville County in fourth place, and Cassia County ranking fifth. Then in order came Jerome, Ada, Idaho, Jefferson, Minidoka, Gooding, Owyhee, Latah, Fremont, and Nez Perce counties to make up the big fifteen top-ranking agricultural counties of the state.

We must not suppose, however, that the counties already named are the only important agricultural counties in Idaho. A quick look at the farm products listed in the census shows other counties ranking among the leaders in certain crops.

In wheat production Power County held fourth place, Lewis County stood seventh, and Bannock and Madison counties ranked ninth and tenth. Caribou

Courtesy Twin Falls Chamber of Commerce

AN IDAHO BEAN FIELD

Twin Falls County ranked first in Idaho and fifty-seventh in the United States among the agricultural counties of the nation, as is shown by the 1950 census. Its most famous crop is beans, though this is not its greatest revenue producer.

County, with a little more than 10 per cent of the entire production of the state, held first place in barley, and Lewis, Franklin, and Oneida counties were among the top ten. Leading the state in oats was Boundary County, with Valley County in fourth place and Kootenai and Benewah counties in ninth and tenth places.

Potatoes and sugar beets came mainly from the "big fifteen." However, Franklin, Bannock, Payette, Caribou, and Washington counties contributed liberally to the more than a million tons of sugar beets which Idaho provided to help satisfy the nation's sweet tooth.

Beans, over 236,000,000 pounds of them, came mainly from Magic Valley counties. Lincoln and Elmore counties belonged among the top ten, producing together more than seven million pounds for Idaho's enormous bean pot.

The Clearwater Plateau counties produced more than half the dry peas grown in Idaho. Lewis, Kootenai, and Benewah counties were among the ten leading counties in this crop.

Seven counties produced more than 90 per cent of the state's commercial fruit crop. These, in order of total sales, were Canyon, Gem, Payette, Adams, Twin Falls, Ada, and Nez Perce counties.

In the last two decades, Idaho has become widely known for seed production. This was emphasized by Mrs. Pattison, president of the board of directors of a large international seed company with headquarters in New York City. On a visit to Boise in the 1940's Mrs. Pattison said:

I am here because Idaho is such an important territory in the seed world. And by that I mean the whole seed world. Seeds grown in Idaho are wanted by all countries because they are better. They are better primarily because of irrigation, where you can control the moisture. Idaho has a very favorable climate for the threshing season, which is so important in seeds. Idaho seeds have a better germination, higher purity, and an especially beautiful appearance.

Large quantities of alfalfa, red clover, and alsike and white clover seed were grown in the counties of the Magic Valley, the Lower Snake River Valley, and the Clearwater Plateau. Bingham County, in the Upper Snake River Valley, and Valley County were also important in this production, the last also being the leading county in the nation in growing brome grass seed. A new seed crop, safflower, is proving successful in Power County, the seed being valuable for the oil they yield.

Garden seeds are very important in Idaho. Twin Falls County is the leading county in the United States in the production of seed beans, as Latah County is for seed peas. Idaho also produces more than 80 per cent of the nation's hybrid sweet corn seed, 75 per cent of its turnip seed, 50 per cent of its onion and carrot seed, and a large part of its rape seed. In general, about 25 per cent of the nation's garden seed is grown here. These are nearly all from the counties of the Lower Snake River Valley and Twin Falls County.

Livestock and Dairy Counties. The value of livestock and livestock products sold in Idaho in 1949 amounted in round numbers to $126,000,000. The livestock industry, like the other important occupations, is mainly centered in certain sections and counties of the state.

SHEEP RANCH IN SNAKE RIVER VALLEY

The large numbers of sheep in the counties of the Snake River Valley help Idaho to stand seventh among the states as a producer of sheep and wool.

Cattle. The 1950 census showed just under a million cattle in Idaho. These included both beef and dairy animals. Canyon County led all others with 66,274 head. Its 24,037 milk cows also placed it first in the dairy cattle division. In all cattle, Twin Falls County was second, followed by Bingham, Ada, Cassia, Lemhi, Owyhee, Idaho, Gooding, and Washington counties in that order. In the number of milk cows Ada County was second, followed by Twin Falls, Bingham, Franklin, Gooding, Bonneville, Jefferson, Caribou, and Payette counties to make up the top ten counties of the state.

Several counties with a small population are important livestock counties. They have large upland grazing areas for summer use. They also have enough good hay land in the valleys and basins to produce the feed needed for the cold season. Most of the mountain and plateau counties of southern Idaho and those of the Clearwater Plateau are good open-range districts. Counties leading in range cattle, as shown by the 1951 report of the State Tax Commission, were Owyhee, Lemhi, Custer, Idaho, Cassia, Washington, Twin Falls, Oneida, Bear Lake, and Bingham counties in that order as the top-ranking ten counties. Together, they had considerably more than half the range cattle of the state.

Dairy Products. Measured by the yearly volume of dairy products sold, several counties ran their sales into the millions of dollars. In 1949, Canyon and Ada counties alone sold more than eight million dollars' worth of dairy products. What cities in those counties provide good markets for dairy foods?

Other counties with sales above a million dollars each were Twin Falls, Bingham, and Franklin. Selling between a half million and a million dollars' worth each were Payette, Gooding, Gem, Bonneville, Cassia, Jefferson, Kootenai, Bannock, Bonner, Minidoka, Bear Lake, and Jerome counties.

Sheep and Wool. The last census re-

DAIRY COWS IN THE LOWER SNAKE RIVER VALLEY

Because of several cities and towns that provide good markets, dairying is of special importance in this part of Idaho.

Courtesy U.S. Bureau of Reclamation, Region No. 1, Boise

vealed that Idaho had 1,580,690 sheep and lambs, and that in 1949 over eight million pounds of wool were sheared. In sheep population Twin Falls County was in the lead, with more than 125,000 head. Others with large numbers of sheep were Gooding, Blaine, Elmore, Bonneville, Bingham, Owyhee, Minidoka, Jerome, and Gem counties.

Hogs. It is well known that pigs like milk and thrive on it the same as humans do. It should not surprise us to learn that the leading dairy counties also have a large swine population. In 1949 Canyon and Ada counties held first and second rank. These were followed by Idaho, Washington, Bingham, Jefferson, Bonneville, Twin Falls, Cassia, and Latah counties in that order. Do you think that the fact that Idaho and Latah counties are noted grain counties has anything to do with their having large numbers of swine?

Horses. Once noted for the number and quality of its horses, Idaho has largely turned to automobiles, trucks, and tractors for its motive power. But there were still about 88,000 horses in the state in 1949. Bingham County led, with Canyon, Twin Falls, Owyhee, and Idaho counties close behind. Most of the mountain counties had more horses in proportion to human population than the well-settled farming counties. Can you tell why?

Poultry and Bees. Chickens, eggs, and turkeys are good old stand-bys on many an Idaho farm. In the number of chickens Canyon County scored another first, but Franklin County crowded it closely. Also adding heavily to the poultry population were Ada, Twin Falls, Bingham, Kootenai, Bonneville, and Jefferson counties. Nearly all counties, however, had a considerable number of chickens. Turkeys were most plentiful in Franklin, Canyon, Gooding, and Gem counties.

The 1951 tax rolls of the state showed that there were then nearly twenty-five thousand stands (hives) of bees in the

TRIUMPH MINE IN WOOD RIVER DISTRICT

Though not seriously rivaling Shoshone County, the counties of the Upland Empire have, nevertheless, an impressive record in mineral production.

Courtesy U.S. Bureau of Reclamation, Region No. 1, Boise

state. Bingham County led all others that year. Other counties in which the people stood a good chance of getting stung were Jerome, Cassia, Madison, Blaine, Oneida, Lemhi, Nez Perce, Ada, Fremont, and Gem counties. Wendell, near the Jerome-Gooding county line, advertises itself as the honey capital of Idaho, as it has the largest honey processing plant in the state.

Mining Counties. Do you recall reading in an earlier unit about buried treasure in Idaho? If so, you remember, no doubt, that the richest treasures of all are in the Coeur d'Alene mining district. Most of this extremely rich lead-silver-zinc district is in Shoshone County, one of the great mining counties of the United States. This county alone has produced more mineral wealth than all the rest of the state combined.

But this does not mean that other counties are lacking in mineral resources. Caribou, Bear Lake, and Bingham counties are now producing large quantities of phosphate rock, with the promise of

greater production in the near future. The mines at Stibnite, in Valley County, produced most of the antimony mined in the United States until recently, when foreign mines with low-cost labor flooded the American market with antimony and forced the Valley County mines to close, at least for the time being. Lemhi County is now producing a good share of the tungsten and cobalt the nation needs to keep its war materials factories at work. Gold, copper, and several other minerals are mined in Idaho, Custer, Lemhi, Blaine, Elmore, and Valley counties. There are only a few counties in the state that do not hold promise for future developments in mining.

Lumbering Counties. Lumbering, our third great basic industry, is, of course, most important in the Panhandle counties though it is by no means neglected in a number of counties south of the Salmon River.

Without attempting to list them in order of importance, the counties of Benewah, Bonner, Boundary, Clearwater,

WHITE PINE LOGS ON THE WAY TO THE MILL

The Panhandle counties hold first rank among the lumbering regions of Idaho.

IDAHO'S ONLY PORTLAND CEMENT FACTORY

In this factory at Inkom is produced the only Portland cement manufactured in Idaho. Huge limestone reserves near by date far back in the geological history of the state. Other commercial deposits are found in many Idaho counties, notably in the Seven Devils region of western Idaho.

Idaho, Kootenai, and Shoshone are the leading timber and timber-products counties of northern Idaho. South of the Salmon River, Adams, Boise, Gem, Valley, and Washington counties supply much commercial timber, the bulk of which is cut into lumber. Other counties add to the total, but the counties named are the leaders. Huge timber resources are held in national and state forests in the counties of the Panhandle and the Upland Empire in northern and central Idaho.

Manufacturing Counties. Though manufacturing is not of such great relative importance in Idaho as it is in many states, it is steadily growing. In the agricultural sections of the state, most of the manufacturing is based on products of the farms, ranches, and orchards. Meat-packing plants, creameries, cheese factories, flour mills, and beet-sugar factories are leaders in such work.

In the mining counties, such as Shoshone County, the smelting and refining of ores are the most important manufacturing processes. These are not exactly true manufacturing industries, since they do not in themselves turn the raw products of the mines into finished goods ready for general use as they come from the mills. They are, however, necessary steps in the manufacturing process. The plants in southern Idaho that turn out fertilizers and elemental phosphorus are good examples of true manufacturing based on mineral resources. In the forested areas of the state, lumber and other forest products are the most important manufactured goods.

The *Idaho Industrial Directory* for 1952, prepared by the Idaho State Chamber of Commerce, listed nearly eight hundred establishments engaged in manufacturing, processing, or fabricating goods and materials of many kinds. In a recent year products manufactured in Idaho were valued at close to sixty-five million dollars, with the counties of Ada, Bannock, Bonner, Bonneville, Canyon, Clearwater, Kootenai, Latah, Nez Perce, and Twin Falls accounting for about four fifths of the manufacturing in the state. Which of these probably made food products? Which were engaged in making lumber and forest products?

Business and Commercial Interests. The business census of 1948, compiled by the United States Department of Commerce, showed that Idaho had 1,152 wholesale and 7,332 retail establishments. Total sales of these establishments amounted to just under a billion dollars, or a little more than $1,700 for each man, woman, and child in the state.

To round out the business picture in Idaho, let us examine the total income of the people of the state as reported in 1951 by the Office of Business Economics, United States Department of Commerce. The total income was given in round numbers as $763,800,000. Broken down, it showed an average per capita income of $1,436 for each man, woman, and child in Idaho. If your own family had received this amount for each person in the family, what would have been your family income for that year?

III. IDAHO CITIES AND TOWNS

THE UNITED STATES CENSUS BUREAU lists as a city any municipality having a population of 2,500 or more. According to this classification, Idaho had twenty-nine cities in 1950. These were distributed in twenty-five counties. Only four counties, Bannock, Canyon, Shoshone, and Twin Falls, had two cities each. Nineteen counties had no cities at all, if we follow the Census Bureau listing.

The Ten Largest Cities. It would take many more pages than this book can spare to allow a detailed discussion of Idaho cities. We may, however, take a brief look at the largest ten. These are named in the following table.

Table No. 3

TEN TOP CITIES OF IDAHO—1950 CENSUS

Rank	City	Population, 1950	County in which located
1	Boise	34,393	Ada
2	Pocatello	26,131	Bannock
3	Idaho Falls	19,218	Bonneville
4	Twin Falls	17,600	Twin Falls
5	Nampa	16,185	Canyon
6	Lewiston	12,985	Nez Perce
7	Coeur d'Alene	12,198	Kootenai
8	Moscow	10,593	Latah
9	Caldwell	10,487	Canyon
10	Burley	5,924	Cassia

Boise. Four main factors have caused Boise to grow quite rapidly. (1) It is the capital of the state and as such naturally attracts many people who like to live in or near the nerve center of the state, the place where state affairs are planned and from which they are administered. (2) It is located in Boise Valley, one of the state's richest agricultural regions. (3) It has a fine all-year climate, warmer than most parts of the state, but healthful and invigorating. (4) Its location in the western end of the Snake River Valley makes it a gateway city through which flows a large part of the east-west travel, traffic, and transportation moving between the East and the Middle West and the Pacific Northwest.

Boise is rapidly becoming an important industrial and commercial city, but its proudest boast is that it still remains principally a city of homes, where friendship and neighborliness are the rule. Its excellent public-school system, capped by Boise Junior College, its many churches and other social and cultural institutions, its nearness to mountains and recreational areas, and its railroads, highways, and airlines give its people exceptional opportunities for wholesome living in the best American tradition.

Pocatello. The "Gate City" is the metropolis or chief city of southeastern Idaho. It is best described as a transportation, industrial, and commercial city standing at the crossing of natural routes of travel and transportation. It is very favorably located to draw raw materials from the surrounding regions for a variety of manufacturing enterprises and to ship the finished products north, south, east, and west over transcontinental railroads and fine highways to markets. It is a rail, truck, bus, and airline hub of constantly growing importance. Its Union Pacific Railroad repair shops and its recently completed ultramodern railroad yards are among the largest and best between the Mississippi River and the Pacific Ocean. Idaho State College and a fine public-school system offer excellent educational opportunities to the people living in and near Pocatello.

Idaho Falls. Sharing importance with

Pocatello in eastern Idaho is Idaho Falls, third city of the state. Center of a large and extremely productive irrigated agricultural district in the Upper Snake River Valley, the city naturally has characteristics typical of prosperous farming communities. It has a large manufacturing and processing business founded on the products of the surrounding farms and ranches. The picturesquely beautiful and unusual Latter-day Saints Temple is making the city a center of Mormon interests, though other church denominations are well represented. Here is the headquarters for the Atomic Energy Commission's atomic reactor station, where extensive and extremely important developments in the field of atomic energy are being worked out.

Twin Falls. The "Magic City," as it is called, is the chief commercial and industrial city of south central Idaho and the most important cultural and trade center of Magic Valley. Like Idaho Falls, it owes its importance chiefly to the extensive and fertile irrigated region which surrounds it. Its industries are mainly based on the agricultural products of the Magic Valley counties. Though not on a main railroad, it is served by an important branch line of the Union Pacific which extends southward into Nevada and connects with the main line of the Southern Pacific from Chicago to the San Francisco Bay area. Near Twin Falls are the magnificent Shoshone Falls and the Shoshone Gorge of the Snake River, both among the noted scenic wonders of the West.

Nampa and Caldwell. Fifth and ninth in size, respectively, among Idaho cities are these two Canyon County cities in the heart of fertile Boise Valley. Their steadily expanding industries are based largely on the products of the superior irrigated lands that surround them. Beet-sugar manufacturing, milk canning, meat packing, dairying, and processing and packing fruits and vegetables are typical industries. At Caldwell is located the College of Idaho. There, too, is the home of The Caxton Printers, Ltd., leading book publishers of the intermountain West. At Nampa is the Northwest Nazarene College.

Lewiston. Sometimes called Idaho's seaport, because it is reached by steamboats, this is the chief city of the Clearwater Valley and Plateau. Surrounded by extensive and fertile farming and grazing lands, the city is largely supported by agricultural interests and its industries are largely based on agricultural products. But it is also the location of one of the world's large lumber mills. Recently a large pulp and paper mill was finished and put into operation. Until it was closed in 1950, the Northern Idaho College of Education was maintained as a state school for training teachers. The 1955 legislature reactivated the school as a two-year college for training teachers, naming it the Lewis-Clark Normal School and placing it under the supervision of the University of Idaho.

Coeur d'Alene. The "City of Recreation," seventh in size among Idaho cities, is located at the northern end of Lake Coeur d'Alene. Though there are some good agricultural lands close by, the city depends largely on forest and recreational industries. It is an important supply point for the great Coeur d'Alene mining district located a few miles to the east. The

North Idaho Junior College is located there.

Moscow. The home of the University of Idaho and the seed-pea capital of the United States is located among the rolling Palouse Hills of Latah County. The city is best known for its educational opportunities, but it is also an important commercial center for the northern section of the Clearwater Plateau. Here are located large grain elevators and flour mills. The leading seed-pea district of the United States is centered here. Three railroads provide outlets to outside markets. Outstanding clay deposits are the basis of a considerable brick and clay-products industry.

Burley. Though tenth among the cities of Idaho in 1950, Burley does not closely rival any of the others in size. It is much like the other agricultural cities of the Snake River Valley, depending mainly on the products of surrounding irrigated farming and grazing sections for most of its industrial and commercial activities.

The Smaller Cities of Idaho. The nineteen smaller cities of Idaho, as classified by the United States census of 1950, are nearly all located in irrigated farming and livestock sections. The three exceptions are the Panhandle cities of Sandpoint, Kellogg, and Wallace. The first depends upon the forests, a limited agricultural industry, and outstanding recreational activities for its chief sources of employment. The last two depend almost wholly on mining. Appendix Table 6 lists these cities in order of size, names the counties in which they are located, and shows the basic industries most important to their economic life. Do you live in one of these cities?

By state law Idaho provides that any place with a population of one thousand or more may incorporate as a city. In 1950 there were twenty-three other incorporated cities besides those shown in the table on page 182 and Appendix Table No. 6. Only two, Mullan and St. Maries, had more than two thousand residents.

Idaho, then, counting the incorporated places with one thousand or more people, had fifty-two cities in 1950. Thirty-three of them are county seats. This has, of course, been a help to their growth and development. In general, however, the business interests of all these cities are closely related to the natural resources of the counties and regions in which they are located. What are the principal natural resources on which your own or your nearest city depends?

Villages and Incorporated Towns. In 1950 there were 136 incorporated villages in Idaho. Among these are some of the oldest towns in the state. Ten of our county seats are in such incorporated villages. Only one county seat in the state, Murphy, in Owyhee County, is not in an incorporated city or village.

Shoestring Villages. In 1947 the Idaho Legislature enacted laws permitting the sale of intoxicating liquors in incorporated cities and villages. As a result of these laws, Idaho has some of the longest villages on earth. The village of Island Park, in Fremont County, stretches along both sides of Highway 191, the Yellowstone Highway, for a distance of thirty-three miles. Advertising itself as the "village with the longest main street in the world," it consists of several small pleasure resorts scattered along the highway.

A similar village in Kootenai County reaches from near the Coeur d'Alene city limits north almost to the boundary line between Kootenai and Bonner counties. Still another of these shoestring villages, North Fork, in Lemhi County, is close to thirty miles in length.

Unincorporated Towns. Several places in Idaho are large enough to be cities and villages in a legal sense but have never organized. Most of them are residential districts which have grown up as suburbs adjoining our principal cities. The people living in them are close enough to enjoy the benefits offered by the cities, yet escape some of the burden of taxation. Many people in the cities whose taxes make possible the comforts and conveniences of city life speak of such suburban communities as "parasite towns," drawing their substance from the cities but not contributing in fair measure to their support. Do you agree with this line of reasoning?

IV. HOW OUR COUNTIES WERE NAMED

DO YOU KNOW how your county got its name? Nine of our counties have names of Indian origin or connected with Indian history. Seventeen are named for historical characters or persons connected in some manner with the counties bearing their names. The remaining sixteen counties received their names from various sources.

Counties with Indian Names. Five counties, Bannock, Kootenai, Lemhi, Nez Perce, and Shoshone, were named for Indian tribes that lived in Idaho.

Benewah County bears the name of Chief Benewah, a leader in the Coeur d'Alene tribe.

Camas County received its name from the abundance of camas plants once growing in the Malade Basin, now Big Camas Prairie, in the southern part of the county. The bulblike roots of this plant were a favorite food of practically all Idaho Indians.

Latah County's name was formed from the first syllables of two Nez Perce words, *la-koh,* a pine tree, and *tah-ol,* a kind of stone used by the Indians in making pestles for pounding or pulverizing food.

The name of Minidoka County was chosen from an Indian word meaning "broad expanse," therefore, a wide plain or valley.

County Names Honoring People. Ada County was named for Ada Riggs, the first white child born in the county.

Adams, Jefferson, Lincoln, Madison, and Washington counties honor Presidents of the United States.

Bingham County bears the name of Congressman Bingham of Pennsylvania. Bingham was a friend of Governor Bunn, who was territorial governor of Idaho when the county was organized.

Blaine County was named for James G. Blaine, once United States Secretary of State and for many years a leading member of Congress.

Bonner County recalls Edwin L. Bonner, who operated an early-day ferry over Kootenai River where the city of Bonners Ferry is now located.

Bonneville County keeps alive the memory of Captain B. L. E. Bonneville, an army officer, explorer, and fur trader who spent several years in what is now southern Idaho.

Clark County was named for Sam Clark, an early cattleman of eastern Idaho.

Franklin County was named for Franklin Richards, a leader among the Mormons who established Franklin, the first permanent settlement in Idaho.

Fremont County's name is a tribute to General John C. Fremont, explorer and map maker who surveyed the Oregon Trail across southern Idaho in 1843.

Gooding County was named for Frank R. Gooding, an Idaho governor and member of Congress.

Jerome County took its name from Jerome C. Hill, who helped develop irrigation projects in Magic Valley.

Lewis County honors Captain Meriwether Lewis, one of the leaders of the Lewis and Clark Expedition.

Francis Payette, early Hudson's Bay man at Old Fort Boise, gave his name to Payette County, the smallest county in the state.

Counties Named for Places and Things. Eight counties in this group were named for physical features of the country or region. The rest derived their names in various ways.

Boise County was named for the Boise River. The word is from the French, *les bois,* meaning "trees" or "woods." It is said to have been a reference to cottonwood trees once growing plentifully along the stream.

Boundary County was so named because it lies along the international boundary line between Canada and the United States; or, more specifically, the line between Idaho and British Columbia.

Butte County was named for Big Butte, a prominent landmark and travelers' guide in the desert region of the Snake River Plains in the southern part of the county.

Canyon County's name is a reference to canyons along the Snake and Boise rivers.

Caribou Fairchild discovered gold near a high peak east of Grays Lake. The mountain was named for him and, it is said, the peak gave its name to Caribou County. It may, however, have been named for the man instead of the mountain.

Cassia is the name of a kind of plant that grew in abundance along a tributary creek of Raft River. Both the creek and Cassia County bear the name of the plant.

Clearwater County was named for the Clearwater River, in whose drainage basin the county is located. The Indians called the river *koos-koos-kia,* meaning "clear water." Do you think the Indian word would have been a more fitting name for the county?

The Ida Elmore was a famous gold mine on the upper reaches of the Boise River. Elmore County was named for the mine.

Gem County is taken from "Gem of the Mountains," Idaho's symbolic name.

Idaho County was named for the *Idaho,* an early river steamer on the Snake.

Oneida, New York, was the former home of many early settlers in the Little Malad River valley. In memory of their former home, the settlers named Oneida County.

Owyhee is said to be a corruption of

the word Hawaii. No one seems to know just why the name was selected for Owyhee County, though legend has it that two Hawaiians were killed there during the mining frenzy of 1863. However, the name was not new. In the poem *Evangeline,* Henry Wadsworth Longfellow wrote, before Idaho Territory was created:

Far in the West there lies a desert land, where the mountains
Lift, through perpetual snows, their lofty and luminous summits.
Down from their jagged, deep ravines, where the gorge, like a gateway,
Opens a passage rude to the wheels of the emigrant's wagon,
Westward the Oregon flows and the Walleway and Owyhee.

Power County was so named because of the power possibilities at the American Falls on the Snake River. The falls were so named, according to generally accepted accounts, because some American trappers were drowned there in the early days when the fur trade was an active industry in the West. The city of American Falls is now located there.

Valley County took its name from Long Valley, a picturesque, mountain-bound valley along the North Fork of Payette River.

*   *   *   *   *

The increase in counties from eighteen to forty-four and the more than half a hundred incorporated cities give proof of Idaho's rapid growth since statehood. This growth came about principally through the development of the abundant natural resources of the respective counties. These counties differ in so many respects that practically any way of living is possible in them, from primitive conditions of pioneer life to the advantages and conveniences of modern cities. In most counties rich natural resources still await their fullest use. With the richness and variety of these resources, we in Idaho have unusual opportunities of living in almost any manner we, as individuals, may choose. This is one of the things that makes our state such an interesting and attractive place in which to live, a place where dreams often do come true.

Educational and Social Progress

How Idaho has kept pace with the nation in providing educational opportunities for children and young people; and how social and welfare agencies make possible a richer and better life.

HOW HAS IDAHO KEPT PACE with the rest of the nation in caring for the educational and social needs of our people? How is our educational system organized and managed? What care do we take of our aged and unfortunate citizens? How have we tried to solve some of the problems related to our safety and morality, or right living? What local institutions and organizations serve the social needs of the people? As we try to find answers to such questions as these, we shall gain a clearer picture of life in Idaho as it affects all of us who live here.

I. THE PUBLIC SCHOOLS

IDAHO HAS BEEN GENERALLY RECOGNIZED as being among the most progressive states in the excellence of its public schools. Recent developments in this field are outstanding, and if they accomplish what is expected, Idaho will rank even higher among the top states of the Union in public education.

Between statehood in 1890 and the year 1912, several forward steps were taken. County superintendents were given wider powers and duties. The office of State Superintendent of Public Instruction brought about closer unity and cooperation among the schools by preparing courses of study to guide the work of teachers in both elementary and high schools.

The State Board of Education. In 1912 the legislature authorized and the people adopted a constitutional amendment creating the State Board of Education to supervise and direct all phases of public education in Idaho. This board, whose five members are appointed by the governor for five-year terms, has been the directing force responsible for a large share of the success of our school system, both the public schools and the institutions of higher education.

The Idaho Plan and the Equalization Act. The educational system of the state was greatly improved in 1933 when the legislature adopted the Unified Plan, more commonly called the Idaho Plan, for the public schools. This plan provided a new method of appropriating school funds on a classroom-unit basis and set aside more funds for low-valuation districts. It gave a more nearly equal opportunity for the pupils of all the schools to benefit under the new law. Under this plan our schools improved until they were rated among the best of the nation.

Some of its provisions are still in effect, though changed in many respects by later laws.

No other important changes in the educational system occurred until 1933. Then the whole country was suffering from the depression. A large share of taxes were unpaid because the people had little money. Schools were hard hit and could not raise enough revenue to operate in a satisfactory manner.

These conditions caused the state legislature to enact a new law in 1933 known as the Equalization Act. Under this law the state greatly increased the amount of money it paid to local school districts so that girls and boys attending school in poorer districts could have better paid teachers and better equipment and supplies, and so have more of the educational advantages of children living in richer districts. This law brought great educational improvement by giving to all children a more nearly equal opportunity to secure good elementary and high-school training.

Teachers' Retirement Law. On December 7, 1941, came Japan's "sneak attack" on Pearl Harbor in the Hawaiian Islands. This immediately plunged the United States into the second World War, which had already broken out in Europe. The entire nation at once went all out for war. Great numbers of Idahoans joined the armed forces and others took employment in war factories, where top wages and salaries were being paid to hurry up the production of war equipment and supplies. Many teachers left the classrooms to join the Army, Navy, Air Force, and women's war organizations. Many became workers in war factories. Many

schools found it difficult or impossible to secure satisfactory teachers.

To deal with the teacher shortage, Governor Arnold Williams called a special session of the state legislature in 1945. The lawmakers passed the Teachers' Retirement Law, which permits a teacher to retire and receive a pension after reaching the age of sixty years. Teachers are required to retire when reaching the age of seventy. All the states in the Union now have similar laws.

This law is having a good effect on our schools. It is drawing a high class of young men and women into the teaching profession and, what is more important, is keeping a considerable number of them there. For the first time in our state's history, Idaho boys and girls can look forward to teaching not only as a high type of public service but also as a profession in which they may be reasonably sure of a fairly satisfactory income and of security in their old age.

The Peabody Survey. Recognizing the importance of the public schools and the need for progressive laws affecting them, the legislature appropriated fifty thousand dollars to have an outside agency make a study of our entire public-school system. The contract for doing this was awarded to the George Peabody College for Teachers of Nashville, Tennessee. A group of outstanding authorities in the field of public education spent several months in 1946 in studying the Idaho school system and submitted their recommendations to the 1947 legislature as a basis for new school laws.

School Reorganization Act. The legislature, acting on the recommendations contained in the Peabody Survey, passed

CIVIC AUDITORIUM AND HIGH SCHOOL, IDAHO FALLS

This picture of the new civic auditorium and high school at Idaho Falls was taken early in 1953. Increased school enrollment in rapidly growing cities such as Idaho Falls has caused millions of tax dollars to be invested in new school buildings and equipment in Idaho in recent years, and millions more are seriously needed.

far-reaching school legislation which is commonly spoken of as the Reorganization Act. These laws are now being put into general effect in the state. School districts numbered 1,112 when the new laws became effective. On July 1, 1954, they had been reduced by consolidation to 190 districts, of which eighteen did not maintain schools but sent their pupils to conveniently located consolidated schools.

Important provisions of the Consolidation Act are: (1) Three kinds of school districts are authorized, Class A, Class B, and Class C districts. Their difference is mainly one of size rather than of quality, a small district often maintaining as good a school as a larger district. (2) A state-supervised and state-assisted school transportation system takes pupils to and from school. (3) Class A and Class B schools must employ specially trained superintendents holding college degrees in school administration. (4) The supervision of Class C districts was under the county superintendent of schools until 1955, when the office of county superintendent was abolished by action of the legislature. (5) District boards of school trustees consisting of five members are elected by

the people of the districts. (6) A five-member county board of education for each county was authorized to exercise general supervision over the schools of the county. (7) An improved and better balanced plan of financing the public schools requires the state to provide a large portion of school money and to exercise a somewhat larger control over its expenditure. (8) The educational requirements for teachers' certificates were raised so that teachers entering the profession after September 1, 1955, shall have at least four years of college training. Recent legislative action has slightly modified this provision.

Recent School Laws. Educational matters received much attention in the 1953 session of the state legislature. (1) The largest school appropriation in state history was passed, largely to enable school districts to pay higher salaries to teachers. (2) The State Teachers' Retirement System was placed on a sound financial basis. (3) The offices of county superintendent and the county board of education were abolished in completely reorganized counties. (4) A law was passed to give provisional teaching certificates to persons completing two years of college work, thus enabling more young people to become teachers and to help to overcome the teacher shortage which has for several years been a serious school problem in Idaho. These laws, as you can see, made some changes in the requirements provided in the original Reorganization Act.

Though not provided for by law, the United Education Council, consisting of the State Trustees' Association, the Idaho Congress of Parents and Teachers, and the Idaho Education Association, has a great deal to do with school legislation. The members of the state legislature give very careful consideration to bills which have the support of the United Education Council.

Kinds of Public Schools. Most of the larger school districts now maintain elementary schools for grades 1 to 6, junior high schools for grades 7 and 8 or grades 7, 8, and 9, and senior high schools. A few also have kindergartens for children under six years of age, but this is not common. How are the schools in your district organized?

There are still quite a number of one-room and two-room schools in rural areas where it is not convenient for children to attend larger schools. However, as we have already seen, the number of the small schools has been greatly reduced as a result of the Reorganization Law. Nearly all the counties of the state are now either wholly or partly reorganized into larger school districts.

Chart No. 2

IDAHO INCREASES THE STATE'S SHARE OF THE EDUCATIONAL COSTS*

(A 380 per cent increase)

(Courtesy Idaho Department of Education)

		Legislative Appropriations for Idaho School Equalization Program
1943–45	$2,500,000	
1945–47	$3,025,000	
1947–49	$8,000,000	
1949–51	$7,160,000	
1951–53	$8,250,000	
1953–55	$12,000,000	

*This was further increased by $15,000,000 by the 1955 legislature.

II. EDUCATIONAL INSTITUTIONS

EVERY PERSON IN IDAHO who desires to do so should have the opportunity to attend college after completing his elementary and high-school education.

Idaho makes this possible by tax-supported institutions of higher education. At present these are the University of Idaho, Idaho State College, the Boise Junior College, the North Idaho Junior College, and the Lewis-Clark Normal School.

University of Idaho. The first institution of higher education in the state was the University of Idaho. Authorized in 1889 by the last territorial legislature, it opened its doors in 1892. Today the university has about seventy-five buildings on a campus of three hundred acres at Moscow and a near-by university farm of eight hundred acres. In addition, there are about a score of student-operated fraternity and sorority houses for honor societies and other student organizations.

Instruction is provided in nearly half a hundred fields of learning. About two thousand separate courses are taught by a faculty of highly trained instructors. To provide this great variety of instruction, the university has nine separate colleges and schools, as follows:

College of Letters and Sciences
College of Agriculture
College of Engineering
School of Mines
College of Law
School of Forestry
School of Education
School of Business Education
Graduate School

In connection with instruction, research work is carried on in practically all the colleges as well as in experimental and field stations scattered over the state. The map that follows on page 194 shows the location of most of the experiment stations and indicates some of the kinds of work carried on by them.

The research work in connection with the College of Agriculture, College of Engineering, School of Mines, School of Forestry, and School of Business Administration have been of special value in increasing crop yields, controlling plant and animal diseases and pests, developing improved varieties of farm crops and fruits, improving methods of mining, and improving and making fuller use of the forests. Such work has increased the

Courtesy Moscow Chamber of Commerce

AIR VIEW, UNIVERSITY OF IDAHO

The University of Idaho, established by the legislature in 1889, consists of nine colleges and schools located on a beautiful three-hundred-acre campus at Moscow, in the rolling Palouse Hills of Latah County.

ADMINISTRATION BUILDING, IDAHO STATE COLLEGE

"In fact as well as in theory, a thoroughly democratic institution."—Carl W. McIntosh, President.

Courtesy ISC News Bureau, Pocatello

state's wealth by millions of dollars and offers great promise for the future.

Idaho State College. Located at Pocatello is Idaho State College, second only to the University of Idaho in size and importance. As the Academy of Idaho it was created by the legislature in 1901. It operated as a state academy, or high school, until 1915, when it was changed to a two-year college and renamed the Idaho Technical Institute.

In 1927 another change was made. The legislature placed it under the control of the University of Idaho and again changed its name, this time calling it the Southern Branch of the University of Idaho, but continuing it as a two-year college except for the School of Pharmacy, which had already been raised to four years, with power to grant the degree of bachelor of science in pharmacy.

The last change occurred in 1947. That year, in response to a popular demand by the people of southern Idaho, the legislature created Idaho State College as a full four-year degree-granting college and made it independent of any control by the University of Idaho. A law enacted by the 1955 legislature authorizes the granting of advanced degrees under rules of the Board of Education.

The campus now consists of 350 acres. There are more than a score of major buildings and almost as many temporary buildings. There are, also, about 150 apartment units for the use of students who do not have other living quarters.

Study courses leading to the bachelor of arts, the bachelor of science, and advanced degrees are similar to those offered by colleges elsewhere. But in the School of Trades and Industrial Education, students are given an opportunity to secure practical training in such fields as auto mechanics, auto painting and body repairs, carpentry, plumbing and pipe fitting, diesel mechanics, cosmetology, machine shop, upholstering, aviation, refrigeration, sheet metal work, secretarial training, printing, radio and

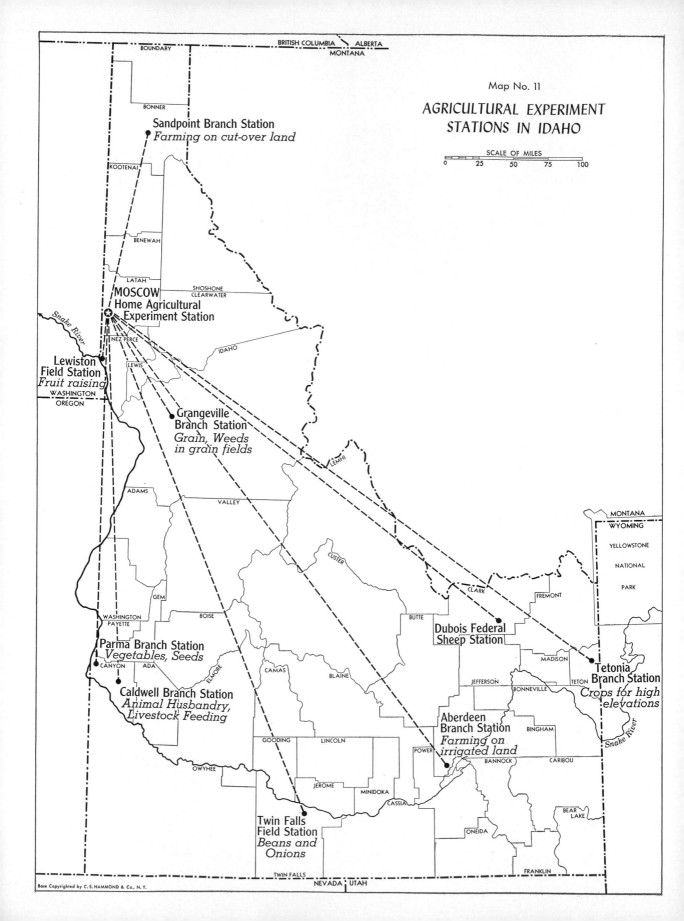

Map No. 11

AGRICULTURAL EXPERIMENT
STATIONS IN IDAHO

SCALE OF MILES
0   25   50   75   100

BRITISH COLUMBIA   ALBERTA
MONTANA

BOUNDARY

BONNER

Sandpoint Branch Station
Farming on cut-over land

KOOTENAI

BENEWAH

LATAH

SHOSHONE
CLEARWATER

MOSCOW
Home Agricultural
Experiment Station

Snake River

NEZ PERCE

IDAHO

Lewiston
Field Station
Fruit raising

LEWIS

WASHINGTON
OREGON

Grangeville
Branch Station
*Grain, Weeds
in grain fields*

LEMHI

ADAMS

VALLEY

MONTANA
WYOMING

YELLOWSTONE

NATIONAL

PARK

CUSTER

GEM

BOISE

CLARK

FREMONT

WASHINGTON
PAYETTE

BUTTE

Dubois Federal
Sheep Station

MADISON

Parma Branch Station
Vegetables, Seeds

CANYON   ADA

ELMORE

CAMAS

BLAINE

JEFFERSON

BONNEVILLE

TETON

Tetonia
Branch Station
*Crops for high
elevations*

Caldwell Branch Station
*Animal Husbandry,
Livestock Feeding*

Aberdeen
Branch Station
*Farming on
irrigated land*

BINGHAM

Snake River

GOODING   LINCOLN

POWER

BANNOCK

CARIBOU

OWYHEE

JEROME

MINIDOKA

CASSIA

BEAR
LAKE

Twin Falls
Field Station
*Beans and
Onions*

ONEIDA

FRANKLIN

TWIN FALLS   NEVADA   UTAH

THE ADMINISTRATION BUILDING FORMS THE CENTER OF CAMPUS LIFE AT THE UNIVERSITY OF IDAHO

The Gothic tower with its clock is the "trade-mark" of the university

electronics, and electricity. It is now rated high among such schools in the United States.

Junior Colleges. In 1939 the state legislature passed a law permitting the organization of junior college districts to give two years of work above the high school level. So far, two public, tax-supported junior colleges are operating in Idaho, though they are not state schools.

Boise Junior College. This institution began in 1932 as a church school sponsored by the Episcopal Church. When the law permitting the organization of junior college districts became effective, the Boise Junior College district was formed and the college became a public institution.

The college provides two years of instruction in these fields: art, business, education, engineering, forestry, home economics, music, prelegal, premedical, prenursing, and semiprofessional and vocational shop courses. The work is planned both to meet the demands of the first two years of regular college work and to prepare students who do not intend to do more college work for positions in various occupations and professions.

North Idaho Junior College. Like Boise Junior College, this began as a private school. Opened in 1933 as the Coeur d'Alene Junior College, it became a public, tax-supported school in 1939. It offers major courses of study that meet the first two years' requirements for bachelor of arts and bachelor of science degrees. The major courses are in education, engineering, business administration, commercial, journalism, speech, premedical, preveterinary, predental,

and music studies, and include the usual subjects found in such courses.

Private Colleges. Besides the public institutions of higher education there are in Idaho three excellent private colleges. The College of Idaho at Caldwell is under the general supervision of the Presbyterian Church. The Latter-day Saints Church operates Ricks College at Rexburg. The Church of the Nazarene maintains the Northwest Nazarene College at Nampa. All three offer most of the courses generally given in four-year colleges and all meet the general requirements of the State Board of Education, which has for many years rated them as accredited four-year colleges. They do not, however, receive any money from state funds or tax sources.

Teachers' Colleges. Until 1950 two colleges for training teachers were maintained by the state. The Northern Idaho College of Education, formerly the Lewiston Normal, was located at Lewiston, while at Albion, near Burley, was the Southern Idaho College of Education, formerly the Albion Normal. Neither of these schools was operated from 1950 to 1954 because the state legislature did not set aside sufficient funds. However, the buildings were maintained and both colleges are still listed as part of the educational system of Idaho. In fact, as we have seen, the Northern Idaho College of Education was reactivated and renamed by the 1955 legislature as a two-year college for the training of elementary teachers.

Special Schools. Idaho has not neglected its boys and girls who are in need of special instruction and help because of handicaps or unfavorable home

Map No. 12

IDAHO STATE EDUCATIONAL
AND
WELFARE INSTITUTIONS
1954

SCALE OF MILES
0   25   50   75   100

or community conditions. To provide for such cases, two special schools are operated under the general supervision of the State Board of Education. These are the Industrial Training School at St. Anthony and the School for the Deaf and Blind at Gooding.

The Industrial Training School. It is a sad fact that children and youth under the age of eighteen occasionally violate the law and find themselves in trouble. To care for such juvenile delinquents, as they are usually called, the state legislature created in 1903 a special school to train and educate them for useful citizenship.

The aim of the Industrial Training School is to give the pupils an opportunity to change their habits and gain knowledge and skills that will enable them to become useful citizens. Elementary and high-school subjects are taught. Both boys and girls receive sound instruction and practice in trades and occupations, homemaking skills, and character-building activities. Physical training and music are important parts of the youth program. The fact that more than three fourths of them make good after leaving the school indicates that the Idaho Industrial Training School serves the purpose for which it was mainly established.

State School for the Deaf and Blind. First opened in Boise in 1906, the State School for the Deaf and Blind was transferred to Gooding in 1910 when the building in Boise was destroyed by fire. By special methods of instruction, handicapped children and youth between the ages of six and twenty-one are taught the fundamentals of elementary education. The blind use the Braille System, learning the raised symbols by using their finger tips to recognize letters, words, and numbers.

The school, with its farm, is so managed that many of the students are able to become wholly or partly self-supporting. The faculty members of the school are specially trained for their work, and the school is now a very valuable part of Idaho's educational system.

III. CORRECTIONAL AND WELFARE INSTITUTIONS

THE STANDARDS OF DECENT SOCIETY demand that the unfortunate shall be aided and the lawless restrained. Even in territorial days, as we learned in earlier units, Idaho met these obligations to her people. The care thus given them has been widened and improved since statehood, and today we have several such institutions, all provided and maintained wholly or in part by legislative appropriations.

The State Penitentiary. The protection of life and property is a major duty of the state. Persons who offend against laws enacted for our protection must, if their offenses are serious or habitual, be placed where they can no longer continue such practices.

Among our institutions is one we would never voluntarily choose as a residence or stopping place, even temporarily. Our penitentiary, located at Boise, was a gift from the Federal government when Idaho became a state. It has proven of great value, both in protecting our people and in rebuilding the lives of many who went astray. Persons convicted of felonies, which means serious crimes such as murder and manslaughter, burglary, forgery, and many others, are confined in the penitentiary until their sentences are completed or until they are paroled or pardoned.

The penitentiary is managed by the State Board of Correction. The board has two principal aims. The first is to reform the prisoners, if possible, and prepare them to be useful and law-abiding citizens after leaving prison. In carrying out this aim, they keep first offenders separated from habitual criminals of a vicious kind. The convicts who show promise are given training in various occupational skills so that they will be able to support themselves after their release. The large prison farm near the penitentiary and a number of plants that do special kinds of work aid in carrying out the reform purposes.

The second aim, that of protecting society and punishing lawbreakers, is accomplished by holding hardened criminals and repeaters, those serving second or even third and fourth terms for felonious crimes, in closer confinement for the duration of their sentences. This may seem harsh, but we must recognize that there are certain types of criminals whose release is unwise and who, if released, nearly always commit other crimes as soon as favorable opportunities to do so arise.

State Hospitals. The people of Idaho take pride in the fact that the state has a well-rounded system of caring for its handicapped citizens. Five special hospitals serve the needs of the people in special ways. Four of these are under the management of the newly created State Board of Health, authorized by the 1955 legislature. The new board has charge of two state mental hospitals, the Nampa State School, the State Tuberculosis Hospital, and also of the Youth Conservation Program, organized to deal with the rehabilitation of certain types of juvenile delinquents and with special youth problems. The board also has supervision of the State Health Department.

Mental Hospitals. Idaho has two hospitals to care for mental and nervous patients who are not able to lead normal home and community lives. They are among our oldest institutions. The State Hospital South, located at Blackfoot, dates from late territorial years. The State Hospital North, near Orofino in Clearwater County, was opened for use in 1906. Both are under the management of the State Board of Health.

Both hospitals are under the direct supervision of trained physicians, assisted by specialists and nurses trained in the field of mental and nervous disorders. Farms belonging to the hospitals give an opportunity for healthful outdoor exercise and work suitable for those physically able to profit from such activity, and at the same time enable the hospitals to produce a part of their food supplies. The hospitals are successful in restoring the health of many of their patients, who are then returned to normal life in their own homes.

Nampa State School. Nampa is the location of an institution for another class of unfortunates. To Nampa State School are sent those who were born so lacking in mental ability that they are unable to properly care for themselves. The school provides training, chiefly in manual work, that is of considerable value. Some of the girls and women learn simple household tasks, such as washing dishes, sweeping, easy sewing, and similar chores. The boys and men who are able are taught to work in gardens, take care of lawns, make simple articles of wood, and do other things easy to learn and perform. In this way some inmates become so nearly self-supporting that they are able to return to their families. Those who stay are able to earn a portion of their care and at the same time enjoy the satisfaction that exercise and work provide.

State Tuberculosis Hospital. Tuberculosis, sometimes called consumption, is a dreaded disease of the lungs that annually kills hundreds of thousands of people. Though Idaho is not a major tuberculosis area, there are, nevertheless, hundreds of Idaho people who get this disease, which seems to attack those of high-school and college age more than any other age group. The disease can be cured if discovered in time. This is why tuberculosis tests and X-ray chest examinations are so important.

Home treatment of the disease is usually not satisfactory because special care and diet under highly trained doctors and nurses are required, usually over long periods of time. At Gooding is located Idaho's State Tuberculosis Hospital, where victims of the disease can secure the expert care and treatment needed for their recovery.

Veterans' Hospital. Supported jointly by the state and the Federal government is the Veterans' Hospital, located at Boise. To this institution go many former Idaho servicemen who have injuries or an illness resulting from military service in the armed forces of the United States. A large tract of land in the northern part of Boise is used for hospitals and other buildings adapted to the needs of the patients. Unlike the other state hospitals, the Veterans' Hospital is not managed by the State Board of Health, but has its own director and staff of administrators and workers.

Other State Welfare Institutions. In other special ways, Idaho extends its care and protection to its people. Three institutions for such special services are the Soldiers' Home, the Children's Home Finding and Aid Society, and the Lava Hot Springs Sanitarium.

Soldiers' Home. In our territorial period many veterans of the Union or Federal forces during the Civil War settled in Idaho. Some of them became unable to care for themselves, so in 1893 the legislature provided money for building the Soldiers' Home near Boise. The legislature also set aside twenty-five thousand acres of state land to help support the home.

No longer are the aged veterans of the G.A.R., Grand Army of the Republic, seen under the spreading trees, for they have all answered the final roll call and have been mustered in with the shadowy ranks of comrades long since gone. But the Soldiers' Home lives on, an enduring emblem of our state's care for those who serve when the supreme need arises. Open to veterans of the Indian wars, the Spanish-American War, World War I and II, and the Korean war, it still provides a home for former soldiers, sailors, and Marines who need or desire its refuge.

Children's Homes. Homeless children are not neglected in Idaho. In co-operation with the National Home Finding Society, the Children's Home Finding and Aid Society was organized in Idaho. The first home was established in Boise in 1908. Two years later the present Children's Home in Boise was dedicated, and in 1912 the Lewiston branch children's home was opened. The society cares for orphans and abandoned children, as well as for some who are legally taken away from their parents and turned over to the society. These children are cared for and educated and, when possible, placed by adoption in homes where the new parents will love and care for them.

Lava Hot Springs Sanitarium. Perhaps the state's most unusual welfare and social institution is located at Lava Hot Springs in Bannock County in southeastern Idaho. There a group of hot springs supply a huge volume of water heavily charged with a variety of minerals. The sanitarium maintained there by the state is a popular recreational area. The curative qualities of the waters are useful in the treatment of several diseases and large numbers of people are benefited. This institution is largely self-supporting, but the legislature makes appropriations from time to time for buildings and other improvements, under the direction of a managing board, the Lava Hot Springs Foundation, whose members are appointed by the governor.

IV. OTHER SERVICE ORGANIZATIONS

IDAHO IS JUSTLY PROUD of its many fine service organizations which provide a wide variety of services for the people of the state. Though not supported by public funds, they are among the most useful of our institutions.

Churches. The fine spiritual leadership of churches is too well known to need special attention here. All the leading Christian denominations have churches in Idaho. Hardly a village is so small that it does not have a church house in which the people may gather to worship in complete freedom according to their own religious preference. Most of the well-settled rural communities also have one or more churches to serve the spiritual and social needs of the people. What churches are found in your own city, town, or community?

Youth Organizations. Boys and girls in practically all parts of Idaho have the opportunity of belonging to 4-H Clubs, Boy Scouts, Girl Scouts, Campfire Girls, and similar organizations. Most churches also have special service and social groups in which youth is served, as do the Grange and several other fraternal societies.

The largest boys' service organization is the Boy Scouts of America. There are seven Boy Scout councils in Idaho. The Boise Area Council, Boise, and the Oregon-Idaho Council, Nampa, serve boyhood in southwestern Idaho and eastern Oregon. The Snake River Council, Twin Falls, includes the scout troops of Magic Valley. Scouts of southeastern Idaho belong to the Tendoy Council, Pocatello. Scouts of the Upper Snake

A CONSERVATION PROJECT

4-H club members with baby ring-necked pheasants.

Courtesy Idaho Fish and Game Department

River Valley, the Lost River Valley, and the Salmon area are under the Teton Peaks Council at Idaho Falls. The Lewis and Clark Council, Lewiston, and Idaho Panhandle Council, Coeur d'Alene, look after scout interests in northern Idaho. Together, these councils usually have between twelve thousand and fifteen thousand Idaho boys enrolled in local scout troops in the state. Do you belong to the Boy Scouts, Girl Scouts, or Campfire Girls?

Almost all the important agricultural counties have active 4-H Clubs. These are part of the field agricultural services maintained by the Extension Division of the University of Idaho. Activities are supervised by county club leaders, county agents, and local adult leaders in the communities.

Fraternal Societies and Service Organizations. All these are well distributed in Idaho. Among the fraternal societies are the Masons, Odd Fellows, Elks, and Moose. All these carry on welfare programs which include charities, hospitals for crippled children, and other social and welfare work. Both the Masons and the Elks have crippled children's hospitals in Boise.

The Red Cross has chapters in almost every county in the state. The Salvation Army gives help and encouragement to the underprivileged and the down-and-outers in the larger cities. The Y.M.C.A. and the Y.W.C.A. are semi-charitable organizations that render useful services.

Commercial clubs are found in practically all Idaho cities. At the top of these businessmen's groups are the Idaho State Chamber of Commerce and the Junior Chamber of Commerce, with headquarters in Boise. Rotary Clubs, Kiwanis Clubs, Lions Clubs, and other special organizations are also found in the leading cities.

The Parent-Teacher Association is a very active organization in Idaho. Its purpose is the improvement of youth and childhood through better schools, better home conditions, and better community living.

Women's clubs are important and render many worth-while services. Among the leaders in this field are the Business and Professional Women, the P.E.O., the Delta Kappa Gamma, War Mothers, American Association of University Women, and a dozen or so others, all useful in their respective fields.

Farmers' Organizations. Two organizations of farm folk are strong and important in Idaho. The Grange has been active since mid-territorial years and has local groups in most of the farming sections of the state. The Farm Bureau, though not so strong as the Grange, has much influence, especially in political and business policies affecting farm income.

Livestock associations have been organized in many counties. The Cattlemen's Association is especially active in range management and in protecting ranchers against rustling, or the stealing of range stock.

V. PROBLEMS CONNECTED WITH INTOXICATING LIQUORS, NARCOTICS, AND GAMBLING

MAYBE THE EARLY CAVE MAN DIDN'T DISCOVER how to make intoxicating liquors, but certainly they were first prepared far back in the dim beginnings of human life. The use or, rather, the *abuse* of alcoholic drinks has brought great misery to mankind. The control of the liquor business and its sister evils, narcotics and gambling, has provided organized government with some of its most difficult problems.

Idaho's Liquor Problem. Our state legislature has tried in several ways to control the liquor business in Idaho. In early statehood liquor sellers were licensed and allowed to operate saloons. Then counties were given the right to control the sale of intoxicating liquors under a system of local option, or home rule. Some counties permitted liquor sales and others did not. Finally, in 1915, the legislature passed a law forbidding the manufacture or sale of intoxicating beverages in the state.

In 1919 the Eighteenth Amendment to the Constitution of the United States outlawed liquor in the entire nation. Moonshining, the making of illegal liquors, and bootlegging, the sale of illegal liquors, then became common in many parts of the country, especially in the larger cities. Finally, in 1933, the Twenty-first Amendment was adopted, repealing the Eighteenth Amendment, and Idaho was again faced with the necessity of making new laws to regulate the sale and use of intoxicants.

State Liquor Dispensary System. In 1935 the Idaho Legislature created a system of state liquor stores. Under this plan, all intoxicating drinks[1] bought or sold in the state must be secured through the state stores.

In 1947 the legislature passed a law permitting the sale of liquor by the drink in taverns, as they are generally called. But tavern operators must secure a liquor license and must purchase their supply of "wet goods" through the state dispensary system. Further, such taverns are

[1]Beer is not classed under Idaho law as an intoxicating liquor.

not permitted to operate outside incorporated cities and villages, so that they will be under police supervision.

Narcotic Drugs. A narcotic drug is one that causes sleep, stupor, or dullness, chiefly by its effect on the brain and nerves. The use of opiates, or narcotic drugs, is harmful and dangerous to the user, and sometimes to others as well. These drugs injure the health, deaden the senses, slow down mental and muscular reactions, increase accidents, and sometimes lead to the committing of crimes. Taken in large quantities or over long periods of time, they may cause insanity and death. All are habit-forming in greater or lesser degree. Among them are alcoholic liquors, opium, morphine, cocaine, and marihuana, usually pronounced merry-wanna.

Gambling, Slot Machines, and Punchboards. Various forms of gambling, including slot machines, have at various times been permitted in Idaho. When licensed by the state and municipalities, they bring in a steady stream of revenue. For this reason, some Idaho cities have depended upon such devices to produce income needed for civic improvements and for other purposes.

After prolonged debate, the 1953 legislature passed a law making slot machines illegal in Idaho. The law was challenged in the courts and in 1954 the issue was carried to the Idaho Supreme Court.

This court ruled that slot machines, punchboards, and other devices that sometimes pay off in cash to lucky winners are lotteries and as such are forbidden by the state constitution. That seems to have settled the matter for the time being, but attempts may be made later to change the constitution so such devices can again be legally operated. Whether we are for slot machines and similar devices or against them, we can at least enjoy this clever rhyme contributed by "M. D." to the *Pocatello Tribune,* now the *Idaho State Journal:*

> Sing a song of sixpence,
> A pocket full of dough,
> Four and twenty slot machines
> Standing in a row.
> Now your pocket's empty,
> You'll never get it back.
> Wasn't that a silly way
> To spend your hard-earned jack?

* * * * *

The people of Idaho, as this unit shows, have given a great deal of attention to improving their educational, social, and spiritual opportunities and in caring for the needy and unfortunate citizens. This regard for others and the many organizations and agencies enriching life in the state are as important as our great natural resources in making Idaho such a delightful place in which to live.

Courtesy Idaho Power Company, Boise

MOST OF IDAHO'S AGRICULTURE DEPENDS UPON THE WATERS STORED BY VARIOUS IRRIGATION PROJECTS

Significant Events in State and Nation

How progress and developments in Idaho have kept pace with national affairs; and how national and world events have made themselves felt in Idaho.

NATIONAL AND WORLD EVENTS often have far-reaching effects in the states that make up our Federal Republic. Not only national affairs but world affairs as well have deeply influenced our way of life and the course of history in Idaho. Organized labor and labor problems, economic conditions at home and abroad, wars among the nations, Federal activities within the states—all these and many others are conditions affecting the people of Idaho and the other states in the Union. In this unit we shall notice briefly some of the most important conditions and events which have influenced the course of affairs here in our own state.

I. ORGANIZED LABOR AND LABOR PROBLEMS

THOUGH ONE MURDER in Idaho that shocked the entire nation was the outgrowth of labor troubles, the state as a whole has been but little disturbed by disputes between employers and workers. Strikes and violence have been rare, mainly because we are principally an agricultural state and a state of small business establishments. We have had few large employers, comparatively little manufacturing, and not many large-scale industrial enterprises. We have, however, sometimes felt the effects of labor disturbances in other places and, on a few occasions, have had labor difficulties of our own.

Riots in the Mining Districts. Our most serious labor troubles occurred in the Wood River mines of southern Idaho and in the Coeur d'Alene mines of the Panhandle. Miners, dissatisfied with wages and working conditions, armed themselves and seized some of the mines by force. The trouble in the Wood River district was soon settled, but it lasted for several years in the Coeur d'Alene mining section of the Panhandle. In a pitched battle at Gem between miners and guards, six men were killed and several more wounded. Finally, striking miners seized a Northern Pacific train, loaded it with dynamite, and blew up the Bunker Hill and Sullivan mine. At last conditions became so out of hand that Governor Steunenberg placed the Coeur d'Alene district under martial law. National guardsmen and United States soldiers took control and order was gradually restored.

A labor union, the International Workers of the World, usually called the I.W.W., had grown very strong. The members spread through the Northwest and led a series of bloody strikes, not only among the miners but in lumber camps and along the water fronts of important Pacific coast cities.

Murder of a Former Governor. The leaders of the "Wobblies," as the I.W.W. members were commonly called, had never forgiven the Idaho governor for using force in stopping riots in the Coeur d'Alene mining region. After his second term as governor, Steunenberg retired to his home in Caldwell. There, in 1905, he was murdered by a bomb that had been attached to his front gate so that it would explode when the gate was opened.

This cowardly murder aroused Idaho as no crime before or since has ever done. Governor Frank Gooding immediately offered a state reward of $5,000 for the arrest of the murderer, and other sources quickly raised the total reward to $25,000.

A stranger, registered in a Caldwell hotel under the name of Thomas Hogan, was suspected. After his arrest, Harry Orchard, for that is the name by which he was known, confessed the crime, and said that he had been employed for the purpose by William ("Big Bill") Haywood, Charles H. Moyer, and George A. Pettibone, all formerly connected with the Coeur d'Alene riots. The three men Orchard named as his bosses were arrested in Colorado and brought to Idaho for trial.

Seldom has a trial anywhere in the United States attracted more attention. More than half a hundred reporters representing several of the largest newspapers of the nation were on hand to keep the public informed. Clarence Darrow, then America's most noted criminal lawyer, came from Chicago to conduct the defense. He was assisted by Edgar Wilson, John F. Nugent, and K. I. Perky, all able Idaho attorneys and all at some time in their lives members of Congress. The prosecution was headed by James H. Hawley, later to fill the governor's chair. His chief assistant was a brilliant young Boise lawyer named William E. Borah, whose powerful address to the jury gave him a national reputation as an orator and paved the way for his early election to the United States Senate.

Since there was little to connect Haywood, Moyer, and Pettibone with the murder except Harry Orchard's unsupported testimony, they were not convicted, though there was little doubt of their guilt. Orchard, who confessed not only the Steunenberg murder but many others, was sentenced to death. Because he turned state's evidence, his sentence was changed to life imprisonment in the state penitentiary at Boise. There, until his death in 1954, when he was an old, gray-haired man, he paid the penalty for his terrible crime.

Idaho Labor Unions and Labor Warfare. Today, organized labor in Idaho, especially strong in the Pocatello area and the lumbering and mining sections of northern Idaho, works through its local unions. Most of these union groups are a part of the American Federation of Labor, the AF of L, with headquarters in Boise. A few local unions are part of the CIO, the Congress of Industrial Organizations, and of the United Mine, Mill, and Smelter Workers. Labor unions have done much to secure higher wages and better working conditions for wage earners.

The welfare of working people in Idaho is now promoted in several ways.

There is a State Department of Labor, headed by a commissioner appointed by the governor to administer state labor laws and co-operate with the office of the United States Secretary of Labor.

II. BUSINESS UPS AND DOWNS

BOOMS AND PANICS, also called periods of inflation and periods of depression, have occurred from time to time in our history. During booms, or periods of inflation, there is plenty of money in circulation. Business is good, factories are busy, wages are high. During panics, or depressions, the opposite is true. Money is scarce, business is poor, factories are often closed, and prices and wages are low. Both conditions may have many causes, some of which are usually nation-wide, or even world wide.

Good Times and Hard Times in Idaho. As we learned in earlier units, times were not always good during Idaho's territorial years. You remember, no doubt, that a period of hard times forced the silver mines to close during the 1870's, a disaster from which the Silver City mining district never fully recovered.

When the state was only three years old, another very severe depression gripped the United States. Factories closed, large numbers of banks failed, and millions of people were without work. Farmers and stockmen could hardly give their products away. The depression lasted two years or more and Idaho, along with the rest of the nation, suffered severely.

By 1898 general business conditions

had become good again in the United States. For three decades there was a great and steady business growth in the nation, which was further stimulated by two wars which occurred during this period, the Spanish-American War and World War I.

Idaho shared the general progress of these thirty years. Our population increased from less than 160,000 to more than 440,000 and twenty-three new counties were organized. Most main roads in our present system of highways were laid out and largely constructed, except for modern hard-surfacing, and many miles of railroads, especially branch lines, were built. Hundreds of thousands of acres were placed under irrigation and other types of farming added to Idaho's importance as an agricultural state. All in all, this was a very favorable period in Idaho's history.

The Great Depression. The long period of good times for the nation and for Idaho ended in 1929. Almost without warning, stocks, bonds, and similar forms of investments took a tremendous drop in Wall Street and other financial centers. Fortunes were wiped out and thousands of speculators and investors were ruined. This was followed swiftly by widespread bank failures. Thousands of business and manufacturing establishments closed their doors. Prices of nearly everything dropped rapidly and soon millions of people were without work.

The Great Depression, as it is known, lasted for about ten years. In fact, not until the United States was forced into the second World War did it completely end. The history of the depression in Idaho is so closely tied up with national and world events that it deserves a special section of its own, which will follow soon.

Inflation Period of World War II. When the United States went to war against Japan, Germany, and Italy in 1941, business immediately became very active and prices and wages began to rise sharply. These conditions were caused by a number of things: (1) Large numbers of men left industry to enter the armed forces, creating a shortage of workers. (2) The government bought huge quantities of many kinds of goods and materials needed by the Army, Navy, and Air

Force. (3) War factories offered high wages to get the workers they needed to prepare the nation for an all-out war in the shortest possible time. (4) There was a great decrease in food production in the war-torn countries of Europe and Asia, creating a good market for practically all agricultural products of the United States and other countries in the Western Hemisphere.

The surrender of the nations against which we were at war did not end the war boom of the 1940's. Soon the war in Korea began, causing a still higher rise in prices and wages. As these lines are written, in 1955, the period of inflation which began with the second World War is still continuing, though prices and wages are apparently leveling off and becoming more stable. Idaho, along with the rest of the nation, is feeling the effects in higher prices and in the higher taxes we must pay to keep our nation strong.

III. THE "NEW DEAL" AND THE "FAIR DEAL" IN IDAHO

THE ELECTION OF FRANKLIN D. ROOSEVELT AS PRESIDENT in 1932 introduced a new era in government, an era in which peacetime spending and the increase in government services rose to a higher point than ever before in our history. Efforts of President Hoover to check the depression had not succeeded. With Roosevelt, the Democrats came into complete control of the national government. Idaho had also chosen a Democratic administration, headed by Governor C. Ben Ross, and so was in a position to co-operate fully with national plans to fight the

depression and attempt to restore normal conditions.

The Banking Holiday. The first action taken by President Roosevelt was to close all banks for a time until their condition could be investigated. People could not use their bank accounts and most of them had a difficult time carrying on. Business came to a virtual standstill.

As rapidly as banks could be examined, they were allowed to open again for business, if found in good financial condition. Only a very few banks in Idaho were compelled to close permanently, and business of all kinds soon began to operate again as well as conditions allowed.

Alphabetical Government Agencies. Beginning in 1933 and continuing for several years, Congress enacted a series of laws planned to overcome, or at least lessen, the evils of the depression. The government organizations set up to accomplish this purpose became known as "alphabetical agencies" because they were usually designated by the first letters of their names.

Nearly all these alphabetical agencies of the Federal government operated in Idaho, as they did in the other states of the nation. The National Industrial Recovery Act (NIRA) imposed a rigid control over business and the relations between employers and employees. The Public Works Administration (PWA) and the Works Progress Administration (WPA) provided employment through public building and improvement projects, such as building schoolhouses, constructing and improving roads, streets, water systems, sewer systems, airports and airfields, and so on. The Civilian Conservation Corps (CCC) employed young men between eighteen and twenty-five years of age in making improvements in the national forests and on public lands. The Agricultural Adjustment Administration (AAA), the Farm Credit Administration (FCA), and the Home Owners' Loan Corporation (HOLC) were organized to aid farmers and home owners. These and other agencies were aimed at ending the depression and bringing back better times. Nearly all of them were discontinued when they had

Courtesy U.S. Forest Service   *Photo by Paul S. Bieler*

PUBLIC CAMPGROUND IMPROVED BY THE CCC

Among New Deal agencies in Idaho, one of the most useful was the Civilian Conservation Corps. By their conservation and improvement work in the national forests and on public lands, they did much to benefit forestry, grazing, recreation, roads, streams, and wildlife in Idaho.

either done what they were organized to do or had proven unsuccessful.

Foreign Policies. In foreign affairs Franklin D. Roosevelt's administration, generally called the "New Deal," began to give American aid of many kinds to so-called "backward nations" and to countries left in a poor condition by the outbreak of World War II. When President Roosevelt died in 1945 and was succeeded by Vice-President Harry S Truman, the same general policies were followed both at home and abroad. The "Fair Deal," as Truman called his administration, even enlarged some of the New Deal policies. Vast sums of money were required by the government to meet our problems in the United States and aid in foreign activities. The net result in Idaho was to raise already high taxes to a still higher level.

New Pilots for the Ship of State. The New Deal–Fair Deal era of Democratic control of the national government came to at least a temporary end after the elections of 1952. The Republican candidate, General Dwight D. Eisenhower, was elected President and both houses of Congress were given Republican majorities by a very narrow margin. Idaho, too, elected nearly all Republican candidates for state offices, including strong Republican majorities in both branches of the state legislature.

In the 1954 off-year election, so called because the Presidency was not at stake, the voters elected a Democratic Congress, though the margin of Democratic control was small, especially in the Senate. In Idaho, however, Robert E. Smylie, the Republican candidate for governor, was elected and the Republicans retained control of both branches of the state legislature.

During the twenty years that the Democrats had the responsibility of leading in the management of national affairs, from 1933 to 1953, the Republicans and the Democrats were fairly even in strength in Idaho. As a result, both political parties have shared in the management of state affairs. That this management has generally been sound is proven by the fact that Idaho was, in 1954, one of the very few states that was out of debt and that operated its state government on a cash basis. This is a matter of pride to us at a time when many state governments have gone deeply into debt and when our huge national debt has climbed to more than two hundred and seventy billion dollars.

IV. IDAHO AT WAR

IDAHO, AS ONE OF THE FORTY-EIGHT STATES, has four times had the unpleasant duty of going to war. Hating war and loving peace, we have had no other choice when our national security has been threatened.

The Spanish-American War. When our country went to war against Spain in 1898, an Idaho regiment was quickly recruited and sent to the Philippine Islands. Following the defeat of Spain and our purchase of the islands, some of the Filipinos refused to yield to American authority. The First Idaho Regiment was part of the forces called upon to put down the revolt.

In the first engagement Major Edward McConville, the regimental commander, was killed almost as the battle began. Enraged, the Idaho regiment launched a savage charge against great odds and quickly drove the Filipinos from the field, inflicting heavy losses upon them. The wild charge prompted General King, the American commander, to say, "There go the Idaho savages and all ———— can't stop them."

After a few months' fighting, the

Philippine insurrection ended and the Idahoans returned home. Among them was a young officer, Captain Frank W. Hunt, who soon thereafter was elected governor of the state.

The First World War. Less than twenty years passed before Idaho was again called on to send its sons to war. This time the conflict was a desperate, bloody, and gigantic struggle involving almost all of Europe, much of Asia and Africa, and most of North America. It began in Europe in 1914 but the United States was not drawn into the struggle for nearly three years. However, in 1917, Congress declared war on Germany, and Idaho, along with the other states, was automatically involved in the conflict.

Idahoans in the War. During World War I, 105,337 Idaho men registered for service and about 20,000 of them served in the Army, Navy, and Marine Corps, more than half of them being sent to Europe. Other thousands volunteered for the various services.

Thousands of Idahoans took part in the fierce battles that occurred in the last two years of the war. Finally the Central Powers, as Germany and her allies were called, were beaten. On November 11, 1918, at eleven o'clock in the morning, an armistice was declared and the war was over.

The end of the war brought delirious joy. In every city, town, and hamlet in Idaho, as in every other part of our land, wildly cheering throngs quickly gathered. The whole population of our state, it seemed, stopped whatever tasks they were engaged in and assembled in hundreds of impromptu celebrations. Ever

since that time Armistice Day, changed in 1954 to "Veterans' Day," has been one of our national holidays.

But all was not joy. The terrible war took a heavy toll. Of the thousands of Idahoans answering the call to the colors, 783 paid the supreme sacrifice and hundreds more suffered from disease and battle wounds.

On the Home Front. Not on battlefields alone did Idaho serve. The people purchased millions of dollars' worth of war bonds and thrift and savings stamps. They gave liberally to the Red Cross, the Salvation Army, the Y.M.C.A., and other organizations serving our men in the armed forces. Even the schools were active in various wartime activities and most school children of the state bought savings stamps to help support the war effort.

Veterans' Welfare Bureau and Servicemen's Organizations. In 1919 the Idaho Legislature created the Veterans' Welfare Bureau to serve wounded and former servicemen who became ill. This organization, as we learned in the preceding unit, maintains a Veterans' Hospital at Boise and still serves the needs of war veterans, whose numbers have been greatly increased as a result of the second World War and the Korean war.

Following the first World War, returned servicemen created several organizations to keep alive their spirit of unity, to serve the interests of their members, and to give more effective peacetime services to their states and their country. The largest and most effective of these is the American Legion. Posts of this nationwide organization are found in

Courtesy Veterans' Administration, Boise, Idaho

many cities and towns in Idaho. From
the ranks of the Legion have come several of our recent Idaho governors and
other state officers. Perhaps your own
father or someone closely related to you is
a Legionnaire. Ask him to tell you how
this organization serves in the community, the state, and the nation.

The Second World War. After the
first World War, conditions in Europe
remained unsettled. In Germany political
changes brought Adolf Hitler into power
as a dictator. A similar development in
Italy made Mussolini the real ruler in
that nation. The two dictators formed an
alliance and the stage was set for World
War II, the mightiest conflict of all time.

As in the first World War, the United
States hoped to keep clear of the trouble.
Japan, however, had entered the war on
the side of Germany and Italy, and,
without warning, suddenly sent a fleet of
airplanes to bomb Pearl Harbor, the
great American naval base in the Hawaiian Islands, destroying 19 American
naval vessels, 127 airplanes, and killing

more than 2,000 men. This happened
December 7, 1941, and we had no course
left except to defend ourselves. Congress
declared war and once more Idahoans
answered the call and rallied to the defense of our country.

From the beginning to the end of the
gigantic struggle, Idahoans worked un-
tiringly in the war effort. Several military
establishments were set up in the state.
Our young men and women answered
the call to arms by the thousands. Other
thousands served in the factories making
ships, airplanes, weapons, munitions,
and all sorts of war materials and supplies. A huge sum of Idaho money was
spent to help bring the war to a victorious
end.

In the Armed Services. More than
60,000 Idaho men and women wore the
uniforms of the various branches of the
armed services, including women's aux-
iliaries. Records show that 1,279 of them
lost their lives in military action, while
hundreds more died of disease and other
causes. Many more were wholly or

partially disabled as a result of wounds or sickness. The table which follows shows the number of Idahoans in the various services during the war.

opposed to any further spread of Communism and President Truman immediately ordered United States forces to go to the aid of the South Koreans. Amer-

Table No. 4

IDAHO IN WORLD WAR II*

Branch of Service	Army and Air Forces	Women's Auxiliaries	Total
Army Department	39,000	799	39,799
Navy Department	17,440		17,440
Marines	3,136	570	3,706
Coast Guard	402		402
Totals	59,978	1,369	61,347

*Sources: War Department, report to July 31, 1946, as released April 10, 1947.
Department of the Army, Office of Adjutant General, January 31, 1946.
Compiled by Bureau of Naval Personnel for December 1, 1941, to January 1, 1947.
Compiled by Casualty Section, Office of Public Information, Navy Department.

Idaho Support for the War. Besides the men and women in the military services, Idahoans served in many other ways to make the war effort successful. They invested a total of $215,000,000 in war bonds, exceeding our state's quota in each of the eight campaigns to sell bonds to the people. Thousands of Idaho people worked in war factories. The production of food crops and livestock was greatly increased. Children in all parts of the state tended war gardens and helped in salvage drives to collect scrap metal and paper. In every way possible the people on the home front demonstrated their patriotism and their willingness to serve their communities, the state, and the nation during the war crisis.

War in Korea. In 1950 Communist armies of North Korea suddenly invaded South Korea. The United States was opposed to any further spread of Communism and President Truman immediately ordered United States forces to go to the aid of the South Koreans. Americans, with some help from other countries belonging to the United Nations, continued to resist the North Korean and Chinese Communist armies until 1953. A truce between the opposing forces was then arranged and, in 1954, details of a possible peaceful ending of the conflict, which has cost hundreds of thousands of lives, began to be slowly worked out, though no actual treaty of peace has as yet been agreed upon by the two opposing sides in the conflict.

Idaho War Heroes. War and the crisis of battle almost always bring outstanding examples of remarkable self-sacrifice and heroism. In recognition of such brave acts, the Congressional Medal of Honor, our highest military award, is sometimes given. To the close of 1954, records show that eight Idahoans have received this distinguished award, as follows:

"For conspicuous gallantry and intrepidity at the risk of his life
above and beyond the call of duty."

Thomas C. Neibaur, Sugar City	World War I
*Leonard C. Brostrom, Preston	World War II
*Nathan Van Noy, Jr., Preston	World War II
Lloyd G. McCarter, St. Maries	World War II
David B. Bleak, Shelley	Korean War
*James E. Johnson, Pocatello	Korean War
*Dan D. Schoonover, Boise	Korean War
Reginald R. Myers, formerly of Boise	Korean War

*Killed in action and medal awarded posthumously to closest living relative.

Senator Henry Dworshak called attention to the fact that of seventy-one Congressional Medals of Honor awarded to those taking part in the Korean war, four were to Idaho heroes.

Without subtracting anything from the glory and valor of the other Medal of Honor winners, let us look at the story of Junior Van Noy, as published in the Pacific Edition of *Yank,* the army newspaper. Van Noy had the reputation of being a quiet, retiring sort of boy who said little and that without the use of profane language so common among soldiers. In fact, a sergeant in his outfit said, "We kind of figured him as a mama's boy—which just goes to show how wrong you can be."

Junior was suffering from an infection in both ears and was being treated at the first-aid station three times a day. The doctors tried to send him away for treatment but, knowing how short his company was of gunners, he refused to go and stuck to his gun position on Scarlet Beach landing near Finschhafen, in New Guinea. Before the action in which he lost his life, he shot down a low-level Jap bomber which came within reach of his

Browning 50-caliber machine gun, and about this time he received five shrapnel wounds. Still he refused to give up his post. The rest of the story, which began when three Japanese landing barges appeared off Scarlet Beach, is as it was published in *Yank:*

Two barges landed right in front of Pvt. Van Noy's 50-caliber position. They beached just 15 yards away. The barges' ramps slowly began to fall. Japs started throwing out grenades by the handful. Pvt. Van Noy held his fire.

When the ramps were all the way down, when the Japs blew their bugles and began to charge, Pvt. Van Noy pressed his finger on the trigger and cut loose. The first to fall were two Jap officers trying to scorch Van Noy out of his position with flame throwers. The remaining Japs fell on their faces and continued throwing grenades and firing.

Aussie Bren gunners some yards behind Van Noy's pit began shouting to him to "Get the — out of there, you bloody fool." Seeing the grenades burst all about the pit, Sgt. Fuina yelled, too, ordering him to get out of his exposed position.

Pvt. Van Noy's loader, Cpl. Poppa, crawled from the pit with a shattered leg trailing behind him. He thought Van Noy would follow. But Pvt. Van Noy changed belts and kept on firing.

Sgt. Fuina saw a grenade land squarely in the pit. Van Noy's stream of tracers continued to rake up and down the water's edge, where by this time the Japs were frantically trying to dig into the sand.

Then there were other flashes and Van Noy's gun ceased firing.

Until dawn the firing crackled around the beached barges. . . . When the sun rose out of the Bismarck Sea, a skirmish line of infantrymen moved down to the beach to mop up the remnants. There weren't any remnants to mop. Junior's Browning had accounted for at least half of the 40 who landed. Aussie gunners and Sgt. Fuina's 37 did the rest. . . .

It was a sad lot of victorious soldiers who finally went over to Pvt. Van Noy's weapon pit. Pvt. Van Noy was the only Allied soldier killed in the action. The first grenade in the pit had torn off his left leg. It took a rifle bullet between his eyes to stop him. Even then, the men wondered if he hadn't continued to fire after death. Every bullet in his gun had been fired. All his American buddies and the 20 Australians who fought with Junior Van Noy agreed with Sgt. Fuina, when he looked down at the dead soldier's body and said:

"That kid had more guts than all the rest of the d—— army put together."

That seems to about size it up.

V. GOVERNMENT INSTALLATIONS IN IDAHO

As war gripped our nation, our problems of national defense and safety became more acute. The government found more establishments of special kinds were needed to train our military forces and to make and assemble the huge quantities of equipment and supplies to carry on the war.

Several establishments of this kind were located in Idaho. Two are still in use. Others have been disposed of or abandoned, as the need for them no longer justified their cost.

Naval Ordnance Plant. Most important of these establishments built during the second World War was the Naval Ordnance Plant at Pocatello. Costing about $35,000,000, this was at first used to repair and manufacture guns for our naval vessels. At present it is doing special work, some of it of a secret kind. It also serves as a storage depot for large quantities of naval equipment and supplies of many kinds. Commanded by naval officers, it normally employs hundreds of workers, most of them former servicemen.

Mountain Home Air Base. In the Elmore County desert southwest of Mountain Home has been constructed one of the nation's largest military air bases. This great airfield has some of the longest runways in the world. It is connected with the city of Mountain Home by a government-built railroad and an oiled highway. Several thousand military and civilian personnel are regularly stationed at this important base. Former servicemen are given preference in the employment of needed workers.

Temporary Installations. Many temporary establishments, located in various parts of the United States, were needed for special purposes during World War II. Several of these were located in Idaho but are no longer needed for their original purposes. Some of them have been completely abandoned.

The Farragut Naval Base at the southern end of Lake Pend Oreille, used to give Navy men their "boot," or first, training, is now a wildlife research center and preserve, supervised by the Idaho Fish and Game Department, with the assistance of the United States Fish and Wildlife Service. The Pocatello Army Air Base, now Phillips Field, is Pocatello's municipal airport and landing field. Gowen Field Army Air Base, near Boise, is also an airport and an industrial area belonging to Boise. The United States Department of Defense has, however, reserved certain military rights at both Phillips Field and Gowen Field.

The Hunt Japanese Relocation Camp in Jerome County once housed about ten thousand displaced Japanese and Americans of Japanese ancestry who were temporarily placed there for security reasons while our nation was at war with Japan. The area is now the center of a newly developed irrigated farming district.

A camp for German prisoners of war was located west of Rupert in Minidoka County. Two prison camps for conscientious objectors, as we call people who refuse to enter military service for religious reasons, were located in Bannock County and Valley County.

National Reactor Testing Station. Latest and greatest of the Federal installations in Idaho is the National Reactor Testing Station of the Atomic Energy Commission. Located on a huge reserve, most of which was formerly the testing range of the Naval Ordnance Plant, the area includes 439,000 acres in the desert southeast of Arco. It is one of a national chain of establishments engaged in atomic energy research and experimental work. The Idaho Operations Office of the U.S. Atomic Energy Commission is located at Idaho Falls. In operation in 1954 were four reactors and a chemical processing plant.

The Experimental Breeder Reactor uses enriched uranium as a fuel. It has already been proven in this plant that fuel (uranium) as it is used up will produce more fuel (plutonium) than was originally consumed. This is considered one of the greatest scientific discoveries of all time and promises an inexhaustible supply of fuel for future use.

The Materials Testing Reactor is used to test the effect of atomic radiation on various materials needed in building sundry types of reactors and other atomic installations.

The Submarine Thermal Reactor experiments in the development of nuclear engines to provide power for submarines. As a result of experiments here and in other similar plants, the United States has already launched the *Nautilus,* the world's first atomic-powered submarine. This reactor station is also experimenting in power for industrial use, and has employed atomic or nuclear processes in the production of electricity.

The Aircraft Nuclear Propulsion Reactor carries on experiments in developing atomic power for aircraft. If successfully worked out, this promises to open a new era in air travel and transportation.

The Chemical Processing Plant is designed to recover or reclaim nuclear fuel from used fuel materials. It also conducts experiments in finding ways and materials for safely building and operating atomic plants in areas of dense population.

The map which follows shows the location of the atomic preserve. For reasons of safety, the various plants and buildings needed in carrying on the activities of

HEADQUARTERS BUILDING OF THE IDAHO OPERATIONS, U.S. ATOMIC ENERGY COMMISSION

The National Reactor Testing Station is located about forty miles west of Idaho Falls, on U.S. Highway 20.

Courtesy Idaho Falls Chamber of Commerce and Melville's Studio

the National Reactor Testing Station are placed at some distance from each other. Both the grounds and the various estab-lishments are closed to the public except for officially approved and planned visits to the station.

VI. TRANSPORTATION AND COMMUNICATION GO MODERN

IDAHO IN 1890 was a child of the frontier, with frontier facilities for travel, transportation, and communication. There were, as we learned in Unit 8, railroads crossing southern and eastern Idaho and the Northern Pacific had completed its main line across the Panhandle. Wagon roads of poor quality existed in the settled communities and a few bridges spanned the main streams. As a whole, both travelers and shippers faced many hardships and difficulties. Our present transportation facilities, however, are part of a nationwide network of railroads, highways, and airlines.

A geographical factor was originally responsible for railroads entering Idaho. The state reaches south from Canada almost five hundred miles, and railroads from the East and Middle West leading to the great seaports of the Northwest simply couldn't go around Idaho. Also, nature placed within the borders of Idaho two of the best natural transportation routes in the West: the Snake River Valley in southern Idaho and the Purcell Trench in the northern part of the state. Most of the railroads of Idaho are shown on Map No. 1.

Panhandle Railroads. Two years after Idaho became a state, the Great Northern Railway extended its main line across the Panhandle and pushed on to the Puget Sound seaports. A few years later the Chicago, Milwaukee, St. Paul and Pacific completed its main line to the Pacific, crossing the Idaho Panhandle south of the Great Northern line. A fourth important railroad, the Spokane International Railway, also built many

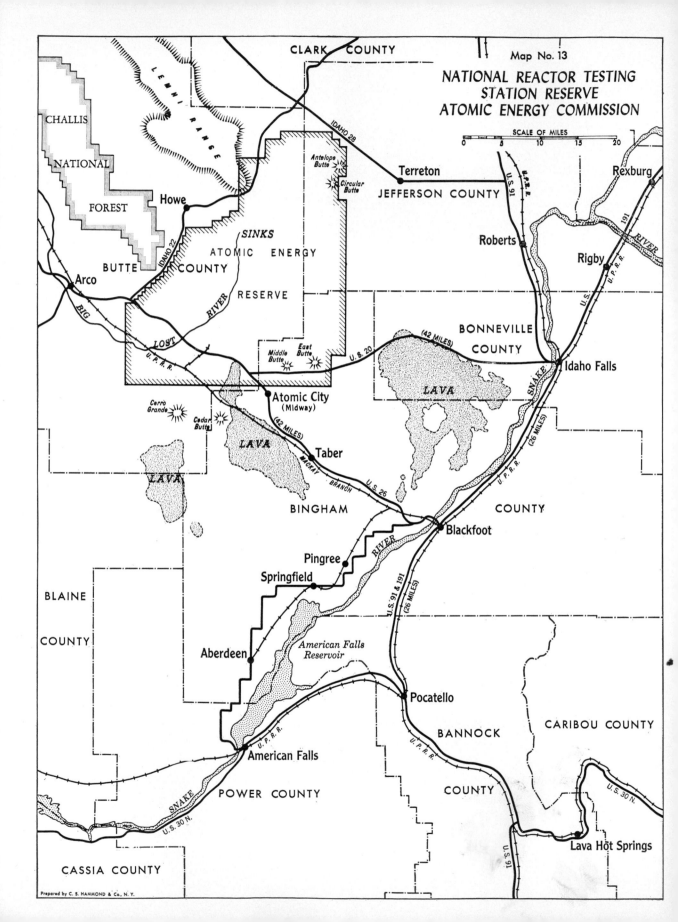

miles of rail lines through some of the finest forests of the Panhandle. In addition to opening northern Idaho to settlement and industrial development, these railroads tapped the vast timber resources of the region and made lumbering one of the major industries of the Panhandle.

Several important branch railroads also serve northern Idaho. The Camas Prairie Railroad, owned jointly by the Union Pacific and the Northern Pacific, extends from Lewiston to Grangeville through the fine agricultural lands of the Nez Perce Prairie and Camas Prairie. A branch line to Stites on the Clearwater River, and one to Orofino and Headquarters, handles a large volume of saw logs and other forest products. Other short lines reach east and west to Nezperce and Winchester. Another comparatively short railroad, the Washington, Idaho, and Montana Railway, extends from Palouse, Washington, to Bovill, in Latah County, nearly all of its forty-nine miles passing through a combination region of forests and farmlands that is part of the famous Palouse country.

Union Pacific Lines. The Union Pacific System is the leader among Idaho railroads, with a total mileage in the state many times as large as all other lines combined. Not only does it serve all of southern Idaho, but its lines from the state of Washington reach into the famed Coeur d'Alene mining district in Shoshone County and into the fertile Palouse country around Moscow. We recall, too, that the Union Pacific is also joint owner of the Camas Prairie lines.

The Idaho railroads now part of the Union Pacific were the original Utah & Northern from Ogden, Utah, to Helena, Montana; the Oregon Short Line, connecting Granger, Wyoming, with Huntington, Oregon; and the North Idaho lines of the Oregon-Washington Railroad and Navigation Company.

To the east the Union Pacific System gives direct connections from Idaho to Chicago, Omaha, Kansas City, and Denver. Western lines reach Los Angeles, Portland, and Seattle. The main north-south line across eastern Idaho connects Salt Lake City and Ogden with Butte by way of Pocatello and Idaho Falls.

Besides the main lines, the following branch lines in southern and eastern Idaho, all part of the Union Pacific, serve most of the Snake River region: Boise and Nampa to McCall; Weiser to New Meadows; Payette to Emmett; Caldwell to Wilder; Nyssa, Oregon, to Homedale and Marsing; Shoshone to Ketchum and Sun Valley; Shoshone to Hill City; North Side Branch, Minidoka to Bliss; South Side Branch, Minidoka to Rupert, Burley, Twin Falls, and Buhl; Twin Falls to Wells, Nevada; Blackfoot to Aberdeen; Blackfoot to Mackay; Idaho Falls to West Yellowstone; Idaho Falls to Victor. Other short branch lines that do not operate regularly serve agricultural districts in the upper Snake River Valley and Magic Valley. The newest branch line was constructed in Bingham County in 1948 from Fort Hall to the Simplot phosphate mines on the Fort Hall Indian Reservation, where one of Idaho's newest towns, Gay, is growing up.

Among Union Pacific projects in Idaho in recent years, two are outstanding: (1) the development of the internationally famous Sun Valley resort, which has be-

POCATELLO

Air view of the Gate City showing Union Pacific yards, among the largest railroad repair and maintenance shops between the Mississippi and the Pacific coast.

Courtesy Pocatello Chamber of Commerce

come one of the country's finest winter sports areas and one of the West's most popular meeting places for conventions of all kinds; (2) the retarder yards in Pocatello, among the most modern and efficient switching yards in the United States, completed at a cost of more than $3,000,000 and which have recently been further enlarged.

Public Utilities in Idaho's Economy. It would be almost impossible to overemphasize the importance of railroads in Idaho's business life. Not only does long-distance transportation and travel, as well as much local business of that kind, depend mainly on the railroads, but their share in the economic life of the state is very great. They give employment to thousands of workers and their payrolls are an important factor in maintaining business. They move Idaho products to outside markets rapidly and efficiently. Their tax valuation of nearly seventy million dollars enables the state, counties, municipalities, and school districts to lean heavily on the railroads for tax revenue to meet their expenses.

This is true, as well, of other public utilities, such as power and light companies and similar service organizations. As shown by the 1953 *Annual Report of the Idaho State Tax Commission,* railroads and other utilities were assessed at slightly more than $139,000,000. The total assessed value of all property in the state was just over $581,000,000. Thus we see that the public utilities pay approximately one fourth of all property taxes collected in Idaho. The two largest taxpayers in this group were the Union Pacific Railroad and the Idaho Power Company, which together had an assessed value of nearly $85,000,000.

Idaho Highways. Our system of highways really had its beginning in 1919 when a Bureau of Highways was established in the State Department of Public Works. Motor cars were then coming into general use in the state and there was a growing demand for more and better roads.

Our State Highway System. Federal aid in highway construction began in the United States in 1917. From that time to

December 31, 1953, direct Federal aid amounted to $57,967,185.71 to the Federal Aid Primary, Secondary, and Urban road systems of Idaho. In addition, Federal funds to national forest highways of the state have totaled $29,811,437. Also appropriated to Idaho for various special road funds were $24,069,302. Together, Idaho has received in total Federal money, from 1919 to 1953, the grand total of $111,847,923.99.

In general, regular Federal-aid funds to the state's Federal-aid highways cannot be used unless the state puts up its share of road money. In recent years not far from half of Idaho's road money has come from the Federal government and the rest has been supplied by the state, the counties, and the highway districts. These proportions, however, are only approximate and vary considerably for the different kinds of roads and construction projects.

Roads belonging to the state highway system at the close of 1953 are shown on the map which follows. This, of course, does not give county and special highway district roads.

As of December 31, 1953, there were 40,324.8 miles of public highways in Idaho, classified as follows:

Of the state highways shown on Map No. 14, 3,768 miles were paved or oiled by the close of 1953. Approximately two thousand miles of county and special road district highways were also paved or oiled. Somewhat less than eight thousand miles of the total road mileage in the state were classed as primitive and unimproved roads.

Money for the Highways. Finding money for road construction and maintenance is the main problem confronting the Department of Highways. Except for Federal aid, the entire road fund comes from special sources. For the year 1953, total receipts amounted to somewhat less than twenty million dollars. Approximately 60 per cent of this came from a state tax of six cents per gallon on gasoline sales, 15 per cent from motor vehicle licenses, 10 per cent from motor vehicle gross weight fees, and the remaining 15 per cent from miscellaneous sources.

To bring in more money for the highways, it has been suggested that license fees should be raised. For several years automobile licenses have cost a flat five dollars each. The 1955 legislature repealed this law and imposed a graduated scale of license fees based mainly on the age of the vehicle. This will, of course, in-

Table No. 5

IDAHO HIGHWAY MILEAGE

Classification	Mileage
State Highways	4,741.0
County Roads	17,664.2
Highway District Roads	9,518.5
National Forest Development Roads	7,869.8
National Indian Reservation Roads	511.8
National and State Parks, Military Roads	19.5

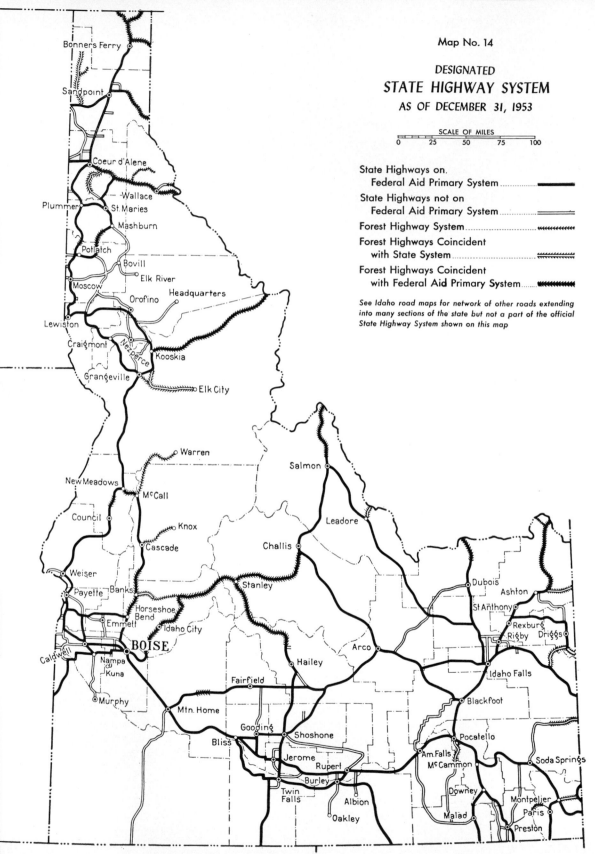

Map No. 14

DESIGNATED
STATE HIGHWAY SYSTEM
AS OF DECEMBER 31, 1953

SCALE OF MILES

0   25   50   75   100

State Highways on.
Federal Aid Primary System..............

State Highways not on
Federal Aid Primary System..............

Forest Highway System.........................

Forest Highways Coincident
with State System.........................

Forest Highways Coincident
with Federal Aid Primary System.......

See Idaho road maps for network of other roads extending
into many sections of the state but not a part of the official
State Highway System shown on this map

crease the amount of money available for road construction and maintenance.

The Highway Administration Act. In 1951 the state legislature passed a law known as the Highway Administration Act. The law created the Department of Highways and the office of State Highway Engineer. To aid and advise the State Highway Engineer, a Board of Highway Directors was provided, consisting of three members appointed by the governor, one from each of the three highway districts into which the state is divided. The purpose of the law was to place the highway system on a permanent basis, as free as possible from political interference, and make a long-range planning and construction program possible.

Some Important Highways in Idaho. Heavily traveled east-west highways that cross Idaho are U.S. 20 from Boston, Massachusetts, to Albany in western Oregon; U.S. 30, called locally the Oregon Trail Highway, from Atlantic City, New Jersey, to Astoria, Oregon, at the mouth of the Columbia River; U.S. 10, from Detroit, Michigan, to Seattle, Washington; and U.S. 2 from Sault Sainte Marie, Michigan, to Bonners Ferry, Idaho. The Lewis and Clark Highway, which crosses Idaho by way of the Clearwater Valley, is now under construction.

Several important north-south highways also traverse portions of Idaho. U.S. 91 passes through eastern Idaho on its course from Los Angeles to Canada. U.S. 93 lays a crooked course through central Idaho, from its junction with U.S. 66 in Arizona, to Canada. In western Idaho is U.S. 95, the North and South Highway or Panoramic Highway, reaching from southern Arizona to Canada.

State highways are not generally so well known or well improved as the Federal highways. Connected as they usually are with the Federal system of highways, they help tie together nearly all parts of the state, except the more rugged mountain sections, into a fairly satisfactory but far from complete network of public roads.

Safety on the Highways. Do you sometimes go with your family on motor trips and vacations? Has anyone you ever knew started on such a trip and failed to return safely? Do you think such trips are safer and more enjoyable if everyone knows the meaning of road signs and the driver is always careful and courteous on the road?

In its report for 1953, the State Department of Highways announced that there was one death in Idaho from road accidents every $41\frac{1}{2}$ hours, one person injured every $4\frac{1}{2}$ hours, and a traffic accident every 58 minutes for the entire year. The economic loss was over twenty million dollars, more than twice as much as the state spent that year for highway construction. This loss was equal to the complete destruction of 2,004 homes, worth, on an average, ten thousand dollars each. And, of course, the suffering and sorrow these accidents caused were beyond price. The following topics will point out ways in which most of the accidents could have been prevented.

The enforcement of traffic laws and regulations in the state, especially outside cities having their own police force, rests mainly with the State Highway Patrol. But there have been too few officers for them properly to patrol the thousands of miles of highway that should be policed. In 1954, however, radar speed control was instituted, which should do much to check excessive speed, the cause of more highway deaths than any other single factor.

Road Signs. Idaho highways are well marked for your information and safety as you travel. There are three general kinds of such signs, those that warn of danger, those that give information, and those that identify the highways.

Idaho, with most other states, is now using uniform traffic control signs approved by the Bureau of Public Roads and the American Association of State Highway Officials, Washington, D.C. Briefly, these traffic control signs depend on both shape and color, as indicated here:

1. Warning signs. These are usually diamond-shaped, with black markings on a highway-yellow background. They are also made up in black and white.

2. Group regulatory signs. Intended to supply information, these signs are usually square or rectangular, with black lettering on a white background.

3. Guide group. These are highway identification signs. Those on Federal highways are uniform throughout the nation, while state highway signs vary. Idaho, as you no doubt already know, uses the highway number on a background showing the state in outline.

Lines painted on the pavement also have special meanings. Probably most important from a safety standpoint is a solid white line painted on the driver's side of a broken center line. Such a line warns the driver not to attempt to pass a driver ahead of him traveling in the same direction until both drivers have passed the solid white warning line.

Hand Signals and Blinker Lights. Until recently hand signals were generally used by drivers to indicate intention. The left hand extended straight out means that the driver intends to make a left turn. If the hand points sharply upward, the driver intends to make a right turn; and if the hand is dropped down, the driver intends to slow down or stop.

Most of the newer cars have lights on both front and rear with which the driver signals his intention by flashing the lights. Flashing lights on the right side of the car, the driver's right, indicate a right turn. Similar lights blinking on the left side indicate a left turn. If both rear lights go on, the driver intends to stop or to slow down.

1. WARNING SIGNS
BLACK ON YELLOW BACKGROUND

TURN   CURVE   SIDE ROAD   CROSS ROADS

SIGNALS AHEAD   STOP AHEAD   NARROW BRIDGE   PAVEMENT ENDS

NARROW ROAD   MEN WORKING   HILL   SCHOOL

ROUND   OCTAGONAL   SQUARE   RECTANGULAR

2. REGULATORY AND INFORMATION SIGNS

USUALLY SQUARE OR RECTANGULAR, BLACK LETTERING ON WHITE BACKGROUND

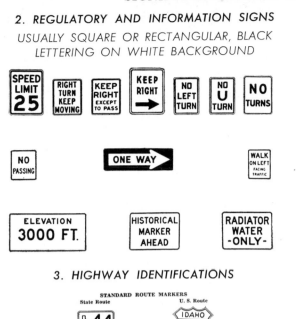

3. HIGHWAY IDENTIFICATIONS

Traffic Lights. Three colors are used for traffic lights: green, red, and yellow or amber. On a steady green light, the driver may go ahead or make a turn. A steady red light means stop, unless green arrows indicate that the driver may proceed. A flashing red light requires the driver to come to a complete stop, then proceed with caution if the way is clear. A yellow or amber light warns a driver to proceed cautiously.

Some people claim they don't believe in signs. Motor vehicle drivers, however, should be an exception. They should not only believe in signs; they should also understand what the signs mean and should carefully follow the instructions they convey.

Rules for Safe Driving. Here are given some of the most important rules for you to know and practice in order to be a safe driver (and no other kind should be allowed on the highways):

1. Do not drive without a license or permit.
2. Drive as closely as practicable to the right-hand edge of the street or highway.
3. Always signal for stops and turns before you reach them, showing signal continuously for the last one hundred feet before the turn or stop is made.
4. Obey all traffic signs and signals.
5. Do not exceed posted speed limits.
6. Drive at a speed that keeps your car under perfect control at all times.
7. Reduce ordinary speed when driving at night.
8. Dim lights when meeting other cars at night.
9. Do not follow the car ahead of you too closely.
10. Always pass the car ahead of you safely (if at all) and do not try to pass on curves and hills or where you do not have clear sight ahead at least five hundred feet.
11. Yield right of way to pedestrians and cars on a through street or highway.
12. Above all, don't be a show-off. Remember that you are handling the most dangerous machine in the world when you are at the wheel of an automobile, truck, or bus.

Don't be an accidental murderer. It's an experience you can never forget or outlive.

The Air Age in Idaho. Idaho's State Department of Aeronautics is recognition of the value of air travel and transport in a state such as ours, where the usual rail

THE FOUR MOST DEADLY DRIVERS

and highway facilities are lacking over extensive areas.

The State Department of Aeronautics, in its 1952 report, *Idaho Airport Facilities,* listed 119 airports in the state. About 75 of these were owned by municipalities, counties, and the state of Idaho. The United States Forest Service maintains 27. Also listed are nearly 50 emergency landing fields. A seaplane base is operated at Coeur d'Alene. These do not include the large Mountain Home Air Base, which is not used by civilian flyers except, perhaps, for emergencies.

Airports with hard-surfaced runways long enough for the use of larger planes are located at the Boise Air Terminal, Burley Municipal Airport, Caldwell Municipal Airport, Coeur d'Alene Air Terminal, Gooding Municipal Airport, Idaho Falls Municipal Airport, Nez Perce County Airport at Lewiston, Moscow-Pullman Airport, Pocatello Munici-

pal Airport, and Joslin Field, the Twin Falls Municipal Airport.

Regular air transport service is supplied by three airlines: Empire Air Lines maintains regular flight schedules to Coeur d'Alene and Moscow in northern Idaho and at Boise, Gooding, Twin Falls, Burley, Pocatello, and Idaho Falls in southern Idaho. The United Air Lines serve Boise and Twin Falls. Western Air Lines have regular service to Idaho Falls and Pocatello.

The Civil Aeronautics Administration said in a recent report that there were then 545 registered civil aircraft in the state. Ada and Canyon counties had 191 of these. Twin Falls County, with 39 registered aircraft, stood third. The CAA is a volunteer organization serving as a special aid to the military air services in times of national emergencies.

Quite a number of private operators make special flights into Idaho's mountain regions, taking mail and supplies of many kinds to the few people living in remote places not easily reached by ordinary means of transportation. Many sportsmen also use this method to reach choice hunting and fishing sections. Forest Service landing fields are generally used on these flights.

Modern Communication. Idaho shares, of course, in the miracle of modern communication. Before statehood, Idaho had limited telegraph and telephone services in addition to the post office facilities. But not until 1898 did Idaho have direct long-distance telephone connections with distant points. That year a direct long-distance line was opened from Boise to cities on the West Coast.

Today communication is no longer a problem. Telephone lines reach into all parts of the state and nation, and long-distance calls are made to foreign lands. The Forest Service has telephone connections with remote portions of the national forests, where fire control is a constant summer problem. Radios are plentiful. Walkie-talkies are in use where fast communication is imperative and where telephone service cannot be depended on. A police radio network protects many parts of the state from law violators, being particularly valuable as an aid in intercepting criminals trying to get out of the state in fast automobiles.

Most of the larger cities of Idaho have radio broadcasting stations. A complete list of them is given in Appendix Table 7 in the Statistical Appendix in this book. Which one is your favorite station? What other stations in Idaho and bordering states can you bring in on your radio?

Television is the newest form of communication to be used in Idaho. In the southern part of the state there are television facilities near Boise, Idaho Falls, and Pocatello which provide a limited number of programs. In northern Idaho, broadcasts are received from outside the state, chiefly from Spokane. If you will examine Appendix Table 7, you will see the list of stations that provide television outlets at this time (1955). No doubt the facilities for this form of communication will be greatly expanded in the near future.

* * * * *

As a state, Idaho does not stand alone. Almost every community and every activity in the state are tied in many ways to other communities and other activities in other parts of the nation and the world. Let us, as citizens, continue to develop Idaho in harmony with the high ideals of our own people and for effective cooperation with the nation of which we are a part and with the modern world in which we live.

News released to the world in August, 1955, at the meeting of the International Conference on Peaceful Uses of Atomic Energy, told that Arco, Idaho, had been test lighted on July 17, 1955, by electricity produced at the National Testing Station near that city. Thus, to an Idaho city go the honor and distinction of being the first city in the world to be lighted by atomic power.

I Speak for Democracy

By ELIZABETH ELLEN EVANS

I am an American.

Listen to my words, Fascist, Communist.

Listen well, for my country is a strong country, and my message is a strong message.

I am an American, and I speak for democracy.

My ancestors have left their blood on the green at Lexington and the snow at Valley Forge

. . . on the walls of Fort Sumter and the fields at Gettysburg

. . . on the waters of the River Marne and in the shadows of the Argonne Forest

. . . on the beachheads of Salerno and Normandy and the sands of Okinawa

. . . on the bare, bleak hills called Pork Chop and Old Baldy and Heartbreak Ridge.

A million and more of my countrymen have died for freedom.

My country is their eternal monument.

They live on in the laughter of a small boy as he watches a circus clown's antics

. . . and in the sweet, delicious coldness of the first bite of peppermint ice cream on the Fourth of July

. . . in the little tenseness of a baseball crowd as the umpire calls "Batter up!"

. . . and in the high school band's rendition of "Stars and Stripes Forever" in the Memorial Day parade

. . . in the clear, sharp ring of a school bell on a fall morning

. . . and in the triumph of a six-year-old as he reads aloud for the first time.

They live on in the eyes of an Ohio farmer surveying his acres of corn and potatoes and pasture

. . . and in the brilliant gold of hundreds of acres of wheat stretching across the flat miles of Kansas

. . . in the milling of cattle in the stockyards of Chicago

. . . the precision of an assembly line in an automobile factory in Detroit

. . . and the perpetual red glow of the nocturnal skylines of Pittsburgh and Birmingham and Gary.

They live on in the voice of a young Jewish boy saying the sacred words from the Torah: "Hear O Israel: the Lord our God, the Lord is One. Thou shalt love the Lord thy God with all thy heart and with all thy soul and with all thy might."

. . . and in the voice of a Catholic girl praying: "Hail, Mary, full of grace, the Lord is with thee . . ."

. . . and in the voice of a Protestant boy singing: "A mighty Fortress is our God, A Bulwark never failing . . ."

An American named Carl Sandburg wrote these words:

"I know a Jew fishcrier down on Maxwell Street with a voice like a north wind blowing over corn stubble in January.

He dangles herring before prospective customers evincing a joy identical with that of Pavlova dancing.

His face is that of a man terribly glad to be selling fish, terribly glad that God made fish, and customers to whom he may call his wares from a pushcart."

There is a voice in the soul of every human being that cries out to be free. America has answered that voice.

America has offered freedom and opportunity such as no land before her has ever known, to a Jew fishcrier down on Maxwell Street with the face of a man terribly glad to be selling fish.

She has given him the right to own his pushcart, to sell his herring on Maxwell Street,

. . . she has given him an education for his children, and a tremendous faith in the nation that has made these things his.

Multiply that fishcrier by 160,000,000—160,000,000 mechanics and farmers and housewives and coal miners and truck drivers and chemists and lawyers and plumbers and priests—all glad, terribly glad to be what they are, terribly glad to be free to work and eat and sleep and speak and love and pray and live as they desire, as they believe!

And those 160,000,000 Americans—those 160,000,000 free Americans—have more roast beef and mashed potatoes,

the yield of American labor and land;

. . . more automobiles and telephones,

. . . more safety razors and bathtubs,

. . . more Orlon sweaters and aureomycin, the fruits of American initiative and enterprise;

. . . more public schools and life insurance policies, the symbols of American security and faith in the future;

. . . more laughter and song—
than any other people on earth!

This is my answer, Fascist, Communist!

Show me a country greater than our country, show me a people more energetic, creative, progressive— bigger-hearted and happier than our people, not until then will I consider your way of life.

For I am an American, and I speak for democracy.

*　　*　　*　　*　　*

Our Constitutional
Freedoms, Rights, and Duties

How the people of Idaho co-operate in the privileges and duties of self-government, and how they pay the costs of their chosen form of government.

HOW WOULD YOU LIKE TO LIVE under a form of government where you had no rights or liberties? Where you would not be permitted to go on a trip unless you first secured permission from the police or some governmental official? Where you could be arrested, thrown into prison, and held without trial for months or years, perhaps forever, if it suited the leaders to treat you in that fashion? Where, if you did own any property, the taxes you paid would be whatever the tax collector could frighten you into paying? Where you could not vote or hold public office? Where you could not belong to the church of your own choice? Where you could not even read anything but gov-ernment-published newspapers or listen openly to a radio broadcast unless it was government approved?

Any or all of these conditions could, and would, affect your life if you happened to live in one of many countries in the world today which do not have constitutional self-government. We use that term to describe a form of government in which the rights, privileges, and duties of the people are plainly set forth in published constitutions or codes of law. Such governments are recognized as governments by law instead of governments by men. They are not subject to the sudden whims of the rulers who happen to be in power at the moment.

I. CONSTITUTIONAL GUARANTEES OF FREEDOM

A CENTURY BEFORE IDAHO became a state, constitutional freedom was firmly established as a part of the American way of life. The first ten amendments to the Constitution of the United States were a bill of rights for the American people, our insurance that one of the first and greatest duties of our national government was to establish securely the liberties we had won as a result of the Revolutionary War.

The Constitution of Idaho. The constitution of Idaho, like the Constitution of the United States, provided for the American three-way plan of government. The three departments, legislative, executive, and judicial, were set up in our state government, giving us the same system of checks and balances that had proven so effective in the government of the United States and the other states of the Union.

The *legislative department* is given the responsibility of making laws for governing the state. The *executive department* sees to it that these laws are put to work and made effective. It carries on the actual work of government. The *judicial department* provides courts and judges to see that those who disregard the laws are punished and that justice is administered fairly to all on equal terms. By making the three departments separate in their duties and more or less independent of each other, we use the checks and balances that tend to check and balance each department's powers and thus prevent any one department of government from becoming so strong that it can control the others and threaten the liberties of the people.

Declaration of Rights. Our state constitution clearly recognizes that all responsible citizens of Idaho are "by nature free and equal and have certain inalienable rights, among which are enjoying and defending life and liberty, acquiring, possessing and protecting property, pursuing happiness, and securing safety."

These are, in general, the rights and freedoms guaranteed to the people under the first ten amendments, the so-called "bill of rights" in the Constitution of the United States. By restating these rights, our state constitution gives the people of Idaho double assurance that their liberties will be protected under the laws of the state as well as under Federal laws. Briefly stated, the Idaho constitution makes these provisions for the protection of Idaho citizens:

1. All political power belongs to the people, to the citizens of Idaho.

2. Idaho is an inseparable part of the American Union.

3. Religious freedom is guaranteed.

4. The writ of habeas corpus, which is a legal method by which persons accused of crime must be released or given a quick trial, shall not be suspended except under extraordinary circumstances.

5. Every accused person shall have the right to a speedy and public trial by jury.

6. No person can be arrested or confined to await trial except on indictment (in-DITE-ment), or charge, by a grand jury, or on information legally given by the public prosecutor, the prosecuting attorney.

7. Every person is guaranteed freedom of speech and press. (But this does not give a person freedom to speak or write falsely in such manner as to damage the character or reputation of another person.)

8. The people have the right to assemble in a peaceable manner for their common good.

9. The people have the right to instruct their elected representatives in public office, and may send petitions to the legislature asking that body to correct wrongs that may exist.

10. The people have the right to own and bear arms (weapons) for their security and defense.

11. The civil powers of the people shall be above the military power, meaning that military courts or officers cannot control the state and the local courts provided for by law. (The President or the governor may, however, declare martial law in an emergency that threatens public safety, thus placing control temporarily in the hands of military authorities.)

12. Under the power called eminent domain, the government (Federal, state, or local) may take private property that is needed for the public good, but only by paying a just price for such property.

13. No person may be imprisoned for debt.

14. No law shall be passed that interferes with or destroys contracts that have been legally made.

15. The homes, properties, and persons of citizens cannot be searched or seized unless the officers performing that work have search warrants or other legal authority for such search or seizure.

16. Courts of justice shall be open to every person on equal terms, and justice shall be administered without delay, prejudice, or sale.

17. No power, either civil or military, can interfere with or deny any citizen the right of suffrage (the right to vote).

Do you now see how the constitution of Idaho protects you in your rights and liberties? The main difference between the American way of life and life in many other countries is that here in the United

The Ever-Lengthening Shadow

Fiscal year ending June 30, 1929
Federal expenditures were less than two thirds of total income payments to individuals in California.

Fiscal year ending June 30, 1939
Federal expenditures were equal to total income payments to all individuals in the Pacific and Mountain states as well as in North Dakota, South Dakota, and 42 percent of Nebraska.

LEGEND

■ Federal expenditures equal to income payments of states in blackened area.

▨ State and local expenditures equal to income payments of states in cross-hatched area.

© 1952, By The First National Bank of Boston.

Fiscal year ending June 30, 1953
Estimated Federal expenditures for the fiscal year ending June 30, 1953, equal estimated total income payments to all individuals west of the Mississippi River, and in addition, all of the income to individuals in Mississippi and 55 percent of the income of Alabama. Total state and local expenditures of the entire country are shown in the cross-hatched area. The two shaded areas account for 95 percent of the nation's crude petroleum production, 85 percent of the lumber output, 70 percent of the total value of mineral production, and 71 percent of the total value of all farm crop production.

Courtesy The First National Bank of Boston

States the citizen is first and the government is second. In our country government exists only to serve and protect you and me and every other citizen. As long as we keep our constitutional form of government, the government can never become the master of the people, as it is in so many parts of the earth.

Keeping the Constitution Up with Changing Times. At the time the Idaho constitution became the foundation law of the state in 1890, it was strictly a frontier land, with only eighteen counties, fewer than ninety thousand people, and with only two towns having more than a thousand residents. Naturally, a constitution suited to conditions which then prevailed would need to be changed from time to time as conditions changed. The framers of our constitution knew this and provided a method for amending it when it seemed wise to do so.

A proposed amendment to the state constitution is first acted upon by the state legislature just as other bills are, but first it must receive a two-thirds vote, or more, in each branch of the lawmaking body. It is then submitted to the voters of the state at the next regular election and, if approved by a majority of the voters, it becomes part of the constitution of Idaho. There are other ways in which changes could be made, but this is the only method so far used in amending the Idaho constitution, and it is both simple and democratic.

II. WHAT OUR GOVERNMENT DOES FOR US AND HOW THE COSTS ARE PAID

NOBODY REALLY ENJOYS paying taxes, but if we remind ourselves of a few of the many things our taxes pay for, it will, at least, put a sugar coating on the tax pill and enable us to swallow it with better grace. These are some of the things our tax dollars buy and that government, our own government, does for us.

Protection. One of the finest things about living in America and Idaho is that we are protected by our government in many important ways. Here are some of them.

1. We are *protected from armed enemies* in certain other countries who might, if they felt able, try to change our way of life or come into possession of the great resources of our nation and the many good things that we enjoy.

2. We are *protected in our persons,* because the police and other peace officers are alert and watchful to guard us from violence and lawbreakers. Our governor has the power to call out the state militia to protect us if mob action or other widespread disorder proves too much for local peace agencies to handle.

3. We are *protected in our homes and our property,* because both the Federal and state constitutions guarantee us against unlawful search and seizure. Our homes may not be entered against our will except by an officer armed with a legal search warrant. Further, our property cannot be taken from us without due process of law.

4. We are *protected in our citizenship,* because the right to vote, to belong to whatever religious faith we may choose,

to speak and write freely, to hold public office, and to enjoy many other privileges of citizenship are all guaranteed and protected under the laws of our nation and state.

5. Our *health and safety are protected* by laws guarding us in a great many ways: from polluted, or impure, water; from adulterated foods and unclean food factories, packing houses, processing plants, and markets; from unsanitary dairies; from filthy streets and alleys; from contagious diseases in schools and other public places; from dangerous working conditions in mines and factories; from unsafe streets and highways; from dangerous driving practices; and in scores of other ways.

Unfortunately, the laws cannot always protect us, especially *against our own carelessness and neglect.* Each one of us must help uphold the laws by obeying them and by personally assuming responsibility for our own actions. If, by disobeying the law we put ourselves outside its protection, who is usually to blame when something goes wrong?

Liberty. As you know, in the United States we are free to do almost anything that does not interfere with the rights and the welfare of someone else. We have liberty of action. We may go almost anywhere we choose within our own country. We may engage in any work, business, or profession we choose. We may belong to whatever church, political party, club, organization, or social group we wish to join. We may vote, hold office, and take part in other governmental activities without hindrance or control. Can you think of a single freedom you do not

have except the freedom to harm or interfere with someone else?

Services. In our country, the various units of the government serve us in a multitude of ways. They build and operate our schools. They construct streets and highways. They maintain forests, parks, and recreational areas for our use and pleasure and conserve our fish and game. They guard us against fire. They construct or aid in constructing irrigation and drainage projects. They supply information about the weather. They regulate traffic for our safety. They provide water for our cities and towns. They establish and maintain colleges and universities. How many other services can you think of that are provided by some branch or department of government?

Paying the Costs of Government. The most urgent problem that constantly faces our government is that of raising and spending the money necessary to carry on the work of government on the various levels: national, state, and local. This will grow even more critical as population increases, as civilization becomes more complex, and as the people demand more and more services from their government.

Since taxation in one form or another is the method by which nearly all government revenue is provided, every citizen naturally feels a keen interest in this tremendous problem. It touches also the earnings, the purse, and the bank account of every taxpayer and, indirectly, all the rest of us. After all, it is well said that "Government has nothing except what the taxpayer gives it."

Why Government Now Costs More. We need to understand that the people of

Idaho, as well as those in other states, have to support or help to support government at five levels: (1) the Federal government, (2) state government, (3) county government, (4) municipal and other forms of local government, and (5) since 1945, the United Nations. It is true, of course, that we do not pay taxes directly to the United Nations, but it is also true that the international organization of half a hundred countries that comprise the United Nations depends on the United States for quite a substantial share of the money necessary to meet UN expenses.

For many years there have been large increases in nearly all the costs of government. The greatest increases are on the national level, where taxes have multiplied about ten times as much as state taxes, and more than twenty times as much as local taxes, in the last few years. How the total tax payments to the Federal government mounted between 1940 and 1952 is shown in the opposite graph.

Perhaps at your age you aren't interested in taxes. However, your parents are, and you will be, too, when you become old enough to pay the taxes instead of just reading about them. Therefore, let us notice some of the reasons why taxes and the costs of government have increased so greatly in the last four decades. Space will permit only a brief mention of them, but no doubt your parents, teachers, or some of your grown-up friends will explain things you do not understand if you will ask them to do so. Here are some of the reasons why taxes now take roughly one third of every dollar earned in the United States.

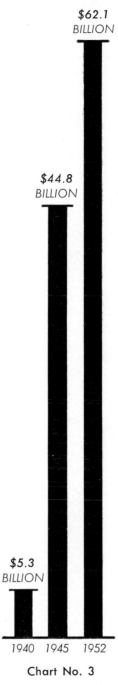

Chart No. 3

RISE IN FEDERAL TAXES IN U.S.

In the twelve years from 1940 to 1952 the Federal tax bill of Americans increased almost 1,200 per cent.

(Based on U.S. Treasury Reports.)

1. *Wars—Past, Present, and Future.* Our need to maintain a large army, navy, and air force to fight the wars that may be thrust upon us, and to keep us strong enough to protect ourselves against possible enemy nations, requires more tax dollars than any other single governmental expense. Hospital and medical care and other services needed by our sick and disabled servicemen and servicewomen further increase the costs of war. So does the large amount of interest the government must pay on our huge national debt, a large part of which was made necessary by war and the threat of war.

2. *Other Important Reasons.* There are, of course, many other reasons why government, all government, now costs more.

a) Our population, both in Idaho and in the nation, has increased rapidly, requiring more government services for the people and more officers and other workers to provide those services.

b) Attendance in public schools and higher institutions of learning has increased by leaps and bounds, calling for many new buildings, new equipment, and many more teachers and other workers to provide elementary, high-school, and college students with the education they need and to which they are entitled.

c) In most parts of the nation, including our own state, highways need rebuilding and extending to carry more traffic and heavier loads. Larger and better airports and landing fields must be constructed for expanding air travel and transportation.

d) Billions of dollars have already been spent and a great deal more may be needed to help friendly nations that have been weakened by war or held back by poverty, disease, ignorance, and lack of properly developed natural resources.

e) New theories of government in the widening fields of social security now protect workers by paying them unemployment insurance, and by paying pensions to disabled and elderly citizens who need assistance.

f) Payments to farmers and livestock growers to maintain prices of their products at a satisfactory level have cost the government billions of dollars, as have similar subsidies[1] in other fields of activity.

g) Inflation,[2] brought on by war and other causes, has decreased the purchasing power of the dollar so much in recent years that wages and prices have been pushed sharply upward in an effort to maintain our high standard of living. As a result, much larger sums have been necessary to meet practically all costs, including, of course, the costs of government.

In all these ways and many more, the costs of all government have gone ever higher. Taxes have become so high that they are a heavy burden upon practically everyone, and forward-looking men and women are hunting for ways to reduce them. Whether ways can be found to do so will depend to a great extent upon

[1]Subsidy. Government payments made to individuals and business establishments to guarantee them against losses and to encourage greater production.

[2]Inflation. A condition in which money is so plentiful that prices and wages rise above a reasonable level.

whether there is peace or war in the world in the years that lie ahead, and whether we, the people, are willing to get along with fewer services and less aid from government than we have become accustomed to receiving.

Sources of Public Revenue. Now that we understand that there must be a vast, continuous flow of money to pay the costs of government, let us see from what sources this money comes. Most of it is secured by various kinds of taxes paid by the people. We do need to remember, however, that a great deal of the money

sixty-five billion dollars of revenue collected by our national government in one year is beyond our understanding. But we can understand it when we know that it equaled a little more than an average of $420 collected from every man, woman, and child living in the United States in 1952. Of this vast sum, Idahoans paid $117,674,165 into the Federal treasury.

As we can see from the table, income taxes paid by our parents and the other people of the nation is by far the largest single source of revenue. But, in a small

Table No. 6

SOURCES OF FEDERAL INCOME

Source	Amount
Corporation income and profits taxes	$21,466,910,019
Individual income and employment taxes	33,738,370,243
Alcohol and tobacco taxes	4,114,282,002
Manufacturers' and retailers' excise taxes	2,824,443,832
Miscellaneous taxes	2,865,579,464
Grand Total	$65,009,585,560

that leaves the taxpayers' pockets to support the government finds its way back into circulation as salaries and wages for government workers, in purchases of equipment and supplies, in interest to owners of government bonds, and in various other ways. If this were not true, the costs of government in a nation so large as ours would soon bankrupt the people.

Federal Revenue. To the United States Treasury comes revenue from many sources. The 1953 *World Almanac* shows the chief sources of revenue for the fiscal year ending in 1952.

A sum so great as the approximate

way, you yourself help to make up this huge total. When you attend a picture show or other form of public entertainment, you pay a Federal tax on the ticket that admits you. If you purchase jewelry and many other kinds of goods, a Federal tax is part of the price you pay. When you buy a United States Savings Bond, you loan your money to Uncle Sam. So, you see, every one of us helps in some way to pay the costs of maintaining this great nation of ours. However, instead of thinking of this as a burden, let us regard it as a privilege, as indeed it truly is, when taxes are kept at a reasonable level. In that way, each of us has a direct interest and share in the financial welfare of our country.

Idaho State Revenue. Revenues from all sources for the operation of our state government are quite modest when compared with the scores of billions of dollars annually required by Uncle Sam. Nevertheless, the total is a hearty sum indeed, amounting to well over $50,000,000 a year. Total revenue paid to the Idaho state government from all sources in a recent biennium, or two-year period, as shown by a report prepared by the Idaho State Tax Commission, amounted to $120,000,000 in round numbers. The largest single source of general-fund revenue coming to the state is from the state income tax. About $26,000,000 came from the Federal government, leaving approximately $93,500,000 that came from taxes, fees, licenses, and similar sources paid by the citizens of Idaho and by various companies and corporations doing business in the state. This amounted to about $110 a year for each man, woman, and child living in Idaho. If your own family paid at the average rate, how much did your family pay into the state treasury?

County Revenue. The sources from which a county in Idaho gets the money to pay the costs of county government depend a great deal on what kind of county it is. If it has several cities and incorporated villages, its revenue will come from several sources:

1. Property taxes on real estate, public utilities like railroads and power and light companies, merchandise, and other taxable property.

2. Licenses paid by operators of certain kinds of business, such as taverns and establishments selling beer.

3. State funds apportioned to the counties for road building and other purposes.

4. Federal grants for such special purposes as building hospitals and other welfare institutions.

5. Fees of various kinds charged by county officers.

6. A share of the profit on liquor sold by the state liquor stores.

7. A share of national forest income if the county contains any national forest lands.

8. Miscellaneous sources such as rents, interest, sales of county property, fines, and other sources.

The more thinly populated counties must lean heavily on property taxes, though they share in some other sources of revenue. However, the cost of county government is much less in such counties, so the tax load of the people is usually lighter than in the more densely populated counties where the people expect more services from county government.

Municipal Revenue. Cities and villages in Idaho obtain their revenue in much the same ways that the counties get their funds. They collect property taxes, fees for licenses of various kinds, and share in some county, state, and Federal funds under certain conditions. In addition to such sources, cities and most villages charge their residents for water, this source usually bringing in quite large sums. A few Idaho cities have their own electric power plants and depend quite heavily on light and power income to help pay the cost of city government. Another source of revenue in most of the larger cities is the money taken in by parking meters. Sometimes state laws have permitted slot machines, punchboards, and similar devices to be operated in Idaho. When this was done, cities and villages, as well as counties, shared in the money taken in this manner. However, the 1953 legislature passed laws making the operation of slot machines unlawful after January 1, 1954, so that source of revenue is no longer available.

There are a few other sources from which municipalities secure revenue but those named account for nearly all the money raised to pay the costs of local government. Can you suggest some reasons why city government costs more in proportion than state and county government? What are some of the important ways in which municipal governments serve their people?

School Revenues. Schools get their money principally from two sources, by far the largest part coming from taxes. The local district levies a tax, the county levies a county school tax, and the state legislature appropriates money to help support the schools. The state and county school funds are apportioned to the local districts according to law. The local district levy must be large enough to pay all operating costs not covered by state and county apportionments. In most districts in Idaho the local tax levy is higher than either the state or county levy, and it is often higher than the combined state and county levies.

The second important source of school revenue is interest on the Permanent Endowment Fund. When Idaho was admitted as a state, the Federal government gave a large amount of public land to the state to help support the public schools. As those lands were sold, the money received was put into a special fund known as the Permanent Endowment Fund, with the provision that only the interest earned by the fund could be used.

The Permanent Endowment Fund, in the fall of 1953, amounted to $44,481,719.59. This large fund was credited to the various state institutions as follows:

THE PERMANENT ENDOWMENT FUND

Public Schools	$29,391,232.59
State Charitable Institutions	2,898,437.20
School of Science, University of Idaho	2,624,723.38
Northern and Southern Idaho Colleges of Education	2,456,440.49
University of Idaho	2,351,980.37
State Penitentiary	1,791,560.88
Agricultural College, University of Idaho	1,668,889.67
State Hospital South	1,298,456.20

(Figures supplied by State Auditor)

BUILDING A MOUNTAIN HIGHWAY

Constructing and maintaining highways in a mountainous state like Idaho costs our state government millions of dollars annually.

Courtesy Idaho State Chamber of Commerce, Boise

Since only the interest on the Permanent Endowment Fund may be used, the fund steadily grows larger as state endowment lands are sold or leased and the money received is added to the fund. How fortunate the schools and institutions of Idaho are! In many states poor management and dishonest public officials have robbed the endowment funds of much and, in some cases, of all the money that was once held in trust in those funds.

The school districts get smaller amounts from other sources. For example, we saw that the various counties having national forest lands get a share of the money earned by the forests. The schools get 15 per cent of the national forest money given to the counties. Schools also have a small revenue obtained from fees, rentals, the sale of surplus school property and supplies, and so on, but the total sum obtained from such sources pays only a very small part of school expenses. The larger part, as already stated, comes from taxes.

III. WHO IS A CITIZEN IN IDAHO?

NOT EVERYONE has all the rights, privileges, and duties of citizenship in our own state. There are excellent reasons for this. Do you think, for example, that young children should be allowed to vote, to hold office, and to manage their own affairs? Should persons confined in prison be allowed all the rights that other people have? Perhaps you can think of others who, in your opinion, should not have all the rights of citizenship.

Full Citizenship. The Fourteenth Amendment to the Constitution of the United States says, "All persons born or naturalized in the United States, and subject to the jurisdiction[3] thereof, are

[3]Jurisdiction (JU-ris-DIK'shun). Lawful authority and control.

citizens of the United States and of the State wherein they reside." The states, however, have the power to make laws that have the effect of placing certain restrictions or limits upon the citizenship of the people of the state.

The Right to Vote. The most precious privilege of complete citizenship in the United States is the right to vote. The constitution of Idaho gives this privilege only to United States citizens who are at least twenty-one years old and who have lived six months or more in the state and thirty days or more in the county before election day, and who are registered as legal voters in the precinct, or voting district, in which they are entitled to vote. Of course, with the right to vote goes the right to hold public office and to serve on juries. Thus, all citizens of Idaho, both men and women, who are twenty-one years of age, or older, are of legal, or lawful age.

Legal age and United States citizenship do not, however, always give complete citizenship in Idaho. Persons found guilty of crime and who, as a result, are confined in prison, do not have the right to vote, nor do insane persons and idiots,

or persons not legally competent to manage their own affairs. Until recently, Indians did not have the right to vote in Idaho, but in 1950 an amendment to the state constitution was adopted granting full citizenship to our Indians who are of legal age.

Limited Citizenship. All residents of Idaho, whether United States citizens or not, are protected by the laws of the state and the nation. They also have most other rights of citizenship, including the right to live anywhere in the state they please, to travel anywhere in the state and nation, to attend our public schools and institutions of higher learning, to engage in business, to work at whatever lawful occupations they prefer. Children and youth, though protected by the laws of the state, are legally under the control of their parents or guardians until they become of age or are married.

Citizenship: Privileges and Duties. As a citizen of your school, do you think it is your duty to do all you can to make the school a success? As a citizen of the community, should you do whatever you can to make the community a better place in which to live? As a citizen of

Courtesy Post-Register, Idaho Falls

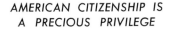

AMERICAN CITIZENSHIP IS A PRECIOUS PRIVILEGE

Group of fifty-three (standing) foreign-born men and women taking their oath as naturalized American citizens at special ceremonies in the municipal auditorium at Idaho Falls, November 19, 1954.

Idaho, is it your duty to obey the laws of the state?

Do you think that the *right* to vote really carries with it the *duty* of voting? Of course, no one has to vote. That is entirely one's own business. If, however, the people who have the right to vote do not do so when they have the opportunity, they probably have only themselves to blame if local, state, and national affairs are not run to suit them. At least, if they have voted, they have done their best to see that what President Lincoln called "government of the people, by the people, and for the people" has been given its best chance to succeed. In a republic such as ours, freedom really is everybody's business, and if we ever lose that freedom, we, the people, will be the ones who allow that sad fate to overtake us.

*   *   *   *   *

We gain most from the experiences we share. Our government will have rich meaning for us when we understand how impossible our American way of life would be without it. So let us share in both the privileges and the duties of our homes, our schools, our churches, our clubs, and our communities, so that when the mantle of complete citizenship in Idaho and the United States falls upon our shoulders, we shall be able to share fully and gladly in the greater privileges and duties that citizenship will bring.

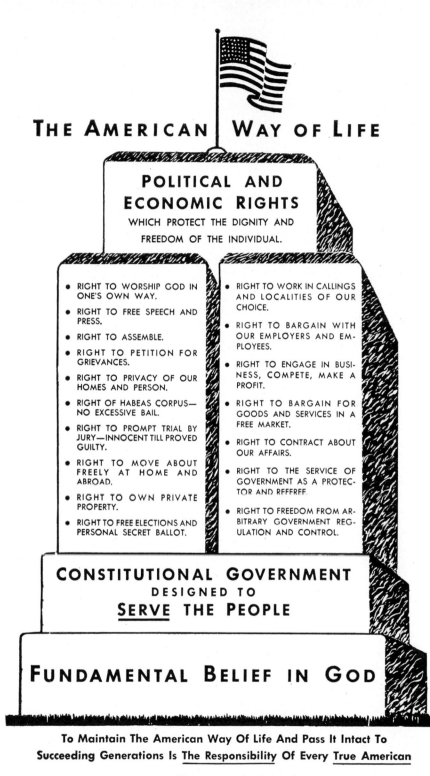

THE AMERICAN WAY OF LIFE

POLITICAL AND ECONOMIC RIGHTS
WHICH PROTECT THE DIGNITY AND FREEDOM OF THE INDIVIDUAL.

- RIGHT TO WORSHIP GOD IN ONE'S OWN WAY.
- RIGHT TO FREE SPEECH AND PRESS.
- RIGHT TO ASSEMBLE.
- RIGHT TO PETITION FOR GRIEVANCES.
- RIGHT TO PRIVACY OF OUR HOMES AND PERSON.
- RIGHT OF HABEAS CORPUS— NO EXCESSIVE BAIL.
- RIGHT TO PROMPT TRIAL BY JURY—INNOCENT TILL PROVED GUILTY.
- RIGHT TO MOVE ABOUT FREELY AT HOME AND ABROAD.
- RIGHT TO OWN PRIVATE PROPERTY.
- RIGHT TO FREE ELECTIONS AND PERSONAL SECRET BALLOT.

- RIGHT TO WORK IN CALLINGS AND LOCALITIES OF OUR CHOICE.
- RIGHT TO BARGAIN WITH OUR EMPLOYERS AND EMPLOYEES.
- RIGHT TO ENGAGE IN BUSINESS, COMPETE, MAKE A PROFIT.
- RIGHT TO BARGAIN FOR GOODS AND SERVICES IN A FREE MARKET.
- RIGHT TO CONTRACT ABOUT OUR AFFAIRS.
- RIGHT TO THE SERVICE OF GOVERNMENT AS A PROTECTOR AND REFEREE.
- RIGHT TO FREEDOM FROM ARBITRARY GOVERNMENT REGULATION AND CONTROL.

CONSTITUTIONAL GOVERNMENT
DESIGNED TO
SERVE THE PEOPLE

FUNDAMENTAL BELIEF IN GOD

To Maintain The American Way Of Life And Pass It Intact To
Succeeding Generations Is The Responsibility Of Every True American

(Courtesy *Freedom's Foundation*, Valley Forge, Pennsylvania)

Our Three-Way Plan
of Representative Government

*How the people of Idaho govern themselves as a sovereign state in co-
operation with the national government and the other states comprising
our Federal Union.*

*I believe in the United States of Amer-
ica as a Government of the people, by
the people, for the people; whose just
powers are derived from the consent of
the governed; a democracy in a republic;
a sovereign Nation of many sovereign
States; a perfect union, one and inseparable; established upon those principles of
freedom, equality, justice, and humanity
for which American patriots sacrificed
their lives and fortunes.*

*I therefore believe it is my duty to my
country to love it; to support its Constitution; to obey its laws; to respect its flag,
and to defend it against all enemies.*

Written in 1917 by WILLIAM TYLER
PAGE, *Clerk of the U.S. House of Representatives.*

THE AMERICAN'S CREED describes the
United States as a "sovereign nation of
many sovereign states." When so used
the word sovereign means supreme, or
possessing the highest authority. As a
nation the United States is completely
independent of any other country and,
as a state, Idaho is completely independent of any other state, being subject only
to the laws and regulations of the United
States in exactly the same manner and
to the same extent that the other states

are. Such a plan of government naturally
calls for close agreement and harmony
between the government of Idaho and
the national government.

The Founding Fathers who drew up
our American plan of government were
determined to prevent that government
from ever becoming so strongly central-
ized that it could seize the power belonging to the people and thus become so
powerful itself that it could destroy the
people's liberty. To guard against such a
possibility, our three-way plan of government was adopted, the duties of government being divided among the three departments named in the preceding unit.
What are these three departments?

The sovereign states that together
make the nation must, of course, have
plans of government that are in general
quite similar to the national plan. Any
other arrangement would probably cause
so much confusion that the work of government could not be done efficiently,
if at all. Idaho, we shall find, has followed the national plan quite closely.
Now let us see how the national plan
and the Idaho plan are similar, and how
the people of Idaho govern themselves
as a sovereign state. Before reading
further, examine the chart that follows.

Chart No. 4

THE AMERICAN PLAN OF GOVERNMENT: NATIONAL, STATE, COUNTY, AND LOCAL

(How the three departments of government compare at all levels)

Department	National Government	State Government	County Government	Local Government
The Legislative or Law-making Department	Congress, composed of the Senate and the House of Representatives, elected by the people of the states	The State Legislature, composed of state senators and representatives, elected by the people of the counties	Board of County Commissioners, elected by the people of the counties	City Council or Commissioners, elected by the people of the city; Village Board of Trustees elected by the people of incorporated villages
The Executive or Administrative Department, which carries on the actual details of government work	President; Vice-President; President's Cabinet; Administrative commissions, boards, bureaus, and other agencies needed to perform the many duties of government	Governor; Lieutenant Governor; Elected state officers; Civil Administrative Department, usually called the Governor's Cabinet; Other commissions, boards, and similar agencies needed to carry on the work of state government	Elected county officers; Special officers and boards, usually appointed, needed to carry on the work of county government	Mayor or City Manager in cities; Chairman of the Village Board in villages; Administrative officers and boards, usually appointed, needed to carry on the work of local government
The Judicial Department (Courts and Judges)	Supreme Court; Circuit Court of Appeals; Federal District Courts; Special Courts	Idaho Supreme Court; District Courts	District Courts also serve the counties	Courts of Justice of the Peace; Municipal Police Courts

Notice that the national government, state government, county government, and community government are all set up on similar plans and that all have the three departments of government: legislative, executive, and judicial.

I. THE LEGISLATIVE DEPARTMENT OF GOVERNMENT

WHEN MANY PEOPLE live and work together, rules are needed to prevent trouble and settle differences. In our form of government, such rules are called *laws,* and the making of these laws is the duty of the *legislative department* of government.

The legislative department is not limited to the nation and the state. The counties, too, must have rules or laws, and so must the cities, towns, and villages. Think what your own school would be like if there were no rules, each pupil being free to do exactly as he liked, without regard for the welfare of anyone else. Do you think you would like to live in a society that had no rules of conduct for its members?

The State Legislature. Idaho's legislative or lawmaking body is the state legislature. It does for the state much the same kind of work that Congress does for the nation.

How the Legislature Is Made Up. The legislature of Idaho, like Congress, consists of two chambers or branches. The upper chamber is the State Senate, consisting of one senator from each county. The lower chamber is the House of Representatives, made up of from one to four members from each county as determined by the population of the counties. At present, based on the 1950 census, Ada County has four representatives in the Idaho House of Representatives; Bannock, Canyon, and Twin Falls counties have three members each; Bingham, Bonneville, Kootenai, Latah, Nez Perce, and Shoshone counties have two members each; and all the rest of the counties have only one member each.

Both senators and representatives in the state legislature are elected for two-year terms. Each member is allowed a salary of ten dollars a day for the first sixty days of a regular session and the same for the first twenty days of a special session. If the legislature remains in session longer than sixty days in a regular session, or for more than twenty days in a special session, the members must serve without pay for such extra time as is required. In addition to salary, the members are allowed travel expenses of ten cents a mile each way from their homes to Boise, and an additional allowance of five dollars per day while serving on committees.

The Senate is presided over by the Lieutenant Governor of the state. The presiding officer of the House of Representatives is the Speaker, elected from its own membership by the House.

The Legislature at Work. Regular sessions of the legislature meet early in January of every odd-numbered year. Each new legislature spends considerable time at the beginning of its session in organizing for work. Both branches of the legislature choose certain officers for special duties. Then committees are named and actual work gets under way.

A majority of the members of each house constitute a *quorum,* or the number of members that must be present when laws are enacted. Bills may be introduced in either house, after which they are referred to suitable committees for further study.

The committee, after studying a bill, may report it back to the house in which it was first introduced with one of two recommendations: (1) that it pass, or (2) that it does not pass. It may also return the bill without any recommendation at all. The committee also has power to *table a bill,* which means that the committee keeps the bill, thus giving the legislature no opportunity even to vote on the measure. This procedure is often used with bills which the committee members agree are unwise or unimportant.

The law requires that before a bill may be voted on, it must be read three times in the house considering it, each time on a different day. This is so that members will be familiar with the bill, and so that they will avoid passing laws in a hasty or ill-considered manner. However, if the bill is urgent, two thirds of the members may vote to dispense with the three readings usually observed.

If, when the measure comes to a vote, it receives a majority of the votes cast, it is then sent to the other house, where the same procedure is followed. If the two houses fail to agree, the bill is then sent to a joint committee of both houses to iron out the causes of disagreement. Then the amended bill is again sent on its way through the legislature.

When a bill has finally been passed by both houses, it is sent to the governor, who may follow one of three courses: (1) sign the bill, thus making it a law; (2) veto the bill and return it to the legislature with his objections; (3) keep the bill without either signing it or vetoing it. If he keeps it more than five days, it becomes a law without his signature unless the legislature has adjourned. If it has adjourned, the governor may veto the bill by filing it, with his objections, with the Secretary of State within ten days. Unless he does so, it becomes a law without his signature.

Laws passed by the legislature usually go into force sixty days after the session adjourns. Sometimes, however, the legislature declares an emergency and puts the law into effect either at once or at the end of a specified time.

Local Legislative Bodies. The three-way plan, as we have seen, is carried all through American government from the highest to the lowest levels. Operating at the local level are counties, cities and villages, school districts, and, occasionally, other incorporated civic bodies.

Board of County Commissioners. Do your parents pay taxes on their property? Do you have a public road passing your home? Is there a voting precinct in your locality? Do you have a county hospital? Of course, there is the school which you attend.

With all these affairs and many others, the Board of County Commissioners has much authority in the county. The County Commissioners have a considerable number of *legislative* duties which the laws of Idaho require them to perform, as well as *executive* duties. Among the legislative duties of the County Commissioners, these are of greatest importance:

1. The commissioners levy county taxes, fix license fees for certain occupations and services, and in other ways secure the money necessary to operate the county government. This duty parallels that of the legislature at the state level and of Congress at the national level.

2. Like Congress and the legislature, the County Commissioners adopt a budget showing the estimated expense of government for the current year.

3. Though the Board of County Commissioners does not, like Congress and the legislature, pass appropriation bills controlling the spending of public money, the board must approve purchases and unusual spending projects in advance, and bills to be paid by the county are usually examined and allowed by the commissioners before payment is made.

4. Public works are not usually started by the nation or state until Congress or the legislature has given approval and provided the necessary funds. In the same way the Board of County Commissioners sets up such work projects as public roads, bridges, public buildings, and similar undertakings on the county level.

The four examples shown do not by any means include all the legislative duties of the Board of County Commissioners. The board divides the county into districts for voting in elections, establishes courts of justice of the peace, provides for organizing school districts and operating schools, and authorizes the building and maintaining of roads. It equalizes tax assessments within the county. It makes rules and regulations for conducting both its own affairs and those of the other county offices unless the law prescribes the methods to be followed. In short, it does the things necessary to keep the county operating as a going concern, both financially and otherwise.

For the purpose of choosing county commissioners, each county is divided into three districts. One commissioner is elected from each district, but he is elected by the voters of the whole county rather than by those of his district alone. This provision of the law insures that the three sections of the county will be represented on the board and, also, that each commissioner will work for the welfare of the entire county rather than for just a limited portion of it.

Municipal Councils. Cities and villages are known as municipalities, and certain powers have been conferred on them by state law. Like the larger governmental units, they are organized and operated under the three departments of government: legislative, executive, and judicial.

The municipality in or near which you live has certain laws, known as *ordinances,* which are binding upon the people living or visiting there. Among these ordinances are regulations for such things as traffic; curfew hours, after which children are not permitted on the street unattended; keeping streets, alleys, parks, and other public places free from accumulations of waste and rubbish; inspection of restaurants, bakeries, food stores, and other places serving the public; parking restrictions; and scores of other rules in the interest of public health and safety. All such ordinances are enacted by elected *city councils* or by *village boards of trustees.*

SNAKE RIVER PARKWAY AT IDAHO FALLS

Falls of the Snake River, near the heart of downtown Idaho Falls, showing part of the River Parkway. Buildings in background are, left to right: Latterday Saints Temple, Nurses' Home, and Hospital. Such public improvements as streets, water and sewer systems, and parks and playgrounds are authorized by city councils and require a large share of municipal revenues.

Courtesy Idaho Falls Chamber of Commerce and Melville's Studio

Another important duty of municipal councils is to authorize the construction and maintenance of public improvements such as streets, water and sewer systems, public parks and playgrounds, and similar projects. Such improvements require a large share of the public revenue of municipalities.

Classes of Municipalities. Idaho law permits villages and cities to organize as corporations in order to carry on the business of local government. Such incorporated places are classed as villages, cities of the second class, and cities of the first class, depending on their size.

Villages. Any community having a population of 125 to 1,000 people may incorporate itself as a village. The lawmaking or legislative group in a village is the village board of trustees, which consists of five members elected for four-year terms of office.

The board of trustees has, among others, the following legislative powers: to levy taxes; to employ a clerk, treasurer, marshal, and such other officers and workers as may be necessary; to license certain kinds of business and service establishments; to enact local laws known as ordinances; to set up annual budgets; to provide streets and alleys, water systems, parks, and other public improvements; to create local improvement districts; to inspect and regulate bakeries, meat markets, grocery stores, confectioneries, and similar establishments in the interest of public health; to control motor traffic; and to make other rules and regulations for the public welfare.

Cities of the Second Class. Cities of the second class in Idaho are those having 1,000, but less than 15,000 people. Idaho cities of the second class have an organization somewhat different from other municipalities in the state. Such cities must be divided into not less than two or more than six districts known as wards, something not done in either villages or cities of the first class. From each ward two council members are elected for four-year terms.

The city council of second-class cities

has about the same duties as a village board of trustees, plus additional powers to enable it to meet the larger needs of a larger community. The three important powers that are most necessary for all legislative groups are, as we already know, raising revenue, directing and controlling public spending, and making laws, known in municipalities as ordinances.

Cities of the First Class. In 1950 five Idaho cities—Boise, Pocatello, Idaho Falls, Twin Falls, and Nampa—were large enough to be cities of the first class, each having a population of fifteen thousand or more. The main points of difference, except size, between these and cities of the second class are the number of officers, lack of wards, and enlarged powers of the mayor and council. If the city has adopted the city-manager form of government, legislative duties are performed by the city commissioners and the executive duties by the city manager and his assistants.

The city council (or the commissioners) in cities of the first class has all the powers given to village trustees and councils of second-class cities, plus these additional powers: to establish a board of health; to enact ordinances providing for initiative, recall, and referendum elections; to collect from the county one half of all county road taxes paid by residents of the city; and to establish a civil-service system for members of the fire and police departments. They have other additional powers, but the ones named are the most important.

School Boards. Who makes the rules for your school or your classroom? Sometimes this is done by the teachers or the superintendent and principals. Sometimes the pupils make the rules, or at least help to make them. But if either of these plans is used it is because the school board has delegated that authority, for under the laws of Idaho the school trustees have the duty and the power to make rules for the schools to follow, and they also have the power to enforce the rules.

Thus school boards, like boards of county commissioners, have both legislative and executive powers. In actual practice they usually leave most of these powers in the hands of the school faculty.

But there are some powers the school trustees cannot leave to others. The most important legislative powers they have are the same powers that belong to other legislative bodies, namely: (1) to levy taxes and use other legal methods of raising money; (2) to make budgets and control the spending of school money; and (3) to make general rules and policies for managing the affairs of the districts.

Do you now see that the legislative or lawmaking branch of government is one of the three great divisions in our American plan of government? In the Congress of the United States, in the state legislature, in the Board of County Commissioners, in the city council, in the village board of trustees, and in the school board of our own district, we find at work the fundamental principle that the laws of the land should be made by the elected representatives of the people themselves. In that way the people keep under their own control the government that serves them. Can you think of a better way in which we might govern ourselves?

Direct Legislation. The constitution

of Idaho, Article III, Section 1, reserves to the people the three powers of direct legislation: the *initiative,* the *referendum,* and the *recall.* Let us see how those direct powers do or might operate.

The Initiative. If the people of Idaho desire a certain law, do they have to depend upon the state legislature to enact it? Suppose the legislature neglects or refuses to enact a law the people want. What can be done about it?

In such a case, a petition is drawn up and when signed by 10 per cent of the voters of the state, it is filed with the Secretary of State. The proposition is then placed on ballots, to be voted upon at the next general election. If a majority of voters favor the proposal, it becomes a law of the state. This direct power of the people is known as the initiative.

The Referendum. If the state legislature passes a bill and it is signed by the governor, the bill becomes a law. If the law is unpopular, it may be rejected by a direct vote of the people.

An example of this occurred after a special session of the legislature, in 1935, had passed the sales-tax law urged by Governor Ross. In a referendum vote the sales tax was defeated by the direct legislative power of the people of Idaho and that source of state revenue was closed.

The Recall. If an elected official of the state of Idaho should neglect or refuse to render satisfactory service, or should prove to be unfit or corrupt in office, the people may, by petition, take action to remove him from office. Though such power has been seldom used, the recall law is a strong aid to good government, since elected officers know that the people have the power to remove them from office by holding an election to put the matter to a vote.

II. THE EXECUTIVE DEPARTMENT OF GOVERNMENT

AFTER LAWS ARE ENACTED, they must be put into operation if they are to be of any use. To apply the laws, to put the wheels of government in motion, is the task of the *executive department.* Like the legislative branch, it extends all the way through our government, from the President's office to the smallest unit of government in the local community. The executive department is the working part of government.

The Idaho Executive Department. The government of Idaho serves the people of the state in many ways. In the way it is organized and operates, our state executive department is very much like that of the national government. If you will turn back to the chart on page 245 and compare the executive departments on the national and state levels, you will see how closely they resemble each other in their organization and their work. The work of the executive department is the responsibility of the governor and the many hundreds of assistants who aid him in the performance of the administration of the laws of Idaho.

The Governor. "The supreme executive power of the State is vested in the governor, who shall see that the laws are faithfully executed." In these words the constitution of Idaho briefly but clearly defines the position, the authority, and the duty of the governor. His position in the state is similar to that of the President of the nation, though, of course, on a much smaller scale.

Since 1946 Idaho governors have been elected to four-year terms and may not be elected twice in succession. The office pays a salary of ten thousand dollars a year, and certain travel and other allowances are made to cover necessary expenses.

The governor must be at least thirty years of age, a citizen of the United States, and must have lived in the state two years or more preceding his election. Though Idaho has never had a woman governor, there is nothing in the law to prevent electing one to the state's highest office.

includes the Governors' Conference, the Conference of (State) Chief Justices of the Supreme Courts, the National Association of (State) Attorneys General, the National Association of (State) Secretaries of State, the National Association of State Budget Officers, and the National Association of State Purchasing Agents.

State and Federal co-operation is especially important in the field of Federal grants-in-aid, the name given to Federal participation in programs shared in and paid for jointly by the states and the Federal government. In 1952, for example, such grants-in-aid,[1] as shown to the nearest million dollars, were as follows, of which Idaho received about $14,728,000:

Public Welfare and Assistance	$1,149,000,000
Education	293,000,000
Highways	413,000,000
Health and Hospitals	114,000,000
Employment Security Administration	187,000,000
Other Grants-in-Aid	174,000,000

Unit 9 explained some of the ways in which the governor's work and influence are important. He has many duties, serves on a number of administrative and supervisory boards, and from his office in the Statehouse in Boise carries on his main task, which is seeing that the "laws of the state are faithfully executed."

As we saw earlier, the governor's office is the connecting link between Idaho and the Federal government and between the state and other states in matters of co-operative welfare. Idaho, through the office of the governor and his administrative assistants, holds membership in the Council of State Governments. This

Idaho also participates in interstate compacts or agreements with other states on such matters as sharing the waters of Snake River and other important streams partly in Idaho and partly in other states. Through the Western Interstate Commission for Higher Education, Idaho helps in planning studies and research programs in colleges and universities and joins in the mutual recognition of credits earned in such institutions. The state also has reciprocity (res-i-PROS-i-ti) agreements with many states on such matters

[1] Council of State Governments, *Book of the States, 1954–55; the Standard Biennial Reference Work on State Government* [ed. by Frank A. Smothers and M. Clair Cotterill] (Vol. 10) (Chicago, 1954).

PICTURE FRAMED BY MOTHER NATURE

The Idaho State Board of Publicity, under the supervision of the Secretary of State, was created by the legislature to advertise the many advantages and attractions possessed by Idaho. It was one of the scores of agencies that make up the executive department of government in Idaho.

as highway usage, professional licenses, and similar matters. In all such co-operative agreements the governor and his executive aides share responsibility.

Other Elected Executive Officers. To assist the governor in his work, seven state officers are elected every four years. These are Lieutenant Governor, Secretary of State, State Auditor, State Treasurer, Attorney General, State Superintendent of Public Instruction, and State Inspector of Mines. Each of these officers heads a special executive department of state government. Among them, they have thousands of duties to perform, but the main task of each is briefly stated in the following paragraph.

The Lieutenant Governor presides over the sessions of the State Senate and acts as governor when that officer is out of the state or when, for any reason, he is unable to carry on his work. The Secretary of State is the important record officer, keeping the official records of state affairs. The Auditor is the state's

head bookkeeper, making very careful and accurate records of the state's financial transactions. The Treasurer has charge of the money belonging to the state, paying it out according to law to meet the necessary expenses of state government. The Attorney General is the state's lawyer and the legal advisor of the other state officers. The Superintendent of Public Instruction has general charge of the public schools of the state and is the executive officer of the State Board of Education. The State Inspector of Mines has supervisory duties in connection with mining and minerals in Idaho, safety in the mines being a duty of major importance.

The Governor's Cabinet. In an earlier unit (Unit 9) we learned that Governor Davis recommended a reorganization of the administrative department, which the legislature made into law as the Administration Consolidation Act in 1919. This law is the basis for our present system of civil administrative departments which assist the governor in performing his many duties. Most departments are headed by a commissioner or a director appointed by the governor and responsible to him. The table that follows lists these departments and gives a brief summary of duties connected with each.

Other Administrative and Executive Agencies. Several other state agencies have important duties to perform in connection with the state government and its services to the people of Idaho. Some of them were created by constitutional amendments voted on by the people themselves and can be changed only by changing the state constitution. Some have been discussed in other units of our story of Idaho. Some may be of special value or interest in your own community and might well be made the subject of class reports or talks by people who know of their work.

Among these agencies are the Board of Correction, State Board of Health, State Board of Land Commissioners, State Board of Education, Idaho Fish and Game Commission, State Board of Highway Directors, Public Utilities Commission, State Tax Commission, State Library Board, State Historical Society, State Planning Board, State Land Board, State Board of Publicity, and many others. On some of these agencies the governor and other elected state officers serve, while some are entirely separate from other departments of state government. Do you think the names of these agencies suggest, for most of them, the kind of work they do and the services they perform?

The Executive Department in Local Government. Now that we have seen how the executive departments of the Federal and state government are organized and do their work, let us see how the same plan of organization is carried into the counties and municipalities of Idaho. It is on the local levels, perhaps, that government touches us most closely.

Executive Department of County Government. Both elected and appointed officers make up the executive or administrative branch of county government. Most of these are provided for in the state constitution, but some have been authorized under laws enacted by the state legislature.

Though the Board of County Commissioners has some executive duties, we have seen that a good part of its work belongs to the legislative rather than the executive department. Most of the routine or ordinary work of county government is performed by seven elected executive officers. These are: (1) the sheriff, (2) prosecuting attorney, (3) clerk, auditor, and recorder, (4) treasurer and tax collector, (5) assessor, (6) coroner, and (7) surveyor. It would take a whole unit or more to give a detailed account of the many tasks these officers perform, but a short statement will give a general idea of their work.

The *sheriff* is the peace officer of the county, his main duties being to enforce the laws, preserve order, and protect life and property. Prisoners in the county jail are in his charge. A special duty under his supervision is the examination required by law for all persons in his county who wish to obtain a license permitting them to drive automobiles.

Table No. 7

IDAHO CIVIL ADMINISTRATIVE DEPARTMENTS

(Sometimes called the Governor's Cabinet)

DEPARTMENT	HEADED BY	SUMMARY OF IMPORTANT DUTIES
Aeronautics	Director of Aeronautics	All matters pertaining to air transportation, flying fields, air education, and other general aeronautic affairs
Agriculture	Commissioner of Agriculture	Agricultural and livestock affairs; noxious weeds; agricultural warehouses; weights and measures; co-operates with the U.S. Department of Agriculture; plant and animal diseases and insect pests; marketing rules and regulations; inspection service; plant and animal quarantine
Finance	Commissioner of Finance	Banks and banking; bureau of public accounts; uniform system of bookkeeping for state and county officers; inspection of securities, etc.
Insurance	Commissioner of Insurance	General supervision of insurance companies operating in Idaho, etc.
Labor	Commissioner of Labor	Statistical labor office; represents Idaho in dealing with Federal Mediation and Conciliation Service; co-operates with U.S. Department of Labor and with Industrial Accident Board; aids in arbitration of labor disputes, etc.
Law Enforcement	Commissioner of Law Enforcement	Motor vehicles in general; liquor control; licensing of special occupations; highway patrol; safety on highways, etc.
Public Assistance	Commissioner of Public Assistance	Old-age pensions; the blind; dependent children; co-operates with Federal social security and county public assistance agencies, etc.
Public Health (now under supervision of State Board of Health)	Director of Public Health	Drugs, food, and food products; health regulations; milk and milk products; tuberculosis; water supplies; bureau of child hygiene; co-operates with Federal and local agencies; industrial hygiene, juvenile problems, etc.
Public Investments	Commissioner of Public Investments	Invests special funds and other public funds of the state so they will earn income instead of lying idle, etc.
Public Works	Commissioner of Public Works	State public buildings, except those under the control of the Board of Regents of the University of Idaho
Reclamation	State Reclamation Engineer	Irrigation; water rights; drainage; water agreements with other states; small co-operative and community reservoirs, etc.

The *prosecuting attorney* is the county lawyer. He is the legal adviser of the county commissioners and other county officers. He also prosecutes, or conducts, the trials of persons accused of violating the laws of the state or county.

The *clerk, auditor, and recorder* is really four offices in one. As clerk of the district court, he keeps a complete record of court trials and other court business. As county clerk he makes a record of the official acts of the Board of County Commissioners. As auditor, he keeps the financial records of the county and issues written orders, called warrants, in payment of county expenses. As recorder he keeps a record of deeds, mortgages, and other legal papers relating to the ownership of land and other property. You young people may be interested to know that this office issues marriage licenses, a service that you may some day desire yourselves!

The *treasurer and tax collector's* office collects taxes and other county revenue and sees that these funds are kept securely and used only in a lawful manner. Bills owed by the county are paid by the treasurer on warrants issued by the office of the auditor, the two offices thus serving as a check on each other and lessening the chances of errors or the misuse of public funds.

To the *assessor* is given the duty of assessing or placing a value on property in the county for purposes of taxation. Such property includes real estate; personal property of nearly all kinds; and railroads, telephone and telegraph lines, power plants, and similar public utilities, so called because they serve the public. The assessor also has the special duty of issuing licenses for cars, trucks, and other motor vehicles.

The *coroner* investigates deaths that occur under circumstances that may indicate murder, suicide, or criminal carelessness. To assist in this work, the coroner may call a jury of six persons to hear the testimony of witnesses and examine other evidence that may explain the cause of the death. The coroner may also serve as sheriff if that officer is out of the county or unable to perform the duties of his office.

The principal duties of the *surveyor* are to establish boundary lines for land, survey rights of way for roads and streets, and do other surveying, or land-measuring work, that may be done on the instructions of the Board of County Commissioners. This office also keeps maps and plats relating to lands in the county.

Most counties in Idaho have other officers in addition to those elected by the people. These have become necessary because changed conditions under which Idaho people now live have created needs for services that the elected officers have neither the duty nor the right to provide. As you go through the list of such special officers, see which ones your county provides.

These additional officers may include: (1) a *county board of education,* required in all counties whose schools are not all consolidated under the provisions of the School Reorganization Act, to exercise general supervision over school affairs; (2) a *probation* or *attendance officer* to see that children of the county attend school as required by law; (3) a *county physician,* who serves alone or as part of a health department, to improve

NEW COURTHOUSE
AT POCATELLO

Completed in 1954, the simplicity of design and practical interior arrangement of Bannock County's new courthouse make this one of Idaho's most attractive seats of county government.

IDAHO'S OLDEST AND NEWEST COURTHOUSES

IDAHO'S FIRST COURTHOUSE

At Pierce still stands the first courthouse ever built in Idaho. At the time Pierce City was the county seat of Shoshone County, created by the legislature of Washington Territory before Idaho Territory was organized. The building is now used as a meeting place for various clubs and other local groups.

health conditions in the county; (4) a *county agricultural agent,* who assists farmers and ranchers with their problems; (5) a *county club leader,* who organizes and supervises girls' and boys' 4-H Clubs; (6) a *home demonstration agent,* who aids women in problems of homemaking and home improvement; and (7) a *welfare officer,* who takes care of relief cases and other types of public assistance for needy citizens.

Executive Department of Municipal Government. Nearly all Idaho cities elect a chief executive officer called the *mayor.* It is the mayor's duty to see that the city government serves the people as efficiently as the funds available will allow.

The mayor is assisted by other administrative officers, usually appointed by the mayor with the consent and approval of the city council. The *fire chief* is head of the fire department. The police department is under the *chief of police.* A *street superintendent* manages the construction and maintenance of streets, bridges, and other public thoroughfares. The water supply is supervised by the *water superin-*

tendent. Parks and playgrounds are sometimes a separate department under the supervision of a special department head. The *city engineer* has general charge of many public improvements, such as streets and sewers, water mains, bridges, new additions, and many other projects, his office working out the details for such construction and similar projects. City moneys are handled by the *treasurer.* The *clerk* keeps a record of the official acts of the city council and other officers.

Besides the mayor-council type of government used in most Idaho cities, two other plans of government are permitted under the laws of the state. These are the *commission* form and the *city-manager* form of municipal government.

The commission form is not used in any Idaho city. But the city-manager plan was adopted a few years ago by the people of Twin Falls. A short time later Pocatello adopted the plan, and it is now being considered by the people of several other cities. Under this plan the people elect several *commissioners,* usually seven. The commissioners then employ a *city manager,* frequently a person especially fitted by training or experience to manage city affairs. The manager, with the approval of the commissioners, employs heads for the various departments of city government. Under this plan the commissioners are the legislative body, planning the over-all policies to be adopted. The plans thus made are turned over to the city manager and his assistants to be carried out in the service of the people.

III. THE JUDICIAL DEPARTMENT OF GOVERNMENT

To "ESTABLISH JUSTICE" is one of the principal purposes for which the Constitution of the United States made provision. To carry out that purpose, courts of justice have been established for the United States, for each of the states, and for the counties and local communities throughout the nation. This very important part of our government is the *judicial department.*

State Courts. The state constitution of Idaho recognized the necessity for law and order and authorized courts and judges as a judicial department of state government. Article V, Section 2, of the constitution reads as follows:

The judicial power of the State shall be vested in a court for the trial of impeachments, a supreme court, district courts, probate courts, courts of justices of the peace, and such other courts inferior to the supreme court as may be established by law for any incorporated city or town.

Impeachment. When any officer, from the governor down, neglects or refuses to carry out his duties, he may be removed from office by *impeachment.* The House of Representatives of the state legislature has the sole right to impeach an officer; that is, officially charge him with unfitness and neglect of duty.

After an impeachment is voted by the House of Representatives, the trial is conducted by the State Senate. In order to be adjudged guilty, two thirds of the Senate must so vote. If the governor is impeached, the Senate trial is presided over by the Chief Justice of the Idaho Supreme Court.

The Supreme Court. This is the highest court of the state. It is composed of five justices elected for six-year terms by the people of the state. The names of candidates for Justice of the Supreme Court and judges of the district courts must be on a nonpartisan ballot, which means that there is nothing on the ballot to show the political party to which the candidate belongs. Can you suggest a reason for this?

The Supreme Court must hold at least five terms of court each year, two terms being held in Boise. At least one term each year must be held in Coeur d'Alene, Lewiston, and Pocatello.

The Supreme Court is not a trial court. It reviews cases carried to it by appeal from the district courts. In such appeals the court makes three kinds of decisions: (1) It may affirm the judgment of the district court. (2) It may reverse the decision of the district court. (3) It may order the district court to conduct a new trial. Whatever decision the Supreme Court makes is final.

The Supreme Court also performs other duties and services. It gives examinations to persons who desire to be admitted to the bar; that is, to be given the right to practice law in Idaho. It may recommend that the state legislature appropriate money to pay just claims against the state. This court also has supervision over the State Law Library.

The Supreme Court also has the power to issue four kinds of special writs: (1) *habeas corpus,* a legal order by which an accused person must be given a prompt trial or be released; (2) *mandamus,* a court order requiring an officer to perform his legal duty; (3) *certiorari,* an order to a lower court to send its records

to the Supreme Court; and (4) an *injunction,* or court order, forbidding any action that threatens danger or damage to a person or to property.

District Courts and Judges. The *district courts* are the principal trial courts of the state. Usually several counties are combined into a single judicial district, each presided over by a district judge who holds sessions of the district court in the county seat of each county in his district.

The state legislature has divided Idaho into eleven judicial districts. The district court of each district is presided over by one or more district judges, elected on a nonpartisan ballot by the people of the district. The table that follows shows the judicial districts of Idaho. In which district do you live?

By law, there must be at least two sessions of the district court in each county of the district annually. In the more densely populated counties sessions are usually held oftener than twice a year. In these sessions the district judge, assisted by the prosecuting attorney, the sheriff, and, usually, a jury of twelve citizens, conducts *criminal trials.* If the jury hearing the evidence finds the accused person guilty, it is the judge's duty to sentence the prisoner; or, if not guilty, to order his release.

Many *civil cases* are also tried in the district court. Civil cases are usually disputes over property, such as the title to land, suits to collect past-due debts, suits for damages to persons or property, and similar matters not of a criminal nature. Such cases are not always tried before juries, but either party to a civil suit has the right to demand a jury trial.

Table No. 8

JUDICIAL DISTRICTS OF IDAHO

JUDICIAL DISTRICT	COUNTIES COMPRISING	NUMBER OF JUDGES
First District	Shoshone	I
Second District	Clearwater, Latah	I
Third District	Ada, Boise, Elmore, Owyhee	2
Fourth District	Blaine, Camas, Gooding, Lincoln	I
Fifth District	Bannock, Bear Lake, Caribou, Franklin, Power, Oneida	2
Sixth District	Bingham, Butte, Custer, Lemhi	I
Seventh District	Adams, Canyon, Gem, Payette, Valley, Washington	2
Eighth District	Benewah, Bonner, Boundary, Kootenai	2
Ninth District	Bonneville, Clark, Fremont, Jefferson, Madison, Teton	I
Tenth District	Idaho, Lewis, Nez Perce	I
Eleventh District	Cassia, Jerome, Minidoka, Twin Falls	2

This method of administering justice and protecting life and property is very old in civilization. It was developed in England in very early times. It crossed the Atlantic with the English settlers and has from earliest colonial days been a part of self-government among the people of the United States and Canada. One of the most interesting and instructive things your class could do would be to visit the courthouse while district court is in session and see for yourselves how justice is decided, how wrongdoers are punished, and how the people of your county protect themselves and their property in a just, lawful, and sensible manner.

County and Local Courts. As we have already seen, the district courts of Idaho must hold at least two sessions of court

JURY READY FOR A TRIAL

Justice under the law, with equal rights for all, is best assured by having the guilt or innocence of every person on trial decided by a jury of citizens chosen in the community where the trial is conducted.

yearly in each county seat of the state. Each county also has a probate court for special kinds of work. Other courts serve the needs of local communities in the counties.

Probate Court and Probate Judge. The *probate court* is presided over by a probate judge elected by the people of the county. Among the important duties of the *probate judge* are: (1) to settle the estates of deceased (dead) persons, passing the property on according to law and to the legal heirs or to those who may lawfully inherit the estate; (2) to appoint guardians and trustees to look after the welfare of children who are orphaned or are without proper care and for other persons not competent or able to manage their own affairs; (3) to conduct trials of civil cases involving not more than three hundred dollars; (4) to preside as trial judge in criminal cases classed as *misdemeanors,* minor offenses punishable by small fines or terms in jail; and (5) to handle cases involving *juvenile delinquents,* as we call children and young people under eighteen years of age who find themselves in difficulties with the law. A law enacted by the 1953 legislature also gives the prosecuting attorney special powers to deal with juvenile offenders.

Justices of the Peace. To provide courts for smaller areas than counties, Idaho has officers called *justices of the peace* in each voting precinct of the state. These courts may try civil cases involving not more than three hundred dollars and criminal misdemeanor cases in which fines cannot exceed three hundred dollars or jail sentences be for more than six months. Justices of the peace may also conduct hearings in the cases of persons suspected of having committed more serious crimes and, if the evidence seems sufficient, order such persons to be held for trial in the district court.

To assist the courts of justices of the peace, a peace officer called the *constable* is elected in each precinct. Besides his connection with the justices of the peace, the constable has the responsibility of seeing that elections are conducted legally, this being perhaps his most important duty in a nation where the people rule through a system of free and secret elections.

Municipal Courts. Incorporated cities and villages in Idaho have municipal courts, usually called *police courts,* to hear cases in which persons have been arrested by the police for alleged violations of city and village ordinances. Such courts are presided over by *police judges,* who may fine offenders or sentence them to terms in the municipal jail. They have no authority except in the enforcement of local ordinances.

Federal Courts in Idaho. Idaho is represented in this system of courts by a United States District Court, presided over by a Federal judge appointed by the President. In order to serve all parts of the state, sessions of the court are held at stated times in Boise, Coeur d'Alene, Moscow, and Pocatello. The judge's chambers and principal office are in the Federal Building in Boise. The 1954 session of Congress enacted a law providing for thirty additional Federal judges. One of these is assigned to Idaho, so some changes in the sessions of Federal Court will probably be made.

Cases tried in the Federal District

Court are those to which Federal laws apply. The court has nothing to do with laws enacted by Idaho. Cases tried in the Federal District Court of Idaho may be carried by appeal to the Circuit Court of Appeals for the Ninth Judicial District, in which Idaho is located, and from that court, if desired, to the Supreme Court of the United States, which is the highest court of the land.

IV. CAN FREEDOM BE LOST?

YOU HAVE SEEN, in Units 13 and 14, something of the way in which our people govern themselves and maintain their liberty. Freedom has been lost in many lands and in many periods of history, and if it dies in the rest of America, it will die in Idaho. To remind us that "eternal vigilance is the price of liberty," the American Heritage Foundation sent the Freedom Train on a tour of the United States in 1947. The train stopped in several cities of Idaho to display copies of the immortal documents of human liberty that go to make up the foundations on which our own American Republic is built. Among the documents were copies of the Magna Carta, the Mayflower Compact, the Declaration of Independence, the Constitution of the United States, the Bill of Rights, the Emancipation Proclamation, and the United Nations Charter. Does your school have any copies of these famous documents on display?

The quotation that follows is part of the American Heritage Foundation program which the Freedom Train demonstrated. It shows clearly that we, all of us, must share in the program or run the risk of losing our precious heritage of freedom.

Whether you call it a Democracy or a Republic, whether you judge its benefits by the car in your garage or by the freedom to worship at the church of your choice, by the food on your table or by your freedom to speak out in public without fear, you are a member of a system of government based on the dignity and freedom of the individual and moral equality among human beings.

This system of living together has been achieved only after many generations of struggle against the doctrine that some men have the right to rule others. It is based on the oldest written constitution in the world still in force. It has been preserved through great idealism— great human sacrifice.

Like the sun in the sky and the cream in your coffee, the continuation of this system is too often taken for granted.

Let us be warned: today its flaws are being exaggerated and its benefits minimized in other parts of the world.

At home, its blood stream is weakened by indifference, neglect, and even cynicism.

The time for rededication has arrived! Personal, active participation in the affairs of the nation, the state, the city, and the community by all people of good will and public spirit is our only safeguard for the freedom we have so dearly won.

FREEDOM IS EVERYBODY'S JOB!

*   *   *   *   *

The short story of our American plan of government given in Units 13 and 14

Color photo by Ansgar Johnson

THE CATTLE INDUSTRY IS IMPORTANT TO IDAHO'S ECONOMY

This picture was taken on the Gordon MacGregor ranch in Round Valley

should have made several important things clear: (1) The plan safeguards our liberties because it is based on constitutional law rather than on the personal desires of rulers. (2) The powers of government rest in the hands of the people themselves and are carried out by the elected representatives of the people. (3) The three separate departments of government serve as a system of checks and balances that prevent any one department from becoming strong enough to seriously threaten our liberties. So simple, yet so logical and reasonable our plan of government is! If we cherish it, if we all share in it as we should, it will preserve our freedom and the freedom of countless generations yet unborn. It is truly a precious heritage of our America, a heritage we in Idaho fully share.

Using Our Land and Water Resources

How the people of Idaho have used the natural resources of land and water to make agriculture the top-ranking industry of the state; and how the utilization of water power provides a developing source of electricity.

OUR FERTILE SOILS have, for three quarters of a century or more, been Idaho's greatest natural resource. In the last territorial decade agriculture forged ahead of mining to become the most important Idaho industry, a rank it still holds. In fact, the annual agricultural income is more than the combined incomes from forests and minerals, the other two great wealth-producing natural resources of the state.

However, the soil alone could never have paid such rich rewards. Water, and its wide and abundant use in irrigation, has provided the magic touch that has made Idaho, particularly southern Idaho, one of the outstanding agricultural regions of the West.

I. IDAHO'S GOOD EARTH

THE PEOPLE OF IDAHO own, roughly, one third of the state. Approximately two thirds of its 52,972,160 acres are the property of the United States. The federally owned or managed lands are chiefly national forests and the public domain.

Types of Soil. In *Soils and Man,* the 1938 Yearbook of the United States Department of Agriculture, the soils of Idaho are classified in five groups or types. These are: (1) mountain soils, (2) gray desert soils, (3) prairie soils, (4) alluvial soils, and (5) glacial soils.

The *mountain soils* are, as a rule, lacking in fertility of the kind necessary for ordinary crops. They are, nevertheless, of great value for they nourish our extensive forests, provide summer range for livestock, and furnish the food supply for the wild animals that subsist on vegetation of various kinds.

The *gray desert soils* are the soils of the Snake River Valley, the plateaus and foothills bordering the valley, and the tablelands, benches, and some valleys of the Great Basin. Formed of decomposed lava, or lava ash, alluvial wash, and loess deposited by the westerly winds, these loams, or mixed sand and clay containing vegetable matter, are among the most fertile soils of the nation. When placed under irrigation or when they obtain sufficient moisture from precipitation, they produce high yields of all kinds of crops suited to southern Idaho.

Millions of acres of gray desert soils are not capable of being irrigated. By dry-farm methods some of this land is

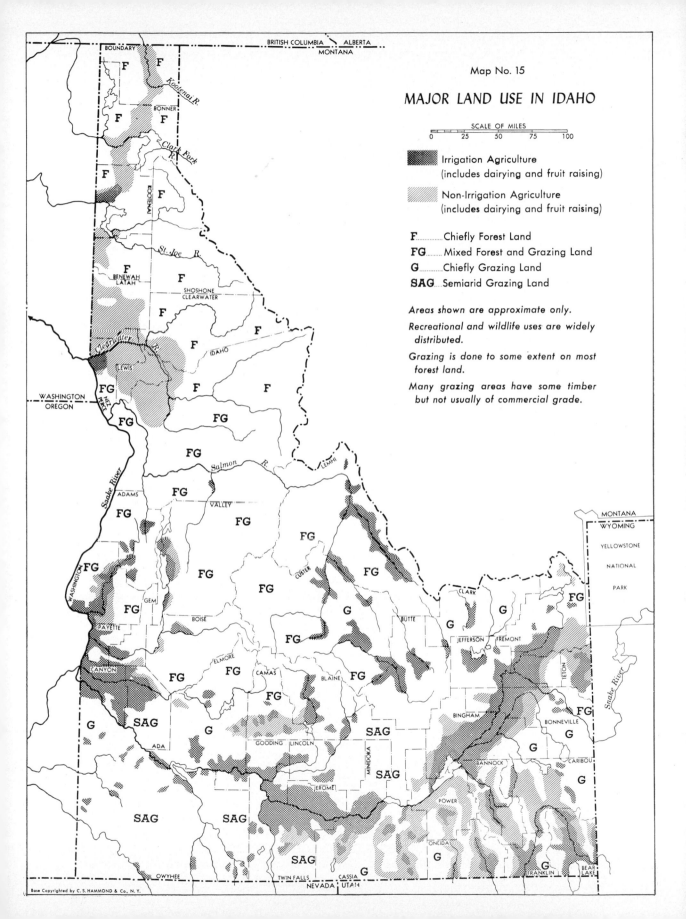

Map No. 15

MAJOR LAND USE IN IDAHO

SCALE OF MILES
0   25   50   75   100

Irrigation Agriculture
(includes dairying and fruit raising)

Non-Irrigation Agriculture
(includes dairying and fruit raising)

F........Chiefly Forest Land

FG....Mixed Forest and Grazing Land

G........Chiefly Grazing Land

SAG...Semiarid Grazing Land

Areas shown are approximate only.

Recreational and wildlife uses are widely
distributed.

Grazing is done to some extent on most
forest land.

Many grazing areas have some timber
but not usually of commercial grade.

Base Copyrighted by C. S. Hammond & Co., N. Y.

GENERAL VIEW OF A FARMING AREA ON THE OWYHEE PROJECT

The region is well known for the fine quality of its fruits, and vegetables of nearly all kinds grow here in abundance

FORESTS AND WILD PASTURES

More of Idaho's soils are used for growing trees and as natural pasture land than for any other use, giving us high rank in forestry, lumbering, and livestock production.

made to yield profitable crops. Some of our best wheatland is in such dry-farm areas. Most of this soil, however, that cannot be irrigated, grows native grasses and herbage on which great numbers of livestock are pastured.

The *prairie soils* are nearly all in the Clearwater Plateau. They are deep, rich, mellow loams of a darkish color, composed chiefly of volcanic ash deposited over the region by winds from the Columbian Plains to the westward. These natural grasslands are excellent pastures. Placed under cultivation, they produce large crops and have the advantage of being in the part of the state where irrigation is not necessary.

The *alluvial soils* have been washed down from mountain slopes and deposited in the valleys and basins. Old lake beds, about which we read in an earlier unit, are also made up largely of alluvial sediments. Most of these lands, naturally very fertile, have been brought under irrigation except where no water is available or where they lie too high for successful farming. The greater part of these soils

is in mountain valleys and basins, and the uncultivated areas are grazing sections or sections which support wildlife adapted to the region.

The *glacial soils* are found principally in northern Idaho. There the continental glacier spread pulverized glacial drift over considerable areas, notably the Purcell Trench and the plateau district to the west and north of Lake Coeur d'Alene. These gravelly loams are open, porous soils which produce well but which require more moisture than is generally supplied by natural precipitation. This explains why the principal irrigated section of the Panhandle is the Rathdrum Prairie and bordering lands.

Uses of the Soils. In general the soils of Idaho have two main uses: (1) agricultural uses, including the growing of livestock, and (2) the production of trees and other natural vegetation. The use that is of the most value to the people depends on the natural conditions prevailing in the various sections of the state. Which of these uses is most important in your own section of Idaho?

Courtesy Pocatello Chamber of Commerce

Ever since Idaho became a state, the agricultural uses of the soil have provided the major source of income for our people. Even the forested portions of the state have immense agricultural values, since they provide natural pastures for livestock and in them are the sources of most of the streams that furnish irrigation water for the semiarid plains and valleys that would, without water, be of little value for raising crops.

Principal Agricultural Regions. In Units 5 and 6 we learned the locations and resources of the natural regions of Idaho. Unit 10 made us acquainted with the leading agricultural counties. Now let us consider briefly the chief farming regions and their advantages and see how they contribute to the agricultural economy of the state. (See map, page 265)

The Upper Snake River Valley. This great agricultural section extends from the vicinity of American Falls northeastward up the Snake River Valley and its tributary valleys to the Boundary Ranges of the Continental Divide and the Wyoming border. It includes all or a major part of Bannock, Bingham, Bonneville, Clark, Fremont, Jefferson, Madison, Power, and Teton counties. With a total area of nearly 8,000,000 acres, it includes approximately 3,316,000 acres of farmlands, of which close to 600,000 acres are under irrigation.

Elevations in the Upper Snake River Valley farming areas range from about 4,300 feet at American Falls to slightly more than 6,000 feet in the highest cultivated sections of Teton Basin and the mountain valleys along the northern border of the Upper Snake River Valley. The average annual precipitation varies from nine to sixteen inches, depending mainly on elevation. The length of the growing season is from about four and a half months in the lower elevations to less than three months in the highest cultivated districts.

The principal crops of the Upper Snake River Valley are potatoes, wheat,

GROWING IDAHO'S MOST
NOTED CROP

World-famous potatoes are
grown in great quantities on the
fertile irrigated lands of the
Upper Snake River Valley.

Courtesy U.S. Bureau of Reclamation, Region No. 1, Boise

alfalfa hay, sugar beets, barley, and red clover and field peas grown for seed. Here is the chosen home of the Idaho Russet potatoes, farmed throughout the nation and in many foreign lands for superior flavor and cooking qualities. Wheat is grown extensively on both the irrigated valley lands and on the dry-farm lands of benches and foothills bordering the valleys.

Some vegetables are raised for market, particularly carrots and green peas, though not in very large quantities. Apples, raspberries, and strawberries are grown commercially on a small scale in certain favored localities. Certified seed, mainly Russet potatoes and alfalfa, bring premium prices. Most hardy green vegetables do well on irrigated land.

Ranked in order of size, the principal cities of this region are Pocatello, Idaho Falls, Blackfoot, Rexburg, St. Anthony, and Rigby. All except Pocatello depend almost entirely upon the agricultural products of the region for their business

success, and even Pocatello would not prosper if deprived of the income based on the crops and livestock of surrounding areas.

Magic Valley. Elevation and climate are somewhat more favorable in Magic Valley than in the Upper Snake River Valley. General elevation is approximately from three thousand to five thousand feet and annual precipitation from eight inches to fifteen inches. The growing season varies from three to five months, depending on elevation.

The chief crops are the same as those of the Upper Snake River Valley, with the addition of beans, onions, and tree fruits. As we have already learned, this part of Idaho is one of the most important bean-growing sections of the United States.

The eight counties of Blaine, Camas, Cassia, Gooding, Jerome, Lincoln, Minidoka, and Twin Falls, which are geographically located in the Magic Valley agricultural section, have a total area of

Courtesy Idaho Falls Chamber of Commerce

WALKING MILK FACTORIES AT WORK

Dairy cows helped Dwight Disney, dairyman near Idaho Falls, win the title of "Idaho Grassman of 1952." The Upper Snake River Valley is one of Idaho's many fine dairying sections.

ONIONS GROWN FOR SEED

The Magic Valley region of Snake River Valley produces bumper crops of onions, beans, potatoes, wheat, alfalfa, and other crops.

Courtesy U.S. Bureau of Reclamation, Region No. 1, Boise

more than 7,000,000 acres, of which about 660,000 acres are under irrigation.

Ranked in order of size, the principal Magic Valley cities are Twin Falls, Burley, Jerome, Gooding, Rupert, Buhl, and Filer. Without exception, these owe their success to the products of the agricultural lands of this fertile region.

The Lower Snake River Valley. Another group of eight counties makes up the Idaho sections of the Lower Snake River Valley. These are Ada, Adams, Canyon, Elmore, Gem, Owyhee, Payette, and Washington counties. Of the total of 3,055,000 acres in farms, about 550,-

000 acres were under irrigation in 1950.

In this great farming section is found the greatest diversity of crops in Idaho. The soils are no better, but elevation, climate, and length of growing season all combine to make possible the raising of nearly all kinds of middle Temperate Zone crops. The elevation ranges from a little more than two thousand feet in the lower end of the valley to slightly over three thousand feet on the Mountain Home Plateau, and the growing season ranges in general from about four to five and one half months. Precipitation, mostly in the winter and spring, averages

SUGAR FROM THE SOIL

This Idaho field of sugar beets helped fill the sugar bins of the nation. Both climate and soil are well adapted to the growing of this important crop.

SUNNY SLOPE ORCHARD

The Lower Snake River Valley is ideally suited to the production of tree fruit, apples, prunes, peaches, cherries, and apricots being most important.

from about ten inches to twenty inches annually in the various parts of the valley region.

Among the field crops, wheat, alfalfa, clover, oats, barley, corn, potatoes, sugar beets, beans, and onions all return heavy yields. Vegetables of nearly all kinds thrive. Lettuce, sweet corn, green peas, carrots, early potatoes, melons, cantaloupes, and other crops of the truck farmer and market gardener move to market in great quantities.

Fruit growing is so important that Idaho is well known in the West for the fine quality of its fruits, most of which are raised in the Lower Snake River Valley section. Apples and prunes are the leading fruits, but cherries, apricots, peaches, plums, pears, grapes, and berries are all grown commercially. According to figures compiled by the Idaho Public Utilities Commission, our state's orchards annually load for shipment about five thousand carloads of fruit. This does not take into account the large quantities of fruit supplied to home markets and hauled by truck to other states.

Seed growing and marketing has become a $20,000,000-a-year industry in

WHEAT FOR A MILLION
LOAVES

Wheat is the most important crop of the Clearwater Plateau, which ranks among the best farming regions of the Pacific Northwest.

Courtesy Lewiston Chamber of Commerce

Idaho. We have seen that certain kinds of seed, notably potatoes, beans, wheat, barley, alfalfa, and red clover, are produced in the Upper Snake River Valley and Magic Valley. As we learned in Unit 10, seed production is even more important in the Lower Snake River Valley. Every state and more than a score of foreign countries now use Idaho-grown seed of many kinds.

The chief cities of this region, in order of size, are Boise, Nampa, Caldwell, Payette, Weiser, and Emmett. Like the cities in other parts of the Snake River Valley, these owe their prosperity mainly to the fine agricultural lands with which they are surrounded. They also draw heavily from the Oregon section of the Lower Snake River Valley, which lies just across the Snake from this region of Idaho.

The Clearwater Plateau. The agricultural lands of the Clearwater Plateau are located in Latah, Nez Perce, Idaho, Lewis, and Clearwater counties. The best lands are the Palouse Hills, Camas Prairie, Nez Perce Prairie, and small areas in the Clearwater Valley.

The plateau lands lie at elevations between 2,500 and 3,500 feet, and the lands in the valley proper are in general from 800 to 1,200 feet above sea level. Precipitation in most parts of the region is more than twenty inches a year, making irrigation unnecessary except in the main valley and on low benchlands around Lewiston. The growing season is from four to five months in most parts of the plateau and from five to seven months in the valleys. These factors, plus the fertile soils, account for the high position the Clearwater Plateau holds in the Northwest as an outstanding agricultural region.

The leading crops of this region are wheat and field peas, with barley, oats, potatoes, beans, alfalfa, and sweet clover raised in considerable quantities. Red clover, alsike clover, and rape are grown for seed. In the lower Clearwater Valley, near Lewiston, fruits and vegetables are extensively raised, favored by the Mediterranean-type climate much like that in the Valley of California. Apples, cherries, and peaches are the main fruit crops, with some grapes produced commercially.

Lewiston, Moscow, Grangeville, and Orofino are the chief cities of the Clearwater Plateau, though Lewiston and Orofino are really valley cities. All depend heavily on agricultural products, though not to the same extent as the cities of the Snake River Valley except, possibly, Moscow.

Bear River Basin. Following the Clearwater Plateau in importance as an agricultural region is the Bear River Basin in southeastern Idaho, the only part of the state not in the drainage basin of the Columbia River. The basin contains the agricultural lands of all of Bear Lake, Franklin, and Oneida counties, and a large part of the farmland of Caribou County.

Most of the farmlands of this region are located in Upper Cache Valley in Franklin County, Bear Lake Valley in Bear Lake County, and the Soda Springs Plateau, Gem Valley, and Upper Portneuf Valley in Caribou County, the last named not being geographically a part of the Bear River Basin. Only 146,000 acres in this region were irrigated in 1950, a much smaller percentage than in the Snake River Valley regions.

Among crops wheat is easily first in value. Barley and oats are important grain crops. Alfalfa is the most important hay crop, but wild hay yields close to one fourth of all hay cut in the basin. Potatoes and sugar beets are also important crops. The latter is especially valuable in Franklin County, which also ranks high in

HARVESTING PEAS NEAR MOSCOW

Agriculture is the principal industry of the Palouse country around Moscow, the seed pea capital of the United States and dry pea capital of the world.

Courtesy U.S. Bureau of Reclamation, Region No. 1, Boise

RANGE CATTLE NEAR NEW MEADOWS

About 75 per cent of the agricultural income of the Upland Empire is derived from livestock. This district is the home range of the Circle-C Ranch, one of Idaho's large cattle outfits.

growing vegetables for the market. Strawberries and raspberries are produced in considerable quantities in Bear Lake Valley.

Preston, Malad City, Montpelier, and Soda Springs are the leading cities of this part of Idaho. Agriculture accounts for most of their total trade and income, though Montpelier is a division point on the Union Pacific Railroad and Soda Springs is an important center in phosphate mining and in the manufacture of chemicals derived from phosphate.

The Little Panhandle. Benewah, Bonner, Boundary, Kootenai, and Shoshone counties make up the "Little Panhandle" of northern Idaho. The chief agricultural sections of this region are the Lakes Plateau, containing Rathdrum Prairie, and the rich Kootenai Valley in Boundary County.

Wheat is the chief crop of this region, followed closely by oats. Field peas, barley, alfalfa, clover, and timothy are the other leading crops. Alfalfa and clover seed are of value, especially in Boundary County. Does the nearness of Spokane, the principal city of eastern Washington, explain the importance of dairying in this region?

Coeur d'Alene, Sandpoint, Wallace, Kellogg, Mullan, and Bonners Ferry are the chief cities of the Little Panhandle. Unlike most cities of southern Idaho, these do not depend so largely on agriculture for their business, since lumbering, mining, and recreational occupations are very important in this part of the state.

The Upland Empire. Belonging mainly in the Upland Empire of central Idaho so far as their agricultural regions are concerned are Butte and Custer counties, with Big and Little Lost River valleys, Round Valley, and scattered valleys and basins in the upper Salmon River country; Lemhi County, with the Lemhi-Salmon Valley and small agricultural sections along the smaller tributaries of the Salmon; Valley County, with Long Valley on the North Fork of Payette River and scattered farms and ranches along other streams; and Boise County, with Garden Valley, on the South Fork of Payette River, and a few ranches in other

of various kinds of seed. Taken from the *Agricultural Statistics 1951* published by the United States Department of Agriculture, we find these comparisons covering the ten-year period from 1939 to 1948:

Table No. 9
HOW IDAHO RANKS IN AGRICULTURE

Rank Among States	Products
First	Seed: sweet corn, brome grass, rape, carrot, onion, turnip, etc.
Second	Potatoes (Maine first); dry field peas (Washington first)
Third	Dry beans; alsike clover seed
Fourth	Sugar beets; prunes; hops
Fifth	Alfalfa hay
Sixth	Cherries
Seventh	Dry onions; red clover seed
Eighth	Certified seed potatoes
Ninth	Alfalfa seed; wool; head lettuce
Tenth	Barley; sheep
Eleventh	Wheat; green peas; honey

The Bureau of Agricultural Economics, until recently a division of the United States Department of Agriculture, gave the agricultural income of Idaho in 1949, the year on which 1950 census figures were based, approximately as follows:

All livestock and livestock products	$145,577,000
All crops harvested	204,419,000
Federal agricultural payments	5,059,000
Total agricultural income	$355,055,000

parts of the county. About 75 per cent of the agricultural income of the Upland Empire is derived from livestock.

Idaho's Place in Agriculture. While not, as a whole, seriously challenging the greatest farming states, Idaho, nevertheless, holds an important place in the agricultural economy of the nation. Here are some interesting facts to prove it.

We have already seen that we hold first place among the states in the production

Our agricultural rank in 1949 was thirty-third among the states. For a state only a little more than a half century old, with a total population of less than six hundred thousand and whose surface is largely mountainous, this is a record of which we may justly be proud. Idaho will undoubtedly continue to forge ahead in the output of agricultural and dairy products as better and more convenient markets develop.

II. HOW IRRIGATION DEVELOPED IN IDAHO

THE LIFEBLOOD OF IDAHO is water, and our greatness as an agricultural state is due mainly to irrigation, though we must not forget the rich agricultural lands of the Clearwater Plateau, where irrigation has but a small role in farm and ranch life. As shown by the 1950 census, irrigation was practiced on 29,413 Idaho farms, with 2,156,730 acres watered artificially. Slightly less than 10,000 acres in the Panhandle were irrigated, mainly in Kootenai, Nez Perce, and Idaho counties.

In southern Idaho, Twin Falls County led with 238,762 acres under irrigation. Six other counties, Canyon, Bingham, Bonneville, Ada, Jefferson, and Cassia, each had between 100,000 and 200,000 acres of irrigated land. Which of these are in the Upper Snake River Valley? Magic Valley? The Lower Snake River Valley?

With the exception of small irrigated tracts in the Panhandle and about 350,-000 acres in the Bear River Basin and the mountain valleys of the Upland Empire, all of Idaho's irrigated lands lie in the Snake River Valley. It is chiefly these fertile acres that give Idaho its favored position among the great irrigated regions of the earth.

Early Progress in Irrigation. Mormon settlers at Franklin constructed the first permanent irrigation works in Idaho. They dug a ditch from Spring Creek to the fort at Franklin in 1860. Thereafter irrigation was a standard practice wherever the Latter-day Saints settled in southern Idaho and Mormon ditches

were soon a commonplace sight in that part of the territory.

The farming settlements that sprang up in the Boise, Payette, and Weiser valleys in the 1860's were not far behind the Mormons in building canals for irrigation. Small tracts along streams where ditches were easily and cheaply dug came quickly under cultivation, though the work was often carried on by single individuals and families rather than by community co-operation such as was common in the Mormon settlements.

Soon irrigation companies were formed to construct works on a larger scale. They rented water to farmers or made outright sales. This plan had a rapid development and was soon in use in many parts of southern Idaho.

In 1881 the territorial legislature enacted laws permitting water users to file on water rights and record their claims. This established for the first time in Idaho a legal method for securing private ownership of irrigation water and gave a great boost to the practice of irrigation.

As mining declined in importance, people turned more and more to agricultural pursuits. Before the end of the territorial period, in 1890, Idaho had about 800,000 acres under irrigation. This was truly a remarkable accomplishment to be achieved in less than thirty years and without state and Federal aid such as was available shortly after Idaho became a state.

Carey Act Projects. In 1894 Congress passed the Carey Act. Under this law each state in the West, where irrigation

Courtesy U.S. Bureau of Reclamation, Region No. 1, Boise

IRRIGATION MAKES THE DIFFERENCE

Before. *Sagebrush Plains of Southern Idaho*
After. *The Man with the Shovel*

was needed, was given one million acres of suitable land. In 1895 Idaho accepted the terms of this act and several important irrigation projects were soon started. In 1903 work began on the South Side Twin Falls Project, the first large Carey Act project in the state. The North Side Twin Falls Project, under the same act, was started in 1907. Several other Carey Act projects were developed, but no others equaled the Twin Falls project in size or importance.

Reclamation Act. The National Irrigation Law or Reclamation Act, passed by Congress in 1902, marked the real beginning of large-scale irrigation in the West. Under this law the United States Department of the Interior, through its Bureau of Reclamation, could construct or aid in constructing irrigation projects too large and expensive to be undertaken by the states or by private capital. The Bureau of Reclamation constructed the Minidoka and the Boise-Payette projects in Idaho and has sold storage rights in its various Idaho reservoirs to previously ex-

isting canal companies and irrigation districts in need of supplemental water.

Agencies Concerned with Irrigation and Storage. In Idaho three Federal agencies and one state agency are concerned with various responsibilities connected with the use of water, one of our greatest natural resources. These are the Bureau of Reclamation, the United States Corps of Engineers, the Indian Service, and our State Department of Reclamation.

To the Bureau of Reclamation is given the task of building dams, reservoirs, and canal systems for irrigation projects that are constructed under the authority of Congress and paid for by congressional appropriations. The United States Corps of Engineers is primarily engaged in flood control and the improvement of navigation. The Office of Indian Affairs constructs irrigation works to provide irrigation water for the Indian reservations. The Idaho State Department of Reclamation has general supervision of irrigation in Idaho under our own laws, as enacted from time to time by the state legislature.

Ideally, all these agencies co-operate with each other for the general welfare of our people. Local water users' associations have been organized in most irrigated sections of the state to manage irrigation matters in the local communities.

III. OUR IRRIGATION STREAMS AND THEIR USE[1]

THE STORY OF IRRIGATION in Idaho today is the story of our rivers and river basins and their development to serve the needs of the people who live there. We shall probably gain the clearest understanding of irrigation in our state by a study of our rivers to see just what part each plays in the total story. The two sources most depended on for information are the Bureau of Reclamation report recently published, *The Columbia River,* and watermasters' papers in the reports of the Idaho State Department of Reclamation.

From the point where the Snake River crosses the line from Wyoming into Idaho to where it enters the mighty slash in the earth which soon becomes Hell's Canyon, it spreads its life-giving waters over more than a million acres of fertile fields. These fields, with another million or more acres watered by other streams, are the foundation on which the state's con-

tinuing prosperity so largely depends.

Upper Snake River Projects and Storage. In Idaho, Snake River water begins its great irrigation work a short distance upstream from the village of Ririe in the eastern end of Jefferson County. There, near Heise Hot Springs, where the river emerges from its upper canyon, the Great Feeder Canal, one of the world's large irrigation canals, diverts a large part of the natural flow of the river to feed an extensive network of lesser canals that carry the water to the thirsty fields awaiting its magic touch. Altogether about 437,000 acres are watered directly by the Snake River between that point and American Falls.

These lands all lie in the main Snake River Valley and are part of the 760,000 acres of irrigated land which, collectively, are known as the Upper Snake River Projects. Twelve main canals, which carry from 10,000 to 61,000 acre-feet of water each, and forty-two smaller canals, each carrying less than 10,000 acre-feet, water the 437,000 acres extending down the valley from near Rexburg to Pocatello, American Falls, and Aberdeen.

In addition to the lands irrigated directly from Snake River, there are approximately 210,000 acres in Idaho which receive their water from other Upper Snake River Valley streams. These streams, and the lands they irrigate, are shown in the table that follows:

[1]Statistics used in this unit were compiled from the following sources: *The Columbia River* (1947), by the U.S. Bureau of Reclamation; the *Seventeenth Biennial Report* of the State Department of Reclamation; *Surface Water Supply of the United States, Part 13, Snake River Basin* and *Surface Water Supply of the United States, Part 10, The Great Basin,* both by the U.S. Geological Survey; *Columbia River and Tributaries, Appendix O, Power Generation and Transmission,* by the Corps of Engineers, Department of the Army, North Pacific Division; *Reclamation Handbook, Conservation Bulletin No. 32,* the *Minidoka Irrigation Project,* the *Boise, Idaho, Federal Reclamation Project,* and the *Payette Division of the Boise Federal Reclamation Project,* all by the U.S. Bureau of Reclamation; various Watermasters' Reports; and the United States Census Reports, 1950.

Table No. 10

TRIBUTARIES ABOVE AMERICAN FALLS*

Streams	Acres Irrigated
Willow Creek and Blackfoot River (excluding Fort Hall Project, which is under Snake River)	22,000
Fall River and tributaries	44,000
Henrys Fork below Ashton	45,000
Henrys Fork above Ashton	17,000
Teton River and tributaries	66,000
Snake River and tributaries in Idaho above Heise	16,000
Approximate Total Acreage	210,000

*Salt River in Wyoming also irrigates about four thousand acres in the Idaho portion of Salt River Valley.

NOTE. Tables 10 and 11 were prepared by Lynn Crandall, Watermaster, Irrigation District No. 36.

Included among the Upper Snake River Projects is the Fort Hall Indian Reservation Project, consisting of 47,000 acres. This land is served by the Reservation Canal, which can take water from either Snake River or Blackfoot River and Willow Creek. Constructed by the Indian Service, Grays Lake Reservoir and Blackfoot Reservoir hold storage water in reserve to irrigate the Indian lands and Tyhee Flats, a body of fertile soil lying between the Fort Hall Indian Reservation and the city of Pocatello.

All the Upper Snake River Projects, except the Fort Hall Project, were developed by the co-operative efforts of the

Courtesy U.S. Bureau of Reclamation, Region No. 1, Boise

AMERICAN FALLS DAM AND RESERVOIR

Largest of all reclamation projects in Idaho is the huge American Falls Project, whose lake impounds 1,700,000 acre-feet of life-giving water.

water users, most of them between 1880 and 1900. In the earlier period there were often years when the natural flow of the streams was not sufficient to supply all the water needed. To overcome this handicap, the Bureau of Reclamation has constructed three reservoirs and has a fourth under way at the present time. These regulate stream flow and provide supplemental water for the projects. With the Indian Service and private storage, these, together, provide sufficient water for most of the upper valley land, as is

Except the Upper Cache Valley in Franklin County and Gem Valley in Caribou County, both on Bear River, all these irrigated districts produce mainly hay and livestock. Dairying is especially important in the Bear River irrigated districts. In Gem Valley, Black-and-White Day, featuring Holstein dairy cattle and products, is an important annual event.

Magic Valley Projects. Between American Falls and the western boundary of Twin Falls and Gooding counties

Table No. 11

OTHER EAST IDAHO IRRIGATION STREAMS

Stream or Source	Acres Irrigated
Bear River and tributaries	146,000
Portneuf River and tributaries	34,000
Minor tributaries to American Falls Reservoir, including Bannock Creek and springs	9,000
Mud Lake and tributaries	55,000
Little Lost River	12,000
Big Lost River and tributaries	42,000
Approximate Total Acreage	298,000

shown in Appendix Table 8 in the Statistical Appendix at the back of this book.

In addition to the Upper Snake River Projects proper, there are smaller projects in southeastern and eastern Idaho which, together, total about 298,000 acres of irrigated land, as shown by the table given above. These include Bear River Basin districts, the Portneuf River–Marsh Creek district, the Mud Lake district, Big Lost River Valley, and other small sections in the "lost rivers" region bordering the northern part of the Upper Snake River Valley.

lie the irrigation projects of Magic Valley. These include the Minidoka Project, the Twin Falls projects, and smaller projects along the northern and southern borders of Snake River Valley. The main stem of Snake River, which supplies water for about 535,000 acres, is the principal source of water for the Magic Valley projects.

Irrigation from the main stream below American Falls began in 1905 when water was first diverted to the South Side Twin Falls Project. Soon afterward the North Side Twin Falls Project was

MILNER DAM IN MAGIC VALLEY

Water stored behind Milner Dam, built where the Wilson Price Hunt Expedition came to grief in 1811, serves the North Side and South Side Twin Falls projects and a large district near Shoshone and Gooding.

Courtesy U.S. Bureau of Reclamation, Region No. 1, Boise

opened. Both of these were Carey Act projects, receiving water through diversion canals from the Milner Dam, which raised the water level of Snake River about forty feet. Lake Wilson, a reservoir for the North Side Twin Falls Project, also receives water through a canal from Milner Dam. Together the South Side and North Side Twin Falls projects include about 365,000 acres, which are among the most productive lands in the world.

The Minidoka Project, authorized by Congress in 1904, is the first Federal reclamation project in Idaho and one of the first in the West. It consists of about 212,000 acres, distributed as follows: (1) about 72,000 acres in Minidoka County on the north side of Snake River, with Rupert as a center; (2) 48,000 acres south of the river in Cassia County, centering around Burley; (3) the Gooding Division north of Snake River, containing about 55,000 acres in Gooding and Lincoln counties, supplied by a large canal

from Milner Dam; and (4) a large district in Minidoka and Jerome counties north of the present project, which is to be irrigated from deep wells tapping the enormous water reserves underlying the valley. In fact, a substantial beginning has already been made in deep-well irrigation in this project, which will eventually irrigate more than 115,000 acres.

The Minidoka Project is served by two Snake River reservoirs. Completed in 1909, the Minidoka Dam created the Lake Walcott Reservoir, which has a storage capacity of 95,000 acre-feet. But the key structure is the huge American Falls Dam and Reservoir. Finished in 1927, the reservoir has a storage capacity of 1,700,000 acre-feet. Its water supply serves, directly or by exchange, canal companies and irrigation districts in the Snake River Valley from the Wyoming border to the lower end of Hagerman Valley and provides direct and supplemental water for nearly 700,000 acres of irrigated land.

The King Hill Project was built by private interests in 1909. It was later reconstructed by the Bureau of Reclamation, which found that it was not possible to collect all the construction costs. Therefore, the project was given to the water users and most of the uncollected costs were charged off. The total project, of about 6,500 acres, lies in scattered tracts on both sides of the Snake River, extending from the lower end of Hagerman Valley downstream for about thirty miles. The lands produce mainly alfalfa, wheat, fruits, melons, beans, and both early and late potatoes.

South of Snake River in the Magic Valley section there are about 103,000 acres irrigated by streams flowing north to the river. The largest of these projects are the Salmon Falls Creek Project in Twin Falls County and the Goose Creek Project in Cassia County. Raft River and its tributaries irrigate about 22,000 acres. The remaining irrigated lands are supplied by various small creeks rising in the mountainous sections of Cassia and Twin Falls counties. All these projects were constructed through the co-operative efforts of the water users themselves. The Oakley (Goose Creek) and Salmon Falls districts began as Carey Act projects.

In the northern part of the Magic Valley section of Snake River Valley, Big Wood River, Little Wood River, and their tributaries provide water for approximately 80,000 acres. Part of the Big Wood River water is used on the Minidoka Project near Gooding and Shoshone. The rest is used farther upstream in the vicinity of Richfield in Lincoln County and Bellevue, Picabo, and Carey

in Blaine County. Close to 6,000 acres in Big Camas Prairie in the southern part of Camas County is watered by Camas Creek.

Appendix Table 9 in the Statistical Appendix gives a list of the principal reservoirs storing irrigation water for use in Magic Valley. Though the American Falls Reservoir is located in the Upper Snake River Valley, its stored waters are used almost entirely on Magic Valley irrigation projects.

Between Milner Dam and the lower end of Hagerman Valley, many large springs break from the lava canyon walls north of the Snake. Their annual flow of approximately 5,600,000 acre-feet varies hardly at all from year to year. Together, they irrigate about 16,000 acres in Hagerman Valley and small scattered tracts on the floor of Shoshone Canyon upstream almost to Milner Dam. They could, of course, irrigate a much larger area if land were available.

Lower Snake River Valley Projects. For most of its downstream course between Hagerman Valley and the south, or upper, end of the Grand Canyon of Snake River, the Snake flows at the bottom of a trench that lies considerably lower than the plateau lands on either side of the river. Because of this and the lack of suitable land along the canyon floor, water from the Snake River is used for only about 40,000 acres in the Lower Snake River Valley. The rest of this great irrigated region in Idaho is watered by Snake River tributaries, the Boise, Payette, and Weiser rivers from the east, and the Bruneau and Owyhee rivers from the south.

Most important of the Lower Snake

Courtesy U.S. Bureau of Reclamation, Region No. 1, Boise

BOISE RIVER STORAGE PROJECTS

ARROWROCK DAM AND RESERVOIR   *ANDERSON RANCH DAM AND RESERVOIR*

These great dams, both among the high dams of the world, impound Boise River water to irrigate part of the Boise Irrigation Project.

River tributaries from an irrigation standpoint is the Boise River, Idaho's second most valuable irrigation stream. This river now provides the big drink for 340,000 thirsty acres, and may, within a few years, through exchange with Payette River or Snake River waters, be diverted in part to lands on the proposed Mountain Home project. At present, however, all its irrigation water is used on the Boise Project, one of the great irrigation projects of the West.

Irrigation began in the Boise Valley in 1864 and by 1900 most of the low areas were under ditch. The plateaus on either side of the valley proper could not, however, be reached by ditches from the river. The cost of construction of necessary reclamation works to reach this land was too much for private capital to undertake. Congress passed the Reclamation Act in 1902, following which the United States Bureau of Rec-

lamation set up the Boise Project in 1906.

Lake Lowell, or Deer Flat Reservoir, in the southern part of Canyon County, was the first work undertaken by the Bureau of Reclamation in the Lower Snake River Valley. Water was diverted from the Boise River to this natural reservoir basin by the forty-five-mile New York Canal. Then, in 1915, the notable Arrowrock Dam was constructed just below the junction of the North and South forks of the Boise River. Arrowrock Reservoir and Lake Lowell together provide water for the Arrowrock Division, which includes the great irrigated region south of the Boise River and extends all the way to the Snake River, fifty miles to the west.

To provide additional water for the Boise Project and to regulate stream flow on the Boise River, the Anderson Ranch Dam on the South Fork of Boise River has recently been completed.

PAYETTE RIVER STORAGE PROJECTS

BLACK CANYON DAM AND RESERVOIR   CASCADE DAM

These dams hold back Payette River water for use on the Boise Irrigation Project

This dam, the highest earth-fill dam in the world at this time, is 336 feet in height, approximately 2,900 feet long, and more than a half mile thick at the base. It creates a reservoir in Elmore County with a storage capacity of 500,000 acre-feet. Its completion in 1952 assures an ample supply of irrigation water for the Boise Project. With the older Arrowrock Reservoir and the newly constructed Lucky Peak Dam between Arrowrock and Boise, it gives protection against annual spring floods which have heretofore overflowed low-lying parts of the Boise Valley and caused much damage.

The Payette River serves about 160,000 acres of land, of which 112,000 acres are in the lower section of the Payette Valley. These lands were all placed under irrigation by private owners. However, an additional 52,000 acres of benchlands between the Boise and Payette rivers are part of the Boise Project.

In order to bring lands on the Payette Division of the Boise Project under irri-

gation and to provide additional water for lands already under ditch, the Bureau of Reclamation built the Black Canyon Dam, near Emmett, the Deadwood Dam on Deadwood River, and the Cascade Dam on the North Fork of the Payette River.

The Weiser River is, by comparison, far less important for irrigation than the Boise and Payette rivers. Its numerous tributaries and the lack of a broad valley along the main stream have caused the development of several small irrigation projects which, together, contain about 41,000 acres. Of these, about 27,000 acres are watered by the Weiser River and 14,000 acres by tributary streams. These lands lie in the lower part of Weiser Valley near the city of Weiser, in the Middle Valley around Midvale and Cambridge, and in the Upper Valley in the general vicinity of Council, the county seat of Adams County. These lands produce chiefly wheat and other small grains, hay, fruit, vegetables, and livestock.

For much of their length both the Bruneau River and its tributaries flow through very deep and rugged lava canyons which make the use of their waters on the bordering plateaus almost impossible. Only about 21,000 acres are now irrigated by these streams, most of the land being in the lower Bruneau Valley, the "Valley of Tall Grass" described in Mrs. Hawes's recent book about that region.

Though the Owyhee Project is one of the large Bureau of Reclamation projects in the Lower Snake River Valley, and irrigates about 114,000 acres, only about 30,000 acres are in Idaho. The rest of the lands are in eastern Oregon across Snake River from the Boise Project. Water for this project is stored in the Owyhee Reservoir, a huge artificial lake on the Owyhee River in eastern Oregon. Of the 30,000 Idaho acres in this project lying in the northwest part of Owyhee County from Marsing to Homedale, two thirds are irrigated by water pumped from the Snake River and one third by water from the Owyhee Reservoir.

About 12,000 acres on the Duck Valley Indian Reservation in Nevada and Idaho are watered from the Owyhee River. Storage is in Wildhorse Reservoir in Nevada. This project, like the Fort Hall Project, was constructed by the Office of Indian Affairs.

A few small pumping projects along the main valley of the Snake River have been developed between Hammett in Elmore County and Marsing in Owyhee County. Indian Cove, Eagle Cove, and Grandview are the largest of these. Since the completion of the Strike Dam of the Idaho Power Company in 1953, a canal from the dam to Grandview has dis-

placed the former pumping project. Altogether, these small projects serve only from 12,000 to 15,000 acres, largely used to grow hay for livestock. They also supply irrigation water to some land on the north side of the Snake River.

Appendix Table 10, in the Statistical Appendix, shows the main storage projects that hold water for the Lower Snake River Valley.

Irrigation in the Upland Empire. The Salmon River and its tributaries and the North Fork of Payette River are the streams most used for irrigation in the valleys and basins of the central Idaho mountains. The 1950 census reported about 24,000 acres irrigated in Valley County, nearly all of which were in Long Valley along the North Fork of Payette River. In the Salmon River Basin as a whole, approximately 106,000 acres are normally under irrigation.

In the Upper Salmon River Basin approximately 35,000 acres are irrigated in Lemhi Valley, 18,500 acres in Pahsime-

DEADWOOD DAM AND RESERVOIR ON DEADWOOD RIVER

Courtesy U.S. Bureau of Reclamation, Region No. 1, Boise

roi Valley, 7,000 acres in Round Valley near Challis, and approximately 14,000 acres in the Salmon Valley just above and below the city of Salmon, including Big Flats and the Carmen Creek district. Minor tributaries account for the remaining 6,000 acres irrigated in the upper basin.

The principal irrigated section of the lower Salmon River Basin is in Meadows Valley at the head of Little Salmon River. There about 14,000 acres are under irrigation, including close to 8,000 acres of subirrigated pasture land. This is one of the best beef-cattle sections of Idaho and the home range of the famous Circle-C Ranch.

Irrigation in the Panhandle. Irrigation is little used north of the Salmon River in Idaho. Though the water resources are great, there is but little land that needs or is suitable for irrigation. In the Rathdrum Prairie district northward from the city of Coeur d'Alene are five small irrigation districts totaling less than 10,000 acres. The Bureau of Reclamation has undertaken the enlargement and improvement of this project, which may, in time, irrigate approximately 35,000 acres, most of which is now dry-farmed. The Bureau has also aided the Lewiston Orchards Project, where about 3,300 acres, mainly in small tracts, is watered by small tributary streams.

There are, of course, other places in Idaho where irrigation is carried on. In fact, there is hardly a valley, especially in southern Idaho, that is totally lacking in irrigation if suitable land and water are available. In such locations are found a goodly number of small farms and ranches which are watered by turning onto the fields the small streams so plentiful in the mountainous districts. Would you expect such remote farms and ranches to be given over mainly to hay and livestock? Why?

Idaho Needs a Reclamation Program. The Idaho State Reclamation Association, with offices in Boise, listed in the *Idaho Reclamation News* these reasons why a sound reclamation program is needed in Idaho and the Columbia River Basin:

1. Supplemental water would be provided for 1,163,000 acres of land in Idaho now under irrigation which suffer from periodic water shortages.

2. The nation needs 4,000,000 acres of new land a year if we are to maintain our present standard of living. Irrigation projects help supply those acres.

3. New irrigated acreage totaling 1,300,000 acres could be added in Idaho, providing 16,250 new farms of eighty acres each, and homes for 75,000 to 100,000 people.

4. Annual farm income would be increased about $52,000,000 a year, based on 1940 figures.

5. Flood control, an urgent problem in some lower valleys of Idaho, would be provided.

6. Work provided by new reclamation projects would help prevent large-scale unemployment if a depression should bring hard times.

7. Reclamation developments would repay their costs. There is now less than 1 per cent of repayments to the government past due in Idaho.

8. Population of the state would prob-

ably be increased by about 260,000 persons.

9. New cities and villages growing up as a result of reclamation development could provide a means of livelihood for business and professional people, tradesmen, mechanics, and craftsmen. Records show that for every new person on a farm, two others are supported in cities and towns on or near reclamation projects.

10. The assessed valuation of the state would be increased by more than $150,-000,000.

11. More than 5,000 new business and industrial enterprises would be established.

12. The development of the 10,000,-000 acres in the West capable of being irrigated would allow submarginal land now being unwisely used for crops to be put into pastures and woodland, helping to control soil erosion, one of the nation's most serious problems.

In 1946 the Agricultural Department of the Northern Pacific Railroad cited these facts to prove the value of irrigation to the West: Up to that time the United States government had invested about $312,000,000 in irrigation projects. About $67,000,000, or one fifth of the investment, had already been repaid. These irrigation projects yielded, in 1946, products valued in round numbers at $411,000,000, *thus producing in a single year more in new wealth than the entire original cost of building the projects.*

IV. HYDROELECTRIC POWER

"WATER RESOURCE POTENTIAL PUTS IDAHO SIXTH

"Idaho, with a potential 3,170,000 horsepower[2] in water resources is the sixth ranking state, the U.S. Geological Survey reported."

THE NEWSPAPER HEADLINE and paragraph above shows that our state is particularly fortunate in its water resources available for making electricity. The six leading water-power states, as listed by the Geological Survey, are Washington, Oregon, California, New York, Arizona, and Idaho, in that order.

Water-Power Rivers. Because of their large volume and rapid flow, practically all of our principal streams could be used to produce large quantities of electricity. The table that follows gives the annual flow of these streams, measured in acre-feet. (See Table No. 12)

The total volume of these twelve rivers is approximately seventy-five million acre-feet of water yearly. There are also many smaller streams which could, if need should arise, be used for small hydroelectric plants.

The Snake River, Bear River in southern Idaho, and the Clark Fork–Pend Oreille River in northern Idaho are now the chief producers of electricity in the state. The mighty turbines and humming dynamos of these and other streams make the electricity needed to light our cities

[2]Horsepower. The force required to lift a weight of 33,000 pounds one foot in one minute.

Table No. 12

AVERAGE ANNUAL FLOW OF PRINCIPAL IDAHO RIVERS

Stream	Where Measured	Acre-Feet of Annual Run-off
Snake River	(Below Weiser	10,626,000
	(Above Lewiston	19,270,000
Clark Fork–Pend Oreille River	Priest River	16,390,000
Kootenai River	Canada Line	10,500,000
Clearwater River	Spalding	9,691,000
St. Joe–Coeur d'Alene–Spokane System	Post Falls	4,313,000
Salmon River	White Bird	6,393,000
Payette River	Emmett	1,903,000
Boise River	Below Arrowrock	1,584,000
Henrys Fork (North Fork) of Snake River	Near St. Anthony	826,000
Weiser River	Mouth of River	567,000
Bear River (Oct. 1950–Sept. 1951)	Alexander	888,000
Bruneau River	Near Mouth	293,000

(Compiled from U.S. Bureau of Reclamation, U.S. Geological Survey, and Watermasters' Reports.)

and rural homes and to furnish economical and convenient power to turn the wheels of industry.

Electricity on the Farm. "Idaho is among the six top states in the nation in percentage of farms served with electric power," according to the project director for the Idaho Farm Electrification Committee in 1952. More than 97 per cent of Idaho's farms have electricity, provided by private power companies or rural co-operative electrical associations. The University of Idaho, in co-operation with the Idaho Power Company, the Utah Power and Light Company, and the Washington Water Power Company, has carried on a program of electrical research and development in Idaho for more than a quarter of a century. This has been of great aid in placing Idaho in such a favorable position in rural electrification.

Electricity in Industry. More and more, industry is turning to hydroelectricity as a source of cheap power in Idaho. This is largely because our rapid mountain streams are almost ideally adapted to this use. The larger rivers supply a huge volume of water in both winter and summer. By means of dams this water can be used for generating immense quantities of hydroelectricity which, by building power lines, can be carried anywhere in the state to furnish the power needed in manufacturing and for other industrial uses.

Examples of these uses are found in the great mines and smelters in the Coeur d'Alene mining district, the enormous sawmills and the wood pulp mills of the northern part of the state, and the recently built fertilizer factories and great chemical plants in southeastern Idaho. The electric furnaces of the Westvaco plant, for example, require more electricity than is used by the combined cities of Boise, Pocatello, Twin Falls, and Nampa. There are, of course, thousands of ways in which business establishments, large and small, use electricity in Idaho. Can you name some of them?

Hydroelectric Plants in Idaho. At present "white coal," or electricity, made in Idaho by means of water power, exceeds a half million kilowatts. Most of this is produced in plants owned and operated by private power companies and corporations. An almost complete list of hydroelectric plants in Idaho is given in Appendix Table 11 in the Statistical Appendix.

There are more than a dozen rural and co-operative associations which purchase electricity from private companies to serve their communities. The Montana Power Company sells some electricity in the Coeur d'Alene district and the California Pacific Utilities Company extends transmission lines into Oneida County, but neither company has power plants in the state.

* * * * *

The brief glimpses we have had into how our people use the land and water resources of Idaho shows us how greatly we depend on the bountiful gifts of Mother Nature. Wisely used and properly conserved, these resources will grow in value through the years and continue

Courtesy Washington Water Power Company, Spokane

NEW POWER DAM AT CABINET GORGE

On Clark Fork River at Cabinet Gorge the Washington Water Power Company has the spectacular dam shown here. It is capable of producing 200,000 watts of hydroelectric energy, most of which will be used in northern Idaho and eastern Washington.

to serve future generations in our state, nation, and world. Surely, the least we can do is to resolve that we shall never knowingly or willfully do anything to impair the usefulness of these great gifts.

Using Our Forest and Mineral Resources

How Idaho's extensive forest and mineral resources are being developed and used, and how they hold great promise for the future welfare of the state and its people.

THE FOREST AND MINERAL RESOURCES of Idaho are the basis of two of our three major industries. Next to agriculture, they give employment and a livelihood to more Idaho people than any other basic industry. Both are so valuable that special departments of our state government have been created to assist in their management. These are the offices of the State Inspector of Mines and the State Forester, executive officer of the Forestry Department.

I. IDAHO'S LIVING CARPET

WHAT IS SO PLEASANT on a warm summer day as the cool shade and the fragrance of evergreen trees? What is more pleasing to the sight than a mountain slope or a native meadow dappled with wild flowers in full bloom?

The green forests of our mountains, the smaller trees and shrubs of our more open slopes and valleys, the purple sage of our plains and plateaus, the grasses that spread from border to border—all these are Idaho's living carpet, a magic carpet more enchanting than that on which Ali Baba made his wonderful journeys long ago.

Two Kinds of Forests. Our forests,

Courtesy U.S. Forest Service

FOREST SCENE IN THE IDAHO PANHANDLE

Altogether, forests cover about 22,000,000 acres in Idaho, approximately 40 per cent of the state's total area. Commercial forests occupy about 14,000-000 acres and noncommercial forests about 8,000,000 acres. The most valuable commercial forests are in the northern and central parts of the state.

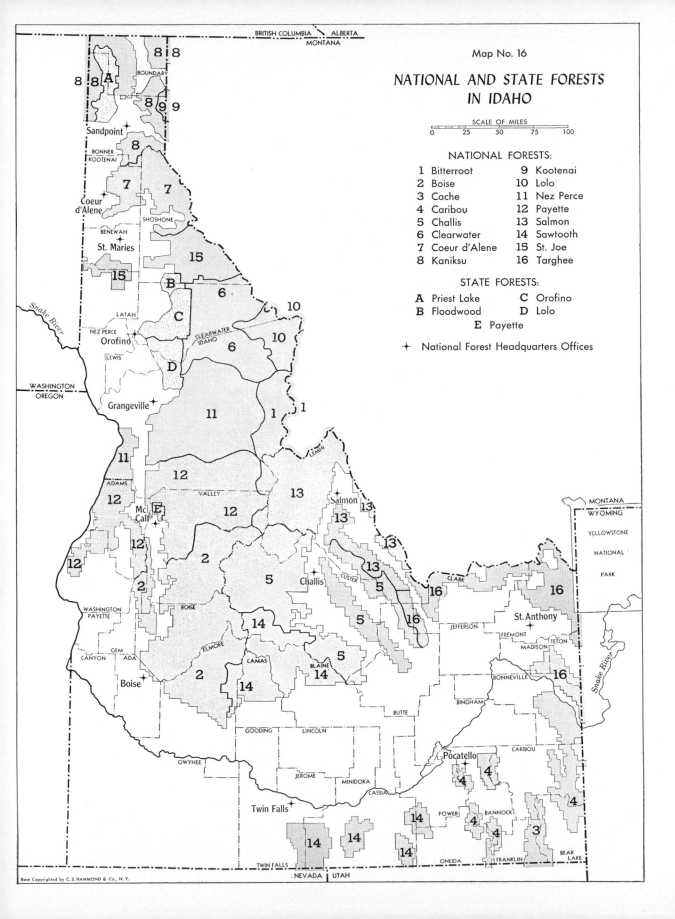

Map No. 16

NATIONAL AND STATE FORESTS IN IDAHO

SCALE OF MILES

0   25   50   75   100

NATIONAL FORESTS:

1	Bitterroot	9	Kootenai
2	Boise	10	Lolo
3	Cache	11	Nez Perce
4	Caribou	12	Payette
5	Challis	13	Salmon
6	Clearwater	14	Sawtooth
7	Coeur d'Alene	15	St. Joe
8	Kaniksu	16	Targhee

STATE FORESTS:

A Priest Lake   C Orofino
B Floodwood   D Lolo
        E Payette

+ National Forest Headquarters Offices

Base Copyrighted by C. S. HAMMOND & Co., N.Y.

A VIEW OF THE RUTLEDGE UNIT, POTLATCH FORESTS, INC., AT COEUR d'ALENE

Tugs tow the huge log rafts down Lake Coeur d'Alene from St. Maries

on which we are dependent for lumber, fuel, and many kinds of forest products, as well as for a cover for our uplands to store and slow down the melting of snow and to prevent erosion, are of two general kinds, as classified by our State Forestry Department: commercial forests and noncommercial forests. Together they comprise an area of about 21,814,-000 acres, approximately two fifths of the state's total area. However, only a little more than 18,000,000 acres of the forest areas are timbered now.

Commercial Forests. From our commercial forests, most of which are in northern and central Idaho, come the forest products whose combined output makes forestry one of the three major industries of the state. According to the 1950 census, Idaho held eleventh place among the states in the total value of timber products.

Noncommercial Forests. A little less than one sixth of Idaho's living carpet comprises the noncommercial forests. In these timbered areas the forest growth is not generally suitable for industrial uses at present. Later on some of this timber will no doubt be utilized in industry. The huge total lies in scattered areas in all the subareas of the state, but it is mainly in central Idaho.

Lacking great industrial value, the noncommercial forests are, nevertheless, of great value. They cover watersheds, conserving winter snowfall and regulating spring and summer runoff. They prevent erosion that, without the forest cover, would soon strip the slopes of their soil. They provide pasturage for large numbers of livestock. They conserve and protect wildlife. They yield large quantities of cheap fuel and considerable material for certain farm needs, such as poles for building corrals, temporary fence posts, and other similar articles not required to be of commercial-grade timber.

Nonforested Lands. These make up about three fifths of the total area of the

PACK TRIP TO THE PRIMITIVE AREA

Recreation is a valuable use of the Idaho forests. A pack trip into the Idaho Primitive Area, or into another section of mountain wilderness, is a never-to-be-forgotten adventure.

state. The cause is lack of moisture, the annual precipitation being well below the twenty inches generally considered necessary for satisfactory forest growth. Most of these lands are south of the Salmon River.

Most of the irrigated and dry-farm regions are in the nonforested part of Idaho. But by far the larger portion of these lands consist of sagebrush plains, with an undercarpet of grasses and other small vegetation that can withstand the semiarid climate of most of southern Idaho.

The chief values of this desert-type vegetation are grazing, soil cover, preventing erosion, and regulating spring and summer runoff of melting snow and rain. Too, they furnish shelter and food for species of wildlife that prefer to live in such surroundings.

Owners and Users of Idaho Forests. The users of our forests in Idaho are the hundreds of thousands of people who live in and depend on the forests for a living

or who visit them for rest and recreation. The owners or managers of these forests are of five kinds: (1) the national forests, managed by the United States Forest Service; (2) the state forests, under the general supervision of the Board of Land Commissioners working through the office of the State Forester; (3) the counties of the state; (4) private owners, both corporations or companies and individuals; and (5) the public domain, administered by the Bureau of Land Management, a division of the United States Department of the Interior. How all these share responsibility in the conservation of Idaho's forest resources we shall see in later topics, and in Unit 18.

Economic Value of the Forests. A large number of our people depend upon forest work and products for their livelihood, especially in northern and central Idaho, where most of our forests are located. Thousands of men work in lumber camps and sawmills. Others are employed in factories making wood products. Many find a place in professional forestry in national, state, and private forests, in fire protection work, and in the control of forest diseases and insect pests.

National, state and local governments lean heavily on forest industries and resources for revenue to carry on the work of government. Privately owned timberlands, industries using raw materials from the forests, and workers who earn their living in forest occupations all pay taxes which help to support local, state, and national government. Railroads and truck lines in forest areas draw a considerable part of their income from transporting logs, lumber, and other timber products. These in turn give employment to many people, thus increasing incomes among their workers.

There are revenue-producing uses of forest lands that prove that sometimes we "can have our cake and eat it, too." At least, we can use the forests as important sources of revenue without cutting down the trees. This revenue comes from the recreational use of forest lands. Since the 1920's, good roads have opened up many forest areas, resulting in an astonishing increase in the number of vacationists using the forest. As one observer wrote:

Recreationists are a free-flowing source of income, and local residents, from gas-station attendants to hunting guides, have shared in the earnings from scenic lakes and forests. The recreational use of forests, wildlife, and waters of Idaho has covered the full range of summer and winter outdoor pastimes from skiing and picnicking to hunting and packing trips.

Only a rough estimate is possible concerning the increased income because of recreational forest uses, but the most conservative estimates place the amount at many millions of dollars annually. Do you think this amount will increase as population increases in the Northwest?

Another important revenue use of the forest which does not materially damage

Courtesy U.S. Forest Service, Missoula, Montana

LOGS IN THE CLEAR-WATER RIVER AT LEWISTON

Making lumber, wood pulp, paper, and other wood products, the Lewiston mills of the Potlatch Forests, Inc., make that city one of the important lumbering centers of the Northwest.

or reduce the forests is grazing. Grazing fees for livestock using the forests of Idaho amount to more than a quarter million dollars a year.

Varieties, Distribution, and Uses of Trees. Nearly all our trees belong to the coniferous, or cone-bearing, softwoods. These blanket the mountains of central Idaho, most of the Panhandle, and mountainous sections of the southeastern part of the state.

Cottonwoods grow in valleys where moisture is sufficient for their needs, and quaking aspens are plentiful on mountain slopes and in the higher valleys and basins. Willows and birches grow along mountain streams. In parts of the semi-arid regions of southern Idaho junipers provide a pleasing contrast with the treeless expanse that is the general rule.

White Pine. The most valuable tree in Idaho is the Idaho white pine, a member of the western white pine family. It is found mainly north of the Clearwater River. Between the Clearwater and St. Joe rivers is said to be the largest stand of virgin white pine now left in the United States. Timber from this forest supplies logs for the world's largest white pine sawmill at Lewiston.

Yellow Pine and Douglas Fir. Next to the white pine in value are the ponderosa or western yellow pine and the Douglas fir. These are most plentiful in the mountainous regions from the Clearwater River to the Snake River but they are also found in smaller quantities in other sections of the state. They provide approximately one fourth of the saw timber cut in Idaho and nearly all the lumber milled south of the Clearwater River.

Other Useful Trees. Western red cedar, larch or tamarack, and hemlock, all plentiful in parts of northern Idaho, are used for lumber and special products. Engelmann's spruce and white fir or balsam fir are found in higher valleys and basins. Lodgepole pine is especially abundant in parts of the central Idaho mountains and most timbered sections of eastern and southern Idaho. The table that follows gives much useful information about the trees of Idaho, where they are mainly found, and how they are used.

There are, of course, other kinds of trees in Idaho. Along the watercourses cottonwoods were once common and are still found in a good many places. In fact, one of the largest areas of uncut cottonwood in the United States is found in the Wood River section of south central Idaho. The wood is used in a Jerome plant for making food containers of various kinds and for wood veneer. Another common softwood tree is the quaking aspen, having little commercial use, but nonetheless it is a source of fuel, posts, and poles where better varieties of timber are lacking.

In Idaho much timber is used for fuel, but the cash value of this fuel is far less than for many other timber products. Much of the fuel is from noncommercial forests, dead timber, and trimmings and other wastes from sawmills and factories making lumber products.

From a business standpoint, lumber stands far above all other commercial products of Idaho forests. The bulk of the lumber is shipped to other states. As we have seen, western white pine, western yellow pine or ponderosa pine, and Douglas fir provide most of the timber cut for saw logs.

Table No. 13

IDAHO TREES AND THEIR USES

Kind of Trees	Main Distribution	Some Important Uses
Idaho (Western) White Pine	Eight northern counties	Finish lumber, furniture, cabinets, matches, ceiling, doorframes, boxes, specialties, plywood
Western Yellow (Ponderosa) Pine	Mountains of central and northern Idaho	Lumber, framing, subfloors, siding, columns, boxes, crates, furniture, ship timbers, shingles, plywood
Douglas Fir	General	Lumber, dimension and mine timbers, framing, ties, posts, fuel, lath
Western Larch (Tamarack)	Mainly Panhandle	Lumber, dimension and structural timbers, mine timbers, fuel, ties, posts, lath, piling, poles
Lodgepole Pine	General	Rough construction, ties, cordwood, farm and mine timbers, poles, posts, plywood
Engelmann's Spruce	Along high lakes and streams	Lumber, cabinets, shelving, food containers, linings, tanks, rough lumber, pulpwood
White Fir	Mainly Panhandle	Sidings, ceiling, moldings, shiplap, pulpwood
Western Red Cedar	Scattered areas in northern Idaho	Power and telephone poles, ship timbers, posts, shingles, caskets, tanks, silos, boxes, furniture
Western Hemlock	Principally North Idaho	Joists, siding, flooring, ceiling, lath, boxes, pulpwood

According to the American Tree Association's *Forestry Directory* for 1949, the average lumber production in Idaho is close to eight hundred million board feet annually. About two hundred million board feet a year, or one fourth the annual cut, is used in the state, while three fourths, or six hundred million board feet, are shipped out of the state. These figures, of course, vary from year to year as business conditions change. Since 1949, the trend has been upward, perhaps to a billion feet per year.

Idaho forests produce great numbers of telephone and telegraph poles, fence posts, and pole timbers used as piling for wharves and other construction. Most of these come from the cedar stands of northern Idaho, particularly from the Clearwater, St. Joe, Coeur d'Alene, and Kaniksu National Forests. In recent years, because of new kinds of timber preservatives, the lodgepole forests are becoming fairly heavy producers of pole-type timber.

Pulp and paper mills in Spokane, Washington, have obtained about ten million board feet annually from the fir, spruce, hemlock, and cottonwood stands of northern Idaho. The Potlatch Forests, Inc., has built a large paper and pulp mill at Lewiston and similar mills are being considered in other sections to make use of inferior timber unfit for lumber.

The Diamond Match Company and

WOOD FOR MILLIONS OF MATCHES

In this mill at Post Falls, and at other mills in northern Idaho, the match manufacturers use Idaho lumber as the source of their products, which are distributed all over the world.

the Ohio Match Company take a large volume of white pine match blocks annually. Millions of shingles are cut, chiefly from cedar logs. There are several box factories in northern and southwestern Idaho. Other timber products range from furniture, cabinets, caskets, and water tanks to ironing boards, food containers, and toys.

Most of the cities in northern Idaho lean heavily on timber for their industries. Coeur d'Alene, Sandpoint, and Lewiston are the most important lumbering and wood-products manufacturing centers. Others of importance are St. Maries, Bonners Ferry, Grangeville, Orofino, Priest River, Potlatch, Winchester, and several other small cities and towns.

Already there are more than four thousand uses of wood, and science is constantly finding new and improving old uses. We have already named the principal uses in Idaho, but these only scratch

the surface here. For example, almost two thirds of wood is cellulose fiber. Taken from trees, this fiber can be made into a kind of cloth called rayon. Our trees can also be converted into explosives, plastics, chemicals, and even feed to fatten cattle. These are some illustrations that show a few of the many ways in which our forests can be made to supply some of our future needs.

Rivals of the California Redwoods. Not very many Idahoans know that there are giant cedars in northern Idaho that approach the great California redwoods in size and age. Ranging up to sixteen feet in diameter and as much as 150 feet in height, these cedars are an impressive sight. Their age is estimated at from two thousand to three thousand years. Earl Murphy, secretary of the Idaho Chamber of Commerce, said of them: "Those trees were seedlings when ancient Greece was at the height of its power."

II. NATIONAL AND STATE FORESTS IN IDAHO

Sixteen national forests and five state forests include most of the government-owned and government-managed forest lands in Idaho. Together they contain about twenty-one million acres, approximately 39 per cent of the total area of the state. In them are found most of the commercial forests that have not yet been cut over, as well as extensive areas of noncommercial forests used mainly for livestock and wildlife pastures and for watershed protection.

National Forests. Eight of our sixteen national forests are in the Panhandle. They are part of National Forest Region No. 1, whose head offices are in Missoula, Montana. The remaining eight are south of the Salmon River in Region No. 4, with regional offices in Ogden, Utah. California has a larger number of national forests than Idaho, but in total area Idaho ranks first among the states.

The table that follows contains important facts about the national forests that are wholly or partly in Idaho. In or near which national forest do you live? See Map No. 16, which accompanies this unit.

Table No. 14

NATIONAL FORESTS IN IDAHO

(Compiled from *Forestry Directory* of the American Tree Association)

National Forests in Idaho		Headquarters Offices	Approximate Acreage in Idaho
Bitterroot*		Hamilton, Montana	829,000
Clearwater		Orofino, Idaho	1,103,000
Coeur d'Alene		Coeur d'Alene, Idaho	724,000
Kaniksu†	Region No. 1,	Sandpoint, Idaho	867,000
Kootenai*	Missoula, Mont.	Libby, Montana	49,000
Lolo*		Missoula, Montana	399,000
Nez Perce		Grangeville, Idaho	1,931,000
St. Joe		St. Maries, Idaho	962,000
Boise		Boise, Idaho	2,612,000
Caribou‡		Pocatello, Idaho	955,000
Cache§		Logan, Utah	268,000
Challis	Region No. 4,	Challis, Idaho	2,448,000
Payette	Ogden, Utah	McCall, Idaho	2,308,000
Salmon		Salmon, Idaho	2,049,000
Sawtooth‖		Twin Falls, Idaho	1,732,000
Targhee✳		St. Anthony, Idaho	1,024,000
		Total Acreage in Idaho	20,160,000

*In Idaho and Montana.
†In Idaho, Montana, and Washington.
‖In Idaho and Utah. Absorbed the Minidoka National Forest in 1953.
✳In Idaho and Wyoming.

‡In Idaho, Utah, and Wyoming.
§In Idaho and Utah.

Courtesy Grangeville Chamber of Commerce and Shira Studio

LOG TRAMWAY OVER THE SALMON RIVER

The deep Salmon River Canyon is a serious obstacle to transportation. Here the lumbermen have employed an unusual method of getting saw logs across this natural barrier, as the bridge is not strong enough to support heavily loaded trucks.

How the National Forests Are Organized. Each of the national forests is under the general supervision of a Forest Supervisor. The offices of the supervisor and his assistants are in a city located in or conveniently near the forest.

The national forests, in turn, are divided into smaller divisions called districts. Each district is under a forest ranger, who is not only the guardian but the manager as well of a great timberland often consisting of a quarter-million acres or more. These rangers supervise timber sales, grazing, watershed protection, forest-fire protection, telephone lines, forest roads and trails, recreational development and uses, and assist in wildlife protection in their districts. During the warm season they live in homes located conveniently in their districts. In winter they generally live in the headquarters cities and do the planning and paper work for their summer assignments.

Income from National Forests. Created mainly for conservation purposes, the national forests are used for the benefit of the people. From this use the national forests of Idaho realize an income not far from a million dollars a year, earned principally from timber sales and grazing fees. This money is used largely for forest improvements such as roads, trails, telephone lines, and similar protective purposes, as appropriated by Congress. However, 25 per cent of the national forest income is turned over to the counties in which the forests are situated, where part of it goes to help support the public schools and the rest is used for road building and maintenance.

There is considerable income on some forests from the lease of mineral rights, including oil and natural gas. In recent years oil companies have leased large areas on the national forests of southeastern Idaho, where exploration is under way to determine whether oil and gas exist in commercial quantities. But any money derived from such sources goes to the United States Department of the Interior, which has title to all mineral rights on the national forests.

State Forests. When Idaho Territory was organized and at other times, certain Federal lands were given the territory

Courtesy Idaho State Forestry Department

ANCIENT CEDAR OF NORTH IDAHO

Former Governor Len Jordan and A. B. Curtis, Chief Fire Warden of the Clearwater Timber Protective Association, measure what is believed to be the largest living tree in Idaho. It is growing in the Land Board State Park near Elk River, Idaho.

and state for the support of schools, colleges, charitable and welfare institutions, and for other purposes. Among these lands were valuable forested areas.

Our state forest lands are managed by the State Board of Land Commissioners, working through the office of the State Forester. It is the State Forester's job to develop plans for forest management, and he is responsible for carrying out the plans with due regard for all users of the state forests: lumbermen, ranchers and farmers, conservationists, people using the forests for recreation, the native wildlife, and all other forest users.

To aid in management, some of the

best of the state forest lands have been placed in state forests, similar in some ways to national forests. Created in 1950, the five state forests are listed in the following table. They are also shown on Map No. 16.

Table No. 15

IDAHO STATE FORESTS

In the state forests north of the Salmon River are some of our finest stands of white pine. The ponderosa or yellow pine is the most valuable species in the Payette Forest.

State Forest	County in Which Located	Approximate Area (Acres)
Priest Lake	Bonner-Boundary	193,000
Floodwood	Clearwater-Shoshone	60,000
Orofino	Clearwater	96,000
Lolo	Clearwater-Idaho	60,000
Payette	Valley	13,000
	Total	422,000

Courtesy Tommy Barrett's Camera Shop, Pocatello

McGEE RANGER STATION, COEUR d'ALENE NATIONAL FOREST

In scores of ranger stations live the forest rangers of Idaho's national forests. Timber sales, grazing, fire protection, range and watershed improvement, and wildlife conservation are among the important duties they perform.

Courtesy Idaho State Chamber of Commerce, Boise

IDAHO DUDE RANCH

Dude ranches are located in many parts of the national forests and other remote areas of Idaho and the West. These offer attractive opportunities for summer and fall activities in inspiring and healthful surroundings.

Courtesy U.S. Forest Service

SHEEP GRAZING IN A NATIONAL FOREST

National and state forests in Idaho provide summer range for hundreds of thousands of sheep and cattle.

Courtesy Idaho State Chamber of Commerce, Boise

BEEF CATTLE "REFLECTING" ON THEIR GRAZING ADVANTAGES

You can see the contentment in the expressions of these beef cattle, and their contentment is reflected in the clear water in the foreground of this unusual photograph, taken in the great Upland Empire of central Idaho.

Privately Owned Forest Lands. Several million acres of forest lands in Idaho are owned by individuals, railroads, and lumber companies and corporations. It is from such lands that the lumbermen secure saw timber for most of the approximately a billion board feet of lumber which the state yields annually. Sawmill operators, however, also purchase timber from the state lands and national forests. These sources are becoming increasingly important as the good privately owned timber grows scarcer.

In the production of lumber, Idaho ranked eleventh among the states in 1950. With proper attention to forest conservation, discussed in our last unit, Idaho should continue to benefit enormously from our great forest resources for centuries still to come.

III. USING IDAHO'S MINERALS

THE FORTY-SEVENTH ANNUAL REPORT OF THE MINING INDUSTRY OF IDAHO gave the following summary of Idaho minerals and mining:

Idaho is divided into 44 counties, 36 of which can be classed as having minerals of commercial importance. In the past, practically all mining has been confined to the five principal metals: Lead, silver, gold, zinc, and copper. In addition to these a great variety of uncommon metals and minerals occur in sufficient extent to be of commercial importance. This great diversity of mineral wealth establishes Idaho as one of the principal mining states of the Union.

Idaho's Variety of Minerals. From A to Z, every letter in the alphabet can be used to begin the name of a mineral which can be found somewhere within the boundaries of our great state of Idaho. For proof of this fact, just look over the names of the minerals which are given in the following list (this includes the names of stones used in construction and industry):

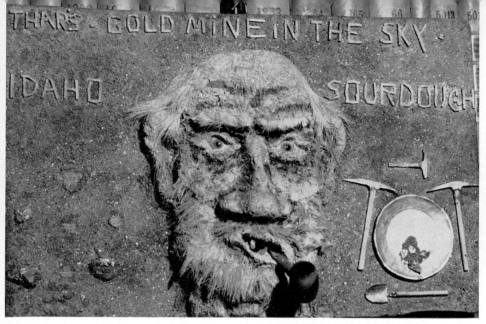

IDAHO SOURDOUGH

Original plaque made by "Red" Fisk, himself a genuine "sourdough" prospector of Warren, Idaho.

Courtesy George A. McDowell, Inspector of Mines

Table No. 16

AN ALPHABET OF IDAHO MINERALS

A. Agates, alumina clay, antimony, arsenic, asbestos
B. Barites, basalt, bentonite, beryl, beryllium, bismuth, bloodstones
C. Cerium, chromite, cinnabar, clays, coal, cobalt, copper
D. Diamonds, diatomaceous earth, dolomite
E. Epsomite, electrum
F. Feldspar, fluorite
G. Gallium, garnets, gold, granite, graphite, gypsum
H. Hornblende
I. Ilmenite
J. Jade, jasper
K. Kermesite
L. Lanthanum, lead, limestone
M. Magnesite, manganese, marble, mica, molybdenum, monazite
N. Natural gas, nickel, nitrates, nontronite clay
O. Opals
P. Petrified wood, phosphate rock, pumice, pyrites
Q. Quicksilver (mercury)
R. Rubies, rutile
S. Salt, sandstone, sapphires, silicon, silver, sulphur
T. Talc, tellurides, titanium, thorium, tin, tripoli, tungsten, turquoise
U. Uranium ores
V. Vanadium
W. Wollastonite, wurtzite
X. Xanthoconite
Y. Ytterbium
Z. Zinc, zircon or zirconium

In Bulletin No. 166, United States Department of the Interior, in co-operation with the School of Mines of the University of Idaho, is found this statement:

Idaho contains one of the largest areas of mineralized territory in the United States. The great mountainous area, 50,000 square miles in extent, that extends from the Snake River Plains on the south to British Columbia, is mineralized

Production and Uses of Idaho Minerals. In 1950, according to the *World Almanac,* Idaho produced minerals to the value of seventy-nine million dollars in round numbers. Broken down, the mineral production of a recent year gives a bird's-eye view of Idaho's leading metallic minerals, arranged in order of value:

Table No. 17

PRODUCTION OF LEADING IDAHO MINERALS (EXCEPT PHOSPHATE)

Mineral	Production	Per Cent	Total Value
Lead	177,088,000 lbs.	47%	$31,698,752
Zinc	172,534,000 lbs.	34%	22,947,022
Silver	11,448,875 ozs.	15%	10,361,810
Gold	58,454 ozs.	3%	2,045,890
Copper	3,248,000 lbs.	1%	704,816
		Total	$67,758,290

through most of its entire length. The ores in this belt include gold, silver, copper, lead, zinc, quicksilver, nickel, tungsten, and molybdenum. Among the nonmetallic minerals found in Idaho are coal, phosphate rock, asbestos, tripoli, fire clay, and mica.

Idaho produces seventy-two kinds of precious and semiprecious stones. It is said that Idaho gem beds cannot be duplicated in any other state, and that they are second only to those of Africa. They include agates of every known kind, jade which is equal to that of China, opals from old lava beds, pink, green, and red garnets, and diamonds. In fact, what is said to have been the largest diamond ever found in the United States, weighing 19.5 carats, was found more than a quarter century ago between McCall and New Meadows.

Approximately 80 per cent of Idaho's total mineral production comes from the "billion-dollar triangle," the fabulously rich lead-silver-zinc Coeur d'Alene mining district, located chiefly in Shoshone County. For more than sixty years this district has averaged about nineteen million dollars a year in the production of the five metals in the foregoing table. During the 1940's and early 1950's, its annual output averaged well above forty million dollars.

Among the great mines of this district are the Sunshine Mine, which produces more silver than any other mine in the nation; the Bunker Hill and Sullivan, the largest lead-silver producer, perhaps, in the world; the Hecla Mine, the Federal mines, the Day merger mines, and the Star Mine, largest producer of zinc. The

PHOSPHATES OF SOUTH-
EASTERN IDAHO GIVE THE
STATE NEW INDUSTRIES
*MONSANTO CHEMICAL
PLANT*

Courtesy Soda Springs Chamber of Commerce

WESTVACO ELEMENTAL
PHOSPHORUS PLANT

*The largest phosphate de-
posits in the United States
are the basis for new fertilizer and chemical plants.*

Courtesy U.S. Bureau of Reclamation, Region No. 1, Boise

output of these and other mines provides
the livelihood for the people of Wallace,
Kellogg, and Mullan, the three principal
cities of the Coeur d'Alene triangle, as
well as for the entire district.

Not all of Idaho's mineral wealth,
however, is buried in Shoshone County
and North Idaho. From Stibnite, in Valley County, came about 98 per cent of the
nation's antimony and much of its tungsten in World War II, and this section
also produces much gold. The Bonanza,
Triumph, and other mines in the Wood
River district surrounding Hailey are

heavy producers of galena (lead-silver) ores. The Ima Mine at Patterson in Lemhi County is normally a large producer of tungsten. Gold dredges still operate profitably in the Yankee Fork district, Boise Basin, Elk City district, Warren district, and at other places in the Upland Empire.

Developing rapidly is the phosphate mining and processing industry in southeastern Idaho, where more than half the nation's phosphate reserves are located. *Information Circular 7529* of the Bureau of Mines, a branch of the United States Department of the Interior, gave the following summary of this industry: The five principal companies operating in this field are the Anaconda Copper Mining Company, with mines at Conda near Soda Springs; the Simplot Fertilizer Company, whose mines are east of Fort Hall on the Fort Hall Indian Reservation; the Waterloo Company, with mines in Montpelier Canyon in Bear Lake County; the Westvaco Company at Pocatello; and the Monsanto Chemical Company at Soda Springs. Together, these use approximately a million tons of phosphate rock annually, valued at close to five million dollars. The Anaconda Copper and Simplot interests are manufacturers of phosphate fertilizer and the Westvaco and Monsanto companies produce elemental phosphorus, a violent liquid that bursts into flame when exposed to the air and which has many uses in modern industry. The entire phosphate industry in southeastern Idaho is expanding so rapidly that figures concerning its development are often outdated within a short time following their publication.

At Conda, a few miles from Soda Springs, in Caribou County, is the Intermountain West's most continuous phosphate rock mining development. Mining started there in 1920 and since that time more than two million tons of phosphate rock have been shipped by the Anaconda Copper Mining Company, which owns the mines, to Pacific coast points and to the Hawaiian Islands. Production is now in excess of two hundred thousand tons annually, but apparently the amount of phosphate still in reserve in this mine is sufficient to insure heavy production for many years to come.

A copper-cobalt district is being developed in the western part of Lemhi County, where Cobalt, one of Idaho's newest towns, has been built on Panther Creek below Forney. The cobalt deposits here are said to be the largest in the United States. The metal is used to make alloys capable of withstanding tremendous heat and it is of special value in the construction of jet engines for airplanes. It also has many other important uses in industry.

The newest important mining development in Idaho is the growing use of monazite, the black sand that was such an annoyance to placer miners in early Idaho. Monazite beds extend from the Boise Basin northward through the Cascade district to the Warren meadows. They contain several rare earths of special value. These beds yield thorium, a product useful in the atomic energy field; ilmenite; titanium, the "wonder metal" that is similar to aluminum; and zirconium, used in the ceramics industry, steel foundries, and chemical industries. Special uses of monazite are in the manufacture of jet engines, cigarette lighter fluids, and movie projection lights. The best monazite ores sell as high as $375 a ton, with some special rare-earth metals worth one dollar a milligram, about enough to cover the head of a pin. These monazite beds in Idaho are almost the only important source for the United States, since supplies formerly received from Brazil and India have largely been shut off.

There are great coal deposits in Teton County, which are as yet largely undeveloped. As better transportation is provided, these will play an increasingly important role in the state's economy. At present their use is mainly restricted to communities located reasonably near the deposits.

Copper, lead, zinc, silver, and gold are used in hundreds of ways, many of which you already know. To name some of the uses of other Idaho minerals is to hint at industries based on our mineral wealth that will some day help to make Idaho an important industrial section.

Antimony, also called stibnite, of which our state produces a large share of the nation's supply, is an alloy for mixing with and hardening other metals. It is classed as a strategic war metal and for that reason the Idaho deposits are a particularly valuable resource. Asbestos is used in making fireproof fabrics and in the manufacture of shingles, insulating material, paper, cement, and paints. Bentonite is used in beauty clays, in refining petroleum, and in making drugs and candies. Clays are basic raw materials for brick, tile, pottery, tableware, and sanitary ware. From coal we derive many things, such as synthetic gasoline, drugs, dyes, and many other items. Diatomaceous earth contributes to insulating materials, filters, concrete mixtures, polishing powders, and so on. Graphite is a substance needed in making paints, stove

Courtesy George A. McDowell Inspector of Mines

BRADLEY MINE AT STIBNITE

Here, during World War II, was produced more than 90 per cent of the antimony mined in the United States. Antimony, a strategic war metal, is of special value in wartime. This district also produces gold and mercury, the latter another strategic war mineral.

polish, electrical appliances, and lead pencils. Gypsum is a base in wall plaster, blocks and tiles, and portland cement. Mica is much used in electrical industries, wallpaper, tile and concrete, roofing ma- portland cement. The table which follows, showing Idaho's high rank among the states in certain minerals and mineral products, gives some interesting comparisons.

Table No. 18

IDAHO'S RANK (1953) IN CERTAIN MINERALS

(Compiled from various reliable sources)

Rank	Minerals and Products
First	Zinc, silver, antimony, cobalt, monazite
Second	Lead, abrasive garnets, cadmium
Third	Phosphate rock and elemental phosphorus
Fourth	Tungsten concentrates
Fifth (estimated)	Gold
Sixth (estimated)	Copper

terials, rubber goods, and lubricants. Nickel is a hard metal much used in industry for many purposes. Mercury, or quicksilver, is another strategic war mineral which Idaho furnished the nation in large amounts in World War II. Tungsten is a hardening material for alloys and another of Idaho's strategic metals. Limestone is chiefly important in making portland cement, but many other uses are possible.

The list of uses for our Idaho mineral resources could go on at great length. But surely you can now see how extremely valuable these are to us, and particularly to future Idahoans, whose privilege it will be to put them into service for themselves and for the use and benefit of all mankind.

Rated in the order of value, the minerals now of most worth in Idaho are: (1) lead, (2) zinc, (3) silver, (4) phosphate, (5) gold, (6) antimony, (7) copper, and (8) limestone in the form of

What of the Future? No other basic occupation seems to hold the fascination that mining does. Once it was gold that drew the eyes of the world to Idaho. Next, silver occupied the spotlight, which it soon shared with lead and zinc. In the last decade phosphate came into its own. Now the possibility of finding uranium in paying quantities is drawing prospectors into the mountains and deserts, testing with their Geiger counters, hopefully listening for the telltale clicks that may herald a new and epoch-making discovery. Now, too, the oil geologists are scanning the surface formations that may indicate deep-lying pools of "black gold" hidden in sands lying deep in Mother Earth.

No matter what the magnet that draws prospectors and mining men afield, one thing is certain: Our state has already yielded a huge sum in mineral wealth and will, through future years, continue to reward the efforts of those who are daring enough and ingenious enough to reclaim the buried treasures Mother Nature has concealed beneath the surface of Idaho.

*   *   *   *   *

Forest industries and mining, together with agriculture, are the great basic industries on which Idaho so greatly depends for the welfare and prosperity of the people. As these industries are expanded, the state should have a steady and continuous growth, especially if our hydroelectric possibilities are also expanded to provide cheap and abundant power. Idaho seems destined in the not too distant future to become an industrial state of much importance in our national economy.

FUN AT PAYETTE LAKE, THE "MILE HIGH PLAYGROUND"

Using Our Wildlife
and Recreational Resources

How the great wildlife and recreational advantages of Idaho add to our welfare, and why our fame in these respects has spread to many other states and countries.

IN *Wildlife of Idaho*, Chase A. Clark, then governor of the state, wrote:

The wildlife is yours. It belongs to the boys and girls of Idaho. . . . You must see to it that the wild creatures are well taken care of, that they have good homes with plenty to eat, whether it be in the forests, fields or waters. You should have more animals, rather than less, so that there will be wildlife to pass on to your children and grandchildren.

Never kill any living thing just for the sake of killing. . . . Harmful pests must be controlled. . . . Be sure that a bird or mammal really is harmful before you kill it. Learn its habits and be sure.

By all means hunt. Learn to be a good hunter. Shoot and shoot straight. By all means fish.

Learn to do it well. Above all though, learn to be a good sportsman, and that means to be fair, honest and liberal with all the wild things. A good sportsman grows into a good citizen. . . .

Our splendid recreational resources include other things than fish and game. Our mountain scenery, our woodlands, our running streams and sparkling lakes, our parks and picnic grounds—these, too, are part of our Idaho heritage, more precious, it may be, than our sources of material wealth. How well are we acquainted with the great out of doors that Idaho offers for our enjoyment, good health, and welfare?

I. WHAT IDAHO OFFERS THE HUNTER AND FISHERMAN

IT WAS NOT BY ACCIDENT that Idaho has become a famous hunting and fishing state. Nature endowed her with conditions very favorable to an abundant and varied wildlife. We have already seen that a large part of the state is mountainous, a forest wilderness well fitted to shelter and feed a host of wild animals.

In the *Idaho Little Blue Book,* published by the State Board of Publicity, we are told that our state has 6,500 streams offering more than 12,000 miles

of trout fishing, and 1,763 lakes, nearly all of which contain fish. Many of the forests and waters are in rugged back country so hard to reach that they are seldom visited. This is good, because it helps preserve wildlife for future Idahoans to enjoy.

Big Game. Few states can match Idaho in varieties of big game. These include deer, elk, moose, antelope, both mountain sheep and mountain goats, bear, and cougars or mountain lions. A few wood-

MONARCH OF THE FOREST

Moose are not plentiful in Idaho, but are found in limited numbers in the Island Park country of eastern Idaho and in a few other parts of the state.

land caribou live in the extreme northern part of the state.

Deer, our most abundant game animals, are found in practically every county. Black-tailed or mule deer are most plentiful south of the Salmon River. The smaller white-tailed deer are very much at home in the Panhandle. Both kinds of deer, however, are found to some extent in nearly all parts of the state.

Elk are found in the mountains of eastern Idaho, the rugged central Idaho country, and the Clearwater wilderness. The largest elk herds roam the wild crags, ridges, and canyons of the Selway-Bitterroot Primitive Area. Life holds few greater thrills than to stand on some high point and listen to the bugling of great bull elk, literally monarchs of their wild domain.

Beginning with the 1954 hunting season, the Fish and Game Department started a survey to make as accurate a count as possible of the number of elk ranging in the Clearwater drainage area. Estimates have placed the number at somewhere between twenty-five thousand and thirty thousand head. If true, this is

DEER AT HOME

ELK ON SOUTH FORK, PAYETTE RIVER

Deer and elk are Idaho's most plentiful big-game animals. The former are found in all parts of the state. Elk are most abundant in the Selway-Bitterroot Primitive Area in the eastern part of Idaho County; they are fairly plentiful in other areas of the state.

the area in the days of Lewis and Clark, the expedition might have been spared much of the suffering and starvation that it faced along the Lolo Trail.

Moose, largest members of the American deer family, prefer brushy and swampy areas. They are most plentiful in the Island Park district of the North Fork of the Snake River. Smaller numbers are found in central and northern Idaho. Not many of these noble animals remain in the state, so that hunting them is not generally permitted, except in very limited areas.

Antelope, mountain sheep or bighorns, and mountain goats are quite choosey in selecting homes. Most of our antelope and pronghorns are in the Pahsimeroi district of Lemhi and Custer counties, the Lost River–Birch Creek country in Butte, Clark, Custer, and Lemhi counties, and

the largest elk herd in North America and, possibly, in the entire world. Incidentally, this also explains why elk hunters from many parts of the nation come to Idaho each year to try to bag one of these noble game animals. If even a fraction of this great herd had been in

on the semiarid plateaus of Owyhee County. Both bighorns and mountain goats, the few that still exist, live among the highest and ruggedest crags of the Selkirk, Bitterroot, Sawtooth, Clearwater and Salmon River Mountains.

The large meat-eating animals stay

among the mountains. Black and brown bear, both of the black bear family, are found in limited numbers in most of the mountainous districts. They are, however, more numerous in central and northern Idaho. An occasional grizzly still roams the region adjoining Yellowstone National Park. There may be a few grizzlies in the Nelson Range of the Selkirk Mountains and in the Bitterroot Range. These great bears are now nearly extinct in the state.

There are a good many cougars in the mountains of central and northern Idaho. Because they kill many deer and, occasionally, domestic animals, they have had a bounty placed on them and have been thinned out by hunters who wanted both the thrill of taking them and the price placed on their luckless heads.

In its annual report, the Idaho Fish and Game Department reported that hunters bagged a total of 41,354 big-game animals in 1952, divided as shown in the following table:

Courtesy U.S. Bureau of Reclamation, Region No. 1, Boise

WAITING, BUT WATCHFUL

The "Chink" or Chinese pheasant is Idaho's most abundant upland game bird. This trio seems about ready to take off for a less public spot.

Table No. 19

IDAHO BIG GAME

(*Twenty-Fourth Biennial Report,* Idaho Fish and Game Department, July 1, 1950, to June 30, 1952)

Animals	Number Reported Killed	Estimated Number in State
Deer	55,828	140,550
Elk	14,657	43,600
Bear	Grizzly—Closed season	38
	Black —1,000 (est.)	6,470
Mountain Goat	8	3,570
Bighorn Sheep	Closed season	2,500
Pronghorn Antelope	1,888	13,447
Moose	58	1,317

HONKERS AREN'T ALWAYS WILD

These Canada geese, usually wild and wary birds, seem to have lost their fear of man. Could they be waiting for a handout? Probably not, for the truth is they are only molting, at which time they cannot fly.

The Game Department census for 1953 gave Idaho a deer population of approximately 153,000 and 45,000 elk.

Upland Game Birds. These include five species of grouse, Chinese pheasants, two kinds of partridges, and some varieties of quails. Only the grouse are native to Idaho, all the rest having originally been brought into the state from other places.

Members of the grouse family are the blue grouse, ruffed grouse, also called willow grouse, Franklin's grouse or fool hens, sharp-tailed grouse or prairie chickens, ptarmigan, and sage grouse or sage hens, as they are usually called.

Blue grouse live in timbered areas in the mountains and are usually found quite well up. Ruffed grouse are more widespread, and in Idaho are often found along the mountain streams. Both the prairie chickens and ptarmigan are extremely scarce, the latter living in the highest elevations of the Panhandle mountains. Franklin's grouse is also growing quite scarce, probably because they are so stupid and unwary that they can sometimes be killed with a stick or club.

Sage grouse are at home in the sagebrush regions of Idaho and other western states. Though Idaho was once the home of countless thousands of sage grouse, only limited numbers remain except on bird preserves where they are protected. Short hunting seasons with very small bag limits are sometimes permitted for sage grouse, blue grouse, ruffed grouse, and Franklin's grouse. Hunting is not permitted at any time for other species of grouse.

Idaho's most abundant game bird is the Chinese pheasant, the ringneck or Chink. It is widely distributed throughout the agricultural sections of the state but is most plentiful in parts of the Snake River Valley and the Clearwater Plateau. Bag limits are more liberal and hunting seasons longer on these than on any other of our upland game birds.

Hungarian and Chukar partridges and quail have been planted where conditions seemed most favorable for them. Their increase, however, has not been as great as hoped for. They do provide some shooting, and further study and research may find a way to make them succeed better in areas where they have been introduced. Mourning doves are among the game birds of Idaho, but popular interest in hunting them has not been high.

Migratory Waterfowl. For sportsmen these are mainly limited to wild ducks and geese. Idaho is located on a main flyway traveled by migratory waterfowl from nesting grounds in Canada and Alaska to southern latitudes where these birds winter. For that reason we have heavy fall flights of ducks and geese, many of which stop here to rest and feed on their way south.

There are also thousands of these birds that nest and rear their young in Idaho. Many of these refuse to migrate. Thus we may see resident flocks at any time of the year in parts of the state, notably in the Snake River Valley.

Unusually interesting among the migratory waterfowl are whistling swans and trumpeter swans. Both are scarce, the trumpeters being at one time considered on the verge of extinction. Both kinds of these stately birds visit Idaho waters from time to time, and both seem to be slowly increasing in number. Shooting them is strictly forbidden.

Fish. What varieties of fish does our state have that call one Idahoan in every three to our fishing waters and attract thousands of nimrods from other places? Space will allow only a few short paragraphs instead of the many pages the answer to this question deserves.

More trout are caught than any other kind of game fish. The trout include the rainbow, Eastern brook, brown or Loch Leven, native or cutthroat, Dolly Varden or charr, steelhead, Mackinaw or lake trout, and the famed Kamloops of Lake Pend Oreille. These range from the pan-fish size of small streams to giant trout occasionally thirty pounds or more in weight. The size of what is caught depends on lady luck and the location of the fishing hole.

The salmon species include the splendid chinook, or king salmon, and the kokanee or sockeye, also called blueback and landlocked salmon. The chinook are hatched high up on the headwaters of the streams of central and northern Idaho. Then they go down to the ocean to grow large and powerful. When four to six years old, they migrate back to the waters in which they first saw life. There they spawn and start a new generation of

RIDE HIM, COWBOY!

The Kamloops trout grow big in Lake Pend Oreille.

A SNAKE RIVER "WHALE"

The sturgeon has descended almost unchanged from ancient ages. Today's fishermen are fishing for them with rod and reel. Sometimes they land them and sometimes they don't. This husky specimen could probably not have been landed by the modern method.

chinooks and then die, completing one of the strangest and most interesting life cycles of our earth. The Salmon River and its tributaries are the state's favorite salmon streams.

The mightiest of all our fish is the armored, boneless sturgeon, caught in Snake River from Shoshone Falls down. These strange fish have survived from past geological epochs. They often range in size up to three hundred pounds, but occasionally fishermen have taken "Snake River whales," as they are sometimes called, weighing well above the half-ton mark.

Another unusual fish is the ling or lake lawyer, caught only in the Kootenai River and its tributaries. This is a freshwater codfish, usually taken only in the winter months.

Other fish include the whitefish, grayling, bluegill, crappie, perch, bass, and catfish. Most of these, except the whitefish, have been brought in from other places and planted in Idaho waters. They now provide thousands of fishermen with both sport and food, and are gradually being introduced in waters not suitable for trout and salmon.

Fur Bearers. The first white explorers to pass through the Rocky Mountains were amazed at the abundance of furbearing animals along the streams. Beavers were, as you know, the lure that drew the French Canadians and the mountain men to the streams of Idaho. They still provide more furs for industry than any other Idaho fur bearer. There are, however, muskrats, minks, foxes, martens, skunks, raccoons, and occasional fishers still to be found. Otters, among the finest of our fur animals, were once common in the state but are now seldom seen. Coyotes, cougars, and wildcats, all classed as predatory animals, those that prey on other animals, provide pelts and sport. Trapping is carefully regulated by state laws enforced by the Fish and Game Department and by the Federal Fish and Wildlife Service.

CHINCHILLAS AT HOME

These natives of the high Andes are among the aristocrats of the fur-bearers. Only the wealthy can now afford to wear their glorious coats.

Courtesy Imperial Chinchilla Ranch, Idaho Falls, Idaho

Fur farming is comparatively new in Idaho, but minks, foxes, and chinchillas are raised in several parts of the state. Chinchillas, small imported animals from the high Andes, are now at home in several parts of the Snake River Plains. The Imperial Chinchilla Ranch at Idaho Falls is probably the largest of its kind in the United States. Chinchilla furs are so expensive that little effort has been made to pelt the animals, though a beginning in that direction is now being made.

II. SCENIC AND RECREATIONAL AREAS

WITHIN THE BORDERS OF IDAHO are many famed scenic and recreational areas which, altogether, number their visitors by millions of persons annually. Many of us who live in Idaho have not taken the time to visit places that out-of-state visitors travel hundreds, even thousands, of miles to see. Most of these have been mentioned elsewhere in this book but let us take a quick look at them here to remind ourselves how fortunate we are to live in a state so favored by nature in the number of outdoor attractions.

National Parks and Monuments. Idaho shares in Yellowstone National Park, though only a small part of that world-famous region is inside our borders. Nowhere else on earth can be found so many amazing sights as are grouped close together in this wonderland of nature. Open through the months of June, July, August, and September, Yellowstone draws more than a million visitors a year, among them people from every state and from many countries beyond our national boundaries. If you have not seen Yellowstone National Park, you have a rare treat awaiting you. Be sure to visit it during your next summer vacation. You will never forget the marvels you see there.

A park noted for glorious scenery is Teton National Park. Just south of Yel-

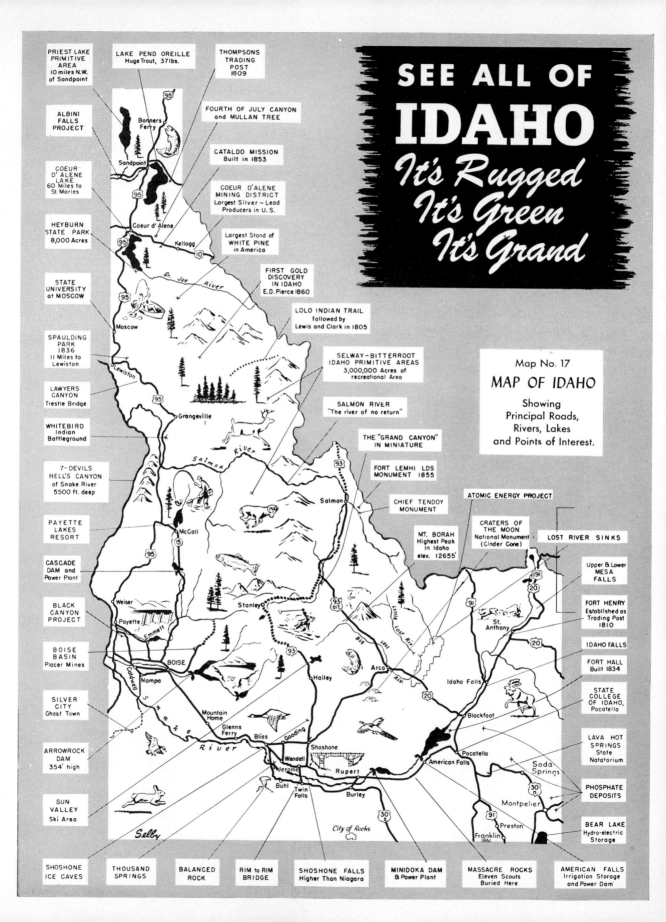

SEE ALL OF
IDAHO
It's Rugged
It's Green
It's Grand

Map No. 17

MAP OF IDAHO

Showing
Principal Roads,
Rivers, Lakes
and Points of Interest.

PRIEST LAKE
PRIMITIVE
AREA
10 miles N.W.
of Sandpoint

LAKE PEND OREILLE
Huge Trout, 37 lbs.

THOMPSONS
TRADING
POST
1809

ALBINI
FALLS
PROJECT

FOURTH OF JULY CANYON
and MULLAN TREE

CATALDO MISSION
Built in 1853

COEUR
D' ALENE
LAKE
60 Miles to
St. Maries

COEUR D'ALENE
MINING DISTRICT
Largest Silver — Lead
Producers in U. S.

HEYBURN
STATE PARK
8,000 Acres

Largest Stand of
WHITE PINE
in America

FIRST GOLD
DISCOVERY
IN IDAHO
E.D. Pierce 1860

STATE
UNIVERSITY
at MOSCOW

LOLO INDIAN TRAIL
followed by
Lewis and Clark in 1805

SPAULDING
PARK
1836
11 Miles to
Lewiston

SELWAY—BITTERROOT
IDAHO PRIMITIVE AREAS
3,000,000 Acres of
recreational Area

LAWYERS
CANYON
Trestle Bridge

SALMON RIVER
"The river of no return"

WHITEBIRD
Indian
Battleground

THE "GRAND CANYON"
IN MINIATURE

7–DEVILS
HELL'S CANYON
of Snake River
5500 ft. deep

FORT LEMHI LDS
MONUMENT 1855

ATOMIC ENERGY PROJECT

CHIEF TENDOY
MONUMENT

PAYETTE
LAKES
RESORT

CRATERS OF
THE MOON
National Monument
(Cinder Cone)

LOST RIVER SINKS

MT. BORAH
Highest Peak
In Idaho
elev. 12655'

CASCADE
DAM and
Power Plant

Upper & Lower
MESA
FALLS

BLACK
CANYON
PROJECT

FORT HENRY
Established as
Trading Post
1810

BOISE
BASIN
Placer Mines

IDAHO FALLS

FORT HALL
Built 1834

SILVER
CITY
Ghost Town

STATE
COLLEGE
OF IDAHO,
Pocatello

ARROWROCK
DAM
354' high

LAVA HOT
SPRINGS
State
Natatorium

PHOSPHATE
DEPOSITS

SUN
VALLEY
Ski Area

BEAR LAKE
Hydro-electric
Storage

SHOSHONE
ICE CAVES

THOUSAND
SPRINGS

BALANCED
ROCK

RIM to RIM
BRIDGE

SHOSHONE FALLS
Higher Than Niagara

MINIDOKA DAM
& Power Plant

MASSACRE ROCKS
Eleven Scouts
Buried Here

AMERICAN FALLS
Irrigation Storage
and Power Dam

Bonners
Ferry

Sandpoint

Coeur d' Alene

Kellogg

St. Joe River

Moscow

Lewiston

Grangeville

Salmon River

Salmon

McCall

Weiser

Payette

Emmett

Stanley

BOISE

Caldwell

Nampa

Mountain
Home

Glenns
Ferry

Bliss

Gooding

Wendell

Jerome

Buhl

Twin
Falls

Burley

Rupert

Shoshone

Hailey

Arco

Little Lost Riv.

Big Lost Riv.

St.
Anthony

Idaho Falls

Blackfoot

Pocatello

American Falls

Soda
Springs

Montpelier

Preston

Franklin
1861

Snake River

Selby

City of Rocks

CRATERS OF THE MOON

The weird volcanic region which includes the Craters of the Moon National Monument is one of the most remarkable examples in the world of recent volcanic activity.

lowstone Park, this great scenic region is so close to us, just over the border in the Jackson's Hole country in Wyoming, that we can claim an interest in it, even though it does not enter Idaho. The magnificent Grand Teton, called the Matterhorn of America, is in this park. You can always kill two birds with one stone by visiting both these fine national parks on the same trip.

Another of the world's strange wonderlands is Craters of the Moon National Monument. Located in the northern part of Idaho's Snake River Plains between Lost River and Wood River valleys, its eighty square miles of lava flows, cinder cones, craters, and lava tunnels and caves constitute one of the world's finest displays of recent volcanic activity. A well-equipped public campground serves the thousands of visitors who journey there each summer.

Attention should also be called to the Roosevelt Grove of Ancient Cedars.

This is barely over the line in Washington, but is so nearly in Idaho that we may claim a share in it.

Places to Go in Idaho. The places in Idaho that are well worth seeing and enjoying are almost bewildering in their number and variety. *Idaho, A Guide in Word and Picture,* first published in 1937 by The Caxton Printers, Ltd., of Caldwell, Idaho, required 180 pages to list and describe the state's outstanding attractions. Copies of this book are available in most of our public libraries and in many school libraries. It is an excellent aid in planning where to go and what to see in the state.

Do you wish to see remarkable canyons? Hell's Canyon, between Idaho and Oregon, and the Salmon River Canyon, which slashes a mighty trench east and west across central Idaho, are among the deepest and most spectacular in America. Annual boat trips through these wild gorges offer rare opportunities to lovers

Courtesy Tommy Barrett's Camera Shop, Pocatello

GRANDEUR BEYOND GRANDEUR

In the mountain region of Idaho are wilderness areas so utterly wild and rugged that they defy description. Such a place is this in the Bighorn Crags of the Idaho Primitive Area.

of outdoor adventure. Other spectacular canyons are Snake River's Shoshone Gorge near Twin Falls, the wild canyons of the Middle Fork of the Salmon River and its tributaries, South Fork Canyon on the Payette River, Danskin Canyon on the South Fork of the Boise River, the deep and forbidding Bruneau River Canyon, the beautiful canyon of the Clearwater River, the great Locksa River Canyon, Lawyers Canyon of the Clearwater Plateau, the deep and scenic canyons on the upper St. Joe and Coeur d'Alene rivers, and the Moyie (MŌ-YA) River Canyon in Boundary County. In fact, Idaho specializes in canyons, but many of the most spectacular cannot be visited by automobile.

Do you especially enjoy spending your time in scenic regions where nature has not been much changed by man's interference? Then go to the Primitive Area along the Middle Fork of the Salmon River; the Sawtooth Primitive Area around the headwaters of the Salmon, Boise, and Payette rivers; the great Selway-Bitterroot Primitive Area of the Selway River; the magnificent high country of the Bitterroot Range; the Selkirk Mountains in Bonner and Boundary counties; the Island Park country in Fremont County; the Seven Devils Mountains in Adams and Idaho counties; and the great canyon-gashed plateaus of Owyhee County. These are some of the regions you will be sure to enjoy if you can get there.

Would you prefer a beautiful lake setting where you could make new friends and have the companionship of other recreationists? Among Idaho's notable lakeside recreational areas are the Lake Pend Oreille area near Sandpoint; Lake Coeur d'Alene and the city of Coeur d'Alene; Priest Lake with its encircling forests; the Payette Lakes mile-high playground at McCall; Alturas, Redfish, and the other beautiful lakes of the upper Stanley Basin, rimmed by the majestic Sawtooth peaks; and beautiful Bear Lake, the great recreational area of Bear Lake County and southeastern Idaho. There are scores of lesser lakes that are visited by thousands of fishermen and picnickers. Well over a million visitors a year spend many enjoyable days at these notable attractions.

Do you like the thunderous music and the rainbow mists of waterfalls? Shoshone Falls, near the city of Twin Falls, is Idaho's mightiest cataract, where Snake River drops 280 feet in one mighty

HELL'S CANYON OF SNAKE RIVER

The deepest known canyon in North America, this mighty slash lies along the Idaho-Oregon boundary under the western rim of the Seven Devils Mountains.

Courtesy U.S. Bureau of Reclamation, Region No. 1, Boise

plunge. A few miles upstream are the Twin Falls of the Snake, now changed to a single waterfall by the Idaho Power Company dam. On the road from Ashton to Yellowstone Park is Upper Mesa Falls (or Big Falls) of the North Fork of the Snake River, where the stream makes a sheer drop of 114 feet. A side road near Ashton leads to Cave Falls on Fall River. The most beautiful waterfall in the Panhandle is Moyie Falls on the Moyie River, not far from the city of Bonners Ferry. There are lesser waterfalls on many Idaho streams, among them the beautiful Thousand Springs and other cascades in Hagerman Valley. There are also man-made falls at most of our great irrigation and power dams.

Are you acquainted with the strange rock formations found in our state? Some of the strangest are in Craters of the Moon National Monument. Others decidedly worth seeing are the Silent City of Rocks in Cassia County, with its imitation mosques, its monoliths and turrets carved by erosion; the Gooding City of Rocks in Gooding County, whose strange shale and sandstone formations are marked with beautiful colors; remarkable Balanced Rock, whose great mushroom crown towers forty feet above the slender column on which it rests; the weird Sucker Creek and Jump Creek canyon formations in Owyhee County; and scores of other formations in various parts of the state.

Would you like to go with the Trail Riders of the Wilderness on one of their annual horseback excursions in the Sawtooth area? Sponsored by the American Forestry Association, of Washington, D.C., two Trail Riders excursions leave Sun Valley each summer and spend about two weeks in the wilder and more remote sections of the Sawtooths, areas which can be reached only on foot or horseback. These are rare treats which can be enjoyed only by special arrangements with the Forestry Association.

Sun Valley deserves a paragraph all its own. This world-famous resort on upper Big Wood River was developed and is owned and operated by the Union Pacific Railroad. A year-round program of winter and summer sports is maintained for the host of visitors constantly arriving there. Many notable people from all parts of the world are guests, and it is becoming one of the most popular convention centers of the West.

State-Owned Recreational Areas. Idaho owns several recreational areas, some of which are outstanding in their fields. Three that we should certainly visit are Lava Hot Springs, Heyburn State Park, and Spalding Memorial Park.

Lava Hot Springs Sanitarium is located in the town of Lava Hot Springs on the Portneuf River in Bannock County. Here a group of remarkable hot springs, each with a different mineral content, discharge about 8,500,000 gallons of water daily. The curative properties of the waters have long been known and thousands of people use the state-managed baths to improve their health. Many more people visit the famed resort to enjoy the recreational advantages offered by both public and private swimming pools and the well-equipped picnic grounds provided by the state. The state pools, sanitarium, and grounds are managed by the Lava Hot Springs Foundation, a board appointed by the governor. Probably more people use this health and recreational area than any other in southern Idaho.

Heyburn State Park, located at the southern end of Lake Coeur d'Alene, includes an area of 7,838 acres, a third of which are water, with most of the land area heavily forested. In it are Lake Chatcolet, Benewah Lake, Round Lake, and a small part of Lake Coeur d'Alene.

Courtesy U.S. Forest Service

TRAIL RIDERS OF THE WILDERNESS

Sponsored by the American Forestry Association, of Washington, D.C., the Trail Riders make journeys into wilderness areas in many parts of the nation. Here the annual trip in the Sawtooth Mountains gets under way.

STANLEY BASIN FROM GALENA SUMMIT

Surrounded by lofty ranges of the Sawtooth and Salmon River mountains, Stanley Basin is one of the most beautiful and picturesque places in Idaho. It is reached by U.S. Highway 93, extending from Las Vegas, Nevada, to Glacier National Park in Montana.

Courtesy Idaho State Board of Publicity

Named for a former senator from Idaho, and set apart for the use and enjoyment of the public, this recreational area is used by scores of thousands of visitors annually. It is a nature preserve in which can be seen most of the plants as well as many of the birds and smaller animals that are found in northern Idaho.

Spalding Memorial Park was established in memory of the Reverend Henry Spalding and the first Christian mission in Idaho. On the Clearwater River a few miles upstream from Lewiston, this historical park contains monuments, buildings, and relics of great historical value. There is located the privately owned Sacajawea Museum, which should, probably, be purchased and maintained by the Idaho State Historical Society because of the many historical and Indian relics it contains.

There are also several picnic areas owned by the state and placed by the 1949 legislature under the general super-vision of the State Department of Highways. These consist of three areas along the Boise–Idaho City highway, one at the Salmon River bridge near Challis, one in Lawyers Canyon between Lewiston and Grangeville on U.S. Highway 95, and two on U.S. Highway 30 at historic points between American Falls and the Raft River. Lakeshore areas have also been developed as public recreational areas at Payette Lake and other Idaho lakes.

* * * * *

Idaho does, indeed, have wildlife and recreational resources probably unexcelled by those of any other state. These are for the enjoyment of all our people and for the many thousands of visitors from other states and countries. We should all realize that carelessness and the misuse of these resources can only result in loss to everyone and damage to these great attractions. Let us act accordingly when we have the opportunity to visit and enjoy them.

Conservation Pledge

I GIVE MY
PLEDGE AS AN AMERICAN
TO SAVE AND FAITHFULLY TO
DEFEND FROM WASTE THE
NATURAL RESOURCES OF
MY COUNTRY – ITS SOIL
AND MINERALS, ITS
FORESTS, WATERS,
AND WILDLIFE

Originated by L. L. Foreman. Used by special permission of *Outdoor Life Magazine*

Kodachrome courtesy Bunker Hill & Sullivan Mining and Concentrating Company

FROM EARLY DAYS MUCH OF IDAHO'S WEALTH HAS COME FROM MINING

This picture shows the Electrolytic Zinc Plant of the Sullivan Mining Company at Kellogg, Idaho

Conservation—Key to Idaho's Future

How the conservation and wise use of our natural resources will improve the American way of life for present and future generations of Idaho citizens.

IDAHO'S MOST IMPORTANT NATURAL RESOURCES are, as you know, the five great natural resources named in the Conservation Pledge with which our final unit begins. Are Idahoans making wise use of these resources? Can we derive full benefit from their use and at the same time manage them so that they will not be lost or seriously damaged? Let us look at some of the problems facing us in the field of conservation and examine some of the suggestions offered for the handling of these problems. As you read, notice particularly the conservation problems which seem to be of most importance in your own section of the state.

I. CONSERVATION OF THE SOIL

"GOOD, PRODUCTIVE SOIL is Idaho's greatest asset. But it is not necessarily a permanent asset. Unless soil is wisely used and given proper care, its value may be impaired, or even lost, in a short time." So says a statement in *10 Keys to Soil and*

Courtesy Grangeville Chamber of Commerce and Shira Studio

PUREBRED BEEF CATTLE NEAR GRANGEVILLE

Natural grasslands of the Clearwater Plateau are superior for livestock production and general farming.

LOGS FROM PANHANDLE FORESTS

Soils and climate combine to make the mountains of northern Idaho well fitted for growing trees.

Water Conservation, a bulletin of the Portneuf Soil Conservation District in southeastern Idaho.

Wise use of the soil means that the soils of Idaho should be put to the use for which they are best fitted. Land that is most suitable for raising crops should be used for that purpose. Other lands are well adapted to tree growth and, in most cases, that is the wisest use to which they can be put. Still other areas are not suitable for either farming or growing timber, but are most useful as pastures for livestock and wildlife, and here natural vegetation should be allowed to flourish.

Soil Conservation Agencies in Idaho. Careful farmers have always tried to keep their lands fertile. However, there are some problems that have to be solved by group co-operation, if they are to be solved at all. As a result, several agencies work together in Idaho to carry on a program of soil conservation.

Congress created the national Soil Conservation Service in 1935. Idaho co-operates in that work with more than a score of conservation districts in the farming sections of the state. These are voluntary organizations of farmers who, with the aid of trained conservation workers, carry on various kinds of conservation projects in the districts and on the various farms. Is your own community part of a soil conservation district?

The county agricultural agents give help in solving soil conservation problems in their counties. Farm youth are learning conservation practices through Future Farmers and 4-H Clubs. The Forest Service and Grazing Service aid in many ways. Important, too, is the work of the College of Agriculture of the University of Idaho and the agricultural experiment stations it operates with the co-operation of the United States Department of Agriculture. The table that follows shows where the experiment stations are located and some of the kinds of work they carry on. (Also see Map No. 11, Unit 11.)

Table No. 20

IDAHO AGRICULTURAL EXPERIMENT STATIONS

Experimental and research work has brought benefits worth many millions of dollars to Idaho agriculture and has greatly aided the agricultural conservation program.

Experimental Stations*	Kinds of Work. Does Not Include All Kinds Done
Moscow, Home Station	All types of agricultural research and experimental work; supervision of branch stations
Aberdeen Branch Station	Irrigation practices and crops; potatoes; alfalfa; grains; leads nation in barley seed improvement
Caldwell Branch Station	Animal feeding; diversified crops; general farm practices; animal husbandry
Grangeville Branch Station	Grain crops; control of noxious weeds in grain fields
Lewiston Field Station	Fruits
Parma Branch Station	Fruits and vegetables; insects; seed production; specializes in onion seed improvement
Sandpoint Branch Station	Crops and farm practices on cutover lands of northern Idaho
Tetonia Branch Station	Crops and farm practices for farming in high elevations
Twin Falls Field Station	Primarily beans and onions; seed improvement; bean diseases

*A Federal sheep experiment station near Dubois in Clark County also co-operates with the state in sheep and wool improvement.

Courtesy U.S. Bureau of Reclamation, Region No. 1, Boise

ONIONS ON THE BOISE PROJECT

The fertile plains, where irrigation water is available, are among our finest farming lands.

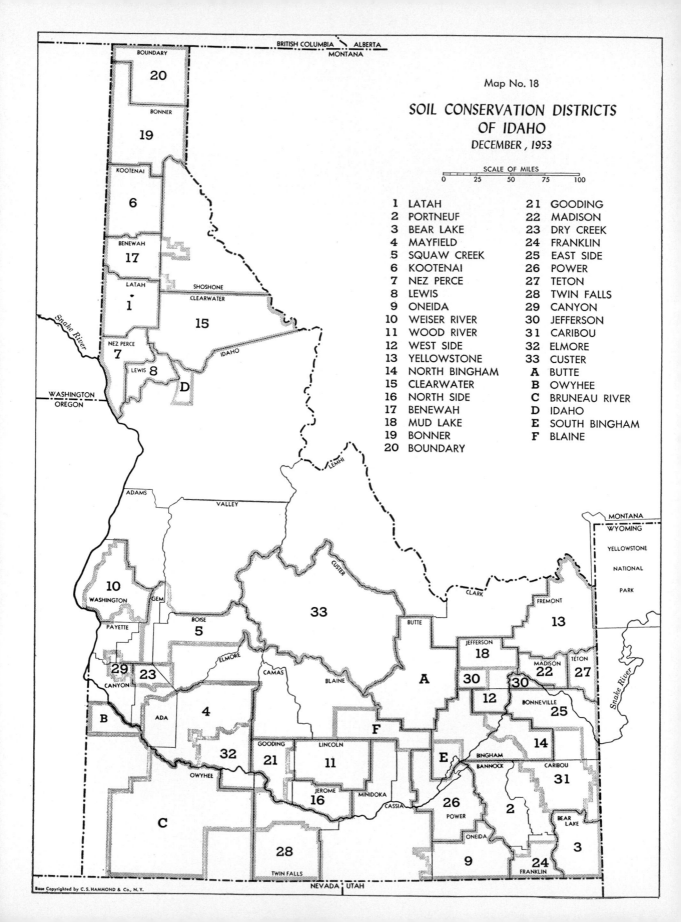

Map No. 18

SOIL CONSERVATION DISTRICTS
OF IDAHO
DECEMBER, 1953

SCALE OF MILES
0   25   50   75   100

1	LATAH	21	GOODING
2	PORTNEUF	22	MADISON
3	BEAR LAKE	23	DRY CREEK
4	MAYFIELD	24	FRANKLIN
5	SQUAW CREEK	25	EAST SIDE
6	KOOTENAI	26	POWER
7	NEZ PERCE	27	TETON
8	LEWIS	28	TWIN FALLS
9	ONEIDA	29	CANYON
10	WEISER RIVER	30	JEFFERSON
11	WOOD RIVER	31	CARIBOU
12	WEST SIDE	32	ELMORE
13	YELLOWSTONE	33	CUSTER
14	NORTH BINGHAM	A	BUTTE
15	CLEARWATER	B	OWYHEE
16	NORTH SIDE	C	BRUNEAU RIVER
17	BENEWAH	D	IDAHO
18	MUD LAKE	E	SOUTH BINGHAM
19	BONNER	F	BLAINE
20	BOUNDARY		

Idaho's Soil Conservation Problems and Practices. Soil conservation in Idaho presents a number of serious problems. Among them four are so important that they deserve special consideration. They are: (1) preventing or checking erosion; (2) maintaining soil fertility; (3) getting rid of noxious, or harmful, weeds; and (4) improving range and pasture lands. Which of these are problems in your own section of Idaho?

Erosion Control. Erosion is a thief! By means of running water and wind it steals our precious topsoil. Every twenty-four hours running water carries away enough soil in the nation to make two hundred farms of forty acres each. Right here in Idaho you yourself have seen running water in tiny rivulets, brooks, creeks, and rivers dark with the load of soil it was carrying. If you live in the open country you have often seen strong winds raising billowing clouds of dust that was once the top layer of fertile Idaho fields.

Chart No. 5

CO-OPERATIVE CONSERVATION AGENCIES

(Compiled from federal, state, and local sources)

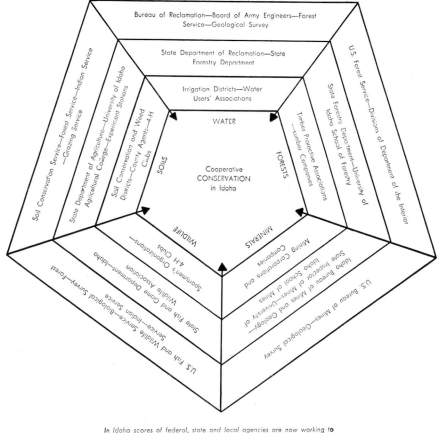

In Idaho scores of federal, state and local agencies are now working to make wiser use of and conserve for future use the natural resources of the state.

RESULTS OF WATER EROSION

Running water quickly carries the soil from unprotected hills and slopes.

While erosion cannot be entirely prevented, several farming practices help in controlling this thief. The most helpful practices are contour and strip farming, terracing, building gully checks, the use of cover crops, planting windbreaks, and using correct methods of cultivation.

On slopes and hilly land, fields are laid out and plowing and cultivating is done on contours, or across the slopes, instead of up and down. This causes water to sink into the land. It is particularly useful in checking *sheet erosion,* in which the top layers of soil are sometimes almost completely lost. Such farming districts as the famous Palouse Hills on the Clearwater Plateau, the rolling lands of the Ashton Plateau, and other sloping and hilly farming districts find *contour farming* particularly helpful.

In the plan known as *strip farming,* fields are laid out in parallel strips which are alternately planted to cultivated and noncultivated crops. For example, one strip might be planted to potatoes, beans, or sugar beets, while the strip next to it might be in hay or wheat or pasture.

This method, especially when used with contour farming, is very effective. It is valuable in checking both water and wind erosion.

The *terracing* plan is widely used on slopes and hillsides. Terraces are built along the contour of the slopes to check water runoff. Spillways at intervals prevent flooding and allow the water to escape slowly without causing heavy damage. By a careful use of terracing, strip farming, and contour plowing and cultivation, water erosion can be quite effectively controlled.

Several other things are helpful in checking erosion. When gullies or small ditches begin to form on sloping land, obstructions should be placed in them at intervals. Cover crops, or close-growing crops that do not require cultivation, such as various kinds of hay and pasture grasses, protect the surface of the land and keep both wind and water from stealing the soil. Windbreaks of trees and shrubbery help check wind erosion. Stubble, straw, and other crop leftovers may remain on the fields as cover protection.

SOIL EROSION IN IDAHO

Lost or strayed! 120 tons of soil per acre near Newdale in Fremont County.

Fall-plowed land may be left rough during the winter so rain and melting snow will sink into the land instead of causing gullies and washing the soil away. Well-planned systems of crop rotation and pastures are especially useful in holding erosion in check, as are land leveling and correct methods of cultivation.

As J. N. ("Ding") Darling, a foremost conservationist, wrote: "This is beefsteak and potatoes, roast duck, ham and eggs, and bread and butter with jam on it that is being washed down our rivers each year in the form of good rich topsoil." And, we might add, that is flying away on the wings of the wind. Let's save Idaho's precious soil.

Keeping the Soil Fertile. Most Idaho soils in farming areas are naturally fertile, but they do not stay that way very long unless they receive proper attention and care. If you live in or have traveled through farming sections, you have probably seen fields that have been abandoned or turned into second-rate pastures because they are no longer productive enough to grow crops at a profit. How to restore such lands to usefulness and save other lands from a similar fate are conservation tasks of the present and future.

Among effective plans for keeping farming land fertile are good systems of crop rotation; the use of both barnyard manure and commercial fertilizers; plowing under such crops as sweet clover and alfalfa as *green manures;* using the fields as part-time pastures; draining naturally heavy and wet lands; and using special methods of cultivation. What are the special problems of maintaining fertility

SOIL SLIP IN THE PALOUSE HILLS NEAR MOSCOW

How do you think erosion such as is shown here might have been prevented?

ADDING HUMUS TO THE SOIL

Plowing under sweet clover and other "green manure" crops helps maintain the fertility of the soil.

Courtesy Jay G. Garner, County Extension Agent, St. Anthony

in your own community, and how are they being solved?

Controlling Noxious Weeds. In his efforts to conserve the soil and harvest profitable crops, man wages a ceaseless war against weeds. According to specialists in this warfare, Idaho's losses from weeds amount to the staggering total of a hundred million dollars a year.

Do you know the worst noxious weeds common in your part of the state? If you live on a farm or cultivate a family or market garden, such knowledge will prove very valuable. The county agent for your county will be glad to give you help in your war against weeds if you will write to him or call at his office.

The nine worst weeds of Idaho are listed as wild morning-glory or bindweed, quack grass, Canadian thistle, whitetop, perennial low thistle, yellow toadflax, perennial ground cherry, Russian knapweed, and leafy mustard. A list of other weeds that cause much damage includes cocklebur, crowfoot or hungerweed, pigweed, ragweed, tumbleweed, water hemlock, wild mustard, wild oats, dodder, plantain, puncture vine, and dandelion. Even these lists do not include all the

harmful weeds, and others enter the state from time to time. Such a newcomer is halogeton (hal-o-JE-ton), a poisonous weed resembling Russian thistle that has now appeared in southern Idaho. It is quite deadly at certain stages of its growth and has already caused heavy losses among sheep and cattle.

Most weed-control projects now enlist the aid of several agencies: the Federal government, the state, the counties, weed control districts, and other agencies. More than three fourths of Idaho's counties now have weed-control projects. Several large noxious weed control districts blanket the best farming sections of the state.

Several plans are used in the war against weeds: (1) Pure seed laws forbid the sale of seed containing noxious weed seeds. (2) Cultivation will keep some weeds under control, especially the annuals, those that grow from seed each year. (3) Certain crops will crowd out and kill some of the less hardy weeds, this being, for instance, the best way yet discovered for getting rid of halogeton. (4) Chemical sprays are effective in controlling many kinds of weeds. (5) Crop rotation is a valuable practice in keeping weeds from getting a start and holding them from spreading rapidly. (6) Counties usually cut the weeds along public roads to get rid of harmful plants that may be growing by the roadside. (7) Railroad workers burn and spray weeds that grow on the railroad right of way. (8) Farmers often burn along the banks of irrigation ditches and fence rows to destroy the seeds of harmful weeds, though this practice may deprive pheasants and other birds of food during the winter unless the burning is delayed until spring.

Improving Rangelands and Pasture Lands. Our rangelands in Idaho consist of about twenty million acres of national forests managed by the United States Forest Service and close to twelve million acres more which are under the supervision of the United States Grazing Service, a division of the Bureau of Land Management. There are also several million more acres of public domain and state lands. On most of these unfenced acres grazing is carried on part of each year.

Range management policies are largely patterned after Federal regulations and practices. These include: (1) No more animals are allowed on the range than it will support without serious damage to vegetation. (2) Sufficient grazing areas and vegetation are reserved for wildlife. (3) Sheep and cattle are usually assigned different grazing areas, since cattle do not thrive on ranges heavily used by sheep. (4) Farmers and ranchmen living close to rangelands are allowed free use of the range for livestock kept for domestic use, such as horses and milk cows.

How can our ranges be improved and preserved? What are the effects of forest and range fires? What will be the result if too many animals are allowed to use the range? Will loss of stock occur if poisonous weeds and plants grow on the range?

Such questions as these suggest certain good-management practices: (1) Prevent forest and range fires. (2) Reseed areas that have been burned over or overgrazed, or keep livestock off until nature has repaired the damage. (3) Replace sagebrush and other inferior vegetation with range grasses and other herbage more useful for grazing animals. (4) Rid the ranges of noxious weeds that crowd out useful plants or poison livestock. (5) Construct water holes in dry sections so that the range areas may be enlarged and made more useful.

Poor Land Use vs. Proper Land Use. It has long been accepted as an axiom, or truth that doesn't need proving, that *poor land makes poor people*. The Soil Conservation Service has well summed up the difference between poor land use and proper land use in the following contrasting statements:

POOR LAND USE

1. Unwise use of the land. Taking crops out of the soil every year without putting anything back into the soil.

PROPER LAND USE

1. Good land use. A crop rotation with clover and grass or alfalfa and grass plowed under to restore fertility and organic matter to the soil.

POOR LAND USE—*Cont'd*

2. Up- and downhill tillage makes gutters for water to run in.

3. Working the soil too much in the fall, which pulverizes it too finely and leaves the field too smooth.

4. Soil left bare has no protection.

5. Burning stubble robs the land of plant food and organic matter.

6. Steep land washes easily. When cultivated each year, steep slopes lose tons of topsoil.

7. Steep slopes are hard and costly to farm.

8. Rilled and gullied slopes are hard on farm machinery and often cause breakage. Some harvest is delayed because combine parts are broken crossing those gullied slopes. Repair bills must be subtracted from profits.

9. Crop yields decline or get poorer as topsoil is allowed to wash away, taking plant food.

10. Without livestock on the farm, the operator is tempted to cultivate every acre for "cash crops" every year.

11. Erosion makes poor land, poor roads, poor schools, poor churches, and poor people.

PROPER LAND USE—*Cont'd*

2. Farming across the slope and strip cropping makes water walk instead of run downhill.

3. Leave fall-worked land rough and cloddy.

4. Vegetation of any kind left on the surface provides a protective cover.

5. Make use of straw. Return it to the soil from which it came.

6. Grass and alfalfa on steep slopes hold the land from washing.

7. Steep slopes will provide hay or pasture for livestock and reduce the hazard of continuous farming on such areas.

8. Protected slopes have no rills and gullies to interfere with farming operations or to break up machinery and delay work. Conservation pays. No repairs mean more profits.

9. Crop yields increase where soil fertility is kept up by a good rotation with sweet clover or alfalfa and grass.

10. With livestock the gentle slopes can be used for grain and steep slopes that are subject to erosion can be used for hay and pasturage.

11. Conservation means better living, good schools and roads through wise land use; churches well supported, thriving communities and happy people.

Mother Nature has been very good to us in Idaho by providing us with a great deal of fertile farming and grazing land. Whether these lands remain fertile or lose their fertility depends almost entirely upon the farming and grazing practices we follow. We should never, through selfishness, greediness, neglect, or ignorance, follow land-use practices that will result in harm to us or those who follow us in future generations. This responsibility is ours.

II. WATER CONSERVATION

THE LIVING WATERS—Idaho's lakes and streams—constitute one of our greatest resources. In agriculture, mining, lumbering, manufacturing, and other industries, water has a multitude of uses. A good share of our recreational activities takes us to the streams and lakes. The wildlife abundance for which our state is noted is closely related to our waterways, our wealth of living waters.

Among the problems that need attention in water conservation, four are especially important: (1) We need to provide as much water as possible for the present and future needs of irrigation. (2) Some parts of the state need protection from occasional or seasonal floods and the constant threat of erosion. (3) We must plan domestic water supplies for our growing cities and towns. (4) Steps need to be taken to protect our waters from becoming dangerously polluted, or impure.

Water Storage and Watershed Protection. As we learned in earlier units, many of our water needs in Idaho have partly been met by the construction of reservoirs. These catch and save huge quantities of water which would ordinarily be lost in the annual spring and early summer runoff when winter snows are melting and our streams run bank full or overflow. The water storage afforded by the reservoirs helps in preventing destructive floods and erosion in our valleys. At the proper time the stored waters are released for irrigation and for making hydroelectricity.

Watershed protection is very important in water conservation. The United States Forest Service lists several ways in which this may be done: (1) Keep at least a third or more of the natural vegetation of the watersheds. (2) Graze livestock on the watersheds only during the proper season and avoid overgrazing. (3) Regulate timber cutting in watershed areas by limiting the amount of timber that may be removed. (4) Guard carefully against forest and range fires. (5) Control timber diseases and forest insect pests. (6) Reforest and reseed watershed areas that have been burned over or overgrazed. In which of these conservation practices can we, all of us, share?

Water Pollution. Would you willingly or knowingly drink water that contains disease germs or that has been poisoned by waste matter from smelters and manufacturing plants? These are examples of water pollution problems that have become very troublesome in many parts of the nation. Even in Idaho there are places where dangerous pollution already exists. As population increases and more industrial establishments are built, such prob-

GOLD DREDGE AT WORK

This cause of water pollution has been practically eliminated by an amendment to the state constitution adopted by the people in the election of 1954.

Courtesy Grangeville Chamber of Commerce and Shira Studio

lems as these will become harder to solve. Here are several things that should receive attention, and in some of them practically all of us can assist.

Cities, towns, and rural homes should not allow sewage to enter our streams, lakes, and canals, as typhoid and other dangerous diseases may be spread by such careless and unsanitary practices. Industrial wastes from smelters and factories may be a very serious source of water pollution, as the wastes often contain harmful substances which make the water unfit for human use and kill fish and other wildlife.

Another cause of water pollution is the dredging of stream beds and adjoining lands to recover minerals. This is the modern method of placer mining in Idaho. It causes water downstream from dredging operations to be very muddy and is sometimes harmful to fish in the streams. It also makes the water unfit for domestic use. On larger streams used for irrigation it causes silt to settle in irrigation canals and ditches. Fortunately,

such work is usually done along mountain streams far from heavily settled areas. Recently, however, requests for dredging permits for portions of the Snake and Boise rivers have aroused the opposition of people living along those streams.

In the 1954 election, the people of Idaho approved an amendment to the state constitution which will place rigorous controls over dredging operations along our streams. Under this law, dredging will not be, now or in the future, a serious cause of water pollution.

The general public, which includes you and me, is far too often guilty of another kind of pollution. Have you ever visited a campground or recreational area and found it littered by wastes carelessly left by campers and picnickers? Nothing is more disgusting than to drive to such a place to spend a holiday only to find an ugly, unsanitary litter left by previous users! We all know that such wastes should either be burned or buried or placed for collection in containers provided for that purpose. Unless we care enough not to be guilty of similar offenses, we do not deserve to enjoy the splendid recreational advantages our state offers in such full measure.

Waste of Irrigation Water. The United States Bureau of Reclamation estimates that only about 50 per cent to 60 per cent of the water released into ditches and canals for irrigation ever reaches the land for which it was intended. The rest is lost, either by sinking into the ground, leaking through the canal banks, or by evaporating. If these estimates are accurate, enough water is lost in irrigating an eighty-acre farm to supply the needs of an additional fifteen acres or more if the water had all reached the land.

Waste of irrigation water can be decreased in several ways: (1) by the proper construction of canals and ditches; (2) by the use of shrubbery, grasses, and even small trees along the canal banks; (3) by proper preparation of the land surface; (4) by avoiding overirrigation and too frequent watering, both of which may cause damage to the soil and to growing crops; (5) by returning waste water to streams and canals wherever possible; and (6) by closing the canals when the irrigation season ends and holding the water in storage until it is again needed.

Domestic Water Supply. Have you read or heard radio announcements about water shortages in great cities like New York and Los Angeles? Idaho, of course, has no really large cities as yet. But even here we need to make careful plans to insure sufficient water for the home, for industrial uses, for fire protection, and for the sanitary needs of our cities and towns, not only now but in the future. Both streams and underground waters are used for these purposes. No matter what the source, such water should be provided in ample quantity and be of a high quality. If we do not plan such water supplies now for both city and rural needs, we may one day find that we have waited too long and that no suitable sources are left from which we can draw the water we require. What steps have been taken in your own city or home to insure the water you may need in the future?

Idaho Water Users. Have you ever stopped to think how much water is used in Idaho every day? Here are some facts, prepared by the United States Forest Service, that may surprise you.

1. Idahoans consume 27,500,000 gallons of water per day for home use, drinking, cooking, laundering, bathing, and cleaning.

2. 150,000 home owners or occupants need three feet of water per acre annually for watering lawns and home gardens.

3. 52,000 Idaho farmers, ranchers, orchardists, and truck gardeners use 9,400,000 acre-feet of water annually to produce agricultural crops valued in excess of $190,000,000.

4. More than 70,000 workers, with a payroll of over $127,000,000, annually are employed in Idaho industries directly or indirectly dependent on water: mining, construction, manufacturing, transportation, communications, utilities, and wholesale and retail trade are the major industrial groups involved.

5. Constant supplies of water are necessary for the operation of seventy-two hydroelectric power plants which furnish 346,000 kilowatts of electricity for Idaho homes, communities, and industries.

6. Seven eighths of the lands that produce Idaho's usable water are inside Idaho's sixteen national forests.

7. In addition to water, Idaho's national forests also produce sport and recreation for 220,000 fishermen, 73,000 hunters, 50,000 ski enthusiasts, and 550,000 picnickers and campers; a home for 130,000 deer, 30,000 elk, and thousands of other wild birds and animals; a sustained annual cut of 825,000,000 board feet of timber; summer feed for 900,000 sheep and 100,000 cattle in Idaho; and revenue for the state, direct and indirect, amounting to hundreds of thousands of dollars each year.

Is there anything we can do to reduce the amount of water we use? Do you think people should begin to plan now to assure themselves an ample water supply for future needs?

III. FOREST CONSERVATION

OUR NATIONAL CONSERVATION POLICY really began with forest conservation. As early as 1876 the United States Department of Agriculture appointed a special agent to study forest conditions, because it was in the forests that waste was most noticeable and alarming. Fifteen years later, in 1891, Congress authorized the President to set aside public forest lands as reserves. Under this law, President Benjamin Harrison created the Yellowstone Park Timberland Reserve, now the Shoshone National Forest. This was the first Federal forest reserve in the United States, created to save the public timber resources of the nation.

Conservation in the National Forests. By far the largest and most active conservation agency in Idaho is the United States Forest Service. Its general policy was clearly stated in 1905 by Gifford Pinchot, one of our greatest conservationists, who was then chief of the Forest Service. He said:

In the administration of the forest reserves it must be clearly borne in mind that all land is to be devoted to its most productive use for the permanent good of the whole people, and not for the temporary benefit of individuals or companies. . . . The water, wood, and forage of the reserves must be conserved and wisely used for the benefit of the home builder, first of all, upon whom depends the best permanent use of lands and resources alike. The continued interest is directly dependent upon a permanent and accessible supply of water, wood, and forage, as well as upon the present and future use of these resources.

The conservation of the forests calls for answers to six main problems: (1) prevention of forest fires; (2) control of timber diseases; (3) getting rid of forest insect pests; (4) proper methods of timber removal; (5) supervision of grazing; and (6) protecting the water supply.

Forest Fires. Most dreaded of all forest dangers are forest fires. Over the nation as a whole, forest fires in an average year burn an area as large as the state of New York. They destroy enough saw timber to build more than 80,000 five-room houses and enough smaller timber to make 3,000,000 tons of newsprint. They bring death to great numbers of wild animals and upland game birds. They cause heavy erosion of the burned-over areas and contribute to destructive floods by destroying the timber and vegetation that protect the watersheds.

Do you know the three main causes of forest fires in the United States: Well, here they are: *men, women, and children!* Yes, the nation over, man is the big bad wolf of the forests so far as forest fires are concerned. Figures show that about ninety forest and range fires in every hundred are caused by people.

In Idaho, man's guilt is not so great. Here lightning starts more forest fires than all other causes combined, but more range fires are started by people than by lightning. Our Idaho forest regions are not usually heavily populated and most people who visit the forests keep to main traveled or access roads and stay in public campgrounds. But even in our state man-caused fires are all too frequent. Nearly all of these could be prevented if forest users would only be careful with matches, cigarettes and cigars, and campfires.

The forest officials who have supervision of national forests, as well as those in charge of state and private forest lands, are especially watchful during the fire season, and improved methods of fire control have been developed. Roads have been constructed to key areas, and a network of trails penetrates most parts of the forests. Landing fields for small airplanes have been built in many parts of the forests. When fires break out in re-mote areas that cannot be quickly reached by other means, trained firefighters dropped by parachute usually get the fires under control before they have time to cause much damage. Lookouts, or watchtowers, built on high summits, are occupied during the summer months by watchers called lookouts, or "smoke chasers." These are constantly on duty and report by telephone or radio any suspicious curl of smoke rising from the evergreen cover that clothes the mountains and valleys. Air patrols are now becoming increasingly common and have taken over much of the detection work formerly done by lookouts.

What life on an Idaho forest lookout is like is well told in the following letter from a lookout, or smoke chaser, to her mother.

Dear Mother,

We were wishing yesterday that there was some way of getting you up to our lookout. What a spot! You've heard the caution to people who live in glass houses. Ours is almost that. It is cement floored, rock walled up to about waist high, with windows on up to the ceiling. Along the west wall is our stove, work cupboards, and table. The bunks are along the north and south walls. In the center of the room are the alidade[1] and telephone, and our map drops down from the ceiling.

Every window frames a picture. To the east is our favorite etching: Rainbow Basin, studded with sapphire lakes carved in granite and surrounded by the living emerald of pine and fir— Big Rainbow, Heart, Lark, Three-Lakes, and many others nameless to us. To the south is the sawmill area, with its densely timbered slopes. Smiths Prairie sprawls in a basin to the south-west, and beyond it barren mountains may be seen. To the north and northeast are lovely roll-

[1]Alidade (AL-i-dade). An instrument like a surveyor's compass for measuring degrees on a map or circle.

ing meadows landscaped by a Master Hand, and in the background are sharp, rugged peaks receding crest after crest to the majesty that is the Sawtooths, until finally lost in the faint blue haze of far horizons.

In front of the cabin is the triangle-shaped dirt and rock yard about twenty feet long, from which the trail leads down to three levels: the wood yard, the unloading area, and the hitching rack. Our garbage pit is unlimited—just walk to the edge of the cliff, lean back, and heave.

Our days are pretty uniformly patterned: Breakfast from seven to eight; lunch from twelve to one; dinner from six to seven. One of us must be on call, meaning in reach of the telephone, at all times. Our territory is divided into segments, each of which must be carefully and systematically studied at frequent intervals for any sign of smoke. We make a morning report to Idaho City about 7:15 a.m. and get the weather report from there about 11:00. We make a night check before going to bed.

We have been pretty lucky so far. The weather has been favorable, and we have had only a few small fires, all set by lightning. We have some real electric storms up here, but everything is well protected against danger from that source by a maze of lightning rods all grounded in the earth, or rather the stone, on which our cabin rests.

It is now almost time for the weather call, so: This is Trinity Mountain, elevation 9,473 feet, signing off, with a very special bit of love to Mother.

As ever,
B.

Living in a forest lookout on some high summit of the Idaho Rockies during the summer months sounds rather interesting, doesn't it? Perhaps, when you get a little older, you may want to do your bit serving as "the eyes of the forest." Your nearest forest ranger or district fire warden will be glad to tell you how you can secure an appointment.

Courtesy U.S. Forest Service

FOREST SERVICE SMOKE JUMPER

Air-borne fire fighters reach their destinations so quickly as a rule that they are able to bring most forest fires under control while they are still small.

What can you and I do to help prevent forest fires? Here are six important precautions the Forest Service gives us:

MATCHES. Be sure your match is out. Break it in two before you throw it away.

TOBACCO. Be certain that your pipe ashes and cigar and cigarette stubs are dead before throwing them away. Never throw them into brush, leaves, needles, or dry grass.

MAKING CAMP. Before building a fire scrape away all inflammable material

EYES OF THE FOREST

In lookouts located at strategic points in the forest, watchers keep constant vigil during the fire season.

from a spot about five feet in diameter. Dig a hole in the center and in the hole build your fire. Keep your fire small. Never build it against a tree or logs or near brush.

BREAKING CAMP. Never break camp until your fire is out—dead out.

BURNING BRUSH. Never burn slash or brush in windy weather or while there is the slightest danger that the fire will get away.

HOW TO PUT OUT A CAMPFIRE. Stir the coals while soaking them with water. Turn small sticks and drench both sides. Wet ground around the fire. If you can't get water, stir in dirt and tread it down until tightly packed over and around the fire. Be sure the last spark is dead.

Forest Diseases. Did you ever see a sick tree? The leaves or needles turn pale and soon drop off. Sometimes sap oozes from the bark or fungus growth appears. The U.S. Forest Service, the State Forestry Department, and private timber owners are constantly on the alert, and in the last quarter of a century they have spent millions of dollars in combating two

IN THE WAKE OF A FOREST FIRE

This picture needs no comment, since it tells its own tragic story.

WHITE-PINE BLISTER RUST CONTROL

White-pine blister rust may be controlled by destroying wild gooseberry and wild currant bushes in the forest. Can you tell why? (Courtesy U.S. Department of Agriculture, Bureau of Entomology and Plant Quarantine.)

serious forest diseases, both attacking the white pine forests. These are *white-pine blister rust* and *pole blight*.

Blister rust is a fungus disease that is spread by means of spores, or minute dustlike particles scattered by the fungus when it ripens. The spores spread from a diseased white pine tree to wild gooseberry or wild currant bushes, which it attacks. Then it goes from the diseased bushes back to another pine tree, which then develops the sickness.

Since blister rust cannot spread from one tree to another, it may be controlled by finding and destroying the gooseberry and currant bushes in the forests. This has been extensively done in northern Idaho, with great improvement in the situation. But much work still remains to be done before this forest murderer is completely under control.

Little is known at present about the second white pine disease, pole blight, as it is called, because it usually attacks younger trees in the pole stage of growth. The Forest Service and the University of Idaho are now carrying on extensive studies that, it is hoped, will reveal both the cause and the cure for this new disease which is spreading into the valuable white pine forests of the Idaho Panhandle.

Forest Insect Pests. The dollar losses in timber caused by insects of various kinds are in some districts greater than the fire losses. James C. Evenden, former Senior Entomologist[2] for the United States Forest Service in Region 1, describes the situation as being so grave that

there is no place in forestry for the destruction of timber by insects. . . . It is fully realized by all who are familiar with existing conditions that the loss of timber that has occurred and is still occurring can no longer be endured if proper benefits are to be derived from forest lands.

Insects that cause forest damage are of two general kinds: those that eat the foliage, or leaves and needles, and the borers and tunnelers that attack the inner layers of bark and the wood. Both kinds

[2]Entomologist (en-to-MOL′o-jist). A scientist who specializes in the study of insects.

OPERATION FLIT GUN

Spraying a forest in northern Idaho to control Douglas fir tussock moths. (Courtesy U.S. Department of Agriculture, Bureau of Entomology and Plant Quarantine.)

cause damage in Idaho forests, and their control is both difficult and costly.

Among the foliage eaters, the Douglas fir tussock moth and the spruce bud worm have been the most destructive. In 1947 a very heavy infestation of the moths threatened trees on over four hundred thousand acres of forests in Latah, Benewah, and Clearwater counties. In a fight against them, airplane crews rained a deadly spray of DDT and fuel oil over the threatened areas with satisfactory results.

A similar fight against pine butterflies was carried on by the Boise National Forest in 1954 over an area of approximately two hundred and fifty-five thousand acres. Both operations checked the ravages of the insects and resulted in saving millions of feet of timber.

More destructive than the foliage eaters are the bark beetles. Various kinds of these insects attack the western yellow pine, western white fir, Douglas fir, Engelmann's spruce, and lodgepole pine. Since 1910 bark beetles have caused enormous losses in Idaho and neighboring states. The beetles kill the trees by tunneling around the trunks in the sap layers of bark, thus stopping the return flow of food manufactured in the needles and eventually destroying the trees.

Since 1947 the U.S. Forest Service, the State Forestry Department, and private owners of forest lands have made determined efforts to check the destruction caused by beetles. In recent years large infested areas in the forests of Idaho, Wyoming, and Montana have been worked over. While control has not yet been fully attained, new spray machines and new kinds of chemicals and oils offer new and more effective ways of fighting the insects. Private industry has made a great contribution in this work by logging millions of feet of infested timber.

Mistletoe, a parasite plant drawing its sustenance from growing trees, causes heavy damage to Douglas fir and lodgepole pine forests of Idaho. Research work is now going on to discover the best methods of controlling this parasite.

Methods of Lumbering. As the better stands of timber on privately owned lands were cut or greatly reduced, operators began turning to the national and state forests. To be sure that there would be as little waste as possible, the Forest Service and the State Forestry Department have laid down certain rules considered necessary from a conservation standpoint.

1. Timber cutting is on a *sustained yield* basis, which merely means that timber will not be cut at a faster rate than new timber can be grown.
2. *Selective cutting* is practiced, taking only such trees as are mature enough to be cut without permanent loss to the forest.
3. *Slash,* which is the top and branches of trees, is piled for burning when conditions are right, thus keeping the danger of forest fires low. Sometimes slash is scattered to add humus to the soil, decrease the fire danger, and check erosion.
4. Cutting must be done carefully so that near-by trees and young timber are little damaged by falling trunks.
5. Occasional cone-bearing mature trees are left to restock the cutover areas.
6. If most of the timber is removed, young trees are set out to start a new forest.
7. On watersheds that are main sources of water for irrigation and domestic use, sufficient timber is left standing to slow down the melting of snow and to prevent erosion.

Conservation in State and Privately Owned Forests. You have learned that much timberland in Idaho is owned by the colleges, schools, and other state institutions. These lands are managed by the State Forestry Department along the same lines as the national forests are managed.

To protect and improve Idaho forests, timber protective associations have been organized. The Timber Protective Association of South Idaho and the Timber Protective Association of North Idaho are the leaders. The national forests, state forests, and private owners all co-operate in carrying on fire protection and insect and disease control work done by the protective associations.

Among most of the lumber companies,

SOUTH IDAHO TIMBER PROTECTIVE ASSOCIATION HEADQUARTERS

Here is centered the work of various agencies concerned with forest protection.

Courtesy U.S. Forest Service   Photo by K. D. Swan

conservation has become part of their operating policy. They are cutting largely
on a sustained yield basis, following the
practice of selective cutting, and working
on plans to use as much of the timber cut
as possible.

One stumbling block stands in the way
of true conservation. In remote parts of
both the national and state forests there
are no roads. As a result, trees are getting
so old they are losing much of their value.
Like any other crop, timber should be
harvested when it is at its prime. Both
the Federal government and the state are
losing money because vast quantities of
good timber cannot be reached for cutting. Do you think it might be a wise plan
in the long run if more access roads were
built into the heavily timbered areas so
the trees could be cut before they lose so
much of their value for lumber?

**Other Conservation Work in For-
estry.** Reforestation work is carried out
on a large scale in Idaho. Large numbers
of young seedling trees are grown in forest nurseries and are set out where fires
and wasteful methods of lumbering have
not left enough standing timber to renew
the forests by natural means.

The *tree-farm* plan is making rapid
headway in Idaho. This is a comparatively new movement, aimed at growing
trees for the future. An increasing number of tree farms, ranging from wood-lot
size to huge tracts, are being put into operation. On these tree farms, timber is
considered a crop to be grown and harvested like any other crop. Trees are cut
when ready for use and others set out
to take their places. The forest is thinned
by cutting out weaklings and deformed
trees and every effort is made to have a
crop of some kind ready to place on the
market every year or at short intervals.
With scores of tree farms embracing
more than half a million acres, Idaho

GROWING YOUNG TREES
FOR IDAHO FORESTS

A plantation of ponderosa pine planted by CCC boys near Kalispell Bay, Priest Lake, in Kaniksu National Forest.

now leads all other western states in the number of tree farms, almost three hundred, following approved conservation methods.

IV. CONSERVATION OF MINERAL RESOURCES

Our buried treasures, the mineral resources of the state, differ from other natural resources in one respect: when they have once been used, they cannot be replaced. Only in nature, through processes usually requiring very long periods of time, can minerals be made, though some gems are now manufactured synthetically.

Maybe you are wondering, since minerals once mined cannot be renewed, just how we can apply a conservation policy to our mineral resources. Shall they be left in the earth merely for the sake of saving them? Common sense tells us that such a course would be foolish.

Some Principles of Mineral Conservation. A number of things can be done in the field of mining and using our minerals that will be of great value in conserving these resources: (1) Waste should be reduced as much as possible by better methods of mining and smelting. (2) More uses in industry should be found for minerals that Idaho does or can produce. (3) Improved transportation facilities are needed so that low-grade ore bodies can be worked at a profit. (4) We should try to find substitutes for minerals that are scarce or expensive. In this work, research being carried on at the University of Idaho and by some of the large mining companies is of great value, as it is, too, in improving methods of mining and smelting. (5) Minerals found mixed with ores of other minerals, many of which have heretofore been cast aside, should be saved as byproducts and put to use. (6) Mineral surveys, many already made by the United States Geological Survey and the Idaho Bureau of Mines and Geology,

MINE RESCUE TEAM READY FOR ACTION

Work in underground mines is dangerous, and crews must be ready at any time for emergency rescue work.

Courtesy George A. McDowell, Inspector of Mines

should be extended to include other areas in the state. (7) New industries based on our mineral resources should be developed in the state.

More Knowledge About Idaho Minerals. More general knowledge about our Idaho mineral resources will help increase our interest in them and strengthen a program of conservation in their development and wiser use. Textbooks should bring these resources more forcefully to the attention of our school population and give us simple information concerning them. Do you think a collection of rocks and minerals in your school, all properly labeled, might be a good beginning for a conservation project along this line? By writing to the Idaho Bureau of Mines and Geology at Moscow, schools can obtain a box of twenty-five Idaho minerals free. That would be a good way to start your own collection.

V. WILDLIFE CONSERVATION

"RECREATION DEPENDING UPON WILDLIFE is already the greatest sporting proposition in the nation in terms of dollars and cents and public participation." In these words Dick d'Easum, until recently public relations representative of the Idaho Fish and Game Department, pointed to the danger facing Idaho's wildlife. Dr. Gerald Wendt, a scientist of national reputation, emphasized the same danger when he foretold a time in the future when the population of the Northwest would be ten times as great as it is now. This means, of course, that there will be a great increase in the number of hunters and fishermen who will be out in season trying to take the limit of fish and game allowed them under the law. Too, in industry, more leisure time is available, and this many people use by turning to hunting, fishing, and other outdoor activities.

Can Idaho, in the face of these odds, continue to be a great hunting and fishing state? Certainly a very active wildlife conservation program must be kept in force if we are to retain our present rank as one of the great wildlife states of the nation.

Fish and Game Department and Conservation. To lead our conservation program, the Idaho Fish and Game Department was created. The state is divided into five districts, with one commissioner from each district appointed by the governor. These five men make up the Fish and Game Commission, which is the policy-making body of the Fish and Game Department. These men also determine, to a large extent, how the money available for the department shall be used for the control and improvement of the wildlife resources of the state. The five districts are shown in the following table.

amendment to the state constitution, leaves no doubt that conservation is one of the main tasks of the Fish and Game Department:

All wildlife, including all wild animals, wild birds, and fish, within the State of Idaho, is hereby declared to be the property of the State of Idaho. It shall be preserved, protected, perpetuated, and managed. It shall be captured or taken only by such means, or in such manner, as will preserve, protect, and perpetuate such wildlife, and provide for the citizens of this state, and as by law permitted to others, continued supplies of such wildlife for hunting, fishing, and trapping.

The work of the department is carried on under a director appointed by the Fish and Game Commission. The work is organized in five sections: Conservation Enforcement, Fisheries Management, Game Management, Information and Education, and Business Administration. Each district is also under a district conservation supervisor. A force of field men, formerly called game wardens but now

Table No. 21

IDAHO FISH AND GAME DISTRICTS

One commissioner from each district makes up the Idaho Fish and Game Commission

Number	Counties Comprising District
One	Benewah, Bonner, Boundary, Kootenai, Shoshone
Two	Clearwater, Idaho, Latah, Lewis, Nez Perce
Three	Ada, Adams, Boise, Canyon, Elmore, Gem, Owyhee, Payette, Valley, Washington
Four	Blaine, Butte, Camas, Cassia, Custer, Gooding, Jerome, Lemhi, Lincoln, Minidoka, Twin Falls
Five	Bannock, Bear Lake, Bingham, Bonneville, Caribou, Clark, Franklin, Fremont, Jefferson, Madison, Oneida, Power, Teton

The language of the Fish and Game Act, adopted by the people of Idaho as an

known as conservation officers, patrol and check their respective areas to pro-

LAPWAI BIRD FARM

On Idaho's two game-bird farms are raised thousands of young birds annually, which are released in suitable areas for the benefit of hunters.

Courtesy Idaho Fish and Game Department

tect wildlife and see that fish and game laws are not violated.

Other Wildlife Conservation Agencies and Practices. Besides the Fish and Game Department, other agencies play a part in wildlife planning. Among these are the Fish and Wildlife Service of the United States Department of the Interior; the Forest Service of the United States Department of Agriculture; the co-operative wildlife research unit of the University of Idaho; the Idaho Wildlife Federation; 4-H Clubs enrolled in wildlife conservation work; local organizations of sportsmen; and the many thousands of Idaho citizens who actively aid in this work.

All the agencies co-operating in wildlife management depend in general on ten methods. These fall into the following groups: (1) fishing and hunting licenses; (2) regulation of hunting and fishing seasons; (3) bag limits; (4) game and bird management areas; (5) game bird farms; (6) range improvement and feeding programs; (7) fish hatcheries; (8) stream improvement and control of trash fish; (9) research projects; and (10) control of predatory animals.

Hunting and Fishing Licenses. State laws require hunters and fishermen, with certain exceptions, to purchase licenses. The fees for these licenses are used by the Fish and Game Department to carry on conservation work for the protection and improvement of the wildlife resources of the state.

Regulation of Hunting and Fishing. The dates for hunting and fishing and the length of the seasons are established by the commission on the recommendation of the Fish and Game Department. They vary in different parts of the state and for the various kinds of animals and birds that may be taken. In the interest of conservation, every person who visits the woods, fields, and fishing waters should know and strictly obey these laws and regulations.

Bag Limits. Like closed seasons, the number of game animals and birds that may be taken is regulated by the Fish and Game Department. The relative abundance or scarcity of the game generally

FISH HATCHERY NEAR
TWIN FALLS

In hatcheries such as this, located in various parts of Idaho, the Fish and Game Department raises millions of young fish to keep up the supply in Idaho streams and lakes.

Courtesy Idaho Fish and Game Department

decides what bag limits to set. Every person who hunts or fishes will, if he believes at all in wildlife conservation, voluntarily keep within the legal limits set by the authorities.

Game and Bird Management Areas. These are areas in which no hunting is allowed unless birds and animals become so plentiful that there is danger of diseases attacking them or that the food supply will no longer be sufficient to properly support the number on the preserve. Then "special hunts" may be allowed in order to reduce the oversupply of game.

Game management areas, more commonly referred to as refuges, are established by the state legislature on the recommendation of the Fish and Game Department. They are changed from time to time to meet changing conditions, and are distributed through the state so that practically all species of game animals and birds have reserves in which they are not disturbed by people. Our national and state parks and monuments are also game and bird refuges. From the preserves game spreads to surrounding areas, thus helping supply wildlife to all parts of the state.

There are, too, several migratory waterfowl refuges in the state. These are under the joint management of the United States Fish and Wildlife Service and the State Fish and Game Department. Most of them are on rivers and lakes where geese, ducks, swans, and other waterfowl nest and raise their young. They also serve as rest and feeding stations on the flyways of migrating birds.

Game and Bird Farms. The Fish and Game Department has purchased a number of ranches in big-game districts. These serve primarily as winter range, thereby producing feed for wild animals when the winter snows become so deep that the animals have difficulty getting enough natural food to stay alive and healthy. Winter feeding is resorted to only as an emergency measure under extreme or unusual conditions.

Two upland game-bird farms are operated by the Fish and Game Department, one near Lapwai in Nez Perce

County and the other near Jerome in Jerome County. These raise several kinds of game birds, but far more Chinese, or ring-necked, pheasants than any other species. The young birds are later released in areas suitable for them.

Fish Hatcheries. Most waters of the state are fished so heavily during the fishing season that the natural supply of fish is not enough to keep the waters stocked. To stock our streams and lakes, the Fish and Game Department operates fish hatcheries in various parts of the state. In the biennium from November 1, 1950, to October 31, 1952, sixteen hatcheries were in operation, which, together, produced more than thirty-one million fish, mainly trout. For the location of these hatcheries and the number of fish each produced, see Appendix Table 12.

Stream Improvement and Trash Fish. The method of raising fish in hatcheries is expensive and is not wholly satisfactory. To increase the natural supply of fish and to provide better living and food conditions in our waterways, there is carried on a program of stream improvement. Among conditions favorable to an increased supply of fish in the streams are: (1) crooked and obstructed channels to give the fish better chances to escape their natural enemies; (2) abundant supply of water insect life and other food; and (3) suitable spawning places. Stream improvement attempts to supply such conditions on streams where they may be lacking.

Lakes and streams often have so many trash fish, or worthless fish, that game fish can no longer thrive. Then the Fish and Game Department carries on projects to get rid of the trash fish and replace them with suitable kinds of game and food fish.

Other Wildlife Conservation Work. Research work and planning is carried on

Courtesy Idaho Fish and Game Department

PLANTING FISH BY AIR

Remote lakes far back in the mountains of Idaho receive periodic supplies of young fish dropped from low-flying airplanes.

by the Fish and Game Department, the United States Fish and Wildlife Service, the University of Idaho, and other agencies. Under the Pitman-Robinson Act of Congress, Federal funds are used to aid in research work. The Forest Service aids in fire prevention, wildlife range improvement, wildlife census counts, and other ways. Such predatory animals as coyotes, cougars, and wildcats are controlled by professional hunters, the use of poison, and the payment of bounties. The United States Fish and Wildlife Service is of much assistance in this work. Rod and gun clubs and other organizations of sportsmen co-operate in many ways to protect and conserve our wildlife resources.

Your Share and Mine in Wildlife Conservation. We who have the good fortune to live in Idaho must share the responsibility for wildlife conservation. Among the things we can do are these: guard against forest and range fires by always being extra careful when picnicking, camping, hunting, and fishing; observe strictly all fish and game regulations; when hunting and fishing, take only what we need and can use, even though the law allows us more; return unharmed all undersize fish we catch; if we live on a farm or ranch, mark the location of pheasant nests and the nests of other useful birds so they may be left undisturbed until the young hatch and are able to care for themselves; plant or leave vegetation which provides food and shelter for pheasants and other birds; belong to 4-H Clubs that are engaged in wildlife conservation projects; join, and encourage our parents and friends to join, in the co-operative game-farm movement, which is quite new in Idaho, and about which the county agent or county club leader can tell you. Can you think of other ways in which we can help in wildlife conservation activities in our own communities?

VI. USING CONSERVATION KEYS TO UNLOCK THE FUTURE

OUR IMMEDIATE WELFARE is, as we have seen, based primarily on the use of the natural resources Idaho possesses. But what of the future? Will it be possible to use these resources to expand our present industries and build new industries? Of course it will, and conservation, which includes wise and careful use of our resources, is the key that will open the doors to future opportunities in Idaho.

Keys in Agriculture. We know that the full use of our water resources for irrigation will add hundreds of thousands of acres to our cultivated areas. Huge additions to crop production, agricultural income, taxable wealth, supplemental industries and occupations, and a large increase in population will result. Reclamation, the irrigation of new lands, thus becomes one of the important keys for opening the door to a greater agricultural life.

There are, however, other keys, some of which have already been suggested: flood control, checking erosion, drainage, improving soil fertility, increasing the value of our ranges for livestock and wildlife. There are cutover lands in certain areas, particularly in the Panhandle. Research and experimentation will show us how to use such lands to the best advantage and so increase our agricultural possibilities. This, too, is reclamation and true conservation.

Along with agricultural expansion will come rich industrial possibilities. New industries based on raw materials and waste products of the farms and ranches will undoubtedly be developed. Making alcohol and starch from cull potatoes, both fairly recent developments in Idaho, are examples of this kind of development. Chemurgic farming[3] has already made a beginning in Magic Valley and the Lower Snake River Valley. There are almost limitless possibilities in these fields.

Already under serious consideration is the building of wool-washing establishments, since Idaho is one of the important sheep states. Factories for making woolen goods and others for converting hides and skins into leather and leather goods seem entirely logical and practical. No doubt the day will come when there will be many factories and processing establishments scattered through the better farming sections of Idaho to use agricultural products in making many things useful to mankind and giving employment to thousands of people.

Keys in Forestry. Opportunities for new industries based on our forest resources are many. The Potlatch Forests Inc. have already pioneered in this field by converting sawdust into a fuel called Pres-to-logs. That company and the Diamond Match Company have started the manufacture of wood pulp for paper.

Plywood, plastics, textiles, chemicals, excelsior, insulating materials, paper, furniture, toys—these and a host of other products suggest that the time is not far distant when, through conservation, Idaho forests will be contributing much more richly to living in our state.

Keys in Minerals. Since Idaho is especially rich in minerals, these offer many opportunities for the future. Cutting tools made from diamonds and garnets, pottery and building materials, chemicals and fertilizers, abrasives, scouring and polishing agents, ornaments and jewelry, alloys, filters, insulators, glass, even uranium from central Idaho's vast deposits of monazite sand—these are but a fraction of the possibilities in this direction. It seems a safe prophecy that Idaho will one day have a more extensive industry based on our mineral resources.

Water Keys. Irrigation and hydroelectric power are the two keys that will open the doors to the full use of our great water resources. Idaho cannot fail to become in the future a great industrial state. Power in tremendous quantities will be needed to operate the smelters, factories, and processing plants needed in industry. Electric power now seems the answer, and Idaho has the huge water resources needed to produce it. When the need arises, the power will be produced.

Wildlife and Recreation Keys. Idaho is already widely known for the variety and abundance of its wildlife and for its great scenic attractions. Its annual income from these sources, including money spent for all phases of hunting and fishing activities, already runs into many millions of dollars annually. This income will greatly increase as our population grows and as more people and establishments

[3]Chemurgic (ke-MUR'jik) farming. Growing crops to be used in making drugs, chemicals, and for other similar uses.

are needed to care for the increasing number of tourists and sportsmen drawn here by our wildlife resources.

Our recreational resources, aside from wildlife, offer in themselves very great possibilities. We have seen how Sun Valley, Island Park, the Payette Lakes and the Panhandle lakes have already developed a large industry in supplying the recreational needs of our own residents and of tourists from other states. When we consider the many undeveloped scenic and recreational areas in Idaho, we can see that these keys may unlock the doors to many opportunities as people turn in ever greater numbers to Idaho, Gem of the Mountains, for their outdoor pleasures and adventures.

Conservation must become a part of our personal, community, and state pol-icy if Idaho is finally to reach the future that is possible. If we become conservation conscious, we may confidently expect that the resources of our state will be used to the best advantage and will, at the same time, be so carefully conserved that they will provide a firm foundation for the future prosperity of Idaho's people.

*   *   *   *   *

And now we have come to the end of our story, the final page of our book. But the story of Idaho has not ended; it never will end. We ourselves will help write the future pages and chapters by the way in which we live, the manner in which we carry out our responsibilities as citizens. Let us so shape its future that Idaho may indeed prove its splendid motto: *Esto Perpetua,* meaning "It is forever!"

IDAHO

1950 Total Population 588,637

COUNTIES

Ada (B6) 70,649
Adams (B5) 3,347
Bannock (F7) 41,745
Bear Lake (G7) 6,834
Benewah (B2) 6,173
Bingham (F6) 23,271
Blaine (D6) 5,384
Boise (C6) 1,776

Bonner (B1) 14,853
Bonneville (G6) 30,210
Boundary (B1) 5,908
Butte (E6) 2,722
Camas (D6) 1,079
Canyon (B6) 53,597
Caribou (G7) 5,576
Cassia (E7) 14,629
Clark (F5) 918
Clearwater (C3) 8,217

Custer (D5) 3,318
Elmore (C6) 6,687
Franklin (G7) 9,867
Fremont (G5) 9,351
Gem (B6) 8,730
Gooding (D6) 11,101
Idaho (C4) 11,423
Jefferson (F6) 10,495
Jerome (D7) 12,080
Kootenai (B2) 24,947

Latah (B3) 20,971
Lemhi (D4) 6,278
Lewis (B3) 4,208
Lincoln (D6) 4,256
Madison (G6) 9,156
Minidoka (E7) 9,785
Nez Perce
  (B3) 22,658
Oneida (F7) 4,387
Owyhee (B7) 6,307

Payette (B5) 11,921
Power (F7) 3,988
Shoshone (B2) 22,806
Teton (G6) 3,204
Twin Falls
  (D7) 40,979
Valley (C5) 4,270
Washington (B5) 8,576
Yellowstone Nat'l.
  Park (G5) ....

Aberdeen (F7) 1,486
Acequia (E7) 125
Addie (B1) 15
Ahsahka (B3) ....
Alameda (F7) 4,694
Albion (E7) 610
Albion (mts.)(E7) ...
Alexander (G7) ....
Allan (mt.) (D4) .....
Almo (E7) ....
Alpha (C5) ....
Alpine (G6) 172
Alridge (G6) ....
American Falls◉
  (E7) 1,874
American Falls
  (res.) (F6) ....
Ammon (G6) 447
Amsterdam (D7) 100
Anderson Ranch
  (res.) (C6) ....
Archer (G6) 400
Arco◉ (E6) 961
Arimo (F7) 337
Arrowrock
  (res.) (C6) ....
Ashton (G5) 1,256
Athol (B2) 226
Atlanta (C6) 300
Atomic City (F6) 500
Auger (falls) (D7) ..
Avery (C2) 350
Avon (B3) 6
Baker (B4) 150
Bald (mt.) (D5) ......
Bancroft (G7) 495
Banida (G7) 140
Banks (B5) ....
Bannock (mts.)(F7) ...
Bannock (peak)(F7) ...
Basalt (F6) 227
Bayview (B2) 150
Bear (B4) ....
Bear (lake) (G7) .....
Bear (riv.) (G7) .....
Beaverhead
  (mts.) (E4) ....
Bellevue (D6) 528
Benewah (B2) 50
Bennett (C6) 10
Bennington (G7) 200
Berger (D7) ....
Bern (G7) 140
Big Creek (C4) 24
Big Lost (riv.) (E6).
Big Southern
  (butte) (E6) ....
Big Springs (G5) 5
Big Wood (riv.)(D6)
Bitterroot
  (mts.) (D3) ....
Black Pine (mts.)
  (E7) ....
Black Pine
  (peak) (E7) ....
  ◉ County Seat

Blackfoot◉ (F6) 5,180
Blackfoot (riv.)(G6)
Blackfoot River
  (res.) (G7) ....
Blanchard (A1) 200
Bliss (D7) 126
Bloomington (G7) 302
BOISE (B6) 34,393
Boise (mts.) (B6)...
Boise (riv.) (B6)...
Boles (B4) 25
Bone (G6) 50
Bonners Ferry◉
  (B1) 1,776
Borah (peak) (E5)..
Boulder (mts.)(D6).
Bovill (B3) 437
Bowmont (B6) ....
Bridge (E7) ....
Broten (B1) 30
Bruneau (C7) 100
Bruneau (riv.) (C7).
Buhl (D7) 2,870
Burgdorf (R4) ....
Burke (C2) 800
Burley◉ (E7) 5,924
Burmah (D6) ....
Cabinet (B1) 60
Calder (B2) 65
Caldwell◉ (B6) 10,487
Camas (F5) 40
Cambridge (B5) 354
Cameron (B3) 83
Canfield (B4) ....
Carey (E6) 1,100
Careywood (B1) 50
Caribou (mt.) (G6).
Caribou (mts.) (G6)
Carmen (F4) ....
Cascade◉ (C5) 943
Cascade (res.) (C5).
Castle (peak) (D5)..
Castleford (C7) 500
Cavendish (B3) ....
Cedar Creek
  (res.) (D7) ....
Cedar Creek
  (peak) (E7) ....
Centennial (mts.)
  (G5) ....
Centerville (C6) 25
Central (G7) 120
Challis◉ (D5) 728
Chatcolet (B2) 92
Chester (G5) 247
Chesterfield (G7)..
Chilco (B2) 45
Chilly (E5) 84
Chubbuck (F7) 120
Churchill (D7) ....
C. J. Strike
  (res.) (C7) ....
Clagstone (B1) 15
Clark Fork (B1) 387
Clarkia (B2) 150

Clawson (G6) 34
Clayton (D5) 75
Clearwater (C3) 53
Clearwater (mts.)
  (C3) ....
Clearwater
  (riv.) (B3) ....
Clementsville (G6)...... 38
Cleveland (G7) 135
Cliffs (B7) 32
Clifton (E7) 201
Coeur d'Alene◉
  (B2) 12,198
Coer d' Alene
  (lake) (B2) ....
Coeur d' Alene
  (mts.) (B2) ....
Conda (F7) 330
Coolin (B1) ....
Copeland (B1) 11
Corral (D6) 157
Cottonwood (B3) 689
Council◉ (B5) 748
Craigmont (B3) 594
Crane Creek
  (res.) (B5) ....
Craters of the Moon
  Nat'l Mon. (E6)...
Crouch (B5) 60
Crystal (F7) ....
Culdesac (B3) 175
Cuprum (B4) 20
Darlington (E6) 200
Dayton (F7) 287
Deadwood(res.)(C5)
De Lamar (B6) ....
Deary (B3) 320
Declo (E7) 219
Deep Creek (mts.)
  (F7) ....
Dent (B3) ....
Denver (B4) 29
Desmet (B2) ....
Diamond
  (peak) (E5) ....
Dietrich (D7) 160
Dingle (G7) ....
Dixie (C4) 56
Donnelly (C5) 595
Dover (B1) 385
Downey (F7) 748
Driggs◉ (G6) 941
Drummond (G5) 59
Dubois◉ (F5) 430
Duck Valley Ind.
  Res. (B7) ....
Dudley (B2) ....
Eagle (B6) 500
East Hope (B1) 149
East Sister
  (peak) (C2) ....
Eastport (B1) 108
Eden (D7) 456
Edgemere (B1) 96
Elba (E7) 180

Elk City (C4) 300
Elk River (B3) 312
Ellis (D5) ....
Elmira (B1) 128
Emida (B2) 125
Emmett◉ (B6) 3,067
Enaville (B2) 60
Fairfield◉ (D6) 502
Fairview (G7) 398
Felt (G6) 120
Fenn (B4) 57
Ferdinand (B3) 206
Fernwood (B2) 200
Filer (D7) 1,425
Firth (F6) 293
Fish Creek
  (res.) (E6) ....
Fish Haven (G7) .....
Forest (B3) ....
Forney (D4) ....
Fort Hall (F6) ......
Fort Hall Ind.
  Res. (F6) ....
Franklin (G7) 467
French Creek (B4)..... 65
Fruitland (B6) 573
Fruitvale (B5) 125
Gannett (D6) 43
Garden City (B6) 764
Garden Valley (C5)..... 210
Gardena (B5) ....
Gardner (F6) ....
Gem (C2) 500
Genesee (B3) 552
Geneva (G7) ....
Georgetown (G7) 404
Gibbonsville (E4)..... 200
Gibbs (B2) 35
Gifford (B3) 51
Gilmore (E5) 50
Glengary (B1) ....
Glens Ferry (C7) 1,515
Goldburg (E5) ....
Golden (C4) 100
Gooding◉ (D7) 3,099
Goodrich (B5) 16
Goose Creek
  (res.) (D7) ....
Goose Creek
  (mts.) (E7) ....
Goldstone (mt.)(E4)
Grace (G7) 761
Grainville (G5) 30
Grand View (B7) .....
Grangemont (C3) 130
Grangeville◉ (B4) ...2,544
Granite (B1) 150
Gray (G6) ....
Grays (lake) (G6)...
Greencreek (B3) 51
Greenleaf (B6) ....
Greer (B3) 127
Grimes Pass (C5)....
Grouse (E6) 43
Hagerman (D7) 520

Hailey◉ (D6) 1,464
Hamer (F6) ....
Hammett (C7) 350
Hansen (D7) 463
Harpster (C4) ....
Harrison (B2) 322
Harvard (B3) 102
Hauser (B2) 70
Hayden Lake (B2).. 39
Hazelton (E7) 429
Headquarters (C3).. 300
Heath (B5) 15
Heglar (E7) 10
Heise (G6) 87
Henry (lake) (G5)..
Heyburn (E7) 539
Hibbard (G6) 400
Hill City (D6) 15
Holbrook (F7) ....
Hollister (D7) 80
Homedale (A6) 1,411
Hope (B1) 111
Horse Shoe Bend
  (B6) 401
Howe (F6) 200
Huetter (B2) 84
Humphrey (E5) 35
Hunter (peak) (D3)
Hyndman
  (peak) (D6) ....
Idaho City◉ (C6) 246
Idaho Falls◉ (F6)..19,218
Idahome (E7) ....
Indian Valley (B5).. 50
Inkom (F7) 434
Iona (G6) 502
Irwin (G6) 147
Island Park (G5) ...
Jerome◉ (D7) 4,523
Joseph (B4) 23
Juliaetta (B3) 365
Juniper (F7) ....
Kamiah (B3) 812
Kellogg (B2) 4,913
Kendrick (B3) 409
Ketchum (D6) 757
Keuterville (B3) 25
Kilgore (G5) 160
Kimberly (D7) 1,347
Kingston (B2) ....
Kooskia (C3) 629
Kootenai (B1) 199
Kootenai (riv.) (C1)
Kuna (B6) 534
Laclede (B1) 200
Lago (G7) 250
Lake (G5) 8
Lake Fork (B5) 11
Lakeview (B2) ....
Lamont (G6) 50
Lane (B2) ....
Lapwai (B3) 480
Lava Hot Springs
  (F7) 591
Leadore (E5) 159

Place	Pop.
Leesburg (D4)	
Lemhi (E5)	150
Lemhi (mts.) (E5)	
Lemhi (riv.) (E5)	
Leonia (B1)	
Leslie (E6)	40
Letha (B6)	376
Lewiston◉ (A3)	12,985
Lewisville (F6)	402
Liberty (G7)	
Lincoln (F6)	
Little Lost (riv.) (E5)	
Little Owyhee (riv.) (B7)	
Little Weiser (riv.) (B5)	
Little Wood (riv.) (D6)	
Lochsa (riv.) (C3)	
Lorenzo (G6)	250
Lost River (E6)	37
Lost River (mts.) (E5)	
Lowell (C3)	
Lowell (lake) (B6)	
Lowman (C5)	30
Lucile (B4)	13
Lund (G7)	103
Mackay (E6)	760
Mackay (res.) (E6)	
Macks Inn (G5)	100
Magic (res.) (D6)	
Malad City◉ (F7)	2,715
Malta (E7)	518
Marble Creek (C2)	6
Marsing (B6)	643
Marysville (G5)	190
May (E5)	75
Mayfield (B6)	
Mc Call (C5)	1,173
Mc Cammon (F7)	578
Mc Guire (mt.) (D4)	
Meade Peak (mt.) (G7)	
Meadow Creek (B1)	15
Meadows (B5)	190
Melba (B6)	203
Melrose (B3)	5
Menan (F6)	430
Meridian (B6)	1,810
Mesa (B5)	179
Middleton (B6)	496
Midvale (B5)	231
Milner (D7)	
Minidoka (E7)	113
Minkcreek (G7)	124
Monteview (F6)	
Montour (B6)	155
Montpelier (G7)	2,682
Monument (peak) (B4)	
Moore (E6)	256
Moravia (B1)	
Moreland (F6)	250
Moscow◉ (B3)	10,593
Mountain Home◉ (C6)	1,887
Mountain Home Air F. Base (C6)	
Moyie (riv.) (B1)	
Moyie Springs (B1)	109
Mud (lake) (F6)	
Muldoon (E6)	
Mullan (C2)	2,036
Murphy◉ (B6)	37
Murray (C2)	158
Murtaugh (D7)	239
Myrtle (B3)	20
Naf (E7)	
Nampa (B6)	16,185
Naples (B1)	300
New Meadows (B4)	621
New Plymouth (B6)	942
Newdale (G6)	312
Nezperce◉ (B3)	543
Nordman (B1)	18
North Fork (D4)	100
North Fork Payette (riv.) (B5)	
North Pocatello (F7)	575
Norton (peak) (D6)	
Norwood (C5)	
Notus (B6)	313
Nounan (G7)	
Oakley (D7)	684
Obsidian (D6)	11
Ola (B5)	300
Oldtown (A1)	358
Onaway (B3)	81
Orchard (B6)	
Orchards (A3)	4,494
Oreana (B6)	100
Orofino◉ (B3)	1,656
Orograde (C4)	12
Ovid (G7)	200
Owyhee (mts.)(B6)	
Owyhee (riv.) (B7)	
Oxford (F7)	110
Palouse (riv.) (B3)	
Pardee (B3)	
Paris◉ (G7)	774
Parker (G6)	306
Parma (B6)	1,369
Patterson (E5)	112
Paul (E7)	560
Payette◉ (B5)	4,032
Payette (mts.)(B5)	
Payette (riv.) (B6)	
Peale (mts.)(G7)	
Pearl (B6)	38
Peck (B3)	170
Pegram (G7)	75
Pend Oreille (lake) (B1)	
Pend Oreille (mt.) (B1)	
Pend Oreille (riv.) (A1)	
Picabo (D6)	100
Pierce (C3)	544
Pilot Knob(mt.)(C4)	
Pine (C6)	
Pingree (F6)	102
Pinyon (peak) (C5)	
Pioneer (mts.) (D6)	
Pioneerville (C6)	8
Placerville (C6)	17
Plano (G6)	403
Plummer (B2)	395
Pocatello◉ (F7)	26,131
Pollock (B4)	
Ponderay (B1)	248
Porthill (B1)	68
Portneuf (F7)	65
Portneuf (riv.) (F7)	
Post Falls (A2)	1,069
Potlatch (A3)	1,024
Potlatch (riv.) (B3)	
Prairie (C6)	150
Preston◉ (G7)	4,045
Prichard (B2)	40
Priest (lake) (B1)	
Priest River (A1)	1,592
Princeton (B3)	84
Purcell (mts.)(C1)	
Pyramid (peak)(E4)	
Raft (riv.) (E7)	
Rainbow (peak)(C4)	
Ranger (peak) (D3)	
Rathdrum (A2)	610
Raymond (G7)	88
Red (riv.) (C4)	
Red River Hot Springs (C4)	12
Regena (C6)	
Reno (F5)	
Reubens (B3)	116
Rexburg◉ (G6)	4,253
Rhodes (peak) (D3)	
Richfield (D6)	429
Riddle (B7)	35
Rigby◉ (G6)	1,826
Riggins (B4)	287
Ririe (G6)	527
Riverside (F6)	
Roberts (F6)	341
Robin (F7)	165
Rockford (F6)	
Rockford Bay (B2)	27
Rockland (F7)	277
Rocky Bar (C6)	
Rocky Ridge (mt.) (C3)	
Rogerson (D7)	75
Roseberry (C5)	
Roselake (B2)	212
Roswell (A6)	92
Roy (F7)	25
Rupert◉ (E7)	3,098
Ryan (peak) (D6)	
Sagle (B1)	75
St. Anthony◉ (G6)	2,695
St. Charles (G7)	363
St. Joe (B2)	75
St. Joe (riv.) (B2)	
St. Maries◉ (B2)	2,220
Salmon◉ (D4)	2,648
Salmon (falls) (D7)	
Salmon (riv.) (B4)	
Salmon River (mts.) (C5)	
Salmon River (res.) (D7)	
Samaria (F7)	
Samuels (B1)	
Sanders (B2)	25
Sandpoint◉ (B1)	4,265
Santa (B2)	
Sawtooth (mts.)(D6)	
Sawtooth (mts.)(C6)	
Selkirk (mts.)(B1)	
Selway (riv.) (C3)	
Seven Devils (mts.) (B4)	
Shafer (butte) (B6)	
Shelley (F6)	1,856
Shoshone◉ (D7)	1,420
Shoshone(falls) (D7)	
Shoup (D4)	
Silver City (B6)	2
Sleeping Deer (mt.) (D5)	
Small (F5)	
Smelterville (B2)	76
Smiths Ferry (C5)	
Smoky (mts.) (D6)	
Snake (riv.) (A3)	
Snake River (mts.) (G6)	
Snake River (plain) (D7)	
Soda Springs◉ (G7)	
Southwick (B3)	200
Spencer (F5)	70
Spirit Lake (A2)	823
Springfield (F6)	435
Springston (B2)	57
Squaw (peak) (D4)	
Squirrel (G5)	
Stanley (D5)	33
Star (B6)	525
Starkey (B5)	3
Steel (mt.) (C6)	
Sterling (F6)	
Stewart (mts.)(E7)	
Stibnite (C5)	717
Stites (C3)	227
Stone (F7)	170
Strevell (E7)	25
Sublett (E7)	10
Sugar City (G6)	684
Sun Valley (D6)	428
Sunbeam (D5)	6
Swan Valley (G6)	203
Swanlake (F7)	250
Sweet (B6)	200
Sweetwater (B3)	80
Taber (F6)	
Tamarack (B5)	
Taylor (mt.) (D5)	
Tendoy (E5)	
Tensed (B2)	189
Terreton (F6)	35
Teton (G6)	463
Teton (riv.) (G6)	
Tetonia (G6)	232
Thatcher (G7)	50
Thompson (peak) (C5)	
Thornton (G6)	300
Three Creek (C7)	65
Tindall (C7)	5
Treasureton (G7)	
Triangle (B7)	35
Triumph (D6)	97
Troy (B3)	531
Tuttle (D7)	15
Twin (falls) (D7)	
Twin (peaks) (D5)	
Twin Falls◉ (D7)	17,600
Twin Lakes (B2)	225
Twin Springs (C6)	
Tyhee (F7)	350
Ucon (F6)	356
Ustick (B6)	200
Vay (B1)	80
Victor (G6)	431
Viola (B3)	150
Virginia (F7)	245
Walcott (lake) (E7)	
Wallace◉ (C2)	3,140
Wapello (F6)	
Wardner (B2)	772
Warm Lake (C5)	500
Warren (C4)	30
Wasatch (mts.)(G7)	
Waugh (mt.) (D4)	
Wayan (G7)	
Weippe (C3)	1,000
Weiser◉ (B5)	3,961
Weiser (riv.) (B5)	
Wendell (D7)	1,483
Westlake (B3)	35
Weston (F7)	382
White Bird (B4)	
White Knob (mts.) (E6)	
Wilder (A6)	555
Wildhorse (B5)	18
Wilson Lake (res.) (D7)	
Winchester (B3)	488
Winona (B3)	
Winsper (F5)	
Wood (riv.) (D6)	
Woodland (C3)	
Worley (B2)	233
Yellow Pine (C4)	35
Yellowstone Nat'l Park (H5)	

◉ County Seat

Statistical Appendix

Appendix Table 1

IDAHO PEAKS 10,000 FEET OR MORE IN HEIGHT

	Name of Peak	County Location	Mountain Location	Elevation
1.	Mt. Borah	Custer	Lost River Range	12,655
2.	Leatherman	Custer	Lost River Range	12,230
3.	Hawley	Custer	Lost River Range	12,130
4.	Bell	Lemhi	Lemhi Range	12,125
5.	Hyndman	Blaine-Custer	Pioneer (Sawtooth) Rn.	12,078
6.	Dorion	Custer	Lost River Range	12,016
7.	Ryan	Blaine-Custer	Boulder (Sawtooth) Mts.	11,900
8.	Castle	Custer	White Cloud (Sawtooth) Mts.	11,820
9.	Standhope	Blaine-Custer	Pioneer (Sawtooth) Mts.	11,700
10.	McCaleb	Custer	Lost River Range	11,599
11.	Glassford	Custer	Boulder (Sawtooth) Mts.	11,500
12.	Big Black Dome	Custer	White Knob Mts.	11,357
13.	Invisible	Custer	Lost River Range	11,343
14.	Gunsight	Lemhi	Lemhi Range	11,324
15.	Dickey	Custer	Lost River Range	11,140
16.	Galena	Blaine-Custer	Boulder (Sawtooth) Mts.	11,118
17.	Grouse Creek	Custer	Pahsimeroi (Lost Riv.) Rn.	11,105
18.	Easley	Blaine-Custer	Boulder (Sawtooth) Mts.	11,093
19.	Flatiron	Lemhi	Lemhi Range	11,025
20.	Freeman	Lemhi-Montana	Beaverhead Range	11,002
21.	Devil's Bedstead	Blaine-Custer	Pioneer (Sawtooth) Mts.	11,000
22.	Eldorado	Lemhi-Montana	Beaverhead Range	11,000
23.	Boulder	Blaine-Custer	Boulder (Sawtooth) Mts.	10,966
24.	Sheep	Custer	Boulder (Sawtooth) Mts.	10,915
25.	Patterson	Custer	White Cloud (Sawtooth)	10,882
26.	Copper Basin Knob	Custer	White Knob Mts.	10,779
27.	Thompson	Boise-Custer	Sawtooth Range	10,776
28.	Cramer	Boise-Custer	Sawtooth Range	10,720
29.	Redfish Lake	Custer	Sawtooth Range	10,689
30.	Snowyside	Blaine-Boise-Custer-Elmore	Sawtooth Range	10,659
31.	Elk	Boise-Custer	Sawtooth Range	10,605
32.	Washington	Custer	White Cloud (Sawtooth)	10,527

NOTE.—There are sixty-five named peaks 9,000 to 10,000 feet, thirty peaks 8,000 to 9,000 feet, and hundreds of peaks and summits below 8,000 feet.
Sources: *Idaho Encyclopedia*, U.S. Geological Survey, and U.S. Forest Service.

Appendix Table 1—*Cont'd*

	Name of Peak	County Location	Mountain Location	Elevation
33.	Sawtelle	Fremont	Centennial Mts.	10,500
34.	Independence	Cassia	Albion Mts.	10,360
35.	Cache	Cassia	Albion Mts.	10,340
36.	Twin Peaks	Custer	Salmon River Mts.	10,328
37.	General	Custer	Salmon River Mts.	10,325
38.	Bald	Custer	Salmon River Mts.	10,314
39.	Baron	Boise-Custer	Sawtooth Range	10,307
40.	Blackman	Custer	White Cloud (Sawtooth) Pks.	10,307
41.	Heyburn	Custer	Sawtooth Range	10,229
42.	Jefferson	Fremont-Montana	Centennial Mts.	10,211
43.	Norton	Blaine	Smoky (Sawtooth) Mts.	10,200
44.	Slide	Clark-Montana	Centennial Mts.	10,200
45.	Reward	Boise-Custer	Sawtooth Range	10,115
46.	Porphyry	Custer	White Knob Mts.	10,087
47.	McGuire	Lemhi	Bighorn Crags (Salmon Riv. Mts.)	10,070
48.	Glens	Boise-Elmore	Sawtooth Range	10,065
49.	Jordan	Custer	Salmon River Mts.	10,054
50.	Baird	Bonneville	Snake River Range	10,040
51.	Big	Camas	Smoky (Sawtooth) Mts.	10,000
52.	Tango	Custer	Salmon River Mts.	10,000

Appendix Table 2

TERRITORIAL NEWSPAPERS OF IDAHO

(For use with Unit 8)

Year Estab.	Original Name	Place Published	Remarks
1862	*The Golden Age*	Lewiston	Suspended 1865; Idaho's first newspaper
1863	*The Boise News*	Bannack City (later Idaho City)	Later (1864) *Idaho World;* suspended 1918
1864	*Idaho Statesman*	Boise	Now *Idaho Daily Statesman*
1865	*Owyhee Avalanche*	Ruby City; to Silver City, 1866	Suspended 1932(?). Only known early-day file in Bancroft Library, Univ. of Calif., Berkeley
1867	*Journal*	Lewiston	Suspended
1880	*Tribune*	Lewiston	Sold, 1889; now *Lewiston Tribune*
1880	*Idaho Register*	Blackfoot, to Idaho Falls	Now the *Post-Register*
1881	*Bear Lake Democrat*	Paris	Now *Paris Post*
1881	*Challis Messenger*	Challis	Still published
1881	*Ketchum Keystone*	Ketchum	Suspended; old files purchased by Univ. of Idaho
1881	*Wood River Times*	Hailey	Now *Hailey-Wood River Times*
1882	*Kootenai Courier*	Rathdrum	Suspended
1882	*Moscow Mirror*	Moscow	Later *Star-Mirror;* suspended
1882	*The Signal*	Weiser	Still published
1883	*News-Miner*	Hailey	Combined with *Hailey Times*
1883	*The Journal*	Shoshone	Still published
1883	*The Tribune*	Caldwell	Now the *Caldwell News-Tribune*
1885	*Idaho Herald*	Pocatello	Merged with *Pocatello Tribune*
1885	*Idaho Press*	Wallace	Now *Wallace Press-Times*
1886	*Albion Nugget*	Albion	Suspended
1886	*The Enterprise*	Malad City	Now the *Idaho Enterprise*
1886	*Idaho County Free Press*	Grangeville	Still published
1886	*Idaho Recorder*	Salmon	Now the *Recorder Herald*
1886	*The News*	Kellogg	Still published
1887	*Blackfoot News*	Blackfoot	Suspended
1887	*Idaho State Tribune*	Wallace	Merged with *Wallace Press-Times*
1888	*The Bulletin*	Mountain Home	Merged with *Mountain Home News*
1888	*The News*	Genesee	Still published
1889	*Pocatello Tribune*	Pocatello	Now the *Idaho State Journal*
1889	*The Republican*	Mountain Home	Merged with *Mountain Home News*
1889	*Rexburg Journal*	Rexburg	Still published

AUTHOR'S NOTE.—Because of research difficulties, it is not possible to know for a certainty if all the above listings are entirely correct. Corrections, if any, will be welcomed.

Appendix Table 3
DELEGATES TO THE IDAHO CONSTITUTIONAL CONVENTION, JULY 4 TO AUGUST 6, 1889
(Use with Unit 9)

Ada County:
  John S. Gray
  A. B. Moss
  Edgar Wilson
  John Lemp
  W. C. Maxey
  Chas. A. Clark
  I. N. Coston
  P. J. Pefley
  Frank Steunenberg
Alturas County:
  Jas. H. Beatty
  A. J. Pinkham
  O. B. Batten
  L. Vineyard
  P. McMahon
  J. W. Ballentine
Bear Lake County:
  J. L. Underwood
Bingham County:
  W. H. Savidge
  F. W. Beane
  H. B. Kinport
  J. T. Morgan
  H. O. Harkness
  Robert Anderson
  Sam F. Taylor
Boise County:
  Fred Campbell
  George Ainslie
  John H. Myer
Cassia County:
  H. S. Hampton
  J. W. Lamoreaux
Custer County:
  O. J. Salisbury
  A. J. Pierce
  A. J. Crook
  Jas. M. Shoup
Elmore County:
  F. P. Cavanah
  A. M. Sinnott
  Homer Stull

Idaho County:
  A. F. Parker
Kootenai County:*
  Henry Melder
  Albert Hagan
Latah County:
  Willis Sweet
  W. J. McConnell
  J. W. Brigham
  W. D. Robbins
  W. B. Blake
  A. S. Chaney
Lemhi County:
  N. I. Andrews
  Thos. Pyeatt
  John Hagan
  J. M. Howe
Nez Perce County:
  Jas. W. Reed
  J. W. Poe
Logan County:
  J. S. Whitton
  Henry Armstrong
  W. C. B. Allen
Oneida County:
  John Lewis
  D. W. Standrod
Owyhee County:
  S. J. Pritchard
  C. M. Hays
  J. I. Crutcher
Shoshone County:
  W. B. Heyburn
  W. H. Clagett†
  Wm. H. Hammel
  S. S. Glidden
  W. W. Woods
  A. B. Bevan
  A. E. Mayhew
  G. W. King
Washington County:
  Sol Hasbrouck
  E. S. Jewel
  Frank Harris

*W. A. Hendryx, of Kootenai County, did not take his convention seat.
†Served as Convention Chairman.
List checked for correctness by State Historian Mrs. Gertrude McDevitt and Mrs. Mathews, Assistant.

Appendix Table 4

IDAHO'S MEMBERS OF CONGRESS SINCE STATEHOOD
(Use with Unit 9)

I. SENATORS: (R for Republican, D for Democrat, P for Populist)

William J. McConnell—R	1891
George L. Shoup—R	1891–1895 and 1895–1901
Fred T. Dubois—R	1891–1897 and 1901–1907
Henry Heitfield—P	1897–1903
Weldon B. Heyburn—R	1903–1909 and 1909–1912†
William E. Borah—R	1907–1940†
Kirtland I. Perky—D	1912–1913
James H. Brady—R	1913–1918†
John F. Nugent—D	1918–1921
Frank R. Gooding—R	1921–1928†
John Thomas—R	1928–1933 and 1940–1945†
James P. Pope—D	1933–1939
D. Worth Clark—D	1939–1945
Glen H. Taylor—D	1945–1951
Charles C. Gossett—D	1945–1947
Henry C. Dworshak—R	1946–1947 and 1949–*
Bert H. Miller—D	1949–†
Herman Welker—R	1951–‡

II. REPRESENTATIVES

Willis Sweet—R	1890–1895
Edgar Wilson—D	1895–1897 and 1899–1901
James Gunn—P	1897–1899
Thomas L. Glenn—P	1901–1903
Burton L. French—R	1903–1909, 1911–1915 and 1917–1933
Thomas R. Hamer—R	1909–1911
Addison T. Smith—R	1913–1933
Robert M. McCracken—R	1915–1917
Thomas C. Coffin—D	1933–1934†
Compton I. White—D	1933–1947 and 1949–1951
D. Worth Clark—D	1935–1939
Henry C. Dworshak—R	1939–1945
Abe McGregor Goff—R	1947–1949
John Sanborn—R	1947–1951
John T. Wood—R	1951–1953
Hamer Budge—R	1951–*
Mrs. Gracie Pfost—D	1953–*

*Present incumbent. Re-elected in 1954.
†Died during term of office.
‡Term expires in 1957.

Appendix Table 5

IDAHO'S GOVERNORS SINCE STATEHOOD

(To use with Unit 9)

R indicates Republican, D indicates Democrat

Governor	Terms	Dates of Service
George L. Shoup—R	–1*	–1890
Norman B. Willey—R	1	1890–1893
William J. McConnell—R	2	1893–1897
Frank Steunenberg—D	2	1897–1901
Frank W. Hunt—D	1	1901–1903
John T. Morrison—R	1	1903–1905
Frank R. Gooding—R	2	1905–1909
James H. Brady—R	1	1909–1911
James H. Hawley—D	1	1911–1913
John M. Haines—R	1	1913–1915
Moses Alexander—D	2	1915–1919
D. W. Davis—R	2	1919–1923
Charles C. Moore—R	2	1923–1927
H. C. Baldridge—R	2	1927–1931
C. Ben Ross—D	3	1931–1937
Barzilla W. Clark—D	1	1937–1939
C. A. Bottolfsen—R	2	1939–1941; 1943–1945
Chase A. Clark—D	1	1941–1943
Charles C. Gossett—D	–1*	–1945
Arnold Williams—D	1	1945–1947
C. A. Robins—R	1	1947–1951
Len B. Jordan—R	1	1951–1955
Robert E. Smylie—R	1†	1955–

*Resigned to accept seat in U.S. Senate.
†Present incumbent, elected Nov. 2, 1954.

Appendix Table 6

SMALLER CITIES OF IDAHO

(Use with Unit 10)

	City	1950 Pop.	County in Which Located	Basic Industries
1	Blackfoot	5,180	Bingham	Agriculture
2	Kellogg	4,913	Shoshone	Mining; forestry
3	Alameda	4,694	Bannock	Agriculture
4	Jerome	4,523	Jerome	Agriculture
5	Sandpoint	4,265	Bonner	Forestry; recreations; agriculture
6	Rexburg	4,253	Madison	Agriculture
7	Preston	4,045	Franklin	Agriculture
8	Payette	4,032	Payette	Agriculture
9	Weiser	3,961	Washington	Agriculture
10	Wallace	3,140	Shoshone	Mining; forestry
11	Gooding	3,099	Gooding	Agriculture
12	Rupert	3,098	Minidoka	Agriculture
13	Emmett	3,067	Gem	Agriculture; forestry
14	Buhl	2,870	Twin Falls	Agriculture
15	Malad City	2,715	Oneida	Agriculture
16	St. Anthony	2,695	Fremont	Agriculture
17	Montpelier	2,682	Bear Lake	Agriculture
18	Salmon	2,648	Lemhi	Agriculture; forestry; mining
19	Grangeville	2,544	Idaho	Agriculture; forestry; mining

NOTE.—Agriculture includes all kinds of farming and stock raising. Forestry includes lumbering as well as professional forestry. Mining includes both mining and smelting.

Appendix Table 7

BROADCASTING STATIONS IN IDAHO—1955 LISTING

(For use in Unit 12)

City in Which Located	Station	Dial Number	Principal Network	Television
Blackfoot	KBLI	1490	——	
Boise	KBOI	950	CBS	KBOI–TV
	KGEM	1140	ABC; KBS	
	KIDO	630	NBC	KIDO–TV
Burley	KBAR	1230	ABC	
Caldwell	KCID	1490	——	
Coeur d'Alene	KVNI	1240	MBS	
Idaho Falls	KID	590	CBS	KID–TV
	KIFI	1400	ABC; MBS; KBS	KIFI–TV
Lewiston	KLER	740	——	
	KRLC	1350	MBS	
Moscow	KRPL	1400	KBS	
Nampa	KFXD	580	MBS	
Pocatello	KSEI	930	NBC	
	KSEI–FM	Chan. 243		
	KWIK	1240	ABC; MBS; KBS	KWIK–TV
Preston	KPST	1340	KBS	
Rexburg	KRXK	1230	——	
	KRXK–FM	Chan. 229		
Sandpoint	KSPT	1400	KBS	
Twin Falls	KEEP	1450	CBS	
	KLIX	1310	ABC; MBC	KLIX–TV
	KTFI	1270	NBC	
	KTFI–FM	——		
Wallace	KWAL	620	MBS	
Weiser	KWEI	1240	——	

Appendix Table 8

UPPER SNAKE RIVER VALLEY RESERVOIRS
(For use with Unit 15)

Reservoir and Dam	Source of Water	County in Which Located	Storage, Acre Feet
Chesterfield (1911) (Pvt.)	Portneuf River	Caribou	16,000
Grays Lake (1914) (IS)	Lake tributaries	Bonneville	40,000
Jackson Lake (1916) (BR)	Snake River	(Wyoming)	847,000
Henrys Lake (1922) (Pvt.)	Lake tributaries	Fremont	79,000
Blackfoot (1924) (IS)	Blackfoot River	Caribou	410,000
Island Park (1939) (BR)	Henrys Fork	Fremont	128,000
Grassy Lake (1940) (BR)	Fall River trib.	Yellowstone Park	15,000
Mackay (Pvt.)	Big Lost River	Custer	38,000
Mud Lake (Pvt.)	Lake tributaries	Jefferson	40,000
Palisades (BR) (project now under construction)	South Fork of Snake River	Bonneville	1,400,000

Pvt.—Built under private direction, usually co-operating groups of farmers.
IS—Built by the U.S. Indian Service.
BR—Built by the Bureau of Reclamation.

Appendix Table 9

MAGIC VALLEY RESERVOIRS

(For use with Unit 15)

Reservoir and Dam	Source of Water	County in Which Located	Storage, Acre Feet
Milner (1905) (Pvt.)*	Snake River	Jerome–Twin Falls	80,000
Lake Walcott, Minidoka Dam (1909) (BR)	Snake River	Cassia–Minidoka	95,000
Lake Wilson (1909) (Pvt.)	Canal leading from Milner Dam	Jerome	18,000
Salmon (1911) (Pvt.)	Salmon Falls Creek	Twin Falls	183,000
Oakley (Goose Creek Dam) (1912) (Pvt.)	Goose Creek	Cassia	74,000
Twin Lakes (1915) (Pvt.)	Camas Creek tributaries	Camas	31,000
Magic (1917) (Pvt.)	Camas Creek and Big Wood River	Blaine	192,000
Cedar Creek (1920) (Pvt.)	Cedar Creek and tributaries	Twin Falls	28,000
Fish Creek (1922) (Pvt.)	Fish Creek tributary Little Wood River	Blaine	18,000
American Falls† (1927) (BR)	Snake River	Power	1,700,000
Little Wood (1940) (Pvt.)	Little Wood River	Blaine	10,000

*Now maintained and operated by Bureau of Reclamation.
†Located in Upper Snake River Valley but water used mainly in Magic Valley. Some water exchanged for rights in Jackson Lake and other Upper Valley reservoirs.
Pvt.—Built under private direction, usually co-operating groups of farmers.
BR—Built by the Bureau of Reclamation.

Appendix Table 10

LOWER SNAKE RIVER VALLEY RESERVOIRS

(For use with Unit 15)

	Reservoir and Dam	Source of Water	County in Which Located	Storage, Acre Feet
Boise Basin	Lake Lowell, the Deer Flat Reservoir (1908) (BR)	Long canal from Boise River	Canyon	177,000
	Arrowrock (1915) (BR)	Boise River	Boise–Elmore	286,000
	Anderson Ranch (1949) (BR)	South Fork of Boise River	Elmore	500,000
Owyhee Basin	Owyhee (1932) (BR)*	Owyhee River	(Oregon)	1,120,000
	Wildhorse (IS)†	Owyhee River	(Nevada)	32,000
	About forty small, scattered reservoirs (Pvt.)‡	Tributaries of Owyhee River	Owyhee Co., Ore. and Nev.	78,000, combined
	Black Canyon (1924) (BR)	Payette River	Gem	Mainly a diversion dam
	Deadwood (1930) (BR)	Deadwood River and tributaries	Valley	164,000
Payette Basin	Cascade (1948) (BR)	North Fork of Payette River	Valley	703,200
	Nine reservoirs in Weiser Basin (Mainly Pvt.)	Weiser River and tributaries	Adams and Washington	64,000, combined

*Water used mainly in Oregon portion of the Lower Snake River Valley.

†Water used on Duck Valley Indian Reservation in Idaho and Nevada.

‡Water used mainly in Lower Snake River Valley area of southeastern Oregon and northern Nevada, but largely connected economically with Lower Snake River Valley.

BR—Built by the Bureau of Reclamation.

Pvt.—Built under private direction, usually co-operating groups of farmers.

NOTE.—Storage capacity of reservoirs is approximate and not all references agree fully because some use gross storage figures and others use live storage capacity. Here, as well as in Appendix Tables 8 and 9, the live storage capacity is used when possible.

Appendix Table 11
HYDROELECTRIC PLANTS IN IDAHO
(For use with Unit 15)

Owned or Operated By	Location, At or Near	Source of Power	Approximate Kilowatt Capacity
Idaho Power Company	American Falls	Snake River	27,000
	Bellevue	Big Wood River	600
	Bliss	Snake River	80,000
	Cascade	N. Fork Payette R.	275
	Clear Lake	Snake River Springs	2,100
	Horse Shoe Bend	Payette River	1,800
	Malad, Lower	Malad River	8,000
	Malad, Upper	Malad River	14,000
	Salmon	Salmon River	675
	Salmon Falls, Lower	Snake River	65,000
	Salmon Falls, Upper	Snake River	34,500
	Shoshone Falls	Snake River	12,500
	Strike Dam	Snake River	90,000
	Swan Falls	Snake River	11,000
	Thousand Springs	Hagerman Val. Spgs.	7,500
	Twin Falls	Snake River	9,375
Municipal Plants	Idaho Falls	Snake River	7,100
	Bonners Ferry	Moyie River	1,475
United States Agencies	Albeni Falls	Pend Oreille River	140,000
	Anderson Ranch Dam	South Boise River	40,500
	Black Canyon Dam	Payette River	8,000
	Boise Diversion Dam	Boise River	1,500
	Minidoka Dam	Snake River	13,400
	Palisades Dam, under construction	Snake River	30,000
Utah Power & Light Company	Ashton	Henrys Fork	5,800
	Cove	Bear River	7,500
	Grace	Bear River	44,000
	Oneida	Bear River	30,000
	Soda Springs	Bear River	14,000

Appendix Table 12
IDAHO FISH HATCHERIES
(Use with Unit 18)

(November 1, 1950, to October 31, 1952)

Hatchery Location	County	Fish Produced (to nearest thousand)
American Falls	Power	1,828,000
Ashton	Fremont	2,804,000
Clark Fork	Bonner	2,764,000
Coeur d'Alene	Kootenai	1,327,000
Eagle	Ada	1,989,000
Grace (Whiskey Creek)	Caribou	2,409,000
Grangeville	Idaho	979,000
Hagerman*	Gooding	2,250,000
Hayspur	Blaine	2,322,000
Henrys Lake	Fremont	2,770,000
Mackay	Custer	1,287,000
McCall	Valley	2,074,000
Mullan	Shoshone	1,575,000
Sandpoint	Bonner	2,992,000
Twin Falls	Twin Falls	1,362,000
Warm River	Fremont	627,000
	Total	31,359,000

*Road sign by U.S. Highway 30 N, in Hagerman Valley, in 1954, advertised the Hagerman Fish Hatchery as the largest in the world.

Appendix Table 13
ASSESSED VALUATION OF IDAHO
COUNTIES, 1954
(State Tax Commission)

County	Total Valuation For Tax Base 1954	County	Total Valuation For Tax Base 1954
Ada	$65,591,773.29	Gooding	14,290,580.54
Adams	3,815,378.19	Idaho	13,320,161.96
Bannock	27,340,201.18	Jefferson	10,584,841.28
Bear Lake	8,672,223.74	Jerome	11,397,655.03
Benewah	5,558,237.47	Kootenai	17,858,196.67
Bingham	21,261,352.27	Latah	16,622,581.57
Blaine	7,380,884.47	Lemhi	6,618,501.00
Boise	2,958,390.80	Lewis	8,030,393.79
Bonner	18,842,593.26	Lincoln	6,201,686.58
Bonneville	30,200,907.16	Madison	6,670,945.88
Boundary	6,258,582.11	Minidoka	9,061,927.05
Butte	3,436,567.75	Nez Perce	24,329,212.28
Camas	3,560,796.15	Oneida	5,530,927.89
Canyon	37,325,505.82	Owyhee	8,798,640.42
Caribou	13,984,534.49	Payette	8,702,167.70
Cassia	11,547,697.63	Power	11,517,728.70
Clark	3,645,759.07	Shoshone	26,835,046.99
Clearwater	8,668,330.44	Teton	2,721,084.82
Custer	4,075,087.20	Twin Falls	37,375,496.03
Elmore	12,135,456.36	Valley	5,336,101.43
Franklin	9,218,391.12	Washington	9,301,128.32
Fremont	9,258,146.95		
Gem	7,134,988.33	TOTAL	$582,976,791.18

Bibliography

and Related Readings

This is more than a bibliography inasmuch as it contains many titles included for general reading as well as for research purposes.

Explanatory Note:

1. Sources are arranged under twenty-two headings on the basis of subject matter. Some, of course, could be listed in more than one group, but, if given in only one group, they have been placed where, in the opinion of the authors, they most logically belong.
2. The alphabetical arrangement is by title under the respective headings.
3. Each listing is arranged as follows: (1) title; (2) author, if given; (3) publisher, if given; and (4) explanatory comments, if any.

1. AGRICULTURE AND IRRIGATION

After Fifty Years—Irene Welch Grissom. The Caxton Printers, Ltd., Caldwell, Idaho. In verse and story the account of a Scandinavian irrigation project in eastern Idaho.

Boise Federal Reclamation Project. Conservation Bulletin No. 26, Bureau of Reclamation, U.S. Department of the Interior, Washington, D.C.

Boise Federal Reclamation Project, Payette Division. Bureau of Reclamation, U.S. Department of the Interior, Washington, D.C.

Columbia River. Bureau of Reclamation, U.S. Department of the Interior, Washington, D.C. This report, in two volumes, is an unusually valuable source of information on the water resources, geography, and economic development of the Columbia Basin in Idaho.

Conservation Irrigation—McCulloch and Criddle. Agricultural Information Bulletin No. 8, Soil Conservation Service, Idaho Office, Yates Building, Boise, Idaho.

Desert to Abundance. Scenic Idaho, Third Quarter, 1950. Belcher Publishing Company, Boise, Idaho. Story of the Black Canyon irrigation district near Emmett.

Ground Water Flows—Lynn Crandall. Bureau of Reclamation Office, Idaho Falls, Idaho. Mimeographed report prepared by Lynn Crandall, Watermaster, Irrigation District No. 36.

History of Irrigation Development in the Snake River Valley—Lynn Crandall. Bureau of Reclamation Office, Idaho Falls, Idaho. Mimeographed report.

Idaho Made the Desert Bloom—D. Worth Clark. National Geographic Magazine, June, 1944. National Geographic Society, Washington, D.C.

Idaho Reclamation News. Official publication of the Idaho Reclamation Association, Boise, Idaho. Published periodically. Free upon request.

Idaho State Department of Reclamation.

Biennial reports contain much valuable information as well as statistical data. May be obtained free upon request by writing the department at Boise, Idaho.

Irrigation Agriculture in the West. Miscellaneous Publication No. 670, Bureau of Reclamation, U.S. Department of the Interior, Washington, D.C.

Minidoka Federal Reclamation Project. Bureau of Reclamation, U.S. Department of the Interior, Washington, D.C. Story of the Minidoka Project in south-central Idaho.

Reclamation Handbook. Conservation Bulletin No. 32. Bureau of Reclamation, U.S. Department of the Interior, Washington, D.C.

Reclamation Project Data. Bureau of Reclamation, U.S. Department of the Interior, Washington, D.C. Information about Federal reclamation projects in the West.

Saga of American Falls Dam—Irvin E. Rockwell. Hobson Book Press, New York. Story of the building of American Falls Dam, Idaho's largest irrigation work.

Swan Valley Bustling with Construction—Harry Meredith Chagnon. Scenic Idaho, Spring Issue, 1954. Belcher Publishing Company, Boise, Idaho. Story of the building of Palisades Dam in eastern Idaho.

University of Idaho, Moscow, Idaho. Write the Office of Information for lists of bulletins, reports, etc., issued by the College of Agriculture and the Agricultural Experiment Stations. These are nearly all free for the asking.

Water Supply of the United States. Water-Supply Paper No. 1244, Part 10, Bear River Basin. 1952. Geological Survey, U.S. Department of the Interior, Washington, D.C. Statistical data about Bear River and its tributaries in southeastern Idaho.

Water Supply of the United States. Water-Supply Paper No. 1217, Part 13, Snake River Basin. 1951. Geological Survey, U.S. Department of the Interior, Washington, D.C. Statistical data about the Snake River and its tributaries in Idaho.

We Harness a River—Irene Welch Grissom. The Caxton Printers, Ltd., Caldwell, Idaho. In short story, verse, and autobiography, Idaho's former poet laureate tells of the miracle wrought by irrigation.

2. BIOGRAPHY
(Not Listed Elsewhere)

Adventures of Captain Bonneville—Washington Irving. There are several different editions of this famous old book.

And There Were Men—Russell Blankenship. Alfred A. Knopf, New York.

Bird Girl: Sacajawea—Flora Warren Seymour. The Bobbs-Merrill Company, Indianapolis, Ind.

Bonneville the Bold—Walter E. Meacham. Binfords & Mort, Portland, Oregon.

Boys' Life of Fremont—Flora Warren Seymour. Appleton-Century Company, New York.

Broken Hand, the Life Story of Thomas Fitzpatrick—LeRoy R. Hafen and W. J. Ghent. Old West Publishing Company, Denver, Colo.

Busy Life of Eighty-Five Years—Ezra Meeker. Privately printed, Seattle.

Fabulous Colonel Dewey. Scenic Idaho, March-April, 1953. Belcher Publishing Company, Boise, Idaho.

Famous Pioneers for Young People—Ramon P. Coffman and Nathan G.

Goodman. Dodd, Mead & Company, Inc., New York.

Finn Burnett, Frontiersman—Robert Beebe David. The Arthur H. Clark Company, Glendale, California.

James Bridger—J. Cecil Alter. Shepard Book Co., Salt Lake City, Utah.

Jedediah Smith and the Opening of the West—Dale L. Morgan. The Bobbs-Merrill Company, Indianapolis, Indiana. This authoritative new book presents not only the story of the "Praying Trapper" but also much valuable information about the fur era of the Pacific Northwest.

Jim Bridger—Shannon Garst. Houghton Mifflin Company, Boston. For juvenile readers.

Jim Bridger, American Frontiersman—Sanford Tousey. Albert Whitman & Company, Chicago. A well-known writer of juvenile stories tells the tale.

Jim Bridger: Mountain Man—Stanley Vestal. William Morrow & Co., Inc., New York. Vestal is one of the best-known writers in the Western field.

Joe Meek, the Merry Mountain Man—Stanley Vestal. The Caxton Printers, Ltd., Caldwell, Idaho. Few men of his time led a more adventurous life or played a more active part in the Northwest than this famous mountain man.

John Colter, Discoverer of Yellowstone Park—Stallo Vinton. Edward Eberstadt, New York.

John Colter, His Years in the Rockies—Burton Harris. Charles Scribner's Sons, New York. Colter, a member of the Lewis and Clark Expedition, was one of the earliest trappers in the general Upper Missouri–Yellowstone region.

Kit Carson, American Scout—Sanford Tousey. Albert Whitman & Company, Chicago. This famous scout was with Fremont during the official survey of the Oregon Trail.

Kit Carson, Happy Warrior of the Old West—Stanley Vestal. Houghton Mifflin Company, Boston.

Kit Carson, Trail Blazer and Scout—Shannon Garst. Julian Messner, Inc., Publishers, New York. Another favorite writer of juveniles tells the story.

Kit Carson's Own Story—B. C. Grant, ed. Taos, New Mexico. Now out of print, this autobiography is found in some libraries.

Man Unafraid—Herbert Bashford and Harr Wagner. Harr Wagner Publishing Company, San Francisco. The story of John C. Fremont.

McLoughlin and Old Oregon—Eva Emery Dye. Doubleday & Company, Inc., Garden City, New York.

Men Who Built the West—Arthur A. Gray. The Caxton Printers, Ltd., Caldwell, Idaho. A general Western history for junior high school age.

Picture Maker of the Old West—Clarence S. Jackson, ed. Charles Scribner's Sons, New York. Beautifully illustrated with copies of William Henry Jackson's famous pictures.

Ranald MacDonald, Adventurer—Marie Leona Nichols. The Caxton Printers, Ltd., Caldwell, Idaho. An adventurer in the Pacific Northwest during the fur period.

Sacajawea, a Guide and Interpreter of the Lewis and Clark Expedition—Grace Raymond Hebard. The Arthur H. Clark Company, Glendale, Calif. This authoritative book by Wyoming's most noted historian can be found in many libraries.

Sacajawea, the Bird Woman—James Willard Schultz. Houghton Mifflin Company, Boston. Schultz lived for many years among the Blackfeet and wrote with authority about Indians and their lives.

Washakie—Grace Raymond Hebard. The Arthur H. Clark Company, Glendale, Calif. The story of a noted Shoshone Indian chief of southeastern Idaho.

White-Headed Eagle—Richard G. Montgomery. The Macmillan Company, New York. The story of Dr. John McLoughlin.

Yellowstone Kelly—Luther S. Kelly. Yale University Press, New Haven, Conn.

3. CIVICS, CITIZENSHIP, GOVERNMENT, AND LAWS

American City Government and Administration—Austin F. Macdonald. Thomas Y. Crowell Company, New York.

American Government: National, State and Local—Claudius O. Johnson. Thomas Y. Crowell Company, New York.

Associated Taxpayers of Idaho, Boise, Idaho. Write for special bulletins and information on taxation and its problems in Idaho.

Behave Yourself—Betty Allen and M. P. Briggs. J. B. Lippincott Company, Philadelphia.

Book of the States. 1954–55 edition. Council of State Governments, Chicago, Illinois. New edition every two years.

City Government—Richard W. Bardwell and others. Row, Peterson & Company, Evanston, Illinois.

County Government in Idaho. Booklet prepared by the W.P.A. Found in some city, school, and college libraries.

Democracy—Richard W. Bardwell and others. Row, Peterson & Company, Evanston, Ill.

Democracy in America—William M. Muthard. D. Van Nostrand Company, New York.

Democracy in Idaho—Horatio Hamilton Miller. The Caxton Printers, Ltd., Caldwell, Idaho.

Democratic Citizenship in Today's World—A. Elwood Adams and Edward E. Walker. Charles Scribner's Sons, New York.

Footnotes on the Capital Dispute in Idaho—Annie Laurie Bird. Pacific Northwest Quarterly, Vol. XXXVI, 1945.

Frontier Justice—Wayne Gard. University of Oklahoma Press, Norman, Okla.

Frontier Law—William J. McConnell and Howard R. Driggs. World Book Company, Yonkers, New York. An interesting account of early justice in Idaho.

Fundamentals of Citizenship—G. L. Blough and D. S. Switzer. Laidlaw Brothers, Inc., Chicago, Ill.

Governors of Idaho. Twenty-first Biennial Report, 1947–1948, Idaho State Historical Society, Boise, Idaho. From Wallace to Robins.

Governors and Secretaries of State of Idaho Territory—George H. Curtis. Office of Secretary of State, Boise, Idaho. Booklet containing brief biographical sketches.

Growth of Democracy—Prudence Cutright and W. W. Charters. The Macmillan Company, New York.

History of the Organization of Idaho Territory—Henry L. Talkington, ed. Vol. 1, No. 4, January 1, 1909. Idaho State Historical Society, Boise, Idaho.

Idaho Citizen—Fred E. Lukens. The Caxton Printers, Ltd., Caldwell,

Idaho. Formerly an adopted textbook in Idaho civics.

Idaho Civics—Deborah Davis. Syms-York Company, Boise, Idaho. Formerly an adopted textbook in Idaho civics.

Idaho-Montana Boundary Line—Richard U. Good. National Geographic Magazine, January, 1900. National Geographic Society, Washington, D.C.

Idaho State Capital. Twenty-first Biennial Report, 1947–1948. Idaho State Historical Society, Boise, Idaho.

Idaho State Seal. National Geographic Magazine, July, 1946. National Geographic Society, Washington, D.C.

Idaho's Senator Borah—Annie Laurie Bird. Seeing Idaho, May, 1937. A magazine published about 1937–38 by Graves & Potter, Pocatello, Idaho. Files in a few libraries.

Lawless Land—Mark J. Boesch. The John C. Winston Company, Philadelphia. Story of the vigilantes.

Living in Our Communities—Edward Krug and I. James Quillen. Scott, Foresman and Company, Chicago.

Living in Our Democracy—V. N. Devereaux and Homer F. Aker. Harr Wagner Publishing Company, San Francisco. An Idaho adoption.

Living with Others—Laurence E. Goodrich. American Book Company, New York.

Men Who Were Given the Honor to Go to Congress for Idaho—Edith B. Mathews. Twenty-Second Biennial Report, 1949–1950. Idaho State Historical Society, Boise, Idaho.

Municipal and Other Local Governments—M. J. Fisher and D. G. Bishop. Prentice-Hall, Inc., New York.

Our Constitution and What It Means—William Kottmeyer. Webster Publishing Co., St. Louis, Missouri.

Our Federal Government—Richard W. Bardwell and others. Row, Peterson & Company, Evanston, Ill.

Our Independence and the Constitution—Dorothea Frances Fisher. E. M. Hale and Company, Publishers, Eau Claire, Wis. A Landmark Book.

Perpetual War for Perpetual Peace—Harry Elmer Barnes. The Caxton Printers, Ltd., Caldwell, Idaho.

Pictorial History of the Wild West—James D. Horan and Paul Sann. Crown Publishers, Inc., New York. Struggle by peace officers against Western bad men, largely told in pictures.

Political Clash Between North and South Idaho over the Capital—Eugene B. Chaffee. Pacific Northwest Quarterly, Vol. XIX, July, 1938.

Proceedings and Debates of the Constitutional Convention of Idaho—I. W. Hart. The Caxton Printers, Ltd., Caldwell, Idaho. In two volumes, the official story of a very important event in Idaho history and government.

Rocky Mountain Politics—Thomas C. Donnelly. University of New Mexico Press, Albuquerque, N. M. A section devoted to Idaho.

Sagebrush Lawyer—John Fisher Maclane. Pandick Press, New York. A new biography of James H. Hawley, Idaho's "Grand Old Man."

Session Laws of Idaho. The official publication of the laws enacted by the sessions of the Idaho State Legislatures. Found in many offices and libraries.

State and Local Government—Claudius O. Johnson. Thomas Y. Crowell Company, New York.

State and Local Government in the United States—William Anderson and E. W. Weidner. Henry Holt and Company, New York.

State Government—Richard W. Bard-well and others. Row, Peterson & Company, Evanston, Ill.

Story of American Democracy—M. B. Cassner. Harcourt, Brace & Company, New York.

That Word Idaho—Erl H. Ellis. University of Denver Press, Denver, Colo. Booklet compiled from official sources.

Vengeance for Magruder—R. M. Roberts. Scenic Idaho, First Quarter, 1951. Belcher Publishing Company, Boise, Idaho.

Vigilante Days and Ways—Nathaniel Pitt Langford. A. C. McClurg & Co., Chicago.

Vigilantes of Montana—Thomas J. Dimsdale. University of Oklahoma Press, Norman, Okla. The retold story of how vigilantes brought law and order to Idaho and Montana territories in early mining days.

Working for Democracy—Prudence Cutright and W. W. Charters. The Macmillan Company, New York.

You and Democracy—Dorothy Lerner Gordon. E. P. Dutton & Co., New York.

You and Your Community—Lawrence James O'Rourke. D. C. Heath & Company, Boston.

Your Life as a Citizen—Harriet F. Smith and others. Ginn and Company, Boston.

Youth Under Dictators—Orvil Brown. Row, Peterson & Company, Evanston, Ill.

4. CONSERVATION AND NATURAL RESOURCES

American Conservation; in Picture and Story—Ovid McOvat Butler. American Forestry Association, Washington, D.C.

Better Living Through Wise Use of Conservation. Soil Conservation Service, U.S. Department of Agriculture, Washington, D.C.

Conservation and Nevada. State Department of Education, Carson City, Nevada. The conservation problems of Nevada are similar to those of southern Idaho.

Conservation Education in Rural Schools. National Education Association, Department of Rural Education, Washington, D.C.

Conservation Excursions. Bulletin 13. Soil Conservation Service, Washington, D.C.

Conservation Handbook—Samuel Hanson Ordway. Conservation Foundation, New York.

Conservation Handbook for Idaho Teachers. State Department of Education, Boise, Idaho.

Conservation in America—Mary Isabel Curtis. Lyons & Carnahan, Chicago.

Conservation of American Resources—C. N. Elliott. Turner E. Smith & Co., Atlanta, Ga.

Conservation of Forest Resources—K. Decker. University of California, Bureau of Public Administration, Berkeley, Calif.

Conservation of Natural Resources—Conway L. Rhyne and E. E. Lory. Charles E. Merrill Company, Inc., Columbus, Ohio.

Conservation of Northwest Resources—Margaret H. Thompson and O. W. Freeman. Address authors at Prosser, Washington.

County Agricultural Agents. Call at these offices in the courthouse for a great variety of material on conservation.

Cover Crops for Soil Conservation—Kell and McKee. Farmers' Bulletin No.

1758. Soil Conservation Service, U.S. Department of Agriculture, Washington, D.C.

Curriculum Units on Conservation of Natural Resources. California State Department of Education, Sacramento, Calif.

Elements of Soil Conservation—Hugh Hammond Bennett. McGraw-Hill Book Company, New York.

Fish and Wildlife Service, Washington, D.C. Bulletins and information.

Forest Service, U.S. Department of Agriculture, Washington, D.C. Write for conservation material. See Group 19 for regional and district national forest offices.

Graded Curriculum Units in Conservation—Harry H. Caldwell, ed. University of Idaho, Moscow, Idaho.

Idaho Conservation Source Book—Harry H. Caldwell. University of Idaho, Moscow, Idaho.

Land Capability for Soil and Water Conservation in Idaho—Perrott and Baker. Station Bulletin No. 286, Extension Division, University of Idaho, Moscow, Idaho.

Land Renewed—William Richard Van Dersal and Edward H. Graham. Oxford University Press, New York.

Land We Live On—Carroll Lane Fenton and M. R. Fenton. Doubleday, Doran & Company, Inc., Garden City, N.Y.

Large Was Our Bounty: Natural Resources and the Schools. National Education Association, Washington, D.C.

Muddy Waters—Henrie A. Howell. American Association of Colleges for Teacher Education, New York.

National Wildlife Federation, Washington, D.C. Material for the study of wildlife conservation. Write for lists.

Nature's Bank—the Soil. National Wildlife Federation, Washington, D.C.

Oceans in the Sky—Vera Edelstadt. E. M. Hale and Company, Publishers, Eau Claire, Wis. The story of water. A Cadmus Book.

Our American Land—Hugh Hammond Bennett. Miscellaneous Publication No. 596. Soil Conservation Service, U.S. Department of Agriculture, Washington, D.C.

Our Land and Our Living—John C. Caldwell and others. L. W. Singer Company, Syracuse, New York.

Outlines for Teaching Conservation in Elementary Schools. Soil Conservation Service, U.S. Department of Agriculture, Washington, D.C.

Resources and the American Dream—Samuel Hanson Ordway. The Ronald Press Company, New York.

Soil and Water Conservation in the Pacific Northwest. Farmers' Bulletin No. 1775. United States Department of Agriculture, Washington, D.C.

Soil Conservation in Idaho. Soil Conservation Service, U.S. Department of Agriculture, Washington, D.C., or Yates Building, Boise, Idaho.

Soil Conservation Service, U.S. Department of Agriculture, Washington, D.C., Idaho office, Yates Building, Boise, Idaho. Local offices in chief cities of Idaho. Call or write for conservation material of many kinds, most of which is for free distribution.

Teachers' Bibliography, Soil Conservation in Idaho. Soil Conservation Service, Yates Building, Boise, Idaho.

Teaching Conservation—Ward Powers Beard. American Forestry Association, Washington, D.C.

This Is Our Land—Edward G. Cheney and Thorvald Schantz-Hansen. Webb Book Publishing Company, St. Paul, Minn.

Use Without Waste—Margaret Riggs

and George E. Hafstad. Webster Publishing Co., St. Louis, Missouri.

Wildlife Management Institute, Washington, D.C. Information.

5. COUNTIES AND LOCAL REGIONS; CITIES AND TOWNS

NOTE: *Scenic Idaho,* published by the Belcher Publishing Company, Boise, is the source of much material included in this section. To avoid repeating this source so many times, all articles from the magazine are arranged in alphabetical order under the heading *Scenic Idaho,* which see. All other material is arranged in the usual alphabetical order by title.

Boise, the Peace Valley—Annie Laurie Bird. The Caxton Printers, Ltd., Caldwell, Idaho. A scholarly and comprehensive account of the development of the Lower Snake River Valley.

Bonneville County in the Making—Barzilla W. Clark. A former governor of Idaho, now deceased, wrote and published this interesting story of the Upper Snake River Valley. Copies are probably available only in libraries.

Brief History of Camas Prairie—Lucy M. Nelson. The Caxton Printers, Ltd., Caldwell, Idaho. Locale is Big Camas Prairie, chiefly in Camas County.

Caribou County Chronology—Verna Irene Shupe. Print Craft Press, Colorado Springs, Colorado. Probably available only in libraries. Try Soda Springs, Idaho, Public Library.

Counties of Idaho—C. A. Bridges. Pacific Northwest Quarterly, April, 1940.

Elmore County, Its Historical Gleanings—Olive DeEtte Groefsema. Published by Mountain Home News, Mountain Home, Idaho. Try Mountain Home, Idaho, Public Library.

Gems of Thought and History of Shoshone County—G. C. Hobson. Published by the Allied Fraternities Council, Shoshone County. Rare. Write Wallace Public Library for information as to possible sources.

Ghost Towns—Ira H. Masters. Twentieth Biennial Report, 1945–1946. Idaho State Historical Society, Boise, Idaho.

Highlights of Lewiston. Bailey Publishing Co., Lewiston, Idaho. History of the city.

History of Alturas and Blaine Counties—George A. McLeod. Published by Hailey Times, Hailey, Idaho. Try Hailey, Idaho, Public Library.

History of Bannock County—Arthur C. Saunders. Published by the Tribune Company, Ltd., now The Idaho State Journal, Pocatello, Idaho. Try Pocatello, Idaho, Public Library.

History of Custer County—Jesse R. Black. Published by Challis Messenger, Challis, Idaho. Try Public Library, Challis, Idaho.

History of Leesburg Pioneers—Orion E. Kirkpatrick. Pyramid Press, Salt Lake City, Utah. Found in libraries of southern Idaho. Try Public Library, Salmon, Idaho.

History of Lemhi County—John E. Rees. Unpublished manuscript, Idaho State Historical Society, Boise, Idaho.

History of Oneida County—Norman B. Crowther. Mimeographed booklet. Write Norman B. Crowther, Malad City, Idaho.

History of Southeastern Idaho—Merrill D. Beal. The Caxton Printers, Ltd., Caldwell, Idaho. This is an excellent source for material about the southeastern portion of the state and makes interesting reading.

History of Teton Valley—Benjamin

Woodbury Driggs. The Caxton Printers, Ltd., Caldwell, Idaho. Found in many schools and public libraries.

History of Washington and Adams Counties—Judge Frank Harris. Published by the Weiser American, Weiser, Idaho. Try the school and public libraries in Weiser and Council, Idaho.

Idaho Encyclopedia—Vardis Fisher, Director. The Caxton Printers, Ltd., Caldwell, Idaho. Section VI, "Counties," pp. 209–344; Section VII, "Cities, Towns, and Villages," pp. 345–430; "Ghost Towns," pp. 98–114. This valuable book is still available in most good school and public libraries in Idaho.

Idaho Town Names—Fritz L. Kramer. Twenty-Third Biennial Report, 1951–1952. Idaho State Historical Society, Boise, Idaho.

Illustrated History of North Idaho. Western Historical Publishing Co., San Francisco.

Little Bits of Lost River History—C. A. Bottolfsen. Published by Arco Advertiser, Arco, Idaho. Try Public Library, Arco, Idaho.

Magic Valley Yesterdays: Souvenir Book. Magic Valley Yesterdays Committee, Twin Falls, Idaho.

North Idaho Scenic-Land Association, Sandpoint, Idaho, has material of various kinds about the Panhandle, available for free distribution.

Owyhee Bluebook. This is a rare book. Try writing to the County Superintendent of Schools, Murphy, Idaho, or the Public Library, Homedale, Idaho.

Pioneer Days in Idaho County—Sister M. Alfreda Elsensohn. Vols. I–II. The Caxton Printers, Ltd., Caldwell, Idaho. Sister Elsensohn has prepared a voluminous and interesting story which often reaches beyond the present boundaries of Idaho County. Volume I is chiefly historical and Volume II goes into the geographical aspects and the social and industrial development of the region.

Raft River in Idaho History—Leslie L. Sudweeks. Pacific Northwest Quarterly, XXXII.

Scenic Idaho, published by Belcher Publishing Company, Boise, Idaho, has the following articles (arranged in alphabetical order, though not always under the exact titles as listed):

Ashton, Rexburg, St. Anthony, and Idaho Falls—March–April, 1953

Bannock County, Industrial Capital of Idaho—Charles M. Sorenson—Vol. 5, No. 2, 1948

Bear Lake County, Gateway to Southeastern Idaho—Summer Issue, 1954

Boise, City of Trees—Second Quarter, 1950

Boise Valley, Land of Irrigation—Summer Issue, 1954

Canyon County—Vol. 3, No. 1, 1949

Canyon and Ada Counties—September–October, 1953

Cassia County—Vol. 1, 1949

Central Idaho (C. A. Bottolfsen) Vol. 3, No. 2, 1948

Clark County, One of Idaho's Most Wealthy Counties—Spring Issue, 1954

Clearwater County, Orofino, and Historic Old Pierce—September–October, 1953

Council, Gateway to Hell's Canyon—Winter Issue, 1954

Elmore County, Future Breadbasket of the Nation—Summer Issue, 1954

Fabulous Wood River Country—Fourth Quarter, 1951

Gem, Gooding, and Valley Counties—Winter Issue, 1954

Grangeville, Gateway to Idaho's Great Primitive Area—Florence Northway—May–June, 1953

Here is North Idaho—Jim Parsons—Winter Issue, 1948

Historical Elmore County—Olive De-Ette Groefsema—First Quarter, 1952

Historic Idaho City—Utahna Hall—Second Quarter, 1951

Idaho Falls and the Upper Snake River Valley—Third Quarter, 1952

Idaho's Magic Valley— Vol. 3, No. 2, 1948

Idaho Towns: Cascade, New Plymouth, Eagle, Donnelly, Horseshoe Bend, Meridian—Fourth Quarter, 1951

Idaho Towns: Fruitland, Eden, Hazelton, Notus, Melba, Parma, Middleton—First Quarter, 1952

Idaho Towns: Weiser, Council, New Meadows—Fourth Quarter, 1952

Island Park, Home of Rampagin' Rainbows—Algenia McCrea—March–April, 1953

Jerome County, Yesterday and Today—March–April, 1953

Land of Contrasts (Stanley Basin, Sawtooth Mountains)—Ernst C. Peterson—First Quarter, 1951

Legend of Payette—Mae Gilmore—Fourth Quarter, 1952

Lewiston, Idaho's Only Seaport—Gladys Mae Swank—May–June, 1953

Magic Valley Golden Jubilee—Spring Issue, 1954

Mr. and Mrs. Traveler See Camas County—Mildred Robinson—First Quarter, 1952

Owyhee County, Virgin Land of Opportunity—Fall Issue, 1954

Power County, the Hospitality County—Spring Issue, 1954

Southcast Gateways to the Great Northwest—Al Alexander—First Quarter, 1951

Towns of Southeastern Idaho—First Quarter, 1951

Towns on the Oregon Trail: Middleton, Notus, Parma—Martha McKenzie—Third Quarter, 1950

Where the Desert Ends: Marsing, Homedale, Wilder—H. G. Peckham—First Quarter, 1951

Shadow of the Squaw—Compiled by New Plymouth high-school pupils under the direction of Mrs. Clara Goldsmith and recommended as an example of the fine work possible when there is sufficient interest in the local history and development of a community. Rare. Try the school or public library, New Plymouth, Idaho.

Snake River Fork Country—Samuel M. Beal. Published by the Rexburg, Idaho, Journal. Try the public library or the Ricks College Library, Rexburg, Idaho.

Valley of the Tall Grass—Adelaide T. Hawes. The Caxton Printers, Ltd., Caldwell, Idaho. Special edition, found only in a few private and public libraries. Try the school and public libraries in Mountain Home, Glenns Ferry, and Bruneau.

6. ECONOMIC, INDUSTRIAL, AND SOCIAL DEVELOPMENT

Atoms at Work—George P. Bischoff. Harcourt, Brace & Company, Inc., New York.

Atomic Energy Commission's Activities in Idaho—Johnson. Fifty-Third Annual Report, Idaho Mining Industry. State Inspector of Mines, Boise, Idaho.

Atomic Energy Yearbook—John Tutin. Prentice-Hall, Inc., New York.

Beet-Sugar Economics—R. H. Cottrell. The Caxton Printers, Ltd., Caldwell, Idaho.

Columbia River, Vol. I. Bureau of Reclamation Report. Bureau of Reclamation, U.S. Department of the Interior, Washington, D.C. The opening pages of the three sections devoted mainly to Idaho (Upper Snake River Basin, Middle Snake River Basin, and Clark Fork–Clearwater Subdivision) have much valuable material.

Economic Beginnings of the Far West—Katherine Coman. The Macmillan Company, New York.

Economic Resources of the Pacific Northwest—Howard T. Lewis and Stephen I. Millen. Lowman & Hanford Company, Seattle, Wash.

Economic Surveys of Idaho. University of Idaho, School of Business Administration, Moscow, Idaho. A series of reports compiled by the Idaho State Planning Board and the School of Business Administration. Published by Syms-York Company, Boise, Idaho.

Elementary Phosphorus and Its Importance to Idaho Chemical Industries—Miller. Fifty-First Annual Report, Idaho Mining Industry. State Inspector of Mines, Boise, Idaho.

Idaho Encyclopedia—W.P.A. Writers' Project, Vardis Fisher, Director. The Caxton Printers, Ltd., Caldwell, Idaho. See Sections III and IV, pp. 115–68.

Idaho Industries—J. D. "Cy" Price. Booklet prepared in office of Secretary of State, Boise, Idaho, 1950.

Idaho State Chamber of Commerce, Boise, Idaho. Write for information about Idaho business and industry in your special fields of interest.

Industries and Resources of Idaho. Union Pacific Railroad Company, Boise, Idaho.

Let's Visit the Atoms—I. J. Alexander. Brown Book Co., New York.

Our Industrial World—J. Russell Smith and Frank E. Sorenson. The John C. Winston Company, Philadelphia.

Pacific Northwest, Its Resources and Industries—William A. King and Elmer D. Fullenwider. South Western Publishing Company, Inc., Cincinnati, Ohio.

Public Education in Idaho. George Peabody College for Teachers, Nashville, Tenn. The official Peabody Survey Report authorized by the state legislature.

Thorium Is Metal for Future Power and Atomic Weapons—Patterson. Fifty-Third Annual Report, Idaho Mining Industry. State Inspector of Mines, Boise, Idaho.

You and Atomic Energy—John Bryan Lewellen. Children's Press, Inc., Chicago. The wonderful uses of atomic energy told for youthful readers.

7. EMIGRATION; TRAILS AND TRAVEL; THE WESTWARD MOVEMENT

Beyond the Mississippi—Albert D. Richardson. American Publishing Company, Hartford, Conn.

Big Wheels Rolling—Eugenia Stone. The Caxton Printers, Ltd., Caldwell, Idaho. An exciting story of the covered-wagon trail for boys and girls.

Breaking the Wilderness—Frederick S. Dellenbaugh. G. P. Putnam's Sons, New York.

Caravans to the Northwest—John Blanchard. Houghton Mifflin Company, Boston.

Children of the Covered Wagon—Mary

Jane Carr. Thomas Y. Crowell Company, New York.

Coming of the Mormons—James Arthur Kjelgaard. Random House, New York. A Landmark Book.

Continent for Sale—Arthur William Groom. The John C. Winston Company, Philadelphia. The Louisiana Purchase.

Covered Wagon Centennial—Howard R. Driggs and Arthur W. Proctor. World Book Company, New York. Produced under the direction of the Oregon Trail Memorial Association.

Covered Wagon Days—Arthur Jerome Dickson. The Arthur H. Clark Company, Cleveland, Ohio.

Discovery of the Oregon Trail—Philip Ashton Rollins, ed. Charles Scribner's Sons, New York. The Robert Stuart Narrative.

Early Western Travels—Reuben Gold Thwaites, ed. The Arthur H. Clark Company, Cleveland, Ohio. One volume of this thirty-two volume set contains Joel Palmer's *Travels Over the Rocky Mountains,* a journal of a trip to the Oregon Country in 1845–46.

Here Rolled the Covered Wagons—Albert and Jane Salisbury. Superior Publishing Company, Seattle, Wash. Largely told in pictures, as the authors retraveled old trails and visited historic places in the Northwest.

Historical Trails of Idaho—Ora B. Hawkins. Eighteenth Biennial Report, 1941–42. Idaho State Historical Society, Boise, Idaho.

Journal of the Birmingham Emigrating Company—Leander V. Loomis. Edited by Edward M. Ledyard. Legal Printing Company, Salt Lake City, Utah.

Keep the Wagons Moving—West Lathrop. Random House, New York.

On the Oregon Trail—Gina Allen. Row, Peterson & Company, Evanston, Ill. Basic social studies education series.

On the Oregon Trail—Kenneth A. Spaulding, ed. University of Oklahoma Press, Norman, Okla. Based on journal of Robert Stuart, credited with being the first white man to use the route now known as the Oregon Trail.

On the Trail of the Pioneers—John T. Faris. George H. Doran Company, New York.

On to Oregon—Honoré Willsie Morrow. William Morrow & Company, New York.

Oregon Trail. Federal Writers' Project. Hastings House, New York. A log of Federal Highway 30, the Oregon Trail Highway.

Oregon Trail—Francis Parkman. There are several editions of this noted early history of the Oregon Trail.

Overland to the Pacific—Archie Butler Hulbert and Dorothy Printup Hulbert, eds. Stewart Commission of Colorado College and the Denver Public Library. In four volumes. This is an excellent reference work on early trails of the West.

Overland Trail—Reginald Wright Kaufmann. David McKay Company, New York.

Ox-Team Days on the Oregon Trail—Ezra Meeker. There are several publications of this book of the experiences of Ezra Meeker, probably the most famous of the early emigrants.

Rediscovering the Old Oregon Trail. Scenic Idaho, Vol. 3, No. 2, 1948. Belcher Publishing Co., Boise, Idaho.

Road to Oregon—W. J. Ghent. Longmans, Green & Co., New York.

Splendid Wayfaring—John G. Neihardt. The Macmillan Company, New York.

Stories of the Far West—Joseph G. Masters. Ginn and Company, Boston. This interesting book was written by the brother of Ira Masters, several times Idaho's Secretary of State.

This Reckless Breed of Men; The Trappers and Fur Traders of the Southwest—Robert Glass Cleland. Alfred A. Knopf, New York.

Toward Oregon—E. H. Steffelbach. Macrea Smith Co., Philadelphia.

Trail Blazers of Southeastern Idaho—Ver Dene Christiansen. Scenic Idaho, First Quarter, 1951. Belcher Publishing Co., Boise, Idaho.

Trailmakers of the Northwest—Paul Leland Haworth. Harcourt, Brace & Company, New York.

Trails of Early Idaho—Abraham C. Anderson and George W. Goodhart. The Caxton Printers, Ltd., Caldwell, Idaho. George Goodhart, early Idaho pioneer, and his life in southern Idaho.

Trails West and the Men Who Made Them—Edith Dorian and W. N. Wilson. McGraw-Hill Book Co., Inc., New York. A very recent book on Western trails.

Val Rides the Oregon Trail—Sanford Tousey. Doubleday, Doran & Company, Garden City, N.Y. Formerly an Idaho Reading Circle Book.

Wagon Train West—Rhoda Louise Nelson. Thomas Y. Crowell Company, New York.

Wagons West—Elizabeth Page. Farrar & Rinehart, Inc., New York.

Wake of the Prairie Schooner—Irene D. Paden. The Macmillan Company, New York. The Paden family spent nine summers rediscovering the Old Oregon Trail and mapping it.

West of the River—Dorothy Gardiner. Thomas Y. Crowell Company, New York.

Westward America—Howard R. Driggs. G. P. Putnam's Sons, New York. The author has for many years been an official in the American Pioneer Trails Association. Book is beautifully illustrated with color plates of William Henry Jackson's famous western pictures.

Westward the Course; a Story of the Lewis and Clark Expedition—Hildegarde Hawthorne. Longmans, Green & Company, New York.

Wheels Towards the West—Hildegarde Hawthorne. Longmans, Green & Company, New York.

Willamette Way—Margot Austin. E. M. Hale & Company, Eau Claire, Wis.

Winning Oregon—Melvin Clay Jacobs. The Caxton Printers, Ltd., Caldwell, Idaho. Story of legislation and political moves that made Oregon part of the United States.

Young Mr. Meeker and His Exciting Journey to Oregon—Miriam E. Mason. The Bobbs-Merrill Company, Indianapolis, Ind.

8. EXPLORATION AND DISCOVERY

Across the Wide Missouri—Bernard DeVoto. Houghton Mifflin Company, Boston.

Ashley-Smith Exploration and Discovery of a Central Route to the Pacific—Harrison C. Dale. The Arthur H. Clark Company, Cleveland, Ohio.

Before the Covered Wagon—Philip H. Parrish. Metropolitan Press, Portland, Ore.

Bill Clark, American Explorer—Sanford Tousey. Albert Whitman & Company, Chicago. A juvenile.

Buckskin Brigade—James Arthur Kjelgaard. Holiday House, Inc., New York.

Scouts, fur traders, and mountain men.
For youthful readers.

Conquest—Eva Emery Dye. Wilson-Erickson, Inc., Elmira, N.Y. Lewis and Clark.

Course of Empire—Bernard DeVoto. Houghton Mifflin Company, Boston.

Early Far West—W. J. Ghent. Longmans, Green & Co., New York. The West to 1850.

Exploring Expedition to the Rocky Mountains 1842–1844—John C. Fremont. Government Printing Office, Washington, D.C. Official account of Fremont's expedition. Found in a few libraries.

Following the Trail of Lewis and Clark—Ralph Gray. National Geographic Magazine, June, 1953. With map. National Geographic Society, Washington, D.C.

Forward the Nation—Donald Culross Peattie. G. P. Putnam's Sons, New York. Lewis and Clark.

Fremont and '49—Frederick S. Dellenbaugh. G. P. Putnam's Sons, New York.

Fremont, Pathfinder of the West—Allan Nevins. D. Appleton-Century Company, Inc., New York.

Hidden Heroes of the Rockies—Isaac K. Russell and Howard R. Driggs. World Book Company, Yonkers, N.Y.

Jed Smith, Trail Blazer—Frank B. Latham. American Book Company, Yonkers, N.Y. Told for youthful readers.

Journals of Lewis and Clark—Bernard DeVoto. Houghton Mifflin Company, Boston. A noted writer edits the journals for modern readers.

Lewis and Clark Expedition—Richard L. Neuberger. Random House, New York. Story told for teen-agers by the new senator from Oregon.

Lewis and Clark Journals. Record kept by members of the expedition. Usually in three to eight volumes. Sets found in most good libraries.

Lewis and Clark, Partners in Discovery—John Edwin Bakeless. William Morrow & Company, Inc., New York.

Life in the Far West—George F. Ruxton. Edited by LeRoy R. Hafen. University of Oklahoma Press, Norman, Okla. A recent book about the Rocky Mountain fur trade, etc.

Meriwether Lewis—Charles Morrow Wilson. Thomas Y. Crowell Company, New York.

Meriwether Lewis, Boy Explorer—Charlotte M. Bebenroth. The Bobbs-Merrill Company, Indianapolis, Ind.

Meriwether Lewis, Trail Blazer—Flora Warren Seymour. D. Appleton-Century Company, New York.

No Other White Men—Julia Davis. E. P. Dutton & Co., Inc., New York. Outstanding events of the Lewis and Clark Expedition.

Of Courage Undaunted—James H. Daugherty. Viking Press, New York. Lewis and Clark.

On the Trail with Lewis and Clark—Bonnie C. Howard and Ruth Higgins. Silver, Burdett Company, New York.

Opening the West with Lewis and Clark—Edwin L. Sabin. J. B. Lippincott Company, Philadelphia.

Pathbreakers from River to Ocean—Grace Raymond Hebard. University Publishing Company, Chicago.

Pathfinders of the West—Agnes C. Laut. The Macmillan Company, New York.

Pioneers of the Rocky Mountains and the West—Charles A. McMurry. The Macmillan Company, New York.

Pioneers West—Joseph Lewis French. Garden City Publishing Co., Garden City, N.Y.

Star of the West—Ethel Hueston. A. L. Burt Company, Inc., New York. A story of Lewis and Clark.

Thirty-One Years on the Plains and in the Mountains—William F. Drannan. Jackson Book Co., Kansas City, Mo. Found in some libraries.

Trail of Lewis and Clark—Olin D. Wheeler. G. P. Putnam's Sons, New York.

Trails of the Pathfinders—George Bird Grinnell. Charles Scribner's Sons, New York.

Trail to Oregon—Frederick B. Coons. Binfords and Mort, Portland, Oregon.

Two Captains West—Albert and Jane Salisbury. Superior Publishing Company, Seattle, Wash. Another picture story, this time about Lewis and Clark, by the authors of *Here Rolled the Covered Wagons*. (See Group 7.)

Westward Crossing—Jeannette Mirskey. Alfred A. Knopf, New York. Lewis and Clark.

Young Shannon, Scout with Lewis and Clark—Grace Voris Curl. Harper & Brothers, New York.

9. FORESTS, FORESTRY, AND FOREST PRODUCTS

American Forest Products Industries, Inc., Washington, D.C. Write for lists of materials, bulletins, etc., for free distribution.

Annual Forestry Directory. American Forestry Association, Washington, D.C. Write for lists of available material. Published annually.

First Book of Tree Identification—Matilda Rogers. Random House, New York.

First Book of Trees—Mirabelle Cormack. Franklin Watts, New York.

Forest Outings. Forest Service, U.S. Department of Agriculture, Washington, D.C.

Forestry for 4-H Clubs. Bulletin HH-53. Forest Service, U.S. Department of Agriculture, Washington, D.C.

Forest Trees and Forest Regions of the United States. Map V-1. Forest Service, U.S. Department of Agriculture, Washington, D.C. Wall map.

Forests and Men—William B. Greeley. Doubleday & Company, Inc., Garden City, N.Y.

Great Forest—Richard Gordon Lillard. Alfred A. Knopf, New York.

Highlights in the History of Forest Conservation. Bulletin AIB-85. Forest Service, U.S. Department of Agriculture, Washington, D.C.

How to Know the Trees of the Intermountain Region. U.S. Forest Service, Region 4, Forest Service Building, Ogden, Utah.

Idaho Forest and Timber Handbook—Miller. University of Idaho, Moscow, Idaho.

Idaho Forests, Their Care and Preservation. Idaho State Forestry Department, Boise, Idaho.

Idaho Loggers Battle a River—Ross Hall. National Geographic Magazine, July, 1951. National Geographic Society, Washington, D.C.

Idaho State Forestry Department, Boise, Idaho. Free material of many kinds available for distribution.

Kingdom of Trees—Erle Kaufmann. Reilly & Lee Company, Chicago, Ill.

Know Your Watersheds. Bulletin L. Forest Service, U.S. Department of Agriculture, Washington, D.C.

Living and Forest Lands. Bulletin HP-388. Forest Service, U.S. Department of Agriculture, Washington, D.C.

Lookout Wife—Jeanne Kellar Beaty. Random House, New York, N.Y. A very readable and humorous book about the experiences of a forest lookout and his wife on the Salmon National Forest in Idaho.

National Forest Facts, Intermountain Region. U.S. Forest Service, Region 4, Forest Service Building, Ogden, Utah.

National Forest Facts, Northern Region. U.S. Forest Service, Region 1, Federal Building, Missoula, Montana.

(Map) *National Forests of Region 1.* U.S. Forest Service, Region 1, Federal Building, Missoula, Montana.

(Map) *National Forests of Region 4.* U.S. Forest Service, Region 4, Forest Service Building, Ogden, Utah.

New Forest Frontiers. Miscellaneous Bulletin No. 414. Forest Service, U.S. Department of Agriculture, Washington, D.C.

Northern Idaho's Forest Problems. Northern Rocky Mountain Forest and Range Experiment Station, Missoula, Montana.

Northern Idaho Forest Resources and Industries. Miscellaneous Publication No. 508. U.S. Forest Service, Region 1, Federal Building, Missoula, Mont.

Nose for Trouble—James Arthur Kjelgaard. Holiday House, Inc., New York.

Our Forests, What They Are and What They Mean to Us. Miscellaneous Publication No. 162. Forest Service, U.S. Department of Agriculture, Washington, D.C.

Our National Forests. Bulletin AIB-49. Forest Service, U.S. Department of Agriculture, Washington, D.C.

Plain Facts About Our Forests. Miscellaneous Publication No. 543. Forest Service, U.S. Department of Agriculture, Washington, D.C.

Products of American Forests. Forest Service, U.S. Department of Agriculture, Washington, D.C.

10. FUR TRADERS AND TRAPPERS; TRADING POSTS; MOUNTAIN MEN

American Fur Trade and Far Western Exploration—Hiram M. Chittenden. Rufus Rockwell Wilson, New York. Comprehensive story of the fur business in western America, in two volumes.

Astoria—Washington Irving. There are several publications of this famous old book.

Correspondence and Journals of Nathaniel Wyeth, 1831–1836. F. G. Young, ed. University of Oregon, Eugene, Ore. Published by the Oregon Historical Society.

David Thompson's Journals Relating to Montana and Adjacent Regions—Catherine White, ed. University of Montana, Missoula, Montana.

"Doctor" Robert Newell—Elliott. Oregon Historical Quarterly, Vol. 9.

Donald MacKenzie, "King of the Northwest"—Cecil W. MacKenzie. Ivan Deach, Jr., Los Angeles.

Empire of Fur—August William Derleth. Aladdin Books, New York.

Fort Hall on the Oregon Trail—Jennie Broughton Brown. The Caxton Printers, Ltd., Caldwell, Idaho. A comprehensive and scholarly work by a former Pocatello teacher.

Fort Hall on the Saptin (Snake) River—Miles Cannon. Washington Historical Society Quarterly, July, 1916.

Forty Years a Fur Trader on the Upper Missouri—Charles Larpenteur. Francis P. Harper, New York.

Fur Brigade—Mary Reynolds, pseud. (Dickson Reynolds). Funk & Wagnalls Co., New York.

Fur Hunters of the Far West—Alexander Ross. Available in some libraries.

Furs to Furrows—Sydney Greenbie. The Caxton Printers, Ltd., Caldwell, Idaho. A vivid reappraisal of the historic drama of the fur trade.

Fur-Trade and Early Western Exploration—Clarence A. Vandiveer. The Arthur H. Clark Company, Cleveland, Ohio.

Fur Trade and Empire; George Simpson's Journal—Frederick Merk, ed. Harvard University Press, Cambridge, Mass.

Fur Trappers of the Old West—Anita Melva Anderson. Wheeler Publishing Company, Chicago. Very easy reading, mainly about Jim Bridger and associates.

History of Fort Henry—Samuel M. Beal. *Seeing Idaho,* September, 1937. A magazine published about 1937–38 by Graves & Potter, Pocatello, Idaho. Files in a few libraries.

Hudson's Bay Company. Hudson's Bay House, London. Found in some libraries.

Hudson's Bay Company—Maloney. Oregon Historical Society Quarterly, Vol. 37.

Hudson's Bay Express—Robert Davis. Holiday House, New York.

Important Results from the Explorations of John Jacob Astor. Oregon Historical Quarterly, Vol. 12.

Jedediah Smith and the Opening of the West—Dale L. Morgan. See Group 2.

Jedediah Smith, Fur Trapper of the Old West—Olive Burt. Julian Messner, Inc., New York.

Jed Smith, Trail Blazer—Frank B. Latham. Aladdin Books, New York. American Heritage Series.

Jim Bridger, Historic Old Man of the Mountains—Margaret Hawkes Lindsley. Scenic Idaho, Second Quarter,

1950. Belcher Publishing Company, Boise, Idaho.

Journal of a Trapper—Osborne Russell. Syms-York Company, Inc., Boise, Idaho.

Journal of John Work—John Work. The Arthur H. Clark Company, Cleveland, Ohio.

Kullyspell House—Robert G. Bailey. In *Seeing Idaho,* February, 1938. Published during 1937–38, a few files of this old magazine are found in libraries.

Letters of Dr. John McLoughlin—Burt B. Barker, ed. Binfords & Mort, Portland, Oregon.

North West Company—Gordon C. Davidson. University of California Press, Berkeley, Calif.

Peter Skene Ogden's Diary. Oregon Historical Society Quarterly, Vol. 10.

River of the West—Francis Fuller Victor. Columbian Book Co., Hartford, Conn. About the fur trade of the Columbia region, this book is found in some libraries.

Russian Fur Trade—Raymond Henry Fisher. University of California Press, Berkeley, Calif.

Sitka—Clarence Leroy Andrews. The Caxton Printers, Ltd., Caldwell, Idaho. Of interest to students of Idaho history chiefly because Sitka was the center of early Russian fur trade in the Pacific Northwest.

Sons of the West—Lorah B. Chaffin. The Caxton Printers, Ltd., Caldwell, Idaho. Story of the early fur trade in Wyoming and eastern Idaho.

Story of the Trapper—Agnes C. Laut. D. Appleton & Co., New York.

Trapper Days—Beulah V. Hunkins and R. H. Allen. American Book Company, New York.

Trappers and Traders of the Far West—

James Henry Daugherty. Random House, New York. A Landmark Book.

Up the Columbia for Furs—Cecil Dryden. The Caxton Printers, Ltd., Caldwell, Idaho. Based on the journals of Alexander Ross and Ross Cox, two of the early fur-gatherers of the Oregon Country.

11. GENERAL LIST

(Histories, reference sets, and other books not belonging under special lists.)

America, Land of Freedom—Gertrude Hartman. D. C. Heath & Company, Boston. An Idaho adoption.

American History—John V. and Gertrude Southworth. Iroquois Publishing Company, Syracuse, New York.

American Nation Yesterday and Today—Rolla M. Tryon and others. Ginn and Company, Boston.

American Story—Ruth Wood Gavian and W. A. Hamm. D. C. Heath & Company, Boston.

Atlas of American History—James Truslow Adams. Charles Scribner's Sons, New York. Maps: Plates 100–101; 102; 112–113; 117–119; 130–131; 138–139; 142–143; 145.

Building America. Americana Corporation, New York. Volumes I–VIII.

Building of Our Nation—Eugene C. Barker and others. Row, Peterson & Company, Evanston, Ill.

Building Our America—Clyde B. Moore and others. Charles Scribner's Sons, New York.

Caravans to the Northwest. Houghton Mifflin Company, Boston. Northwest Regional Council for groups studying Northwest problems.

Child's Idaho—Claire Boyle Bracken. Syms-York Company, Boise, Idaho.

Stories of Idaho history written for children of the elementary grades.

Early Days in the New World—John V. and Gertrude Southworth. Iroquois Publishing Company, Syracuse, New York.

Early History of Idaho—William J. McConnell. The Caxton Printers, Ltd., Caldwell, Idaho. No longer in print, this is an interesting history of early Idaho written by a man who served as governor of the state and in the United States Senate.

Heroes and Heroic Deeds of the Pacific Northwest—Henry L. Talkington. The Caxton Printers, Ltd., Caldwell, Idaho. In two volumes. Volume I is more concerned with early Idaho history while Volume II deals more generally with Oregon and Washington and with pioneer life.

History of Idaho—Hiram T. French. Lewis Publishing Company, Chicago. Now out of print but available in many libraries. Volume I is the historical volume.

History of Idaho—John Hailey. Syms-York Company, Boise, Idaho. Out of print, but available in many libraries.

History of Idaho, Gem of the Mountains—James H. Hawley. S. J. Clarke Publishing Company, Chicago. Out of print but available in many libraries. Volume I is historical.

History of Idaho Territory—W. H. Elliott. Wallace H. Elliott & Company, San Francisco. Out of print, but available in some libraries.

History of Oregon—W. H. Gray. Published by the author. Out of print, but found in some libraries.

History of Oregon—Horace D. Lyman. North Pacific Publishing Society, New York, N.Y. In four volumes.

History of Oregon, Washington, and

Idaho—Hubert Howe Bancroft. The History Company, Publishers, San Francisco. *Bancroft's Works,* Vols. XXIX, XXX, XXXI.

History of the Pacific Northwest—George W. Fuller. Alfred A. Knopf, New York, N.Y.

History of the Pacific Northwest—Joseph Schafer. The Macmillan Company, New York.

History of the State of Idaho—Cornelius J. Brosnan. Charles Scribner's Sons, New York. Revised edition published in 1948.

History of World Peoples—R. W. Cordier and E. B. Robert. Rand McNally & Company, Chicago.

History of Young America—R. W. Cordier and E. B. Robert. Rand McNally & Company, Chicago.

Idaho. Idaho State Board of Publicity, Office of the Secretary of State, Boise, Idaho. A booklet of pertinent facts about Idaho.

Idaho: A Guide in Word and Picture. Prepared by the Federal Writers' Projects of the Works Progress Administration. (American Guide Series.) Second edition. Oxford University Press, New York. See "An Essay in Idaho History," pp. 3–19.

Idaho; the Place and Its People—Byron Defenbach. American Historical Society, New York. Volume I is Idaho history.

Idaho Bibliography—Professor Maralyn Morton. Idaho State College, Pocatello, Idaho. This recent compilation of source material by Professor Morton is by far the most complete bibliography of its kind in existence.

Idaho Chronology, Nomenclature, Bibliography—John E. Rees. W. B. Conkey Company, Chicago.

Idaho Encyclopedia—Federal Writers' Project, Vardis Fisher, Director. The Caxton Printers, Ltd., Caldwell, Idaho. Section II, pp. 77–114.

Idaho of Yesterday—Thomas B. Donaldson. The Caxton Printers, Ltd., Caldwell, Idaho. Reminiscences of an Idaho pioneer about the lively early days in Idaho.

Idaho Official Publication Commemorating Fifty Years of Statehood. Fred York Printing Company, Boise, Idaho.

Idaho Yesterday and Today. Graves and Potter, Pocatello, Idaho. 1934. Souvenir Handbook of Fort Hall Centennial celebrating the hundredth anniversary of the founding of Old Fort Hall. Found in some libraries.

Illustrated History of the State of Idaho. Lewis Publishing Company, Chicago. 1899. Now out of print, this rare book is a history of Idaho Territory rather than a history of the state.

Living in Idaho—Thelma M. Rea. The Caxton Printers, Ltd., Caldwell, Idaho. Prepared by a Boise teacher as a textbook in Idaho social studies for the lower elementary grades.

Living in Our America—I. James Quillen and Edward Krug. Scott, Foresman and Company, Chicago.

My America—M. M. Ames and others. Webster Publishing Company, St. Louis, Mo.

My Country—M. M. Ames and others. Webster Publishing Company, St. Louis, Mo.

My Country's Growth—M. M. Ames and others. Webster Publishing Company, St. Louis, Mo.

New World and Its Growth—J. G. Meyer and O. S. Hamer. Follett Publishing Company, Chicago.

Once Upon a Time in America—Gertrude E. Eastman. State Department of Education, Boise, Idaho. Miss Eastman of the State Department of Education has prepared a late bibliography of social studies material for Idaho schools.

Our Great Northwest—Arthur S. Taylor and others. Harr Wagner Publishing Company, San Francisco, California.

Our New Nation—Eugene C. Barker and others. Row, Peterson & Company, Evanston, Illinois.

Pageant of America. Yale University Press, New Haven, Conn. Each volume in this valuable reference set deals with special phases of American history and development. See Index and Table of Contents.

Pioneer Days of Oregon History—S. A. Clarke. J. K. Gill Company, Portland, Ore.

Readings in Pacific Northwest History—Charles Marvin Gates, ed. University Book Store, Seattle, Wash. Valuable general source book.

Rise of Our Free Nation—Edna McGuire and T. B. Portwood. The Macmillan Company, New York.

Snake River in History—Miles Cannon. Oregon Historical Society, Vol. XX, March, 1919.

Social Studies Guide. State Department of Education, Boise, Idaho. Prepared by the Curriculum Committee as a general guide to the study of history in Idaho.

Some Idaho Monuments, Markers, and Memorials—Mary L. Smith. Eleventh Biennial Report, 1927–1928, Idaho State Historical Society, Boise, Idaho.

State We Live In—Byron Defenbach. The Caxton Printers, Ltd., Caldwell, Idaho. Out of print but found in many libraries.

Story of America—Ralph V. Harlow. Henry Holt and Company, New York.

Story of Idaho—Francis Haines. Syms-York Company, Boise, Idaho. Idaho history told in brief chapters by a former history teacher in Northern Idaho College of Education, now the Lewis-Clark Normal School.

Story of Life in America—Mary G. Kelty. Ginn and Company, Boston.

Story of Our Country—Eugene C. Barker and others. Row, Peterson & Company, Evanston, Ill.

Story of Our Country—Ruth and Willis M. West. Allyn & Bacon, Boston.

Story of Our Land and People—Glenn William Moon. Henry Holt and Company, New York.

This Is America's Story—Howard B. Wilder and others. Houghton Mifflin Company, Boston. An Idaho adoption.

Your Country and Mine—Gertrude S. Brown and others. Ginn and Company, Boston.

12. GEOGRAPHY AND GEOLOGY

American Continents—Harlan H. Barrows and others. Silver Burdett Company, New York. An Idaho adoption, grades 7–8.

American History and Its Geographic Conditions—Ellen Churchill Semple. Houghton Mifflin Company, Boston.

American Nations—Wallace W. Atwood and Helen Goss Thomas. Ginn and Company, Boston.

At Home on Our Earth—Gertrude Whipple and Preston E. James. The Macmillan Company, New York. An Idaho adoption, grades 7–8.

Blazing Trails in Rugged Idaho. State Board of Publicity, Office of the Secretary of State, Boise, Idaho. Publicity booklet.

Columbia River—Horace D. Lyman. G. P. Putnam's Sons, New York.

Columbia River. Bureau of Reclamation,

U.S. Department of the Interior, Washington, D.C. Also listed in Groups 1 and 6, this 1947 report gives much valuable information concerning the geography of the Snake River Basin and the Clark Fork-Clearwater Subdivision of Idaho.

Down the River of No Return—Robert G. Bailey. R. G. Bailey Printing Company, Lewiston, Idaho. Good account of the Salmon River.

Down the River of No Return—Philip J. Shenon and John C. Reed. National Geographic Magazine, July, 1936. National Geographic Society, Washington, D.C.

Geography and World Affairs—Stephen B. Jones and Marion F. Murphy. Rand McNally & Company, Chicago.

Geography of a Working World—Wallace R. McConnell and Helen Harter. Rand McNally & Company, Chicago.

Geography of American Peoples—Wallace R. McConnell. Rand McNally & Company, Chicago.

Geography of Idaho—Ernest E. Holmes. The Macmillan Company, New York. This booklet is found in a few libraries.

Geology and Mineral Resources of Southeastern Idaho—George Rogers. Superintendent of Documents, Government Printing Office, Washington, D.C.

Hell's Canyon—Robert G. Bailey. R. G. Bailey Printing Company, Lewiston, Idaho. The Snake River Canyon between Oregon and Idaho, of special interest because of its power possibilities.

Idaho: A Guide in Word and Picture. Prepared by the Federal Writers' Projects of the Works Progress Administration. (American Guide Series.) Second edition. Oxford University Press, New York. See "Idaho from the Air," beginning on page 41; and Part III,

"The Primitive Area," beginning on page 235.

Idaho Boundary Survey. Geological Survey Bulletin No. 170. U.S. Geological Survey, U.S. Department of the Interior, Washington, D.C.

Idaho Encyclopedia—Vardis Fisher, Director. The Caxton Printers, Ltd., Caldwell, Idaho. Section I, "The Physical State," pp. 15–76.

Idaho Little Blue Book. Idaho State Board of Publicity, Office of the Secretary of State, Boise, Idaho. Booklet of physical features and facts.

Idaho the Gem State. Scenic Idaho, No. 2, 1949. Belcher Publishing Company, Boise, Idaho.

Incredible Idaho—Dorine Goertzen. Scenic Idaho, Fall Issue, 1954. Belcher Publishing Company, Boise, Idaho.

Journeys Through the Americas—DeForest Stull and Roy W. Hatch. Allyn and Bacon, Boston.

Life in America: The West—Dale L. Morgan. Fideler Company, Grand Rapids, Mich.

Neighbors on Our Earth—Gertrude Whipple and Preston E. James. The Macmillan Company, New York. An Idaho adoption, grades 7–8.

Our American Neighbors—J. G. Meyer and others. Follett Publishing Company, Chicago.

Our Home, State, and Continent—Albert P. Brigham and Charles T. McFarlane. American Book Company, New York. Edition containing the Idaho Supplement. Former Idaho adoption.

Physiography of the Western United States—Nevin M. Fenneman. McGraw-Hill Book Company, New York.

Pioneer Days in Idaho County—Sister M. Alfreda Elsensohn. The Caxton Printers, Ltd., Caldwell, Idaho. Volume II contains much geographical material about this section of the state.

Prehistoric America—Anna Terry White. E. M. Hale Company, Eau Claire, Wis. A Landmark Book.

Rocks and Their Stories—Carroll Lane Fenton and M. A. Fenton. Doubleday & Company, Inc., Garden City, New York.

Rocky Mountains—Wallace W. Atwood. Vanguard Press, Inc., New York.

Romance of the Rivers—John T. Faris. Harper & Brothers, New York. Includes the Columbia River.

Sketches of Idaho Geology—Edward F. Rhodenbaugh. The Caxton Printers, Ltd., Caldwell, Idaho. A former professor at Idaho State College has told the fascinating story of Idaho's strange geology.

Tetons, The—Fritiof Fryxell. University of California Press, Berkeley, Calif. Though the Tetons are actually just over the boundary in Wyoming, the region is of great interest to the people of Idaho.

United States in the Western World—Wallace W. Atwood. Ginn and Company, Boston.

Western United States—Harold Wellman Fairbanks. D. C. Heath & Company, Boston.

World View—Clarence W. Sorensen. Silver, Burdett Company, New York.

13. INDIANS AND INDIAN LIFE

Bannock Indian War of 1878—George Francis Brimlow. The Caxton Printers, Ltd., Caldwell, Idaho. Based largely on official records of the War Department.

Battle of Bear River—Leslie Sudweeks. Seeing Idaho, May, 1937. Files of this old magazine, published in 1937–38, found in a few libraries.

Battle of Pierre's Hole. Seeing Idaho, August, 1937. Files of this old magazine, published 1937–38, found in a few libraries.

Book of Indian Crafts and Costumes—Bernard S. Mason. A. S. Barnes & Co., New York.

Chief Joseph—Chester Anders Fee. Wilson-Erickson, Incorporated, New York.

Chief Joseph of the Nez Perces—Shannon Garst. Julian Messner, Inc., New York.

Dorion Woman—J. Neilson Barry. Seeing Idaho, August, 1937. A few libraries have old files of this magazine.

First Book of Indians—Mary Elting. Franklin Watts, Inc., New York. A juvenile book.

Handbook of American Indians—Frederick Webb Hodge, ed. Government Printing Office, Washington, D.C. This is Bulletin No. 30, Parts 1–2, of the Smithsonian Institution, Bureau of American Ethnology.

Hear Me, My Chiefs!—Lucullus Virgil McWhorter. The Caxton Printers, Ltd., Caldwell, Idaho. The story of Chief Joseph and the Nez Perce War.

Heroism of Timothy—Fred Ulen. Seeing Idaho, January, 1938. Files of this old magazine found in a few libraries.

How the Great Chief Tyhee Was Buried—Alfred M. Grubb. Seeing Idaho, January, 1938. Files of this old magazine found in a few libraries.

Indian Art of the Americas—Le Roy H. Appleton. Charles Scribner's Sons, New York.

Indian Cradle Boards—Ora B. Hawkins. Eighteenth Biennial Report, 1941–1942, Idaho State Historical Society, Boise, Idaho.

Indian Experiences—DeCost Smith. The Caxton Printers, Ltd., Caldwell, Idaho.

An artist tells of his experiences among Indian tribes of the West.

Indian Forest and Range—Jay P. Kinney. Forest Enterprises, Washington, D.C.

Indian Legends of the Pacific Northwest—Ella E. Clark. University of California Press, Berkeley, Calif.

Indian Picture Writing—John E. Rees. Eleventh Biennial Report, 1926–27, State Historical Society, Boise, Idaho.

Indian Rock Writing in Idaho—Richard P. Erwin. Twelfth Biennial Report, 1929–30, State Historical Society, Boise, Idaho.

Indian Tribes of North America—John R. Swanton. Bulletin No. 145, Smithsonian Institution, Bureau of American Ethnology, Government Printing Office, Washington, D.C.

Indian Wars of Idaho—Royal Ross Arnold. The Caxton Printers, Ltd., Caldwell, Idaho. Now out of print, this book is found in most good libraries in Idaho.

Indians at Work. U.S. Bureau of Indian Affairs, Washington, D.C. No longer published, files of this magazine may sometimes be borrowed by writing to the Indian Service, U.S. Department of the Interior, Washington, D.C.

Indians of the United States—Clark Wissler. Doubleday, Page & Co., New York. The dean of the American Museum of Natural History writes with considerable emphasis on Indian life of today.

Massacre of the Ward Family—William M. Ward. In the Sixth Biennial Report, 1917–1918, State Historical Society, Boise, Idaho.

My Life and Experiences among Our Hostile Indians—Major-General O. O. Howard. A. D. Worthington & Co., Hartford, Conn. General Howard's own story, including his account of the Indian wars in Idaho.

Myths and Legends of the Pacific Northwest—Katherine B. Judson. A. C. McClurg & Co., Chicago.

Nez Perce Delegation to St. Louis in 1831—Francis Haines. Pacific Historical Society, March, 1937.

Nez Perces Since Lewis and Clark—Kate C. McBeth. Fleming H. Revell Company, Chicago.

Nez Perce War Letters—Eugene B. Chaffee. In Fifteenth Biennial Report, 1935–36, State Historical Society, Boise, Idaho.

North American Indians—Rose Amelia Palmer. Government Printing Office, Washington, D.C. A publication of the Smithsonian Institution, Washington, D.C.

Otter Massacre—George H. Abbott. In Reports, Vol. I, No. 3, October, 1908, State Historical Society, Boise, Idaho.

Pioneer Boy among the Indians—E. N. Wilson and Howard R. Driggs. Aladdin Books, New York. This is the book formerly called *The White Indian Boy,* and is the story of Uncle Nick Wilson and his boyhood among the Indians of southeastern Idaho and northern Utah.

Real Book About Indians—Michael Gorham. Garden City Books, New York.

Red Eagles of the Northwest—Francis Haines. Bookhaven Press, Los Angeles, Calif. About the Nez Perce Indians and Chief Joseph.

Red Heroines of the Northwest—Byron Defenbach. The Caxton Printers, Ltd., Caldwell, Idaho. Now out of print, this book tells the stories of Sacajawea, Madame Dorion, and Jane.

Sheepeater Campaign—Col. W. C. Brown. Tenth Biennial Report, 1925–26, State Historical Society, Boise, Idaho.

Sinopah the Indian Boy—James Willard Schultz. Houghton Mifflin Company, Boston.

Treaty Rock at Post Falls, Idaho. Seventeenth Biennial Report, 1939–1940, Idaho State Historical Society, Boise, Idaho.

U.S. Indian Service, Washington, D.C. Write for special information you may desire.

War Chief Joseph—Helen Addison Howard and Dan McGrath. The Caxton Printers, Ltd., Caldwell, Idaho. Biography of the great Nez Perce war chief.

With the Indains in the Rockies—James Willard Schultz. Houghton Mifflin Company, Boston.

Yellow Wolf: His Own Story—Lucullus Virgil McWhorter. The Caxton Printers, Ltd., Caldwell, Idaho. These stories are told from the Indian's point of view.

14. LIVESTOCK AND RANCHING

Adventures of an Idaho Lamb. Scenic Idaho, No. 1, 1949, Belcher Publishing Company, Boise, Idaho.

Album of Horses—Marguerite Henry. Rand McNally & Company, Chicago.

America's Sheep Trails—Edward N. Wentworth. Iowa State College Press, Ames, Iowa.

Approved Practices in Beef Production—Elwood M. Juergenson. Interstate Printers and Publishers, Inc., Danville, Ill.

Approved Practices in Dairying—Elwood M. Juergenson. Interstate Printers & Publishers, Inc., Danville, Ill.

Back Trailing on Open Range—Luke D. Sweetman. The Caxton Printers, Ltd., Caldwell, Idaho, 1951. Experiences on the open range, 1885 to 1900.

Cow Country Cavalcade—Maurice Frink. Johnson Publishing Co., Boulder, Colo. Of general interest to cattlemen and ranchmen.

Cowboy Encyclopedia—Bruce Grant. Rand McNally & Company, Chicago.

Cowboys and Cattle Kings—C. L. Sonnichsen. University of Oklahoma Press, Norman, Okla.

Cowboys and Cattle Trails—Shannon Garst. Wheeler Publishing Company, Chicago.

Cowboys of America—Sanford Tousey. Rand McNally & Company, Chicago.

Day of the Cattleman—Ernest Staples Osgood. University of Minnesota Press, Minneapolis, Minn.

Golden Fleece—Hughie (Florence) Call. Houghton Mifflin Company, Boston. Life on a sheep ranch.

Home Below Hell's Canyon—Grace Jordan. Thomas Y. Crowell Company, New York. The wife of Idaho's recent governor describes their family life on a sheep ranch in the famous Hell's Canyon country.

Horses Across America—Jeanne Mellin. E. P. Dutton & Co., Inc., New York. Colored illustrations add to the interest of this book.

Horses Are for Warriors—William E. Sanderson. The Caxton Printers, Ltd., Caldwell, Idaho. Adventures of Lame Wolf, a young Nez Perce warrior, who brings about the use of horses by his tribe. These horses were the ancestors of the Appaloosas, the spotted horses now so popular among horse fanciers of the Northwest.

Irrigated Pastures—Hamilton and others. Farmers' Bulletin No. 1973. Soil Conservation Service, Yates Building, Boise, Idaho.

Log of a Cowboy—Andy Adams. Houghton Mifflin Company, Boston.

Probably the most famous of all books about cowboys and range life.

More Pounds of Meat—More Pounds of Wool—White. Soil Conservation Service, Yates Building, Boise, Idaho.

Now Ninety and Nine Plus—Julia Arthur. Scenic Idaho, Spring Issue, 1954. Belcher Publishing Company, Boise, Idaho.

Palomino and Other Horses—Wesley Dennis. World Book Company, New York.

Pinnacle Jake—Albert Benton Snyder. The Caxton Printers, Ltd., Caldwell, Idaho. A humorous story of life in the cattle country of the Northwest.

Rebuilding the Federal Range. Bureau of Land Management, U.S. Department of the Interior, Washington, D.C.

Regrassing Southern Idaho Ranges—Hall. Extension Bulletin No. 146. University of Idaho, Extension Division, Moscow, Idaho.

Rodeo—Glen Rounds. Holiday House, Inc., New York. Juvenile.

So This Is Ranching!—Inez Puckett McEwen. The Caxton Printers, Ltd., Caldwell, Idaho. This famous story tells about life on an Idaho ranch with mingled humor and wisdom.

Trail Driving Days—Dee Brown and Martin F. Schmitt. Charles Scribner's Sons, New York. Superbly illustrated book of the cattle country—trails, driving, marketing, and other phases of the cattle business.

Trail Tales—James David Gillilan. Abingdon Press, New York.

Trails Plowed Under—Charles M. Russell. Doubleday, Page & Co., New York. Wyoming and Montana cattle country, described and illustrated by the famous "Cowboy Artist." Conditions described are similar in many ways to the early cattle industry in southern Idaho.

When the Long Horned Cattle of Texas Came to Idaho—James R. Keith. Sixteenth Biennial Report, 1937-1938, Idaho State Historical Society, Boise, Idaho.

Wild Horse of the West—Walker D. Wyman. The Caxton Printers, Ltd., Caldwell, Idaho. All the adventure and color associated with the wild horses of the West tingles this comprehensive history of the noblest of mammals.

Wild Horses—Suzanne Taylor. Scenic Idaho, Third Quarter, 1950. Belcher Publishing Company, Boise, Idaho.

Wyoming Cattle Trails—John K. Rollinson. The Caxton Printers, Ltd., Caldwell, Idaho. This story of the western cattle industry tells, among other things, of the movement of Oregon cattle eastward. Also stories of the long trail drives told in range lingo. Conditions described were, no doubt, quite similar to those on the great territorial cattle ranches of southern Idaho.

15. MINERALS AND MINING

Blackbird, Most Unusual Mine in the United States—George Young and Don Haash. Scenic Idaho, Third Quarter, 1952. Belcher Publishing Company, Boise, Idaho.

Bonanza Trail—Muriel V. S. Wolle. Indiana University, Bloomington, Ind. Ghost towns and mining camps of the West.

Cobalt Deposits in the Blackbird District of Lemhi County. Idaho Bureau of Mines and Geology, Pamphlet No. 61, University of Idaho, Moscow, Idaho.

Coeur d'Alenes, Idaho's Fantastic Min-

ing Area—Betty Spencer. Scenic Idaho, Third Quarter, 1950. Belcher Publishing Company, Boise, Idaho.

Early and Recent Mining Activity in Central Idaho—John C. Reed. Press Bulletin No. 18. University of Idaho, Moscow, Idaho.

Elementary Methods of Placer Mining. Pamphlet No. 35. Idaho Bureau of Mines and Geology, University of Idaho, Moscow, Idaho.

Field Book of Common Rocks and Minerals—Frederick Brewster Loomis. G. P. Putnam's Sons, New York.

Field Guide to Rocks and Minerals—F. H. Pough. Houghton Mifflin Company, Boston.

Geography, Geology and Mineral Resources of Southeastern Idaho—George R. Mansfield. See Group 12.

Geology and Gold Resources of North-Central Idaho. Bulletin No. 7. Idaho Bureau of Mines and Geology, University of Idaho, Moscow, Idaho.

Geology and Mining Resources of Part of Southeastern Idaho. Professional Paper No. 152. U.S. Geological Survey, Department of the Interior, Washington, D.C.

Geology and Ore Deposits, Alturas Quadrangle. Bulletin No. 5. Idaho Bureau of Mines and Geology, University of Idaho, Moscow, Idaho.

Geology and Ore Deposits, Atlanta District. Pamphlet No. 49. Idaho Bureau of Mines and Geology, University of Idaho, Moscow, Idaho.

Geology and Ore Deposits, Bayhorse Region of Custer County. Bulletin No. 877. U.S. Geological Survey, Department of the Interior, Washington, D.C.

Geology and Ore Deposits, Boise County. Bulletin 944C. U.S. Geological Survey, Department of the Interior, Washington, D.C.

Geology and Ore Deposits, Dixie Mining District—Livingstone. Vol. IX, No. 2. School of Mines, University of Idaho, Moscow, Idaho.

Geology and Ore Deposits, Elk City District in Idaho County. Circular 9. U.S. Geological Survey, Department of the Interior, Washington, D.C.

Geology and Ore Deposits, Florence Mining District. Pamphlet No. 46. Idaho Bureau of Mines and Geology, University of Idaho, Moscow, Idaho.

Geology and Ore Deposits, Lemhi County. Bulletin 528. U.S. Geological Survey, Department of the Interior, Washington, D.C.

Geology and Ore Deposits, Mackay Region. Bulletin 97. U.S. Geological Survey, Department of the Interior, Washington, D.C.

Geology and Ore Deposits Near Murray. Pamphlet No. 47. Idaho Bureau of Mines and Geology, University of Idaho, Moscow, Idaho.

Geology and Ore Deposits, Rocky Bar Quadrangle. Pamphlet No. 26. Idaho Bureau of Mines and Geology, University of Idaho, Moscow, Idaho.

Geology and Ore Deposits, Shoshone County. Bulletin 732. U.S. Geological Survey, Department of the Interior, Washington, D.C.

Geology and Ore Deposits, Warren Mining District. Pamphlet No. 45. Idaho Bureau of Mines and Geology, University of Idaho, Moscow, Idaho.

Geology and Ore Deposits, Wood River Region. Bulletin 814. U.S. Geological Survey, Department of the Interior, Washington, D.C.

Geology and Ore Resources, Boise Basin. Bulletin No. 9. Idaho Bureau of Mines and Geology, University of Idaho, Moscow, Idaho.

Geology and Ore Resources, Clark Fork

District. Bulletin No. 12. Idaho Bureau of Mines and Geology, University of Idaho, Moscow, Idaho.

Gold in Idaho. Pamphlet No. 68. Idaho Bureau of Mines and Geology, University of Idaho, Moscow, Idaho.

Handbook of Fluorescent Gems and Minerals—Jack A. DeMent. Mineralogist Publishing Co., Portland, Ore.

Handbook of Uranium Minerals—Jack A. DeMent and H. C. Dake. Mineralogist Publishing Co., Portland, Ore.

Idaho: A Guide in Word and Picture. Prepared by the Federal Writers' Projects of the Works Progress Administration. (American Guide Series.) Second edition. Oxford University Press, New York. See Part IV, "Idaho Lore": "Buried Treasure," beginning on page 251, and "Ghost Towns," beginning on page 260.

Idaho Building Stone. Idaho State Inspector of Mines, Boise, Idaho. Published in the Twenty-Sixth Annual Report, Idaho Mining Industry.

Idaho Encyclopedia—Vardis Fisher. The Caxton Printers, Ltd., Caldwell, Idaho. "Mining," Section III, pp. 126–31; "Minerals," Section III, pp. 131–33.

Idaho's Glory of Gold and Men—Historic Old Pierce—Wilma Merrill. Scenic Idaho, September–October, 1953.

Idaho's Monazite Industry. Scenic Idaho, Vol. 4, No. 2, 1949.

Idaho State Inspector of Mines, Boise, Idaho. This office issues an annual report of the Idaho Mining Industry, and Biennial Reports every two years. These are very valuable sources about mining and minerals in Idaho.

Lead-Silver Deposits of Clark Fork District of Bonner County. Bulletin 944B. U.S. Geological Survey, Department of the Interior, Washington, D.C.

Metal and Coal Mining Districts of Idaho. Pamphlet No. 57. Idaho Bureau of Mines and Geology, University of Idaho, Moscow, Idaho. This also contains notes on the nonmetallic mineral resources of the state.

Mineral Deposits of Idaho. Mining Industry of Idaho, Fifty-First Annual Report, 1949. Office of the State Inspector of Mines, Boise, Idaho.

Minerals and How to Study Them—Edward Salisbury Dana. John Wiley & Sons, Inc., New York.

Minerals, Metals, and Gems—Alpheus Hyatt Verrill. L. C. Page and Company, Boston.

Mining Salutes Idaho's Fifty Years of Statehood, 1890–1940. Idaho Mining Association, Boise, Idaho. A booklet.

Nonmetallic Minerals—R. B. Ladoo. McGraw-Hill Book Company, New York.

Ore Deposits in Tertiary Lavas in the Salmon River Mountains. Pamphlet No. 25. Idaho Bureau of Mines and Geology, University of Idaho, Moscow, Idaho.

Phosphate. Mining Industry of Idaho, Thirty-Eighth Annual Report, 1936. Office of State Inspector of Mines, Boise, Idaho.

Phosphate Deposits in Idaho—Kirkham. University of Idaho, Moscow, Idaho. Reprint No. 1.

Placer Mining Districts in Boise County. Bulletin 7028. U.S. Geological Survey, Department of the Interior, Washington, D.C.

Placer Mining Districts of Idaho County. Bulletin 7023. U.S. Geological Survey, Department of the Interior, Washington, D.C.

Portland Cement Material Near Pocatello. Pamphlet No. 28. Idaho Bureau of Mines and Geology, University of Idaho, Moscow, Idaho.

Quicksilver in Idaho. Mining Industry of Idaho, Forty-Eighth Annual Report, 1946. Office of State Inspector of Mines, Boise, Idaho.

Reminiscences of Early Mining Camps—McPherson. Pacific Northwest Quarterly, July, 1938.

Riches from the Earth—Carroll Lane Fenton and M. A. Fenton. Longmans, Green & Co., New York. A juvenile book.

Rocket of the Comstock—Ethel V. Manter. The Caxton Printers, Ltd., Caldwell, Idaho. "An exciting blend of the story of the Comstock Lode and of its famous bonanza king, John W. Mackay," for whom Mackay, Idaho, was named. This famous mining district in Nevada was much like that of our own Silver City district in Idaho.

Silver and Gold Deposits of the Yankee Fork District. Pamphlet No. 83. Idaho Bureau of Mines and Geology, University of Idaho, Moscow, Idaho.

Silver Strike—William T. Stoll and H. W. Whicker. Little, Brown & Company, Boston. Story of the Coeur d'Alene Mining District.

Soda Springs, Idaho's New Industrial Midget. Scenic Idaho, Vacation Issue, 1953.

Strategic Minerals of Idaho—Arthur William Fahrenwald. Press Bulletin No. 20. University of Idaho, Moscow, Idaho.

Tungsten, Cinnabar, Manganese, Molybdenum and Tin Deposits in Idaho—Livingstone. School of Mines Bulletins, Vol. 14, No. 2. University of Idaho, Moscow, Idaho.

16. MISSIONARIES AND MISSIONS

Elkanah and Mary Walker, Pioneers Among the Spokanes—Clifford Merrill Drury. The Caxton Printers, Ltd., Caldwell, Idaho.

Henry Harmon Spalding, Pioneer of Old Oregon—Clifford Merrill Drury. The Caxton Printers, Ltd., Caldwell, Idaho. Story of the Spalding Mission near Lewiston.

History of the Coeur d'Alene Mission of the Sacred Heart—Rev. Edmund R. Cody. The Caxton Printers, Ltd., Caldwell, Idaho.

Home Missions on the American Frontier—Colin B. Goodykoontz. The Caxton Printers, Ltd., Caldwell, Idaho.

How Marcus Whitman Saved Oregon—Oliver W. Nixon. Star Publishing Company, Chicago.

Idaho's First Mill—Clifford Merrill Drury. Seeing Idaho. Files of this old magazine, formerly published by Graves and Potter, Pocatello, Idaho, are found in a few libraries.

Indian Missions of the Pacific Coast—Rev. Myron Eells. Union Press, Philadelphia.

Jason Lee, Prophet of New Oregon—Cornelius J. Brosnan. The Macmillan Company, New York.

Jason Lee's Diary. Oregon Historical Society Quarterly, Volume 17. Diary written while going to the Oregon Country in 1834.

Jesuits in Old Oregon—William Norbert Bischoff. The Caxton Printers, Ltd., Caldwell, Idaho.

Life, Letters and Travels of Father Pierre-Jean de Smet—Hiram M. Chittenden and Alfred T. Richardson. Francis P. Harper, New York.

Marcus and Narcissa Whitman, Pioneers of Oregon—James H. Daugherty. Viking Press, New York.

Marcus Whitman, Pathfinder and Patriot—Rev. Myron Eells. Lowman & Hanford, Seattle, Wash.

Marcus Whitman, Pioneer and Martyr—Clifford Merrill Drury. The Caxton Printers, Ltd., Caldwell, Idaho.

Memoirs of the West—Eliza Spalding Warren. Marsh Printing Company, Portland, Ore. The first white child born in Idaho tells her own story of life at Spalding Mission and in the West.

Narcissa Whitman, Pioneer—Jeannette Easton. Harcourt, Brace & Company, New York.

Oregon Missions—James W. Bashford. Abingdon Press, New York.

Oregon Missions and Travels over the Rocky Mountains in 1845–46—Pierre Jean de Smet, edited by Reuben Gold Thwaites. Vols. 28 and 29, *Early Western Travels*. The Arthur H. Clark Company, Cleveland, Ohio. These two volumes are found in most good libraries in the West.

Reminiscences of a Missionary Bishop—Daniel S. Tuttle. Thomas Whittaker, New York. Bishop Tuttle, Idaho Territory's well-loved missionary, tells his own story.

Salmon River Mission—Samuel M. Beal. Seeing Idaho, May, 1937. Files of this old magazine, no longer published, found in a few libraries.

Spalding Mission—Byron Defenbach. Seventeenth Biennial Report, 1939–1940, Idaho State Historical Society, Boise, Idaho.

Whitman's Ride Through Savage Lands—Oliver W. Nixon. Winona Publishing Company, Chicago.

17. PIONEER LIFE

Boise, the Peace Valley—Bird. See Group 5.

Bonneville County in the Making—Clark. See Group 5.

Busy Life of Eighty-Five Years—Meeker. See Group 2.

Early Days in Old Oregon—Katherine B. Judson. Metropolitan Press, Portland, Ore.

Early History of Idaho—McConnell. See Group 11.

Early Reminiscences of "Uncle" Tom Beale. Fifth Biennial Report, 1915–1916, Idaho State Historical Society, Boise, Idaho.

Frontier Law—McConnell and Driggs. See Group 3.

Heroes and Heroic Deeds of the Pacific Northwest—Talkington. See Group 11.

History of Southeastern Idaho—Beal. See Group 5.

History of Teton Valley—Driggs. See Group 5.

Idaho of Yesterday—Donaldson. See Group 11.

Letters of Long Ago—Agnes Just Reid. The Caxton Printers, Ltd., Caldwell, Idaho. A pioneer of Bingham County writes of early life in southeastern Idaho.

Life and Adventures of Alex Toponce—Alexander Toponce. Century Printing Co., Salt Lake City, Utah, 1923. Another pioneer of southeastern Idaho tells the story of his life.

My Adventures in the Far West—Charles Nelson Teeter. Thirteenth Biennial Report, 1931–1932, Idaho State Historical Society, Boise, Idaho.

Pioneer Days in Idaho County—Elsensohn. See Group 5.

Pioneer Days of Oregon History—S. A. Clarke. Vol. I–II. J. K. Gill Company, Portland, Oregon.

Reminiscences of a Pioneer—W. A. Goulder. Timothy Regan, Boise, Idaho.

Reminiscences of Early Idaho—Charles Shirley Walgamott. The Caxton Printers, Ltd., Caldwell, Idaho. Early life in southern Idaho.

Reminiscences of Francis Mylon Redfield. Printed privately by Ethel Redfield, Pocatello, Idaho.

Six Decades Back—Charles Shirley Walgamott. The Caxton Printers, Ltd., Caldwell, Idaho. Early life in the Magic Valley section of southern Idaho.

Stories of Early Times in the Great West for Young Readers—M. Florence Bass. The Bobbs-Merrill Company, Indianapolis, Ind.

Trails of Early Idaho—Anderson and Goodhart. See Group 7.

Valiant Seven—Netta Sheldon Phelps. The Caxton Printers, Ltd., Caldwell, Idaho. The story of the Sager children, who were orphaned on a wild frontier.

Valley of the Tall Grass—Hawes. See Group 5.

We Sagebrush Folks—Annie Pike Greenwood. D. Appleton-Century Company, New York.

Western Galaxy—Tullidge. Juvenile Instructor Office, Salt Lake City, Utah. An old magazine with articles on the early West.

18. READING FOR PLEASURE AND PROFIT

NOTE: This list contains the titles of books recommended more for entertainment than for information, though many of them are valuable for their historic backgrounds and their pictures of life in the Northwest.

Arrowrock—Earl Wayland Bowman. The Caxton Printers, Ltd., Caldwell, Idaho. Collection of poems and stories.

Beavers, Kings and Cabins—Constance Lindsay Skinner. The Macmillan Company, New York.

Black Feather—La Verne Harriet Fitzgerald. The Caxton Printers, Ltd., Caldwell, Idaho. Stories of the Sheepeater Indians in the Yellowstone.

Boy, Grizzly, and Wolf—Peter Gray Wolf. The Caxton Printers, Ltd., Caldwell, Idaho. Peter Gray Wolf's stories of Indians of the Northwest.

Broken Fang—Rutherford Montgomery. The Caxton Printers, Ltd., Caldwell, Idaho. Story of a half-dog and half-wolf, set in the Rocky Mountain Northwest.

Bunch Quitter—Don Patton. The Caxton Printers, Ltd., Caldwell, Idaho. Story of a Western cow pony that refused to be submissive to men who misunderstood him.

Capture of the Golden Stallion—Rutherford Montgomery. Little, Brown & Company, Boston.

Carcajou—Rutherford Montgomery. The Caxton Printers, Ltd., Caldwell, Idaho. Formerly on the Idaho Reading Circle list.

Christmas Horse—Glenn Balch. Thomas Y. Crowell Company, New York.

Covered Wagon—Emerson Hough. Grosset & Dunlap, New York. A novel of the Oregon Trail.

Cowboy Boots—Shannon Garst. Abingdon-Cokesbury Press, Nashville, Tenn. Juvenile.

Cowboy Tommy's Roundup—Sanford Tousey. Doubleday, Doran & Company, Inc., New York.

54-40 or Fight—Emerson Hough. A. L. Burt Company, New York. Historical novel of the struggle between England and the United States for the Oregon Country.

Fighting Sheepman—Ray Palmer Tracy. Little, Brown & Company, Boston. Northwest sheep ranch.

From Honeymoon to Massacre—Stella

Parker Peterson. Review & Herald Publishing Association, Washington, D.C. Romantic and tragic story of the Whitmans.

Gotch, the Story of a Cowhorse—Luke D. Sweetman. The Caxton Printers, Ltd., Caldwell, Idaho. Story of old cattle trails of the Middle West.

High Trail—Elers Koch. The Caxton Printers, Ltd., Caldwell, Idaho. Thrilling adventures on a pack trip into the Clearwater wilderness in Idaho.

Idaho Lore—Federal Writers' Project. The Caxton Printers, Ltd., Caldwell, Idaho.

Idaho Sprout—John Baumann. William Morrow & Company, New York. Story of a boyhood in the Big Camas Prairie country of the Wood River section of southern Idaho.

Indian Fur—Glenn Balch. Thomas Y. Crowell Company, New York. Idaho's own Glenn Balch tells an interesting story of a boy's adventures among the Blackfeet and Shoshones.

Indian Paint—Glenn Balch. Grosset & Dunlap, New York. Story of an Indian pony.

Indian Saddle Up—Glenn Balch. Thomas Y. Crowell Company, New York. Indians and their horses.

Indians and Cowboys—Sanford Tousey. E. M. Hale & Company, Publishers, Eau Claire, Wis. A Cadmus Book.

Josie and Joe—Ruth Gipson Plowhead. The Caxton Printers, Ltd., Caldwell, Idaho. Adventures of an Idaho tomboy and her brother. A Junior Literary Guild selection.

Josie and Joe Carry On—Ruth Gipson Plowhead. The Caxton Printers, Ltd., Caldwell, Idaho. Adventures of Idaho twins.

Last of the Sea Otters—Harold Mc-Cracken. Frederick A. Stokes Company, Philadelphia. Story of the famous fur animals of the Northwest Coast which led the Russians into the fur trade.

Lone Bull's Mistake—James Willard Schultz. Grosset & Dunlap, New York. Famous Indian story by a man who lived much of his life among the Blackfeet.

Lord Grizzly—Frederick E. Manfred. McGraw-Hill Book Company, New York. The romantic story of Hugh Glass, a famous mountain man.

Lost Horse—Glenn Balch. Thomas Y. Crowell Company, New York. For youthful readers.

Louisiana Purchase—Robert Tallant. Random House, New York. A Landmark Book.

Lucretia Ann in the Golden West—Ruth Gipson Plowhead. The Caxton Printers, Ltd., Caldwell, Idaho. Formerly an Idaho Reading Circle book.

Lucretia Ann on the Oregon Trail—Ruth Gipson Plowhead. The Caxton Printers, Ltd., Caldwell, Idaho. Formerly an Idaho Reading Circle selection.

Lucretia Ann on the Sagebrush Plains—Ruth Gipson Plowhead. The Caxton Printers, Ltd., Caldwell, Idaho. One of the well-known Lucretia Ann series.

Midnight Colt—Glenn Balch. Thomas Y. Crowell Company, New York. A ranch story by Idaho's well-known writer of juvenile stories.

Mile High Cabin—Ruth Gipson Plowhead. The Caxton Printers, Ltd., Caldwell, Idaho. The story of four talented youngsters transplanted to Idaho, where they built a new life for themselves.

Oak's Long Shadow—Olive Burt. The John C. Winston Company, Philadelphia. Story of the Basques in south-western Idaho.

Old Man Crow's Boy—John Baumann. William Morrow & Company, New York. A youth's adventures in early days in the Wood River country of southern Idaho.

Ol' Paul, the Mighty Logger—Glen Rounds. E. M. Hale & Company, Publishers, Eau Claire, Wis. A Cadmus Book.

Paul Bunyan Swings His Axe—Dell J. McCormick. The Caxton Printers, Ltd., Caldwell, Idaho. Story of the fabulous deeds of Paul Bunyan, mythical lumberjack giant.

Real Book About the Wild West—C. A. Regli. Garden City Books, New York. One of the Doubleday Real Book Series.

Ride, Cowboy, Ride—William Stephen Warren. E. M. Hale & Company, Publishers, Eau Claire, Wis. Story of a boy on the spring roundup. A Cadmus Book.

Rogue's Valley—Evelyn L. Bronson. J. B. Lippincott Company, Philadelphia. The story of the Rogue River Indians in southwestern Oregon.

Sacajawea of the Shoshones—Delia Florence Emmons. Binfords & Mort, Portland, Ore.

Seek the Dark Gold—Jo Evalin Lundy. The John C. Winston Company, Philadelphia. Fur traders and trappers in the Northwest.

Stories of Idaho—Lyda Hoffman Bruneau. Bailey Printing Co., Lewiston, Idaho. An interesting collection found in listings by the State Department of Education.

Story of Man in Yellowstone—Merrill D. Beal. The Caxton Printers, Ltd., Caldwell, Idaho. History, reference and guidebook of Yellowstone National Park by an Idaho State College professor who spends many of his summers in the park.

Swede Homestead—Nancy Mae Anderson. The Caxton Printers, Ltd., Caldwell, Idaho. A sincere picture of homesteading in northern Idaho.

Tall Timber Tales—Dell J. McCormick. The Caxton Printers, Ltd., Caldwell, Idaho. A collection of rollicking Paul Bunyan stories for children of all ages.

Trail of the Spanish Horse—James Willard Schultz. Houghton Mifflin Company, Boston. According to history, the first horses were brought to America by early Spanish invaders.

Trailer Trio—Emma Atkins Jacobs. The John C. Winston Company, Philadelphia.

Wilderness River—Marguerite Isabel Ross. Harper & Brothers, New York. A boy's adventures during the fur era.

Winter Horse—Glenn Balch. Thomas Y. Crowell Company, New York. Another horse story by Idaho's writer of juvenile stories.

Young Mac of Vancouver—Mary Jane Carr. Thomas Y. Crowell Company, New York.

19. RECREATIONS, SCENERY AND SCENIC ATTRACTIONS

Among the "Craters of the Moon"—R. W. Limbert. National Geographic Magazine, March, 1924. National Geographic Society, Washington, D.C.

Craters of the Moon National Monument—Harold T. Stearns. Bulletin No. 13. Idaho Bureau of Mines and Geology, University of Idaho, Moscow, Idaho.

Exploring our National Parks and Monuments—Devereaux Butcher. Houghton

Mifflin Company, Boston. Includes Yellowstone Park and Craters of the Moon National Monument.

Golden Road to Adventure—This is the title of a beautifully illustrated periodical issued by the Brink-and-a-Half Club. Published in Lewiston, Idaho, it describes and pictures outstanding attractions of northern Idaho.

Guide to Craters of the Moon National Monument—Harold T. Stearns. The Caxton Printers, Ltd., Caldwell, Idaho. Now out of print, this guidebook is found in some libraries.

Hell's Canyon—Bailey. See Group 12.

Idaho: A Guide in Word and Picture. Prepared by the Federal Writers' Projects of the Works Progress Administration. (American Guide Series.) Second edition. Oxford University Press, New York. See Part II, "Tours," beginning on page 129; also Part III, "The Primitive Area," beginning on page 235; and "A Trip into the Area," beginning on page 242.

Idaho Encyclopedia—Vardis Fisher. The Caxton Printers, Ltd., Caldwell, Idaho. See Section I, "The Physical State," pp. 25–76.

Let's Go Camping—Harry Zarchy. Alfred A. Knopf, New York.

Let's Visit Our National Parks—Bryon Steel. Robert M. McBride & Company, New York. Motor guidebook.

North Idaho Scenic-Land Association, Sandpoint, Idaho. This organization has a great deal of material concerning recreational advantages and scenic attractions of the Panhandle.

Our Country's National Parks—Irving Robert Melbo. The Bobbs-Merrill Company, Indianapolis, Ind. Two volumes.

Principles of Canoeing—Albert Van Sic-
len ("Pierre") Pulling. The Macmillan Company, New York. A new outdoors book by an Idaho State College professor.

River of No Return—Bailey. See Group 12.

Scenic Idaho—Published by Belcher Publishing Company, Boise. Idaho. The following articles in alphabetical order describe and picture some of Idaho's recreational and scenic areas:

Bruneau Canyon. Al Alexander
        Third Quarter, 1950
Exploring the Bighorn Crags. C. M. "Chet" Belcher   Vol. 2, No. 2, 1947
Hell's Canyon, America's Deepest Gorge. John Advent
        Winter Issue, 1948
Idaho, Center of America's Rodeo
        Summer Issue, 1954
Idaho's Primitive Areas
        Vol. I, No. 1, 1946
Incredible Idaho. Dorine Goertzen
        Fall Issue, 1954
Lake Pend Oreille, North Idaho Mecca. Jim Parsons
        Vacation Issue, 1953
McCall and Payette Lakes
        No. 2, 1948
Silent City of Rocks. Harry Harpster
        Fall Issue, 1954
Thousand Springs Valley. Vardis Fisher   Third Quarter, 1952

Seeing Idaho—Published about two years, 1937–38, by Graves and Potter, Pocatello, Idaho. A few libraries have files of the old magazine. Articles describing recreational and scenic areas are in alphabetical order:

Down the River of No Return. Robert G. Bailey   July, 1937
Exploring Idaho's Clinker Box. Willard Adams and Clyde Ormond
        October, 1937

Heyburn State Park. Charles Sowder
January, 1938
Hiking Over the Selkirks. Winnifred
E. Drake   October, 1937
Seeing Idaho from Borah Peak. Robert
Fulton   Summer Edition, 1938
That Monument to Monumental.
Glenn Balch   January, 1938
Vacation Trails: North Idaho; Central Idaho; South-Central Idaho.
Eb. Fulton and others   July, 1937
State Board of Publicity, Office of the
Secretary of State, Boise, Idaho. The
Secretary of State has in his files some
material prepared by the State Board
of Publicity. Inquire.
Tourist Charter Services in Idaho—
Harry H. Caldwell and Cornelis Visser.
University of Idaho, Moscow, Idaho,
1952.
U.S. Forest Service. Maps and descriptive material may be obtained free
from the offices of the different national
forests in Idaho, as follows:
Bitterroot National Forest, Hamilton,
Montana
Boise National Forest, Boise, Idaho
Cache National Forest, Logan, Utah
Caribou National Forest, Pocatello,
Idaho
Challis National Forest, Challis, Idaho
Clearwater National Forest, Orofino,
Idaho
Coeur d'Alene National Forest, Coeur
d'Alene, Idaho
Kaniksu National Forest, Sandpoint,
Idaho
Kootenai National Forest, Libby, Montana
Lolo National Forest, Missoula, Montana
Nez Perce National Forest, Grangeville, Idaho
Payette National Forest, McCall,
Idaho

Salmon National Forest, Salmon,
Idaho
Sawtooth National Forest, Twin Falls,
Idaho
St. Joe National Forest, St. Maries,
Idaho
Targhee National Forest, St. Anthony,
Idaho

20. REFERENCE BOOKS AND ENCYCLOPEDIAS

NOTE: Some of these have been listed
under other groups, where it seemed
pertinent to include them, but titles
are repeated here.
American People's Encyclopedia. Spencer Press, Inc., Chicago.
Book of Knowledge. Grolier Society, Inc.,
New York.
Britannica Junior. Encyclopaedia Britannica, Inc., Chicago, Ill.
Collier's Encyclopedia. New York, N.Y.
Compton's Pictured Encyclopedia. F. E.
Compton & Company, Chicago, Ill.
Encyclopedia Americana. Americana
Corporation, New York and Chicago.
Encyclopaedia Britannica. Encyclopaedia
Britannica, Inc., Chicago, Ill.
Grolier Encyclopedia. Grolier Society,
Inc., New York, N.Y.
Idaho: A Guide in Word and Picture.
Prepared by the Federal Writers' Projects of the Works Progress Administration. (American Guide Series.)
Second edition. Oxford University
Press, New York.
Idaho Digest and Blue Book. Hobson.
The Caxton Printers, Ltd., Caldwell,
Idaho, 1935.
Idaho Encyclopedia—Fisher. The Caxton Printers, Ltd., Caldwell, Idaho,
1938.
Lands and People. Grolier Society, Inc.,
New York, N.Y.

Richards Topical Encyclopedia. Grolier Society, Inc., New York, N.Y.

World Almanac. Published annually by *New York World-Telegram,* New York.

World Book Encyclopedia. Field Enterprises, Inc., Chicago, Ill.

21. TRANSPORTATION AND COMMUNICATION

NOTE: Most of the Idaho histories listed in Group 11 have chapters on transportation and communications.

Ben Holladay, the Stagecoach King—J. V. Frederick. The Arthur H. Clark Company, Glendale, Calif.

Building of the First Transcontinental Railroad—Adele Nathan. Random House, New York.

Butterfield Overland Mail—Watterman L. Ormsby. Huntington Library and Art Gallery, San Marino, Calif.

Discovery of Marias Pass—Grace Flandrau. Great Northern Railway, Spokane, Wash.

First Overland Mail—Robert E. Pinkerton. Random House, New York. A Landmark Book.

Historic Adventure Land of the Northwest—Grace Flandrau. Great Northern Railway, Spokane, Wash.

Idaho State Department of Aeronautics, Boise, Idaho. This department has supervision of airlines and air travel in Idaho. Write if information is desired.

Idaho State Highway Department, Boise, Idaho. This department has charge of the system of state highways, including the Federal-aid roads. Write if information is desired. Free road maps on request.

Jerry and the Pony Express—Sanford Tousey. Doubleday, Doran & Company, Inc., Garden City, N.Y. A noted writer of juvenile stories is the author.

Old Ferries—Foster. Twentieth Biennial Report, 1945–1946, Idaho State Historical Society, Boise, Idaho.

Overland Mail—LeRoy R. Hafen. The Arthur H. Clark Company, Cleveland, Ohio.

Pony Express—Samuel Hopkins Adams. Random House, New York. A Landmark Book.

Pony Express Goes Through—Howard R. Driggs. Frederick A. Stokes Company, New York. Formerly on the Idaho Reading Circle list.

Popular Mechanics Picture History of American Transportation—Edward L. Throm. Simon and Schuster, New York.

Riding West on the Pony Express—C. L. Shelton. The Macmillan Company, New York.

Romance of the Rails—Agnes C. Laut. Tudor Publishing Company, New York.

Steamboats in the Timber—Ruby El Hult. The Caxton Printers, Ltd., Caldwell, Idaho. The story of early steamboat transportation in northern Idaho.

Story of American Roads—Virginia Hart. William Sloane Associates, Inc., New York.

Tall Timber Pilots—Dale White and Larry Florek. The Viking Press, Inc., New York. Thrilling new book about the daring flyers who daily risk their lives flying into the wild country of the intermountain Northwest.

Thrilling and Truthful History of the Pony Express—William Lightfoot Visscher. The Charles T. Powner Co., Chicago.

Travel in Early Days in Idaho—John Hailey. Idaho State Historical Society, Vol. I, No. 1, April, 1908.

22. WILDLIFE AND NATURAL HISTORY

Beasts of the Tar Pits—W. W. Robinson. The Macmillan Company, New York. About ancient animals of the West, many of which also lived in what is now Idaho.

Chisel-Tooth Tribes—Winnifred Bronson. E. M. Hale & Co., Eau Claire, Wis. Includes the story of the beaver. A Cadmus Book.

Cougar, Killer and Coward—Carl Hayden. Scenic Idaho, Fourth Quarter, 1952. Belcher Publishing Company, Boise, Idaho.

Coyotes—Winnifred Bronson. Harcourt, Brace & Company, New York.

Flora of Idaho—Ray J. Davis. William Brown, Dubuque, Iowa. Dr. Davis, on the faculty of Idaho State College, has a beautifully illustrated book about the plant life of Idaho.

From an Old Hunter and Guide—Paul Swayne. Scenic Idaho, Vol. 4, No. 2, 1949. Belcher Publishing Company, Boise, Idaho.

Game Management—Aldo S. Leopold. Charles Scribner's Sons, New York.

Hunting in the Northwest—Clyde Ormond. Alfred A. Knopf, New York. One of Idaho's best-known sportsman-writers tells of hunting and caring for various kinds of game in Idaho.

Idaho Fish and Game Department, Boise, Idaho. This department can supply information on nearly any phase of wildlife in Idaho. Write for information desired.

Idaho's Primitive Area. U.S. Forest Service, Region 4, Ogden, Utah.

Idaho Sportsman. Published in Twin Falls, Idaho, this is the official publication of the Idaho Wildlife Federation.

Idaho Wildlife Review. Idaho Fish and Game Department, Boise, Idaho. Published bi-monthly, this little magazine is a valuable source of information. Free.

Making Land Produce Useful Wildlife. Farmers' Bulletin No. 2035. Soil Conservation Service, Yates Building, Boise, Idaho.

Mammals of the Pocatello Region of Southeastern Idaho—Wayne B. Whitlow and E. Raymond Hall. University of California Press, Berkeley, Calif.

Mountain Lakes in Idaho. Idaho Fish and Game Department, Boise, Idaho.

National Wildlife Federation, Washington, D.C. Bulletins and information.

Our Great Out-of-Doors—J. N. "Ding" Darling. Izaak Walton League of America, Dubuque, Iowa.

Prehistoric America—Anna Terry White. Random House, New York.

Recent Mammals of Idaho—William B. Davis. The Caxton Printers, Ltd., Caldwell, Idaho. Distribution and conservation of Idaho mammals.

Return to the River—Roderick L. Haig-Brown. William Morrow & Company, New York. The strange story of the Chinook salmon run, in which the rivers of central and northern Idaho have an important share.

Sportsman's Guide. Edward W. Pulver and Son, Seattle, Wash. A set of detailed maps of each section of Idaho, with information pertinent to sportsmen. Often on sale by local stores dealing in hunting equipment and supplies.

Upland Game Birds of Idaho. Idaho Fish and Game Department, Boise, Idaho.

U.S. Fish and Wildlife Service, Department of the Interior, Washington, D.C. Write for information about any matter in which you are interested concerning migratory waterfowl, control of predatory animals, fish and game preserves (Federal), and other wildlife matters in which this service has a share.

Western Wild Life—Allen Chaffee. The Caxton Printers, Ltd., Caldwell, Idaho. A fund of stories and information written for youthful readers.

Wildlife in Idaho—Plastino. Scenic Idaho, Fourth Quarter, 1952. Belcher Publishing Company, Boise, Idaho.

Wildlife Management Institute, Washington, D.C. General and special information.

Wildlife of Idaho—William M. Rush. Idaho Fish and Game Department, Boise, Idaho. An interesting and valuable book about Idaho wildlife. Free if still available. Has been distributed to most schools in the state.

Wolf in North American History—Stanley P. Young. The Caxton Printers, Ltd., Caldwell, Idaho. A study of the wolf from the fur period of the West to the present by a biologist who has spent a quarter of a century with the Fish and Wildlife Service of the Department of the Interior. Though wolves are all but extinct in Idaho (except the coyote) there is much in this book to interest the reader.

Index